On the Dignity

Catholic Social Teaching and Natural Law

F. Russell Hittinger

Edited by Scott J. Roniger

Foreword by Mary Ann Glendon

The Catholic University of America Press
Washington, D.C.

The following chapters were previously published by Russell Hittinger as essays in the following locations and are reproduced with permission:

Chapter 1: "The Coherence of the Four Basic Principles of Catholic Social Doctrine: An Interpretation." *Nova et Vetera*, English Edition 7, no. 4 (2009): 791–838.

Chapter 2: "Toward an Adequate Anthropology: Social Aspects of *Imago Dei* in Catholic Theology," in *Imago Dei: Human Dignity in Ecumenical Perspective*, ed. Thomas Albert Howard (Washington, DC: The Catholic University of America Press, 2012), 39–78.

Chapter 3: "Social Roles and Ruling Virtues in Catholic Social Doctrine," *Annales Theologici* 16 (2002): 295–318.

Chapter 4: "The Three Necessary Societies: Russell Hittinger Outlines the Social Vision of Pope Leo XIII," *First Things*, 274 (June–July 2017): 19–27.

Chapter 5: Originally published in *The Teachings of Modern Roman Catholicism: On Law, Politics, and Human Nature*, edited by John Witte Jr. and Frank S. Alexander. Copyright © 2007 Columbia University Press. Reprinted with permission of Columbia University Press.

Chapter 6: "Two Modernisms, Two Thomisms: Reflections on the Centenary of Pius X's Letter Against the Modernists." *Nova et Vetera*, English Edition 5, no. 4 (2007): 843–79.

Chapter 7: "Yves R. Simon on Natural Law and Reason," in *Acquaintance with the Absolute: The Philosophy of Yves R. Simon*, ed. Anthony O. Simon (New York: Fordham University Press, 1998), 101–27.

Chapter 8: "*Quinquagesimo Ante*: Reflections on *Pacem in Terris* Fifty Years Later," in *The Global Quest for Tranquillitas Ordinis. Pacem in Terris, Fifty Years Later* (Pontifical Academy of Social Sciences, Acta 18, 2013), www.pass.va/content/dam/scienzesociali/pdf/acta18/acta18-hittinger.pdf

Chapter 9: "Human Nature and States of Nature in John Paul II's Theological Anthropology," in *Human Nature in Its Wholeness: A Roman Catholic Perspective*, ed. Daniel Robinson (Washington, DC: The Catholic University of America Press, 2006), 9–33.

Chapter 10: "Natural Law and Public Discourse: The Legacies of Joseph Ratzinger," *Loyola Law Review* 60 (2014): 241–72.

Chapter 11: "The Situation of Natural Law in Catholic Theology," *Nova et Vetera*, English edition 9, no. 3 (2011): 657–70.

Chapter 12: "Religion, Human Law, and the Virtue of Religion: The Case of *Dignitatis Humanae*," *Nova et Vetera*, English edition 14, no. 1 (2016): 151–77.

Chapter 13: "How to Inherit a Kingdom: Reflections on the Situation of Catholic Political Thought," co-authored with Scott Roniger, *Nova et Vetera*, English edition 21, no. 3 (2023): 971–90.

Chapter 14: "What St. Benedict Taught His Dark Ages—and Ours," in *Renewal of Catholic Higher Education: Essays on Catholic Studies in Honor of Don J. Briel*, ed. Matthew T. Gerlach (Bismarck, ND: University of Mary Press, 2017), 58–79.

Cataloging-in-Publication Data is available from the Library of Congress

ISBN: 978-0-8132-3851-7
eISBN: 978-0-8132-3824-1
Paperback ISBN: 978-0-8132-3823-4

On the Dignity of Society

For the Family:
JH (RIP), FRH4, MAH, BH, LH, FRH5, DH.
And my editor and colleague, SR

Contents

Foreword

MARY ANN GLENDON
Learned Hand Professor of Law Emeritus, Harvard University

POPE SAINT JOHN PAUL II, as a major contributor to the social teachings of the Catholic Church, was keenly aware both of the need to keep the Church's social teaching in close touch with the human sciences and of the increasing difficulty in doing so. He frequently stressed the importance of the social sciences, philosophy, and theology ("particularly moral theology") to the development of the social doctrine, observing that dialogue with those fields would be more essential than ever in meeting the economic, social, and political challenges of the third millennium.[1] While it is not the Church's task to offer technical solutions to social problems, he wrote, "she still feels obliged to make her contribution to preserving peace and to building a society worthy of man. To do this . . . she needs constant and more extensive contact with the modern social sciences, with their research and with their findings."[2]

Those exhortations to interdisciplinary dialogue would be unremarkable were it not for the fact that their author was one of the twentieth century's foremost critics of a constellation of views that are pervasive among philosophers, theologians, economists, lawyers, sociologists, and students of politics—views that embrace the deconstruction of all moral norms and proclaim the socially constructed character of truth, reality, and human nature. "Nowadays," John Paul II wrote in *Centesimus Annus*, "there is a tendency to claim that agnosticism and skeptical relativism are the philosophy and the basic attitude which correspond to the democratic forms of life."[3] Time and again, he pointed out that if truth is entirely subjective, there can be no sure principle for justly ordering social relations. If there is no truth, he warned, the force of power takes over, people become means and objects to be exploited, there is no basis for human dignity, and no basis for human rights.[4] Why then, a curious person might ask, did the philosopher-pope encourage dialogue with the disciplines

---

1. John Paul II, Encyclical Letter *Sollicitudo Rei Socialis* (December 30, 1987), §3; John Paul II, Encyclical Letter *Centesiumus Annus* (May 1, 1991), §§55, 59; John Paul II, Motu Proprio *Socialium scientiarum* (January 1, 1994).

2. John Paul II, *Socialium scientiarum.*

3. John Paul II, *Centesimus Annus,* §46.

4. See John Paul II, *Centesimus Annus,* §44.

that have been the chief diffusers of reductionist accounts of human nature and society and relativistic accounts of moral reasoning and norms?

John Paul II provided two answers, both of which are challenging for those who hope that the principles of Catholic social thought might help to shift probabilities in favor of human flourishing in today's world. The first concerns what Catholic social thought can contribute to the human sciences. By entering into "dialogue with the various disciplines concerned with man," he wrote, the social doctrine "assimilates what these disciplines have to contribute, and helps them to open themselves to a broader horizon."[5] He himself frequently urged social scientists to be open to reexamining some of their most fundamental presuppositions; to be mindful of the unity that underlies their fragmented disciplines; to question their assumptions about personhood; and to "be not afraid" in the quest for truth.

The second answer concerns how dialogue with the human sciences can benefit the social doctrine (besides assisting the effort to keep well-informed about the changing social manifold). On this point, John Paul II sounds much like John Stuart Mill. The process can aid us in examining our own assumptions, making them more "real, relevant and personal, distinguishing the valid elements in the tradition from false and erroneous ones, or from obsolete forms which can be usefully replaced by others more suited to the times."[6] Given the present state of the human sciences, and given that contemporary Catholic social thought suffers from many of the same confusions and controversies that mark the various disciplines, our curious person might be forgiven for thinking that the dialogue has not been going too well.

How timely, therefore, are these lucid essays by Russell Hittinger. Hittinger's historical sense and rare command of the relevant disciplines enable him to illuminate each major step in the development of Catholic social thought by situating it in the context of social, political, and intellectual history. Even readers who know the field well will find an abundance of thought–provoking insights in this eminently readable and informative volume.

Reminding us that Catholic social doctrine did not begin with the industrial revolution and the plight of workers in that period, Hittinger locates the origins of its modern form in the need to defend the institutions of the Church in the wake of the French Revolution. That need spurred efforts to establish the principle that societies other than the state should be recognized as having dignity and authority within their proper sphere of action. The relevance of these efforts has persisted through the rise of totalitarian regimes and the extension of state control deep into civil society under liberal democracies.

---

5. John Paul II, *Centesimus Annus*, §59.
6. John Paul II, *Centesimus Annus*, §50.

Hittinger traces how Pope Leo XIII, writing in the midst of the social, economic, and political transformations of the late nineteenth century, produced a remarkably structured, evolving body of social doctrine that survived well into the twentieth century as a "different kind of liberalism." Through his eyes we see the protagonists of Catholic social thought in their own times and places struggling with the issues of their day. Along the way, he clarifies much of the confusion surrounding the concepts of subjectivity, solidarity, and subsidiarity.

With regard to the present state of affairs, Hittinger wryly notes that "the great hope of Catholic social doctrine was that, once the state is properly limited, we would see a flourishing of other societies and modes of solidarity. But it is not evident that this has happened or is about to happen any time soon."

Looking to the future, Hittinger draws inspiration from Pope Benedict XVI. When young Joseph Ratzinger came on the academic scene, he writes, "Moral theology was a half-lit moon in the firmament of theology." Pope Leo XIII's revival of Thomism had made natural law "a common coin of discourse and exposition. But the coin came in different denominations." Given the persistent differences of opinion over the grounding of natural law today, Hittinger endorses the view often expressed by Pope Benedict that discourse about natural law in the public square needs the Enlightenment. He comments:

> The quandary is ironical, to say the least. The Church needs the voice of its former opponent, the voice that declared the rights of man and the dignity of reason. But this is not the first time the Church has found itself on the terrain of such historical irony.

As for Lenin's question, "What is to be done?" Hittinger offers no simple answers. Instead he concludes this collection of essays by saying: "In the end the one infallible 'solution' to the new Dark Age upon us would be to address the darkness in ourselves and turn again and again back to Him who is the 'true Light' coming into the world, the One who brings us the light, joy and peace of Easter through patient suffering in the desert, of the Cross."

Without detracting from that affirmation, one may nevertheless applaud the light that Hittinger has brought to a body of thought greatly in need of *aggiornamento*.

The Dignity of Society in History

Introduction to Russell Hittinger's Essays on Catholic Social Teaching and Natural Law

SCOTT J. RONIGER

Loyola Marymount University

> For on whatever place one has fallen, on that place he must find support that he may rise again.
>
> —St. Augustine, *De Vera Religione*

FRANCIS RUSSELL HITTINGER III has been the leading scholar of Catholic social doctrine for some time now. The essays presented here are the fruit of his thinking on the topic over the course of many years, and I suggest that a serious reading of this collection will reveal that it is without rival in the field. Because these essays present much of Hittinger's mature thought as he has articulated it in the past twenty-five years, I wish to begin by charting the historical development of Hittinger's work. Situating his essays this way will enable us to appreciate the continuity of his thought as it has deepened over the course of his career, which will in turn reveal something of the nature of the central object of that thinking: the Church's teaching on social matters and the place of natural law theory within it.

I. THE DEVELOPMENT OF HITTINGER'S THOUGHT

Hittinger's career can be roughly divided into three interconnected phases, each marked by its own particular foci and apex, and each preparing the way for that which followed it. After undergraduate studies in philosophy, Church history, and theology at the University of Notre Dame and graduate studies in philosophy at St. Louis University, the first phase of his career stretched from the mid-1980s until the beginning of the third millennium after Christ. Hittinger began this period by making a lasting contribution to the field of natural law thinking with the publication of his first major work, *A Critique of the New Natural Law Theory* (1987). In fact, Hittinger is the source of the now-standard title "new natural law theory" to designate a school of thinking about the topic. This book has long been widely recognized as fundamental reading for those who wish to understand the differences between the approach of the new natural lawyers and that of the more classical, Thomistic philosophers, with a focus on the philosophical shortcomings of the former. After the publication of *A Critique of the New Natural Law Theory*, Hittinger published widely on issues in ethics, legal theory, and political philosophy. His work from this phase culminated in the appearance of *The First Grace: Rediscovering the Natural Law in a Post-Christian Age*, which was published in 2003 and contained essays originally composed between 1987 and 2001. *The First Grace* is a significant achievement that remains in the upper echelon of books on Thomistic natural law theory, as well as on moral and legal philosophy more generally.

Bookended by two significant and influential works, this initial phase in Hittinger's career is marked by deep engagement with (a) the sources of Catholic ethical and political philosophy, especially St. Thomas Aquinas's natural law theory, and (b) historical developments in American political, legal, and judicial spheres, with the sources of Catholic thought being mined for their own sake and being made to shed light on contemporary trends in the United States. These two intellectual foci bore fruit in the practical realm, where Hittinger was among the leading Catholic intellectuals giving voice to the cause of unborn children in our nation. It is also important to highlight an essay that appeared in 1992 entitled "The Problem of the State in *Centesimus Annus*."[1] This publication marked Hittinger's first sustained academic engagement with Catholic social teaching and helped to sow the seeds of a deep and prolonged reflection upon the Church's teaching on social issues. Ch. 7 of this collection is taken from the first stage of Hittinger's work.

The second phase of Hittinger's career spanned roughly the first twelve years of the twenty-first century and evidenced the initial flowering of his interest in Catholic social doctrine. At the beginning of this period, Hittinger spent a sabbatical year split between Rome and the University of Notre Dame, during which time he read extensively from the sources of Catholic social teaching and studied its historical development through the nineteenth and twentieth centuries. His publications during this second phase are the fruit of this engagement with the sources and history of Catholic social thought, but they also reveal a deep continuity with his earlier studies of St. Thomas, natural law, ethics and political philosophy, and legal theory. This continuity between moral philosophy and social doctrine manifests a central aspect of Catholic social teaching itself, which is a dimension of Catholic moral theology. As Pope St. John Paul II says,

---

1. See Hittinger, "The Problem of the State in *Centesimus Annus*," *Fordham International Law Journal* 15 (1992): 952–96.

The Church's social doctrine is not a "third way" between liberal capitalism and Marxist collectivism, nor even a possible alternative to other solutions less radically opposed to one another: rather, it constitutes a category of its own. Nor is it an ideology, but rather the accurate formulation of the results of a careful reflection on the complex realities of human existence, in society and in the international order, in the light of faith and of the Church's tradition. Its main aim is to interpret these realities, determining their conformity with or divergence from the lines of the Gospel teaching on man and his vocation, a vocation which is at once earthly and transcendent; its aim is thus to guide Christian behavior. *It therefore belongs to the field, not of ideology, but of theology and particularly of moral theology.*[2]

Just as grace imitates nature, so too does moral theology, including social doctrine, imitate philosophical ethics and natural law theory.[3] Hittinger says that moral philosophy and moral theology overlap insofar as "they study the right ordering of human action to ends. Social doctrine is particularly interested in the social virtues of charity and justice by which the person is right with God and neighbor. But being right with God and neighbor includes membership in societies which need to be rightly ordered both within and without." Therefore, he draws the conclusion that "the reader who tries to distill the purely theological elements of social doctrine while leaving behind the philosophical instruments will understand something of the magisterial tradition, but not very much." The development of Hittinger's work tracks this relationship between philosophy, theology, and social theory and thus helps to disclose it.

The second phase of Hittinger's career therefore represents more than a consistent development of the first, but rather the first serves as the necessary foundation for its completion in the second. It integrates historical studies of the development of Catholic social teaching with systematic exposition of the theological coherence of that tradition, while also articulating the essential role of philosophy and natural law within both. This period culminates in the publication of the essay "The Coherence of the Four Basic Principles of Catholic Social Doctrine: An Interpretation," which is something of a modern classic and has become required reading for anyone interested in the Church's teaching on social issues. For this reason, we have placed it as the opening chapter of this collection. In addition to the opening essay, Chs. 2, 3, 5, 6, 9, and 11 are taken from this phase of Hittinger's work.

---

2. John Paul II, Encyclical Letter *Sollicitudo Rei Socialis* (December 30, 1987), §41. Italics added.

3. For the claim that grace imitates nature, see Aquinas, *Summa Theologiae (ST)*, II-II, q. 31, a. 3. He says, "Grace and virtue imitate the order of nature, which has been instituted by divine wisdom" (trans. mine).

The third phase of Hittinger's career has covered roughly the previous decade and continues to the present day. In his publications during this time, Hittinger's continued research on natural law is wedded to an increasingly detailed engagement with the historical development of Catholic social teaching that facilitates the process of getting to the deepest metaphysical and Christological roots of that tradition. The third phase culminates in two essays, each of which represents the apex of these interconnected aspects of Hittinger's research. In a work that will be published separately from this collection and tentatively entitled "A Lasting Paradigm? Reflections on the Development of Catholic Social Teaching," Hittinger tracks the major historical shifts that have taken place from Pope Leo XIII in the nineteenth century to Pope Francis in the twenty-first. In the penultimate chapter of this volume, entitled "How to Inherit a Kingdom: Reflections on the Situation of Catholic Political Thought," Hittinger and the present author manifest the most fundamental truth and thus the deepest root of the tradition of Catholic social teaching: Jesus Christ, as God Incarnate acting in our history for our salvation, founded a supernatural kingdom that is not of this world. In this essay and during this period generally, we see a fecund engagement with the thought of Joseph Ratzinger, which complements Hittinger's Thomism and strengthens his integration of historical sensibility and theological depth. Hittinger's study of Ratzinger also allows him to show the importance of eschatology for Catholic social teaching, which represents an organic deepening of his integration of philosophy, history, and theology witnessed in the second phase. In addition to the penultimate essay, Chs. 4, 8, 10, 12, and 14 are taken from this third period.

With these three phases distinguished, a profound unity emerges that serves to manifest something of the essence of Catholic social teaching. Hittinger's is a historically important body of work on Catholic moral and social philosophy and theology that is rooted in natural law theory and Thomistic philosophy, but also animated by St. Augustine's thought and thus consistently sensitive to historical contexts and arenas for moral and theological disputation. Due in part to this philosophical infrastructure, Hittinger's sensitivity to historical developments both in society and in the Church's applications of her teaching in response to social movements does not lead to relativism or historicism; rather, it enables him to penetrate ever deeper into the Church's teaching in order finally to arrive at the historical and metaphysical root of the entire tradition: Jesus Christ established a supernatural kingdom that is not of this world. The eschatological dimension of Christian faith is therefore fundamental for understanding Catholic social doctrine, for eschatology is not merely a reflection upon the four last things, nor is it a quietistic longing for a future state of being free from the struggles of earthly life; rather, it is the supernatural presence here and now in history of the ultimate reality of the kingdom of God that will be definitively completed when Christ returns in glory. Eschatology is the adherence to Christ made possible by grace and faith that structures the entire being and action of Christian life, and thus Christ's establishment of a supernatural kingdom not of this world is the "fundamental principle that can serve as a light—not at the end of the tunnel of contingencies but one that illuminates our path at the very beginning." In sum, the development of Hittinger's work reflects the intellectual and spiritual architecture of Catholic social doctrine.

II. THE CONTENT OF THE ESSAYS

Having outlined the development of Hittinger's thinking, let us now give a precis of the essays in this collection and attempt to draw out some of the major themes and distinctions at work in them. This volume is divided into three parts. The first part is comprised of six essays on Catholic social teaching, the second part is made up of six essays on natural law and its role in social doctrine, and the third part includes two essays discussing the first principles of the Church's teaching on social issues.

A. Part One: Essays on Catholic Social Teaching

The first essay of Part One, entitled "The Coherence of the Four Basic Principles of Catholic Social Doctrine: An Interpretation," is a tour de force in which Hittinger synthesizes the major themes of Catholic social teaching—human dignity, solidarity, subsidiarity, and common good—by articulating their philosophical foundations and showing the historical challenges that led to the development of social doctrine. He points out that, historically, it was the French Revolution and the subsequent Church-state crisis that posed the most fundamental challenges to the Church and her teaching and necessitated the development of social doctrine, not simply the developments of the Industrial Revolution, although the latter did in fact raise new problems and exacerbate old issues.[4] He shows that the philosophical key to achieving a coherent understanding of this tradition is the proper grasp of social ontology, the theorizing of the matter, form, being, and ends of various societies. In a development of

---

4. As Hittinger says, "The post-1789 Church-state crisis is what gave the Church real incentive to develop a body of social doctrine. On this score it is important to understand that the social doctrine did not begin with the industrial revolution and the problems of benighted and dislocated workers. It began with the need to defend the institutions of the Church. Catholic social doctrine, accordingly, emerged in defense of two propositions: first, that the state does not enjoy a monopoly over group-personhood; second, that societies other than the state not only possess real dignity as rights-and-duties bearing unities, but that they also enjoy modes of authority proper to their own society."

the classical metaphysical insight that being and being one are coextensive, Hittinger manifests the being of social groups by working out the relationships between parts and wholes and by distinguishing the different kinds of unity obtaining in different forms of human association. In so doing, he shows how classical metaphysics is at work in human affairs, and he enables us to understand the nature and dignity of society in all its analogical instantiations. I would like to suggest that his articulation of the nature and dignity of society is perhaps Hittinger's most important philosophical achievement, one that sets him apart from other scholars working in the tradition of Catholic social teaching. In Hittinger's lexicon, society is the keyword, the word rejected by the modern builders but the one that remains the cornerstone of the Church's teaching on the communal life and happiness of man.

One of the many strategic distinctions drawn in this chapter is that between a partnership and a society, with a society constituted as a unity of order in which the members pursue common ends through common actions structured by shared ways of life. Societies, as unities of order, stand mid-way between mere aggregates, on the one hand, and instances of substantial unity, on the other hand. Societies can therefore be called "group-persons." Partnerships, however, fail to achieve this unity of order because the goods to be achieved through the partnership are private—that is, are lessened when shared—and because the ways of achieving such goods do not necessitate common action. In a partnership, as distinct from a society, the ends pursued by the partners are not the result of common actions for common goods, both of which are goods that cannot be lessened when shared, but to the individual actions of the partners extrinsically linked with a view of the private yield of each. A society is a community constituted by the unification of persons (a "group-person") in view of common goods, but a partnership is a coordination of individuals marked not by a unity of persons but rather by a collection of things, often so collected for the sake of individual profit. In a true society, the members want the bond itself that unifies them as an essential aspect of pursuing the common end of their common action.

This fundamental distinction allows Hittinger to show that a polity, properly understood, is a society of societies, or a community of communities, and therefore he is able to show how subsidiarity is demanded by the very nature of political life, existing as it does as a kind of hierarchical complementarity. In order to make this point, Hittinger shows how the Church's principle of subsidiarity is distinct from devolution theories and, one might add, from any form of libertarianism. Subsidiarity is founded upon the recognition that there are analogous realizations of true societies and that each society is a (partial) completion of the human person's natural inclination to social and political life; it "assumes" that each society has its inherent, natural dignity and proper sphere of authority, not merely an instrumental value as an intermediate buffer against or curb of state power. Subsidiarity is therefore fitting for human political life because it shows that political authority must recognize, protect, and promote the natural dignity and authority manifest in societies such as families, schools, and trade unions, to name only a few. This principle shows that it is of the nature of political authority to unify unities by nesting them in a way that respects their ontological status as unities of order, drawing them into higher modes of communion with each other so as to perfect and not absorb them. That is, subsidiarity is a dimension of natural justice founded upon the dignity and authority of myriad social forms, and therefore "the sin of the modern state is the injustice of its claiming a monopoly over group-personhood."

The second essay, "Toward an Adequate Anthropology: Social Aspects of *Imago Dei* in Catholic Theology," poses the intriguing question: "Can social entities be said to exist in the image of God?" In response, Hittinger argues that a Catholic understanding of the human person as made unto the image of God rests upon two distinct but related philosophical insights that can be considered "preambles" of a Catholic theology of *imago dei*. First, the human person possesses a "unity of being and operation that manifests certain excellences," especially the divine-like excellences of knowing truth and loving others, and, second, human societies are distinct in kind, unity, and excellence from mere aggregations of human persons. Thus, the philosophical foundation for Catholic thinking about human persons as created to God's image is a hendiadys, a one through two: it is the truth that the unity and excellence of the human person is perfected, manifested, and poured out into societies marked by an analogous unity, dignity, and excellence.

Based upon these insights, Hittinger distinguishes two modes of imitating God. "First, a diversity of created things, each having a good according to its participated being. Second, a diversity of created things imitating God insofar as they cause goodness in others—insofar as they bring into existence, through secondary causality, additional modes of participation among themselves and others. The superabundance of what exists in God *simply* is, in creation, most perfectly expressed in a varied manifold." Both the diversity of created being and the activities of those beings as they interact with each other make manifest something of the infinite being and goodness of God. For our part, human beings imitate God by knowing and loving (God) and by loving goodness into others, especially within societies. The best human life, the life of happiness in virtue, is therefore the mixed life of contemplation and action because both of these forms of human activity can rightly be understood as ways of imitating God. Hittinger is therefore able to show that Pope Leo XIII "and his successors were advancing an argument for normative social pluralism based upon a social imitation of God." These arguments also set the stage for an excellent discussion of Christian marriage, which can now be understood as "a social entity that is not just a perfection of the individual image [of God], but one that is itself the bearer of an image." Again, we are made to see the social dimension of Christian anthropology and the dignity of social union as distinct from its mere utility.[5]

The third essay, "Social Roles and Ruling Virtues in Catholic Social Doctrine," investigates "the idea of the *munus regale*—the function, mission, gift, or vocation of ruling" in order to show "why the liberal conception of liberties, rights, and social pluralism needs to be preserved and corrected by an ontology of the human person as a 'royal creature' who participates in divine ruling powers." Hittinger reflects upon the Church's teaching that all Christians, through baptism, participate in the *tria munera Christi*, the "functions" of priest, prophet, and king, and he argues that these *munera* should be understood as gifts of service given to human persons for the development of self and others in view of the common good. Basing his argument largely on the work of Pius XI and John Paul II, Hittinger shows that the *munus regale* perfects a natural dimension of human persons: our inclination to social and political life, which includes the aspect of ruling and being ruled. Neither the natural substrate nor the theological form of the *munus regale* should be understood as a right to dominate others, but rather as the vocation to self-mastery in the life of virtue and to self-gift in the life of service to others. Thus, Hittinger uses Catholic social teaching to recapitulate and to extend an ancient insight from Plato and Aristotle—namely, that the ruler must first rule himself by inculcating virtue before he will be able to govern others prudently.[6]

The fourth essay discusses the eponymous three necessary societies of marriage-family, polity, and Church. Hittinger draws attention to the ways in which Catholic social doctrine has presented these societies as necessary for human happiness; they are seats of eudaimonia. After describing what Pope Leo XIII called the "Great Conflagration" of society accomplished by the French Revolution and its aftermath, Hittinger shows that Leo responded, not with his own rendition of the *Syllabus of Errors*, but with questions that are "at once more philosophical and more practical: How do we *civilize* this situation? What is our proposal for social order? What can we work with in social matters, and how do we measure what's been lost and what might be regained?" Reflection upon the three necessary societies and their relationships to each other provides

---

5. As Hittinger says, "In its deepest pattern, Catholic social doctrine was a defense of the individual *in* society; more specifically, it was chiefly an articulation of the dignity of society and a defense of societies against the state's ambition to exercise a monopoly on fraternity. Arguments drawn from the economy of creation, such as natural law, and arguments drawn from the economy of redemption were thus marshaled, usually in tandem, to buttress this explicitly anti-Rousseauvian conception of social orders representing divine things."

6. See, *inter alia*, Plato, *Gorgias*, 491a–e; Aristotle, *Nicomachean Ethics*, VI, Chs. 5–13 and *Politics*, VII, especially Chs. 1 and 15.

a sturdy framework for answering these questions. The societies of marriage-family, polity, and Church are necessary for human happiness because "the human person is a domestic (matrimonial-familial) animal, a political animal, and an ecclesial animal." Thus, Catholic social thought has shown that the dignity of the human person will be truncated if one does not properly understand the dignity of the three necessary societies in which we find the perfection of our nature, which constitutes our happiness. Hittinger shows that these societies have in common (analogically) three properties: (a) their respective forms and ends are not arbitrary or purely voluntary, but natural or supernatural; (b) they are not disposable or transitory associations because we dwell in each one; and (c) they are subsidiary to one another. Finally, Hittinger argues that the demise of the three necessary societies represents a truly catastrophic social situation, and he distinguishes two ways in which such a social calamity has come about in recent history: *from above* by events such as the French Revolution and the two world wars, and *from below* by the cultural, economic, and technological revolutions that began during the 1960s and have gained considerable steam since. Despite their differences, both directions of social disaster are based upon inadequate understandings of what it is to be human, and thus the truth of the human person as created to the image of God, redeemed by Christ, and perfected in the three necessary societies is once again shown to be fundamental for Catholic faith and social teaching.

The fifth essay, "The Accomplishment of Leo XIII," is an authoritative presentation of the Leo XIII's contribution to Catholic social teaching and is a must-read for anyone interested in the topic. It begins with an impressive survey of the history of the political and social crisis that reached its nadir in the nineteenth century and that prompted the Church to develop her modern social doctrine before turning to a discussion of the synthesis developed by Leo XIII and his team of philosophers and theologians in response to their historical situation. Hittinger's discussion of this Leonine synthesis also includes important reflections on Leo's life and experience, which provide the context for his doctrinal accomplishment. It is worth noting here that Hittinger identifies a crucial aspect of the formal structure of Leo's thought: "Throughout his letters, Leo used a twofold pedagogy to situate the human agent who participates in divine providence both through the natural law and through the law of the Gospel. . . . The distinctions related to this double pedagogy—reason and faith, general and particular providence, nature and grace—represent two ways that the human knower participates in God's ordering wisdom." Hittinger shows how this double pedagogy textures Leo's rich teaching on many issues, including philosophy's relation to Catholic faith and theology, the nature of law, the proper understanding of human liberty under law, the origin of political authority, and the various forms of prudence. The chapter ends with a brief overview of the considerable influence of Leo's teaching in the twentieth century before concluding that "Leo's chief legacy is to have prompted the papal magisterium to think, and to think at levels deeper than diplomacy and public policy."

The sixth essay, "Two Modernisms, Two Thomisms: Reflections on Pius X's Letter against the Modernists," was written in 2007 to mark the centenary of Pope Pius X's condemnation of modernism. Hittinger takes the occasion as an opportunity to contrast Pius X's condemnation, put forth in the Roman Inquisition's decretum *Lamentabili Sane* and in his encyclical *Pascendi Dominci Gregis*, with Pope Leo XIII's *Aeterni Patris* (1879). He shows that Leo's call for a revival of scholastic philosophy and theology, above all the thought of St. Thomas Aquinas, initiated a program that "looked backward, from the traditions to the original [system of St. Thomas himself], and forward toward a constructive engagement with modern philosophy and science." By contrast, Pius X moved "directly to a disciplinary matter" whose tone can be perceived by listening to Pius's decrees that seminary professors may not disparage or set aside Thomas's teaching "especially in metaphysical questions" and that "to be heard 'carping' (*carpendo*) at Scholasticism was a ground for dismissing either faculty or administrators in ecclesiastical schools."

However, Hittinger argues that the tension between these two Thomisms—Leo's constructive and synthetic form and Pius's legislated and disciplinary form—manifests the deeper tension "between two different aspects of modernity with which Catholicism had to reckon." The first aspect of modernity included its social, economic, political, and legal machinations that necessitated the development of Catholic social teaching, and the second aspect included the philosophical systems of modernity, as well as the popular ideologies they spawned, that challenged the *praeambula fidei*, especially those truths knowable by natural reason concerning the existence and nature of God. Broadly stated, Leo's Thomism was a response to the first aspect of modernity, and Pius's Thomism was a response to the second. Thus, "the Leonine revival was motivated by the search for an adequate *doctrina civilis*," while Pius X, responding as he was to a "different sort of Modernism," used Thomism to distinguish true from false philosophy and "to detect true from false churchmen" in an attempt to protect sacred doctrine and to promote orthodox systematic theology. Hittinger acknowledges the nuances of both modernisms and both Thomisms, and he recognizes the ways in which these two sets of issues—the social-political and the metaphysical-theological—are necessarily intertwined. He is therefore able to give a balanced and learned presentation of a complex and important episode in the Church's modern history, a presentation from which he draws serious conclusions. This essay is a vivid example of Hittinger's historical learning and the way it allows him to illuminate philosophical and theological disputes.

B. Part Two: Essays on Natural Law

Part Two begins with the essay "Yves R. Simon on Natural Law and Practical Reason." Of the great neo-scholastics of the twentieth century, Yves Simon is too often neglected or given short shrift, and it is my hope that Hittinger's essay will stimulate a deeper engagement with Simon's thought. Hittinger begins by pointing out Simon's understanding of the three foci of natural law thinking: (1) order in human practical thinking, (2) order in the natural world, and (3) the transcendent activity of divine providence as responsible for the orders in (1) and (2). Serious treatments of natural law must take account of all three foci, the questions each raises, and the ways all three are interconnected. These three foci help us to understand Simon's claim that there is an "eternal return" of natural law thinking, and Hittinger argues that this eternal return is due to "the daunting challenge of explaining away the notion that there are things to be distributed and owed to persons on grounds other than those made by positive ordinances." That is, it seems plain to human experience that there are sources of order deeper than or prior to a given polity's cultural norms and legislative activities, and the philosopher's task is to contemplate these sources, not explain them away. To search philosophically for the "prior premises" of human action and positive law is ultimately to search for natural law.

According to Hittinger, Simon understood that natural law thinking is "Janus-faced," as it must contemplate the ways that practical thinking is based upon the prior premises of natural law, and it must also consider how natural law can be "extended" or made "effective" in contingent circumstances. Hittinger argues that "Simon thought that the problem of natural law is best discussed not exclusively as a regression to first premises, but prospectively toward the distinct ways that the first premises are made effective." This distinction allows Hittinger to give an interesting exposition of three philosophical issues that occupied Simon and that "tend to be submerged in the practical and institutional discourse": (1) the relation of law to practical reasoning, (2) the ways that law differs from authority and individual prudence, and (3) the question as to the legal status of natural law—that is, whether or not natural law can be understood to be anything more than a metaphorical "law."

Via Simon, Hittinger shows that law—especially natural law—functions as a premise for actions, which are the conclusions of practical thinking. While the natural law provides the deepest foundation for human action, it is prudence— the virtue of practical wisdom—that enables one to deliberate, to judge, and to act well in the midst of contingent circumstances that permit multiple ways of pursuing an end. For "prudence comes into its own when there is something contingent or variable about the relation" between acts for the sake of an end and the end for the sake of which one acts. Prudence allows human agents to achieve the ends toward which natural law directs them.

One must, however, be attentive to the distinction between the various kinds of prudence (personal, familial, political, and regnative) and the ways that each one is able to make the natural law "effective" in human life. Regnative or legislative prudence issues in positive laws, which serve as premises for human action founded on the prior premises of natural law, and therefore legislative prudence tends of its very nature toward generality or universality. These points allow Hittinger to highlight Simon's excellent distinction between the two ways authority can be active. Simon argues that authority is a natural necessity and that it is active both in law, which tends toward generality, and in "particularized commands" directing particular, concrete, and contingent situations; in fact, authority is more at home in directing a multitude confronting particular contingencies, where unanimity cannot be consistently achieved. Thus, all legitimate positive law requires authority, but not all authority is legislative. In other words, even though all activities of practical reason and all species of prudence are rooted in law, not all practical measures and prudential decisions are laws; so, the proper sphere of positive law does not exhaust the realm of authority and prudence. The essay concludes with a discussion of Simon's attempt to offer a way of arguing to the existence of God as legislator of the natural law, which is necessary to establish its full legality. Such metaphysical arguments present what is first in the order of being but last in the order of discovery.

In both its content and its structure, Ch. 8, "Reflections on Natural Law in *Pacem in Terris*," continues the discussion of natural law, right order, and prudence. Hittinger argues that "the interpretive key" of Pope John XXIII's *Pacem in Terris* is to be found "in the organization of the encyclical itself," and I suggest that the interpretive key to Hittinger's essay on the encyclical is to be found in the organization of the essay itself. After a brief introduction, this chapter is divided into three sections, respectively entitled "Looking Back," "Looking Around (in the Encyclical)," and "Looking Ahead: Signs of the Times." This tripartite structure is just that of the virtue of prudence, as Aquinas says, "Providence is the principal part of prudence, and the other two parts—viz., memory of what is past and understanding of what is present—are ordered toward it. For it is from the past as remembered and the present as understood that we judge about future things that have to be provided for."[7] Prudence is founded upon and brings to perfection the natural order that pertains to human

---

7. Aquinas, *ST*, I, q. 22, a. 1. See Scott Roniger, "Prudence as Command Across Presence and Absence," *Review of Metaphysics* 47, no. 4 (2021): 577–619. Cicero also claims that the parts of prudence are memory of things past, intelligence or knowledge of things present, and foresight of things future. See *De Inventione*, Book II, LIII. See also *The Iliad of Homer*, trans. Alexander Pope (New Haven, CT: Yale University Press, 1967), Book I, 83–96, and Book III, 145–52.

persons created in the image and likeness of the God whom they seek. Founded upon the natural law, prudence orders future contingents toward good ends by recalling the lessons of the past and understanding the contours of the present, so this essay is a "prudential" look at that which makes prudence possible.

While the essay is structured "prudentially," its content is an exposition of the natural law thinking presented in *Pacem in Terris*, including a discussion of the intellectual sources and historical developments that led to John XXIII's encyclical and the way in which the encyclical identified the issues that would become stumbling blocks in the decades after its promulgation. Hittinger shows that St. Augustine's understanding of peace as the tranquility of order is the key philosophical insight in Pope John XXIII's thinking, and he gives a memorable formulation of Roncalli's Augustinian understanding of a perennial task of a bishop: "to discern the signs of the times according to the deeper patterns of history, and the still deeper principles of order which ought to inform it."

Hittinger says it is "nonsense" to argue, as some have done, that *Pacem in Terris* turns natural law upside down by subordinating natural law to subjective human rights. Rather, the core of the encyclical is its integration of "justice as rights and justice as right order." The encyclical presents rights and right order as an integral unity, and attending to the structure of the encyclical helps us to see this unity. In *Pacem in Terris*, Pope John XXIII articulates six modes of order, and his charter of human rights stands between two discussions of divinely created order. Holding in view both the structure of the encyclical and its content enables us to see that peace is "richly textured" and requires a proper order amongst the many kinds of order themselves. Thus, the encyclical teaches that "if there are natural rights then there is order prior to, and distinct from, the orders we construct or confer."

Human rights and right order to human goods are necessarily integrated with each other, and their unity can be seen by focusing on the word "endowment." Human persons are naturally endowed with intellect and will, so the human endowment is the dignity of being made to the image and likeness of God, being open to reality as a whole, and thus participating in the order of the eternal law. The natural anthropological endowment entails that human persons are not only "part of a vast created order" but also capable of "appreciating and appropriating that order" and are thus called to achieve the tranquility of moral order by being properly subject to God and to each other. Our natural human endowment is the source both of our natural order to goods and of the rights that accrue to us in view of this natural order. Interestingly, Hittinger shows that both John XXIII and Dr. Martin Luther King Jr., in his *Letter from a Birmingham Jail*, agree on these points, for "each shared the conviction that authentic rights claims and right order are co-implicates rather than opposites, and that the nucleus of both is the anthropological endowment." I suggest that Hittinger's essay shows how *Pacem in Terris* can be understood as a modern recapitulation of the classical philosophical insight that the human being's substantial form (the rational soul or "human endowment") unfolds itself in our proper *ergon* (openness to the whole of reality, truth, and love), and thus "gives" us our natural order to our *telos* (perfection in happiness, joy in truth).[8] These three dimensions of human nature—form, function, and *telos*—cannot be separated from each other, and their natural integration provides the necessary context for properly understanding natural law as the foundation for human rights.

In Ch. 9, "Human Nature and States of Nature in John Paul II's Theological Anthropology," we move from an explication of the rights and right order of man as rooted in the human endowment to a discussion of this endowment itself. Hittinger locates John Paul II's work historically by tracing the shift in emphasis in Catholic social teaching from responding to an "institutional crisis" toward responding to an "anthropological crisis." As Hittinger points out, when Wojtyła was elected pope in 1978, every previous pontiff since 1775 had written an inaugural encyclical on the problem of political order. However, John Paul II's first encyclical, *Redemptor Hominis*, announced his shift in emphasis from the institutional crisis, which had dominated Catholic social teaching until that time, to the anthropological crisis, which was to occupy much of his thinking. With John Paul II, the central question shifts from "Quid est Caesar?" to "Quid est Homo?"

John Paul II's answer is of course contained *in nucleo* in *Gaudium et spes*, 22: "It is only in the mystery of the Word incarnate that light is shed on the *mysterium hominis*. For Adam, the first human being, was a figure of the future—namely, of Christ the lord. It is Christ, the last Adam, who fully discloses man to himself and unfolds his noble calling by revealing the mystery of the Father and the Father's love." Hittinger astutely recognizes that the key word is *fully*, for "Adam could not be a 'type' were he bereft of certain human dignities, such as rationality, freedom, sociality. If the old Adam were evacuated of anthropological content, the Christian message about Christ could not probe and broaden anthropological questions; rather, it would stand merely as another 'construction' alongside others." John Paul II understood that one of the distinctive marks of our age is "negative anthropology"—namely, the "ready affirmation of what man is not combined with a deep-seated reluctance to affirm normative anthropological content." Such negative anthropologies are ultimately rooted in the modern reinterpretations of Genesis, especially those developed by Hobbes, Locke, Kant, and

---

8. According to Aristotle, an entity's *eidos*, *ergon*, *aretē*, and *telos* are inseparably linked; what a thing is, its nature, determines its characteristic activities, ends, and perfections. See Aristotle, *Nicomachean Ethics*, I.7, 1097b21–1098a21, and *Metaphysics*, IX.8, 1050a10–25.

above all Rousseau. These reduce the human person to a kind of pre-political rubble that can then be constructed artificially solely on the sovereign will of the individual.

In response, John Paul II developed a sophisticated "positive anthropology" that integrates philosophical and theological insights. The key to this teaching is the articulation of what Hittinger calls the four "anthropological thresholds": between man and God, man and beast, good and evil, and man and woman. John Paul II reflects on these four distinct but related experiences by reading scripture, especially Genesis, in a novel way, allowing the Biblical text "to call attention to human experiences often overlooked" and "to relocate [questions] that originally led to a doctrine" of the Church.

The tenth essay, "Natural Law and Public Discourse: The Legacies of Joseph Ratzinger," moves from John Paul II to his successor and argues that Ratzinger found his way to the tradition of natural law theory in his role as a systematic theologian. Hittinger argues that Ratzinger "left the tradition [of natural law] better off than he found it." He shows that Ratzinger's engagements with natural law thinking, coupled with John Paul II's reflections on the topic, were part of an intellectual project that significantly improved moral theology in the post-Vatican II Church and eventually proved fundamental for both *Veritatis Splendor* and *Fides et Ratio*. However, Hittinger says that, in order to understand Ratzinger's contributions to natural law theory, we must recognize that the title "natural law" is used and developed in many different ways and for varied purposes. Hittinger distinguishes three "contexts" in which the natural law is employed: (1) the systematic, (2) the dialectical, and (3) the dialogical.

Hittinger says that natural law thinking within the *systematic* context "is not immediately concerned with making moral arguments, but rather with making coherent the sources of truth, including what is recognized or pre-supposed about the natural habitat of reason." The systematic context is the most comprehensive and contemplative of the three; natural law thinking within this context is concerned with identifying and integrating the sources of knowledge of the natural law. Within the *dialectical* context, philosophers and theologians begin with a concrete, disputed moral question, which is usually occasioned by current cases or moral dilemmas, and attempt to reason to a specific conclusion. Thus, natural law thinking within the dialectical context seeks to answer a pressing moral question by applying the principles of natural law to a concrete case. Finally, interlocutors operating in the *dialogical* context do not search primarily for answers to specific moral questions or for the coherence of the sources of truth; rather, they use the natural law as an aspect of the search for common premises across religious and philosophical traditions. Hittinger says that natural law thinking in the dialogical context is "a search for common and converging pathways of evidence."

In this essay, Hittinger is most concerned with Ratzinger's contributions to the dialogical context of natural law thinking, but he says that all three contexts are intertwined, so a development in one area has consequences for the other two. However, each of these three contexts for reflection on the natural law has its own integrity and proper method of investigation. These distinctions enable Hittinger to give a lucid appraisal of Ratzinger's contributions to the Church's teaching on natural law, and I suggest that they are crucial for any philosopher or theologian interested in studying the tradition of natural law thinking.

The eleventh essay is entitled "The Situation of Natural Law in Catholic Theology" and considers fundamental aspects of natural law theory within both the systematic and the dialogical contexts by turning to *Veritatis Splendor* and to the document of the International Theological Commission (ITC), *In Search of a Universal Ethic: A New Look at the Natural Law*. After placing each document in its proper historical context, Hittinger argues that *Veritatis* shows us that "natural law forms an organic part of moral theology" because "moral truths—in principle accessible to human reason—not only constitute a 'preparation for the Gospel,' but are also situated within it." The natural law is therefore "presupposed" by moral theology in two ways: "first, as principles of moral order are derived from human nature; second, as those very same principles are clarified and integrated in the teachings of Christ." Due to this "double commitment" of moral theology to natural law (natural law as "prior to" and as "integrated within" moral theology), Hittinger concludes that "the theological affirmation of natural law in *Veritatis* makes the moral theologian *more* responsible to the natural law than the moral philosopher."

When he turns to the ITC's study of natural law, Hittinger finds two important places where the document can be bolstered. "First, while the document affirms clearly enough, even insistently, the importance of prudence in judgments that make the natural law effective, its depiction of universal moral norms *prior* to prudence is not very clear. Second, it leaves out of the picture what kind of dialogue can be conducted with secular modernity." While the ITC document speaks of the natural law as "a source of objective inspiration," Hittinger distinguishes "objective inspirations" from properly legal precepts and shows that the natural law must be understood as issuing the latter.

The twelfth essay, "Religion, Human Law, and the Virtue of Religion: The Case of *Dignitatis Humanae*," discusses St. Thomas's treatments of the virtue of religion in order to shed light on the Second Vatican Council's Declaration on Religious Freedom. Hittinger shows that St. Thomas gives us two distinct and complementary discussions of the virtue of religion, one systematic and the other historical, and he says that a key distinction functions in both of Aquinas's treatments. Hittinger distinguishes between what he calls *"the stem [of the virtue of religion] and its branches"* and *"the historical situation of formation* (and deformation) of religious acts." By the religious "stem" and its branches, Hittinger is referring to "Thomas's examination of the rational inclination to know the truth about God and the various practical considerations and acts of religion," and by the historical situation of formation he means "the record of how humans have been educated by laws, customs, and higher causes that include demons and God himself" as to the proper (or improper) mode of executing religious acts and thus of perfecting (or harming) the stem.

While the stem of the virtue of religion remains sturdy and vibrant, human beings apart from God's direction and grace have not been successful regarding the formation of this stem throughout our history. Apart from God's revelation and his action of drawing a people to Himself, our history is one of deforming a sturdy because "divinely instilled" inclination to honor and worship God. Hittinger's discussion of St. Thomas's teaching on the virtue of religion is original and important, and it allows him to shed considerable light on *Dignitatis Humanae* and to make shrewd points concerning the relationship between Church and state.

C. Part Three: First Truths

Ch. 13, "How to Inherit a Kingdom: Reflections on the Situation of Catholic Political Thought," is coauthored by Hittinger and myself and is the most recent essay in this collection. It begins with a discussion of Leonine era "pontifical prudence" as it unfolded within the Church's relations with civil governments in the late nineteenth and early twentieth centuries as a necessary context for understanding the Church's development and application of the principles of Catholic social teaching. In the second section, we draw from the thought of St. Augustine, Pope St. John Paul II, and Joseph Ratzinger to identify "a truly *first* principle" of Catholic social doctrine—namely, that "the Kingdom of Christ is separated both in ordinary human time and eschatologically." Putting to the side the usual spectrum of juridical and moral meanings of separation, we argue that in its primary theological sense "separated is the equivalent of being 'set aside' not only as something holy, but just as importantly something accomplished by a divine rather than a human act." Because the Church is set aside, and set beyond, as something holy and wholly accomplished by God, it is contradicted by the reign of sin which is directly opposed to the truth that the Church embodies and proclaims, but the Church is not directly opposed by politics just as such. Rather, temporal politics is simply "other than" the kingdom of Christ. Ratzinger's reflections on eschatology enable us to develop this point, for he argues that "the message of the Kingdom of God has something very important to say to politics. It is healthy for politics to learn that its own content is not eschatological. The setting asunder of eschatology and politics is one of the fundamental tasks of Christian theology."[9] Finally, we use the work of Étienne Gilson to show the disastrous avatars the Church lets loose in the world, and indeed the avatar that she herself becomes, when she neglects the eschatological dimension of the Incarnation of God in Christ and attempts to substitute for the theological virtues an intra-mundane task or mission.

In the final chapter, "What Saint Benedict Taught the Dark Ages: His and Ours," Hittinger offers four "vignettes" or "nocturnes" that manifest the significance of St. Benedict "for his 'dark age' as well as our own." These four vignettes, each of which is marked by wonderful insights, are titled (1) Owl of Minerva: Wisdom in Twilight, (2) Dark Ages, (3) Curriculum, and (4) Harkening. The essay as a whole is a work of Christian wisdom that manifests what is at the heart of the spiritual life and thus at the core of the life of Christian learning and culture. It demonstrates how the first truth that Jesus's kingdom is not of this world can become the principle for a practical life lived in accordance with this truth, both for the monks of St. Benedict in their dark ages and for lay men and women in our own. The images of light and darkness are superbly deployed throughout the essay, which shows us that Benedict's genius was to found a monastery and a way of life that is nothing other than a school that *"turns prodigals into pilgrims."* Not all are called to join this school, but all are invited to learn from the way it incarnates the saving Truth of the kingdom of God within a society of believers who are in but not of the world. This concluding chapter, along with the book it recapitulates and fittingly brings to a close, is a beacon of light in an increasing dark world.

---

9. Ratzinger, *Eschatology: Death and Eternal Life*, trans. Michael Waldstein (Washington, DC: The Catholic University of America Press, 1988), 59.

PART I

Catholic Social Teaching

CHAPTER 1

The Coherence of the Four Basic Principles of Catholic Social Doctrine

An Interpretation

INTRODUCTION

On Reading the Tradition

PIUS XI (1922–1939) IS THE FIRST POPE to speak of social doctrine as a unified body of teachings which develop by way of clarity and application. In *Quadragesimo Anno*, Pius said that he inherited a "doctrine" handed on from the time of Leo XIII.[1] By any measure, it is a prodigious tradition. Beginning in 1878 with the election of Leo, popes have issued more than 250 encyclicals and other teaching letters. About half are related, broadly, to issues of social thought and doctrine.[2]

This new doctrinal specialty is placed within moral theology because, as John Paul II insisted, it must "reflect on the complex realities of human existence, in society and in the international order, in the light . . . of the Gospel teaching on man and his vocation."[3] Moral philosophy and theology overlap insofar as they study the right ordering of human action to ends. Social doctrine is particularly interested in the social virtues of charity and justice by which the person is right with God and neighbor. But being right with God

---

1. Pius XI, Encyclical Letter *Quadragesimo Anno* (May 15, 1931), §§18–21, *Acta Apostolicae Sedis (AAS)*, vol. 23, 182–84.

2. Only the *litterae encyclicae* and the *epistolae encyclicae* are encyclicals in the strict sense of the term. I use the expression "encyclicals and other teaching letters" to cover more inclusively other species of papal documents containing ordinary magisterial teaching. My enumeration follows the *Enchiridion delle Encicliche*, 8 volumes, edizione bilingue (Bologne: EDB, 1994–1998).

3. John Paul II, Encyclical Letter *Sollicitudo Rei Socialis* (December 30, 1987), §41, *AAS* 80 (1988), 570; see also Encyclical Letter *Centesimus Annus* (May 1, 1991), §54, *AAS* 83, 859–60.

3

and neighbor includes membership in societies which need to be rightly ordered both within and without. Even those actions which modern ethicists take to be self-regarding—actions properly undertaken for one's own good—are nonetheless orderable to a community. In this sense we can speak of being right not merely with one's neighbors as singular persons, but also being rightly ordered to (and within) a community.[4]

Although social doctrine has a specifically theological orientation, it makes use of philosophical instruments. If one reads *Mystici Corporis* (1943), Pius XII's encyclical on the nature of the Church, alongside the three great "social" encyclicals—*Rerum Novarum* (1891), *Quadragesimo Anno* (1931), and *Centesimus Annus* (1991)—it is apparent that the ensemble of teachings shares a common stock of principles on such things as the human person, the different forms of solidarity, subsidiarity, and the common good. The reader who tries to distill the purely theological elements of social doctrine while leaving behind the philosophical instruments will understand something of the magisterial tradition, but not very much.

The project is also complex because of the subject matter. It is one thing to understand the principles drawn from theology and philosophy. It is quite another thing to understand concrete social realities. In his Christmas Message of 1955, Pius XII pointed out that although the principles of social order are natural, the social realities "change over time with social developments."[5] Some changes are brought about by historical forces which cannot be attributed directly to anyone's decision or policy. Other developments arise from within societies, as their members make mutual adjustments to one another and thereby bring about new ways of molding and forming the order of their common goods. Families, associations, markets, political constitutions, and the law of nations are dynamic. They respond both to external forces and to internal actions of their members. Accordingly, social doctrine also must make use of the social sciences.

Whereas in doctrinal theology proper, the revealed data are unfolded with more clarity and richness gradually, as the Church reflects upon the deposit

---

4. See, for, example Aquinas in *Summa theologiae*, I-II, q. 21, a. 3, ad 1. In answer to the objection that "good or evil actions are not all related to another person, for some are related to the person of the agent," Thomas replies: "A man's good or evil actions, although not ordained to the good or evil of another individual, are nevertheless ordained to the good or evil of another, i.e. the community." A social entity is something that can be harmed in the moral sense of the term, and it therefore falls within the domain of justice. English texts from the *Summa theologiae* are taken from the translation of the Fathers of the English Dominican Province (New York: Benzinger Brothers, 1948).

5. Pius XII, "Radio message Col curore aperto," December 24, 1955: "un ordine naturale, anche se le sue forme mutano con gli sviluppi storici e sociali," available at vatican.va.

of faith, in social doctrine the teachings include applications of principles to the contingencies of societies.[6] This makes social doctrine very interesting. By the same token, it can be distorted through ideologies, political policies, and various kinds of jargon used by political parties.

Finally, the project is complex because all three factors—the theological, philosophical, and social scientific—are given different emphasis over the course of decades since 1878. The tradition is not only multi-disciplinary but internally multi-faceted, as one pope introduces new themes even while circling back upon the work of his predecessors. It is the Roman way to introduce new considerations while at the same time tightening their connection to the preceding tradition. Old things are made to look new, and new things look old. John Paul II referred to the scribe trained for the kingdom, who is compared to "a householder who brings out of his treasure what is new and what is old" (Mt 13:52). This is not mere pious sentimentality. The pope meant it as a hermeneutical principle suitable for reading the tradition of social doctrine. Someone who reads the magisterial documents as bits of "news" or as ad hoc pieces of Church policy on particular social issues will understand something, but not very much.

An Approach to the Four Principles: Human Dignity, Solidarity, Subsidiarity, and Common Good

For centuries, Catholics used the term *doctrina civilis*—or teaching(s) about political order. The chief virtue of justice, holding sway over all other species of justice, was called *iustitia legalis*, legal or general justice, which took its name from what is most characteristic of polity, the ordering of law. After the pontificate of Leo XIII (1878–1903), *doctrina civilis* became *doctrina socialis*; for its part, *iustitia legalis* became *iustitia socialis*.

Why did the term "social" come to the fore in Catholic teaching and thought? In order to answer this question, it is necessary to consider the four basic principles which orient the proceedings of the Pontifical Academy of Social Sciences: dignity of the person, solidarity, subsidiarity, and common good. Notice that, while all four principles presuppose the human person, the last three are specifically and irreducibly social. The dignity of the human person cannot be interpreted on the premise of methodological individualism— namely, that social unities and relations among members can be reduced to nonsocial properties of members or composites thereof. Indeed, whether

---

6. Consider, for example, the way in which John Paul II gives an "interpretive rereading [*relegantur*]" of *Rerum Novarum*. At the outset, he contends that it is necessary "to look back [*respectandum*], to look around [*circumspectandum*], and to look ahead [*futura inspectanda*]." *Centesimus Annus*, §3, AAS 83, 794–95.

there are real social entities instantiating real social relations amongst their members is the first and most abiding question.

I will proceed in this fashion.

First, I will explore a few ontological principles which will help us to understand why two or more persons constitute a society. This effort is best accomplished by asking three questions. What makes a social union different than the unity of a substance? What makes a social union different than an aggregation of individuals? What makes a social union different than partnerships which organize private shares? We need a reasonably clear, but also flexible, account of social entities before we tackle the principle of subsidiarity.

Second, I will explore the difference between devolution and subsidiarity. Terms like solidarity, subsidiarity, and devolution have a history. They are used variously by political parties, labor unions, constitutional lawyers, and political theorists. Moreover, they run the gamut from the political-left to the political-right. I shall put these phenomena to one side. Rather, I want to show why solidarity, subsidiarity, and common good depend upon what we mean by a society. Then, and only then, can we ask the question whether plural societies, each with its own distinctive common good, can enjoy a common good that transcends the particular social unions without injustice to or destruction of those groups.

Finally, I will offer some brief reflections on the problem of applying the principles to contemporary societies.

GROUP PERSONS

Basic Social Ontology

Margaret Thatcher famously said that there is "no such thing as society," there are only "individual men and women, and there are families." Lady Thatcher was surely right that groups like families and polities, clubs, teams, and colleges do not possess the unity of an individual substance. The two creation myths of Genesis, for example, clearly distinguish between the one-flesh unity of Adam and Eve (Gn 2:21–25) and the antecedent sequence of natural kinds. Sacred Scripture seems to confirm common sense and untutored observation. Marriage does not have a nature in the same sense as a plant, a bird, or even a human being. When two or more people are constituted in a society, there is not produced a second or third natural kind.

In answer to the question, what is a social entity, the lawyers (civil and canonical) as well as the political philosophers have said that society is a "person." We can recall Aquinas's definition of a person as that which is "distinct by reason of dignity":

For as famous men were represented in comedies and tragedies, the name "person" was given to signify those who held high dignity. . . . And because subsistence in a rational nature is of high dignity, therefore every individual of the rational nature is called a "person." Now the dignity of the divine nature excels every other dignity; and thus the name "person" pre-eminently belongs to God.[7]

Thomas refers to the Latin word *persona*, a mask used by actors to impersonate a well-known character—someone distinct in dignity. In Republican Rome, when a family attained the office of praetor (vice military commanders and judges of the standing courts), it achieved the rank of nobility and was entitled to keep the wax masks of ancestors for family worship and funerals (*ius imaginum* was the right to publicly impersonate those who are distinct in dignity). Roman jurists transferred the right of impersonation to the legal status of person. Person now means the capacity to be effective in the eyes of the law. Playing a certain role for a specific purpose in a legal drama, he becomes something more than a natural person. Only later did theologians and philosophers transfer the idea of impersonation and the person at law to a rational, individual substance—to the very thing personated; to persons, both human and divine.[8]

While lawyers have always been most interested in how to construct and assign the legal "mask," philosophers and theologians have never ceased asking the question, what stands behind the masks? Is legal personhood nothing but the mask, or are the masks somehow attributes of real persons? And who are these real persons? Why should they need masks at all?

The short answer can be put as follows. All natural persons need legal masks because they assist the public manifestation and efficacy of natural capacities. The owner of a vineyard, and a son who stands to inherit the father's vineyard, will find the legal masks very convenient. The status or standing to conduct business at law requires the same natural person to be different persons—as son, as legatee, as citizen, and so forth. As for who are the real persons, they are individuals of a rational nature who are also members of societies that constitute something more than the sum of their members.

Thomas notes in his treatise on justice in the *Summa theologiae* that justice regards actions, and actions belong to "supposits and totalities" (*ST* II-II, q. 58, a. 2), to natural persons and to groups. In sum, justice concerns individual

---

7. *ST*, I, q. 29, a. 3, ad 2.

8. The progression from impersonation to persons is traced by Marcel Mauss, the nephew of Emile Durkheim: "A Category of the Human Mind: The Notion of Person; the Notion of Self," in *The Category of the Person: Anthropology, Philosophy, History*, ed. M. Carrithers, S. Collins, and S. Lukes (Cambridge: Cambridge University Press, 1985), 1–25. See also Otto von Gierke, *Associations and Law: The Classical and Early Christian Stages*, ed and trans. George Heiman (Toronto: University of Toronto Press, 1977).

persons, and then, from a different point of view, individual persons as members of a unity of order that transcends the sum of the parts. There are many Latin names for such an entity—*societas, persona moralis, corpus ex distantibus, colleyium, universitas, communitas*—but for our purposes I will use the more familiar term "society."

In the tradition common to jurists, philosophers, and theologians, the word "person" denotes whoever and whatever is a locus of rights and responsibilities. In this respect, there were at least three kinds of persons. *First*, there are natural persons. Here, the word "natural" is used to denote whoever possesses a unity of a rational substance: human persons, angelic persons, or divine persons sharing the unity of a single substance. *Second*, there are *fictional persons*. As Thomas Hobbes said, "[t]here are few things that are incapable of being represented by fiction."[9] Inanimate things like bridges, hospitals, and houses can receive endowments, and thus bear interests and rights at law. Like Caligula's horse, made a senator by imperial decree, such entities are distinct in dignity not on account of their own nature, virtue, or power, but rather by a *fictio legis*, the construction of law. For a fictional person, there is nothing other than the legally assigned "mask." *Third*, there are what should be called *group* persons, entities having neither the unity of a substance, nor a unity merely imposed upon things in the fashion of a legal or mental fiction.

Such persons—real but neither substantial nor fictional—are called societies. A society possesses what Thomas called a unity of order:

> It must be known that the whole which the political group or the family constitutes has only a unity of order [*habet solam ordinis unitatem*], for it is not something absolutely one. A part of this whole, therefore, can have an operation that is not the operation of the whole, as a soldier in an army has activity that does not belong to the whole army. However, this whole does have an operation that is not proper to its parts but to the whole.[10]

---

9. Thomas Hobbes, *Leviathan*, ed. Richard Tuck (New York: Cambridge University Press, 1996), I, c. 16.

10. *In Eth.* I.5. The collective noun implies a plurality of subjects in some kind of unity (*ST*, I, q. 31, a. 1, ad 2). While only individuals subsist in their own right, society exists in its members by way of order. The order is what substitutes for "form" in a natural unity.

> Now, one way in which one comes from many is the way of order alone; so from many homes a city comes to be, or from many soldiers an army. Another way is that of order and composition; so a house comes to be when they join together its parts and its walls. But neither of these two ways fits the constitution of one nature from a plurality. For things whose form is order or juxtaposition are not natural things. The result is that their unity cannot be called a unity of nature. (*Summa contra Gentiles*, IV, c. 35)

This category, *unitas ordinis*, is taken from Aristotle and Thomas, and was revived by Pope Leo XIII and his philosophical colleagues at the Roman Academy of St. Thomas Aquinas in order to avoid the extremes of nineteenth-century social thought. One extreme depicts society as a kind of super-individual having a single mind or a single body like a biological organism. The other extreme is to think of a society as a purely accidental unity ensuing upon the choices and actions of individuals who follow their own preferences. In this case, the ideal model was a market rather than an organism. Leo and his associates saw that a proper understanding of social entities required a middle course.

Catholic social doctrine began to take shape at the same time that sociology emerged as an academic discipline. When Leo was elected in 1878, he knew relatively little of this fledgling discipline, except perhaps the extreme positions of Compte and Marx.[11] But Leo and his advisors were certainly more

---

Therefore, a society is neither a natural unity nor a mere compositional unity, but rather is *unum per ordinationem*. The unity is characterized as the order itself—*est ordo ipsius*. It is both common end and shared structure.

11. For centuries, a de facto social pluralism was taken for granted. But now that society itself was the thing under dispute, how should the Church speak? In retrospect, we might wonder why the Church did not begin a serious discourse with social scientists, some of whom worried about the problem of social disintegration. In brief, the answer is twofold. First, the Roman authorities did not know very much about this emergent science. Second, what they did know seemed forbidding. I have carefully combed through the major teaching documents of the nineteenth century, and the thinkers typically mentioned are Fourier, Saint-Simon, Rousseau, Marx, and various species of liberalism, without the names of particular thinkers usually being identified. These were called physiocrats in the late eighteenth and early nineteenth centuries, and naturalists at the end of the century. They advocated a social science, to use Henri de Saint-Simon's phrase, that reduced social phenomena to the "physics of organized bodies." Concretely existing social institutions were a false consciousness to be reformed by science. See Georg G. Iggers, "Further Remarks about Early Uses of the Term 'Social Science,'" *Journal of the History of Ideas* 20, no. 3 (1959): 433–36. This is why, even as late as the pontificate of Pius XI, who really was interested in demographics and economics, the magisterial documents refused to utter the two words "social science." Instead, they used circumlocutions, such as *periti in re socialis*—experts in social matters—sometimes with the additional word *disciplina*, to indicate that there are certain methods appropriate to that work. Indeed, it is not until the Vatican II era, and especially during the pontificate of John Paul II, that the social sciences are acknowledged. In the early nineteenth century, Catholic thinkers like Joseph de Maistre and Louis de Bonald adumbrated a social science. See Robert Spaemann, *Der Ursprung der Soziologie aus dem Geist der Restauration. Studien über L. G. A. de Bonald* (Munich: Kösel, 1959). These politically reactionary, though brilliant, first-stirrings of social thought had little purchase in the documents of the Roman Magisterium. Leo XIII wished to develop a social teaching grounded in philosophy, chiefly that of Thomas Aquinas. In doing so, he wanted to keep the foundations relatively clean of anything that sailed too close to the shores of reactionary politics. For this part of the story, see Ch. 6 in this collection. On Leo's suspicion of Romantic reactionaries, see Ch. 5.

than amateurs in law (canonical and civil) and philosophy. Naturally, they reached for a category that was readily available within the orbit of their familiar disciplines. From the New Testament, they were more than a little familiar with the principle of *koinonia*, which is fundamental to ecclesiology and moral theology. From the law they understood the rubric of a group-person, and from philosophy they understood the Aristotelian and scholastic rubric of a unity of order. They chose wisely, because two notions allowed them to develop an analytical framework that was, at once, both sturdy and supple. They took the ancient legal rubric of a *persona moralis* to designate a group having sufficient unity to be a right-and-duty-bearing entity at law; and then they grafted it on to a realistic social ontology of a unity of order that is not reducible either to a natural substance or to a mere aggregate of individuals. Hence, in document after document, from the time of Leo onward, we find the phrase "true society." This relatively simple matrix served both descriptive and normative purposes. Once we have a way to pick out what counts as a "true society," then we can put in place a scheme of rights and responsibilities, depending on the various ends and modes of unity of particular societies.

In a unity of order each member possesses what is individually proper to himself—namely, certain operations and acts not reducible to the commonality, and not dissolved or cancelled by membership in a group. At the same time, a society enjoys a real unity transcending mere aggregation of the members.[12] Unity of order is not an ideal model imposed upon social data. Rather, it only brings into view facts available to common sense: that the individuals in a queue are parts not members of the queue, and they are the members not the parts of St. Rita's parish. The first is an aggregation, the second a unity of order. In the parlance of mereological set theory (the logic of parts and wholes), a group is a non-extensional set because it does not necessarily change its identity whenever the constituent bits or pieces change. For France, or the Catholic Church, or the local labor union, change of constituents can *sustain* rather than *destroy* the identity of the group. In an extensional set, however, the addition or subtraction of one constituent changes the identity of the set. With one exception, this certainly is not true of a social entity.[13]

---

12. See David-Hillel Ruben, "Social Wholes and Parts," *Mind*, New Series 92, no. 366 (1983): 234–38. For aggregative or "extensional" sets—A = B if A and B sare just the same bits or constituents—see also his "The Existence of Social Entities," *The Philosophical Quarterly* 32, no. 129 (1982): 301.

13. Marriage is different, of course, because the union of the two particular persons is more immediately the "common" good. Therefore, marriage really does change with the death or dismissal of a spouse. Polygamy, for example, does not imply a marriage that becomes, by increments, larger with every new spouse. Marriage, however, is ordered to family, and families can persist over time with the inclusion of a new member.

Ordinarily, the law will assume the perpetuity of a society for the good reason that it does not have the mortality of a natural substance.

Wherever there are plural rational agents, aiming at common ends, through united action, *and where the unity is one of the intrinsic goods aimed at*, we have a society—something distinct in dignity. To use once again the traditional terminology, the group is said to have an extrinsic common good (victory for the army) and an intrinsic common good (the common order of its action).[14] Groups differ in terms of the ends and the structure of their respective, internal unity. A faculty, for example, aims to advance learning and to educate students, but, unlike a marriage, its intrinsic unity does not depend upon conjugal relations. Traditionally, a matrimonial society has only one form, a man and a woman, who share life unto perpetuity, as a whole, through a one-flesh act of sexual unity.[15] For its part, a polity can have plural forms—rule by one, by a few, by many, or a mixed form. It can consist of different proportions of men, women, and children. Societies are quite different in their ends and modes of unity.

But any society has this much in common. It possesses an intrinsic common good, which cannot be distributed or cashed-out. The common good never exists as a private good, and therefore when someone exits a marriage or a polity, he cannot take away his private share. Even in our confused legal cultures, courts understand perfectly well that they can divide and distribute the external properties, but not the marriage itself. The matrimonial society, therefore, is not redistributed so much as dissolved or annulled.

A group will hold itself out to the rest of the world as something distinct in dignity,[16] possessing rights and responsibilities.[17] Not *as though* they are

---

14. In any integral whole like a society, common order is the form, analogous to a substantial form that unifies a natural thing. The extrinsic good of the army is the victory. Cf. Aquinas, *In XII Meta.*, lec. 12, no. 2627; and *In I Sent.*, d. 44, q. l, a. 2. Cf. Gregory Froelich, "The Equivocal Status of *Bonum Commune*," *The New Scholasticism* 63, no. 1 (1989): 38–57.

15. As Pius XI emphasized, marriage is not just a partnership to bring about certain ends, but is rather a mode of union by which such ends are achieved. Pius XI, Encyclical Letter *Casti Connubii* (December 31, 1930), §24, *AAS* 22, 548f.: "This mutual molding [*interior conformatio*] of husband and wife, this determined effort to perfect each other, can in a very real sense, as the Roman Catechism teaches, be said to be the chief reason and purpose of matrimony, provided matrimony be looked at not in the restricted sense as instituted for the proper conception and education of the child, but more widely as the blending of life as a whole [*totius vitae communio*] and the mutual interchange and sharing thereof."

16. Take, for example, the American *Declaration of Independence*: "We, therefore, the representatives of the United States of America, in General Congress assembled, appealing to the Supreme Judge of the world for the rectitude of our intentions, do, in the name and by the authority of the good people of these colonies solemnly publish and declare, that these United Colonies are, and of right ought to be, *free and independent states*."

17. The ontology we are developing here is evident in Pius XII, Encyclical Letter *Mystici Corporis* (June 29, 1943). At the outset, Pius argues that the Church is a true society,

one, but rather *as one*. In this sense, a society is called a *persona moralis*, a *corpus moralis*, a *unitas collectiva*, or even a *corpus mysticum*.[18] The word "moral" denotes a unity of action among plural agents, in contradistinction to the term "physical," which denotes a substantial unity. Social entities might be spatially locatable (for example, France, or one's parish, or college), but their unity transcends material aggregation. The same natural persons at once can be members of France, a parish, and a college without confusion, though not always without rivalries and tensions of loyalty.

Thus the scriptural hexaemeron crowns the six days of creation not with another natural kind, much less with an aggregation of material forces, but

---

which is to say that it is something more than a commutation of private things by consent of the parties (§9). Like any society, the Church is a unity of order that transcends aggregation of the members, while at the same time preserving the dignity of what is proper to the parts; see §61, *AAS* 35, 221:

> In a natural body the principle of unity unites the parts in such a manner that each lacks its own individual subsistence; on the contrary, in the Mystical Body the mutual union, though intrinsic, links the members by a bond which leaves to each the complete enjoyment of his own personality [*Dum enim in naturali corpore unitatis principium ita partes iungit, ut propria, quam vocant, subsistentia singulae prorsus careant; contra in mystico Corpore mutuae coniunctionis vis, etiamsi intima, membra ita inter se copulat, ut singula omnino fruantur persona propria*]. Moreover, if we examine the relations existing between the several members and the whole body, in every physical, living body, all the different members are ultimately destined to the good of the whole alone [*unice destinantur*]; while if we look to its ultimate usefulness, every moral association of men [*dum socialis quaelibet hominum compages, si modo ultimum utilitatis finem inspicimus, ad omnium et uniuscuiusque membri profectum, utpote personae sunt, postremum ordinantur*] is in the end directed to the advancement of all in general and of each single member in particular; for they are persons.

See his analogies between various species of societies, differing according to their respective ends and modes of unity (§§63–68, *AAS* 35, 223–27).

18. The term "mystical" does not necessarily refer to supernatural things, but rather designates a society—namely, a person distinct in dignity, but distinguished from a person whose dignity consists in the unity of substance. The transition of usage from the strictly theological to political and juridical contexts has been well studied: in the 1930s and 1940s by Henri de Lubac, SJ, *Corpus Mysticum*, trans. Gemma Simmonds, CJ, with Richard Price and Christopher Stephens (Notre Dame, IN: University of Notre Dame Press, 2006); and more recently by Francis Oakley, "Natural Law, the *Corpus Mysticum*, and Consent in Conciliar Thought from John of Paris to Mattias Ugonius," *Speculum* 56, no. 4 (1981): 786–810; and by Hélène Merlin and Allison Tait, "Fables of the 'Mystical Body' in Seventeenth-Century France," *Yale French Studies*, no. 86, (1994): 126–42. The masterworks, however, are by Ernst Kantorowicz: *The King's Two Bodies: A Study in Mediaeval Political Theology* (Princeton, NJ: Princeton University Press, 1957); and "Mysteries of State," *Harvard Theological Review* 48 (1955): 65–91.

with a society. In Jewish and Christian allegorical exegesis, this society was, in turn, the *type* of another society—Israel or the Church.[19] As Augustine contended in the *Confessions*, creation is for the sake of the Church. For his part, Thomas argued that God declared the unity of order at the sixth day "very good" because he "wished to produce His works in likeness to Himself, as far as possible, in order that they might be perfect, and that He might be known through them. Hence, that He might be portrayed in His works, not only according to what He is in Himself, but also according as He acts on others, He laid this natural law on all things, that last things should be reduced and perfected by middle things, and middle things by the first, as Dionysius says."[20] In other words, we are made unto the image of God not only because the individual person possesses the excellence of a rational nature, but also because we must cause good in others. Virtually all of the modern popes have highlighted this principle for social doctrine. From this twofold imaging of God flows the dignity of the individual and of social order. Notice the two imagings are without rivalry precisely because of the recurring distinction between unity of substance (the rational nature of the human person) and unity of order (a multiplicity of rational beings constituting an order, a "true society").[21] In this twofold imaging, the tradition has also emphasized the unique dignity of the unity of a multiplicity enjoying a common good. Thomas speaks of the created unity of order as "divinity" (*divinitas*), and, in the case of polity, as being "more divine" (*divinius*) than other imagings, whether individual or collective, because "divinity" signifies "the common good which is participated by all."[22]

---

19. On Jewish and Christian readings, see Gary A. Anderson, *The Genesis of Perfection: Adam and Eve in the Jewish and Christian Imagination* (Westminster, KY: John Knox Press, 2003). See, once again, Pius XII, who insists that marriage constitutes a mystical person (*constituere mysticum personam*), *Mystici Corporis*, §67.

20. *ST*, Supplement, q. 34, a. 1. See also Augustine, *Confessions*, XI–XIII. On the completion of the hexaemeron as "very good," see also Thomas, *SCG*, II, c. 45; III, c. 64; *ST*, I, q. 25, a. 6, and q. 47, a. 1. The diversity of entities is not a succession that amounts to a mere quantitative improvement, but rather a diversity exhibiting a unity of order. Goodness, which is simply and uniformly in God, exists in creatures in a multiform manner.

21. Thus Thomas speaks of the "trace" (*vestigium*) of the Trinity in creatures: "And therefore Augustine says (*De Trin.* vi, 10) that the trace of the Trinity is found in every creature, according *as it is one individual*, and according *as it is formed by a species*, and according as it *has a certain relation of order*." *ST*, I, q. 45, a. 7.

22. Here, from *In Rom.*, 1.6 (concerning verse 20 of the Pauline letter), and *De veritate*, q. 5, a. 3. These two terms—*divinitas* and *divinius*—must be distinguished from the term *deitas*, which refers directly to the divine essence. On this theme of the common good as a participational likeness, see Lawrence Dewan, "St. Thomas and the Divinity of the Common Good," in *Ressourcement Thomism: Sacred Doctrine, the Sacraments, and the Moral Life; Essays in Honor of Romanus Cessario, OP*, ed. Reinhard Hütter and Matthew Levering (Washington, DC: The Catholic University of America Press, 2010).

In his seminal essay on "Moral Personality and Legal Personality," the British legal historian F. W. Maitland writes:

> When a body of twenty, or two thousand, or two hundred thousand men bind themselves together to act in a particular way for some common purpose, they create a body, which by no fiction of law, but by the very nature of things, differs from the individuals of whom it is constituted. . . . If the law allows men to form permanently organized groups, those groups will be for common opinion right-and-duty bearing units; and if the law-giver will not openly treat them as such, he will misrepresent, or, as the French say, he will 'denature' the facts. . . . For the morality of common sense the group is a person, is right-and-duty-bearing unity.[23]

When individuals, with a note of permanence,[24] engage in united action for a common purpose, there comes into existence a unity that transcends the aggregation of its parts. That is to say, there comes into existence a group-person (a society) that requires the rest of us to recognize not only the individuals, but, as Maitland puts it, "$n + 1$ persons."[25] It would "denature" the facts, Maitland says, to pretend otherwise.[26] Every society will depend upon individual persons. This is just what Aristotle and Thomas meant by a unity of order, inasmuch as the members are not reducible to the whole as accidents to an underlying substance. *Groups are not ontologically basic in the order of substances.* They are basic, however, in constituting a unity that excels parts (members), which are also wholes (natural persons).

What Maitland calls "$n +1$" persons means that the group or society, and not just its individual members, should morally count as an agent or a patient.[27] As the bearer of rights and responsibilities, a society can harm or be harmed in the moral sense of the term. We morally harm a society when we

---

23. F. W. Maitland, "Moral Personality and Legal Personality," in *State, Trust and Corporation*, ed. D. Runciman (Cambridge: Cambridge University Press, 2003), 63, 68; quoting A. V. Dicey.

24. Thus, a society is not necessarily formed when two or more agents collaborate to lift a box. To be sure, such collaborations can be the beginning of something more. A society, however, requires the intention of stable order, which itself includes the intrinsic good of common action.

25. Maitland, "Moral Personality," 69.

26. On the *genossenschaftliche* character of polity, as a harmony of group-persons, see Otto von Gierke, *Natural Law and the Theory of Society, 1500 to 1800: With a Lecture on the Ideas of Natural Law and Humanity by Ernst Troeltsch*, trans. with an introduction by Ernest Barker (a translation of 5 subsections in vol. 4 of Gierke's *Das deutsche Genossenschaftsrecht*) (Boston: Beacon, 1957).

27. For groups as agents and patients in the moral order, see Nicholas Wolterstorff, *Justice, Rights and Wrongs* (Princeton, NJ: Princeton University Press, 2008).

fail to recognize its common good and its agency as an "$n +1$" person by refusing to give it the proper legal personality or mask. In such cases, we do something more than harm what belongs privately to the individuals; more precisely, we harm what those individuals, as members, hold in common.

Hence John Paul II's use of the term "subjectivity of society." A society is something more than inter-subjectivity. Its inter-subjectivity constitutes a "subject" in its own right.[28] This distinction between mere inter-subjectivity and a society is drawn from ordinary experience. A number of individuals in a shopping mall certainly evince inter-subjectivity without pretending to constitute a society. Regarding this phenomenon, Hobbes speaks of a "mere concourse of the people, without union to any particular design by obligation of one to another, but proceeding only from a similitude of wills and inclinations."[29] Such "concourse," of individual wills or desires, more or less spontaneously converging upon similar objects, is what we might find in the marketplace of a city. It is not harmed, and is quite likely facilitated, when we refuse it the status of a society or group. Spontaneous orders which emerge from inter-subjectivity are not incompatible with a strong ontology of social entities. Economists favor this notion of *catallaxy* or unplanned order for the good reason that it is empirically verifiable and useful for explaining market relations. It is problematical only when used to explain the entirety of social relations.[30]

---

28. John Paul II, *Centesimus Annus*, §13, *AAS* 83, 809–10: "[T]he social nature of man is not completely fulfilled in the State, but is realized in various [intermediary] groups, beginning with the family and including economic, social, political and cultural groups which stem from human nature itself and have their own autonomy. . . . This is what I have called the 'subjectivity' of society which, together with the subjectivity of the individual, was canceled out by 'Real Socialism'." Here he is citing his 1987 encyclical *Sollicitudo Rei Socialis*, §§15, 28, *AAS* 80, 530, 548. Again, he affirms the dignity of two kinds of persons or subjectivities. See also International Theological Commission, *Memory and Reconciliation: The Church and the Faults of the Past*, approved by Prefect Joseph Cardinal Ratzinger (December 1999), 2.1: "The question arises as to why the biblical writers did not feel the need to address requests for forgiveness to present interlocutors for the sins committed by their fathers, given their strong sense of solidarity in good and evil among the generations (one thinks of the notion of 'corporate personality' [*si pensi all'idea della 'personalità corporativa*])."

29. Hobbes, *Leviathan*, II, c. 22. Accomplished more perfectly by animals, for example, by swarms (Hobbes, *De Cive*, 5.5). So, on Hobbesian grounds, we must distinguish (a) peoples united in action, (b) people transitorily touching upon the same object, (c) unified swarms. Only the first needs the *consensus iuris* of the sovereign (*De Cive*, 5.4).

30. In this sphere of spontaneous adjustments and exchanges, we might think of Friedrich Hayek's notion of catallaxy. See Hayek, *The Mirage of Social Justice* (London: Routledge, 1976), 107–9. Nothing in our account of the social ontology of groups denies the existence or importance of catallactic order—an order that ensues upon agents pursuing diverse ends. As Hayek contends, the model of spontaneous, catallactic order pertains especially to a market "through people acting within the rules of the law of property, tort, and

Aristotle famously said that man is naturally a political animal, for men "make common" words, judgments, and deeds.[31] To be sure, not everything can be put in common, for that would be totalitarian. And not everything that is made common can be done so in exactly the same way. Families, voluntary associations, the Church, and the state make different things common in different ways. The Aristotelian-Thomist ontology of unity of order is meant as a point of departure for empirical and moral investigation. It allows us to begin correctly, by not confusing social unity with the unity of a natural organism, a mere compositional unity, or a pattern of inter-subjectivity.

In making things common, societies are to be distinguished not only from what Hobbes called a *concourse* of wills, but also from a more *specific agreement* of wills typical of a partnership. In a partnership, two or more people deliberately and explicitly make a contract with respect to mutually agreeable ends while laying claim to their private shares and yields. Admittedly, this distinction between a partnership and a society is tricky when we examine concrete facts. For one thing, partnerships can become societies, and societies can devolve into mere partnerships—a phenomenon that is familiar to anyone who observes the life of families in an American suburb.[32] Both can be brought into existence through the instrument of a contract. And to make our descriptive ontology all the more complicated, in a commercial society like ours we often speak of societies as partnerships even when we mean something more than that. Moreover, the law is often prepared to treat group-persons rather generically.[33]

---

contract" (109). However, Hayek expands the model to include the broader society in which such market relations take place. He brusquely dismisses the importance of group persons.

31. See Aristotle, *Politics*, trans. Carnes Lord (Chicago: University of Chicago Press, 1984), I, c. 2.

32. Thomas sometimes speaks generically of any kind of unity toward an end, even when the reciprocal actions are only minimally societal, in the sense we've put on that term. *In IV Sent.*, d.27, q. 1, a. l: "A joining denotes a kind of uniting, and so wherever things are united there must be a joining. Now things directed to one purpose are said to be united in their direction thereto [*Ea autem quae ordinantur ad aliquid unum, dicuntur in ordine ad illud adunari*]; thus many men are united in following one military calling or in pursuing one business, in relation to which they are called fellow-soldiers or business partners [*vel socii negotiationis*]." The term *socii* corresponds roughly to what we would call partners or allies. Whenever there is a common end, there will be some kind of "joining" of action. Here, however, Thomas seems to mean by businessmen something akin to what we mean by partners.

33. It is worth considering Frederick Hallis's point:

As we have emphasized on more than one occasion, collectivities do not all require the same treatment. They present an infinite variety in respect of their internal solidarity and the importance of their purposes. It would be idle to maintain that some of these cannot be treated adequately without the conception of

Let us return now to the distinction between a partnership and a society. In mere partnership, the work is traceable to the individual partners but not to the partnership itself.[34] One who supplies Honda with auto parts does not intend to bring into being a society. No corporate personality is aimed at. The reciprocity has no aspect of permanence; it has no united action; indeed, it requires no society whatsoever—except incidentally, perhaps, in the breach of contract, in which case the partners repair to the courts of the political society. "Mere partnership," Yves Simon observes, "does not do anything to put an end to the solitude of the partners."[35] In our example, it is sufficient that one delivers the parts, that Honda assemble the cars, and that various individuals write monthly checks for leasing the equipment. Therefore a partnership corresponds more or less to what used to be called an *universitas rerum*, an organization of things. Each partner contributes and is entitled to yield for his private benefit precisely the parts which belong to him.[36] To be

---

corporate personality. All that we maintain is that in some cases this conception becomes indispensable. Without pretending to draw the exact line in this matter, it is sufficient for the moment to say that the conception of corporate personality is essential in cases where the collectivity in question possesses a certain degree of solidarity and permanence. (Frederick Hallis, *Corporate Personality: A Study in Jurisprudence* [Oxford: Oxford University Press, 1930], 100–101).

34. Yves Simon writes: "In a mere partnership each action is traceable to some partner, e.g., all the work is traceable to the handicraftsman and all the financing to the money-lender, [but] none is traceable to the partnership itself." Simon, *Philosophy of Democratic Government* (Chicago: University of Chicago Press, 1951), 64.

35. Simon, *Philosophy of Democratic Government*, 64.

36. Pius XII said that it would be wrong to think "that every particular enterprise" is a genuine "society of persons." *Speech to UNIAPAC*, May 7, 1949, *AAS* 41, 285. He seemed to have in mind what we have called *partnerships*, which remain strictly at the level of commutative justice. Each part contributes and extracts its private portion of the whole. There is no intrinsic common good distinctive of a society or a communion of persons. Pius was concerned that strict commutative justice, such as workers contracting a just wage, is not always the same as a just distribution within a genuine social whole. The just wage in commutation is sacrificed to a cost-benefit calculus of distribution even though there is no proper whole as a context for the distribution. The justice of partnerships in modern "enterprises" is a very tricky problem for just this reason. Does this partnership, which undoubtedly comes under the justice of commutation, also contain aspects of society (beyond mere inter-subjectivity)? Pius XII reckoned that the business enterprise should be organized not only by the instrumental good of efficiency, but "also and above all by giving it the value of a true community" (*Speech to ACLI*, March 11, 1945, *AAS* 37, 71). The problem of how to characterize the limited partnerships, or *sociétés anonymes*, goes back to the Leonine era. The various philosophies and policies of what was called "corporativism" had the ideal of transforming limited companies into the "moral persons" of true societies or associations. For example, the very influential Fribourg Union, which consisted of an international group of Catholic social thinkers, proposed in 1891 that those who invest in an enterprise as

sure, there can be no such organization without real persons doing their part; the essential point is that it is not the persons but rather the things which are collected.

In the order of justice, we harm a partnership when we prevent the partners from contributing and extracting what is privately their own. It depends principally on what has been called "commutative" justice. In a society, on the other hand (what the canonists call a *universitas personarum*), the individuals are not parts or partners so much as members who enjoy the common order in the manner of "usufructuaries"; each is entitled to enjoy what is

---

anonymous partners ought to receive a reasonable return on their investment after a few years, at which time the company should pass into hands of the members of an organic association. This ideal inevitably ran into problems with the scale and complexity of modern corporations. For a thorough study of the *régime corporatif* developed by the Fribourg Union, and its interaction with the evolution of Catholic social doctrine in the late nineteenth century, see Normand Joseph Paulhus, "The Theological and Political Ideals of the Fribourg Union" (PhD diss., Boston College, 1983).

Pius XI taught that the economy is part of a complex unity of order which includes various kinds of partnerships and societies. But he certainly emphasized the crucial role of self-governing societies; see Pius XI, Encyclical Letter *Quadragesimo Anno*, §83, *AAS* 23, 204:

> But complete cure will not come until this opposition has been abolished and well-ordered members of the social body [*socialis corporis*]—Industries and Professions—are constituted in which men may have their place, not according to the position each has in the labor market but according to the respective social functions which each performs. For under nature's guidance it comes to pass that just as those who are joined together by nearness of habitation establish towns, so those who follow the same industry or profession—whether in the economic or other field [*sive oeconomica est sive alterius generis*]—form guilds or associations [*collegia seu corpora*], so that many are wont to consider these self-governing organizations [*haec consortia iure proprio utentia a multis*], if not essential, at least natural to civil society [*sin minus essentialia societati civili, at saltem naturalia dici consueverint*].

(Note that in the next paragraph [p. 205] Pius goes on to expound Thomas's notion of unity of order in which the order itself counts as the form of unity.) In *Centesimus Annus*, John Paul II appears to take a slightly different approach. Rather than attempting to distinguish which enterprises are societies or mere partnerships, he emphasizes the nature of human action, and how it will naturally expand into various relations of solidarity; *Centesimus Annus*, §43, *AAS* 83, 847: "By means of his work a person commits himself, not only for his own sake but also for others and with others. Each person collaborates in the work of others and for their good. One works in order to provide for the needs of one's family, one's community, one's nation, and ultimately all humanity. Moreover, a person collaborates in the work of his fellow employees, as well as in the work of suppliers and in the customers' use of goods, in a progressively expanding chain of solidarity [*instar coniunctionis continuae, quae gradatim se extendit*]."

common, but not as his or her private part.[37] Importantly, a common good is not opposed to the individual good, but rather to the private good. A partnership is not opposed to private good—indeed, the whole point is to organize private goods (pooling resources) to enhance the private yield. There is nothing inherently suspect about partnerships; in fact, they are as ancient as society itself. But they should not be confused with societies.

Again, let us take the example of a queue in front of a credit union: the individuals are *parts* of the queue, *partners* in the credit union, and perhaps *members* of St. Rita's parish. It is only the latter for which we use the word "society" in something more than a metaphorical sense.

A society does not just aim at a common objective, but intends to have it brought about by united action. Think, for example, of a family, a faculty, a crew-team, or an orchestra. In each case, the reason for action includes the good of common action. Achievement of a mutually agreeable result is not enough. To be sure, an orchestra aims to produce the music, just as a crew-team aims to win the race; for their part, spouses aim to raise children and to send them into a wider world of societies. Yet, for each of these groups, their respective corporate unity is one of *reasons for action*. In the case of a society, unity is an intransitive good—ordinarily, it survives the failure of the crew team to win the race, the failure of a marriage to produce children, or the failure of a polity to negotiate a treaty with another state. Partnerships usually do *not* survive failure of the partners to secure the mutually agreeable ends for which the arrangement was constructed.

In sum, we will find human sociability manifesting itself in a variety of ways: spontaneous inter-subjectivity, deliberate partnerships, and in authentic

---

37. Usufruct, or the right of enjoyment or participation. This important concept is traced out by Heinrich Rommen, *The State in Catholic Thought: A Treatise in Political Philosophy*, 2nd English ed., introduction by Russell Hittinger (Leesburg, VA: Alethes Press, 2008), 139. Every societal common good is usufructory inasmuch as the good of the common order cannot be devolved into private hands or dominion. The issue has surfaced especially in marriage. Leo XIII argues that God "so decreed that man should exercise a sort of royal dominion over beasts and cattle and fish and fowl, but never that men should exercise a like dominion over their fellow men." Encyclical Letter *In Plurimus* (May 5, 1888), *Leonis XIII P.M. Acta (Acta Leonis)*, vol. 8, 171f. The human agent does not stand either to his own body or to the body of another as master to instrument. Once dominion is transferred to the human body, the human person encounters the human world as Adam did the animals (Leo XIII, Encyclical Letter *Sapientia Christianae* [January 10, 1890], §12, *Acta Leonis* 10, 18). Therefore the conjugal union of husband and wife involves differentiation of function (like any unity of order) but never dominion. Its form consists of an order of unity rather than dominion in property. See Leo XIII, Encyclical Letter *Arcanum Divinae* (February 10, 1880), §7, *Acta Leonis* 2, 13f; and Pius XI, Encyclical Letter *Casti Connubii* (December 31, 1930), §84; *AAS* 22, 572f.

societies which have an intrinsic common good. Nevertheless, the order of a society is something more perfect, for it not only has greater unity and durability, but most importantly it has a common good that is intrinsically valuable to each of its members. Thus Cajetan's dictum: *Mihi sed non propter me*—"for me, but not for my sake." As the word "perfection" implies, something is brought to completion. In the case of a society, we can call it solidarity, friendship, or being rightly ordered to one's neighbor. Once we consider a common good, the moral imperative of being rightly ordered to one's neighbor takes on a new note. For we must take into account not merely just exchange or just distributions, but also consider human actions insofar as they adequately contribute to, and participate in, the social common good.

There are three ways to destroy a society. First, by destruction of its members, or its matter. Second, by disintegration of the aim to achieve common ends through united action. Third, by destroying the instrument of authority that coordinates the common action. Partnerships, on the other hand, are destroyed either by destruction of their parts or by the obsolescence of the extrinsic end of the partnership (the yield, as it were). Both can be destroyed by injustice. But the kind of justice that applies to the one is not exactly the kind of justice that applies to the latter. Later, we will introduce the concept "social justice," which pertains to the common good—to the order itself commonly participated and enjoyed by members of a society.

Summary

Societies are unities the order of which cannot be reduced either to substantial unity or to a unity of mere aggregation.

- Societies are constituted not only according to common ends, but also by a shared structure or intrinsic common good. The word "common" is opposed to "private," but certainly not to "individual." Each member shares the common good of order. Nonetheless, what is common cannot be cashed-out and taken as a private share. One who leaves a club, marriage, church, or polity cannot require the common good to be distributed to him or her. This is what marks the difference between a society and a partnership.
- For a social unity of order, the parts are also wholes (individual persons) which retain their own proper operations. Catholic social doctrine has often repeated Thomas's dictum: "Man is not ordained to the body politic, according to all that he is and has."[38] But this

---

38. *ST*, I-II, q. 21, a. 4, ad 3: "Quod homo non ordinatur ad communitatem politicam secundum se totum et secundum omnia sua."

principle holds true of any society. Whatever the dignity of a society, it does not supplant, but rather presupposes, the dignity of the individual person.

- Precisely because every society consists of a diversity of members who retain their own proper operations, human persons can be members of plural societies. Husband and wife are members of a municipality, of a nation, of a church. Children are members of the family and members of a college or a team. Each of these memberships can be referred once again to a wider society at both the level of the state and the international order. Human sociability is not exhausted in a single membership. The chief goal of social justice is the harmonization of these diverse group-persons.

- Therefore the *Catechism of the Catholic Church* teaches: "A *society* is a group of persons bound together organically by a principle of unity that goes beyond each one of them. As an assembly that is at once visible and spiritual, a society endures through time: it gathers up the past and prepares for the future. By means of society, each man is established as an 'heir' and receives certain 'talents' that enrich his identity and whose fruits he must develop. He rightly owes loyalty to the communities of which he is part and respect to those in authority who have charge of the common good" (CCC, §1880).

MODELS OF CIVIL SOCIETY

The diverse set of non-governmental associations called "civil society" includes economic corporations, trusts, schools and faculties, charitable organizations and foundations (both religious and secular), the press, clubs, churches, sodalities, and labor unions. In a free society, these groups will possess juridical personality, their appropriate legal masks. That there be a civil society distinct from the formal organs of the state, and that civil society be recognized at public law, are uncontroversial propositions today. Since the seventeenth century, however, we have inherited quite different understandings of the nature of civil society and the ontology of group-persons upon which it would seem to depend. I will call one the devolution model and the other the subsidiarity model.

Devolution Model: Concessions and Fictions

When we think of modernity we think of the Enlightenment, of the sovereignty of reason, and of ideologies of liberty; we think especially of its technologies. But its greatest and most sustained work was the state. Scholars debate exactly what makes a polity a modern "state," but some criteria will appear on every list: such as territorial homogeneity, monopolies over lethal force, education, police, taxation, and, of course, *sovereignty as indivisible, perpetual, and inalienable power.*[39]

Beginning in the seventeenth century, one of the most urgent questions was how to reconcile the state's monopoly over public authority and power with the myriad of other groups claiming authority, rights, and liberties according to custom, natural law, and ecclesiastical law. How does state sovereignty (which recognizes the state as the pre-eminent, if not the exclusive group-person) comport with what Maitland called the "right-and-duty bearing" unities that we are calling civil society?[40]

Thomas Hobbes (1588–1679) provided an early, and very clear, model for understanding the relationship between groups and the sovereign state. It has been called the "concession" theory. The term concession is traced to the Edict of Gaius in the *Digest of Justinian* 3.4.1, where *collegia* or other social bodies are conceded "on the pattern of the state."[41]

In the *Leviathan*, Hobbes contends that a "person is he whose words or actions are considered either as his own, or as representing the words or actions of another man, or of any other thing to whom they are attributed, whether truly or by fiction."[42] In the natural as well as in the legal world, there are three kinds of "person": (1) natural, individual persons who speak and act for themselves; (2) artificial persons who represent the speech and actions of others; and (3) purely fictional persons, such as bridges, churches, or hospitals. Seeing clearly enough that the state could not count as a natural, individual person, Hobbes concluded that the state is an artificial person, which is to say that the state has a corporate nature by virtue of a multitude being represented. This representative is called the "sovereign."

This division of persons and personations brings us to the crucial issue. Into what category do we place non-governmental entities of this sort? Can they be persons? Hobbes writes: "For power unlimited is absolute sovereignty.

---

39. To mention only a few covered in Christopher Pierson, *The Modern State* (London: Routledge, 1996), 6–34.

40. See Thomas's criticism of Plato's idea that the polity is a homogenous order, *Sententia libri Politicorum*, I.1, §§1–2, 17–18; and his remarks on natural diversity at II.1, §§7–8.

41. *Digest of Justinian*, 3.4.1, at 137. Note the three important verbs in this dictum: *concedere, permittere, confirmare.* The term "concession" is emphasized in the magisterial work of Otto Friedrich von Gierke (1841–1921), who attempted to recover the juristic concept of corporate personality from what he called the "concession" theory. For Gierke, it was Hobbes who gave the most challenging version of it in modern times. See Otto von Gierke, *Natural Law and the Theory of Society, 1500 to 1800.* See also Otto Gierke, *Associations and Law: The Classical and Early Christian Stages,* with an interpretative introduction to Gierke's thought by George Herman (Toronto: University of Toronto Press, 1977).

42. Hobbes, *Leviathan*, I, c. 16.

And the sovereign, in every commonwealth, is the absolute representative of all the subjects; and therefore no other can be representative of any part of them, but so far forth as he shall give leave."[43] For Hobbes, once the sovereign comes into existence, there can be only one legitimate artificial or representing-person. Other group-persons may exist only by the permission or *concession* of the sovereign. At least in passing, it is worth noting that concession theory is not a creation of the modern state, but goes back to Roman law. Nor is there anything inherently wrong with the concession model.[44] So long as the objectives belong to public authority, the state may rightfully outsource the means to the ends. This is true, as well, for corporations other than the state. A university, for example, may make concessions with regard to the production and sale of its logo for the football team.

Here, we must pause to clarify these two legal terms of art, *fiction* and *concession*. The strong version of the fiction-model will hold that there is no group-person of any sort behind the legal mask. John Austin, for instance, described groups as subjects only by "*figment* for sake of brevity of discussion."[45] In philosophy, science, and law it is driven by the premise of methodological individualism—namely, that social unities and relations among members can be reduced to nonsocial properties of members or composites thereof.[46] The

---

43. Hobbes, *Leviathan*, II, c. 22.

44. Aspects of "concession" are well-known in Roman and ecclesiastical law. Associations claiming a share of public authority in the civil or ecclesiastical spheres require permission to so exist. Canon law (CIC 1983), for example, routinely distinguishes between the *moralis personae* of the Catholic Church and the Holy See (Can. 113, §1), which are instituted by divine ordinance, individual persons or *personae physicae* (Can. 113, §2), and a myriad of other *personae iuridicae* which receive a special status by virtue of their useful purposes and their ability to achieve them (Can. 113, §3). Baptized Catholics, for example, enjoy a right to establish and direct associations which serve a charitable or pious purpose, to hold meetings, and to pursue their purposes by common effort (Can. 215). But they cannot claim the title "Catholic" without ecclesiastical concession (Can. 216). Some private associations are merely praised or recommended (Can. 299, §2); or they might be approved when their statutes are reviewed by a competent authority (Can. 299, §3); no association can call itself Catholic without consent of the proper authority (Can. 330, and 312; 803, §3); still others can be regarded as public, acting in the name of the Church, and are said to be "erected" (Can. 301). Canon 116, §1 provides for juridical persons to act in the name of the Church, while §2 provides for an association to act in its own name with ecclesiastical approval. Unfortunately, the Code does not provide a synthetic account of these various *personae*.

45. Lord Coke's famous dictum; *Case of Sutton's Hospital* (1612), 5 Rep. 303; 10 Rep. 32 b: "It is a fiction, a shade, a nonentity, but a reality for legal purposes. A corporation aggregate is only in abstracto—it is invisible, immortal, and rests only in intendment and consideration of the law."

46. The array of contemporary positions on methodological individualism and its alternatives is summarized by Frederick F. Schmitt, "Socializing Metaphysics," in *Socializing*

concession-model, however, refers to societies made legitimate by the law. Concession can remain open to the reality of the group prior to the state's award of jural capacities. Until then, they are regarded either as so unimportant as to receive no notice, or they are regarded as illegitimate. The real group simply moves from being not officially recognized to being publicly capacitated. Both *fiction* and *concession* have been used by the modern state in ways which are prejudicial and harmful to societies other than the state.[47] When these two legal devices are used in tandem, the state will command its lawyers to consider only the state's construction, not the very group that gave rise to the issue in the first place.[48] The state regards and treats all group-persons as outsourced instruments of its own group-personality.

The modern French state began precisely on this note. Consider article 3 of the French *Declaration of the Rights of Man and Citizen* (1789): "The principle of all sovereignty resides essentially in the nation. No body nor individual may exercise any authority which does not proceed directly from the nation."[49] Two years later, the state passed a law against corporations:

> Since the abolition of all kinds of corporations of citizens of the same occupation and profession is one of the fundamental bases of the French Constitution, re-establishment thereof under any pretext or pretence or form whatsoever is forbidden.[50] Citizens of the same occupation or profession . . . may not, when they are together, name either president, secretaries, or trustees, keep accounts, pass decrees of resolutions, or draft regulations concerning their alleged common interests.[51]

Metaphysics: The Nature of Social Reality, ed. F. F. Schmitt (Lanham, MD: Rowman & Littlefield, 2003), 1–37.

47. In 2007, for example, China's State Administration of Religious Affairs announced Order Number 5, a law covering the "Management Measures for the Reincarnation of Living Buddhas in Tibetan Buddhism." The state prohibits Buddhist monks from returning from the dead without government permission. No one outside China can influence the reincarnation process, and only monasteries in China can apply for the concession. See *Harper's Magazine*, March 2008, 20.

48. On the problem of conflating concession and fiction, see Janet McLean, "Personality and Public Law Doctrine," *University of Toronto Law Journal* 49, no. 1 (1999): 129–30.

49. Document 17, in *A Documentary Survey of the French Revolution*, by John Hall Stewart (New York: Macmillan, 1951), 114.

50. Chapelier Law, 14 June 1791, §1; Document 28, in Stewart, *Documentary Survey*, 165.

51. Chapelier Law, 14 June 1791, §2. Indeed, more than a century later, the Third Republic enacted such legislation; French Law of Associations, title III, §13 (1 July 1901): "No religious congregation may be formed without an authorization given by law that determines the conditions of its exercise. . . . The dissolution of a congregation or the closing of any establishment may be declared by a cabinet decree." In his fine study of the

The multi-faceted order of estates, corporations, guilds, clubs—each with its distinctive legal bonds and signs and costumes—is swept aside as alien to the unity of the body politic.

In modern times, most revolutionary regimes will attempt to forbid subsidiary societies. History testifies that even the most brutally centralizing regimes eventually will retreat from the totalitarian ideal. They will make concessions. Why should the sovereign ever grant a concession? For our purposes today we might think of *devolution*, which often has a very strong resemblance to the older concession model. Imagine a homogeneous power formally

---

Revolution's rejection of "the society of orders and *corps*, or corporations," Pierre Rosanvallon emphasizes that Isaac-René-Guy Le Chapelier and his colleagues meant by *régime corporatif* more than the specifically economic institutions. They meant a regime consisting of plural societies, each with its own distinctive legal bonds, usually with its own distinctive signs and costumes, together making up the whole of the body politic: estates, religious corporations (clerical and religious congregations), guilds, clubs, municipalities, and so forth. If property-owning corporations exist, said Jacques-Guillaume Thouret, they differ from natural individuals who possess innate faculties and rights. "Corporations are merely instruments fabricated by the law for the greatest possible good." They are trustees of a public service mission located in the state. Rosanvallon notes: "But the essential question was philosophical: corporate ownership inherently raised the prospect of a rival to public authority. The corporations in a sense threatened the states claim to a 'monopoly on perpetuity,' a perpetuity being in the order of temporality the equivalent of generality in the order of social forms." Pierre Rosanvallon, *The Demands of Liberty: Civil Society in France Since The Revolution*, trans. Arthur Goldhammer (Cambridge, MA: Harvard University Press, 2007), 28.

In this connection, we should bear in mind the original meaning of "solidarity." In France, *solidaires* were those bound together in collective responsibility, according to the semi-autonomous societies called *communautés*. The idea of *solidarité* was drawn remotely from the legal expression *in solidum*, which, in Roman law, was the status of responsibility for another person's debts. Usually, the legal status of *solidaires* presupposed membership in a society (nation, family, etc.) that persists over time and is not exhausted in a single exchange nor characterized as a limited liability partnership. The Napoleonic Code (1804) expressly forbade the presumption of *solidarité* (art. 1202) in order to underscore the ontology of natural persons bound together chiefly, or only, in the state, and secondarily by contracts engaged by individuals. Thus, one becomes a *solidaire* only contractually (arts. 395–96, 1033, 1197–1216, 1442, 1887, 2002). With the revolutions which followed in the wake of the Napoleonic wars, and with the onset of the industrial revolution, the term "solidarity" began to acquire the plethora of meanings it has today: solidarity of workers, political parties, nations, churches, and humanity in general. This was due to the widespread alarm at the disintegration of society and a renewed interest in intermediate associations. The historical evolution of the term is tracked within the Jewish community by Lisa Moses Leff, "Jewish Solidarity in Nineteenth-Century France: The Evolution of a Concept," *The Journal of Modern History* 74, no. 1 (2002), 33–61. The more global history is provided by Steinar Stjernø in *Solidarity in Europe: The History of an Idea* (Cambridge: Cambridge University Press, 2004).

belonging to the state. But the state decides to parcel-out aspects of this power from the top-down, or from the center to the periphery. While the state does not deny its own plenitude of power or sovereignty, it does recognize the contingent fact that it cannot efficiently reach all of the objects within its formal power. Accordingly, the state will out-source power, by way of a quasi-delegation, to other groups for the purpose of efficiently creating and distributing certain goods and services: education, charitable relief of the poor, and the orderly transfer of property or investment, to mention only a few. The complexity and scale of modern states practically guarantee that the sovereign must make concessions. It must, in this sense, *learn to devolve*.[52] While despotic regimes will tend to be stingy, liberal regimes will tend to be generous in giving concessions. England was the model for a liberal regime, jealous of its sovereignty, but ever ready to outsource certain functions to corporations and to unincorporated groups and to trusts, even to pirates acting as auxiliaries of the royal navy.

The golden-age of concession theory was the eighteenth and nineteenth centuries because it was during this time that states were created according to the modern idea of sovereignty. Yet this model is quite durable, never entirely disappearing, even in our time. Take, for example, the debates in Europe and the United States over the issue of marriage. What kind of juridic person is a marriage? In 1992, the Hawaiian Supreme Court defined marriage as "a partnership to which both parties bring their financial resources as well as their individual energies and efforts."[53] This point was reiterated in the controversial 2003 decision of the Massachusetts Supreme Court, which prohibited the legislature from giving legal title of marriage only to one man and one woman. Let's put to one side the moral issue of whether marriage ought to be exclusively heterosexual. This puts the cart before the horse. First, we want to know whether there are group-persons distinct from partnerships, and second, what reason the state has to recognize them.

---

52. The word "devolution" is commonly used in a generic sense, to speak of decentralization. I prefer the standard eighteenth-century sense of the term, as used by Edward Gibbon in *The Decline and Fall of the Roman Empire*, vol. 3, XXXI.1: "The character of the civil and military officers, on whom Rufinus had *devolved* the government of Greece, confirmed the public suspicion, that he had betrayed the ancient seat of freedom and learning to the Gothic invader." Or speaking of Maxentius: "Whilst he passed his indolent life either within the walls of his palace, or in the neighboring gardens of Sallust, he was repeatedly heard to declare, that he alone was emperor, and that the other princes were no more than his lieutenants, on whom he had devolved the defence of the frontier provinces, that he might enjoy without interruption the elegant luxury of the capital" (vol. I, XIV). Hence governments, powers, treasuries are said to *devolve*.

53. Baehr v. Lewin, 852 P. 2d 44, 58 (citing Gussin v. Gussin 73 Hawaii 470, 483, 836 P. 2nd 484, 491) (1992).

We begin by considering the nature of civil marriage itself. Simply put, the government creates civil marriage. . . . *Civil marriage is created and regulated through exercise of the police power.* . . . Civil marriage anchors an ordered society by encouraging stable relationships over transient ones. It is central to the way the Commonwealth identifies individuals, provides for the orderly distribution of property, ensures that children and adults are cared for and supported whenever possible from private rather than public funds, and tracks important epidemiological and demographic data.[54]

We read that the state does not merely regulate, but creates marriage through the exercise of the police power. What aspects of good order move the state to allow married people to be a right-and-duty unity? The Court mentions economic reasons (property), sociological reasons (stable relationships), health reasons (care for the old or indigent), and scientific reasons (collection of epidemiological data). The state breathes into the dust of sexual relationships and private aspirations to intimacy, and creates a "person" at law. This person, then, becomes the site or occasion for bringing about more efficiently certain results which are in the interest of the state.[55] All that remained for the Massachusetts Court to do was to judge that one sex or two sexes are immaterial to the state's interest in having other agents procure the publicly desirable results, and therefore not to favor one arrangement over the other. The Massachusetts decision is a pure example of concession theory. The court leaves untouched the question whether this juridic person is a society or a partnership. The public efficiencies falling within the purview of the positive law could be attached to either a partnership or a society.[56] Indeed, the law

---

54. Goodridge v. Dept. of Public Health, 440 Mass. 309 (2003).

55. Compare to Justice Joseph Story, a jurist from Massachusetts and Chief Justice of the Supreme Court. Joseph Story, *Commentaries on the Conflict of Laws* (Boston, 1834), 100: "[Marriage] may exist between two individuals of different sexes, although no third person existed in the world, as happened in the case of the common ancestors of mankind. It is the parent and not the child of society."

56. The 1801 draft of the French *Code Civil* proposed that "what marriage in itself is was previously unknown, and it is only in recent times that men have acquired precise ideas on marriage." An important response to the draft was undertaken by Viscount Louis de Bonald (1754–1840). Published in 1801 under the title *On Divorce*, this little philosophical and legal brief contributed to the suppression of the law of divorce in 1816, until the Third Republic reinstituted it in 1884. Louis de Bonald, *Du Divorce*, considéré au XIXe siècle, 3rd ed. (Paris: Le Clère, 1818; original edition 1801); translated as *On Divorce*, ed. and trans. Nicholas Davidson (New Brunswick, NJ: Transaction Publishers, 1992). Since social unity is a minimal requirement for law to gain any footing in the question of marriage, Bonald reasons that the issue pivots on "the unity of union and the multiplicity of unions" (*On Divorce*, 63). There are three options. *First*, union of the sexes with

of no-fault divorce guarantees in practice, if not in theory, that a marriage is a partnership.

Devolution Model. Intermediate Powers

While the concession model is by no means dead, its star has been in eclipse during the second part of the twentieth century. Especially after the Second World War, there has been interest in reviving another strand of liberalism on the issue of civil society—one that emerged in the eighteenth and nineteenth centuries in reaction to state absolutism. In France, we think of Montesquieu and Tocqueville—or perhaps James Madison in the United States. Émile Durkheim observed: "If that collective force, the State, is to be the liberator of the individual, it has itself need of some counter balance; it must be restrained by other collective forces, that is, by . . . secondary groups [for] it is out of this conflict of social forces that individual liberties are born."[57]

We may call it the power-checking model, because it estimates the value of groups other than the state chiefly in terms of a check upon untrammeled power. Montesquieu wrote: "Political liberty is found only in moderate governments. . . . It is present only when power is not abused, but it has eternally

---

the intention *not* to form a society, which even the law recognizes as promiscuity rather than marriage. *Second*, union of the sexes *without* an intention to form a society which is concubinage. *Third*, union of the sexes *with* a commitment to form a society. In effect, Bonald outlines the three categories which we have used in this paper: (1) sexual union as a concourse of wills, (2) sexual union as partnership, (3) sexual union constituted in a society.

57. Émile Durkheim, *Professional Ethics and Civic Morals* (New York: Free Press, 1958), 62–63. Hutchins, 6n2. Durkheim's work is a complicated subject. On the one hand, no one labored more strenuously in the nineteenth century to establish the objective reality of *faits sociaux* and the sui generis status of social facts. He vigorously rejected any methodology that would reduce social to non-social facts. Even so, he viewed society in the distinctively modern way of powers, forces, and their equilibrium. Thus the idea *corps intermediaries* was developed in view of the need to check the power of the state, even substituting for the family which, in modern times, had no such clout. Generally, he tended toward a kind of substantialism. Some authors, however, have attempted to put him into an Aristotelian tradition. For his distinction between mechanical (primitive) and organic (modern) solidarity suggested that organic solidarity is just what Aristotle and Thomas meant by a unity of order. The title page of his *Division of Labor* cites Aristotle's *Politics* (I, 1261a24) on the point that the real unity of the polis must include a diversity of elements. While this might indicate the intrinsic value of hierarchical order of social solidarities nested within others, it also comports with the idea of powers limiting other powers. On Durkheim's penchant for describing collective forces along the lines of thermodynamics and electricity, its seeming conflict with organic metaphors, and Durkheim's quest to win a scientific recognition of sociology, see Steven Lukes, *Émile Durkheim: His Life and Work* (New York: Penguin Books, 1973), 215ff.

been observed that any man who has power is led to abuse it; he continues until he finds limits. . . . So that one cannot abuse power, power must check power by the arrangement of things."[58] Hence the famous idea of civil society as "intermediate powers." What interested Montesquieu was not the specifically social landscape, or the *milieu intérieur*, of corporate persons (an ontology that perhaps he took for granted) so much as the general distribution of "powers." Civil society is useful as an arrangement that checks abuse of power and thereby inclines a political society to moderation.

This line of thought concedes to the state its monopoly over public things. Importantly, it differs from the concession model with regard to the end to be achieved. Whereas the concession model seeks to protect and maintain state sovereignty by outsourcing its power to other groups, the power-checking model endeavors to shrink its scope—at least materially and politically. Let the state be sovereign in the "modern" sense of the term; but let this sovereignty be materially diminished by intermediate groups. These groups are not estates in the old sense of the term, for they have no representative power or authority; they do not constitute political bodies. Rather, the intermediate powers constitute a vast sphere of *private* judgments, choices, and actions by individuals and associations. Given that the state is no longer limited from above, it follows that its power is limited either from within (for example, the division of powers), or from below.

The power-checking model treats devolution as *privatization*. It, too, wants the state to devolve for reasons of efficiency, but with a value-added purpose. For example, private schools are useful not only because they efficiently allocate educational resources, but also because they check the untrammeled state power over education. This double efficiency has always proved essential to the liberal social theory. Like the two faces of Janus, it looks in one direction toward private competition, organization, and efficient distribution of resources, and it looks in the other direction toward the negative liberty accruing from private initiative. The state is put in the position of having to justify, on cost-benefit grounds, why the private sphere should not prevail whenever there is a concurrent jurisdiction or interest in a common thing: fisheries, education, capital investment, etc.

In both the United States and Europe, this model is often associated (more or less explicitly) with "subsidiarity."[59] In the next section, I will explain

---

58. Montesquieu, *The Spirit of the Laws*, trans. Anne M. Cohler, Basia Carolyn Miller, Harold Samuel Stone (Cambridge: Cambridge University Press, 1989), 11.4, p. 155.

59. Whether the European Community treaties (and amendments) mean by subsidiarity something more than a rule of social efficiency is difficult to determine because the original language, informed by Catholic social thought (mostly through the German thinkers) was transported to a more lawyerly emphasis on constitutional allocation of powers. The

why we should resist the equation. But for now I call attention to the fact that the intermediate powers analysis is not principally interested in the sociality of diverse group-persons. It focuses rather upon efficiency, which is the common coin of public policy and discourse. It matters little whether the efficiencies have this or that social form. The key insight is that the state be limited by the private sphere. If we ask why the state should be so limited, the answer will be that it increases liberty and that such an arrangement is more efficient.

Along these lines, perhaps the most astute and powerful argument for civil society was made by Ernest Gellner in *Conditions of Liberty: Civil Society and its Rivals*, published in 1994. Gellner points out that "civil society" is ambiguous. From one point of view, civil society can mean the "social residue left when the state is subtracted."[60] Consisting of strong bonds of solidarity in families, tribes, and religious institutions, this "residue" can prove to be very potent. The polycentric nature of traditional societies would be very effective if we were only interested in checking the power of the modern state. In a modern, democratic culture, however, civil society must not only check state power, but must also liberate the individual from the suffocating obligations of common faith and kinship. The "miracle of civil society" requires loose associations which protect individual liberty from the solidaric bonds of the state and traditional communities. Once the strong solidarities from above and below are weakened, we enjoy the kind of society suitable to what he calls the "modular man."

> The [western conception of civil society] has not committed itself either to a set of prescribed roles and relations, or to a set of practices. The same goes for knowledge: conviction can change, without any stigma of apostasy. Yet these highly specific, unsanctified, instrumental, revocable links or bonds are effective. The associations of modular man can be effective without being rigid.[61]

Gellner's work is important because he delineates the full implications of the "counterweight" theory of civil society: *devolution from above and disincorporation from below*. His sociology is at once descriptive and normative—at least for us, who live in a market culture, and who prize the associational life of "modular man." That human nature is sociable and that sociability is

---

difference between the two is intelligently surveyed by Christoph Henkel, "The Allocation of Powers in the European Union: A Closer Look at the Principle of Subsidiary," *Berkeley Journal of International Law* 20 (2002): 359–86.

60. Ernest Gellner, *Conditions of Liberty: Civil Society and its Rivals* (New York: The Penguin Press, 1994), 212.

61. Gellner, *Conditions of Liberty*, 100.

capable of strong solidarities from above and from below are not in question. The question, rather, is whether such strong solidarities are useful and agreeable to the democratic culture. Gellner has emphasized what we have called partnerships rather than a plurality of societies possessing intrinsic common goods. I will now go on to argue that this position, though perhaps descriptively accurate of contemporary society, should not be confused with subsidiarity.

Summary

- The concession-model regards group-persons other than the state as legitimate only insofar as they receive the state's concession or imprimatur. Though it enjoys a monopoly on group-personhood, the state can outsource its power to other groups, depending upon the state's estimation of the public utilities of so doing. This model, therefore, should be called devolution.
- The fiction-model reduces societies to their non-social properties. Whereas the concession-model insists that the group is illegitimate until it receives the legal mask (*persona*), the fiction-model holds that there is nothing but the legal mask. In modern states, these two models often work in tandem.
- The model of intermediate powers holds that the existence of group persons other than the state is useful: (1) for checking the power of the state, (2) for distributing more efficiently certain goods and services, and (3) for checking the power of strong solidarities from below, which tend to restrict individual liberties.[62] It, too, tends to understand subsidiarity as devolution.

THE SUBSIDIARITY MODEL IN CATHOLIC THOUGHT

The existence of social persons distinct in dignity, reducible neither to the individual nor the state, stands at the outset of Catholic social doctrine. As well it should, for the Church claimed to be a *persona moralis* instituted by Christ. Moreover, nested within this trans-jurisdictional ecclesial society were a host of subsidiary societies: families, religious orders and congregations, sodalities, colleges, associations of pilgrims, warrior orders, and a myriad of

---

62. We do not suggest that efficiency is of no importance. The first question, however, is efficient "to whom"? Every genuine society, which, as we have emphasized, has both an intrinsic common good (the order) and an extrinsic common good (the victory of army, to use Aristotle's example), will take interest in the efficiencies touching upon the division of labor and the extrinsic results. Indeed, deliberate mutations of societies often occur because of new estimations of efficiency.

other associations, like guilds, which overlapped with municipal and temporal societies. Even into the eighteenth century, the Catholic Church was an extraordinarily diversified and interdependent social order.

Catholic sovereigns were deemed to be junior apostles, receiving privileges to govern much of the temporal estates and life within their realms. The French Revolution's *Civil Constitution of the Clergy* (1790) unilaterally overturned the common law of political Christendom. Church governance was handed over *not* to the mischievous but familiar Catholic ruling families, but instead was given to the nation. The clergy became civil servants elected by democratic vote. This model spread to the former colonies, particularly in Latin America. Rights once belonging to the Church had been transferred to kings, and now to the nation. The state was no longer governed by anointed laity but by a new doctrine of *laicism*.

Once the modern states asserted their monopoly on group personhood, they were bound to collide with the Church. In Europe and in her former colonies, the Catholic Church not only lost its political privilege in the new nation-states. The Church, along with her religious orders, schools, seminaries, and sodalities, was stripped of juridic personality—except such as remained by concession of the states. A society of monks, for example, could not hold themselves out to the rest of society as monks, but rather as makers of pottery. The monastic society was given the status of a business partnership—which is not only an act of concession but also of fiction. Article 27 of the 1917 Mexican constitution was more severe: "The law recognizes no juridical personality in the religious institutions known as churches."

To be sure, the principles of social order were ancient. But the post-1789 Church-state crisis is what gave the Church real incentive to develop a body of social doctrine. On this score it is important to understand that the social doctrine did not begin with the industrial revolution and the problems of benighted and dislocated workers. It began with the need to defend the institutions of the Church. Catholic social doctrine, accordingly, emerged in defense of two propositions: first, that the state does not enjoy a monopoly over group-personhood; second, that societies other than the state not only possess real dignity as rights-and-duties bearing unities, but that they also enjoy modes of authority proper to their own society.

In his famous encyclical *Rerum Novarum* (1891), Pope Leo XIII defended the right of workers to form associations. The following passage touches the nerve of the issue:

> Private societies, then, although they exist within the body politic, and are severally part of the commonwealth, cannot nevertheless be absolutely, and as such, prohibited by public authority. For, to enter into a "society" of this kind is the natural right of man; and the *civitas* has for its office to protect natural rights, not to destroy them; and, if it

forbid its citizens to form associations, it contradicts the very principle of its own existence, for both they and it exist in virtue of the like principle, namely, the natural tendency of man to dwell in society. There are occasions, doubtless, when it is fitting that the law should intervene to prevent certain associations, as when men join together for purposes which are evidently bad, unlawful, or dangerous to the *respublica*. In such cases, public authority may justly forbid the formation of such associations, and may dissolve them if they already exist. But every precaution should be taken not to violate the rights of individuals and not to impose unreasonable regulations under pretense of public benefit. . . . The State should watch over these societies of citizens banded together in accordance with their rights, but it should not thrust itself into their peculiar concerns and their organization, for things move and live by the spirit inspiring them, and may be killed by the rough grasp of a hand from without.[63]

According to Leo, such societies spring from the same source as the state, the "tendency of man to dwell in society." Society does not devolve from the state or come into existence because of the state's need to outsource powers for socially useful ends. Notice Leo's swipe at the "public benefit" argument, which recalls the problem of concession theory. The key point is that, whatever the differences obtaining among political union, ecclesiastical union, familial union, and the many kinds of voluntary unions about which Leo speaks in this passage, they have something in common: the natural social tendency of the human person. True enough, there are qualitative differences between a state, a church, and a family. Yet no one of these societies uniquely instantiates the genus "social." The state, for example, does not represent the genus "social" under which are arrayed the Church or family as "species." This also holds in the opposite direction. The state is not a species of the Church's solidarity, although the state's unique order may be assisted and inspired by the Church's union.

Every social formation embodies diversity (*pluritas et inaequalitas*), for such is necessary for a unity of order in which the members each enjoy their

---

63. Leo XIII, Encyclical Letter *Rerum Novarum* (May 15, 1891), §§51–53, 55, *Acta Leonis* 11, 135–37. Leo here defends the rights of private associations on the basis of Thomas's defense of mendicant poverty in *Contra impugnantes*, written in 1256. In Thomas's works, every analogous use of the word *societas* is mirrored by uses of the word *communicatio: communicatio oeconomica, communicatio spiritualis, communicatio civilis,* and so forth. The word *communicatio* simply means making something common, one rational agent participating in the life of another. Society, for Thomas, is not a thing, but a communication. He quotes Augustine's *De doctrina christiana*: "Everything that is not lessened by being imparted, is not, if it be possessed without being communicated, possessed as it ought to be possessed." *Contra impugnantes,* 1.4, §14, A83, 1265–70.

own operations. We can think of Durkheim's distinction between (1) a "mechanical" expression of the *conscience collective,* in which the group con-science is co-extensive with, and coincides at all points with, the individual's, and (2) an "organic" solidarity in which individuals are grouped by their dif-ferent activities or functions. The latter kind of solidarity approximates a "unity of order." Yet the same principle holds when we ask what kind of order obtains among qualitatively different societies. This is preeminently a political question. How does the state function as a union of social unions without reducing soci-ety to "powers" which differ only quantitatively? It was precisely on this prob-lem that the "intermediate powers" analysis of the French and the American thinkers stumbled. Social diversity was reduced to thermodynamics of power. Leo puts the issue differently. Even if the state has the special and very august function of ordering its members to a common good, that common good, in turn, must protect the common goods of diverse societies within it.

Leo introduces another issue. He writes: "In order that an association may be carried on with unity of purpose and harmony of action, its adminis-tration and government should be firm and wise. All such societies, being free to exist, have the further right to adopt such rules and organization as may best conduce to the attainment of their respective objects."[64] Wherever a soci-ety is marked by common ends and unity (or harmony) of action, there must be authority. Leo's point is that the state will do an injustice if it allows societies to exist, but denies their capacity for self-government. Where there is no right to group authority, common action will depend entirely on spontaneous una-nimity. This is hardly possible in a family, much less in an economic corpora-tion, a university faculty, a church, or even a sports team. Hence, a state that recognizes the existence of civil society, but not the diverse modes of authority appropriate to those societies, reduces civil society to mere partnerships. Recall our earlier point that partnerships have no inherent need of authority, except accidentally, when breach of contract requires the ministry of the courts.

Now, at last, we can address the principle of subsidiarity and distinguish it from devolution. The term was coined by the nineteenth-century Italian Jesuit Luigi Taparelli. For Taparelli and the tradition of Catholic social doc-trine, subsidiarity is not a free-standing concept. As a principle regulating and coordinating a plurality of group-persons, subsidiarity presupposes a plurality of such persons, each having distinct common ends, kinds of united action, and modes of authority. It is not, therefore, a question of whether there shall be group-persons, or whether they are efficient or immediately useful to the state. Rather, the question is how these groups stand to one another and to

---

64. Leo XIII, *Rerum Novarum,* §56.

the state. In its negative formulation, subsidiarity demands that when assistance (*subsidium*) is given, it be done in such a way that the sociality proper to the group (family, school, corporation, etc.) is not subverted. Taparelli used the term *ipotattico*, taken from the Greek *hypotaxis*: the rules governing the order of clauses within a sentence. Rendered in Latin as *sub sedeo*, subsidiarity evokes the concept not only of subordinate clauses in a sentence, but also of auxiliary troops in the Roman legion which "sat below," ready and duty-bound to render service.

Hence it describes the right (*dritto ipotattico*) of social groups, each enjoying its own proper mode of action. While sometimes identified with the word *subsidium* (help, assistance), the point of subsidiarity is a normative structure of plural social forms, not necessarily a trickling down of power or aid.[65] Taparelli used the expression *associazione ipotattica* to emphasize the interdependence of societies, each maintaining its own unity (*conservare la propria unità*) without prejudice to the whole.[66]

On this view, subsidiarity cannot be construed as judgments, decisions, actions at the "lowest level." The notion of a "lowest" level perverts the concept of subsidiarity. The better term is *proper* level. The term "proper" is taken from the Latin word *proprium*, denoting what belongs to, or what is possessed by, a thing or person. On the modern view of the state, there are only two persons having *propria*: the artificial person of the state, and natural, individual persons. The "lowest" level can only mean the individual, or, perhaps, partnerships. Subsidiarity, on the other hand, presupposes that there are plural authorities and agents having their "proper" (not necessarily, lowest) duties and rights with regard to the common good—immediately, the common good of the particular society, but also the common good of the body politic. Pius XII noted that "every social activity is for its nature subsidiary; it must serve as a support to the members of the social body and never destroy or absorb them."[67] Just as no society should destroy or absorb the individual person, so too no particular society should destroy the personhood of other societies.

To be sure, subsidiarity is often described and deployed in a defensive sense—as to what the state may *not* do or try to accomplish—but the principle is not so much a theory about state institutions, nor of checks and balances,

---

65. The history and philosophy of subsidiarity are covered with unusual clarity by Thomas C. Behr, "Luigi Taparelli D'Azeglio, S.J. (1793–1862) and the Development of Scholastic Natural-Law Thought as a Science of Society and Politics," *Journal of Markets & Morality* 6, no. 1 (2003): 99–115.

66. Luigi Taparelli D'Azeglio, *Saggio teoretico di dritto naturale appogiato sul fatto*, 8th ed. (Rome, 1949), 685, 694.

67. Pius XII, *La elevatezza e la nobilità* (February 20, 1946), *AAS* 38, 144f.

as it is an account of the pluralism and sociality of society.[68] Once we distinguish subsidiarity from the similar but misleading notions of devolution, it is

---

68. As we pointed out earlier, Thomas taught there are two ways to imitate God: as *bonum universale in essendo* (just as he is good in himself) and *bonum universale in causando* (causing goodness in others) (*ST*, I, q. 103, a. 4). In the order of the operations of secondary causes, creatures are executors of providence (*SCG*, I, c. 22, no. 2–3). The more extensively the creature communicates its own goodness to others, the more perfect its participation (*SCG*, III, c. 24). But this presupposes diversity—*pluritas et inaequalitas* (*SCG*, II, c. 45, no. 4):

> Then, too, a thing approaches to God's likeness the more perfectly as it resembles Him in more things. Now, goodness is in God, and the outpouring of goodness into other things. Hence, the creature approaches more perfectly to God's likeness if it is not only good, but can also act for the good of other things, than if it were good only in itself; that which both shines and casts light is more like the sun than that which only shines. But no creature could act for the benefit of another creature unless plurality and inequality existed in created things. For the agent is distinct from the patient and superior to it. In order that there might be in created things a perfect representation of God, the existence of diverse grades among them was therefore necessary.

Thomas is speaking here *not* of the inequality of freedom or humanity, but rather of diverse talents, grades, and functions (*ST*, I, q. 96, a. 4; and see *In II Sent.*, d. 44, q. 1, a. 3 [*solutio*]). The social Magisterium has repeatedly insisted that a society of any kind presupposes such diversity; see, for example, *Rerum Novarum*, §17, *Acta Leonis* 11, 108:

> It must be first of all recognized that the condition of things inherent in human affairs must be borne with, for it is impossible to reduce civil society to one dead level. Socialists may in that intent do their utmost, but all striving against nature is in vain. There naturally exist among mankind manifold differences of the most important kind [*Sunt enim in hominibus maximae plurimaeque natura dissimilitudines*]; people differ in capacity, skill, health, strength; and unequal fortune is a necessary result of unequal condition. Such inequality is far from being disadvantageous either to individuals or to the community. Social and public life can only be maintained by means of various kinds of capacity for business and the playing of many parts [*ad res gerendas facultate diversisque muneribus vita communis*]; and each man, as a rule, chooses the part which suits his own peculiar domestic condition.

And in Pius XI, Encyclical Letter *Divini Redemptoris* (March 19, 1937), §29, *AAS* 29, 79:

> But God has likewise destined man for civil society according to the dictates of his very nature. In the plan of the Creator, society is a natural means which man can and must use to reach his destined end. Society is for man and not vice versa. This must not be understood in the sense of liberalistic individualism, which subordinates society to the selfish use of the individual; but only in the sense that by means of an organic union with society and by mutual collaboration the attainment of earthly happiness is placed within the reach of all. In a further sense, it is society which affords the opportunities for the development of all the individual

easier to grasp why it was introduced in Catholic circles as an aspect of social justice. For Pius XI, social justice is that kind of order that ensues when each person is capacitated to "exercise his social *munus*," to contribute to the common good according to his proper office and role (function).[69] This may or may not require the giving of aid, the correction of a deficiency, or the removal of a barrier to the performance of social duties, but what it always entails is respect for a pluriform social order in which the various societies are intrinsically valuable as "persons" distinct in dignity. The state may award a certain legal mask. Indeed, this can count as an example of aid or *subsidium* required by commutative or distributive justice. But this should not be confused with the doctrine that societies are constructed by the state as outsourced facets of the state's need to devolve.

Now we are prepared to explain why the eighteenth-century category *doctrina civilis* came in the twentieth century to be called *doctrina socialis*—social doctrine. With the triumph of the modern nation-states, equipped with an exaggerated premise of state sovereignty, it was a given that man is a citizen, but it was not so clear how, or whether, he ought to be a member of other societies—from vocational and trade associations to churches, families, sodalities—even to what could be called nations. We cannot forget that Pius XI began to use the terms "social justice" and "social doctrine" just when the totalitarian regimes had the wind at their backs, and when the free polities had to intervene extensively and deeply in their national economies. Both the totalitarians and the imperatives of the post-1929 economic crisis made precarious the predicate "social."

In his encyclical *Centesimus Annus* (1991), Pope John Paul II weaves together the different strands of these ideas:

---

and social gifts bestowed on human nature. These natural gifts have a value surpassing the immediate interests of the moment, for in society they reflect the divine perfection, which would not be true were man to live alone [*divinamque praeferunt in civili ordinatione perfectionem, quod quidem in singulis hominibus contingere ullo modo nequit*].

In §29 of *Divini Redemptoris*, Pius adds the following sentences. "But on final analysis, even in this latter function, society is made for man, that he may recognize this reflection of God's perfection [*ut hanc divinae perfectionis imaginem*], and refer it in praise and adoration to the Creator. Only man, the human person, and not society in any form, is endowed with reason and a morally free will." A decade later, Jacques Maritain argued that the political "madness" of the twentieth century could be traced to the ideology of "substantialism," the doctrine that the state is a moral person in the proper (substantial) sense of the term. Maritain, *Man and the State* (Chicago: University of Chicago Press, 1951), 14, 16n11.

69. Pius XI, *Divini Redemptoris*, §51, *AAS* 29, 92.

[The] primary responsibility in [social justice] belongs not to the State but to individuals and to the various groups and associations which make up society. . . . In addition to the tasks of harmonizing and guiding development, in exceptional circumstances the State can also exercise a *substitute function.* . . . Such supplementary interventions, which are justified by urgent reasons touching the common good, must be as brief as possible, so as to avoid removing permanently from society and business systems the gifts of service which are properly theirs [*propria munera*]. . . . Here again the principle of subsidiarity must be respected: a community of a higher order should not interfere in the internal life of a community of a lower order, depriving it of the functions which properly belong to it [*propriis officiis*].[70]

We must notice that John Paul II speaks of higher and lower *communities.*[71] This passage helps to illuminate how solidarity and subsidiarity, in Catholic thought, stem from the same principle. Both presuppose the existence of a

---

70. John Paul II, *Centesimus Annus,* §48.

71. See Pius XII's speech to the secret consistory of February 18, 1946 (*AAS* 38, 144ff; MA-I, 76ff). Pius says that "every social activity is for its nature subsidiary; it must serve as a support to members of the social body and never destroy or absorb them. These are surely enlightened words, valid for social life *in all its grades* and also *for the life of the Church without prejudice to its hierarchical structure*" (emphasis mine). Pius does refer to "what individual men can do for themselves and by their own forces," which of course "should not be taken from them and assigned to the community." Though this might appear to be a reduction to the lowest level in an individualist sense, the whole context of the discussion suggests otherwise. Pius is speaking of the diverse and complex parts of the social structure; moreover, he does not refer just to individuals but also to "members" of the social body. The whole point of the speech, indeed, was to warn about gigantic organizations with their flattening effect toward uniformity, which by centralizing destroy the equilibrium of social institutions. Calvez and Perrin rightly alert their readers to the fact that Pius XI and Pius XII insisted that society is not a substantial or material body; it cannot have that kind of existence or unity. As Pius XI said, "a society can exercise no personal function save through its members." In *Divini Redemptoris* he reminded his readers that while social order reflects the divine perfection (a diversity of members causing good in others), only "the human person, and not society in any form, is endowed with reason and a morally free will." The letter was written against atheistic communism, so Pius had a special need to deny that society is not a natural or physical person. See *Divini Redemptoris,* §29, *AAS* 29, 79. In his 1956 speech to Catholic physicians, Pius XII reiterated this point. Catholic teaching does not consider man in his relationship with society as if he were put into the "organic mind of the physical organism" (*AAS* 48, 679). All of this depends on keeping in view Thomas's idea of a unity of order. When, by creeping metaphors and political ideology, both man and society are regarded as physical organisms, one or the other must be destroyed if there is to be unity. For several papal admonitions in this regard, see Jean-Yves Calvez, SJ and Jacques Perrin, SJ, *The Church and Social Justice: The Social Teachings of the Popes from Leo XIII to Pius XII (1878–1958)* (London: Burns & Oates, 1961), 123–32.

society—as Maitland said, an "$n+1$" unity, where the unity is an intransitive good. Recall our earlier point that a society ordinarily survives defeat or failure of one or more of its purposes; it does not, however, survive the dissolution of united action. Since united action cannot depend entirely on unanimity, authority has an essential function within a society. This is why the principle of subsidiarity cannot be expressed adequately as the imperative that decisions be made at the *lowest possible level*.

Subsidiarity is nothing other than the principle that, when aid be given, it not remove or destroy the authority or functions (*munera*) proper to the society being assisted.[72] As Pope John Paul noted, in "exceptional circumstances" the state may exercise a "substitute function," but not in such a manner as to deprive the society of its "proper" modes of union.[73] Subsidiarity requires that the sociality of society be preserved. No argument to good results external to the society will suffice, unless one has moral reason to dissolve a society, regime, or party.

But this "aid" must be sharply distinguished from the idea of the state imparting, outsourcing, or conceding the social forms and functions of other groups. In *Mater et Magistra*, John XXIII refers to the state's work as "directing, stimulating, co-ordinating, supplying and integrating" a plurality of societies. "Of its very nature," he concludes, "the true aim of all social activity should be to help members of the social body, but never to destroy or absorb them."[74] These groups "must be really autonomous [*suis legibus re ipsa regantur*], and loyally collaborate in pursuit of their own specific interests and those of the common good. For these groups must themselves necessarily present the form and substance of a true community."[75]

Thus the social Magisterium regarded social justice as a new way of presenting Thomas's understanding of general or legal justice. Thomas held that as charity "may be called a general virtue in so far as it directs the acts of all the virtues to the Divine good, so too is legal justice, in so far as it directs the acts of all the virtues to the common good. Accordingly, just as charity which

---

72. On this notion of *munera* as functions, roles, and offices, and its connection to both Roman law and the sacramental theology of the Roman Church, see Ch. 3.

73. *SCG*, III, c. 71: "In every government the best thing is that provision be made for the things governed, according to their mode: for in this consists the justice of the regime. Consequently, even as it would be contrary to the right notion of human rule if the governor of a state were to forbid men to act according to their various duties—except perhaps for the time being, on account of some particular urgency—so would it be contrary to the notion of God's government, if He did not allow creatures to act in accordance with their respective natures."

74. John XXIII, Encyclical Letter *Mater et Magistra* (May 15, 1961), §53, *AAS* 53, 414.

75. John XXIII, *Mater et Magistra*, §65, *AAS* 53, 417.

regards the Divine good as its proper object, is a special virtue in respect of its essence, so too legal justice is a special virtue in respect of its essence, in so far as it regards the common good as its proper object" (*ST* II-II, q. 58, a. 6).

Every juridical proposition implies an inter-subjective relation, *sub specie alteritatis.* Justice always requires a relation to "the other." Therefore all issues of justice have a social aspect. The cardinal virtue of justice pertains to particular justice, either bilaterally (commutative) or by distribution on the basis of merit or need (distributive). But there is another virtue that orders the myriad acts of the other virtues to the common good. It does not substitute for, or cancel-out, the justice of commutation and distribution. Rather, it is the practice of virtue "looked at from the social point of view"—*sub specie societatis.*[76] We can also describe general justice as the harmonization of a heterogeneous whole, which consists, in a unity of order, of other wholes: both natural persons and social persons. This is what is traditionally meant by polity, but it pertains analogically to every society *ad intra.*

To be sure, these subsidiary "wholes" are the subjects of justice at both the level of commutation and distribution. Recognizing the natural right of parents as the primary educators of their children is not, in the first place, a question of social justice but rather of their rights vis-à-vis other individuals or societies. Strict justice, whether commutative or distributive, has as its object "a person equalized,"[77] whether the person be a natural individual or a society. But whenever we speak of a common good, we are not referring to a private right but rather membership and participation in a social order. Because the order is, itself, the common good, it is not amenable to commutation or distribution. This holds true analogously for any society possessing an intrinsic common good. A family, a church, or a polity cannot rightfully exchange or distribute the common good into private hands. Any relatively complex social unity of order will abound with commutations and distributions; but the common order is *not* divisible in this sense.

> Consequently, the way to get the common good into the possession of the members, the way to share among them the virtuous social life, is to develop that life, to serve the common good. There is no need for another direction to legal justice; what is good for the whole is good for the parts.[78]

No matter how different their respective ends and modes of unity, every society will require its members to learn how to participate rather than divide the common order.

---

76. Jeremiah Newman, *Foundations of Justice* (Cork: Cork University Press, 1954), 5.

77. Leo W. Shields, *The History and Meaning of the Term Social Justice* (Notre Dame, IN: University of Notre Dame Press, 1941), 39.

78. Shields, *History and Meaning*, 39–40.

Social justice is the virtue whereby all persons (not just the state) refer the ensemble of their relations to the common good. This is why subsidiarity is not merely an issue of commutation or distribution, but rather manifests itself in the arranging of things in such wise that the operations of a heterogeneous whole are harmonized with regard to the common good. If the operations proper to the parts are destroyed, one has violated both particular and social justice.[79] At the same time, it is not enough simply to do justice to the parts;

---

79. Within a given polity, any number of things are distributed from the whole to the parts (diverse groups): status, proportional representation, monies, and so forth. These goods are enjoyed privately. Here, however, the term *private* means that this or that particular group is the terminal recipient—this family enjoys the tax relief, or that association enjoys use of the public building, and so forth. These societies themselves are deemed private in comparison to the political "whole." Thomas refers to the sub-political group as a member of the "whole"—a *unitas particularis*, which becomes disruptive insofar as it separates itself from the *unitas principalis* (*ST*, II-II, q. 39, a. 1).

The particular unity of a subordinate group is still referable to a *unitas principalis*. What kind? Thomas is clear: the polity (*civitas vel regnum*) which is constituted as a *unitas iuris*. To disrupt the unity of the political common good is a sin against justice in the sense of legal (or social) justice. Interestingly, Thomas notes that some discord within the polity is licit so long as the disputes are not contrary to the common good of all (*quod discordia ab eo quod non est manifeste bonum potest esse sine peccato*) (*ST*, II-II, q. 42, a. 2, ad 2). In other words, we should expect some friction and issues amongst the particular societies within the body politic. See *Centesimus Annus*, §14: "The Church is well aware that in the course of history conflicts of interest between different social groups inevitably arise, and that in the face of such conflicts Christians must often take a position, honestly and decisively. The Encyclical *Laborem exercens* moreover clearly recognized the positive role of conflict when it takes the form of a 'struggle for social justice'."

There is nothing in the nature of polity, rightly considered, that entails social homogeneity. John Finnis rightly points out that general justice cannot require us to regard "the state (rather than any and every community to which one is related) as the only direct object of general justice." Finnis, *Aquinas* (Oxford: Oxford University Press, 1998), 217. By the same token, there is nothing in the natures of diverse groups, rightly considered, that is opposed to being "referred" once again to the wider unity of order. Again, Finnis points out that the "common good which is the object(ive) of all justice logically cannot be distributed." Finnis, *Natural Law and Natural Rights* (Oxford: Oxford University Press, 1980), 194. As he says, the common good is not "a common stock" (168).

See, for example, Thomas's comparison of the common good of polity and of marriage; see *In IV Sent.*, d. 27, q. 1, a. 1, ad 3:

Just as the civic life denotes not the individual act of this or that one, but the things that concern the common action of the citizens [*sicut vita civilis non importat actum singularem huius vel illius, sed ea quae ad communicationem civilem pertinent*], so the conjugal life is nothing else than a particular kind of companionship pertaining to that common action. Wherefore as regards this same life the partnership of married persons is always indivisible, although it is divisible as regards the act belonging to each party.

that parents enjoy a proper right to raise their children, that corporations have a proper right to organize capital and property, that national communities have a right to retain their traditional forms of unity, and that individuals enjoy a right to religious conscience, are necessary but not sufficient conditions for the common good, which is the object of the virtue of legal or social justice.

John Paul II made a similar point in his *Address to the Fiftieth Assembly of the United Nations* (October 5, 1995). Recalling the rather artificial political boundaries imposed upon the diverse peoples and nations after both great wars of the twentieth century, he quoted the remark of Pope Benedict XV, who in the midst of the First World War reminded everyone that "nations do not die" [*riflettasi che le Nazioni non muoiono*].[80] The sense of this remark is that nations can constitute genuine social entities which may or may not, in the contingency of history, be constituted as states. However they are arranged within the broader juridical and geographical compass of states, they nevertheless have a right to exist in their own unique social forms. Nations are not mere aggregations of individuals or temporary partnerships. The pope went on to say:

> But while the "rights of the nation" express the vital requirements of "particularity," it is no less important to emphasize the requirements of universality, expressed through a clear awareness of the duties which nations have vis-à-vis other nations and humanity as a whole. Foremost among these duties is certainly that of living in a spirit of peace, respect and solidarity with other nations. Thus the exercise of the rights of nations, balanced by the acknowledgement and the practice of duties, promotes a fruitful "exchange of gifts," which strengthens the unity of all mankind.[81]

Importantly, the pope is not suggesting that the social forms of these peoples have an absolute right to resist being ordered toward a broader polity, and with that polity, being harmonized with the other nationalities and groups. Rather, he is putting in play two distinct but interrelated notions of solidarity. On the one hand, the unity-of-order called a "nation" has its own solidarity, and, in the order of strict justice, has a right to be regarded as something "one." On the other hand, the nation, like every other subsidiary unity, is to be referred to the broader order—to the common good enjoyed by all groups

---

Thus, any society consisting of common action for a common end enjoys an indivisible unity of order brought about by diverse actions of its members.

80. John Paul II, *Address to the Fiftieth Assembly of the United Nations*, October 5, 1995, §6; quoting Apostolic Exhortation *Allorché fummo chiamati* (July 28, 1915), *AAS* 7, 367.

81. John Paul II, *Address to the Fiftieth Assembly*, §8.

within the polity. This is nothing other than the solidarity of social justice. Moreover, the pope makes clear that this solidarity is referable once again to an international common good in which each polity enjoys the good of order with a multiplicity of other politics.

In answer to the question of why the traditional term general (or legal) justice was dropped in favor of social justice, at least one thing can be said. In modern times legal justice was confused with the virtue of obedience to the positive law of the state. Given the disposition and organization of the modern states circa 1930, this confusion would have had drastic and grotesque consequences. The state then becomes the exclusive agent of social justice, as though the virtue resides entirely in the state, which then has the right to compel other persons (natural and social) to do what they have no natural inclination to do: namely, to consider their acts in relation to the common good. For his part, Leo XIII never relinquished the older term "general justice." But during the pontificates of Pius XI and Pius XII, many Thomists, having given serious consideration to the situation, agreed that social justice should replace the older rubric.[82] In view of the omnicompetent state of their era, and in view of the pressing need to articulate and defend an organic pluralism of society, it was not an unreasonable position to jettison the term "legal" in favor of "social" lest the common good of order be understood as exclusively the order of the state.[83] In short, it was more necessary to insist that the state is "social" than to insist that the plural societies are "political."

In retrospect, we are entitled to question whether it achieved the right results. For one thing, social justice increasingly became associated with relations which ensue upon economic activity. From there, it became all too easy to regard social justice as chiefly concerned with economic commutations and distributions. Pius XI's dictum "[I]t is of the essence of social justice to demand from each individual all that is necessary for the common good" could only be obscured.[84]

While the common good includes commutations and distributions, the common good cannot, strictly speaking, be distributed but only participated. Undoubtedly, there are common goods distributed into private hands. "Before

---

82. In Encyclical Letter *Studiorum Ducem* (June 29, 1923), Pius XI makes explicit that Thomas is to be studied in order to formulate exactly *de justitia legale aut de sociali, itemque de commutative aut de distributive. AAS* 15, 322.

83. For example, legal justice "would be a most misleading and dangerous term today when the subordination of civil law to natural law is no longer generally recognized." Alfred O'Rahilly, *Aquinas versus Marx* (Cork: Cork University Press, 1948), 36. But also Leo W. Shields, *The History and Meaning of the Term Social Justice*, 47–64; and Jeremiah Newman, *Foundations of Justice*, 99–121.

84. Pius XI, *Quadragesimo Anno*, §51.

distribution such goods are part of the common stock and belong to no one in particular, but after distribution they are private goods. The water, for example, in the city reservoir is neither mine nor yours except indeterminately. But once it flows through my tap it is mine."[85] Traditionally, such utilities have been called *bona communia* (in the plural) in order to distinguish them from the *bonum commune* (the common good). Without common utilities privately used there could be no society. Nonetheless, utilities are "means" for the purpose of a well-ordered community, which is not something private. Unless this point is kept firmly in mind, societies of all kinds will become nothing but stockpiles of resources coordinated and distributed to individuals. This, in turn, is the justice of a partnership, distributing private shares rather than the justice of a common good to which each member is ordered.

SUMMARY

- The sin of the modern state is the injustice of its claiming a monopoly over group-personhood—reserving what is "distinct in dignity" for itself and for individual persons. The Catholic position holds that the political sovereign is limited by the very existence of real group persons, of which the state (or polity) is not an exception. A normal society, then, will evince a multiplication of authorities embedded in group persons.
- Unlike the devolution position(s), subsidiarity is not a policy decision whether there ought to be social pluralism. Subsidiarity depends upon there already being a plurality of group-persons. Take away social plurality and there is nothing that can correspond to the principle of subsidiarity. Devolution, when prudentially called for, is a policy, not the principle, of social unity and diversity. Decentralization might be compatible with, or even advantageous to, subsidiarity; but they should not be confused. In certain cases, decentralization can amount to the same thing as subsidiarity, particularly in polities enjoying a federal system in which the "states" (provinces) have a specifically social and political identity—that is to say, where the "states" are something more than merely convenient administrative units of the polity. Issues of decentralization will depend not only on the living social identity of the "states" but also upon the juridical organization of the constitution. In such cases, there is ordinarily a constitutional law governing the association of these federated polities. However, where the constitution leaves room for prudential policies, the principle of subsidiarity will dictate, very generally, that

---

85. Froelich, "The Equivocal Status of *Bonum Commune*," 54.

when the central or national polity either intervenes in the political life of the "states," or when it for reasons of policy devolves or decentralizes on a particular scope of issues, it should not subvert the polity and sociality of the "states."[86]

- Subsidiarity requires the just treatment of self-governing societies. Since every society seeks not only to achieve certain ends, but also to pursue those ends in their own mode of unity, it is to no avail to argue that some other power can get the job done better or more efficiently. Societies have their own internal agency. Therefore, if aid is to be given to a society, it must be done in such a way that preserves the sociality of the group being assisted.

- Yet there is nothing in the nature of a particular society that makes it incapable of being ordered (and ordering itself) to a wider society. Just as individuals must be right with their neighbor, so too must group-persons be right with other group-persons. If a plurality of group persons is natural, so too is political order in which a number of societies enjoy a common order. And if political order is natural, so too is international order. In each case, we find a diverse "whole" referred once again to a wider common good. The virtue that brings about that wider order is called social justice.

- Because social justice is bringing actions (of individuals and groups) into harmony with a wider common good, it should not be confused with distributive justice lest we fall into the trap of dividing and distributing something common. However, it is permissible to say that a society, of whatever magnitude, will distribute common utilities. In this sense, social justice does involve distribution. Even so, when a state makes available free legal counsel to the indigent, we do not say that the rule of law is distributed to private persons. When the international order distributes resources for the development of peoples, the resources are distributed, not the international order itself.

CONCLUSION

Hence, we have arrived at the coherence of the four principles. There are natural persons and group-persons. In different ways, each is distinct in

---

86. It is important to note that although subsidiarity is usually invoked in the case of a larger or superior society helping a lower one, in our age of devolution outsourcing of power or responsibilities to smaller social units can create great burdens on the lower societies. Not every devolution or decentralization protects social pluralism. For example, in American politics we speak of "unfunded mandates," by which the US government forces its own burdens downward to the states and municipalities without adequate funding.

dignity, possessing rights and responsibilities. The human tendency to "dwell in society," to use Pope Leo's words, cannot be exhausted by membership in a single group. It is not the accidental forces of society and history that alone account for the diversity of group persons, but rather human nature itself. Solidarity is never a single thing, but a multitude of relations. On these facts, subsidiarity counts as an authentic principle of social life. When one power assists another, it must not subvert the solidarity of the group. These particular groups, in turn, need the virtue of ordering themselves in harmony with others, and thus is brought into existence the common good called polity. The ordering of members to a society, and of societies to still wider societies, is called social justice.

The foregoing exposition would seem to be a rather neat picture of the four basic principles. I am fairly confident that I have given an accurate presentation of what they originally meant, and how they are supposed to be configured to one another. In sum, they affirm a *principled pluralism* that respects the rights of individuals in their own dignity, and in their membership within various groups. The principles were never meant to be anything like an "ideal" model proposed by some nineteenth-century sociologists, much less by twentieth-century economists.

At the same time, we must admit that our exposition is philosophical. It is complete only in the sense that the principles of any architecture are complete. Nothing can be built or achieved without returning to the concrete terrain of social reality. Here, a philosopher is not the best guide. Even so, I shall offer a few concluding observations.

Let us assume, for the sake of argument, that we have a correct and coherent understanding of the four basic principles, and that we are prepared to apply them to the concrete social, economic, and political world. The first thing that must be conceded is that social change comes not only from impersonal forces, but also from a myriad of decisions and adjustments made by individuals within communities. For example, no impersonal force of history was solely responsible for the fact that, in most of the Western societies, family is regarded as the so-called nuclear family rather than an extended network of uncles and aunts and cousins. Nor did anyone dictate by law that, in Catholic life, a godparent usually denotes a liturgical rather than an ordinary social function. Because social relations and offices change through the medium of free adaptation, it is the beginning of wisdom to understand that they cannot be changed easily by dictates from on high (of law, social policy, etc.). To be sure, "things" can be organized and reorganized by public policy; but this does not necessarily bring about a social change. The current predicament in Iraq would be the case in point.

Moreover, the social changes with which we must reckon are not uniform. Among some peoples, we see a chronic inability to achieve a common good that transcends tribes, if not organized gangs. They have not achieved the order of polity, and they do not have the luxury of worrying about subsidiarity. Still other peoples have a toe-hold on political order, but lack the utilities for a *bene vivere*, the good life. Without polity, and without adequate utilities, the most rudimentary aspects of social harmony (domestically and internationally) are precarious, to say the least.

Our history in Western societies, however, is marked by the achievement of political order in the state and by the achievement of affluence, which depended to a considerable extent upon the nation-state. This particular political "form" called the nation-state was the engine for the development of modern science and technology, international trade, mandatory education, and the rule of law as we understand it today. But the nation-states and their economies and wars made it difficult for traditional, subsidiary societies to flourish. States used the very awkward legal principles of concession and fiction to situate sub-political societies within the nation-state. Until the 1960s, when the issue of developing peoples became pressing, Catholic social doctrine was formed almost entirely in response to the achievements, but more often to the problems, of relatively advanced Western peoples. This doctrine could take it for granted that these peoples had political order (though much too strong and all-encompassing) and subsidiary societies (which had to struggle for recognition within the nation-state).

To my knowledge, no institution sounded such an early and persistent warning about the state as *Volkskörper* (a nation body) than the Catholic Church. Catholic thought de-substantialized the state in favor of the idea of societies as unities of order. Now, however, we must ask what happens when this modern, omnicompetent state dwindles in authority? This, in fact, was the question posed by John Paul II in *Centesimus Annus*. With the passing of the totalitarian regimes, would society move in the opposite direction, reconstituting itself as a set of market-like relations?

Of the many things which have changed in our life-time, the most notable is the fact that the Western nation-states are not interested in actively persecuting or legally incapacitating associational life—nothing, at least, on the scale of the pre-1945 regimes, and in central and eastern Europe the pre-1989 regimes. Indeed, governments are very reluctant to enforce a "public" morality, preferring instead to leave strong moral notions to the private sphere. Popes from Leo XIII through Pius XII would hardly recognize such a diminished ambition on the part of governments. Think, for example, of Bismarck, Gladstone, and Teddy Roosevelt, and then think of the current crop of political leaders who are more liable to apologize for any notion that the state should be a primary object of loyalty, much less an agent for civilizing the world. Cardinal Ratzinger's remark about the "dictatorship of relativism" applies to this new reality, to societies which are diffident about any assertions of moral order.

The Protestant theologian Karl Barth referred to the post-1945 West as a society of "disillusioned sovereignty."[87] Peoples wanted their nation-states to be more friendly to private life, less belligerent, and more of a coordinating device for enhancing life-styles. Especially in our time of globalization, it becomes quite easy to imagine a good life based upon what Ernest Gellner calls the loose and revocable associations of "modular man." Nowhere does this manifest itself more strongly than in matrimonial and familial societies, which tend to function in the manner of partnerships. In a recent case about gay marriage that came before the California Supreme Court (Mar. 5, 2008), members of the Court expressed astonishment that anyone would worry about the words "marriage" or "partnership" so long as individuals are legally free to have their own relationship.

Finally, I conclude with an empirical question. How is the preference for loose associations related to the decline of the moral authority of the state? The great hope of Catholic social doctrine was that, once the state is properly limited, we would see a flourishing of other societies and modes of solidarity. But it is not evident that this happened, or that it is about to happen any time soon. What is the correlation, if any, between the decline of the nation-state and the rise of partnerships rather than societies?[88] How we situate the principles of solidarity and subsidiarity today will depend upon how we answer this question.

---

87. Karl Barth, *Church Dogmatics*, vol. 3, part 4 (German 467, English 410).

88. We are witnessing what Pierre Manent has dubbed "culture without borders." Markets, globalized communications, and the international aspiration for the rights of man can make polity a bit player on the stage of human happiness. Pierre Manent, *A World beyond Politics? A Defense of the Nation-State*, trans. Marc LePain (Princeton, NJ: Princeton University Press, 2006), 203:

> Commerce, right, morality: these are the three systems, the three empires that promise the exit from the political. Each in its own form: commerce, according to the realism, the prosaic character of interests rightly understood; right, according to the intellectual coherence of a network of rights rigorously deduced from individual autonomy; and finally, morality, according to the sublime aim of pure human dignity to which one is joined by the purely spiritual sentiment of respect.

CHAPTER 2

Toward an Adequate Anthropology

Social Aspects of Imago Dei
in Catholic Theology

IN HIS ENCYCLICAL ON ECUMENISM, *Ut unum sint*, Pope John Paul II
made clear a desire that the Catholic magisterium might serve to enrich
and deepen the faith of all Christians. The reflections that follow on
Catholic social doctrine—a key focus of the magisterium in the modern
age—are offered in this same spirit, inviting Christians of various confessional and denominational loyalties to think *with*—if understandably not
always in full agreement with—the Catholic Church, in the hope that "visible unity" among divided Christians might, in the fullness of time, become
an actual reality.

It is of considerable importance, however, to realize that Catholic social
doctrine was not developed in the intramural quarrels of the Reformation and
Counter-Reformation. Rather, as we discussed in the first chapter, it emerged
in response to the new anthropological and political creed of "man and citizen" that swept from France in 1789 to the rest of Europe and her former
colonies in the late eighteenth and nineteenth centuries. This creed of "liberty,
equality, and fraternity" considered the human person in two ways: first, as a
being of nature, having natural liberties and rights which had been obscured
or broken by the historical social order; second, as a citizen, standing equally
among other citizens before the state. On this model, fraternity was associated
preeminently if not exclusively with citizenship, for as Rousseau among others
had argued, membership in the state reconstitutes the broken relations of
nature and history. Other social memberships claiming their origins in nature,
history, or divine revelation were deemed legitimate only insofar as they were
either the private choice of individuals, or insofar as they were permitted or
"conceded" by the state.

Catholic thinkers, both clerical and lay, quickly targeted the ideal of fraternity as the most troubling part of the new creed. Cardinal Chiaramonti of
Imola (the future Pius VII, later kidnapped and held in solitary confinement
by Napoleon) put on his letterhead: "Liberty, Equality, and Peace in our Lord

Jesus Christ."[1] Throughout the nineteenth century, Catholic thinkers attempted to identify social domains having a sacred solidarity not reducible to state citizenship. During the pontificate of Leo XIII (1878–1903), the pattern for Catholic social doctrine was well established. The Church took a scissors-like approach to the state, limiting and contextualizing citizenship according to higher and lower social orders: from below, by marriage and family, and from above by the Church.

It was an ingenious strategy. In effect, the secular state, which publicly claimed to be desacralized, was pinioned by two facets of a sacramental system. By sacramental we mean not only sacraments in the ordinary sense of the term, like holy orders and marriage, which are instituted by Christ as sacraments of redemption; we also mean by sacrament whatever makes visible the invisible mysteries of God. In both the restricted and the broader sense of the term, sacraments are irreducibly social. There can be no such thing as a private or invisible sacrament. Regarding these social spheres, the Church could say to the state, *noli me tangere*, "don't touch me." In its deepest pattern, Catholic social doctrine was a defense of the individual *in* society; more specifically, it was chiefly an articulation of the dignity of society and a defense of societies against the state's ambition to exercise a monopoly on fraternity. Arguments drawn from the economy of creation, such as natural law, and arguments drawn from the economy of redemption were thus marshaled, usually in tandem, to buttress this explicitly anti-Rousseauvian conception of social orders representing divine things.[2]

Genesis 1:26 teaches that the individual member of the species is a sacrament—speaking now in the broad sense of the term. In the visible order of the hexaemeron, it is the individual man, male and female, who is made unto the image and likeness of God, and thus the individual member of the species is a locus of sacrality in the visible world. This idea, so familiar to Jewish and Christian theology, is much contested, even detested, in the secular world of late modernity. Our culture separates the value of the individual as

---

1. On Chiaramonte, see E. E. Y. Hales, *Revolution and Papacy: 1769–1846* (Notre Dame, IN: University of Notre Dame Press, 1966), 107. For his part, Leo XIII contended that "liberty, equality and fraternity" had its grounding in the relations of the divine Trinity. Encyclical Letter *Humanum genus* (April 20, 1884), §34; and *In plurimis*, §14. By this polemical flourish, Leo did not mean to conflate nature and grace, much less to suggest that Christian Trinitarian theology is merely another way to restate the rights of man and citizen. Rather, he meant to remind his flock that they already have a more adequate understanding of these things.

2. For a compact account of this history, see Ch. 5. There, I put into context the Leonine response to issues of democracy, religion, and public order, especially the question of whether human authority can ever be free-standing without the primary authority of the eternal law.

self-determining from the individual's membership in a certain natural species or kind. A "person" is a pure thisness (as late medieval philosophers suggested, *haecceity*) in his liberty, and is counted as a "member" only by his own choice or consent.[3] The suspicion that membership without consent is a kind of servitude has in our era come to encompass more than what we would count as sociological reality. Choice replaces nature, and gender replaces sex. The late twentieth century champions what has been called a "negative anthropology."[4] We can say what man *is not*, for to affirm what he is limits freedom. Such a view radically upsets our traditional notions of philanthropy, which depend in some way upon our love of what we, as individuals, have in common by way of species. For example, in the Adamic wedding canticle of Genesis 2:23, Eve is recognized not only as an individual but as a fellow human, "bone of my bones, and flesh of my flesh."

The Lutheran theologian Gilbert Meilaender rightly observes that Christianity teaches that the human person is "neither beast nor God." Man cannot be resolved into beast or pure spirit. But this does not imply that the person is a pure individual, deranged from any ranking according to species or kind. In late modernity, therefore, Christians can expect this central anthropological truth about the image of God to be rejected. Interestingly, this rejection is based not only on a denial of what the teaching presupposes in the order of divine revelation and the response of faith; it is also, if not primarily, based on a denial or a doubt about the natural locus of the creature without which a theology of revelation is bereft of its material sign.

Given the contemporary confusion about what belongs respectively to nature or grace, and given radical doubt about the individual's (moral) membership (as person) in a natural species, the question animating this chapter might seem doubly puzzling. Can social entities be said to exist in the image of God? In a theologically serious ecumenical readership such as the present one, I assume for the purpose of this inquiry the basic Christian teaching that the individual *human* person is made unto the image and likeness of God. Although there are a few qualifications to be made along the way, I set aside the need for any polemic or dialectic that gets us back, from scratch so to speak, to the starting point of Genesis 1:26. But with the traditional point of

---

3. As the French philosopher Pierre Manent puts it, human nature for us is a cipher, an "efficacious indetermination" allowing a zone of liberty in which the individual can "affirm himself without knowing himself." Pierre Manent, *The City of Man*, trans. Marc A. LePain, with foreword by Jean Bethke Elshtain (Princeton, NJ: Princeton University Press, 1998), 129.

4. The term "negative anthropology" is taken from Rocco Buttiglione, *Karol Wojtyła: The Thought of the Man Who Became Pope John Paul II* (Grand Rapids, MI: Eerdmans, 1997), 53.

departure fully in view, my theme raises a question of considerable importance. What about social entities? As Paul teaches in Ephesians 5, the great sacrament, or mystery, is the analogical sign of the union of man and woman and of Christ and the Church. While this reality cannot be constituted in the absence of real individual persons, the sign pertains to the union. To use again the example afforded by Genesis 2, Eve is affirmed as a fellow human individual, but, even so, the "union of one flesh" is not reducible to either Eve or Adam.

Doesn't this suggest that a defense of the dignity of the individual human person is a necessary but not a sufficient condition for an "adequate anthropology"?[5] Without its proper complement of social relations and ends, the *humanum* is vulnerable to ideologies and pseudosciences which adopt the principle of methodological individualism: namely, that social unities and relations among members can be reduced to nonsocial properties of members or composites thereof. Following this logic, the matrimonial union is reducible to aggregated individuals, and the individuals are reducible to isolated bits of desire and consciousness stripped of common species. In effect, the property and status of *being a member* would be counted as a mere fiction rather than a great sacrament. Needless to say, this method will not work for Catholic theology, which takes a realistic view of social entities, and what is more, regards social union as the crowning moment in both the orders of creation and redemption—to wit, marriage and church.

The Catholic understanding of "made unto the image and likeness of God" includes two distinct but related ideas—man as an individual member of a common species, and man as a member of a social communion—each in its own way manifesting something of the invisible God. A correct anthropology, then, has not one but rather two tasks. First, to articulate the good of being an individual human being. Second, to articulate how this good is perfected in being a member of a society or societies. Questions of justice and love will inevitably track this twofold aspect of the human good.

My aim in this chapter is not to expound Catholic doctrine in the formal sense of the term. While I limit myself chiefly to sources which have some degree of magisterial authority within the Church—pontifical letters, papal catechesis, conciliar documents, clarifications issued by curial offices—I do so in order to show the evolution and disposition of the questions and to call attention to an emerging pattern of answers. The resources bestride more than one sector of theology: biblical theology, Christology,

---

5. I use the term "adequate anthropology" in the sense given to it by Pope John Paul II, who meant an integral anthropology—one commensurate to the whole human good. The pope used the term in many settings, but a first bevy of meanings is accessible in *Man and Woman He Created Them: A Theology of the Body*, trans. with introduction and index by Michael Waldstein (Boston: Pauline Books, 2006), 678.

sacramental theology, ecclesiology, moral theology (under which Catholic social doctrine is placed), and theological anthropology. This rich panoply of resources itself constitutes a fabric of theology that is recognizably Catholic.

Framing Terms and Questions

At the beginning we need to briefly define some terms. Within the Catholic tradition, *imago* (a copy), *similitudo* (a likeness or perfection of an image), *imitatio* (a representation), *assimulatio* (a similarity in form), *conformatio* (a constitutional character), and *vestigium* (a trace) are theological terms of art.[6] Since Leo XIII, magisterial documents rely chiefly upon Thomas Aquinas's understanding of sacral imaging. I make no apology for using Thomas both in the text and the notes for the purpose of clarifying terms and distinctions. Since the Second Vatican Council, however, the neo-scholastic tradition has had a much looser hold over this subject. While they do not necessarily indicate where the discussion must end, the scholastic terms are often the best place to begin.

It is commonly taught that *imago* pertains in an unqualified sense to Christ, who is *the* (eternal and consubstantial) image of the Father.[7] In the case of the created human person, who is an imperfect likeness, the proper description is drawn from Scripture: *ad imaginem et similitudinem Dei*, unto the image and likeness of God. The preposition indicates that the imprinted image in the human person is not one in being with its source. Thus, *imago* is in man only by an "analogy of proportion." What is the proportion? The proportion signified by *imago* is not just any created effect, but a "likeness in species," or a "likeness in nature."[8] Nothing, of course, participates directly by way of species or nature in divinity except the divine persons. In the human person, the participated likeness consists in acts of knowing and loving which are at the root of human nature—thus counting as likeness in species or nature. This pattern of knowledge and love manifesting from afar in the creature a likeness of divinity has been called the "image of representation."[9] Minimally, it refers to the human aptitude for God as a first principle of being and goodness. These are intimated in the creature's spiritual operations, principally

---

6. Frequently used in conjunction with the pronoun *quaedam* (a certain one), the adverb *quodammodo* (in a certain way or measure), the adjective *conveniens* (harmoniously or fittingly), and the verb *praeferre* (to display).

7. *ST*, I, q. 93, a. 1, ad 2.

8. *ST*, I, q. 93, a. 2, co., ad 4.

9. Here, I rely upon the discussion of image in Romanus Cessario, *Christian Faith & Theological Life* (Washington, DC: The Catholic University of America Press, 1996), 38–48.

self-possession and self-transcendence. From here below, we can see something excellent about the human being that deserves dignity.

It is also commonly taught that although human reason untutored by faith can detect within itself and in other human persons something divine-like in the operations of knowledge and love, the notion that the created person is an analogue of a trinity of divine persons can be grasped only by faith, and by sight only in glory. As Augustine said—and as Thomas reaffirmed—we *see* a trinity within ourselves, but we *believe* a trinity in the godhead.[10] By adoption in baptism, and through actions informed by faith, hope, and charity, we can grasp something of the community of divine persons in the created image. Image of God, in the strict Trinitarian sense, is in the public domain only by virtue of divine revelation and the response of faith. This point always needs to be underscored, for we often confuse a bottom-drawer notion of human dignity (as something divine-like) with the strict idea of being made unto the image and likeness of the Trinitarian God. It needs reemphasis for another reason. As Saint Irenaeus wrote:

> In prior ages it was certainly said that man was made to the image of God, but it had not appeared, since the Word was still invisible, to whose image man had been made, moreover, for this reason the resemblance was easily lost. But when the Word of God became flesh, he confirmed the one and the other; he showed the image in all its truth, becoming himself that which was his image, and restored the resemblance in a stable manner, rendering man completely like the invisible Father by means of the Word, from then on visible.[11]

Finally, it is commonly taught that the term *similitudo* or likeness can mean two things. A likeness can be something more general than an image. All creatures have a certain likeness to God (*similitudo vestigii*) as vestiges or footprints—that is to say, effects which manifest a first cause. *Similitudo* can also mean the perfection of an image. The likeness of the image is more perfect by acquisition or infusion of certain habits. The perfection, whether by nature or grace, is not merely in the capacities to know and love, but in

10. Furthermore, image in human persons is subject to different states or conditions. Man is made unto the image of God (1) by creation, which all have in common, (2) by grace of the New Covenant, and (3) in the likeness of glory. *ST*, I, q. 93, a. 4.

11. See Irenaeus of Lyons, *Against Heresies*, Book V, Ch. 16, no. 2, in *Ante-Nicene Fathers*, Vol. 1, ed. Alexander Roberts, James Donaldson, and A. Cleveland Coxe (Buffalo, NY: Christian Literature Publishing Co., 1885), 544. I refer the reader to International Theological Commission, *In Search of a Universal Ethic: A New Look at the Natural Law* (2009). It explains very nicely how the theme of the image of God is located, in part, but not in its entirety, under natural law. See especially Ch. 5, Section 1, no. 103–9, entitled "*The incarnate Logos, the living Law*," and note 91 on Irenaeus.

operationes—actions.[12] In fact, much depends upon how this distinction is rendered and applied. In this essay, we are usually dealing with the second sense of "likeness," which is to say the (moral) perfection of an image.

Within the scheme of Catholic theology, image falls directly under theological anthropology and Christology, while likeness (as a perfection of the image) falls under moral and sacramental theology, both of which pertain to actions perfecting the image—chiefly, actions in conformity to grace, but not excluding perfections derived from action in accord with the natural law.[13] At least in the Roman model, social doctrine attends to *similitudo*, the actions which perfect an image.

Now, having compressed into a few paragraphs several books of theology, we can begin to address the question whether image and likeness are predicated of a society. At the outset we can remove one option. If we mean that the image and likeness consist directly and properly in an accumulation of social relations, the answer is no. Augustine and Thomas reject, for example, the idea that Adam is not image until Eve, and that neither are images until the child.[14] Made unto the image of God, the human person is, according to Saint John Damascene, an "intelligent being, endowed with free-will and self-movement." This dignity is sacral, because the soul is directly created by and ordered to God. The primary relation, therefore, is the created image entirely to its entire Trinitarian exemplar. As John Paul II has written on Adam's solitude in Genesis: "*Man is 'alone': this is to say that through his own humanity, through what he is, he is at the same time set into a unique, exclusive, and unrepeatable relationship with God himself.*"[15] Society does not confer this

---

12. *ST*, I, q. 93, a. 9, co., ad 1. In the reply to the third objection, Aquinas says: "Nor is it unfitting to use the term 'image' from one point of view and from another the term 'likeness.'"

13. John Paul II, Encyclical Letter *Veritatis splendor* (August 6, 1993), §111: "The service which moral theologians are called to provide at the present time is of the utmost importance, not only for the Church's life and mission, but also for human society and culture. Moral theologians have the task, in close and vital connection with biblical and dogmatic theology, to highlight through their scientific reflection that dynamic aspect which will elicit the response that man must give to the divine call which comes in the process of his growth in love, within a community of salvation. In this way, moral theology will acquire an inner spiritual dimension in response to the need to develop fully the '*imago Dei*' present in man."

14. *ST*, I, q. 93, a. 6, ad 2: "As Augustine says (*De Trin.* xii, 5), some have thought that the image of God was not in man individually, but severally. They held that 'the man represents the Person of the Father; those born of man denote the person of the Son; and that the woman is a third person in likeness to the Holy Ghost, since she so proceeded from man as not to be his son or daughter.' All of this is manifestly absurd."

15. "Solitude and Subjectivity" general audience of October 24, 1979, in *Man and Woman He Created Them*.

primordial dignity. Rather, the face of God, as the Psalmist says, the "light of thy countenance," is signed upon the individual human person. No talk about a social *imago* can disturb this anthropological center nor extinguish its light.

Another hurdle, perhaps more apparent than real, to speaking of a social *imago* is the fact that a human social order does not enjoy a unity of substance. Augustine famously argued that some sign of the Trinity is found in the distinct but unified mental acts of memory, understanding, and love. The key to this argument is that the acts are one in nature, and this cannot be said of two or more human persons in a social union. If we are to speak of a social image, we need a real principle of unity; for where there is no unity, there is nothing to bear an image (not even dimly and from afar) of the exemplary, divine unity. Therefore, we can rule out right away using the term "image" of two or more things which are unified only by way of aggregation or composition. A heap of sand, a mob in the piazza, a queue at the subway stop share a certain propinquity of place and time, but the unity is entirely accidental. It is neither a substantial nor a social unity, and therefore cannot qualify as a natural, created analogue of the divine persons. But this prompts us to ask the question of whether social unions are mere aggregations.

FROM THE TIME OF POPE LEO XIII: NATURAL LAW AND IMITATION OF GOD

To be sure, a social union is nonsubstantial. Members of a society are not stripped of their individual, substantial unity by virtue of their union with others. The issue stands or falls on whether two or more human persons can enjoy a *communio personarum* that stands between a unity of substance and a mere unity of aggregation. Are social unions real without being substantial? The answer is yes, and it provides a toehold into a solution of how we can speak of social entities imaging God.

Leo XIII and his successors fashioned a solution to this problem in two steps. First, they appropriated Aristotle's understanding of a social unity of order, and grafted it onto Pseudo-Dionysius's formula, the good is self-diffusive (*bonum sui diffusivum est*). This step provided a general, natural law framework for understanding the sacral iconicity of social orders, at least insofar as the individual image acquires the perfection of similitude by being rightly ordered in a social body.[16] Second, Leo and his successors turned to sacramental theology in order to show how *some* social orders directly and properly are called *image*.

---

16. As we discussed in the first chapter, the standard Catholic social doctrine principles of solidarity, subsidiarity, and common good are situated within this general scheme, which depends upon the fact that social unities are more than mere aggregations.

We begin with the first context, that of philosophical anthropology and natural theology. A unity of order stands between unity of substance (a man, bird, or plant) and a unity of mere aggregation (a heap of sand, or a queue waiting for the tram). In a social unity of order (a marriage, family, college, or church) each individual retains his own identity and operations; yet the social whole is more than the sum of its parts. It counts as a subject, person, and agent in its own right. Lawyers and philosophers call this kind of entity a "moral person" or a "legal person," or even a "mystical body." John Paul II calls them interpersonal subjectivities. These and other such terms designate the unity of members in a nonsubstantial "body." A social entity has not only a common end, but also an intrinsic common good. Thomas calls it *communicatio in forma*—a shared form that marks its distinctive kind of union.[17] In this case, the "form" is nothing other than an "order" of common action.

Form of order distinguishes a society from other kinds of human intersubjectivity. A crowd at the shopping mall, or an audience at the opera, exhibits intersubjectivity without pursuing a common end through united action. A fully social intersubjectivity can also be distinguished from that of partners. Partners pool their resources for the purpose of increasing profit. But such pooling does not necessarily require common action, and its proximate end is a private yield cashed out to each partner rather than enjoyment of an indivisible common good. To be sure, any temporal society will institute common pools which render more secure certain resources. Nevertheless, even when a common pool is instituted and maintained by a society, the pool is aggregated and made fit for private use in a way that a social union cannot be. The terms of this distinction in canon law are *universitas rerum*, which is an organization of things, and *universitas personarum*, a union of persons. This distinction is clear when we think of a parish, which in one sense is a unity of buildings, lawns, sprinkler systems, and so forth. At least in Catholic theology, a parish is also, and most properly, a union of persons.

When the Catholic social magisterium speaks of a "true society," it means two or more persons communicating in a common good that cannot be distributed or cashed out. The common good never exists as a private good, and therefore when someone exits a marriage or a polity or a church he cannot take away his private share. Courts understand perfectly well that they can divide and distribute the external properties, but not the marriage itself. It is not distributable in a quantitative sense of the term; and whatever is not distributable according to quantity possesses some real unity. In the case of divorce, therefore, the matrimonial society is not redistributed so much as dissolved or annulled.[18]

---

17. *ST*, I, q. 4, a. 3.

18. *In IV Sent.*, d. 37, qu. 1, a. 1, q. 3, ad 3: "Just as the civic life denotes not the *individual* act of this or that one, but the things that concern the common action of the

Take the example of a queue in front of a credit union: the individuals are *parts* of the queue, *partners* in the credit union, and *members* of St. Rita's parish. To be sure, human persons related as parts and partners exhibit sociability, but it is only in their relation as *members* that it is possible to speak of "society." A social union, as John Paul II insisted, is something more than a relation *alter apud alteram*, a side-by-side intersubjectivity. It will enjoy a common good—a form of reciprocal action—that is intrinsically valuable to each of its members. It's not pooled and then consumed so much as it is participated in. Again, this unity is what distinguishes a common good from divisible common utilities.

Following Thomas Aquinas, Leo XIII and his successors took this Aristotelian rubric of a social unity of order and grafted it onto Pseudo-Dionysius. Dionysius held that creatures imitate God in a twofold manner: first insofar as each creature has its own perfection in the order of substance; second insofar as creatures cause good in others. Thus, the famous dictum: *bonum sui diffusivum est*, the good is diffusive of itself. The greater the good, the more it is communicable and shareable.

Leo and Pius XI were quite keen on this formula, and both of them used it frequently to explain the sacred dignity of social orders. Here, one example will suffice. In the first year of his pontificate, Leo issued a letter on the problem of socialism. On the issue of whether diversity and inequality have a social purpose, Leo writes:

> For, He who created and governs all things has, in His wise providence, appointed that the things which are lowest should attain their ends by those which are intermediate, and these again by the highest. Thus, as even in the kingdom of heaven He hath willed that the choirs of angels be distinct and some subject to others, and also in the Church has instituted various orders and a diversity of offices, so that all are not apostles or doctors or pastors, so also has He appointed that there should be various orders in civil society, differing in dignity, rights, and power, whereby the State, like the Church, should be one body, consisting of many members, some nobler than others, but all necessary to each other and solicitous for the common good.[19]

Leo here is paraphrasing Thomas: "God wished to produce His works in likeness to Himself, as far as possible, in order that they might be perfect, and

---

citizens, so the conjugal life is nothing else than a particular kind of companionship pertaining to that common action. Wherefore as regards this same life the partnership of *married persons* is always indivisible, although it is divisible as regards the act belonging to each party."

19. Encyclical Letter *Quod apostolici muneris* (December 28, 1878), §6.

that He might be known through them. Hence, that He might be portrayed [*repraesentaretur*] in His works, not only according to what He is in Himself, but also according as He acts on others, He laid this *natural law* on all things, that last things should be reduced and perfected by middle things, and middle things by the first, as Dionysius says."[20] Notice that Thomas uses the term "natural law" explicitly in connection with the twofold representation of God in creatures. Clearly, this is not the modern epistemological doctrine of natural law but the more ancient metaphysical one based upon *imitation*.

What exists simply in God is communicated to creatures in a multiform manner. Thus, a double *imitation or portrayal*. First, a diversity of created things, each having a good according to its participated being. Second, a diversity of created things imitating God insofar as they cause goodness in others—insofar as they bring into existence, through secondary causality, additional modes of participation among themselves and others. The superabundance of what exists in God *simply* is, in creation, most perfectly expressed in a varied manifold. Charity perfects a social principle embedded in the creation of angels and men: namely, one loves the good not only as it is possessed and owned, but even more as it is poured forth and communicated to many.[21]

According to the exhortation of Ephesians 5:1, "be ye imitators of God," the intellective creature loves the good precisely as it is communicated to many—as it is made common. And without a unity of order, we would have isolated, individual things (each having the good of its own being), but, all together, portraying nothing more than a quantitative accumulation. Against socialism and liberalism, Leo insisted that the natural law requires both the preservation of the individual good *and* the pouring forth [*diffundatur*] of the good in social relations.[22] As Charles de Koninck pointed out, "One cannot love the common good without loving its shareability with others. The fallen angels did not refuse the perfection of that good that was offered them, they refused its community."[23] For his part, Thomas Aquinas argued that one

---

20. He directly cites 1 Cor 12:28–29, but is paraphrasing *ST*, Supplement, q. 34, a. 1.

21. See Aquinas, *De car.*, a. 2.

22. At best, the Dionysian double imitation shows that the plurality of created substances and their reciprocal operations exhibit something of the godhead in two ways: by unity of substance and in new social unities by diffusion of the good. This formula is drawn from natural theology, and therefore does not establish or demonstrate either that God is a trinity of persons or that the intellective creature is an analogue. As a matter of historical fact, the Dionysian-Thomist position on the double imitation was deployed by Catholic thinkers who, of course, had ready to hand the Trinitarian theology in a proper sense of the term.

23. Charles de Koninck, "The Primacy of the Common Good against the Personalists," in *The Writings of Charles De Koninck*, trans. Ralph McInerny, vol. 2 (Notre Dame, IN: University of Notre Dame Press, 2009), 79.

cannot become a citizen in either a temporal or a celestial society without a special virtue pertaining to the good precisely as shareable. Thus the two master virtues, general justice and charity, which pertain to the common good. Thomas held that as charity "may be called a general virtue in so far as it directs the acts of all the virtues to the Divine good, so too is legal justice, in so far as it directs the acts of all the virtues to the common good. Accordingly, just as charity which regards the Divine good as its proper object, is a special virtue in respect of its essence, so too legal justice is a special virtue in respect of its essence, in so far as it regards the common good as its proper object."[24]

The double imitation can also be considered in the light of the Trinity. In the Trinity, a community of persons communicate in a common form. According to revelation, this is a sui generis case of relations which are not accidental but substantial. In the creature, however, communication in a substantial form would obliterate the individuals and remove their ability to cause good in others. Therefore, creaturely imitation of God exhibits two forms which cannot be confused or absolutely separated. Each form represents something of Trinitarian unity. The creature possesses (imperfectly and from afar) a likeness of image in the order of substantial form (the unity of the soul's operations), as well as an additional perfection or similitude insofar as he or she communicates with others in a social form.[25] Thus, two different, but correlative, ideas of unity and good. As Thomas said: "The creature is like God in unity, inasmuch as each creature is one in itself, and all together are one by unity of order."[26]

What would be missing from the world if the state reduced all dignities to individuals and to a single, homogenous social form of citizenship? Leo contended, it would be like angels without choirs—isolated entities which, individually in the order of substance, bear the divine image, but lack a diversity in communicating as a social form whereby gifts are given and received. Society, said Leo in *Rerum novarum* (1891), cannot be reduced to "one dead level."[27]

---

24. *ST*, II-II, q. 58, a. 6; *De car.*, 2.

25. *SCG*, II, c. 45: "Then, too, a thing approaches to God's likeness the more perfectly as it resembles Him in more things. Now, goodness is in God, and the outpouring of goodness into other things. Hence, the creature approaches more perfectly to God's likeness if it is not only good, but can also act for the good of other things, than if it were good only in itself; that which both shines and casts light is more like the sun than that which only shines. But no creature could act for the benefit of another creature unless Plurality and inequality existed in created things. For the agent is distinct from the patient and superior to it. In order that there might be in created things a perfect representation of God, the existence of diverse grades among them was therefore necessary."

26. *De potentia*, q. 3., a. 16, ad 2. The individual person is good by virtue of "kind," but even better according to actions which communicate good to others. This is an ancient trope on the hexaemeron in which the Creator declares the whole to be "very good."

27. *Rerum novarum*, §17, *Acta Leonis* 11, 108.

It was audacious in 1878 not only to pull Dionysius's treatise on angelic hierarchy out of the hat to respond to socialism; even more generally, Leo and his successors were advancing an argument for normative social pluralism based upon a social imitation of God.

Recall that in Genesis the individual acts of creation are deemed "good" one by one. Yet the hexaemeral acts are crowned by the relation of Adam and Eve. This order is deemed "very good." Something new is brought into existence. Not another substance, but a unity of order whereby persons, through action, cause good in one another. This diffusion of the good, in human persons, from the beginning is marked by a matrimonial social union which is a type of the Church.

While Leo and Pius XI sometimes use the term *imago* of this new relation, more often they use the term *similitudo*. Recall that *similitudo* can mean the perfection of an image. The human person is made unto the image and likeness of God, first as regards his very being, and second *sub specie societatis*.[28] In short, social unions are the perfection of the image—they pertain to likeness, presupposing image.[29] But, one might ask, if the social union is not substantial, doesn't this imply that it is accidental? The answer is yes, but perhaps not quite as one might suppose. We read and hear much today about a theology of communion that is "relational." For instance, in *Caritas in veritate*,

---

28. *Quadragesimo anno*, §84. The argument continues through §87, where Pius picks up the thread of Leo's teaching on the diversity of associations. "Because order, as Saint Thomas well explains, is unity arising from the harmonious arrangement of many objects, a true, genuine social order demands that the various members of a society be united together by some strong bond. This unifying force is present not only in the producing of goods or the rendering of services—in which the employers and employees of an identical industry or profession collaborate jointly—but also in that common good, to achieve which all industries and professions together ought, each to the best of its ability, to cooperate amicably. And this unity will be the stronger and more effective, the more faithfully individuals and the industries and professions themselves strive to do their work and excel in it."

Pius's citation takes the reader to two places where Thomas develops the Pseudo-Dionysian theme of a twofold likeness of creatures to God. In the first, taken from *Summa contra gentiles*, Thomas lays out the principle of the *duplex imitatio*, in the order of being and in the order of the good. *SCG*, III, cc. 70–71.

29. *Divini redemptoris*, §29: "It is society which affords the opportunities for the development of all the individual and social gifts bestowed on human nature. These natural gifts have a value surpassing the immediate interests of the moment, for in society they reflect the divine perfection, which would not be true were man to live alone [*divinamque praeferunt in civili ordinatione perfectionem; quod quidem in singulis hominibus contingere ullo modo nequit*]. But on final analysis, even in this latter function, society is made for man, that he may recognize this reflection of God's perfection [*ut hanc divinae perfectionis imaginem*], and refer it in praise and adoration to the Creator. Only man, the human person, and not society in any form is endowed with reason and a morally free will."

Benedict XVI proposes that Catholic social doctrine "requires a *deeper critical evaluation of the category of relation*. This is a task that cannot be undertaken by the social sciences alone, insofar as the contribution of disciplines such as metaphysics and theology is needed if man's transcendent dignity is to be properly understood. . . . The Christian revelation of the unity of the human race presupposes a *metaphysical interpretation of the 'humanum' in which relationality is an essential element*."[30] The recent statement by the Catholic Church's International Theological Commission on man as the image of God asserts that the human person is "an essentially relational being."[31]

We will have more to say about these recent statements later in this chapter. Here, a brief clarification will have to suffice. In the scholastic tradition inherited by the modern popes, the terms "substance," "relation," and "habit" are drawn from Thomas Aquinas, who took and reworked Aristotle's categories. Within this scheme, accidents are not unimportant. For instance, all of the acquired and infused virtues are accidental under the rubric of "habit." One's unity with his or her spouse is accidental under the rubric of "relation." In all beings other than God, perfection depends upon the individual substance having the right accidents.

> From the point of view of its substantial goodness a thing is said to be good in a certain sense, but from that of its accidental goodness it is said to be good without qualification. . . . A thing is called a being inasmuch as it is considered absolutely, but good, as has already been made clear, in relation to other things. Now it is by its essential principles that a thing is fully constituted in itself so that it subsists; but it is not so perfectly constituted as to stand as it should in relation to everything outside itself except by means of accidents added to the essence, because the operations by which one thing is in some sense joined to another proceed from the essence through powers distinct from it. Consequently, nothing achieves goodness absolutely unless it is complete in both its essential and its accidental principles. Any perfection which a creature has from its essential and accidental principles combined, God has in its entirety by his one simple act of being.[32]

A social unity of order is not a substance, but rather an order in which the right relations and habits exist as accidents, which is to say, as perfections, in the individual members. Precisely because social unities are not substances, the same individual can be a member of more than one social body without

---

30. Benedict XVI, Encyclical Letter *Caritas in veritate* (July 7, 2009), §§53, 55.

31. The International Theological Commission's document *Communion and Stewardship: Human Persons Created in the Image of God* (2004), §10.

32. *De Ver.*, q. 21, a. 5.

moving from substance to substance. But he or she certainly needs the appropriate habits and relations to participate as a member in this or that society. This is the key to understanding why social relations and their proper habits come under the notion of *similitudo*—likeness as a moral perfection of what is made unto the image of God.

To return to the main thread of our discussion, Catholic social doctrine contended that by suppressing and homogenizing social relationships other than citizenship, the modern state was at war with a sacred order of things. Insofar as the state permitted the existence of other social entities only by the concession and in the pattern of state sovereignty, the state was implicitly claiming to be the exemplary cause of the good. Social entities are, in effect, icons or copies of the state. We should not underestimate how widely and deeply Catholic thinkers since 1789 depicted the modern state as a neo-pagan expression of state sovereignty.

As for liberalism, the social magisterium typically complained that the second prong of the Dionysian formula is either denied or obscured—diffusion of the good, for liberalism, is only an aggregate result ensuing upon self-interested action, such as the "hidden hand" of the market. Beneficence arises even in the absence of benevolence. We might think again of Hayek's notion of "catallaxy," a spontaneous order in which a general good is attained without anyone intending to do so. This model preserves, perhaps, the dignity of the individual in the abstract, but does not affirm the perfection of the image in social unity. So, if the total state is a demonic rival to the divinity, the liberal state is a demonic rival to the diffusion of the good via social unions which represent, however inchoately, the divine Trinity.

The scissors-like approach positions issues of polity and public order within social sacralities of nature and grace. Except for a few notable exceptions (mostly in the 1960s), magisterial documents will include these three components: 1) a problem touching upon the state, 2) a discussion of what stands higher than the state, and 3) a discussion of what is lower. Take *Dignitatis humanae* (1965), the very tersely worded declaration on religious liberty. The council begins with the question whether the state may legitimately either command or prohibit acts of religion; it then makes a natural law argument for the inviolability of conscience not only as the individual stands before God but also in communal worship, family, and education; and it ends with the liberty of the Church instituted by Christ, which of course goes beyond natural law warrants for liberty from the state. The freedom of the Church "is the fundamental principle in what concerns the relationships between the Church and governments and the whole civil order."[33]

---

33. Preeminently, the Church's freedom is not the *cura religionis* or the *cura iuris* but the care for the salvation of men, *quantum salus hominum curanda requirat (Dignitatis*

The scissor-like approach is important both for what it affirms and what it denies. It denies that any social-political order is legitimate if it proceeds from, or leads inevitably to, social homogeneity. As we have seen, undifferentiated equality can be achieved in two ways: the first by a kind of atomism, where individual persons are recognized but their social memberships are regarded as mere aggregations; the second by a kind of socialism, where individual persons possess no moral standing until and unless they are made members of a politically constructed community. In either way, "democracy" is not sustainable as a legitimate social "form." Pius XII made this clear in his Christmas address of 1944, *Benignitas et humanitas* (True and False Democracy). "If, then, we consider the extent and nature of the sacrifices demanded of all the citizens, especially in our day when the activity of the state is so vast and decisive, the democratic form of government appears to many as a postulate of nature imposed by reason itself." But, he warned, "the state does not contain in itself and does not mechanically bring together in a given territory a shapeless mass of individuals. It is, and should in practice be, the organic and organizing unity of a real people. The people, and a shapeless multitude (or, as it is called, 'the masses') are two distinct concepts."[34] Without adherence to both prongs of the Dionysian understanding of natural law—the good of created persons, and the good diffused in social relationships by free action—there can be no authentic social form at all. Moreover, social forms which privatize what *Dignitatis* calls the "fundamental principle," the social form of the Church, are at odds with both nature and grace.

Image and Sacrament

Now we must move along from the general pattern of imitating God *sub specie societatis*, to a more specific one—*in specie sacramenti*, with respect to a sacramental image. Leo's *Arcanum divinae* (1880) and Pius's *Casti connubii* (1930) were the two most important teachings on matrimony since the Council of Trent. Leo and Pius contended with state laws on civil marriage and divorce which were driven by the proposition that, by nature, marriage is only a collaboration for the purpose of reproduction. Matrimony, on that view, has no fixed, or what Leo called "insculpted," form. Therefore, the form of union falls entirely under the state's law, either by way of a direct imposition or by way of what the law allows individuals to decide.[35] It is not difficult to

---

Humanae, §13). See my paper, "Political Pluralism and Religious Liberty: The Teaching of *Dignitatis Humanae*" (presentation, Meeting of the Pontifical Academy of Social Science, Rome, Italy, April 29, 2011), available at vatican.va.

34. Pius XII, "Benignitas et humanitas [True and False Democracy]," December 24, 1944; *AAS* 37, 13–14.

appreciate why the social form of matrimony was of great interest to Catholics. For without an *insculpted form* marriage cannot be a natural sign of union of Christ and his Church. In short, marriage would not be sacramental in the sense required for the sacramental economy of the New Covenant.

Citing Thomas, Pius XI contends that marriage is not merely a consent to the joining of bodies with a reproductive end in view. Rather, marriage is a consent to a certain union upon which ensue the ends.[36] Marriage is not a free-floating set of ends or purposes, but ends brought about through a specific mode of union. As Thomas taught: "Nor is the direct object of consent a husband but union with a husband on the part of the wife, even as it is union with a wife on the part of the husband."[37] Psychologically, one desires and chooses *this* man or woman. It could also be true that one has in view a mutually agreeable end, such as reproduction, economic security for the wider family, etc. But it is the consent *to the union* that enables the societal form and deserves to be called marriage. The other intentions—to consent to *this* man or woman, and to consent to a common end—can obtain in the absence of matrimony. Indeed, partnerships of various kinds, including partnerships that create a common pool of resources, will often entail a consensus (this person rather than that person) for such and such an end without implying consent to a societal union.[38]

---

35. *Casti connubii*, §49, 558: "To begin at the very source of these evils, their basic principle lies in this, that matrimony is repeatedly declared to be not instituted by the Author of nature nor raised by Christ the Lord to the dignity of a true sacrament, but invented by man. Some confidently assert that they have found no evidence of the existence of matrimony in nature or in her laws, but regard it merely as the means of producing life and of gratifying in one way or another a vehement impulse; on the other hand, others recognize that certain beginnings or, as it were, seeds of true wedlock are found in the nature of man since, unless men were bound together by some form of permanent tie, the dignity of husband and wife or the natural end of propagating and rearing the offspring would not receive satisfactory provision. At the same time they maintain that in all beyond this germinal idea matrimony, through various concurrent causes, is invented solely by the mind of man, established solely by his will."

36. *Arcanum* and *Casti* are interrelated in more than one way. In the first place, Pius XI issued *Casti* as a reprise of Leo XIII's *Arcanum*, which he wished to "affirm" and to "expound more fully" (*Casti connubii*, §4, 540). Thematically their nucleus is identical. As Pius said, Leo meant to vindicate the "divine institution of matrimony" and to defend the "perpetual stability of the marriage bond, its unity and firmness" (§5, 540). Citing Thomas, Pius insisted that marriage is consent to the union (*essentialibus proprietatibus subiciatur*), and should there be anything compatible with the union it is not true matrimony (*non esset verum matrimonium*) for the ends are already contained in the form (§5, 541–42; citing *ST*, III, Suppl., q. 49, a. 3).

37. *In IV Sent.*, d. 27, qu. 1, a. 2, q. 1, ad 3.

38. Thus, Thomas insists, with his typical brevity that reaches to the heart of the question, that matrimony is not merely the joining of minds or bodies, but rather that "the

Reworking these very texts, Pius XI writes that while the begetting and education of children are first in the order of ends, they are not first in the form that makes matrimony: "This mutual molding [*interior conformatio*] of husband and wife, this determined effort to perfect each other, can in a very real sense, as the Roman Catechism teaches, be said to be the chief reason and purpose of matrimony, provided matrimony be looked at not in the restricted sense as instituted for the proper conception and education of the child, but more widely as the blending of life as a whole and the mutual interchange and sharing thereof."[39] He argues that marriage depends upon a "generous surrender of his own person made to another for the whole span of life."[40] Because its social form is instituted by God, Pius asserts that marriage is "more sacred" than the state.[41]

Yet, it is more sacred for another reason. Matrimony is the natural fundament of the sacrament, the sign of the unity of Christ and the Church.[42] In the case of marriage, the material sign is already a social union (it is the only one of the seven sacraments that has a social unity of order as its natural sign). By grace, this social union is called *imago Christi*. Pius calls it a "living image" and an "efficacious" and "mystical image" of the whole Christ, Head and members.[43]

---

joining together of bodies and minds is a result of matrimony." *In IV Sent.*, d. 27, q. 1, a. 1. The essentials: one man and one woman, consenting to a perpetual union, consummated by a one-flesh act of unity.

39. *Casti connubii*, §24, 548f.

40. *Casti connubii*, §9, 543. Marriage is a "union of souls" that makes it entirely different from the "union of animals." In the old *Codex Iuris Canonici* (1917), still in place during Pius's pontificate, canon 1081, §2 defined matrimonial consent as the mutual exchange of "perpetual and exclusive rights to the body [*ius in corpus*], for those actions that are of themselves suitable for the generation of children." In isolation, the canon is perplexing because it does not include the purpose of education; what is more, the phrase *ius in corpus* could suggest the propinquity-of-organs position against which Leo and Pius had been arguing. In fact, the revised *Code* (1983) would rework this canon to reflect Pius's definition of marriage as self-gift: "an act of will by which a man and a woman by an irrevocable covenant mutually give and accept one another for the purpose of establishing a marriage." (CIC [1983], can. 1057, §2.)

41. *Casti connubii*, §69, 565.

42. From the beginning, God "sealed" and "insculpted" in this union the two *proprietates* of unity and indissolubility (*Arcanum*, §5, 12f.). This reference to a law insculpted is taken from Thomas's idea of *lex indita*, which is to say, a law that moves its subject by communicating an inherent form. In the case of marriage, what is indicted or insculpted is not a natural kind but a social form (*vera haec conuigii forma*) amenable to the communication of a new form (*novam quamdam formam*) by the institution of the sacrament (*Arcanum*, §6, 13).

43. "These parties, let it be noted, not fettered but adorned by the golden bond of the sacrament, not hampered but assisted, should strive with all their might to the end that

Importantly, Pius insists that husband and wife bear the image by reciprocation. It has to be done together.[44] At least under the sacrament, neither the husband nor the wife alone are the image, but the union itself. For the sacrament, methodological individualism cannot suffice—namely, that social unities and relations among members can be reduced to nonsocial properties of members or composites thereof. So, here we have at least one instance of a social entity that is not just a perfection of the individual image, but one that is itself the bearer of an image.

We should not be surprised that Catholic social doctrine has regularly and insistently turned to the issue of matrimony. It is not, in the first place, a question of moral theology. Rather, it is the original case of a social union, precisely as a society, bearing the dignity of *imago*. And not just any sacral image, but from a theological standpoint, a plutonium-grade image: namely, *imago Christi*. The "whole Christ" who not only incorporates human nature body and soul, but also concorporates, which is to say, he founds a social body which is the *Christus totus*.[45] We have, in short, an image derived not just from afar, in the processions of the divine persons, but one more immediately in the mission of the incarnate second person. Here, there is a new and distinct ground for affirming *unto the image and likeness*. If we apply the three aspects of Eucharist to marriage, we identify the *sacramentum tantum*, the sign alone, which is a conjugal union of man and woman; the *sacramentum et res*, the sign together with its internal reality, the union of Christ and the Church; and the *res tantum*, communion in a social unity of order.

Even so, it depends in part upon the integrity of the natural sign, which is marriage itself. This is why the legal, political, and philosophical conflict between the modern state and the Church over marriage and divorce was intimately related to both social doctrine and to sacramental theology. Sacramental marriage was the test case for things that are both higher and lower than the state. Marriage is a social entity that not only fits the Dionysian formula, but enjoys a special status. Although it is in one sense lower than the state, in another sense it is, as Pius asserted, more sacred than the state. For its social form is not only directly instituted by God, but is also the natural sign of

---

their wedlock, not only through the power and symbolism of the sacrament, but also through their spirit and manner of life, may be and remain always the living image [*viva imago*] of that most fruitful union of Christ with the Church, which is to be venerated as the sacred token of most perfect love. . . . [Christ] desired marriage to be and made it the mystical image of His own ineffable union with the Church [*qui matrimonium mysticam esse voluit effecitque imaginem suae ineffabilis cum ecclesia coniunctionis*]." Here, splicing together *Casti*, §§42, 129.

44. *Casti connubii*, §29.

45. CCC, §§794–95.

Christ's social body. Here, the social form is called *imago*—the *conformatio* of spouses is a sign of Christ, whose incarnation is not merely an *incorporatio* (God taken flesh) but also a *concorporatio*, the establishment by grace of a social body. This social body is, in the strict sense of the term, *imago Christi*.

ECCLESIOLOGICAL THEMES

In the opening pages of *Lumen gentium*, the Second Vatican Council's constitution on the Church, we read that the ecclesial union is "like a sacrament."[46] In fact, the idea that the Church is in some analogous way a sacramental image is presented so quickly that one might think that it is either a pure assertion or that the argument had already been made. Indeed, it had been made in Pius XII's *Mystici corporis*. Writing in 1943, in the middle of World War II, Pius set out to explain why the primary mission of the Church is to be Christ's social body, and thereby to be the eschatological sign of the unity of the human race.

In *Mystici*, Pius gives a rather thorough survey of the different ways that a social unity transcends the sum of its parts without destruction of its individual members. The Church, he notes, shares many of these predicates: it is a unity of order that does not destroy its individual members, it enjoys an intrinsic common good, functional organicity, and so forth. Unlike other societies, however, the mystical body of Christ has no identity other than being Christ's social body. In the case of marriage we can speak of a natural form that achieves a higher unity by the habilitation of grace. For its part, the Church has no identity other than being grafted onto and conformed to its Head. It has no form other than the actions of its members through the outpouring of charity, the ordering of the Holy Spirit, and sacramental actions. Were the Church only a social and juridical unity, it would be a social entity of some sort (like a club, or association), but it would not be the Church, even if it still shows up in the Yellow Pages.

---

46. "Since the Church is in Christ like a sacrament or as a sign and instrument both of a very closely-knit union with God and of the unity of the whole human race" (§1). Constituted and ordered "as a society" (§8), the church includes what is "suitable for visible and social unity"—a "visible sacrament of this saving unity." For John Paul II's account of the analogous uses of sacrament, see "Man in the Dimension of Gift," general audience of February 29, 1980, in *Man and Woman He Created Them*, 203. The reader should note that John Paul II uses the words "sign" and "sacrament" in analogous ways; see also John Paul II, "Marriage as Figure and as Sacrament of the New Covenant," October 20, 1982; repr., "Marriage as Figure and as Sacrament of the New Covenant," in *Man and Woman He Created Them*, 510–12. On his understanding of restricted and wide senses of sacrament, consult the useful index by Michael Waldstein.

Pius writes that, by sanctifying grace, we are conformed to the image of the Son of God, and renewed according to the image of him who created us.[47] But he goes on to argue, "It is the will of Jesus Christ that the whole body of the Church, no less than the individual members, should resemble Him."[48] Precisely as a society, the Church is Christ's social body expressing "both exterior and interior, a most faithful image of Christ."[49] Citing Bellarmine and Gregory of Nyssa, Pius insists that the Church is a *person*, called Christ.[50] The whole Christ (*Christum totum*) is the head and his social body.[51]

The surprising thing at Vatican II was not *Lumen gentium*, which completed Pius's encyclical on the Church as social *imago Christi*. Rather, the surprising issue was tucked inside of *Gaudium et spes*, where the council treats the (natural) dignity of the individual as *imago Dei*. Early drafts had emphasized Genesis 1:17, "male and female he created them."[52] Rightly so, for traditionally that scriptural verse was referenced for the estate of marriage in the beginning (Mt 19), Christ's prayer for the unity of the Church (Jn 17), and the Pauline teaching about the "great sacrament" of Christ and his Church (Eph 5). All these scriptural passages suppose that a social union is a sign of the sacred. And while the signs differ according to sacramental economies (creation and redemption), the primordial analogue of the human person made unto the image and likeness of God, male and female, is rather important. It stands prominently in both creation and redemption.

At the council, some bishops wanted to say that the social relation is, by creation and not just by grace, a fundamental aspect of the *imago*. Other

---

47. *Mystici corporis* uses the phrase *"imagini Filii dei"* at §46 and cites Rom 8:29 and Col 3:10.

48. *Mystici corporis*, §47.

49. *Mystici corporis*, §48; *Christi imaginem quam perfectissime exprimat*, *Mystici corporis*, §54.

50. See *Mystici corporis*, §53, which describes the Church: *"Ut ipsa quasi altera Christi persona exsistat."* In §52, the document reads: "The social Body of the Church [*sociale Ecclesiae Corpus*] should be honored by the name of Christ—namely, that our Savior Himself sustains in a divine manner the society which He founded."

51. *Mystici corporis*, §77: "Herein we find the reason why, according to the opinion of Augustine already referred to, the mystical Head, which is Christ, and the Church, which here below as another Christ shows forth His person, constitute one new man, in whom heaven and earth are joined together in perpetuating the saving work of the Cross: Christ We mean, the Head and the Body, the whole Christ."

52. My account of the discussion at Vatican II and its implications for the work of John Paul II is indebted to the work of Jaroslav Kupchek, OP, "Komunijny wymiar obrazu Bożego w człowieku w soborowej konstytucji Gaudium et spes," *Studia Theologica Varsaviensia* 44 (2006): 139–58. His full work is his book on John Paul II's theology of *imago Dei*: *Dar i komunia. Teologia ciała w ujęciu Jana Pawła II* (Kraków, 2006).

bishops, however, worried that if the *imago* is predicated on the relation, it would imply that the human person receives the *imago* from a relation to others (*ex relatione ad alios*).[53] This would not only stumble into the heresy that holds that the *imago* is assembled through social relationships; it would also mislead and derogate from the dignity of the individual, under attack in modern times. We recall that in 1965 the totalitarian regimes were still in place. So, they compromised. Here's how the relevant section of *Gaudium et spes*, §24 reads in its final form:

> Indeed, the Lord Jesus, when He prayed to the Father, "that all may be one . . . as we are one" [John 17:21–22] opened up vistas closed to human reason, for He implied a certain likeness between the union of the divine Persons, and the unity of God's sons in truth and charity. This likeness [*similitudo*] reveals that man, who is the only creature on earth which God willed for itself, cannot fully find himself except through a sincere gift of himself.

The council took from *Casti connubii* Pius XI's description of the matrimonial society as a "sincere gift" and then spliced it together with Christ's prayer for the Church's union in the order of grace. Interestingly, rather than dealing straight on with the question of the natural condition of the *imago* in the order of creation, they quote authoritative texts which pertain to how, in the order of grace, matrimony and church are *imagines Christi*. Although the text clearly indicates a natural law position when it proposes that man is perfected by making a sincere gift of himself, the authoritative sources for the social aspects are taken from the New Covenant without the natural fundament drawn from Genesis. Leaving out Genesis, and moving directly to John 17, it seems that the social aspect of the image of God is constituted entirely by grace, which of course is not quite right on the traditional reading of Genesis 1:26 and Ephesians 5.

John Paul II and the Theology of the Body

Upon his election in 1978, John Paul II began to rework *Gaudium et spes*, §24. "The Second Vatican Council, in speaking of the likeness of God, uses extremely significant terms," he noted. "It refers not only to the divine image and likeness which every human being as such already possesses, but also and primarily [*verum etiam et praesertim*] to a certain similarity between the union of the divine persons and the union of God's children in truth and love."[54]

---

53. *Acta Synodolia (AS)*, 1, 4a, s. 720.
54. John Paul II, *Gratissimam Sane* [Letter to Families] (February 2, 1994), §8.

In his lengthy series of Wednesday audiences, the pope argued that Adam's solitude, mythically represented in Genesis 2, confirms the notion that the individual person is the bearer of a divine-like dignity. Everything in the solitude, the pope insists, must be affirmed as that which constitutes *man*.[55] In other words, Adamic solitude represents what the tradition meant by substantial unity—a perfection that cannot be supplanted or cancelled by social relations. In origin, form, and finality the individual is created for God alone, and thus is said to be made unto the image of God. In Genesis, of course, Adamic solitude is resolved by God, who puts Adam into a sleep, from which the original Adam awakes, male and female. Adam's solitude is addressed not by assimilation to another natural substance, nor by the creation of a new substance, but by a *communio personarum*—a sexually differentiated community of persons.

What's important, for our purposes, is John Paul's conclusion to this line of thought:

> If . . . we want to retrieve also from the account of the Yahwist text the concept of "image of God" we can deduce that *man became the image of God not only through his own humanity, but also through the communion of persons*, which man and woman form from the very beginning. The function of the image is that of mirroring the one who is the model, of reproducing its own prototype. Man becomes an image of God not so much in the moment of solitude as in the moment of communion. He is, in fact, "from the beginning" not only an image in which the solitude of one Person, who rules the world, mirrors itself, but also and essentially the image of an inscrutable divine communion of Persons.[56]

Right away we should put aside the idea that the pope means chronological moments. The preceding discussion of Adamic solitude makes clear enough that the created image is not being assembled in time or constituted by adding sociological relations. Perhaps we can interpret the passage as an exegetical deepening of the Dionysian formula of a double imitation: first, the moment of solitude representing the image vested in the substantial nature, and second the gift and communion, representing diffusion of the good. The individual is perfected as a member in union with others by performing acts of giving and receiving, and in this sense "becomes" the image in its perfection. Hence, both the image and its *similitudo*. In fact, John Paul elsewhere refers explicitly to the Dionysian principle in what he calls the double subjectivity of the *imago*.[57]

---

55. John Paul II, "The Meaning of Original Unity," November 14, 1979, in *Man and Woman He Created Them*, 162.

56. John Paul II, "The Meaning of Original Unity," 163.

57. *Letter to Families*, §10: "There is a shortage of people with whom to create and share the common good; and yet that good, by its nature, demands to be created and shared

The human creature, he says, images the Trinity in his own subjectivity and as a member of a social subjectivity—it is in the nature of the created *imago* to diffuse the good through reciprocity of the gift.

There is no question but that he wants to enrich the primordial sign or the sacramentality of the *humanum* precisely in its "unity of the two."[58] For the Catholic tradition, sacramental theology (of marriage) and ecclesiology require this union, "from the beginning." The pope asserts a relational ontology of the created *imago* that *Gaudium et spes*, §24 hesitated to affirm.

Thus, in this dimension, a primordial *sacrament* is constituted, understood as a sign that efficaciously transmits in the visible world the invisible mystery hidden in God from eternity. The sacrament, as a visible sign, is constituted with man, inasmuch as he is a "body," through his "visible" masculinity and femininity. The body, in fact, and only the body, is capable of making visible what is invisible: the spiritual and the divine. It has been created to transfer into the visible reality of the world the mystery hidden from eternity in God, and thus to be a sign of it.[59]

The International Theological Commission for two years studied these issues, and in 2003 submitted to Cardinal Ratzinger, president of the commission, a document entitled *Communion and Stewardship: Human Persons Created in the Image of God*. Referring to Genesis 1:26, the commission states: "God placed the first human beings in relation to one another, each with a partner of the other sex. . . . According to this conception, man is not an isolated individual but a person—an essentially relational being. . . . The fundamentally relational character of the *imago Dei* itself constitutes its ontological structure."[60] The relational nature, they say, "belongs to the specific manner

---

with others, *bonum est diffusivum sui*: 'good is diffusive of itself.' The more 'common' the good, the 'more properly one's own it will also be: mine—yours—ours. This is the logic behind living according to the good, living in truth and charity. If man is able to accept and follow this logic, his life truly becomes a 'sincere gift' [*donum sincerum*]." He is referring here to *Gaudium et spes*, §24.

58. *Sollicitudo rei socialis*, §52: "The fundamental reason [*fundamentalis ratio*] that requires and explains the presence and the collaboration of both men and women is not only, as it was just emphasized, the major source of meaning and efficacy in the pastoral action of the Church, nor *even less is it the simple sociological fact* of sharing a life together as human beings, which is natural for man and woman. It is, rather, the original plan of the Creator who from the 'beginning' willed the human being to be a 'unity of the two,' and willed man and woman to be the prime community of persons, source of every other community, and, at the same time, to be a 'sign' of that interpersonal communion of love which constitutes the mystical, intimate life of God, One in Three."

59. John Paul II, "General Audience," February 20, 1980, in *Man and Woman He Created Them*, 203. Again, for his understanding of restricted and wide senses of sacrament, see the index by Michael Waldstein.

60. *Communion and Stewardship*, §10.

in which the *imago Dei* exists."[61] The commission rejected any sort of dualism that would vest the image only in the psychological capacities to the exclusion of the human body; and it denied any sort of monism that would vest the image only in the actualization of the individual.[62] This language, however, presupposes a distinction between substance and relation so that the latter can truly represent a perfection of the former.

The commission therefore pursued the stronger and broader interpretation of the Trinitarian and relational structure of the created *imago*. It also emphasized the sacramental context of *imago Christi*: "The created image affirmed by the Old Testament is, according to the New Testament, to be completed in the *imago Christi*. In the New Testament development of this theme, two distinctive elements emerge: the Christological and Trinitarian character of the *imago Dei*, and the role of sacramental mediation in the formation of the *imago Christi*."[63] Not surprisingly, marriage is taken to be the chief instance of both the natural and supernaturally elevated situation of the *imago*. Marriage is the foundational example for both the natural and supernatural social principles of man being made unto the image and likeness of God.

---

61. *Communion and Stewardship*, §33. This proposition should be interpreted in the fashion of Thomas (*De Ver.*, q. 21, a. 5), namely that the created human being is not good in every respect it needs to be good without the proper complement of accidents, for example, habits and relations.

62. *Communion and Stewardship*, §9: "Two themes converge to shape the biblical perspective. In the first place, the whole of man is seen as created in the image of God. This perspective excludes interpretations which locate the *imago Dei* in one or another aspect of human nature (for example, his upright stature or his intellect) or in one of his qualities or functions (for example, his sexual nature or his domination of the earth). Avoiding both monism and dualism, the Bible presents a vision of the human being in which the spiritual is understood to be a dimension together with the physical, social and historical dimensions of man." Later, the document notes: "Present-day theology is striving to overcome the influence of dualistic anthropologies that locate the *imago Dei* exclusively with reference to the spiritual aspect of human nature. Partly under the influence first of Platonic and later of Cartesian dualistic anthropologies, Christian theology itself tended to identify the *imago Dei* in human beings with what is the most specific characteristic of human nature, viz., mind or spirit. The recovery both of elements of biblical anthropology and of aspects of the Thomistic synthesis has contributed to the effort in important ways" (§27). The Thomistic synthesis, meaning hylemorphism, the soul as the form of the body. Thomas held that although the created *imago* is chiefly the soul, it also applies to the human body insofar as the rational soul is its "form." See *In III Sent.*, d. 2, q. 1, a. 3, qc. 1, ad 2, where he contends that the living body is *similitudo imaginis*. Also, see his interesting but rather brief thoughts on the comparison of the imprinted *imago* respectively in the angelic and human beings for whom corporeality adds a good that is specific to the human *imago*, in *ST*, I, q. 93, a. 3.

63. *Communion and Stewardship*, §11.

While it is certainly true that union between human beings can be realized in a variety of ways, Catholic theology today affirms that marriage constitutes an elevated form of the communion between human persons and one of the best analogies of the Trinitarian life. When a man and a woman unite their bodies and spirits in an attitude of total openness and self-giving, they form *a new image of God*. Their union as one flesh does not correspond simply to a biological necessity, but to the intention of the Creator in leading them to share the happiness of being made in his image. The Christian tradition speaks of marriage as an eminent way of sanctity.[64]

CONCLUSION

Benedict XVI's first encyclical, *Deus caritas est* (2005), immediately picks up this theme of image and union of persons. The biblical faith shows something new about God and man. God is revealed as capable of a unity of love with the creature "in which both God and man remain themselves and yet become fully one."[65] God not only creates and capacitates the human being, but initiates a society with man. On the anthropological side, the solitude of Adam can be contrasted with the Platonic myth in the *Symposium*, according to which the original *humanum* is a self-sufficient sphere, who, for the sake of punishment, is broken into two. In the Platonic myth, the loss of original self-sufficiency and the ensuing quest for relationship is a penal exercise; in Genesis 2 the communion of Adam and Eve represent a completion in one flesh.[66] Hence, the society is not a diremption but a fulfillment of individual's humanity.

Because the social principle is woven into the deepest mysteries of God and man, Christianity can be said to be a "sacramental mysticism [that] is social in character."[67] It is a doctrine of communion. Properly understood, in charity "the usual contraposition between worship and ethics simply falls apart."[68] Eucharist is communion with God and neighbor, which is the essence of the two great commandments. In his subsequent encyclical, *Spe salvi* (2007), Benedict insists along this same line of thought that individualism

---

64. *Communion and Stewardship*, §38 (emphasis added). And beyond marriage, to the race: "Every individual human being as well as the whole human community are created in the image of God. In its original unity—of which Adam is the symbol—the human race is made in the image of the divine Trinity. Willed by God, it makes its way through the vicissitudes of human history towards a perfect communion, also willed by God, but yet to be fully realized. In this sense, human beings share the solidarity of a unity that both already exists and is still to be attained" (§43).

65. Benedict XVI, Encyclical Letter *Deus caritas est* (December 25, 2005), §10.

66. *Deus caritas est*, §11.

67. *Deus caritas est*, §14.

68. *Deus caritas est*, §14.

obscures the Christian understanding of salvation as a social reality.[69] Here, the pope cites Henri de Lubac, who contended in *Catholicisme: les aspects sociaux du dogme* (Catholicism: The Social Aspects of Doctrine) that the Church's social teachings are nothing less than the Church's self-understanding of the mystery of ecclesial communion. "It is social," he explained, "in the deepest sense of the word: not merely in its applications in the field of natural institutions but first and foremost in itself, in the heart of its mystery, in the essence of its dogma. It is social in a sense which should have made the expression 'social Catholicism' pleonastic."[70] Interestingly, when he was cardinal prefect of the Congregation for the Doctrine of the Faith, Joseph Ratzinger wrote a new foreword to de Lubac's treatise, noting: "The social dimension which de Lubac saw rooted in deepest mystery has often sunk to the merely sociological so that the unique Christian contribution to the right understanding of history and community has disappeared from sight. Instead of a leaven for the age, or its salt, we are often simply its echo."[71]

The mission of the Church is to be the sacrament of *concorporatio*, that is, Christ taking a social body that images the communion of divine persons.[72] In this, Benedict echoes the *Catechism of the Catholic Church*: "The vocation of humanity is to show forth the image of God and to be transformed into the image of the Father's only Son."[73] An adequate anthropology must include, without confusion or reduction, the two memberships—the individual as human person, and as a member of social orders. Both are manifest in the economies of creation and redemption. Individualism not only occludes the dignity of membership in society, but also presents a distorted understanding of the individual.

At the outset I pointed out that the human *imago Dei* as a created analogue of a Trinity of divine persons is in the public domain only by virtue of revelation. Thus, Christians of all stripes constantly need to be reminded that not every dignitarian proposition is the same as the revealed truth that man is made unto the image and likeness of God. The teaching of Genesis and the New Testament about the created and transformed image is not a bottom-drawer garment covering Christian theology and the various humanisms.[74]

---

69. Benedict XVI, Encyclical Letter *Spe salvi* (November 30, 2007), §14.

70. Henri de Lubac, *Catholicism: Christianity and the Common Destiny of Man*, trans. Lancelot C. Sheppard and Sister Elizabeth Englund, OCD, with a foreword by Joseph Cardinal Ratzinger (San Francisco: Ignatius Press, 1988), 15.

71. Ratzinger, foreword to de Lubac, *Catholicism*, 12.

72. See *Caritas in veritate*, §54.

73. CCC, §1877.

74. As Benedict XVI says in *Deus caritas est* (§18), "If I have no contact whatsoever with God in my life, then I cannot see in the other anything more than the other, and I am incapable of seeing in him the image of God."

The same thing must be said for the social and sacramental aspect of the image in the case of marriage and the Church. All of this is something more than a merely "adequate anthropology." It is "adequate" to what Scripture and tradition teach about the whole truth.

Theological anthropology, however, includes common experience and those truths which can be gathered from it. Two seem to be of special importance. First, that the human person possesses a unity of being and operation that manifests certain excellences. This kind of dignity is in the public domain by common experience. Indeed, many wisdom traditions have taken note of the divine-like human capacities. Second, that there is a real and not merely a nominal difference between aggregations of human persons and social unions. The distinction comes from Aristotle, and it hardly depends upon special revelation. These two—the excellence of the human person and the excellence of social unions—are, so to speak, "preambles" of the theology of the image of God. In the modern era, faced with liberal individualism and various statist ideologies of collectivism, the Church has had to make even more clear the two anthropological aspects of the created image.

These and other natural fundaments are not simply a question of apologetics but a question of the coherence of theology. Even if in a certain place and time a culture should obscure these preambles, and even if philosophical, political, and legal debates about the most fundamental aspects of the human being prove intractable, it would not imply that we can ignore the natural estate of the human person by moving to theological anthropology. For revelation itself will not allow us to remain silent about the preambles. As Jesus said about divorce, "In the beginning it was not so." Marriage in the economy of redemption presupposes marriage, however broken the institution might be in a particular society. The ecclesiology of the Mystical Body presupposes a social unity not reducible to aggregated individuals. In sum, the social aspects of *imago Dei* and *imago Christi* would remain a crucial theme in theology simply on its own terms. Surely, this is what de Lubac meant when he asserted that Catholic theology "is social in a sense which should have made the expression 'social Catholicism' pleonastic."

CHAPTER 3

Social Roles and Ruling Virtues in Catholic Social Doctrine

I.

AT THE BEGINNING OF THIS CHAPTER, let us turn once again to Ernest Gellner's work in order to set the stage for our discussion of the *tria munera Christi*, especially the *munus regale*, the kingly or ruling office of Christ.[1] In his *Conditions of Liberty: Civil Society and its Rivals*, Gellner asks why the polities of the West have proved so much more successful than their rivals in the East. He insists that the correct answer is not democracy—nor even a constitutional scheme of legally protected individual liberties—but rather the "miracle of Civil Society."[2] "Civil society," as Gellner defines it, "is that set of diverse nongovernmental institutions which is strong enough to counterbalance the state and, while not preventing the state from fulfilling its role of keeper of the peace . . . can nevertheless prevent it from dominating and atomizing the rest of society."[3]

Civil society here is presented chiefly in its negative function of counterbalancing the state. The idea comes from Montesquieu, who held that liberty is found only in moderate governments, "where power must check power by the arrangement of things."[4] James Madison and Alexis de Tocqueville likewise held that social pluralism, factions, private associations should be valued, among other reasons, because they "check" the despotic tendencies of democratic regimes.

Gellner points out that the power-checking-power model captures only one of the values we assign to civil society: namely, liberty from the extrinsic authority of the state. To say that civil society is the *"social residue left when the state is subtracted"* is descriptively true, but it is not enough.[5] For once we subtract the power of the state, we can be trapped in a suffocating world of social forms and norms. Islamic nations, for example, have rather weak states,

---

1. See Ch. 1, p. 30–48.
2. Ernest Gellner, *Conditions of Liberty: Civil Society and its Rivals* (New York: The Penguin Press, 1994), 32.
3. Gellner, *Conditions of Liberty*, 5.
4. Montesquieu, *Spirit of the Laws*, 11.4.
5. Gellner, *Conditions of Liberty*, 212.

but a strong *Umma* (way of life) that pervades society. In the more fully mature societies of the West, civil society is also valued because it emancipates us from the familial and religious powers which can command our obedience and allegiance. Here, Gellner diverges from Tocqueville's conception of civil society as "intermediate" or "secondary" powers.[6] For Gellner, civil society constitutes a zone of immunity from these secondary (or intermediate) commanding powers. The "miracle" of civil society is the liberty of individuals to freely choose their identities, careers, and associations.

Because civil society is not a sphere of ruling powers of any sort, it must be understood on the model of the economic market.[7] Market order arises not from the commands of the state, but from the choices and preferences of free agents; at the same time, a commercial society will tend to weaken fixed social forms and norms. Thus, the "miracle" of civil society, is what Gellner calls the "modular man."

> The moral order has not committed itself either to a set of prescribed roles and relations, or to a set of practices. The same goes for knowledge: conviction can change, without any stigma of apostasy. Yet these highly specific, unsanctified, *instrumental*, revocable links or bonds are effective. The associations of modular man can be effective without being rigid.[8]

Gellner's account is intended to be both descriptive and normative. This is the way civil society functions in the societies of the West, and this is precisely the order of liberty that liberals ought to defend. One can admit that the modeling of civil society upon the order of the market has enormous appeal. As the French social theorist, Pierre Manent, has pointed out:

> Liberalism eroded social commands and individual will. But it also has a remedy for that erosion. Amid the discrediting of every norm, it retains one: competitiveness. This is one of the principal reasons that liberalism has come back into favor. Everyone in liberal society shrinks at the prospect of giving or receiving a genuine order, since nothing seems to justify commands or obedience. Competition therefore remains the only acceptable candidate for social regulation, since the norm it offers is immanent to social activity. It is imposed on no one, it implies no dogmatism.[9]

---

6. See Tocqueville, *Democracy in America*, II.4.2.

7. Gellner makes this point very crisply; see *Conditions of Liberty*, 88: "political pluralism in terms of independent or autonomous coercive units is out. Local units simply lack adequate weight. Liberty, on the other hand, is impossible without pluralism, without a balance of power. As it cannot be political, it must be economic."

8. Gellner, *Conditions of Liberty*, 100.

9. Pierre Manent, "The Contest for Command," in *New French Thought: Political Philosophy*, ed. Mark Lilla (Princeton, NJ: Princeton University Press, 1994), 185.

Since the mid-nineteenth century, Catholic social thought has intersected with the liberal program on the need to limit and check the powers of the modern state. Indeed, if we study papal social teaching, we will see that popes have been preoccupied with this problem. When John Paul II was elected pope in 1978, his predecessors had already issued 309 encyclicals and other teaching letters, with some 120 encyclicals on the state.[10] From 1775 until 1978, the inaugural encyclical of every pope addressed the problem of the state. Once the popes came to grips with the new state-making regimes which emerged after the Napoleonic Wars, they vigorously defended a principle of social pluralism. To this extent, and by virtue of having a common enemy, Catholic social thought and (what used to be called) liberalism both called attention to the importance of civil society vis-à-vis the state; both developed rights-based arguments in defense of civil society.

Despite these similarities, the Catholic and liberal discourse about social pluralism remained quite different. In the first place, while liberals valued civil society principally for instrumental (the power-checking-power) reasons, Catholic social thought emphasized the intrinsic value of social forms like the family, the private school, churches, and labor unions. In the second place, Catholic social thought has always been suspicious of the market model of social pluralism. Though Catholic thinkers would have no difficulty defending the economic market against Socialism, they remained wary of any effort to make society itself conform to a market. What Gellner celebrates as the "modular man" represents very nearly the opposite of the social pluralism defended in Catholic social thought and teaching.

In order to appreciate how the ideas of social pluralism and subsidiarity can harbor quite different social ontologies, we shall investigate the idea of the *munus regale*—the function, mission, gift, or vocation of ruling. As we shall see, the *munus regale* originated in theological reflection upon the sacred offices of Christ as priest, prophet, and king, and how these *munera* are participated by every baptised person. Since the pontificate of Pius XI (1922–1939), the theme of the *munus regale* was applied beyond its original

---

10. The *AAS* contains twenty-five different kinds of papal pronouncements. During the pontificate of Pius XII, a serious effort was made to standardize the typology. My enumeration of what counts as encyclicals follows the eight-volume *Enchiridion delle Encicliche* (Edizioni Dehoniane 1994–1998), which includes: encyclical letters (*litterae encyclicae*), two kinds of epistles (*epistula encyclica, epistula apostolica*), two species of apostolic letters (*litterae apostolicae: motu proprio, brevia apostolica*), and beginning with Pius XII (1922–1939) a few radio messages (*nuntii radiophonici*) which were intended to do the work of an encyclical. This leaves to one side four other species of papal documents which convey teaching, and which have been used extensively by John Paul II: *adhortatio apostolica, constitutiones apostolicae, homiliae, allocutiones.*

christological and ecclesiological boundaries to the offices, rights, and duties of social institutions. Especially in the social doctrine expounded by this papal magisterium, the idea of the *munus regale* is a keystone for understanding why the liberal conception of civil liberties, rights, and social pluralism needs to be preserved and corrected by an ontology of the human person as a "royal creature" who participates in divine ruling powers.

II.

John Paul expounds the theme of ruling and being ruled in reference to two sections of *Lumen Gentium*, the Dogmatic Constitution on the Church, issued by the Second Vatican Council on 21 November 1964.

The first is *Lumen Gentium*, §36, where the Council fathers speak of Christ constituting his disciples "in a royal freedom" (*in regali libertate*) and teaching them what it means to enjoy the property or virtue of ruling (*regalitas*, which is usually translated "being a king"). Here, *Lumen Gentium* asserts that revelation teaches that "To serve is to reign" (*servire regnare est*). The first and final word of Scripture on ruling power is that whoever rules must serve rather than be served. The second is *Lumen Gentium*, §31, where the laity are said to participate in the *munera Christi*—the priestly, prophetic, and kingly offices of Christ.

Intrigued by repeated use of the word *munus* in the documents of Vatican II, Janet Smith discovered that the word was used at least 248 times by the Council. Though the English translation is sometimes erratic, the Latin typical edition of the *Catechismus Catholicae Ecclesiae* (1997) uses the word *munus* at least 125 times. (Significantly, the principle of subsidiarity is discussed explicitly in the context of the distribution of *munera* by Divine Providence, see especially §§1883–1884). On my count, the 1983 *Code of Canon Law* uses the word 189 times.

The word *munus* is usually, but badly, translated into English as "function." Living as we do in an age of machines and biological reductionism, the word "function" is apt to conjure the wrong meaning. In pre-Christian Rome the word *munus* meant the ancient Etruscan ritual of serving the dead by shedding blood on (or in the vicinity) of ancestral graves. This was the origin of the gladiatorial contest. The earliest recorded *munus* in the city of Rome was given at the Forum Boarium in 264 by Junius Pera in memory of his father. The gladiatorial contest was not called a "game" (*ludus*) but rather a "service" (*munus*) by which the dead are revivified and propitiated by blood. In other contexts it signified a duty or a gift of service. Hence, the word "munificent" is from the Latin *munificus*, generous, bountiful. At law, a *munus* was not to be confused with a *donatio*, which signifies the disposal of property. We can suppose that the word "community," *communitas*, derives from the sharing of gifts, not from the transfer of property.[11] The word *munus* is frequently used in the Vulgate translation—repeatedly, for example, to give the corresponding Latin word for various aspects of Jewish ritual. In Mt 2:11, the Magi give *munera* to the Christ child; the same for the widow's mite in Lk 21:1, and for the sacrifice of the high priest in Heb 8:3. And Christian theologians spoke of the *triplex munus Christi*: priest, prophet, and king.[12]

Pius XI (1922–29), to whom we attribute the teachings on social justice and subsidiarity, is the pope who began to systematically develop the ontology of the *munera*. During his pontificate, individuals, families, corporations, churches, the state itself,[13] and even international authorities,[14] were said to be the bearers not only of *iura* (rights) but also of *munera*—of having roles to play, gifts to give. In the deepest sense, human rights are exemplified in *munera*, whether natural or supernatural.[15] In the Pian encyclicals, the concept

---

11. Or a gift received. As John XXIII says, "Hence, as Leo XIII so wisely taught in *Rerum Novarum*: 'whoever has received from the divine bounty a large share of temporal blessings [*quicumque maiorem copiam bonorum Dei munere accepit*], whether they be external and corporeal, or gifts of the mind, has received them for the purpose of using them for the perfecting of his own nature [*ad perfectionem*], and, at the same time, that he may employ them, as the steward of God's Providence, for the benefit of others.'" John XXIII, *Mater et Magistra*, §119, *AAS* 53, 430; citing *Rerum Novarum*, §22, *Acta Leonis* 11, 114.

12. CCC, §436, §§784–85.

13. Pius XI, *Divini Redemptoris*, §31, *AAS* 29, 81: "We have indicated how a sound prosperity is to be restored according to the true principles of a sane corporative system which respects the proper hierarchic structure of society; and how all the occupational groups should be fused into a harmonious unity inspired by the principle of the common good. And the genuine and chief *munus* of public and civil authority consists precisely in the efficacious furthering of this harmony and coordination of all social forces." And Pius XII, Encyclical Letter *Summi Pontificatus* (October 20, 1939), §59: "it is the noble prerogative and *munus* of the *civitas* to control, aid and direct the private and individual activities of national life that they converge harmoniously towards the common good." *AAS* 31, 433. Designed to assist and coordinate "the natural perfection of man," the *civitas* is said to be *quasi instrumentum*. On the state having an instrumental *munus*, see too John XXIII, Encyclical Letter *Pacem in Terris* (April 11, 1963), §68; *AAS* 55, 276. And linking together *iura* and *munera* of the citizen, see *Pacem in Terris*, §77, *AAS* 55, 279.

14. See, too, John XXIII, *Pacem in Terris*, §141, *AAS* 55, 295: "But it is no part of the duty of universal authority to limit the sphere of action of the public authority of individual States, or to arrogate any of their functions to itself. On the contrary, its essential purpose is to create world conditions in which the public authorities of each nation, its citizens and intermediate groups, can carry out their tasks, fullfill their duties and claim their rights with greater security [*sed etiam singuli homines et interpositi coetus possint tutius sua munera obire, sua praestare officia, sua iura vindicare*]." At §145, the UN is said to have *munera*.

15. On the matrimonial *munus* as a natural and supernatural participation in divine rule, see Pius XI, *Casti Connubii*, §18; *AAS* 22, 546: "Nor must We omit to remark, in fine, that since the duty entrusted to parents for the good of their children [*hoc munus*

of subsidiarity is elucidated first in the idea of a plurality of *munera*, and only secondarily in terms related to the political question of the scope and content of state assistance. Thus, the notion of the *munus* unifies two things which are so often split apart in modern political and social thought: first, what man claims as his own, and second, what man has to give as a gift of service.

We do not know exactly who or what moved Pius XI to bring the sacral language of *munera* into the precincts of ethical and juridical discourse.[16] Pius was formed in the Thomism of the Leonine revival, and was trained under one of Leo's chief teachers, Matteo Liberatore. Liberatore and his mentor, Luigi Taparelli, had adapted Thomism to the political and social disputes of the era. Taparelli is credited with having introduced the term "social justice" and for having made the first systematic case for what Pius XI will later call "subsidiarity."

---

parentibus in bonum prolis commissum] is of such high dignity and of such great importance, every use of the faculty given by God for the procreation of new life is the right and the privilege of the married state alone, by the law of God and of nature, and must be confined absolutely within the sacred limits of that state [*intra sacros connubii limites est omnino continendus*]." And see again how John XXIII works with the same idea; see John XXIII, *Mater et Magistra*, §195, *AAS* 53, 448: "It is of the utmost importance that parents exercise their right and obligation toward the younger generation by securing for their children a sound cultural and religious formation. They must also educate them to a deep sense of responsibility in life, especially in such matters as concern the foundation of a family and the procreation and education of children. They must instill in them an unshakable confidence in Divine Providence and a determination to accept the inescapable sacrifices and hardships involved in so noble and important a task [*munus*] as the co-operation with God in the transmitting of human life and the bringing up of children."

16. My guess is that the impetus came from a relatively little-known encyclical, Leo XIII, *Annum Sacrum* (May 25, 1899). In preparation for the 1900 Jubilee, Leo XIII dedicated the human race to the Sacred Heart of Jesus, claimed to have been miraculously healed by intercessory prayers to the Sacred Heart, and pointed to Christ as the superior model for what it means to rule; in fact, more subsequent encyclicals are written in reference to *Annum Sacrum* than to *Rerum Novarum* (Pius XI will write four encyclicals on the Sacred Heart, and Pius XII will write three). Beginning with this late Leonine encyclical, popes begin to speak more and more of Christ's *munera* and of his ruling powers. In Pius XI, Encyclical Letter *Ubi Arcano* (December 23, 1922), he dedicated his pontificate to the *Regnum Christi*. Then, in a series of encyclicals—*Quas Primas* (December 11, 1925); *Miserentissimus Redemptor* (May 8, 1928); *Rappresentanti in Terra* (December 31, 1929); *Caritate Christi* (May 3, 1932); and *Divini Redemptoris* (March 19, 1937)—he began to explicate the analogies between Christ's *munus regale* and the rights and munera of baptized Christians. Pius XII did the same. Indeed, his first encyclical, *Summi Pontificatus* (October 20, 1939), written to respond to the eruption of the Second World War, begins with an interpretation of Leo's *Annum Sacrum*. In sum, this line of Christological thought became intertwined with "social doctrine." A reminder of this interweave can be seen in *Lumen Gentium*, §36, where the *munera* of the laity are discussed in light of the preface of the Feast of Christ the King, the feast instituted by Pius XI.

Both of the Italian Jesuits developed a Thomistic account of natural rights.[17] During the Leonine period, individuals and associations are usually said to bear *iura et officia*, rights and responsibilities.[18] With Pius XI, however, the *munera* are introduced, and with this term came a new layer of meanings.

My guess is that the idea of *munus* holds together the Aristotelian notion of an *ergon* or characteristic function with the more biblical concept of vocation or mission. In so doing, it gets at something not well developed by conventional Thomism. Let us recall that at the time of Pius XI's pontificate, the overriding issue of social doctrine was not merely whether man is a social animal, naturally ordered to the common good, but more exactly, the status of societies and social roles other than the state.[19] It was these societies—families, youth groups, unions, religious orders—which the totalitarian regimes robbed of their legal personality. Therefore, it wasn't enough to just repeat the standard formulae of commutative, distributive and legal justice. Without social content, these formulae serve no useful purpose. In fact, arguments to the common good can prove counter-productive in the face of the modern state, which is more than happy to make common the entire range of goods.

In any event, Pius XI decided to make clear that rights are not derived from human nature abstractly considered, but rather from human nature as already bearing (implicitly or explicitly) social *munera*. On this view, rights flow from antecedent *munera* (gifts, duties, vocations, missions); hence, it is quite different than the idea of a right as an immunity—*immunitas*, etymologically, implies the absence of a *munus*. It is quite true that immunities are a juridical term of art; every well-developed legal system recognizes immunities of various sorts. Pius XI, however, insisted that principles of social order cannot begin with immunities or with negative rights. We first must understand the *munera* which the immunities protect.

---

17. See R. Jacquin, *Taparelli* (Paris: P. Lethielleux, 1943), 157–243.

18. Sometimes we see the older Leonine formula used side by side with the newer notion of *munera*. For example, John XXIII in *Pacem in Terris*, §60, *AAS* 55, 274: "It is generally accepted today that the common good is best safeguarded when personal rights and duties [*iuribus et officiis*] are guaranteed. The chief concern of civil authorities must therefore be to ensure that these rights are recognized, respected, co-ordinated, defended and promoted, and that each individual is enabled to perform his duties [*officiis*] more easily. For to safeguard the inviolable rights [*inviolabilia iura*] of the human person, and to facilitate the performance of his duties [*ut facilius quisque suis muneribus defungatur*], is the principal duty of every public authority"; citing Pius XII, *Nuntius Radiophonicus*, Pentecost 1941, *AAS* 33, 200.

19. See Pius XII in *Summi Pontificatus*, §61, *AAS* 31, 434: "man and the family are by nature anterior to the State, and that the Creator has given to both of them powers and rights [*iura facultatesque*] and has assigned them a mission [*munus*] and a charge that correspond to undeniable natural requirements."

I might add that one of the reasons commentators have had such problems understanding the term "social justice" is that, for Pius XI, social justice is nothing other than the manifold organicity of the common good; or, to put it in another way, it is the demand that the common good be brought about through organizations, institutions, and groups. According to Pius XI, social justice ensues "when each individual member is given what it needs for the exercise of its proper functions . . . all that is necessary for the exercise of his social *munus*."[20] Social justice, therefore, should not be confused with distributive justice. On the assumption that men and women already have *munera*, indeed, that they are already performing acts which redound to the common good, the role of the political community is facilitative.[21] All issues of social justice encounter *munera* already established in and ordered to a common good. And therefore, when the political authority recognizes and helps to coordinate the social roles and vocations, it is not in the first place a question of distributive justice; for the magistrate does not distribute the *munera* which have been assigned by creation and redemption; rather, by recognizing these *munera* (including the function of the state itself), the magistrate is recognizing a legal justice that neither begins nor terminates in the state.

Subsidiarity, therefore, is a principle derivative from social justice: namely, that when *subsidium* be given either by the parts to the whole or

---

20. Pius XI, Encyclical Letter *Divini Redemptoris*, §51, *AAS* 29, 92: "In reality, *besides commutative justice, there is also social justice* with its own set obligations, from which neither employers nor workingmen can escape. Now it is of the very essence of social justice to demand for each individual all that is necessary for the common good. But just as in the living organism it is impossible to provide for the good of the whole unless each single part and each individual member is given what it needs for the exercise of its proper *function*, so it is impossible to care for the social organism and the good of society as a unit unless each single part and each individual member—that is to say, each individual man in the dignity of his human personality—is supplied with all that is necessary for the exercise of his social *munus* [*ad sociale munus cuiusque suum exercendum*]. If social justice be satisfied, the result will be an intense activity in economic life as a whole, pursued in tranquility and order. This activity will be proof of the health of the social body, just as the health of the human body is recognized in the undisturbed regularity and perfect efficiency of the whole organism."

21. The best case for putting social justice under legal justice is made by Jeremiah Newman, *Foundations of Justice: A Historico-Critical Study in Thomism* (Cork: Cork University Press, 1954). Newman discusses why Catholic thinkers were reluctant to ascribe social justice to the virtue of legal justice. It looked too close to duties to the state. Given the fact that the whole point of social justice was to clarify the limited duties of the state itself, it was understandable that thinkers recoiled from the idea of legal justice. But Newman makes a powerful case for social justice signifying an ordering to common goods which are not reducible to the state. When the state does social justice, it is recognizing the ordering of all society to the divine good.

the whole to the parts the plurality of functions or *munera* should not be destroyed or absorbed.[22]

At the recent Synod of Bishops (Oct. 2001) in Rome, bishops debated the applicability of subsidiarity to ecclesiology. Liberals, of course, contended that Petrine authority is merely a steering device for the activities of local churches, and such churches embody the principle of responsibility discharged at the lowest level. Several bishops responded that subsidiarity is a social and economic doctrine that has no immediate applicability to the constitution of the Church. It seems to me that neither position is quite right.[23] Subsidiarity does not tell us who has which function or *munus*. One has to look elsewhere (natural law, positive law, divine law) for the *munera*. Therefore, subsidiarity cannot be used to settle the debates about the ontology or the distribution of *munera*; rather, it is a principle governing the relations of already-distributed functions. In papal teachings since Pius XI, subsidiarity is proposed as a principle of non-absorption, not a principle that necessarily requires devolution. As it is commonly understood, *devolution* is the opposite of subsidiarity. For devolution presupposes either: (a) an ontological deficiency, measured by a kind of cost-benefit analysis, or (b) that the central government rightly possesses a plenary power that it has now decided to redistribute to other powers and authorities.

First, the principle does not require "lowest possible level" but rather the "proper level." The *proprium* is not determined by size or locality. *Second*, subsidiarity does not *per se* imply a deficiency in the person or office receiving the *subsidium*. The family receives help from the wider political community, but that does not mean that the family is itself "deficient"—rather it means that the family's unique *munus* does not constitute the entirety of the

---

22. Such as craft and work; see Pius XI, *Quadragesimo Anno*, §118; *AAS* 23, 215: "For, according to Christian teaching, man, endowed with a social nature, is placed on this earth so that by leading a life in society and under an authority ordained of God he may fully cultivate and develop all his faculties unto the praise and glory of his Creator; and that by faithfully fulfilling the duties of his craft or other calling he may obtain for himself [*atque artis aliusve vocationis suae munere fideliter*] temporal and at the same time eternal happiness. Socialism, on the other hand, wholly ignoring and indifferent to this sublime end of both man and society, affirms that human association has been instituted for the sake of material advantage alone."

23. See the debate between Cardinal Dulles and Ladislas Orsy (*America*, October 21 and November 25, 2001), which included a brisk exchange about subsidiarity and ecclesiology. Dulles argued: "Subsidiarity as a technical notion can only with great difficulty be applied to the church, since the Petrine office was not founded as a 'subsidiary,' as if to supply for the deficiencies of lower governmental offices." Put in just this way, without further qualification, Dulles is right. The liberals are using "subsidiarity" as a political principle requiring decisions to be made at the lowest possible level. But as I explain, subsidiarity does not have to be construed so narrowly. Questions of scale, locality, and deficiency do not determine the principle, but rather are (or can be) considerations with respect to the application of the principle.

common good, and it is entirely natural for the family to rely upon institutions other than itself. So, too, in Roman Catholic ecclesiology, the Petrine office assists the entire Church in preserving doctrine and maintaining unity, but it's not quite right to use the language of interventions and deficiency. Therefore, the principle of subsidiarity itself protects the special office and *munus* of the Petrine ministry, just as it protects the unique offices and *munera* of all the different vocations. None of this depends immediately upon the issues of scale, locality, or deficiency.[24] *Third*, sometimes there really is a deficiency. A family, for example, can come apart at the seams, and another power has to intervene to assist; or a higher ecclesiastical authority must intervene in the self-governance of a religious order, chapter, or whatever. Subsidiarity in this kind of case demands that the intervention have as its goal the restoration rather than the absorption or elimination of the function, mission, role of the institution being assisted.[25] *Fourth*, as I have already pointed out, subsidiarity does not govern the distribution of offices; rather, the distribution is governed by natural law and divine law (or human positive law). Subsidiarity cannot create a social ontology, and it would be useless or even destructive to make subsidiarity do that kind of work.[26] Any application of the principle of

---

24. In his influential work *Social Ethics: Natural Law in the Western World* (St. Louis: B. Herder Book Co., 1949), J. Messner asserts: "The law of subsidiarity function is the expression of the pluralism as well as of the harmony and hierarchy of the juridical order" (196–97). He notes that subsidiarity is not exclusively a downward moving logic, but can also include obligations of "lower" bodies to the whole (197).

25. In Heinrich Rommen, *The State in Catholic Thought: A Treatise on Political Philosophy* (St. Louis: B. Herder Book Co., 1950), 302f, he observes that Pius XI's *Quadragesimo* emphasizes the non-absorption (rehabilitation) of the *proprium*—what properly belongs to an agent or institution. Therefore, subsidiarity is not in the first place an issue of scale, e.g., the lowest possible power. The new *Catechism of the Catholic Church* follows suit. Quoting Pius XI's *Quadragesimo*, assistance is to be given in light of the *proporiis officiis*, according to the proper offices or stations (CCC, §1883).

26. Thinkers in the Reformed tradition have shrewdly observed that Catholic discussion of subsidiarity sometimes elides over the social ontology of diverse institutions, as though subsidiarity were itself the structural principle of pluralism. See Jonathan Chaplin, "Subsidiarity as a Political Norm," in *Political Theory and Christian Vision*, eds. J. Chaplin and P. Marshall (Lanham, MD: University Press of America, 1994). Chaplin rightly points out that this is a misreading of Catholic social doctrine. See also Chaplin's discussion of the distinction and the relation of "subsidiarity" and "sphere sovereignty" in "Subsidiarity and Sphere Sovereignty: Catholic and Reformed Conceptions of the Role of the State," in *Things Old and New: Catholic Social Teaching Revisited*, eds. F. P. McHugh and S. M. Natale (Lanham, MD: University Press of America, 1993), 175–202. It seems to me that once we attend to the theme of the *munera* we can discover something more than a superficial similarity between the Catholic understanding of subsidiarity and the neo-Calvinist principle of "sphere sovereignty" developed by Abraham Kuyper and Herman Dooyeweerd.

subsidiarity ahead of the distribution of offices and powers is to put the cart before the horse. For the question of just relations between social offices and institutions presupposes the existence of these social forms, each having its own *esse proprium*. And where the nature and scope of these social forms is in doubt, subsidiarity remains a principle without matter.

As I understand it, this is why Pius XI and Pius XII began to apply the idea of *munera* beyond their original meaning in theology. It is worth noting that in some 30 Pian encyclicals, the word *ius* ("right") is used more than 400 times; in 93% of cases, the word is attributed to an authority or to a source of responsibility other than the state. Furthermore, when Pius attributes a "right" to the state it is almost always connected to the responsibility of the state to recognize and protect prior rights—of the family, spouses, children; of God, the Church, local ecclesiastical authority, and its seminaries, schools, and charitable organizations; of property, labor, association.[27] But what organizes the ever accumulating list of rights in the Pian encyclicals are the *munera*, which provide the teleological and social framework for the conception of rights.

III.

The discourse about the *munera*, developed, as I have said, in tandem with the idea of subsidiarity by Pope Pius XI, found its way into work on the Second Vatican Council. *Lumen Gentium* is the immediate source of John Paul's social doctrine.[28] In *Lumen Gentium* the concept of *munera* is made to do at least two things.

First, to explain the political principle of ruling and being ruled within the life of the Church. In this regard, the important text is to be found in the *Note of Explication* appended to *Lumen Gentium*. "[I]t is a question of *munera* which have to be exercised *by a plurality of subjects* cooperating hierarchically by the will of Christ." That is to say, the Church is a communion of diverse agents having different services to render to the whole body. Cardinal Felici explains that this is a better word than *potestates* (powers) because with-

---

27. This word count is in Mary Elsbernd, "Papal Statements on Rights: A historical Contextual Study of Encyclical Teaching From Pius VI–Pius XI (1791–1939)" (PhD diss., Catholic University of Louvain, 1985), 607, 627. Elsbernd unfortunately does not provide the word count for the use of *munera*. She is surely correct to note that the concept of the *munus* is more dynamic, evoking "rights which could only be realized in society and the realization of which perfected the society" (629).

28. Not to overlook the fact that in *Mystici Corporis* (1943) Pius XII adumbrated this move. Notice that Pius begins with the Christology of the Sacred Heart (§8, *AAS* 35, 196). A chief point of the encyclical is that Christ's *munera* are not distributed to the Church merely to create a juridical union (§9, *AAS* 35, 197). The organicity of the Church requires an analogical approach to the *sacra munera* (§§15–18, *AAS* 35, 200–202).

out the *munera* the powers would appear aimless, non-participatory, unilateral, inorganic, anonymous (one might say, precisely those characteristics of the modern state which have proved so troubling over the past four hundred years).[29] The Church is not to be understood either as a modern state in which there obtains a single and undifferentiated sovereign power, nor can it be understood as a devolution of sovereign power.

Second, after treating the initiation of the laity, by baptism, into the *triplex munera Christi*,[30] *Lumen Gentium* (§35) says that the laity have the *munus* (here quoting the disturbing passage in Ephesians 6:12) of wrestling "against the cosmocrats of this dark age, against the spiritual forces of wickedness." The participated royalty of the laity (§36) is expressed, first, in conquering "the reign of sin in themselves," and second, by "serving Christ in their fellow men they might by humility and patience lead their brethren to that King for whom to serve is to reign."

The *munera* are conspicuous in the 1976 Lenten conferences which Cardinal Wojtyła preached for Pope Paul VI. Within the year, these conferences were published under the title *Sign of Contradiction*. The world, Wojtyła proposed, is sorely in need of a "criterion of power." He notes that, as Saint Thomas taught, to be a creature is to be endowed with perfections according to its kind. In the second chapter of Genesis, we see that the created endowment, once received, was a gift immediately communicated. Adam and Eve were "bestowed on the other."[31] Here, he discerns the nucleus of the ontology of the *munera*. Human beings are not just bearers of powers and rights, but of a perfection already poised to act in self-giving. The social function is apparent at the very beginning in the institution of marriage.

Two points deserve attention. First, he contends that *regalitas* (the quality or property of ruling) is "embedded within the structure of the human personality."[32] This point is important because he does not want to argue that the *munera* are merely a theological template laid over the condition of

---

29. Pericle Cardinal Felici goes on to explain that the *munera* signify, first, that there are powers already poised to action (*ad actum expedita*) awaiting canonical and juridical determination; second, a unique ordering (*ex natura rei*) of diverse subjects cooperating in unity. Pericle Cardinal Felici, *Nota Explicativa Praevia*, in *Sacrosanctum Oecumenicum Concilium Vaticanum II: Constitutiones Decreta Declarationes* (Città del Vaticano: Libreria Editrice Vaticana, 1993), 215–16. One cannot fail to notice the similarity between Cardinal Felici's explication of ecclesial *munera* and *communio* and the social doctrine of Pius XI.

30. In *Lumen Gentium*, §31: "These faithful are by baptism made one body with Christ and are constituted among the People of God; they are in their own way made sharers in the priestly, prophetical, and kingly functions of Christ; and they carry out for their own part the mission of the whole Christian people in the Church and in the world."

31. Wojtyła, *Sign of Contradiction* (New York: The Seabury Press, 1979), 55.

32. Wojtyła, *Sign of Contradiction*, 138.

natural man. Second, he emphasizes that the *munus regale* "is not the right to exercise dominion over others."[33] True, he argues, *praxis* is "a manifestation of the 'kingly character' of man"; but this kingship over the world of matter is not to be confused with two other notes of kingship—self-mastery and self-gift.[34] When he promulgated the 1983 *Code of Canon Law*, the Pope remarked: "In the wake of the Second Vatican Council, at the beginning of my pastoral ministry, my aim was to emphasize forcefully the priestly, prophetic and kingly dignity of the entire People of God."[35]

Indeed, in his first encyclical he proposes that human dignity has to be rediscovered as a "kingship" [*regalitas*], a notion, he adds, that is "linked to every sphere of Christian and human morality." Ruling has three characteristic activities. *First*, in the person, *regalitas* means the act of self-mastery made mature by virtue. *Second*, in the world, *regalitas* means the act of dominion over physical things, signifying the priority of spirit over matter. In *Laborem exercens* (1981), for example, he treats the problem of human labor in light of the *triplex munus Christi* (§24)—sorting out how dominion over things relates to ruling oneself and ruling others. *Third*, in the social world, *regalitas* is expressed in acts of service, according to Mt 20:28, serving rather than being served.[36] In his biography of the Pope, George Weigel discusses this

---

33. Wojtyła, *Sign of Contradiction*, 138.

34. Wojtyła, *Sign of Contradiction*, 139.

35. On the *ratio novitatis* see John Paul II, Apostolic Constitution *Sacrae Disciplinae Leges* (January 25, 1983), *AAS* 75, XII; for the pledge to devote his pastoral ministry to the idea, see the Apostolic Exhortation, *Christifideles Laici* (December 30, 1988), §14, *AAS* 81, 410f.

36. In *Redemptor Hominis*, we find all three aspects: "rediscovering in oneself and others the special dignity of our vocation that can be described as 'kingship' [*regalitas*]." This dignity is expressed in readiness to serve, in keeping with the example of Christ, who "came not to be served but to serve" (Mt 20:28). If, in the light of this attitude of Christ's, "being a king" is truly possible only by "being a servant" then "being a servant" also demands so much spiritual maturity that it must really be described as "being a king." In order to be able to serve others worthily and effectively we must be able to master ourselves, possess the virtues that make this mastery possible. Our sharing in Christ's kingly mission—his "kingly function" (*muneris regalis*)—is closely linked with every sphere of both Christian and human morality. John Paul II, Encyclical Letter *Redemptor Hominis*, §21, *AAS* 71, 316. And again at §16, *AAS* 71, 290: "This is expressed by the Second Vatican Council in these beautiful chapters of its teaching that concern man's 'kingship'; that is to say his call to share in the kingly function—the *munus regale* of Christ himself [*ad communicandum cum Christo 'munus regale'*]. The essential meaning of this 'kingship' and 'dominion' (*munus regale illudque dominium*) of man over the visible world, which the Creator himself gave man for his task, consists in the priority of ethics over technology, in the primacy of the person over things, and in the superiority of spirit over matter"; citing *Lumen Gentium*, §§10, 36.

principle as the "Law of the Gift."[37] Although the world knows it not, the most primordial law of ruling is service, which is always the signature of the divine. Not sovereignty as the moderns understand it,[38] but rather a gift communicated for the good of another.[39]

Here, he is not giving a list of *munera*. Rather, by focusing upon the first institution of marriage, he is trying to identify what every vocation, mission, social station has in common. Marriage was instituted to transfer into the visible reality of the world the mystery hidden from eternity in God, and thus to be its sign. "To understand man, it is necessary to enter into the mystery of this *signum*—the human body, which is the visible expression of the *imago dei*, and which at the very beginning discloses a nuptial relationship."[40] So, here in Genesis, we find the original meaning of participated royalty.[41] Divine

---

37. George Weigel, *Witness to Hope: The Biography of Pope John Paul II* (New York: HarperCollins, 1999), 136–37.

38. After World War Two, Catholic thinkers generally avoided the word "sovereignty." In *Man and the State* (Chicago: University of Chicago Press, 1951), Maritain insisted that the term could not be rehabilitated but "scrapped" (see "The Concept of Sovereignty," 28–53). Heinrich Rommen worried that the word was "much tainted," but decided to retain it, albeit with twenty-two pages of qualification. See *The State in Catholic Thought*, Ch. 17. So, too, J. Messner in *Social Ethics*, §§126–35. I can't find any of use of the term in either *Gaudium et Spes* or in *Dignitatis Humanae*. John Paul II uses the word *dominatus* in reference to God's rule (e.g., *Evangelium Vitae*, §66), or in the negative sense to an exaggerated claim of human autonomy (e.g., *Veritatis Splendor*, §35). The phrase *sui iuris* is sometimes used to designate a self-governing political community (e.g., *Centesimus Annus*, §20).

39. It is an idea well known in the medieval world. In *Rerum Novarum*, §51, for example, Leo XIII defended the rights of private associations on the basis of Thomas's defense of Mendicant poverty in *Contra Impugnantes*, written in 1256. In Thomas's works, every analogous use of the word *societas* is mirrored by uses of the word *communicatio: communicatio oeconomica, communicatio spiritualis, communicatio civilis,* and so forth. The word *communicatio* simply means making something common, one rational agent participating in the life of another. Society, for Thomas, is not a thing, but an activity. He quotes Augustine's *De Doctrina Christiana:* "Everything that is not lessened by being imparted, is not, if it be possessed without being communicated, possessed as it ought to be possessed." See Aquinas, *Contra Impugnantes*, I.4.

40. See also Pius XI, *Casti connubii*, §12; *AAS* 22, 544.

41. In John Paul II, *Dominum et Vivificantem* (May 18, 1986), §11, he comments on a passage in *Gaudium et Spes*: "when God is forgotten the creature itself becomes unintelligible." He cites *Gaudium et Spes*, §36. Among the things which become beclouded and distorted is man's vocation to rule and be ruled. The Pope turns to the issue of human conscience, created and redeemed to participate in divine rule. An alert reader will see that many of the themes later explored in *Veritatis Splendor*—the idea of "participated theonomy" and of human conscience as the "herald of a king"—were first explored in the encyclicals on the Trinity. Participated theonomy, *Veritatis Splendor*, §41, *AAS* 85, 1166; the

rule is made visible in (1) mastery over one's own body, (2) dominion over things of the earth, (3) in reciprocal rule over one another's bodies. Interestingly, the first sign of the social *munus regale* is not the state but rather what the Pope calls the "proto-sacramental" institution of matrimony.

In *Mulieris Dignitatem* (1988) he continues this line of inquiry into the difference between ruling things and ruling persons. With sin, the first note of ruling (self-mastery) is eroded, and the second note of ruling (dominion over physical things) is extended to the rule of persons—in Genesis 3:16 ("he shall rule over you") it might look as though Adam now rules Eve by way of dominion appropriate to the rule over the things of the world. Thus, Genesis 3:16 must be compared with 1 Cor 7:3–4, "For the wife does not rule over her own body, but the husband does; likewise, the husband does not rule over his own body, but the wife does." Christ reveals the "royal dignity of service" by teaching that "to serve means to reign."[42] Assuming in his own person "humanity as the inheritance of Adam," Christ decisively answers the question posed in Psalm 8, *quid est homo?*[43] He "fully reveals man to himself," among other ways, by restoring the institution of matrimony, relocating it in the rule of persons rather than the dominion over things. (In passing, we can note that the Pope frequently refers to the threefold concupiscence mentioned in 1 John 2:16—lust, curiosity, and pride; these are the opposites of the three *munera Christi*: lust degrades the priestly offering of the body, curiosity degrades the *munus propheticum*, or the light of teaching, and pride degrades the *munus regale*, the virtue of kingly rule. By the created order, man has some share in these three *munera*, but in the rule of the God-Man, Jesus Christ, these natural endowments are not only clarified and healed by the medicine of grace, but are transfigured and elevated).

Modern political theology was shipwrecked on just this problem of failing to sort out the three kinds of *regalitas*—specifically, in relation to the family. Recall for a moment that modern contract theorists (Hobbes, Locke, Rousseau) assumed that legitimate power requires the location of a sovereign; moreover, they assumed that Christian theologians affirmed with one voice that the evidence or what they called "marks" of sovereignty are to be found chiefly in paternal power given to Adam. Bossuet, for instance, asserted that "all the world agrees that obedience, which is due to public power, is only found (in the Decalogue) in the precept which obliges one to honor his parents. . . . and that the

---

nuncio of a King, §58, *AAS* 85, 1179 (citing Bonaventure, *In II Sent.*, d. 39, a. 1, q. 3); see also his discussion of the *imago dei*, bearing the kingly predicate, §38, *AAS* 85, 1164 (citing Gregory of Nyssa, *De hominis Opificio*, c. 4).

42 John Paul II, Apostolic Letter *Mulieris Dignitatem* (August 15, 1988), §5, *AAS* 80, 1661.

43. *Mulieris Dignitatem*, §11, *AAS* 80, 1679.

name 'king' is a father's name."[44] The Enlightenment thinkers criticized this idea because it seemed to be an ideology of monarchical absolutism.

But rather than asking the question whether the primary analogate of kingship is matrimony rather than paternal power, much less whether paternal power is mere dominion, the debate hurried to the inevitable conclusion that Adam is no king and that Genesis discloses nothing useful about ruling powers. The traditional theology of social roles, or *munera*, could be dismissed as despotism. And to counteract it, Enlightenment thinkers simply transferred the concept of dominion to the individual's relation to himself; on this supposition, it was a small step to propose that legitimate rule of any sort can arise only by consent or contract; the social world, then, is to be built by acts of commutative justice—social forms and norms are mere constructions, legitimated by contractual negotiation.

In the Apostolic Exhortation, *Familiaris Consortio* (1981)—subtitled, "On the *Munera* of the Christian Family[45]—the Pope says that although the "kingly mission" is not to be reduced to politics, the proper and unique vocation of the laity includes what he calls the *munus sociale et politicum*. This Exhortation was issued on the Feast of Christ the King; the preface of that liturgical feast is quoted in *Lumen Gentium*, §36, where we also find the formula *cui servire regnare est* used so often by John Paul. Here, he quotes this formula again."[46] The laity are to order temporal things according to the *regnum Dei*.

> The social role [*Sociale munus*] that belongs to every family pertains by a new and original right to the Christian family, which is based on the sacrament of marriage. By taking up the human reality of the love between husband and wife in all its implications, the sacrament gives to Christian couples and parents a power and a commitment to live their vocation as lay people and therefore to 'seek the kingdom of God by engaging in temporal affairs and by ordering them according to the plan of God.' [*Lumen Gentium*, §31]. The social and political role [*Sociale et policitum munus*] is included in the kingly mission of service in which Christian couples share by virtue of the sacrament of marriage, and they receive both a command which they cannot ignore and a grace which sustains and stimulates them.[47]

---

44. Bossuet, *Politics Drawn from the Very Words of Holy Scripture*, trans. Patrick Riley (Cambridge: Cambridge University Press, 1990), III.3, p. 62. To be sure, Bossuet contends that kingship is service, but from the platform of an absolute power under God.

45. John Paul II, Apostolic Exhortation *Familiaris Consortio: De Familiae Christianae Muneribus* (November 22, 1981), *AAS* 74.

46. *Familiaris Consortio*, §63, *AAS* 74, 156.

47. *Familiaris Consortio*, §47, *AAS* 74, 139.

Here, John Paul follows the ontology first developed by Pius XI. The *iura* are located in the *munera*.

The Pope in *Familaris* is not immediately interested in political constitutions, political parties, or a specific legislative agenda. Rather, he has two points in mind. First, despite the translator, John Paul wanted to make clear that social offices and vocations are not constructed out of abstract rights. Second, that *munus politicum* is properly the service of laity, not priests. The *munus regale* is analogical. The kingly service of a priestly hierarchy must be distinguished from the service of the laity in the temporal order. The virtues of social justice cannot be stripped from social roles.

These thoughts are made even more clear in *Christifideles Laici* (1988):

> A new aspect to the grace and dignity coming from Baptism is here introduced: the lay faithful participate [*participes*], for their part, in the three-fold *muneris* of Christ as Priest, Prophet and King. This aspect has never been forgotten in the living tradition of the Church, as exemplified in the explanation which St. Augustine offers for Psalm 26 [here follows a quote from Augustine]: "David was anointed king. In those days only a king and a priest were anointed. These two persons prefigured the one and only priest and king who was to come, Christ (the name 'Christ' means 'anointed'). Not only has our head been anointed but we, his body, have also been anointed . . . therefore anointing comes to all Christians, even though in Old Testament times it belonged only to two persons. Clearly we are the Body of Christ because we are all 'anointed' and in him are 'christs', that is, 'anointed ones', as well as Christ himself, '*The Anointed One*'."[48]

In medieval political theology, the venerable image of *sponsus* and *sponsa*, Christ and his bride, was diverted from its proper and original context, in the sacrament of baptism, and was made to define the relations between the prince and his state. The King was given a ring to signify his solemn marriage to the realm. Before the age of Absolutism, the office of king exemplified the sanctified laity—these coronation rituals, properly understood, represented the dignities bestowed on every Christian at the time of his baptism. Interestingly, in his panegyric to Constantine, Eusebius of Caesarea contended that when Genesis teaches that man was made in the image and likeness of God it should be inferred that God made Adam and Eve not a political animal, but a *basilikon zoon*, a royal animal; hence, Eusebius reminds the reader that the restoration of the *imago dei* in Christ is a work participated by all baptized persons.[49]

---

48. John Paul II, Apostolic Exhortation *Christifideles Laici* (December 30, 1988), §14; *AAS* 81, 410, *Enchiridion Vaticanum*, vol. 11, 1050.

49. See *Tri. Orat.* IV.

Though never entirely lost, the *munus regale* of the laity had been displaced before the Revolution destroyed the office of anointed kings. In early modernity, political Christendom devolved into an Old Testament model of two anointed rulers. As the Pope remarks, although the *munus regale* of the laity was never entirely forgotten, it was eclipsed, for all practical purposes, by the monarchs and their courts, who jealously guarded what they deemed an exclusive title to the kingly predicate.

From a theological point of view, political modernity did not fix the problem because it did not restore the status of *regalitas* to the people. Modern regimes might accommodate the anointing of priests so long as the *munus regale* of the priest is confined to a private or merely spiritual sphere. For their part, the baptized laity in modern times are considered citizens, whose chief responsibility is to legitimate political power—as a people, however, they reign without ruling. They have an abstract power, but no *munus regale*. Thus, the theological anthropology of participated royalty seems irrelevant to citizenship. Or, to put it in another way, the social residue that remains after we subtract the power of the state is deemed a merely private sphere. In Catholic thought, however, this cannot be true, at least not in the sense ordinarily given to the word "private." For whether the *munera* proceed from natural law or from the roles immediately instituted by Christ, the offices, functions, and powers *are* under law. There is no such thing as a purely private person. Therefore, the state is not limited by a private sphere but rather by a truly, though analogously, public sphere of social forms and norms. This is why modern popes insisted that the plurality of social forms deserves not only immunity from state power but more importantly recognition as public entities having their own *propria*. On this view, the principle of subsidiarity has a social context in which to work.

IV.

John Paul continued the work of Pius XI, Pius XII, and the Vatican Council in putting issues of powers (*potestates*) and rights (*iura*) in the context of *munera*. Here we find perhaps the deepest and most searching element in modern Catholic social thought. It is prominently displayed in the new *Catechism of the Catholic Church*:

> God has not willed to reserve to himself all exercise of power. He entrusts to every creature the *munera* it is capable of performing, according to the capacities of its own nature. This mode of governance ought to be followed in social life. . . . those who govern human communities . . . should behave as ministers of divine providence. (§1884)

The idea of participated royalty, plurified in distinct *munera*, provides the context for the issues of social pluralism and subsidiarity. This social doctrine interweaves social theory, anthropology, political and moral philosophy, and several branches of theology with the ancient metaphysical theme of participation. It is extraordinarily synthetic. But there is a reason for the synthetic approach. By the time of the Second Vatican Council it was clear that Catholicism and liberalism provided converging lines of support for the external organization of liberty: constitutionally limited government, human rights, and the role of free markets (provided that the market be subject to considerations of the common good). At the same time it was clear that anthropological foundations of liberty were quite divergent.

Gellner's "modular man," for example, is a man without *munera*. Civil society is not a theatre in which men freely respond to natural and supernatural *munera*, but quite the opposite; civil society is a zone of immunities from society itself. For good reason, therefore, Catholic social doctrine had to enrich and deepen the Church's understanding of the anthropology and social ontology. This effort practically defines the teachings of the current papal magisterium. If one reads an encyclical like *Centesimus annus* (1992), one will discern what is, by now, a familiar dialectic. On the one hand, the Church affirms the post-1945 Western consensus about the external organization of liberty, while proposing a different conception of man and society. The principles of social pluralism and subsidiarity should be read in light of that dialectic.

CHAPTER 4

The Three Necessary Societies
Family, Polity, and Church

RERUM NOVARUM (1891) begins with this sentence: "That the spirit of new things [revolutionary change], which has long been disturbing the nations of the world, should have passed beyond the sphere of politics and made its influence felt in the cognate sphere of practical economics is not surprising."[1] Since the French Revolution, Catholics had been rethinking the social order—chiefly with regard to the relationship between the Church and the new states, but also in what pertained to "practical economics." When Pope Leo XIII was elected in 1878, "social Catholicism" was flourishing, despite a paucity of magisterial teaching on the subject. This was the era of Catholic circles and associations, led by such luminaries as François-René de La Tour du Pin, Léon Harmel, Albert de Mun, Emmanuel von Ketteler, Frédéric Ozanam, and Adolph Kolping. The Fribourg Union, established in 1884, was the first international organization of Catholic social thinkers. Its representatives urged Leo in 1888 to teach from on high about the cluster of social issues related to economy.

He did so in *Rerum Novarum*. It is not surprising that the opening sentences of that encyclical should refer to the French Revolution. *Rerum Novarum* was written in 1889–1890, during the revolution's centennial celebration. The main celebration was in Paris, of course, where some 32 million visitors found their way to the Exposition Universelle. Its organizing committee accepted architectural drafts for an enormous Centennial Tower. After rejecting several submissions, including a plan for a 300-meter tower in the form of a guillotine, the committee awarded the contract to Gustave Eiffel. Reckoned the tallest building in the world, the Eiffel Tower celebrated French science and economic prosperity. American celebrities like Thomas Edison and Buffalo Bill attended the Hall of Machinery and the Colonial Exhibition, which portrayed the fruits of science and money—especially the mastering of lands and peoples beyond the seas. More than half the funding for the exposition was supplied by a private investors' guaranty association, which yielded

---

1. Leo XIII, Encyclical Letter *Rerum Novarum* (May 15, 1891), §1.

97

a healthy profit. Welcome to modernity: the French Revolution brought to you by Goldman Sachs. The theme song of the exposition included the line "I have destroyed the old laws, I bring hope."

Until the rise of the totalitarian movements in 1917, the French Revolution provided the social vision against which Catholic social thinking sought to define itself. Leo referred to the revolution as the "Great Conflagration," like an event out of the Book of Genesis that had destroyed an original order of things.[2] The revolution had indeed affected a major reorganization of society. Even in its decadent eighteenth-century estate, French Catholic society had been a culture of vows. In 1789 and the years following, that culture swiftly capsized.

In 1790, the revolution issued decrees prohibiting monastic vows then solemn vows, and in their place required a clerical oath to the Civil Constitution of the Church. In 1791, marriage was made only a civil contract, and celibacy for the secular clergy was relaxed. In 1792, two further decrees finished the reorganization of society: The first provided for unilateral and no-fault divorce; the second abolished the monarchy. Thus came about the demise of the two great vows of the laity, that of husband to wife and king to the realm.

Revolutionary change soon spread to the colonies and former colonies. Pope Pius IX played the role of Cassandra, issuing the *Syllabus of Errors* (1864), which included the infamous condemnation of the proposition that "the Roman Pontiff can, and ought to, reconcile himself, and come to terms with progress, liberalism, and recent civilization."[3]

Leo issued no *Syllabus of Errors*. Instead, he asked a question that was at once more philosophical and more practical: How do we *civilize* this situation? What is our proposal for social order? What can we work with in social matters, and how do we measure what's been lost and what might be regained? He remarked: "Nothing is more useful than to look upon the world as it really is."[4] The paradigm of Catholic social teaching formulated by Leo resisted the temptation to utopianism, so seldom resisted elsewhere in the nineteenth and twentieth centuries. The Leonine paradigm for social analysis was simple and sturdy. It was a neo-Aristotelian effort to put the "spirits" of the age into perennial wineskins.

Our framework in social matters should be the three "necessary" societies—that is, societies necessary for human happiness. They include domestic society (marriage and family), polity, and Church. Pius XI, who developed Leo's

---

2. See Pope Leo XIII, Encyclical Letter *Arcanum Divinae* (February 10, 1880), §28.

3. See Pius IX, *Syllabus of Errors*, attached to his Encyclical Letter *Quanta cura* (December 8, 1864), §10.

4. Leo XIII, *Rerum Novarum*, §18.

vision, states: "Now there are three necessary societies, distinct from one another and yet harmoniously combined by God, into which man is born: two, namely the family and civil society, belong to the natural order; the third, the Church, to the supernatural order."[5] There are other associations that enjoy a truly social principle as well. But they are more transient, revisable, and subject to the free designs of human ingenuity. Should these societies wither, we would have social problems. A demise of the necessary societies would mark a social calamity.

To revise the Aristotelian dictum: The human person is a domestic (matrimonial-familial) animal, a political animal, and an ecclesial animal.

Upon his election in 1878, Leo turned immediately to the question of where we stand with respect to these three societies. In *Quod Apostolici* (1878), he argued against the position (of what he took to be socialism) that society can be reduced to equal or self-same bits of the same society. He thus began by establishing that there exist plural societies with quite diverse modes of "membership." He then proceeded to teach about the three necessary societies in turn. In *Aeterni Patris* (1879), he portrayed the Church as a house of wisdom, nourished by philosophical science and divine revelation. In *Arcanum Divinae* (1881), he issued the first formal and synoptic teaching on Christian marriage since the Council of Trent. In *Diuturnum* (1881), he examined the origin of political authority. Leo's simple paradigm of three necessary societies would be used intelligently, flexibly, and effectively by the social magisterium for nearly a century.

In *Arcanum*, Leo argued that it is in the mutual interest of polity and Church to preserve whatever helps persons to live "well and happily." Crucial to the good and happy life is the health of the first necessary society, the domestic order founded upon marriage. Although *Rerum Novarum* includes an important argument for the liberty of voluntary associations, the encyclical's major concern is the rights and obligations of wage-labor pertaining to the support and perfection of the family. To be sure, the dignity of wage-labor reflects the human person as the image-bearer, as Thomas Aquinas said, capable of providing for himself and others—a person who transcends animal instinct, who does not just produce but does so on the basis of rational foresight. And who thus has a right to have at his disposal stable property, as well as an obligation to provide even for social life beyond his natural lifespan. The basis for this case, however, is not a "state of nature" scenario, but rather the rights and obligations of domestic society. It is the right and obligation of political society to respect and protect the social form and ends of marriage and family. It is the right and obligation of the ecclesial society to sanctify and

---

5. Pius XI, Encyclical Letter *Divini Illius Magistri* (December 31, 1929), §11.

teach its members. In *Rerum Novarum*, Leo emphasizes the importance not only of the sacramental bond of matrimony, but of the wisdom of using material goods rightly *sub specie aeternitatis*. "The things of earth cannot be understood or valued aright without taking into consideration the life to come, the life that will know no death. Exclude the idea of futurity, and forthwith the very notion of what is good and right would perish; nay, the whole scheme of the universe would become a dark and unfathomable mystery."[6]

To summarize, the necessary societies have in common (analogically) these three properties:

First, their respective forms and ends are not purely voluntary—not in the fashion of a *societas arbitraria* that can be created, variously reshaped, or dissolved according to transient circumstances. In the case of marriage and Church, the form and ends of the society are instituted by nature or by supernature. Polity is somewhat different, because although its end is given by nature, it has more than one legitimate form (rule by one, rule by a few, rule by many—or what is more likely, a mixed form).

Second, they are not disposable platforms for lifestyle. We are to dwell or to live in them. (One of Leo's favorite verbs is *inhabitere*.) This property of "dwelling in" is analogical. We live in a marriage, a family, a polity, and a church in different ways. Yet they have in common a social principle, let us say a social intention in the strict sense of the term, which is to participate in the union. The union itself is loved. A true society is not an aggregation of exchanges and distributions, even if such divisible things need to be properly exchanged and distributed. We live in societies, not in social movements, political parties, field hospitals, Starbucks, or in Euro-style cultures without boundaries.

Third, they are subsidiary to one another. This follows from the very meaning of necessary societies. Under normal conditions, members who dwell in one society dwell also in the others: Those living in the domestic society are also members of the French Republic and of St. Rita's parish. This principle has been called "hierarchical complementarity." Society is made up of different social orders, among which are relations that are "truly mutual." The different orders need each other, and one cannot replace the others. They exist in themselves as true societies, but exist also for the other dignified orders. It is not sufficient for human happiness to dwell in only one society.

During the Leonine era, which reached into the middle of the twentieth century, the chief problem (anarchists and Bolsheviks put to one side) was not outright rejection of the necessary societies. The problem was getting the right balance according to the complementarity principle. The nation-states insisted that the state had the first and last word in this matter.

---

6. Leo XIII, *Rerum Novarum*, §21.

Therefore, we should not be surprised that the most persistent concrete issue—both in Europe and in the New World—was the schools. The Church historian Roger Aubert has called the school issue "the classic battleground," for the school was the locus of competition between the rights of parents, Church, and state.[7] All three of the necessary societies are, in their own way, nurseries of formation. When Pius XI asserted that "the family is more sacred than the state," his attention was focused chiefly on the issue of education.[8]

What would the Leonine popes—Leo through Pius XI—have considered a calamitous social scenario? It would have been the demise, or something approaching the demise, of the three necessary societies. Such a demise might be instigated from above or from below.

The *scenario from above* was easily imagined by the Leonine social magisterium. After all, the Church had experienced it during the French Revolution. The rise of the totalitarians after World War I provided another frightening instance. On the scenario from above, all three necessary societies, including the political, would be removed from everyday life. Perhaps some aspect of these societies would remain, but only as outsourced emanations of the collective: for example, aspects of administrative authority, aspects of domestic order for breeding purposes, aspects of religion suborned by the collective. Perhaps even well-intentioned states could get halfway down the field of dystopian precarity by overplaying their subsidiary function in times of emergency. This is the gist of *Quadragesimo Anno* (1931). In a condition of perpetual mobilization, the state would absorb the life of the other societies, without formally or legally forbidding their existence. Thus, the principle of subsidiarity was framed as a limit on distributive justice: The polity should respect the unique social forms and ends of Church and family.

As for the *scenario from below*, one example of demise made more than cameo appearances in the letters of Leo and Pius XI. It is the "liberal" utopia, in which the three necessary societies are reduced, in Leo's words, "to the genus of commercial contracts, which can rightly be revoked by the will of those who made them."[9] Leo comprehended the nucleus of the liberal ideology, especially in its relation to marriage and domestic life. Social forms like marriage and family might be determined either by the state or, more likely, by private contract with state sanctions—a *societas arbitraria* whose form is stipulated. Traditionally, distributive justice presupposed a social form, according to which "we" (the polity, the family) owe something to our "members" on the basis of merit or need. But suppose that the net aggregate effects of

---

7. Roger Aubert, *The Church in the Industrial Age*, trans. Margit Resch (New York: Crossroad, 1981), 9:209.

8. See Pius XI, Encyclical Letter *Casti Connubii* (December 31, 1930), §69.

9. Leo XIII, Encyclical Letter *Humanum Genus* (April 20, 1884), §21.

what has been privately exchanged (at any given point in time) count as the virtue of distributive justice. The right thing *could* get into the right person's hands, but it would be completely accidental to a social principle. In a family, for example, the medicine would be not distributed as much as exchanged— let's say, to the child who had saved enough money to buy it.

This warning against liberalism was sounded almost always in reference to reforms of marriage and family law. Again, suppose that there be no (recognized) matrimonial form or ends. It would seem to follow that there are plural forms of matrimony that can be determined by private contract, as Pius XI wrote in *Casti Connubii*:

> Some confidently assert that they have found no evidence of the existence of matrimony in nature or in her laws, but regard it merely as the means of producing life and gratifying in one way or another a vehement impulse; on the other hand, others recognize that certain beginnings or, as it were, seeds of true wedlock are found in the nature of man since, unless men were bound together by some form of permanent tie, the dignity of husband and wife or the natural end of propagating and rearing the offspring would not receive satisfactory provision. At the same time they maintain that in all beyond this germinal idea matrimony, through various concurrent causes, is invented solely by the mind of man, established solely by his will.[10]

Hence, what the state cares about in marriage is reproduction, from which follow its political and legal interests in eugenics, demographics, and the like. The rest, including the form and ends beyond reproduction, can be left to private contract. "Some men," Pius XI averred, "go so far as to concoct new species of unions, suited, as they say, to the present temper of men and the times, which various new forms of matrimony they presume to label 'temporary,' 'experimental,' and 'companionate.'"[11] This sounds like news from a few months ago.

This dystopic revolution from below was imaginable, but unlikely, between 1878 and Pius XI's death in 1939. Even in the case of matrimonial and family law, where the social implications of *homo economicus* surfaced rather sharply, Pius blamed disruptions on overreach from above (albeit abetted by liberal ideas). A true revolution from below would depend on great numbers of people who—from utopian enthusiasm, or perhaps from moral fatigue—truly wanted to abandon the perennial and necessary social forms. Or, what is more likely, it would depend on people who wanted the moral obligations of membership in various societies to be removed or mitigated by

---

10. Pius XI, *Casti Connubii*, §49.
11. Pius XI, *Casti Connubii*, §51.

law. Such abatements might be justified by theories that the perennial social forms are constructed and may be changed arbitrarily—that they are immanent systems without transcendent grounding. But these justifications would have little purchase unless people had experiential reasons for not wanting to inhabit, enjoy, and fulfill the obligations of being political, domestic, and ecclesial animals.

That prospect was not a likely one when Leo and Pius wrote their social letters. State-formation and various species of nationalism were robust. Wars and economic crises kept European humanity (and the rest of the world touched by it) in an almost continual state of mobilization. From the onset of the wars of the twentieth century through the era of postwar recovery in the 1950s, the principle of hierarchical complementarity was intact in practice, even if the social ontology and metaphysics of it were weakened. Simply put, people needed each other, and they needed sustained cooperation among the societies necessary for human flourishing.

The Leonine paradigm had traversed some very choppy historical waters. The social magisterium understood that a social order founded on the three societies could be upset from above or from below. But in retrospect, it is odd that the magisterium (though not Catholics in general) did not give more attention to the "spirit of new things" from below. Competent thinkers, from the Jesuit social theorist Heinrich Pesch to secular economic historians like Karl Polanyi and Joseph Schumpeter, had pointed out that the social relations ensuing upon market competition would tend toward constructed, stipulated, and transient social forms. But from the perspective of what Pius XI called his pontifical "watchtower," the historical and social scene was distinguished by the Church's eking out its ecclesial, social, educational liberties, not to mention its very properties, from states.[12] This admittedly "clerical" experience influenced the Church's general social view, with its emphasis on protection or disruption from above. The social view was not wrong in itself. But it was part of a habit of thinking that would be difficult to break, once the main disruptions came from below.

The wisdom of this paradigm seemed to be confirmed by the deep and sustained cooperation of social institutions after 1945. Notwithstanding what my old friend Richard John Neuhaus said, the "Catholic moment" happened in the decades following World War II. The postwar recovery produced significant economic development and signs of social health. This was the heyday of the so-called *trente glorieuses*, the marvelous down payment of wealth, education, and social energy given to the baby boom. The model of social cooperation at work in Western Europe was given prominence in magisterial and

---

12. See Pius XI, *Casti Connubii*, §3.

conciliar documents (*Pacem in Terris, Populorum Progressio*)—and recommended for the progress of the developing world: social markets without socialism, nation-states without chronic wars, development as "another name for peace." The magisterial optimism of the postwar era did not foresee anything like a post-national (much less post-matrimonial or post-ecclesial) future. It was naively expected that the "friendly hands" of social cooperation could (would?) tame nationalism and overweening ecclesiastical authority without prejudice to the necessary societies situated within an international framework.

Then two revolutions came, which the popes in their "watchtower" had not expected.

In 2004, Cardinal Renato Raffaele Martino, president of the Pontifical Council for Justice and Peace, presented the *Compendium of the Social Doctrine of the Church*. Five years of painstaking work (including on a topical index of 150 pages) had produced a beautiful volume. The authors had compiled several hundred chunks of magisterial texts, sorted according to principles, topics, and applications. There is a vast array of material, running from the Book of Genesis to the Holy See's intervention in Kyoto on the occasion of the Third World Water Forum. The bulk of magisterial texts (pontifical and curial) are drawn from the years between 1958 and 2004. The notable thing is that these several hundred blocks of text are simply juxtaposed under topical headings. There is no argument, no philosophical synthesis, and no historical narrative.

I have had the subversive thought that this enormous compilation, lacking philosophical or historical vectors, represents a tradition that is either sublimely confident in itself, or so overwhelmed that it can only give authoritative blessing to a series of juxtaposed responses to crises—a tradition awaiting synthesis.

What had happened to deprive Catholic social doctrine of its Leonine coherence?

Since the Leonine era ended, we have undergone two revolutions from below. Neither was instigated by higher ruling powers, though political and social authorities surely accommodated them. The revolutions probably had no single cause, but they are interrelated in origin and cumulative in impact. Each is utopic. Each has emerged in real social life. I do not need to describe them in detail, because even if we do not comprehend all of the causes or the future course they might take, we know quite well what the revolutions are.

First, the *cultural revolution of the 1960s*—not the one in China, but the spirit of new things that sprang from the West and manifested itself internationally. It had a generational focus but by no means a generational limit. To put it bluntly, the three necessary societies were deemed unendurable by the better part of two generations. In a paradoxical acknowledgment of the complementarity of the three societies, domestic, ecclesial, and political society were perceived as a single repressive hierarchy in cahoots—the establishment, as it were. I am prepared to admit that this perception was not entirely mistaken. Perhaps the social and institutional authorities had the same thought, because they soon reconfigured themselves as permissive hierarchies.

The Church after *Humanae Vitae* (1968) began to counter the "spirit" of sexual and moral revolution. Pope John Paul II tried to show that marriage and family are not repressive, and as a corollary that polity and Church should not be merely permissive. John Paul was compelled by events to address domestic society—but he had a deeper reason, too. Marriage and family are not only the most vulnerable society, but also the most important one to get right. Whoever shrinks from that society is not well prepared to live in the other two. John Paul came to believe that the crisis of the twentieth century was anthropological, meaning that we are not dealing merely with sporadic spirits of distemper with respect to institutions. The distinctive mark of the age is what John Paul's friend Rocco Buttiglione aptly called *negative anthropology*. This crisis is manifest in the ready affirmation of what man *is not*, combined with a deep-seated reluctance to affirm normative anthropological content.[13]

I will not rehearse all of the theological anthropology that informed John Paul's diagnosis. Let one remark suffice. As pope, he spoke to the Roman Rota (the highest Roman court on matrimonial cases) of anthropologies that regard the "human," given by nature, as raw data, a prolepsis or outline of what man might be when he is made "specifically human" in the "historical and cultural sphere." Behind these anthropologies lies the myth of the proto-man who awaits humanization through the efficacy of culture, a sphere of freedom in which a multiplicity of forms can be imparted to the *proto-humanum*. This myth has made possible a calamity from below.[14]

In *our* modern times, we can imagine polity, marriage, and Church as merely optional—not normative and formative institutions in which we live a life and achieve perfections over generations, so much as instruments we can use to live a life of our own choosing. Negative anthropology construes the three great institutions of human happiness as platforms for self-revision, not the perfection of a nature.

Prior to the cultural revolution, the Church had been accustomed to limits complaints about social order to governments. That custom now needed to be modified. Unlike the law of no-fault divorce legislated by the revolutionary government in France, which was truly a top-down and unilateral act, our cultural revolution was not a creature of the state. Instead, governments permissively accommodated the spirit of the revolution piece by

---

13. For the term "negative anthropology," see Rocco Buttiglione, *Karol Wojtyła: The Thought of the Man Who Became Pope John Paul II* (Grand Rapids, MI: Eerdmans, 1997), 53.

14. See Ch. 9 for a fuller presentation of this topic.

piece. Such governments, by and large, do not think that they have authority to dismantle the cultural revolution. The permissive hierarchies of the post–World War II era do not necessarily intend the destruction of domestic, ecclesial, and political life, so much as they wish to preserve each according to the most minimal normativity.

The second revolution is *techno-economic*, to use Pope Francis's term. Sometimes it is called neoliberalism, but I doubt that the ideology satisfactorily matches the realities of globalized and financialized markets, or the dynamisms of global communications. In late spring of 1992, Justice Anthony Kennedy delivered his famous line about the right to define one's own concept of existence, of meaning, of the universe, and of the mystery of human life. Three months later, Deng Xiaoping proposed an answer to the "meaning of life" that is much less abstract: "To get rich is glorious." Deng explained that there is only "one thought," "one firm rule [hard truth]," namely economic development as it is understood in the West. Some get rich; others lose. But, in the aggregate, people will be happier.

Deng did not invent the expectation that, on the whole, a hot, global, heavily financialized, and speculative economy would be worth the social costs. Despite the fact that almost every nook and cranny of the social order—pensions, university endowments, family savings—is deeply invested in Deng's "one hard truth," few people would be able to describe in concrete *social* terms what that truth "is." What does it mean that the average duration of shareholding in a company amounts to four months? That the life expectancy of a firm in the Fortune 500 is less than fifteen years? That banking assets in a given nation could exceed 500 percent of GDP with only the flimsiest underlying real assets? When allegedly social entities like corporations have lifespans shorter that those of one's pets, to whom do we assess social costs?

In his book *Modern Social Imaginaries*, Charles Taylor argues that in modern times, economic life was the first social imaginary to achieve an identity independent of the political sphere.[15] It is a new "normal order" of mutual enrichment that is at once profoundly social and, let us say, interactive all the way down, but not easily classified under the usual rubric of collective action. A market is social to the extent that it is semiotical, a set of signs regarding prices. Agents reciprocally affect one another in some systematic way, yet the beneficence of the system must be evaluated in light of a concatenation that happens "behind their backs." So imagined, economic life is in tension with the other two modern social imaginaries, the "sovereign people" and "civil society"—for, being based on competition, the economic sphere seems to lack

---

15. See Charles Taylor, *Modern Social Imaginaries* (Durham, NC: Duke University Press, 2004), esp. 69–154.

either the collective action of political life or the many modes of benevolence (however transitory) of voluntary associations.

Taylor is onto something important. Unlike the corporate company towns of yesteryear—Eastman Kodak, Phillips Petroleum—in which diverse people with different skills lived, usually for more than fifteen years, many or most firms today have no obvious social locus. They might treat themselves as having legal personality, but they destroy, and allow themselves to be destroyed, through mergers and acquisitions and such processes. It is hard to see how firms of this type count, on Taylor's view, as either political or civil societies, much less as one of the necessary societies on Leonine terms.

If we are to judge contemporary corporate entities, we need to know something more about them than their effects, be they good or bad. In intrinsic terms, what kind of societies are they?

Since Vatican II, social ontology has included various descriptions and emphases. *Gaudium et Spes* asserts that only the work or labor is human, and all other factors have the nature of tools. John Paul II likewise refers to the necessity of distinguishing work from mechanisms. Economic mechanisms that are not regulated by a juridical framework so that they serve human freedom "in its totality" cannot be approved. This does not exactly answer the most important question, which is whether such things are true social entities gone rogue or mere tools inadequately socialized.

On balance, John Paul II and Benedict XVI have suggested that at least some contemporary economic phenomena genuinely belong to the category "civil society." Hence the use of the term "business economy." Terms like "free" and "market" are appropriate to business, which is thought of as a social solidarity of entrepreneurs and employees who create and distribute real goods and services. Business, in this view, is not one of the necessary societies, but it is an "expanding chain of solidarity" that has social depth.

The 2008 financial crisis made this assignment of "business" to civil society harder to sell. Benedict's *Caritas in Veritate* was a major advance toward recognizing the "new things" in the financial sector. Indeed, it *names* many things that require our serious attention. For the first time, if I am not mistaken, the distinction between a "real" and a "financial" (or "speculative") economy is explicitly addressed; so, too, the problem of aligning short-term and long-term investment, even the problem of no investment at all; also the difference between phantom wealth and disordered growth in contrast to integral development. *Caritas in Veritate* recognizes that the financialized economy has evolved into a system of extraction rather than investment.[16]

---

16. See, *inter alia*, Benedict XVI, Encyclical Letter *Caritas in Veritate* (June 29, 2009), §§21, 40–42.

Even so, there is not much space given in *Caritas in Veritate* to describing, defining, or analyzing the "new things" that are named. Magisterial teaching continues to neglect certain important concepts. For example:

(1) What is the "real" economy, and how does it differ from the "financial" economy? What are the areas of overlap between the two?
(2) What is "speculation"? What are its proper and improper vehicles?
(3) What is "debt"? This question not only has roots in revealed theology but also stands at the center of the financial crisis in domestic and global economies.
(4) Perhaps due to the decline of the older scholastic frame of thought, there is little attention now to what Aristotle called chrematistics, the so-called art of making money divorced from the prudence of household (or other social) management.

The first three can be considered under the category of social tools that are not adequately civilized. The latter, however, raises the specter of an association that perverts even its own social principle.

When Pope Francis was elected, he took as his motto, from Bede's homily on the Gospel of Matthew, *Vidit ergo Jesus publicanum, et quia miserando atque eligendo vidit, ait illi, "Sequere me"* (Jesus therefore saw the tax collector, and since he saw by having mercy and by choosing, he said to him, "Follow me").

To my knowledge, Francis is the first pope to speak explicitly of international capitalism as a "global system." It is a system that renders familiar institutions empty shells of technocracy in the service of the "empire of money."[17]

As many others have noted, Francis almost always speaks of processes rather than institutions; movements rather than political parties; the praxis of those who live and suffer, rather than the boundaries and obligations set by law; and a direct engagement with the people, rather than policies drawn from the abstract models of standard economics. Whereas previous popes emphasized the importance of nation-states and their moral-juridical relations to one another, in Francis's "global system" the nation-state has been suborned, its agency and efficacy compromised.

We have come a long way since Leo XIII's way of proceeding—namely, moderate adjustments of institutions keyed to the three necessary societies. Indeed, in his two magisterial documents, Francis never mentions *Rerum*

---

17. See Pope Francis, Apostolic Exhortation *Evangelii Gaudium* (November 24, 2013), §§55–58; Encyclical Letter *Laudato Si'* (May 24, 2015), §56. For the phrase "empire of money," see Address of Pope Francis to the Participants in the World Meeting of Popular Movements, October 28, 2014.

Novarum. He applies a hermeneutic of suspicion to all intellectually framed social categories.

His hermeneutic of suspicion begins with the Church itself—canon law and curial bureaucracy, doctrines compiled by scholars rather than those purely and simply lived. We are dealing now, to invoke the metaphor of Francis, with field hospitals in which the ministers are not so different from the patients.

The field hospital is an apt metaphor for ministry to a people who cannot live in Leo's three necessary societies. Everyone, to paraphrase Dorothy Day, suffers the precarity of a migrant. Francis seems eager to describe a world in which the three necessary societies are crippled—a dystopia marked by a pervasive sense of homelessness with regard to family, work, nation, and even mother nature.

It is hard to interpret Francis with confidence. *Evangelii Gaudium* and *Laudato Si'* evince a prophetic and poetic and rhetorical ambience that is unique to him. That ambience is meant to move the heart. It is neither philosophy nor policy. Francis does not stand in the pontifical "watchtower," at a distance from the social phenomena he evaluates.

Leo said that "Nothing is more useful than to look upon the world as it really is." Leo and his generation needed the better part of a century to assess what was broken in the aftermath of the "Great Conflagration" and to decide what could be fixed. Francis likewise looks at what is broken in the world system after our two revolutions. To see *this* world as "it really is" requires stepping into the precariousness of the broken, which truly is quite different from what Leo saw in the late nineteenth century. It is one thing to have a theory of institutions, and quite another to know how to live when institutions are decadent. It is something else again to give a properly integrated narrative about these "new things" and to teach how they should be measured by Catholic wisdom.

The insight that I attribute to Francis—that we must learn concretely and humbly, without regurgitating truisms—by the same token suggests the need to go slowly, to learn patiently from the experience of others, and to resist assembling too hastily an over-arching doctrine about "signs of the times." The two revolutions from below are still alive, imprinted on the pages of our time like ink that is still wet. The social magisterium does not need to invent a new doctrine, much less to replace the essential features of Leo's paradigm. But it is a great mercy to learn how to experience and understand social problems afresh.

At the beginning, I pointed out that prior to Leo, nineteenth-century Catholic social thinking on the ground evinced a creative ferment of social theories and experiments in response to the revolutionary disruptions of their times. Perhaps we are re-entering such a revolutionary time, albeit under rather different circumstances. Leo's magnificent teaching from on high depended on the mind and work of the early associations that embodied social Catholicism. He saw clearly enough the dead ends encountered by some of his predecessors, which more often than not were caused by well-intentioned but precipitous teachings and policies. Leo's "paradigm" came from on high, but it summarized and clarified the currents and eddies of social Catholicism in light of a non-negotiable principle. That principle—that we are domestic, political, and ecclesial animals who achieve perfections by rightly dwelling in the perennial societies—is simple enough to understand. But sowing and harvesting the daily bread of this social principle remains a difficult labor.

CHAPTER 5

The Accomplishment of Leo XIII

IN HIS OPENING ALLOCUTION to the Second Vatican Council on October 11, 1962, Pope John XXIII urged the bishops to heed what may be learned from history, "the teacher of life."[1] He recalled, for example, that previous councils were "often held to the accompaniment of the most serious difficulties and sufferings because of the undue interference of civil authorities." The more senior bishops assembled in 1962 could remember that at the papal conclave of 1903, the emperor of Austria effectively exercised the so-called *ius exclusivae*, the right of vetoing a papal candidate. The pope reminded the council that whatever the problems and challenges of the contemporary world, it is not true that in former times "everything was a full triumph for the Christian idea and life and for proper religious liberty."

Many of the intellectual architects of Catholic social teaching were born and came of age prior to the Second Vatican Council and lived through different phases of the problematic history recalled by Pope John. Gioacchino Pecci, the future Pope Leo XIII, was among the oldest of these Catholic "titans." He was born in 1810, as Napoleon's armies were reconstituting the political geography of Europe. Among the youngest is Karol Józef Wojtyła, who would become Pope John Paul II in 1978, exactly a century after Leo's election. Born in 1920, just two years after the end of World War I had swept away the last ruling families of Christendom (Hohenzollerns, Wittelsbachs, Romanovs, and Habsburgs), Wojtyła would live to see the political map drastically change yet again in 1939, 1945, and 1989. Remarkably, Pecci and Wojtyła's respective lives encompass nearly two centuries of lived experience, covering almost the entirety of what we would consider the "modern" situation of Catholicism.

Many of the most influential Catholic thinkers of this era are notable for their contributions to the development of Catholic legal, political, and social thought and doctrine—"social teachings," as they are conventionally called, which have been one of the signal achievements of the Church since the

---

1. John XXIII, "Gaudet Mater," October 11, 1962 in *Sacrosanctum Oecumenicum Concilium Vatican II, Constitutiones, Decreta, Declarationes* (Vatican City: Libreria Editrice Vaticana, 1993), 858.

nineteenth century. This body of thought was not just the doctrinal work of popes and councils, but also the labor of scholars and activists, both clerical and lay. The Catholic mind was formed in a context of struggle with modern ideas and institutions. This conflict was often muddled, chaotic, and sometimes violent, but as so often happens in the history of ideas, it likewise provided the soil for creative advances in the areas of philosophy, theology, and jurisprudence. The problem of the state was the crucible in which the Catholic mind was sharpened. Its importance can be gauged by the fact that when John Paul II was elected pope in 1978, his thirteen predecessors had written some three hundred encyclicals, about half of which were devoted to problems relating to the nature, the ideologies, and the policies of the state.

Political society, of course, was not merely the preoccupation of Catholic thinkers, for the greatest, most sustained, and most troubling work of modernity is the state. If we ask a modern person who or what is sovereign, he or she would not say, "reason," "the individual," or "science," but instead, without hesitation, "the state." The states formed in the wake of the Napoleonic wars at the turn of the nineteenth century were the engines of science and military technology, colonialism, education, and law. Catholics certainly were not unique in having to reckon with the phenomenon of the state. In other respects, however, the Catholic Church had a different and more troubled relationship to the state. The Church's enormous size and international scope, its public law and authority, its educational institutions, and, above all, its refusal to reconfigure itself into national churches, made conflict and rivalry with the modern state almost inevitable. State monopoly over law and, increasingly, education made canon law and the educational system of the Church appear to be an *imperium in imperio*. Religious congregations and orders, with their vast properties, their ancient exemptions from taxation, and their legal privileges drawn from the solicitude of the Roman See and its concordats with temporal sovereigns, offended the new spirit of citizenship.

The rivalry, however, was never anything quite so simple as what is implied by the conventional rubric "church and state." Also at stake was the constitution of society as a spiritual and cultural order that has its own distinct forms of authority and modes of liberty. By the late nineteenth century, it was well understood that society is not a garment that can be divided between civil and ecclesiastical powers. Modern liberalism was also shaped by concern for the liberty of civil society. How to protect and enhance the relationship between three spheres—church, state, and society—is the kernel of what would come to be called "the social question," one that would test the speculative and practical wisdom of Catholicism.

Our historical survey of Catholic legal, political, and social thought begins with the crisis of the nineteenth century. This survey will give us a sense of the events and issues that led to the development of Catholic social teaching and will thereby allow us to understand better Pope Leo XIII's accomplishments. The demise of Catholic political Christendom after the revolutions of 1848 was the matrix for the problems that defined Catholic social thought, even to our own time. We then look at the magisterial effort of Pope Leo XIII to craft a new approach to the issues of church, state, and society. Of particular importance was his *ressourcement* of scholastic Thomism. The so-called Leonine revival of Thomism not only left a deep imprint upon systematic theology and seminary education but also had far-reaching effects upon the way Catholics thought about legal, social, and political issues. Jacques Maritain, John Courtney Murray, and Karol Wojtyła (the future John Paul II) are products of this Leonine revival. Undoubtedly, they appropriated the thought of Saint Thomas in different ways, but the similarities are also quite evident. The case for human rights grounded in natural law, the development of the principle of subsidiarity, and the argument for the integrity and quasi-autonomy of civil prudence are the work of a refurbished Thomism. If Pope John XXIII had good reason in 1962 to celebrate a normalization of relationships between the Catholic Church and temporal authorities, the work of the council certainly did not tie together every loose end. Therefore, we shall need to consider some of the tensions that have arisen within Catholic legal, political, and social thought since the council. Liberation theologians have questioned whether the synthesis of scholastic anthropology and liberal constitutionalism adequately diagnoses the problems of the developing world, and whether it gives proper scope to the prophetic social and political message of the gospel. Within the world of the economically developed Western democracies, that same synthesis of Catholic thought and liberal constitutionalism has become problematical, particularly along the axis of "life" issues concerning human dignity and natural law.

I. THE NINETEENTH-CENTURY CRISIS

After the revolutions of 1848, the Spanish diplomat and political theorist Juan Donoso Cortés asserted, "We cannot know what is religiously affirmed about God without also knowing what is politically affirmed or denied about government."[2] No Catholic could have disagreed with the proposition. Yet, on all sides, the best minds could arrive only at a negative consensus. Within the Catholic Church there was a broad and deep consensus that the Church is not *in* the state. For their part, statesmen in the capitals and courts of Europe could agree that the state is not *in* the Church. But it was far less clear

---

2. Letter to Cardinal Fornari, "Errors of Our Times" (June 19, 1852), in *Juan Donoso Cortés, Selected Works*, trans. and ed. Jeffrey P. Johnson (Westport, CT: Greenwood Press, 2000), 110.

how to formulate affirmative propositions about the relations between religious, political, and social authorities. Beginning with Leo XIII, Catholic theologians, philosophers, and jurists began to supply those missing propositions.

Their work, however, required an understanding of what had become dysfunctional in Catholic political Christendom. Such an understanding was not easily reached, among other reasons, because the political situation from which the Church had to extricate itself was not simply the result of revolutionaries and new secular regimes overtly hostile to the Church. It was also the handiwork of the Church that clung for centuries to the altar-throne order. In *The Things That Are Not Caesar's* (1927), Jacques Maritain insisted that "it was five hundred years ago that we began to die."[3] The problem began in the politico-ecclesiastical soil of a decadent papacy, weakened first by the great schism (1378–1417), and then by the turmoil of the Protestant Reformation (1517). To avoid schism, to create a political climate friendly to the Church's reforms in the Council of Trent (1545–1563), and to facilitate the burgeoning Catholic mission in the New World, the papacy conceded patronal privileges to monarchs. These privileges became a crucial juridical ground for building modern states, and would have a remarkably long-lived career. They survived not only the revolutions of the eighteenth and nineteenth centuries but also the formation of totalitarian states of the twentieth.

Since the sixth century, the temporal estate of the Church had depended upon lay patronage. Prominent laypeople donated properties to the Church and thus acquired certain rights and responsibilities over those properties and their clerical occupants. The cluster of rights and privileges was called the *ius patronatus*, from the word *patronus*, the father of a trust. Most important was the *ius praesentandi*, the right to nominate or present the clerical candidate. By the ninth century, patrons asserted the right to receive feudal homage from their clerical vassals, in exchange for which the layman vested the bishop, priest, or abbot in his temporality, his ecclesiastical property. This infeudation of the Church led to the investiture crisis of the eleventh century. Pope Gregory VII (1015–85) and his successors tried to forbid clerics and religious from giving homage, lest the ecclesiastical office be confused with the fief of a vassal. On the model of the monastery of Cluny, whose monastic charter included immunity from lay control, medieval popes built a church within a church, consisting of religious houses and eventually religious orders, which enjoyed exemptions not only from lay control but also from the authority of local ordinaries. The Gregorian quest for a church independent of royal and lay supervision, autonomous in its own law, and answerable only to Rome was somewhat

---

3. Jacques Maritain, *The Things That Are Not Caesar's*, trans. J. F. Scanlan (London: Sheed & Ward, 1930), 74.

successful with respect to religious orders; but in its quotidian life, the Church was not very effectively extracted from the tangle of patronal rights.

In the modern period, this patchwork of patronal rights came into the hands of royal families intent upon creating sovereign states. This new form of Catholic Christendom began in Spain.[4] As Ferdinand and Isabella completed the final stage of the *reconquista*, the 1486 Bull of Granada conferred on them, "as a reward of their crusade," the right to nominate all major prelacies as well as to hold in trust tithes and endowments in support of religion in Granada.[5] An entire province of the Church thus became a benefice of the crown. When the conquest was complete and the New World was discovered in 1492, Pope Alexander VI issued the bull *Inter caetera* (1493), conceding to the monarchs title to the lands discovered and still to be discovered in the Indies. The grant included the power of the monarchs to license clerics who wished to sail to the Indies. In effect, the monarchs became transatlantic apostolic vicars. In 1508, Pope Julius II's bull *Universalis ecclesiae* conceded a universal patronage over the church in America. After the Anjou-Bourbon house acceded to the Spanish throne in 1700, it won from Pope Benedict XIV in 1753 the patronal right throughout all of Spain. Thus came into existence what was called the *Patronato Real Universal*. Rome had never before conceded, nor had any Catholic prince before received, such a package of delegated authority. The key point, however, is that Madrid did not regard the authority as delegated, but rather interpreted Roman concessions as recognition of authority inherent in state sovereignty.

The development of the modern Gallican church in France paralleled the situation in the Spanish dominions. In 1516 Pope Leo X made a remarkable concession to the king of France, granting Francis I a universal right of nomination to French bishoprics and abbacies.[6] Capitular elections were abolished, and the entire Gallican episcopacy, including some 800 abbeys and 280 priories, became the benefice of the king. Louis XIV astutely used the potentially schismatic Gallican Articles (1682) as a negotiating chip for another deal. Promising in 1690 not to enact the articles into law, Louis won from Pope

---

4. For the legal structure and history the *Patronato Real*, one can rely on studies by W. Eugene Shiels, *King and Church: The Rise and Fall of the Patronato Real* (Chicago: Loyola University Press, 1961), containing important legal instruments in the original languages and English translation, and J. Lloyd Mecham, *Church and State in Latin America: A History of Politico-Ecclesiastical Relations* (Chapel Hill: University of North Carolina Press, 1966).

5. *Orthodoxe fidei* (November 13, 1486); original in Shiels, *King and Church*, 277–82.

6. "Concordat of Bologna (1516)," in *Church and State Through the Centuries: A Collection of Historic Documents with Commentaries*, trans. and ed. Sidney Z. Ehler and John B. Morrall (Westminster, MD: Newman Press, 1954), 134–44.

Innocent XII regalian rights over four southern provinces theretofore exempt from the 1516 concordat. By vowing not to assert in legal theory what he was now entitled to do in practice, Louis XIV completed his hegemony over the church in France. The offices and temporal estates of the church were in effect national property distributed by the king. They flowed from Versailles to a nobility no longer organically tied to (or even present to) the land, the diocese, the monastery; indeed, bishops were consecrated in the royal chapel at Versailles rather than in their own dioceses. When the Estates General met in early summer 1789, every one of the 118 bishops and 18 archbishops was a noble on the state's dole. The architects of the French Revolution of 1789 did not invent, but rather inherited, the principle that the church, as a visible and temporal society, was the property of the state.

This form of Catholic political Christendom proved quite sturdy, lasting for nearly three hundred years. The Church recognized the de facto reality of modern, state-making regimes, while demanding that they remain de jure within the fold of Catholicism. Except in the Papal States, Belgium, and in a handful of Protestant countries (such as the United States), virtually every baptized Catholic in the world lived under a regalist regime at the time of the French Revolution. Impressively, its basic features managed to survive the first wave of revolutions in Europe and in Latin America. In Republican France, royal patronage was swiftly translated into terms of popular sovereignty. The church in all of its temporalities was the property of the state, and all her bishops and clergy were its civil servants. In the former Spanish dominions, the Patronato Real became the Patronato Nacional. Venezuela, for example, would go through twenty-six constitutions without abandoning its law of patronage.

At first reluctantly, but then abruptly, Rome began to separate itself from political Christendom in the decade before the First Vatican Council (1870). Its initial reluctance was due to the Congress of Vienna (1815), where Austria, Russia, Great Britain, and Prussia attempted to arrest the revolutions. Partisans of Catholic order were to be satisfied with the liberation of Pope Pius VII from French captivity, the restoration of the Papal States in Italy and the Bourbon monarchy in France. Thus began the secular and ecclesiastical policy of legitimism. The tangled and tattered relationship between Catholicism and the states was to be solved by obedience to properly constituted authority. No encyclical better exhibits the principles and the failure of legitimism than Pope Gregory XVI's *Cum primum* (1832). The issue at hand was the 1830–32 Polish uprising against Tsar Nicholas I. A regalist par excellence, Nicholas governed his dominions according to the slogan, "Orthodoxy, Autocracy, and Nationality." As part of the political settlement of the Congress of Vienna, Russia won the right of governing the former Kingdom of Poland, comprising the Duchy of Warsaw, bordered on the north and west by Prussian provinces and on the south by the eastern province of Galicia. The uprising was met with brutal Russian repression, begun in Warsaw on November 29, 1830. The constitution was suspended, the universities were closed, and both Roman and Uniate churches were subjected to severe restrictions.

Gregory told the Polish bishops in *Cum primum* that he had no greater hope but that their provinces would be "restored to peace and the rule of legitimate authority." Reminding the bishops of the scriptural warrants for obedience to temporal authority, Gregory wrote:

> "Let everyone," says the Apostle, "be subject to higher authorities, for there exists no authority except from God, and those who exist have been appointed by God. Therefore he who resists the authority resists the ordination of God" (Rom. 13.1–2). . . . Similarly St. Peter (1 Pet. 2:13) teaches all the faithful: "Be subject to every human creature for God's sake, whether to the king as supreme, or to the governors sent through him . . . for (he says) such is the will of God, that by doing good you would silence the ignorance of foolish men." By observing these admonitions the first Christians, even during the persecutions, deserved well of the Roman emperors themselves and of the security of the state.[7]

The Polish bishops were surely puzzled, not to say appalled, by the suggestion that an eight-hundred-year-old church, with a tradition of fierce loyalty to Roman ecclesiastical authority, should abandon its self-government to a schismatic tsar on the model of the obedience owed by early Christians to the Roman emperors.

Undoubtedly, *Cum primum* represented the lowest point of the era of legitimism. However, it had the unintended effect of moving Catholic opinion in favor of a radical reckoning with the dysfunctional remnants of political Christendom. The doyen of the movement was Joseph de Maistre, whose *Du Pape* (1919) stands to nineteenth-century Catholic political theology as Rousseau's *Social Contract* stood to the eighteenth-century ideal of civic republicanism. Though he wrote for the broad project of the restoration, his work would have nearly the opposite effect, for it was de Maistre who insisted that Gregory VII's work be completed in modern times. He remorselessly criticized the ecclesiology of national churches, taunting Gallicans to change the creed to read, "I believe in divided and independent Churches." He insisted that "nothing is accomplished" without overthrowing the "magic castle" of regalism; he accused kings and princes of a "great rebellion."[8] For

---

7. *Cum primum* (June 9, 1832), §§1, 3, in *Acta Gregorii Papae XVI*, ed. Antonius Bernasconi (Rome: S. C. de Propaganda Fide, 1901–1904), 1:143–44.

8. Joseph de Maistre, *The Pope*, trans. Aeneas M. Dawson from the 1819 edition of *Du Pape* (London: C. Dolman, 1850), III.4, 277.

de Maistre, Pope Gregory VII, who declared the freedom of the Church, was "the genius," the man without whom "all was lost, humanly speaking."[9]

It was a most unlikely proposition to declare Gregory VII's policies of the eleventh century to be the model for the Church's relations to the restored crowns of 1815. But Maistre struck a nerve in the Catholic imagination by characterizing the French Revolution as a judgment on the nations, specifically a rod of chastisement for the captivity of Catholic political culture to regalism. De Maistre died in 1821, spurned by Pope Pius VII and the Roman Curia, but predicting a great future for what he called "my greatest work." As the political-ecclesiastical controversy stumbled into one dead end after another, and as the ideas of *Du Pape* were filtered through many different minds, a new generation became convinced that the state cannot co-govern the Church.

Catholic opinion was divided on the question of whether the political and social instability of Europe was due chiefly to an excess of liberty or to an excess of authority. Catholic "liberals," such as Lamennais, Montalembert, and Lacordaire, took the position that the main problem was an excess of authority. The new states were neither Christian nor secular, but exploited the alliance of throne and altar to repress the Church and society. Liberals urged that the Church put its moral authority behind liberty. Catholic "conservatives," such as Louis de Bonald, Joseph de Maistre, and Donoso Cortés, emphasized the pole of authority. The mediation of this dispute would have to await the magisterial encyclicals of Leo XIII and the formation of Catholic social doctrine in subsequent decades. In the middle of the nineteenth century, however, liberals and conservatives could agree on one point. The *ius patronatus*, in every one of its guises, had to be uprooted and the Church restored to the Gregorian ideal of liberty. Almost every major Catholic thinker of the era wrote a treatise or pamphlet on the recovery of the Gregorian reform.[10]

---

9. De Maistre, *The Pope*, II.12, p. 199; III.2, p. 255.

10. Notable works in this genre include Félicité Robert de Lamennais's notes on the history of the Gregorian reform, *Tradition de l'église sur l'institution des évêques* (Paris, 1814); Dom Guéranger, *Affaire de la Légende De Saint Grégoire VII*, in *Institutions liturgiques*, vol. 2, Ch. 21 (Le Mans/Paris, 1841); Henri Lacordaire, *Éloge Funèbre de Daniel O'Connell* (Paris, February 10, 1848); John Henry Newman, *Present Position of Catholics in England* (Notre Dame, IN: University of Notre Dame Press, 2000; first published, 1851); Wilhelm Emmanuel von Ketteler, "Freedom, Authority, and the Church in The Social Teachings of Willhelm Emmanuel Von Ketteler," trans. Rupert J. Ederer (Lanham, MD: University Press of America, 1981; first published, 1862); Donoso Cortés, "Letter to Cardinal Fornari on the Errors of Our Times" in *Selected Works of Juan Donoso Cortés*, trans. and ed. Jeffrey P. Johnson (Westport, CT: Greenwood Press, 2000; first published, 1852); and Antonio Rosmini, *Delle cinque piaghe della Santa Chiesa* (Napoli: 1832, 1848), a scholarly but passionate compendium of arguments against the *ius patronatus*.

This drumbeat of opinion could have only one practical conclusion—some kind of separation of church and state. How this could be accomplished was not clear. Rome was hemmed in by concordats that allowed the states to set and effect ecclesiastical policies. With the exception of Belgium, whose 1832 constitution forbade any use by the government of patronal rights, the former Catholic powers were not interested in relinquishing their titles to supervise religion. Unlike the American constitution, which was unfettered by any history of patronal rights and in any case did not use "separation" as a juridical term of art, separation in the European context was consistent with state authority over ecclesiastical properties, seminaries, and courts. Popes had condemned the principle for that very reason. In his famous speeches at the Malines Congress in August 1863, the Catholic liberal Charles de Montalembert pointed out that separation "can very well be combined with terrible oppression."[11]

The breakthrough did not occur in the serene atmosphere of theory or in the chambers of diplomats, but in Pope Pius IX's rather impulsive decision to issue the *Syllabus of Errors* (1864). Frustrated by the unraveling of the restoration and by the loss of his dominions in Italy, save the city of Rome itself, Pius published a list of eighty erroneous propositions. The eightieth condemned proposition read: "The Roman Pontiff can, and ought to, reconcile himself, and come to terms with progress, liberalism and modern civilization." Public reaction to the *Syllabus* was as furious as the document itself. Though newspapers had fun mocking the pope's quixotic dismissal of modern civilization, political officials understood that something more serious was afoot. For the document contained several other propositions that, if acted upon, would amount to separation initiated from the side of the Church. They carefully noted that seven propositions (§§28–30, 41, 49–51) denied that patronal rights inhere in state sovereignty, that four propositions (§§45–48) denied state monopoly in matters of education, and that four other propositions (§§29–30, 52–53) baldly reasserted the Gregorian position on the legal and economic autonomy of religious orders.

Their anxieties were confirmed four years later when Rome declined to invite nominally Catholic nations to send ambassadors (*oratores*) to the First Vatican Council. This broke with a conciliar custom dating not only to the Council of Trent (1545–63), but also to the Council of Nicaea (325). Presiding at Nicaea, the Emperor Constantine told the assembled bishops: "You, on the one hand, are certainly the bishops inside the Church. I, on the other, might then be the 'bishop' appointed by God of those outside."[12] So, too, in

---

11. Charles de Montalembert, "Malines Address (August 20, 1863)," in *Church and State in the Modern Age: A Documentary History*, ed. J. F. Maclear (New York: Oxford University Press, 1995), 162.

12. *Eusebius's Vita*, 3.12.3, 4.24.

the West, the Catholic sovereign was a kind of *episcopus externus*. The secretary of state, Cardinal Antonelli, refused to extend the invitation on the ground that there could be no principle of selection between "good" and "bad" Catholic sovereigns. Privately, Antonelli said that "exclusively Catholic Governments had virtually ceased to exist."[13]

In France, Émile Ollivier declared in the Chamber of Deputies that the pope had in effect introduced the separation of church and state: "Yes, this is a new fact, a new deed indeed that the disseverance between the laical society and the religious society is put into effect by the pope's own hand."[14] The ever-mischievous ultramontane editor of *L'Univers*, Louis Veuillot, gleefully agreed—princes are now "outside the Church." Moreover, rumor had it that the Jesuits intended to use the First Vatican Council as the occasion to doctrinalize the *Syllabus*. It was in this light that Ollivier would make bold to judge that once deprived of these instruments, the state can be said to be separated from the church. Shrewdly, he went on to say, "Undoubtedly, Gentlemen, I know that Rome earnestly wishes to separate itself from the State, but She does not want the State to separate itself from Her."[15] Count Daru, the French foreign minister, sent a memorandum to Cardinal Antonelli, anxiously pointing out that "all this is nothing else than the consecration of the supreme authority of the Church over society."[16]

Perhaps unwittingly, Count Daru had stated the issue with unusual clarity. Can we imagine a church autonomous in its own sphere, capable of acting upon and through its own members—and thus indirectly upon the wider society—without being an agent of the state (the older confessional model) or requiring the mediation of the state (the newer regalist model)? Such a solution would mean, on the side of the Church, deep revision of the idea that the state has a juridical-political power of *cura religionis*, care of religion. In an 1892 allocution, Leo XIII told his curial cardinals that the Church's temporal mission would center upon "faith embodied in the conscience of peoples rather than restoration of medieval institutions."[17] The much-disputed medieval doctrine of "indirect" ecclesiastical or papal power to suspend acts of states, much less to depose temporal authorities, was abandoned in favor

---

13. "Lord Odo Russell to Earl of C. (March 7, 1870)," in *The Roman Question, Extracts from the Despatches of Odo Russell from Rome, 1858–1870*, ed. Noel Blakiston (London: Chapman and Hall, 1962), 404.

14. Émile Ollivier, "Speech in Chamber of Deputies on July 10, 1868," in Émile Ollivier, *L'Église et l'État au Concile du Vatican*, 3d ed. (Paris: Gamier Frères, 1877), 1:400.

15. Ollivier, "Speech in Chamber of Deputies."

16. "Ministre des Affaires Etranges a M le marquis de Banneville (February 20, 1870)," in Ollivier, *L'Église etl'État*, 1:551–56.

17. Leo XIII, "Onorare le ceneri," March 1, 1892, *Acta Leonis* 12, 384–86.

of an "indirect" authority exercised through the teaching of faith and morals. On the part of the states, the solution would require not only jettisoning the idea that the modern state is *a sanctum* in the medieval sense of the term; it also pointed to the need for what the famous Catholic social theorist and politician Luigi Sturzo (1871–1959) termed a "rhythm of social duality."[18] Society is neither a creature of the state nor the Church. It is not a "depersonalized whole" capacitated to act only through the superstructure of ecclesiastical or civil administration.[19]

The politico-ecclesiastical crisis of the nineteenth century became a lodestone for Catholic social doctrine, the lesson that oriented the work of the next generation of thinkers. Giaocchino Pecci, of course, was a bishop at the council. After becoming Pope Leo XIII in 1878, he would devote his magisterium to understanding the triadic relationship between church, state, and society. Angelo Roncalli, the future Pope John XXIII (1881), Jacques Maritain (1882), Dorothy Day (1897), and John Courtney Murray (1904) were all born in the wake of the crisis. As we saw, John XXIII opened the Second Vatican Council with an admonition to the bishops to recall the lessons of that era. Maritain's first important work in social and political philosophy, *The Things That Are Not Caesar's*, emphasized the Gregorian ideal of church liberty ("Canossa will always remain the consolation of free minds") and examined the new situation of "indirect power" in terms of the moral and prophetic voice of the church acting through society.[20]

No one studied the nineteenth-century crisis more carefully than John Courtney Murray, who invoked its lessons at a crucial stage in the debate over religious liberty at the Second Vatican Council. Bishop de Smedt, the *relator* of the group of bishops charged with formulating a position on the matter, invited Murray to present a summary of the issues disputed up to that point in the discussion. In the summer of 1964, he circulated a brief that was later published under the title "The Problem of Religious Freedom" (1964, 1993). Tracing the crisis through the *Syllabus of Errors* and the letters of Leo XIII, Murray showed why the church-state controversy was irresolvable on monistic grounds, namely the subordination of society to a single, undifferentiated citizenship superintended by the omni-competent state. The crisis called for a recovery of "the Gregorian state of the question of public care of religion," as well as a new discernment of the "growing end" of the tradition.[21]

---

18. Luigi Stuzo, *Church and State* (New York: Longmans, Green, 1939), 563.

19. Stuzo, *Church and State*, 385.

20. Maritain, *The Things That Are Not Caesar's*, 16.

21. John Courtney Murray, "The Problem of Religious Freedom," in *Religious Liberty: Catholic Struggles with Pluralism*, ed. J. Leon Hooper, SJ (Louisville, KY: Westminster John Knox Press, 1993), 165.

II. THE LEONINE SYNTHESIS

Murray's notion of a "growing end" presupposed, of course, a tradition. Pope Pius XI (1922–39) was the first pope to speak of social doctrine as a unified body of teachings that develop by way of clarity and application. He thought of himself as inheriting a "doctrine" (*doctrina*) "handed on" (*tradita*) from the time of Leo XIII. Significantly, he contended that the tradition is communicated not only in the magisterial work of the papal office, but also in the ordinary work of bishops and priests, in the research and writings of lay scholars, as well as in the policies of non-Catholic statesmen.[22] Although it is doubtful that Leo deliberately launched a new doctrinal specialty per se, it cannot be doubted that his work gave a certain cachet to the idea. Indeed, the period from 1878 to 1939 could be called the era of Leonine synthesis. It reached its creative high-water mark in the 1930s between the two world wars, but its effects were consolidated at the Second Vatican Council (1962–65).

The expression "Leonine synthesis" is appropriate for two reasons. First, Leo had to reconcile Pius IX's *Quanta cura* (1864), and its appended *Syllabus of Errors*, with *Dei Filius* (1870), the dogmatic constitution of the Catholic faith adopted at the First Vatican Council. Whereas the *Syllabus* had pungently condemned errors of the Enlightenment, *Dei Filius* affirmed the integrity of reason and its harmony with the propositions of divine revelation to which faith assents. The council affirmed that God, "lord of sciences," is the same God who reveals sacred "mysteries." There is a "twofold order of knowledge," the council maintained, "distinct not only as regards its source, but also as regards its object."[23] The Church does not seek to hinder the advancement of knowledge in the sciences and arts to which natural reason can attain. Leo's many teaching letters represent an extended commentary on the problems listed in the *Syllabus*, but always through the optic of *Dei Filius*, distinguishing the negative and affirmative propositions, and pointing to the different modes of knowledge and wisdoms that apply to a disputed issue.

Second, we can speak of a Leonine synthesis in terms of his ambitious and relentless effort to revive Thomism, for which his encyclical *Aeterni Patris* (1879) is the *magna charta*. His interest in Saint Thomas began at the ripe

---

22. Pius XI, Encyclical Letter *Quadragesimo anno* (May 15, 1931), §§18–21, *AAS* 23, 182–84. On the emergence of the term *doctrina*, see Mary Elsbernd, "Papal Statements on Rights: A Historical Contextual Study of Encyclical Teaching from Pius VI-Pius XI (1791–1939)" (PhD diss., Catholic University of Louvain, 1985), 587n1.

23. Vatican Council I, Dogmatic Constitution *Dei Filius*, IV (April 24, 1870), in *Decrees of the Ecumenical Councils*, ed. Norman P. Tanner (Washington, DC: Georgetown University Press, 1990).

old age of ten, during his training at Viterbo, and continued at the Roman College, where, at the age of fourteen, he became the student assistant of the Jesuit neo-Thomist Luigi Taparelli. In time, he would meet Taparelli's neo-Thomist colleagues Matteo Liberatore and Joseph Kleutgen, who would work on the drafts of *Dei Filius* and *Aeterni Patris*. As bishop of Perugia, Pecci recruited a Thomistic faculty for his Accademia di S. Tommaso, which was an incubator for what became known as the Leonine revival. Once he became pope, Leo swiftly moved to place Thomists into key positions in the curia and in the Roman colleges.

There were practical reasons for Leo's bid to install Thomism as the preferred method for Catholic education. The suppression of the Society of Jesus in 1773 had destroyed an international system of education that was broadly scholastic in orientation. The Napoleonic ideal of the state as teacher (*l'État enseignant*) brought what remained of Catholic schools to the brink of extinction in Europe and South America. Bismarck's *Kulturkampf* was ignited by the issue of church schools. With the more centralized and independent situation of Catholicism after Vatican I, Leo saw the chance to rebuild education, beginning with seminaries. Moreover, the institutions would need a curriculum. Although *Dei Filius* had a scholastic ambience, it did not attempt to settle questions of which particular philosophical schools or theological methods ought to be adopted. For example, *Dei Filius* asserted that the existence of God "can be known with certainty from the consideration of created things"; yet, as Gerald McCool has pointed out, the document did not "specify any definite argument through which the existence and nature of God could be established," nor did it affirm "that purely natural knowledge of God had ever been achieved in fact."[24] Leo seized upon the opportunity to institutionalize Thomism, the only method, in his estimation, capable of protecting positive revelation against modern historicism and naturalism without, at the same time, evacuating the claims of natural reason. Thomism would clarify and unify the internal deposit of faith and doctrine, maintain proper analogies to the discoveries of natural reason and the sciences, and would provide apologetics needed to defend the credibility of Catholicism. In his first encyclical, he made his intentions clear: We must "endeavor that not only a suitable and solid method of education may flourish but above all that this education be wholly in harmony with the Catholic faith in its literature and system of training, and chiefly in philosophy, upon which the direction of other sciences in great measure depends."[25]

24. *Dei Filius*, II; Gerald A. McCool, SJ, *Catholic Theology in the Nineteenth Century* (New York: Seabury, 1977), 219.
25. Leo XIII, Encyclical Letter *Inscrutabili Dei* (April 21, 1878), §13, *Acta Leonis* 1, 53–54.

The institutional and systematic thrust of Leo's program would leave a deep imprint upon the Catholic mind, both clerical and lay, until the 1960s, when Thomistic scholasticism gradually lost its institutional monopoly in the seminaries and universities. The Catholic mind in the 1960s began to gravitate more toward the social sciences than philosophy, and toward personalism rather than the ontology of an Aristotelian natural science. In the area of social thought, however, neo-Thomism both preceded and outlasted Leo's broader institutional aims. In *Aeterni Patris*, he pointedly recommended the teachings of Saint Thomas Aquinas for the "true meaning of liberty" and for the "divine origin of all authority."[26] On these topics, the timeless air of the thirteenth-century scholastic system would not suffice without interpretive bridgework. Middle axioms needed to be devised in order to make a thirteenth-century scholasticism speak to the new social situation. Thomas, after all, had no conception of a modern state or an industrialized economy. Nor in Thomas could there be found a ready-made doctrine of subsidiarity, justiciable natural rights, social justice, political parties, or a lay-based democracy.

The interpretive bridgework began among Leo's Jesuit teachers and colleagues. It is not at all surprising that the intellectual work in the social and political area started with Jesuits. The Jesuits had been expelled first from the Catholic courts in 1759–68 and had been restored only in 1814. They could not fail to be acutely conscious of the political riptides of modern Europe. Pope Pius IX fled the revolution in Rome in 1848, taking refuge in the Kingdom of Naples. There, in exile with the pope, Jesuits began publication of *Civiltá Cattolica* on April 6, 1850. The journal became a venue for Taparelli and Liberatore to mount an aggressive and polemical case for Thomism as the only adequate method for meeting the challenges of the era. Some of their contributions were systematic in nature, covering issues of anthropology, epistemology, and metaphysics. The more controversial pieces, however, dealt with social issues: the nature of the common good, the respective jurisdictions of church and state, the nature and scope of law, and the origin of human authority. No one had seen such a dialectical and polemical Thomism since the sixteenth century, when Baroque-era scholastics in Spain and Portugal—Robert Bellarmine, Francisco de Vitoria, Bartolomé de Las Casas, Francisco Suárez, and Luis de Molina—used Thomas to counter the claims of absolute monarchs. The Jesuit *ressourcement* of sixteenth-century Thomistic political theory was pressed now against Rousseavians and physiocrats who laid the philosophical foundations for laicist republicanism.[27] Interestingly, in 1854

---

26. Leo XIII, Encyclical Letter *Aeterni Patris* (August 4, 1879), §29, *Acta Leonis* 1, 280.

27. Walter T. Odell, "The Political Theory of Civiltà Cattolica From 1850 to 1870" (PhD diss., Georgetown University, 1969).

the Jesuit editors and writers of *Civiltá Cattolica* were expelled from the Kingdom of Naples for daring to assert that the natural law left the institutional form of polities somewhat indeterminate—a position that appeared dangerously subversive in an era of revolution.

At mid-century, neo-Thomists began to chart a middle course between the absolutist claims of monarchy and the absolutist claims of popular sovereignty. Above all, Leo and his neo-Thomist mentors and colleagues were interested in the problem of unity and plurality. In their view, the chief problem of the modern project was not the political "form" of republican or popular government. Thomists had always recognized that a human polity is amenable to plural, legitimate forms, and that such forms can either evolve by custom or change by acts of deliberate constitutional prudence. Thomas himself argued for the prudence of a mixed regime of monarchical, aristocratic, and popular elements, which he believed was embodied in the ancient Jewish state.[28] The problem, rather, lay in what the Jesuit neo-Thomists discerned to be a distinctively modern premise, namely, that unity is achieved only extrinsically by contracts, by the serendipitous outcomes of a market, or, more ominously, by the external application of law as the superior force of the state. Thomists argued that pluralities stem from intrinsic unities, beginning with human nature itself, and including matrimony, family, church, and body politic. The question was not whether there is social pluralism with distinctive modes of authority and freedom, but whether there is an ontological landscape internal to social forms. By nature and supernature, are there norms anterior to, and higher than, the laws imposed by civil law and contract? Indeed, from the nineteenth century to the present day, Catholic social thought has orbited around this issue. The great question of post-1789 Catholicism was whether the modern crisis is to be ameliorated by more or by less public freedom. Neo-Thomists reformulated this problem. It was first necessary, they argued, to understand the anthropological and social grounds of liberty and obligation.

These themes are evident in the great papal letters of Leo XIII, particularly *Rerum novarum* (1891), where Leo distinguished between the rights of obligations of individuals, families, voluntary associations, civil government, and Christian charity. But his work was not a finished product. He had relatively little to say about either the theory or practice of democratic government, and, until the end of his life, remained frustrated by the problem of (Catholic) political parties.[29] While his economic theory represented a

---

28. *ST*, I-II, q. 105, a. 1.

29. See his letter *Graves de communi* (January 18, 1901) on Christian democracy. Leo worried that Catholic associations would become politicized in the fashion of socialist parties.

huge advance in comparison with the thought of his predecessors, it was not well developed in any descriptive or scientific sense. Moreover, while Leo brilliantly delineated the triad of church, state, and society, defending the liberties of church and society vis-à-vis the state, he did not follow through the implications for a fuller doctrine of religious liberty. Nonetheless, Leo imparted to the Catholic world an important precedent. On issues of revealed theology proper, the deposit of faith and tradition would be organized scholastically; but, regarding the "changeable ocean of human affairs," which is to say, "in regard to purely human societies," Leo permitted, even encouraged, new applications of traditional principles.[30] As Thomas had said, the natural law can change by addition, as human prudence discovers new applications beneficial to human life.[31] Leo took inspiration from Luigi Taparelli, who coined the term "social justice," advanced the first philosophically rigorous account of "subsidiarity," and began the work of integrating natural rights with the older doctrine of natural law. Though inspired by the thought of Thomas, little of this could count as a seamless representation of Thomas's own doctrines.

With this historical framework in place, let us examine in more detail Leo's life and accomplishments in the realm of social doctrine.

III. LEO'S ECCLESIASTICAL CAREER

Having barely survived surgery for the removal of a diseased cyst, the ninety-year-old Leo XIII welcomed 350,000 pilgrims to Rome for the Jubilee of 1900. Measured against the past century, the event was a success by virtue of the fact that it took place at all. The jubilees of 1800 and 1850 had been cancelled because the popes were either kidnapped or in exile. Pius IX refused to call a jubilee in 1875 to protest the capture of Rome by the armies of the House of Savoy.

With this history in mind, Pope Leo wrote two encyclicals to put the troubled century into perspective. In *Tametsi futura*, he characterized his pontificate as "difficult and anxious."[32] What "experience constantly shows," he contemplated, is that "all our life on earth is the truthful and exact image of a pilgrimage."[33] In *Annum sacrum*, Leo dedicated the human race to the Sacred Heart of Jesus:

---

30. Leo XIII, Encyclical Letter *Au Milieu* (February 16, 1892), §17, *Acta Leonis* 12, 31.

31. *ST*, I-II, q. 94, a. 5.

32. Leo XIII, Encyclical Letter *Tametsi futura* (November 1, 1900), §2, *Acta Leonis* 20, 295.

33. *Tametsi*, §6, *Acta Leonis* 20, 300.

When the Church, in the days immediately succeeding her institution, was oppressed beneath the yoke of the Caesars, a young Emperor saw in the heavens a cross, which became at once the happy omen and cause of the glorious victory that soon followed. And now, today, behold another blessed and heavenly token is offered to our sight—the most Sacred Heart of Jesus, with a cross rising from it and shining forth with dazzling splendor amidst flames of love. In that Sacred Heart all our hopes should be placed, and from it the salvation of men is to be confidently besought.[34]

Coming just a few years before the tattered monarchies of Europe committed cultural and military suicide in the trenches of World War I, Leo's admonition was prescient. Catholics should prepare themselves for a suffering king rather than a Constantine.

Leo's life bestrode one of the most traumatic centuries in the history of the papacy and the Catholic Church. At the time of Leo's birth in 1810, the French were holding Pope Pius VII, the second pope in less than a decade that they had kidnapped. One of Leo's earliest memories was the triumphant return of Pius to Rome after the fall of Napoleon. Though Leo was a man of aristocratic bearing, one who maintained the ambience of an old-world court inside the Vatican, modern gadgets such as telephones, recording devices, and elevators intrigued him. When he died in 1903, he was buried in the Lateran next to Innocent III, the very epitome of the medieval papal monarchy. Yet Leo spent the last decade of his pontificate trying to reconcile French Catholics to republican government. Before we study his teachings, we need to consider the situation of Catholic Christianity in his own time and place.

Gioacchino Vincenzo Pecci was born on March 2, 1810, at Carpineto in the Latium region, which lies along the ancient road connecting Rome and Naples. For a millennium, this area was part of the Papal States. The Congress of Vienna (1815) restored Latium, then under the sway of Napoleon, to papal governance. Pecci spent most of his adult life as a cleric helping to govern these states, even though he would never be able to do so as pope. Indeed, he would be the first pope since the eighth century not to inherit the papal temporalities in Italy.

Pecci attended the Jesuit college in Viterbo (1818) and then the Roman College (1824). His family background in minor nobility qualified him for admission to the Accademia dei Nobili Ecclesiastici (1832), where he pursued the career track of a Roman lawyer and diplomat. Pecci's training at the Accademia was typical for young men who sought careers in the *prelature*—a quasi-lay bureaucracy governing the Papal States. The prelates were entitled to wear

---

34. Leo XIII, Encyclical Letter *Annum sacrum* (May 25, 1899), §12, *Acta Leonis* 19, 78–79.

violet-colored ecclesiastical dress and to be called *monsignori*. Some prelates, like Cardinal Rampolla, secretary of state under Pius IX, rose to the top of the papal bureaucracy without ever receiving major orders. Others, like Pecci, went on to become priests and bishops.

Although the Papal States constituted the oldest standing temporal monarchy in Europe, their administration at this time was comically incompetent. Having no steady policy of taxation or military conscription, the Papal States could not develop into a modern polity capable of competing with the great state-making regimes north of the Alps. After 1815 the papacy depended upon Austrian or French armies for military protection. In their waning years, the Papal States' only claim to fame was having more opera houses than any country in Europe and possessing the last crop of castrati singers.

Ordained a priest in 1837, Pecci spent forty years as an administrator, diplomat, priest, and bishop in the papal dominions. He fought brigands, established banks and cooperatives for farmers, built hospitals and schools, and supervised the construction of roads. In January 1843, Pope Gregory XVI made Pecci nuncio to Brussels, where he was able to see firsthand the Industrial Revolution in northern Europe. Consecrated archbishop of Perugia in 1846, he spent the next thirty-two years as a reformer in Umbria, notably in the field of education. In 1872 he established the Accademia di S. Tommaso. Appointing his brother Giuseppe Pecci and the Dominican Tommaso Zigliara to the faculty, Bishop Pecci hoped to build a scholastic curriculum of studies. Although there were faint stirrings of Thomism in Italy at this time, it enjoyed only a marginalized position in the Roman schools. The revival of Catholic intellectual life along Thomistic lines was the great passion of Pecci's life—an unusual passion for a pastor and administrator. Immediately after becoming pope, he elevated his brother and Zigliara to the College of Cardinals to spearhead an international reform of Catholic education on the model of Saint Thomas Aquinas.

Pecci was made a cardinal in 1853. The laicist Piedmontese government tested his mettle by occupying Perugia in 1859. Pecci protested the government's suppression of religious orders, absorption of marriage and education by state law, confiscation of church property, and induction of the clergy into the army. Cardinal Pecci managed to stay out of jail even while keeping his diocese intact. As the Papal States crumbled between 1860 and 1870, he remained the loyal servant of Pope Pius IX. Pecci supported, and had a minor role in formulating, the *Syllabus errorum* (1864). On matters political, he was a diplomat and pragmatist, but he rarely conceded ground that he thought rightfully belonged to the Church. Heads of state would soon learn that Pecci was the wiliest pope in centuries.

In 1877 Pius IX called Pecci to Rome, where he was made Cardinal Camerlengo. When Pius died on February 7, 1878, Pecci had the duty of conducting the ceremony that attested the pope's death. The cardinal carried out this task not by applying the silver hammer to the deceased pope's forehead, but rather by putting a veil over Pius's face and lifting it three times with the query, "Giovanni, Giovanni, Giovanni?"[35] For once, the voluble pope had no retort. Pecci was not the front-runner on the list of *papabili* at the conclave of 1878; that dubious position went to Cardinal Bilio, one of the chief architects of the controversial *Syllabus errorum* (1864). But France, Austria, Spain, and Portugal still laid claim to the so-called *ius exclusivae* (the right of vetoing a papal candidate), and they indicated that Bilio was not satisfactory. Indeed, such were the political pressures on the conclave that Cardinal Manning urged the cardinals to retire to Malta under the protection of the British governor. They resolved to stay at the Vatican, where, on the third vote, Pecci was elected on February 30, 1878.

When asked what name he would take, he replied, "That of Leo XIII, out of the deference and gratitude I have always had for Leo XII and the veneration of Saint Leo I which I have had since my youth."[36] Pope Leo I (Leo Magnus) was one of only two popes to be recognized as a Doctor of the Church, and the first pope to be buried in St. Peter's. Perhaps Pecci was inspired by the magnificent marble relief by Alessandro Algardi in St. Peter's, a work that depicted Leo I confronting Attila the Hun outside Rome in 452, for Pecci made a point of mentioning this event in his first encyclical.[37] Leo would take as his pontifical coat of arms the heraldic depiction of a pine tree, two fleurs-de-lis, and a comet, the latter interpreted by his contemporaries as a confirmation of the so-called prophesy of Malachi that this pope would be *lumen in coelo*, a light in the heavens.[38]

IV. A PASSION FOR TEACHING

No one expected the sixty-eight-year-old pope to preside over the 1900 Jubilee. He was an interim pope, elected to solve the dispute between the Church and the Italian state. As it turned out, he never resolved this problem. Popes for another fifty years, in protest against the loss of papal dominions, would call themselves "prisoners in the Vatican." Nor did anyone anticipate that Pecci, who had never written a scholarly treatise, would have the energy and composure to write some 110 encyclicals and other teaching letters—by far the most prodigious output of teaching on the part of any modern

---

35. Francis A. Burkle-Young, *Papal Elections in the Age of Transition, 1878–1922* (Lanham, MD: Lexington Books, 2000), 44.

36. Burkle-Young, *Papal Elections*, 67.

37. *Inscrutabili Dei* (1878), §10, *Acta Leonis* 1, 50.

38. Jacques Martin, *Heraldry in the Vatican* (Gerrards Cross: Van Duren, 1987), 197.

pope.[39] Within twelve months of his election, Leo had already issued four teaching letters.

Leo's letters reveal a relentless drive to diagnose historical contingencies in the light of first principles. Leo did not invent the genre of encyclical letters, nor was he the first pope to make encyclical letters an ordinary means of communication with the universal Church. His predecessor, Pius IX, wrote sixty-six letters during his turbulent pontificate. Leo so perfected the teaching letter that it became a new pedagogical art, best described as applied doctrine. At the same time, his letters effect in the reader a speculative insight that is deeper and more synthetic than that produced by mere policy statements on issues of the day. In this respect, Leo was a public intellectual who took full advantage of the greatest bully pulpit in the world. His achievement is all the more remarkable in that he did not begin writing these letters until he was almost seventy years old. All of his successors have tried, with varying degrees of success, to reduplicate the Leonine art of teaching.

Why did Leo XIII write so many letters? For one thing, the technology of the modern media made it possible for a papal letter to be read in every capital of Europe within hours of its publication. William George Ward (1812–82), the papalist editor of the *Dublin Review*, famously said, "I should like a new papal Bull every morning with my *Times* and breakfast."[40] Leo understood Europe's newfound and seemingly boundless appetite for the newspaper, and he used modern media to transform the arcane papal "bull" into the modern encyclical, which aimed at conveying teaching and information more than rendering legal verdicts.

The most important reason Leo made such extensive use of letters is that by 1878 the Catholic Church had lost (or was in the process of losing) its privileged political status in the Catholic nations of Europe and South America. With the death of Catholic political Christendom, it became impractical to rely upon local political and ecclesiastical elites to maintain the international character of the Church. At the eclipse of the papacy's temporal rule in Italy and the altar-throne alliance in Europe, Leo rediscovered its teaching function.

The gradual, and sometimes violent, dissolution of Catholic political Christendom after 1789 left unresolved problems of a practical and theological nature. Since the early sixteenth century, Catholic sovereigns had acquired

---

39. Only the *litterae encyclicae* and the *epistolae encyclicae* are encyclicals in the strict sense of the term. I use the expression "encyclicals and other teaching letters" to cover more inclusively other species of papal documents containing ordinary magisterial teaching. My enumeration of all species of teaching letters follows the *Enchiridion delle Encicliche*, 8 vols. (Bologna: Edizioni Edhoniane Bologne, 1994–1998).

40. Wilfrid Ward, *William George Ward and the Catholic Revival* (London: Macmillan, 1893), 14.

ecclesiastical privileges to govern the many facets of the Church in their dominions. Originally, Rome conceded these privileges to reward crusades against Islam, to consolidate the Catholic response to the Reformation, and to facilitate missions in the New World. During the era of absolutism, monarchs and their courts in Versailles, Madrid, and Vienna insisted that royal governance of the Church was an inherent right of sovereignty. The revolutions of the late eighteenth and nineteenth centuries, however, did not end the situation of national churches. In France, the royal ecclesiastical prerogatives were swiftly translated into the terms of popular sovereignty. The church in all its temporalities was property of the state, and her bishops and clergy its civil servants. In the former Spanish dominions, the royal Patronato Real became the Patronato Nacional, and Venezuela's first twenty-six constitutions retained its law of state patronage. As late as 1870, the Holy See nominated bishops in only five countries, four of them predominately Protestant.

This juridical and political remnant of Christendom perplexed Leo's nineteenth-century predecessors. After the Congress of Vienna, popes adopted the policy of legitimism, supporting nominally Catholic sovereigns as agents of law and order against the tides of revolution. The revolutions of 1848 demonstrated the obsolescence of this system. Pecci's generation detested state superintendence of the church, with the attendant ministers of cults, confiscation of ecclesiastical property, and monopoly on education. Leo himself called such superintendence *regalismo*, or regalism, a polemical term for the doctrine that the *res sacra in temporalibus* (sacred reality insofar as it is temporal) rightfully belongs to the authority of the civil sovereign.[41]

When the sixty-year-old Pecci attended Vatican Council I in December 1869, churchmen and statesmen understood that the Church would have to extricate itself from captivity to national churches. The bishops debated a draft of a conciliar document *De Ecclesia Christi*, containing five chapters and twenty-one canons on church and state.[42] If adopted, these chapters and canons could mean nothing other than the end of church-state relations as they had existed in the Catholic world. There was talk in European capitals of military intervention to stop the Council. As it turned out, the bishops could not agree on the kind of overarching theory needed to take a decisive position on these chapters and canons. Instead, at the Fourth Session, on July 18, 1870, the Council approved the Dogmatic Constitution *Pastor aeternus*. Politically,

---

41. Leo XIII, Encyclical Letter *Praeclara gratulationis* (June 20, 1894), *Acta Leonis* 14, 207. See John Courtney Murray's commentary on this letter, "Leo XIII: Separation of Church and State," *Theological Studies* 14 (1953): 145–214.

42. Ioannes Dominicus Mansi, ed., *Sacrorum Conciliorum Nova et Amplissima Collectio*, vol. 51 (Arnhem and Leipzig, 1926). *Primum Schema Constitutionis de Ecclesia Christi*, Ch. X–XV, 543–51; canons I–XXI, 551–53.

the definition of papal infallibility was less explosive than the sentence on juris-diction: "Wherefore we teach and declare that, by divine ordinance, the Roman church possesses a pre-eminence of ordinary power over every other church, and that this jurisdictional power of the Roman pontiff is both episcopal and immediate."[43] The local church is not *in* the state but in the universal Church. There would be no more national churches. Thus the bishops had, in effect, endorsed the result of extricating the Church from the states, but they did so indirectly, through the device of papal jurisdictional authority.

The main problem facing Pope Leo was that the Council had put the nail in the coffin of political Christendom but had provided no canon law to legally organize the changes (the Code of Canon Law would not exist until 1917), no solution to the fractured diplomatic relations with governments, and, most important, no picture of what ought to be the normal configuration of church, state, and society. It would be too strong to say that Leo had to invent a new social and political theology from scratch; however, he did have to pick up the pieces of the Church's post-1789 experience and to put together a synoptic view of where Catholicism stood in this new political and social world. What we now call Catholic social teaching emerged in this crisis.

V. A TWOFOLD PEDAGOGY

Throughout his letters, Leo used a twofold pedagogy to situate the human agent who participates in divine providence both through the natural law and through the law of the Gospel. In *Rerum novarum* (1891),[44] for example, he said that the state is "rightly apprehended" according to "right reason congruent with nature" and in light of the "dictates of divine wisdom."[45] The distinctions related to this double pedagogy—reason and faith, general and particular providence, nature and grace—represent two ways that the human knower participates in God's ordering wisdom. For Leo, how-ever, the "natural" does not constitute a zone in which persons or things exist apart from divine providence. It does not track what we usually mean by the "secular." In the nineteenth century, this point was not easily made, for

---

43. Vatican Council I, Dogmatic Constitution *Pastor aeternus* III (July 18, 1870), in *Decrees of the Ecumenical Councils*, ed. Norman P. Tanner, 2 vols. (Washington, DC: Georgetown University Press, 1990), 2:813ff.

44. Leo XIII, Encyclical Letter *Rerum Novarum* (May 15, 1891), §32, *Acta Leonis* 11, 120.

45. The First Vatican Council affirmed a twofold order of cognition, faith, and reason, each with its own "distinct source and object." But this order does not constitute a dualism of truth, "since it is the same God who reveals the mysteries and infuses faith, and who has endowed the human mind with the light of reason." See *Dei Filius* IV, in Tanner, *Decrees*, 2:8.

modern philosophy and science laid claim to a "secular" sphere unfettered from the traditional biblical understanding of authority flowing from either the order of creation or that of redemption. Catholic thinkers, wary of discourse about nature, general providence, and reason, preferred instead to emphasize the perspective of particular providence, scripture, and ecclesiastical history and law. This was the discourse of the older Christendom.

The animus against philosophy arose in reaction to the Enlightenment's critique of particular providence as the abode of superstition and priestcraft. Philosophy meant deism, the doctrine that the natural order is created but not governed by God. In the letter *Christianae reipublicae* (1766), we find Pope Clement XIII castigating philosophers who teach that God is "lazy and indolent."[46] Pius VI, in his first encyclical, criticized philosophy for teaching that particular providence is a "conspiracy against the innate liberty of man."[47] When the Revolution erupted in France, he lamented that the Eldest Daughter of the Church had "commended itself into the counsel of philosophers."[48] The philosophers seek to replace "old, customary, and legitimate constitutions" with novelties based upon abstractions.[49] The most dangerous abstraction is the scenario of a state of nature, espoused in different ways by Spinoza, Kant, and, above all, Rousseau, who said that the state of nature entitles us to consider human nature as "if it had been left to itself."[50] Against this perspective, Pius VI appealed to Genesis 2:17. Placing humanity in the "paradise of delectation," God constituted human liberty under a law.[51] There is no such thing, he concluded, as a human nature or a human condition bereft of a moral (natural) law. Every pope since Clement XIII (1758–69) had issued letters warning about the "virus" and "sects" of philosophy.

Catholic thinkers of the modern period eschewed talk about natural law lest it suggest a human condition untutored by faith and the discipline of the

---

46. Clement XIII, Encyclical Letter *Christianae reipublicae* (November 25, 1766), *Bullarium Romanum*, Cont. (Rome: Camera Apostolica, 1835–1858), 3, 226.

47. Pius VI, Encyclical Letter *Inscrutabile* (December 25, 1775), *Bullarium Romanum*, Cont., 3, no. 5, 178ff.

48. *Communicamus vobiscum* (March 9, 1790), in *Collection générale des brefs et instructions de notre très-saint père le pape Pie VI, relatifs a la Révolution Françoise*, ed. M. N. S. Guillon, 2 vols. (Paris: Chez Le Clere, 1798), 1, 8.

49. Pius VI, Encyclical Letter *Adeo nota* (April 23, 1791), in Guillon, *Collection générale*, 2, 72.

50. Jean-Jacques Rousseau, preface to "Discourse on the Origin and Foundations of Inequality Among Men," in *Discourse on the Origins of Inequality (Second Discourse), Polemics, and Political Economy*, ed. Roger D. Masters and Christopher Kelly, in *The Collected Writings of Rousseau*, 6 vols. (Hanover, NH: University Press of New England, 1992), 3:15.

51. Pius VI, Brief *Quod aliquantum* (March 10, 1791), in Guillon, *Collection générale*, 1, 124–26.

Church. The great Jacques-Bénigne Bossuet, for example, as preceptor and tutor of the dauphin, impressed upon the prince that God's rule should never be understood in the way taught by Deists. "Thus he acted since the beginning of the world. At that time he was the sole king of men, and governed them visibly."[52] In *Mirari vos* (1832), Gregory XVI warned that philosophers make much of natural law in order to cast doubt upon particular providence.[53] Such doubt undermines the claims and titles of the particular ecclesiastical and civil institutions inherited from Christendom, which is to say, from the order of particular providence. The sacral order had to be defended against what the Spanish diplomat Donoso Cortés called "the iron age of philosophical civilization."[54] Perhaps the most influential Catholic writer for Leo's generation was Joseph de Maistre, the doyen of political conservatism, who asserted that "human reason, or what is ignorantly called philosophy," is an "essentially disruptive force."[55] Even a prominent Catholic liberal like Félicité Robert de Lamennais could write that "religion is found near the cradle of all peoples, as philosophy is found near their tomb."[56] Pius IX sometimes referred to natural law, but usually as a defensive measure against hostile state policies.[57] That he would even have to make recourse to natural law and natural rights indicates the much-weakened status of the customary sentiments and instruments by which temporal and ecclesiastical authorities negotiated their differences.

At the risk of oversimplifying, the case against philosophy was twofold. First, philosophy is abstraction that cannot reach, in any useful way, what God teaches through nature and general providence. The "law of history" is the matrix for the teachings of nature, for history discloses concrete relations

---

52. Jacques-Benigne Bossuet, *Politics Drawn from the Very Words of Holy Scripture*, trans. and ed. Patrick Riley (Cambridge: Cambridge University Press, 1990), II.1, prop. 2, 40.

53. Gregory XVI, Encyclical Letter *Mirari vos* (August 15, 1832). Antonius Bernasconi, ed., *Acta Gregorii Papae XVI*, 4 vols. (Rome: S. C. de Propaganda Fide, 1901–1904), 1, 171.

54. Juan Donoso Cortés, "Donoso Cortés to Montalembert (June 4, 1849)," in *Selected Works of Juan Donoso Cortés*, trans. and ed. Jeffrey P. Johnson (Westport, CT: Greenwood Press, 2000), 63.

55. Joseph de Maistre, *Considerations on France*, trans. and ed. Richard A. Lebrun (Cambridge: Cambridge University Press, 1994), 41.

56. Félicité Robert de Lamennais, *Essai sur l'indifférence (1820)*, in *Oeuvres completes de F. de La Mennais*, 12 vols. (Paris: P. Daubrée et Cailleux, 1836–1837), 1:21.

57. Communism is "opposed to the very natural law"; see Pius IX, Encyclical Letter *Qui pluribus* (November 9, 1846), §16, in *Pii IX Pontificis Maximi Acta*, part 1, 7 vols. (Rome: Ex Typographia Bonarum Artium, 185–878), 1, 13; against socialism, he refers to "immutable" and "natural" principles at Encyclical Letter *Nostis et nobiscum* (December 8, 1849), §20, in *Pii IX Acta*, part 1, 1, 211; and he appeals to natural rights in *Syllabus errorum* (December 8, 1864), §§26, 30, 33, 56, 67, in *Pii IX Acta*, part 1, 3, 701–17.

between humanity, society, and God. Thus the French Catholic conservative Louis de Bonald contended that what is "written on the heart" is not the reliable index for "the natural"; rather, the "way of perfection" is shown in the actual evolution of institutions and societies.[58] Philosophers' quest for the primitive, either in nature or in the human mind, never locates something truly original. It locates fundaments that are figments, such as the asocial person and the social contract.[59] Knowledge does not arise from innate ideas, much less by words privately entertained, but by one mind teaching another through speech. Since no one teaches himself or herself to speak, we must admit that knowledge arose from an original speech act, that of God tutoring Adam.[60] In the order of epistemology, socially constituted knowledge was to be the conservative alternative to Cartesian reason (*cogito*). In matters political, it countered the Rousseauvian general will (*volonté généralité*), namely the idea that social relations are rightly constituted only by the fiat of human choice.

While Leo certainly agreed with the polemical thrust of this thought, he refused to consign philosophy to the status of a modern "sect." In an 1892 allocution, Leo explained that the Catholic project should aim at the "conscience of the people" rather than the "restoration of medieval institutions."[61] The Church must enter the marketplace of ideas. He thought that Thomism was useful for something more than propping up historically obsolete institutions. His Jesuit preceptors at Viterbo and Rome had taught the young Pecci that the traditionalists had gone too far in demoting the natural law, the role of human intellection, and philosophy.[62] An adequate Catholic response to philosophers was overdue.

Quoting Matthew 28:19–20, "go and teach all nations," Leo laid out his new agenda in *Aeterni Patris*: "But the natural helps with which the grace of the divine wisdom, strongly and sweetly disposing all things, has supplied the human race are neither to be despised nor neglected, chief among which is evidently the right use of philosophy. For not in vain did God set the light of reason in the human mind; and so far is the super-added light of faith from

---

58. Louis de Bonald, *On Divorce*, trans. and ed. Nicholas Davidson (New Brunswick, NJ: Transaction, 1992), 73.

59. De Maistre, *Considerations*, 49.

60. An early use of this argument is found in Pius VI, *Quod aliquantum* (1791), in Guillon, *Collection générale*, 1:126. A more ambitious use of the argument can be found in Bonald, *On Divorce*, 48ff. On romantic conservatism in Catholic thought, see Ward, *George Ward and the Catholic Revival*, 95–100, and Heinrich A. Rommen, *The State in Catholic Thought: A Treatise in Political Philosophy* (St. Louis: B. Herder, 1950), 238.

61. Leo XIII, "Onorare le ceneri" (March 1, 1892), *Acta Leonis 12*, 384ff.

62. Luigi Taparelli, whose work on natural law very much influenced Leo XIII, broke with the traditionalists on just these points. See Robert Jacquin, *Taparelli* (Paris: P. Lethielleux, 1943), 244.

extinguishing or lessening the power of the intelligence that it completes it rather, and by adding to its strength renders it capable of greater things."[63] "We hold that every word of wisdom," he continued, "every useful thing by whomsoever discovered or planned, ought to be received with a willing and grateful mind."[64] In another document he proclaimed, "The best parent and guardian of liberty amongst men is truth."[65] We misunderstand Leo if we think that he meant that philosophy should overshadow theology; rather, philosophy, like the gold of Egypt, is appropriated by theology and pressed into the service of the true God.[66] The Church should reclaim its role as the "refuge of the liberal arts," a *domus sapientiae*, a "house of wisdom."[67] Both metaphors are interesting. The natural sources of human intellection, if rightly used, lead to natural theology, which considers the relationship between secondary causes and the unrestricted divine cause. So long as it is not short-changed, philosophy is also permeable to the higher wisdom of revelation— hence the twofold pedagogy of creation and revelation. In either register, the intellect does not offer a blind submission to custom, nor indeed to any human authority:

> By obeying Christ with his intellect man by no means acts in a servile manner, but in complete accordance with his reason and his natural dignity. For by his will he yields, not to the authority of any man, but to that of God, the author of his being, and the first principle to Whom he is subject by the very law of his nature. He does not suffer himself to be forced by the theories of any human teacher, but by the eternal and unchangeable truth. Hence he attains at one and the same time the natural good of the intellect and his own liberty. For the truth which proceeds from the teaching of Christ clearly demonstrates the real nature and value of every being; and man, being endowed with this knowledge, if he but obey the truth as perceived, will make all things subject to himself, not himself to them; his appetites to his reason, not his reason to his appetites.[68]

Leo looked to St. Thomas to supply the method for this twofold pedagogy. Thomas "pushed his philosophic inquiry into the reasons and principles of things," but, more important, he developed the analogies between "things

---

63. Leo XIII, Encyclical Letter *Aeterni Patris* (August 4, 1879), §2, *Acta Leonis* 1, 257ff.

64. *Aeterni Patris*, §31, *Acta Leonis* 1, 282.

65. Leo XIII, Encyclical Letter *Immortale Dei* (November 1, 1885), §40, *Acta Leonis* 5, 144.

66. *Aeterni Patris*, §4, *Acta Leonis* 1, 259ff.

67. *Inscrutabili Dei*, §10, *Acta Leonis* 1, 50.

68. *Tametsi futura*, §9, *Acta Leonis* 20, 307.

naturally known" and the theological "mysteries."[69] Leo believed that Thomism is uniquely suitable for affirming the dignity of the human intellect with respect to its natural resources even while showing how human knowledge is open-textured with respect to revelation. It need not be a "sect." Above all, Leo recommended the teachings of Saint Thomas to illuminate the "true meaning of liberty" and the "divine origin of all authority."[70] In the early modern period, Thomists like Francisco Suárez, Robert Bellarmine, and Francisco de Vitoria proved especially agile in the field of legal and political philosophy. Two decades before Leo's election, Jesuits at the *Civiltá Cattolica* had begun to press Thomism into the service of political and legal philosophy. After World War I, during the pontificate of Pius XI, this would be called "social doctrine."

VI. LAW IN DIVINE PROVIDENCE

The theme of law is paramount to Leo's understanding of how human persons and their works stand within God's ordering wisdom. In 1500, there were about five hundred independent political entities in Europe; when Leo wrote his magisterial encyclicals, there were twenty-five. The nation-states that emerged after the Napoleonic Wars had a prodigious capacity for lawmaking as the tool of civil order and uniformity. As state law became more expansive, and as customary law gave way to positive laws, the relation of law to a prior moral, anthropological, and theological order became an issue of the first importance. Who has authority to make law? Are there plural sources of law? What belongs inside or outside the positive law of the state?

Leo followed Thomas's well-known definition of law as a binding precept of reason, promulgated by a competent authority for the common good.[71] This definition can be regarded from two standpoints: from the perspective of the legislator, which is to say, a mind formulating, promulgating, and moving other persons to a common good through a precept of reason; and from the perspective of one subject to law, a mind receiving and acting according to a precept.[72] In the first, we attend to the measuring mind, in the latter to the mind being measured. From either standpoint, Leo argued, law presupposes natural liberty rooted in the intellect:

It is with moral liberty, whether in individuals or in communities, that We proceed at once to deal. But, first of all, it will be well to speak briefly

---

69. *Aeterni Patris*, §18, *Acta Leonis* 1, 273.
70. *Aeterni Patris*, §29, *Acta Leonis* 1, 280.
71. *ST*, I-II, q. 90, a. 1–4.
72. *ST*, I-II, q. 90, a. 1, ad 3.

of natural liberty; for, though it is distinct and separate from moral liberty, natural freedom is the fountainhead from which liberty of whatsoever kind flows. The unanimous consent and judgment of men . . . recognizes this natural liberty in those only who are endowed with intelligence or reason; and it is by his use of this that man is rightly regarded as responsible for his actions. For, while other animate creatures follow their senses, seeking good and avoiding evil only by instinct, man has reason to guide him in each and every act of his life. Reason sees that whatever things that are held to be good upon earth may exist or may not, and discerning that none of them are of necessity for us, it leaves the will free to choose what it pleases. But man can judge of this contingency, as We say, only because he has a soul that is simple, spiritual, and intellectual—a soul, therefore, which is not produced by matter, and does not depend on matter for its existence.[73]

Leo did not say that natural liberty is a law, but a condition of lawmaking and law-abiding action. In its proper sense, law is a binding directive (*vis directiva*), not force (*vis coactiva*). Law imposes not physical but moral necessity, and this condition requires the intellect to grasp both an intelligible good and a term of action by which the good is to be pursued.[74] It is a mistake, therefore, to conceive of human law as an artifact that mimics physical necessities, or the so-called laws of nature investigated by the physical sciences.

Leo also wanted to head off another idea, closely related to the physicalist understanding of the laws of nature: namely, that human liberty consists chiefly in spontaneous instinct and will. For Leo, the intellect is able not only to apprehend particular goods, but also to judge their contingent nature and disposition. No created good is so absolutely good that the very act of knowing it short-circuits liberty. For example, knowing that nutrition is good does not impose a necessity that one take to eating food right there and then. The will freely inclines to different things by virtue of the intellect's various conceptions of the good.[75] Liberty is thus rooted in the intellect in a twofold manner: first, in the intelligible good that makes possible action rather than mere instinct, and second, in the intellect's ability to estimate the good in a variety of dispositions. Together, these elements constitute conditions for law being something more than a projection of force that cancels out human liberty:

---

73. Leo XIII, Encyclical Letter *Libertas* (June 20, 1888), §3, *Acta Leonis* 8, 214.

74. Thomas does not include coercion and punishment in the definition of law; however, it is essential to coercion and punishment that they be acts of law. See *ST*, I-II, q. 92, a. 2.

75. Here, Leo draws from Thomas's distinction of the necessity imposed by the "contact of its action with the object on which it is acting" and the necessity of "obligation" arising from knowledge of a precept. See *De Ver.*, q. 17, a. 3.

In man's free will, therefore, or in the moral necessity of our voluntary acts being in accordance with reason, lies the very root of the necessity of law. Nothing more foolish can be uttered or conceived than the notion that, because man is free by nature, he is therefore exempt from law. Were this the case, it would follow that to become free we must be deprived of reason; whereas the truth is that we are bound to submit to law precisely because we are free by our very nature.[76]

This passage mentions no particular philosophers. It is clear, however, that Leo was arguing against the view, famously advocated by Thomas Hobbes, that the human being is an appetitive mechanism whose instincts are reconditioned or redirected by threat of sanction. Liberty obtains wherever the natural instincts remain unbounded by law. Law and liberty are harmonized, but only at the price of putting both law and liberty within the genus of force and physical necessity; reason itself remains the slave of the passions. Leo argued, to the contrary, that legal motion is not reducible to executive force. The intellect is the term by which a legal authority, first by formulating a plan of action (*ordinatio*) and then by commanding (*imperio*), moves other minds to act; but command is essentially the work of the intellect.[77] Thomas thus contended that the maxim "The will of the prince has the force of law" can make sense only on the supposition that what is promulgated has the *ratio* of justice, which is to say a term of obligation.[78] In modern times the maxim had been revived for purposes of popular sovereignty. Human law is legitimated by an aggregation of wills or preferences that the machinery of state law must represent and then enforce. Leo thought that this conception was a seedbed of despotism—not because of democratic or republican forms of government in and of themselves, but because, according to this philosophy, law does not transcend the artifice of force.

For Leo, natural law is not Rousseau's "voice of nature" (*la voix de la nature*), which speaks to human beings in a state of nature prior to a rule of law. Leo deployed a rather conventional Thomistic understanding of natural law, but he never strayed far from the problem posed by modern social-contract theorists. Does natural law imply a state of nature in which legal predicates are absent because there is no jurisdiction, no legislator? Or does natural law imply that human beings, however they are contingently situated vis-à-vis a particular civil regime, are already under a law? In the first view, natural law is not a "law" except in a metaphorical sense of the term. Law makes its first appearance in

---

76. Leo paraphrases Thomas, who says, "The root of liberty is the will as to its subject, but as to its cause it is reason." *ST*, I-II, q. 17, a. 1, ad 2.

77. *Libertas*, §7, *Acta Leonis* 8, 218.

78. *ST*, I-II, q. 17, a. 1.

an agreement among human agents to provide positive law. Government might arise from the needs and promptings of nature, but not from an antecedent order of obligation. So put, this position thwarts appeal to a normative order of creation. As we said, Catholic traditionalists had countered the state of nature hypothesis in a Burkean fashion by arguing that history discloses no such human condition bereft of social order, and therefore of the predicates of authority. Leo thought that the Church needed an alternative model of natural law that affirms the original jurisdiction of divine providence.

In *Aeterni Patris*, Leo referred to "divine wisdom, strongly and sweetly disposing all things." This image is taken from Wisdom 8:1, where God is said to order creatures "sweetly" (*suaviter*).[79] It was one of Thomas's favorite scriptural texts for creaturely participation in divine governance. "He disposes all things sweetly, because to all things He gives forms and powers inclining them to that which He Himself moves them, so that they tend toward it not by force, but as if it were by their own free accord."[80] For Thomas, the signature effect of divine governance is a multitude of things moving toward the good by inclination, by the exercising of their own natures rather than by force. Every creaturely inclination is an impression from divine wisdom.[81] The human person, however, is the recipient of instilled or impressed law (*lex indita*). The instinctual acts of irrational creatures are directed by God inasmuch as such acts belong to the species, but human actions are directed inasmuch as they belong to the individual: the human being is directed "in his personal actions, and this is what we call law."[82] The natural law is law because God communicates the necessity of obligation; it is called natural because the law is instilled or indicted in us "so as to be known naturally [*naturaliter*]."[83] For Thomas, all human judgment is set within an already existing cosmological, not positivist legal order; natural order arises from a creative act that instills or engrafts rather than imposes the measures of action.[84] In the human soul, the habit of *synderesis* holds the "first precept of law" (*primum praeceptum legis*): "The good is to be done and pursued and evil resisted."[85] By the impression of created light, God induces the creature to share in the rules and measures of the eternal law.[86] The radical implications of Thomas's teaching

---

79. *ST*, I-II, q. 90, a. 1, ad 3.

80. *Aeterni Patris*, §2, *Acta Leonis* 1, 258; *Dei Filius* II, Tanner, *Decrees*, 1:806.

81. *De car.*, 1. For other uses of Wisdom 8:1, see *SCG*, III, c. 97 (on providence); *ST*, II-II, q. 23, a. 2 (on the virtue of charity).

82. *ST*, I, q. 103, a. 8.

83. See *SCG*, III, c. 114.

84. *ST*, I-II, q. 90, a. 4, ad 1.

85. *ST*, I-II, q. 91, a. 1.

86. See Matthew Cuddeback, "Light and Form in St. Thomas Aquinas's Metaphysics of the Knower" (PhD diss., The Catholic University of America, 1998).

should be evident: Every created intelligence has a competence not only to make judgments, but also to make judgments according to a real law—indeed, a law that is the form and pattern of all other laws. The legal order of things thus does not begin with an acquired virtue, possessed by a few; nor does it begin with the offices and statutes of human positive law. God speaks the law, at least in its rudiments, to each intelligent creature. "The right ends of human life are fixed," Thomas explained, and therefore there is a "naturally right judgment about such ends."[87] Thomas grouped these ends under the triad of *to be, to live,* and *to know*—effects of God that are desirable and lovable to all.[88] Thomas also called the new law of grace *lex indita*. By infused grace rather than any written or imposed directive, the soul is inclined to acts of faith, hope, and charity, and thereby to act in accord with the common good of a heavenly polity.[89] The concept of *lex indita* has three important implications. First, in different ways, both the natural law and the new law instill (infuse) terms of action in which the creature partakes personally. Just as the natural law is said to be "written on the heart," so too is the new law "poured out in the hearts" of the faithful. Second, instilled law not only makes known things to be done (*quid sit faciendum*) but also assists the doing (*adiuvans ad implendum*). *Lex indita* does not cancel natural liberty, for human persons are induced through the exercise of their own nature to know and direct themselves freely to goods to which they are inclined by nature or by divine grace. Third, for Leo, as for Thomas, instilled law is a mark of the sacred. *Lex indita* implies creation and recreation and therefore stands outside the orbit of human prudence and legal artifact. We can imitate but not make an instilled law. Human legal authorities cannot pretend to begin from scratch by imposing laws on a supposedly morally motionless human nature.

In his letters, Leo frequently circled back to the theme that human moral and legal judgments, indeed human liberty, depend upon an antecedent divine law:

> All prescriptions of human reason can have force of law only inasmuch as they are the voice and the interpreters of some higher power on which our reason and liberty necessarily depend. For, since the force of law consists in the imposing of obligations and the granting of rights, authority is the one and only foundation of all law—the power, that is, of fixing duties and defining rights, as also of assigning the necessary sanctions of reward and chastisement to each and all of its commands. But all this, clearly, cannot be found in man, if, as his own supreme legislator, he is

---

87. *ST*, II-II, q. 47, a. 15.
88. *ST*, II-II, q. 34, a. 1. The triadic structure of first precepts in I-II, q. 94, a. 2, follows this pattern.
89. *ST*, I-II, q. 106, a. 1.

to be the [supreme] rule of his own actions. It follows, therefore, that the law of nature is the same thing as the eternal law, implanted in rational creatures, and inclining them to their right action and end; and can be nothing else but the eternal reason of God, the Creator and Ruler of all the world. To this rule of action and restraint of evil God has vouchsafed to give special and most suitable aids for strengthening and ordering the human will. The first and most excellent of these is the power of His divine grace, whereby the mind can be enlightened and the will wholesomely invigorated and moved to the constant pursuit of moral good, so that the use of our inborn liberty becomes at once less difficult and less dangerous. Not that the divine assistance hinders in any way the free movement of our will; just the contrary, for grace works inwardly in man and in harmony with his natural inclinations, since it flows from the very Creator of his mind and will, by whom all things are moved in conformity with their nature.[90]

"Laws come before men live together in society," Leo wrote, "and have their origin in the natural, and consequently in the eternal law." The precepts of the natural law, contained materially in the human law, have not merely the force of human law but "possess that higher and more august sanction which belongs to the law of nature and the eternal law." "It is within this very genus of law," he concluded, "that the civil legislator exercises his *munus* [gift of service]."[91] It is not that human law merely replicates in written form the natural law. Even when a legislator devises new laws on the pattern of the natural law, this exercise of *ius facere* is always located "within the perimeter" (*in iusto genere*) of higher law. Rousseau contended that the social order is a "sacred right" (*un droit sacré*) because there can be no other higher law.[92] Leo, however, contended that this assertion offers a misplaced *sanctum* that cannot but do violence against the consciences of citizens who live already under the natural law and, as baptized, under the law of grace.

In this fashion, Leo attempted to provide an adequate interpretation of Romans 13:1 ("Let every person be subject to the governing authorities. For there is no authority except from God, and those that exist are constituted by God"). With respect to natural liberty, he granted the truth of what seemed like a radical premise, that "no man has in himself or of himself the power of constraining the free will of others by fetters of authority."[93] Though it had

---

90. *Libertas*, §8, *Acta Leonis* 8, 219.
91. *Libertas*, §9, *Acta Leonis* 8, 220.
92. Jean-Jacques Rousseau, *The Social Contract and Other Later Political Writings*, ed. and trans. Victor Gourevitch (Cambridge: Cambridge University Press, 1997), LI, 41.
93. Leo XIII, Encyclical Letter *Diuturnum illud* (June 29, 1881), §11, *Acta Leonis* 2, 274.

unimpeachable credentials in earlier Catholic thought, this idea was later obscured by Catholic traditionalists, who thought that it sailed too close to the shores of Rousseau and Enlightenment notions of equality. Leo, on the other hand, contended that from the premise of natural equality we should not conclude that humanity is naturally lawless, or that a social contract constructs a collective title to authority; rather, the idea of natural equality indicates that human authority to bind, sanction, and, if need be, coerce participates in divine authority. God alone "can commit power to a man over his fellow men."[94] Human command dislocated from the scheme of participation in higher law leads, inexorably, to law being "the servitude of man to man."[95] Leo argued that only Christ, the God-human, has *imperium* over other human beings by natural right.[96] Romans 13:1's teaching must therefore be interpreted also in light of Acts 5:29 ("We must obey God rather than men"), because "where the power to command is wanting, or where a law is enacted contrary to reason, or to the eternal law, or to some ordinance of God, obedience is unlawful, lest, while obeying man, we become disobedient to God."[97] From 1791 to 1875, during which time popes issued more than fifty letters, they did not cite Acts 5:29 even once.[98] Instead, the popes continually cited Romans 13:1 ("Let every person be subject to the governing authorities") and 1 Peter 2:13 ("Be subject for the Lord's sake to every human institution"). Beginning with Leo, Acts 5:29 became a frequently quoted scripture in papal social teaching. Indeed, John Paul II cited it no less than eight times in *Evangelium vitae* (1995).

On the social contract, Leo sided with the conservative mainstream of Catholic thought, from Bossuet to the present. Leo's criticism of the social contract must be understood in tandem with his estimation of natural liberty and equality. At issue was not the institutional distribution of authority

---

94. Leo XIII, Encyclical Letter *Sapientiae Christianae* (January 10, 1890), §8, *Acta Leonis* 10, 15.

95. *Immortale Dei*, §18, *Acta Leonis* 5, 130.

96. *Annum sacrum*, §§5–6, *Acta Leonis* 19, 74ff. This refers to Thomas's discussion of the judicial powers of Christ in *ST*, II-II, q. 67, a. 2, ad 2.

97. *Libertas*, §13, *Acta Leonis* 8, 223. See also Leo XIII, Encyclical Letter *Quod Apostolici muneris* (December 28, 1878), §7, *Acta Leonis* 1, 177; *Diuturnum*, §15, *Acta Leonis* 2, 277 (where it is used in connection to Rom 13:1 and Mt 22:21 on the things that are Caesar's); *Sapientiae Christianae*, §7, *Acta Leonis* 10, 15 (on the duty of citizens not to be treasonous to God); *Immortale Dei*, §12, *Acta Leonis* 5, 126 (on the liberty of the Church, but also in light of Rom 13:1 at §3); Leo XIII, Encyclical Letter *Officio sanctissimo* (December 22, 1887), §9, *Acta Leonis* 7, 233 (on Catholic resistance to the Bavarian *Kulturkampf*).

98. After all hope of altar-throne alliance was dashed, Pius IX used Acts 5:29 to trace the boundary of Mt 22:21 regarding the things not owed to Caesar. Pius IX, Encyclical Letter *Quod Nunquam* (February 5, 1875), §10, in *Pii IX Acta*, part 1, 7, 10ff.

(constitutional allocation of powers), at least not in the civil sphere. Leo rather treated the social contract as a theory about the *origin* of authority. From the premise that humanity is naturally lawless, no mere aggregation of wills, however formal the fiat, can explain the emergence of authority to bind—force, yes, but not obligation. Nor can the social contract follow from the opposite premise that each individual is *sui iuris*, a self-constituting law, for this does not explain how that which properly belongs to an individual can be exercised by another. Such a formulation can explain a system of permission-giving but not true authority:

> Those who believe civil society to have risen from the free consent of men, looking for the origin of its authority from the same source, say that each individual has given up something of his right, and that voluntarily every person has put himself into the power of the one man in whose person the whole of those rights has been centered. But it is a great error not to see, what is manifest, that men, as they are not a nomad race, have been created, without their own free will, for a natural community of life. It is plain, moreover, that the pact which they allege is openly a falsehood and a fiction, and that it has no authority to confer on political power such great force, dignity, and firmness as the safety of the State and the common good of the citizens require. Then only will the government have all those ornaments and guarantees, when it is understood to emanate from God as its august and most sacred source.[99]

Leo here is paraphrasing an argument made by the Bishop of Mainz, Wilhelm Emmanuel von Ketteler, whose social and political sermons deeply influenced Leo's mind, particularly on the labor problem. Von Ketteler argued that the general will is the "fiction" that aggregations of force can create society and a true principle of authority.[100] A state erected on this doctrine is entitled to enforce rather than govern the will of the majority; Leo argued that the "doctrine of the supremacy of the greater number, and that all right and all duty reside in the majority" cannot (on its own terms) transcend force.[101]

In sum, Leo's pedagogy of natural law is a doctrine of participated authority as Thomas defined it: "Now among all others the rational creature is

---

99. *Diuturnum*, §12, *Acta Leonis* 2, 275ff.

100. Wilhelm Emmanuel von Ketteler, "The Labor Problem and Christianity," in *The Social Teachings of Wilhelm Emmanuel von Ketteler*, trans. Rupert J. Ederer (Washington, DC: University Press of America, 1981; first published, 1864), 363ff. For his argument that the natural dignity of the human soul under the eternal law requires a structured pluralism of authority, see Wilhelm Emmanuel von Ketteler, "Freedom, Authority and the Church," in *Social Teachings*, 155ff (originally published in 1862).

101. *Libertas*, §15, *Acta Leonis* 8, 224ff. See also *Quod Apostolici*, §2, *Acta Leonis* 1, 173, and *Immortale*, §24, *Acta Leonis* 5, 133ff.

subject to divine providence in the most excellent way, insofar as it partakes of a share of providence by being provident both for itself and for others. . . . This participation of the eternal law in the rational creature is called the natural law." In answer to the objection that it is unnecessary to have two laws, one eternal, the other natural, Thomas responded that "this argument would hold if the natural law were something diverse from the eternal law, whereas it is nothing but a participation thereof."[102] The human intellect is "provident both for itself and for others" because humanity is first measured by a higher law. In recent papal literature this concept is called "participated theonomy."[103] Humanity, Leo said, is a "king by participation" in divine rule. Human beings rule both by obedience to the natural law and by obedience to Christ who fulfills and elevates the natural law.[104]

VII. STRUCTURED PLURALISM

Leo developed the idea of participated authority for purposes similar to those of Abraham Kuyper, who propounded the idea of "sphere sovereignty." Leo and Kuyper were contemporaries. Like Leo, Kuyper insisted that authority does not arise originally through a social contract or the state. "*Higher authority*," he writes, "is of necessity involved" if we are to make sense of plural spheres of society that have real authority and are not reducible one to the other: "In a Calvinistic sense we understand hereby, that the family, the business, science, art and so forth are all social spheres, which do not owe their existence to the state, and which do not derive the law of their life from the superiority of the state, but obey a high authority within their own bosom."[105] Kuyper and his disciples spoke of higher law rather than natural law. Here, we make no effort to effect a superficial reconciliation of "sphere sovereignty" and "participated authority" except to say that both use a theonomic principle to account for a structured pluralism of authority.

For Leo, authority to command is distributed in such a way that, "through the medium of men," plural agents might imitate God's ruling wisdom by bringing about perfection in themselves and others.[106] All human ruling is *ad*

---

102. *ST*, I-II, q. 91, a. 2, ad 1.

103. See John Paul II, Encyclical Letter *Veritatis splendor* (August 6, 1993), §41, *AAS* 85, 1166: "Others speak, and rightly so, of 'theonomy,' or 'participated theonomy,' since man's free obedience to God's law effectively implies that human reason and human will participate in God's wisdom and providence."

104. *Tametsi futura*, §7, *Acta Leonis* 20, 303.

105. Abraham Kuyper, *Lectures on Calvinism* (Grand Rapids, MI: Eerdmans, 1961), 91, 90. Emphasis in original.

106. *Immortale*, §18, *Acta Leonis* 5, 130.

imaginem dei, unto the image of God.[107] Authority to render judgments according to a law does not belong to the civil power alone. "There is," he wrote, "a difference between the political prudence that relates to the general good and that which concerns the good of individuals. This latter is shown forth in the case of private persons who obey the prompting of right reason in the direction of their own conduct; while the former is the characteristic of those who are set over others, and chiefly of rulers of the State, whose duty it is to exercise a preeminent power of command."[108] Judgment and command can be distinguished according to three modes of prudence, each suggesting the ground of a jurisdictional boundary. Individual prudence takes the antecedent (natural) law and renders it efficacious in one's own actions. Such prudence proceeds from the rules and measures of law, rooted in intellect's native capacity to render judgment according to the natural law, and is perfected in self-governance rather than in issuing commands to others. Domestic prudence delivers ordering judgments for a family (but by extension to other societies as well, such as corporations or monasteries). This type of prudence, too, proceeds from law, but its end term is a command that moves others. Thomas calls these commands "ordinances or statutes," but they lack the *ratio* of civil law.[109] When one commands one's children to go to bed, one has not issued a curfew. The kind of prudence that proceeds from law to law is regnative prudence (*prudentia regnativa*). Such prudence is essentially legislative prudence, the capacity to make and impose laws *(leges ponere)*.[110] The chief act of a political authority (*principatus regalis*) is to direct a multitude by law to a political end. What makes this ordering judgment unique is that it remains totally within the genus of law. Having received the (natural or revealed) law, the human intellect makes more law. For Leo, there are two centers of legislative prudence, the state (*civitas*) and the Church (*ecclesia*).

In his letters, Leo repeatedly used the phrase *iura et officia*, rights and duties, with respect to individuals and the various orders of society.[111] There are four main orders, each with its own competence to render judgment: the family, voluntary private associations (which we call civil society), the Church, and the state or *civitas*. The distinction and overlap between these orders was a subject of considerable debate, and none more than marriage and the family, for this institution touches upon all of the others. The married person is at

---

107. *Quod Apostolici*, §6, *Acta Leonis* 1, 176.
108. *Sapientiae Christianae*, §36, *Acta Leonis* 10, 34.
109. *ST*, I-II, q. 90, a. 3, ad 3.
110. *ST*, II-II, q. 50, a. 1, ad 3.
111. Some forty times, according to the word count by Mary Elsbernd, "Papal Statements on Rights: A Historical Contextual Study of Encyclical Teaching from Pius VI–Pius XI (179–939)" (PhD diss., Catholic University of Louvain, 1985), 282n1.

once a citizen, a member of the Church, and, often as not, a member of voluntary societies. Most important for Leo, the material and formal aspects of matrimony have an immediate propinquity to divine providence, both by creation and by sacrament; there is no more evident example of *lex indita* than the society "established for reciprocal affection and for the interchange of duties."[112] Marriage, being "sacred by its own power, in its own nature, and of itself," does not belong to the "*imperio* of civil rulers."[113] No human power—the state, society, the spouses themselves—has authority over marriage as such. Marriage can have different customs, but, unlike political authority, it is not amenable to a prudential introduction of plural forms. The sacrament can introduce a new form, but not by way of derogating from the natural principle.

Regarding marriage, Leo deployed his typical twofold pedagogy. The rights and duties of marriage proceed from the natural order instituted by God (*Deo et natum*) and from Christ's institution of the sacrament (*de sacramentis*).[114] The ordering judgments of domestic prudence include, as a native right, education of children as well as the right to establish free schools.[115] Moreover, the legitimate sphere of domestic judgment embraces the right to possess and order property and the right to form associations.

Leo drew out these implications in his most famous encyclical, *Rerum novarum* (1891). The immediate purpose of *Rerum novarum* was public policy, specifically the question of just wages for laborers and their right to form associations. In no letter do we find Leo writing so ambidextrously with respect to policy and theory. We leave the policy issues to one side in order to see what the encyclical teaches about structured pluralism.[116] As usual, Leo treated property and associations in light of divine providence giving rise to different kinds of human prudence.

Arguments for a natural right of possessing and using private property can be summarized under three anthropological points.[117] First, the human

---

112. Leo XIII, Encyclical Letter *Arcanum divinae* (February 10, 1880), §14, *Acta Leonis* 2, 19.

113. *Arcanum divinae*, §19, *Acta Leonis* 2, 23.

114. *Arcanum divinae*, §§32, 19.

115. By the natural duty and participated authority of the parents, as well as by virtue of their religious obligation. See *Officio sanctissimo*, §11, *Acta Leonis* 7, 235. A good summary of Leo's thought on the school question is provided by Elsbernd, "Papal Statements," 305–9.

116. For an account of the policy issues, see Lillian Parker Wallace, *Leo XIII and the Rise of Socialism* (Durham, NC: Duke University Press, 1966).

117. The complications and finer texture of Leo's arguments are well considered by Matthew Habiger, *Papal Teaching on Private Property, 1891–1981* (Lanham, MD: University Press of America, 1990).

person is an intelligent animal, and hence providential for himself or herself. What is most characteristic of human intelligence is not having but ordering. For this reason, property cannot be possessed in a way that befits human beings if it is merely for "temporary and momentary" use.[118] Second, the ordering wisdom requires the agent to possess something "as his very own," for one cannot dispose and give what one does not have. Moreover, the fruit of the agent's labor bears "the impress of his own personality."[119] Third, because the family is a "true society, governed by an authority peculiar to itself," the father must have a native competence and right to acquire property and to order it according to the needs of the household.[120] Thus Leo concludes: "Provided, therefore, the limits which are prescribed by the very purposes for which it exists be not transgressed . . . the domestic household is antecedent, as well in idea as in fact, to the gathering of men into a community, [and] the family must necessarily have rights and duties which are prior to those of the community, and founded more immediately in nature."[121] Property befits human beings chiefly because of the dignity of intelligent labor and the capacity to make ordering judgments. The "sacred law of nature," in this regard, is not mere preservation, but provident action that freely fulfills duties and social offices.[122] "This great labor question," Leo wrote, "cannot be solved save by assuming as a principle that private ownership is a *ius sanctum*. The law, therefore, should favor ownership, and its policy should be to induce as many as possible of the people to become owners."[123] Although Leo certainly emphasized more than Thomas the right of possession, the overarching argument is possession as a condition of being able to intelligently order and dispose resources for the good of others.[124] The other main issue of *Rerum novarum* is the right of voluntary associations. The following passage deserves to be quoted in full because it is so important for the development of papal social doctrine:

> These lesser societies and the larger society differ in many respects, because their immediate purpose and aim are different. Civil society exists

---

118. *Rerum novarum*, §6, *Acta Leonis* 11, 101.

119. *Rerum novarum*, §§5, 9, *Acta Leonis* 11, 99 and 103.

120. *Rerum novarum*, §13, *Acta Leonis* 11, 105.

121. *Rerum novarum*, §13, *Acta Leonis* 11, 106.

122. *Rerum novarum*, §13, *Acta Leonis,* 105.

123. *Rerum novarum*, §46, see also §13.

124. Some scholars point out that Leo seems to differ markedly from Thomas on the use/possession distinction. See Habiger, *Papal Teaching*, 15–24; Elsbernd, "Papal Statements," 312–25. The most provocative essay on the issue is Ernest L. Fortin's "'Sacred and Inviolable': *Rerum Novarum* and Natural Rights," *Theological Studies* 53 (1992): 203–33.

for the common good, and hence is concerned with the interests of all in general, albeit with individual interests also in their due place and degree. It is therefore called a public society, because by its agency, as St. Thomas of Aquinas says, "Men establish relations in common with one another in the setting up of a commonwealth." But societies which are formed in the bosom of the commonwealth are styled private, and rightly so, since their immediate purpose is the private advantage of the associates. "Now, a private society," says St. Thomas again, "is one which is formed for the purpose of carrying out private objects; as when two or three enter into partnership with the view of trading in common." Private societies, then, although they exist within the body politic, and are severally part of the commonwealth, cannot nevertheless be absolutely, and as such, prohibited by public authority. For, to enter into a "society" of this kind is the natural right of man; and the State has for its office to protect natural rights, not to destroy them; and, if it forbid its citizens to form associations, it contradicts the very principle of its own existence, for both they and it exist in virtue of the like principle, namely, the natural tendency of man to dwell in society.[125]

By "societies of this kind," Leo referred to a wide range of associations, such as labor associations, confraternities, schools, and religious orders that, "by sanction of the law of nature," have legal personality and thus "rights as corporate bodies."[126] They are called "private" in the sense that their nature, purposes, and rights are not constituted by the state. The legal world of private law (*lex privata*) developed from contracts, associations, charters, endowments—and, in the case of religious orders, of course, constitutions under the public law of the Church. What puts private societies into a distinct category from marriage is the fact that their forms are amenable to human prudence. Whereas through birth one can enter a family, a political community, and a church, membership in voluntary associations depends upon choice.

Interestingly, Thomas's tract on the life of voluntary poverty, which comes down to us under the title *Contra impugnantes*, shaped Leo's discussion of the right of association. The tract helps us to understand how Leo adapted medieval notions to contemporary situations. Thomas Aquinas argued that every society is a friendship involving "communications." The word *communicatio* means making something common, one rational agent participating in the life of another.[127] The multiplicity of vocations and avocations are grounded "primarily in Divine Providence, and, secondarily, in

---

125. *Rerum novarum*, §51, *Acta Leonis* 11, 134–35.
126. *Rerum novarum*, §53, *Acta Leonis* 11, 137. On liberty of religious associations, see *Pastoralis vigilantiae* (June 25, 1891), *Acta Leonis* 11, 27ff.
127. See *Contra impugnantes*, I.3–I.5.

natural causes whereby certain men are disposed to the performance of certain functions in preference to others."[128] At issue was laity and religious partaking in a common work of teaching and learning. Thomas contended that "an association of study is a society, established with the object of teaching and of learning; and as not only laymen, but also religious, may lawfully teach and learn, there can be no doubt that, both these classes are able to unite in one society."[129] Competence to perform the common activity rather than one's status should be the measure of voluntary societies. To insist that "religious and laymen ought not, mutually, to communicate their gift of knowledge" is contrary to the scriptures, specifically to 1 Corinthians 12:21: "The eye cannot say to the hand: I need not thy help."[130] The contemplative is not less graced in preaching what he or she receives from God; nor is the teacher less learned when he or she communicates knowledge to the student; nor is anyone less "free" by virtue of imparting a gift to another. Thomas here quoted Augustine's *De doctrina christiana*: "Everything that is not lessened by being imparted, is not, if it be possessed without being communicated, possessed as it ought to be possessed."[131]

But what about authority? Is it not depleted if multiplied? Thomas answered that the free "communications" of a private society are lawful because they proceed from friendship. No human authority can ban friendship, so long as it is for a blameless purpose. Private voluntary societies exhibit authority, but the kind of authority that ensues upon meeting standards inherent to the activities. Such societies are therefore not in competition with civil and ecclesiastical legislators.

Leo's use of this literature calls our attention to two points of capital importance. First, he did not depict civil society in its negative function of counterbalancing the state. That idea comes from Montesquieu, who held that liberty is found only in moderate governments, where "power must check power by the arrangement of things."[132] We notice that Leo did not use the term "intermediate" societies, which suggests not a plurality of inherently valuable social forms but a merely instrumental good, a "buffer" between the individual and the state. Second, his analysis emphasized that these are "real societies" that embody the principle of friendship. The question is not whether they are cost-effective, or whether indeed private action is more efficient than

---

128. *Contra impugnantes*, I.5.
129. *Contra impugnantes*, I.3.
130. *Contra impugnantes*, I.3.
131. *Contra impugnantes*, I.4, citing Augustine, *De doctrina Christiana*, LI.
132. Charles Montesquieu, *The Spirit of the Laws*, trans. and ed. Anne M. Cohler, Basia Carolyn Miller, and Harold Samuel Stone (Cambridge: Cambridge University Press, 1989), 11.4, 155.

the state. No natural right could depend upon such a contingency. The strong claim for these societies is that they bring about mutual perfection by free activity, with the emphasis upon the activity more than the product. Leo insisted that "the State should watch over these societies of citizens banded together in accordance with their rights, but it should not thrust itself into their peculiar concerns and their organization, for things move and live by the spirit inspiring them, and may be killed by the rough grasp of a hand from without."[133] This assertion is the germinal form of the principle of subsidiarity developed by Pius XI.

The situation of the Catholic Church is a more complicated subject. The post-1870 Church, we said, had rejected the ecclesiological and canonical grounds for civil rulers exercising the role of *episcopus externus*. Unbendingly opposed to every trace of *regalismo*, Leo was intent upon drawing a sharp line between the Church and the governments. Considered solely in terms of ecclesiology, this goal was the easiest part of the puzzle, for there was no significant dispute within Catholicism that the Church is directly instituted by Christ with a visible hierarchy and a public law. The First Vatican Council had decisively eliminated the historic option of de facto or de jure national churches. Ongoing persecutions and legal harassment usually clarified rather than obscured the situation. Nor was the bilateral relation of church and state especially difficult to formulate in the abstract. Leo refurbished the ancient two power (*duo sunt*) doctrine of Pope Gelasius: "So there are twin powers," Leo wrote, "both subordinate to the eternal law of nature, and each working for its own ends in matters concerning its own order and domain." Divine providence decrees (1) that these twinned powers operate each in its own order (*in suo ordine*), and (2) that concord (*concordia*) ought to mark their relationship.[134]

The more difficult issue was the triadic relation of church, state, and society. One way to eliminate the tension would be to think of the Church as a private, voluntary society. Under the rubric of "separation," some states attempted to fashion a solution along this line. In the first act of separation in Latin America, Colombia (1853) confiscated church property and transferred it to laity in the parishes. This action was but a prelude to the infamous French laws (1902–5), which transferred church property to cultural associations administered by the laity. Leo wrote repeatedly against such policies and argued not only that they violate Catholic ecclesiology and discipline, but also that these policies implicitly assert that what exists outside the state ceases to

---

133. *Rerum novarum*, §55, *Acta Leonis* 11, 138.
134. Leo XIII, Encyclical Letter *Nobilissima Gallorum* (February 8, 1884), §4, *Acta Leonis* 4, 15ff.

be a true society.[135] John Courtney Murray would call this social form the monistic "society-state"—that is, what is truly social is, or belongs to, the state, all else having the status of individuals temporarily in concert for merely private purposes.[136] Leo saw clearly enough that this solution doomed the Church *and* the principle of voluntary societies.

As the separationist movement gained steam in France, Leo warned that separation is "indifferent to the interests of Christian society, that is to say, of the Church," and has as its aim putting French Catholics "outside of the common law itself [*le droit commun*]."[137] Similarly, with respect to the purported "neutral" marriage laws in Italy, he wrote: "What judgment is to be formed of a Catholic state which throws overboard the sacred principles and the wise enactments of the Christian law on matrimony, and sets about the wretched job of creating a marital morality all its own, purely human in character, under forms and guarantees that are merely legal; and then with all its power goes on forcibly to impose this morality on the consciences of its subjects, substituting it for the religious and sacramental morality."[138] In these passages, Leo was not recommending a state establishment of religion; he rather complained that the state, by refusing to recognize the habits, customs, and conscience of the people, imposes its own morality upon society.[139] In effect, the Church is separated from society.[140]

---

135. *Immortale*, §27, 135; Leo XIII, Encyclical Letter *Iampridem* (January 6, 1886), §6, *Acta Leonis* 6, 7; *Libertas*, §§39–40, 242ff.; Leo XIII, Encyclical Letter *Inimica vis* (December 8, 1892), *Acta Leonis* 12, 325–30. See his warning to Americans not to confuse "the Church, which is a divine society, and all other social human organizations which depend simply on the free will and choice of men." Leo XIII, Apostolic Letter *Testem benevolentiae* (January 22, 1899), *Acta Leonis* 19, 9.

136. Murray, "Leo XIII: Separation," 173. This is first of four essays on Leo, including also John Courtney Murray, "Leo XIII on Church and State: The General Structure of the Controversy," *Theological Studies* 14 (1953): 1–30; John Courtney Murray, "Leo XIII: Two Concepts of Government," *Theological Studies* 14 (1953): 551–67; and John Courtney Murray, "Leo XIII: Two Concepts of Government: II. Government and the Order of Culture," *Theological Studies* 15 (1954): 1–33. Murray's essays are a towering achievement. They are tinged, however, with his polemic against Roman curialists and European thinkers on the church-state issue. A plodding but more careful evaluation of Leo's thought and precedent for Catholic social teaching on church and state is the six-part study by Basile Valuet, *La liberté religieuse et la tradition Catholique: Un cas de développement doctrinal homogène dans le magistère authentique*, 2d rev. ed., 3 vols. (Le Barroux: Abbaye Sainte-Madeleine, 1998).

137. *Au milieu*, §29, *Acta Leonis* 12, 39.

138. *Ci siamo* (June 1, 1879), *Acta Leonis* 1, 240.

139. See Murray, "Leo XIII: Separation," 160, 176.

140. Using a typology that goes back to Leo's time, Roman canonists distinguished *La separazione pura*, in which all churches are treated as private societies and equally

Leo returned time and again to the liberty of the Church,[141] particularly with respect to its sanctifying and teaching missions.[142] In *Quod Apostolici*, he appealed to the governments: "Let them restore that Church to the condition and liberty in which she may exert her healing force for the benefit of all society."[143] The Church's role is to communicate the wisdom of Christ, and, through sacramental action, to impart a supernatural "form" to society.[144] Society needs more than a morality drawn from the natural law, not only because of the deformation of sin, but also because it is a part of human dignity to be open to a supernatural life, without which "it is impossible to please God (Heb. 11:6)."[145] The civil power receives from God no power to sanctify; power to govern souls "excludes altogether the civil authority." The Church "alone in divine matters" exercises a doctrinal magisterium.[146] There are thus two powers, the proximate end of one being "the temporal and worldly good of the human race," the other religious, "whose office it is to lead mankind to that true, heavenly, and everlasting happiness for which we are created."[147] Yet this distinction is not an entirely tidy boundary. With respect to society, the Church is superior to the state not only in the "mixed matters" like marriage and education, but also more generally in the Church's having a superior title to imprint itself upon society. In *Immortale*, Leo asserted, "Whatever, therefore in things human is of a sacred character, whatever belongs either of its own nature or by reason of the end to which it is referred, to the salvation of souls, or to the worship of God, is subject to the power and judgment of the Church."[148]

---

protected by law; *La separazione ostile alia chiesa*, in which the state seeks to deny to the church the right to guide the moral life of her subjects as citizens; and *La separazione parziale*, which concedes to the church some rights proper to a moral person in public law. See Ludovicus Bender, *Chiesa e Stato* (Rome: Editrice A. V. E., 1945).

141. Murray finds the phrase *libertas ecclesiae* or its cognates used in more than sixty Leonine documents. John Courtney Murray, "The Problem of State Religion," *Theological Studies* 12 (1951): 156n3.

142. According to the threefold *munera Christi*—priest, prophet, and king. Leo had much to say about Christ's ruling powers, and by participation, those of the church.

143. *Quod apostolici*, §10, *Acta Leonis* 1, 181.

144. *Diuturnum*, §18, *Acta Leonis* 2, 279 (on the form); Leo XIII, Encyclical Letter *Licet multa* (August 3, 1881), §3, *Acta Leonis* 2, 323 (penetrating all orders of the *civitas*); Leo XIII, Encyclical Letter *Graves de communi* (January 18, 1901), *Acta Leonis* 21, 6ff. (the form impressed by God).

145. *Tametsi futura*, §11, *Acta Leonis* 20, 310.

146. *Sapientiae christianae*, §27, *Acta Leonis* 10, 28; *Arcanum divinae*, §19, *Acta Leonis* 2, 23.

147. *Nobilissima*, §4, *Acta Leonis* 4, 15ff.

148. *Immortale*, §14, *Acta Leonis* 5, 128.

For practical purposes, Leo was happy enough to abide an accommodation where church and state enjoy a kind of equal access to society. On more than one occasion, he warmly noted that the Church thrives in the United States, where the two powers do not "trespass on the rights of the other," and where each can be about its business without "barren quarrels." "The Church," he added, "claims liberty before all else."[149] It is a mistake, however, to think that Leo regarded negative liberty as a perfectly satisfactory situation. He wrote to the American bishops that the Church ought to have the "favor of the laws."[150] In *Immortale*, he insisted that the civil power should "not in any way hinder" but also "in every manner to render as easy as may be the possession of that highest and unchangeable good for which all should seek."[151]

Did Leo believe in the "establishment" of religion? He certainly did not abjure a union of church and the civil commonwealth "as between soul and body."[152] But, with respect to what we mean by establishment, the answer is (a complicated) no. First, he spent his ecclesiastical career trying to protect the Church from the strange "establishments" that survived the revolutions. If he sometimes yearned for the *status quo ante*, it was for the twelfth and not the eighteenth century, and even then he accented the social form rather than the political details.[153] Second, Leo was an antiseparationist. In his world, anti-separationism did not mean a state church. It meant a rather rich and proactive *concordia* in which each power recognizes the other's theological title to rule. Leo did not think that civil authorities ought to be epistemically blind about their place in the order of providence. The state's incompetence to teach doctrine does not entail its incompetence to be taught and to learn; moreover, the concord should include *adiumenta*, assistance, especially on mixed matters such as marriage and education.

Leo's position on the "form" of government departed markedly from that of his predecessors. While "God has always willed that there should be a ruling authority [*principatus*], and they who are invested with it should reflect

149. In an interview given to French journalists, published in *Petit Journal* (February 7, 1892), quoted in Eduardo Soderini, *Leo XIII, Italy and France*, trans. Barbara Barclay Carter (London: Burns, Oates & Washbourne, 1935), 219.

150. Leo XIII, Encyclical Letter *Longinqua oceani* (January 6, 1895), §6, *Acta Leonis* 15, 7: "For the Church amongst you, unopposed by the Constitution and government of your nation, fettered by no hostile legislation, protected against violence by the common laws and the impartiality of the tribunals, is free to live and act without hindrance."

151. *Immortale*, §6, *Acta Leonis* 5, 122ff.

152. *Libertas*, §18, *Acta Leonis* 8, 228.

153. *Immortale*, §21, *Acta Leonis* 5, 132: "There was once a time when civitates were governed by the philosophy of the Gospel. Then it was that the power and divine virtue of Christian wisdom had diffused itself throughout the laws, institutions, and morals of the people, permeating all ranks and relations of civil society."

the divine power and providence in some measure," it is not "necessarily bound up with any particular form of government."[154] Here he suggested two conditions that must inform prudential creation or alteration of political forms. The first is that God has always decreed that human beings come under a visible ruling authority. He dismissed a hypothetical state of nature, the scenario allowing human beings either to invent or to render absent political authority. Second, the word *principatus* signifies a real, active ruling power having authority to bind and loose in a political community. It is not, therefore, merely a power giving executive force to collective decisions. When Leo spoke critically of a "novel conception of law [*ius*]," he referred not to new constitutions but to the idea that there can be law that facilitates liberty but has no authority to bind.[155] The conception, he believes, is "simply a road leading straight to tyranny."[156] The first institutional limit on government is that it be a real government.

The political common good and the principle of *the principatus* are mutually entailed. A mere steering mechanism suggests no political community. It is true, of course, that the civil authority is limited by the presence of other social forms—the Church, family, voluntary associations—each having a different mode of authority. While these entities indicate social goods to be coordinated, they cannot of themselves establish the civil *principatus*. For this reason, we will not find in Leo's thought the notion of an instrumental state, an idea that in fact will emerge (with important qualifications) in Catholic social thought during World War II.[157]

When Leo wrote about the *civitas* "rightly apprehended," his thoughts were never far from the situation in France. This was a nation that suffered a dozen changes of power in Leo's lifetime, that squabbled constantly over the "forms" of government, and that had a pronounced sense of the sacrality of political power. In a letter addressed to all French Catholics, he wrote that while the Church must cross the "changeable ocean of human affairs," it has no legitimate prudence over its "essential constitution," received directly from Christ; but, "in regard to purely human societies, it is an oft-repeated historical fact that time, that great transformer of all things here below, operates

---

154. *Immortale*, §4, *Acta Leonis* 5, 121.

155. *Libertas*, §2, *Acta Leonis* 8, 119.

156. *Libertas*, §16, *Acta Leonis* 8, 225.

157. The first pope to use this language was Pius XII, who spoke of the state as having the role of coordinating action, *quasi-instrumentum*, toward the common good. See Pius XII, Encyclical Letter *Summi pontificatus* (October 20, 1939), §59; *AAS* 31, 433. See also John XXIII, Encyclical Letter *Pacem in terris* (April 11, 1963), §68, *Acta Synodalia Sacrosancti Concilii Oecumenici Vaticani Secundi, Congregatio Generalis CLXIV* (Vatican City: Typis Polyglottis Vaticanis, 1978), 55:276. Jacques Maritain developed the concept extensively in *Man and the State* (Chicago: University of Chicago Press, 1951), 1–27.

great changes in their political institutions."[158] Regarding the temporal regime, it falls legitimately to the human intelligence to make prudential judgments of a constitutional nature—the distribution of authority according to the pattern of one, few, many, or indeed a mixed regime. Leo often made the point that it is not "of itself wrong to prefer a democratic form of government,"[159] that there are "plural forms" of legitimate regime,[160] and that it is not the prudence of the Church "to decide which is the best amongst many diverse forms of government and the civil institutions."[161] Indeed, he even allowed that human prudence extends to the judgment of whether to change a regime midstream, if necessary, to remedy a great evil.[162] All of these assertions are qualified by the proviso that "the respect due to religion and the observance of good morals be upheld."[163]

Did Leo abandon interest in the classical question of what form of government makes the best regime? In one sense, yes. His practical imperative was to extract the Church from the "regime politics" tearing nations apart in the Catholic world. To the French, he wrote:

> By giving one's self up to abstractions, one could at length conclude which is the best of these forms, considered in themselves; and in all truth it may be affirmed that each of them is good, provided it lead straight to its end—that is to say, to the common good for which social authority is constituted; and finally, it may be added that, from a relative point of view, such and such a form of government may be preferable because of being better adapted to the character and customs of such or such a nation. In this order of speculative ideas, Catholics, like all other citizens, are free to prefer one form of government to another precisely because no one of these social forms is, in itself, opposed to the principles of sound reason nor to the maxims of Christian doctrine.[164]

Above all, however, he was interested in the best society, where he thought the mission of the Church is best directed. Important as the issue of political "forms" might be for jurisprudence, Leo thought it was a distraction from the problems of his era. In these senses, his teaching represents not only a post-Christendom but also a postclassical moment for the Catholic mind. His position was well accepted in the United States, where Catholics had a connatural

158. *Au milieu*, §17, *Acta Leonis* 12, 31.
159. *Libertas*, §44, *Acta Leonis* 8, 245.
160. *Immortale*, §36, *Acta Leonis* 5, 141.
161. *Sapientiae christianae*, §28, *Acta Leonis* 10, 28.
162. *Libertas*, §43, *Acta Leonis* 8, 245.
163. *Sapientiae christianae*, §28, *Acta Leonis* 10, 28.
164. *Au milieu*, §14, *Acta Leonis* 12, 28–29.

understanding of how to align political prudence under general providence or "higher law."[165] In France, however, Leo's policy of *ralliement*, rallying Catholics to the Third Republic, fell flat. As he lay on his deathbed, the regime politics of the Dreyfus Affair (1898–1900), which originally targeted a Jewish officer accused of spying for Germany, spilled over into anticlerical laws.

One aspect of the question of political "forms" cannot be passed over in silence because it is so important to Leo's teaching as well as to the subsequent development of Catholic political theory. This is the question of the relation of the "form" and the "power." Leo recognized that the people can establish a form of government, if this be understood as "designating the ruler," but not if it be understood as conferring the very "authority of ruling."[166]

Human beings are free to designate the form (*designatur principes*), which is to say the distribution of offices and holders of office. Human beings are not free to confer the authority (*non conferuntur iura principatus*) by which a multitude is bound by laws and legitimate commands. The immediate background of this distinction is modern contract theories of the origin of political authority. We have seen that Leo held that no human being has a natural right to bind another, for this power is divine, and can only be participated. We have also seen that Catholic conservatives, such as Joseph de Maistre, hold that "human will counts for nothing in the establishing of government."[167] The remote background, however, concerns the arguments of Baroque-era Thomists such as Robert Bellarmine, Francisco Suárez, Tommaso Cajetan, and others. They argued that when the people communicate a new form of government, they do more than merely designate a ruler. To be sure, all authority comes from God, and therefore no human can create the *principatus*; yet Thomists of this time contended that by natural law God vests political authority in the entire people. Any additional specification of the protopopulist form entails what was called a "translation" from the people to the king or the parliament. Mere designation of the office does not settle how political authority is translated whole and complete to the new form. If it is not so translated, whoever holds the office does not possess true authority. Thus emerged a scholastic dispute between "designation" and "translation" theories, both claiming pedigree in the texts of Thomas Aquinas.[168]

---

165. See Bishop John Ireland's sermon "The Catholic Church and Civil Society," given at the Third Plenary Council of Baltimore (1884), in *John Ireland, The Church and Modern Society: Lectures and Addresses*, 2 vols. (Chicago: D. H. McBride, 1896), 1:27–65.

166. *Diuturnum*, §§5–6, *Acta Leonis* 2, 271ff.

167. Joseph de Maistre, *Du Pape*, II.1, 130.

168. And on slender textual reeds. Cardinal Cajetan (1480–1547), in his commentary on *ST*, II-II, q. 50, a. 1, ad 3, introduced the notion of the people translating authority to a king (*potestatem in eum transtulerunt*), and then went on to speculate about a primordial

The translation theory achieved its full elaboration during the struggle against the absolute monarchs, while the designation theory came into vogue during the nineteenth-century struggles against the extreme democrats.[169] Leo and his advisors appeared to side with the designation theory, among other reasons to head off the idea that the Church's own constitution requires a translation from the people. But it is hard to say absolutely, because Leo never addressed the dispute *ex professo*.[170] In fact, it has never been settled by the papal magisterium.[171] The reader may wonder what difference it makes whether a God-given *principatus* is designated or translated by the people. The translation account is a much more powerful ground for the norm of democracy; if the eternal law vests political authority in the people, the specific democratic form of a regime corresponds to the prototype, and, furthermore, it would seem that a principle of consent is crucial for it to be otherwise. Within a generation of Leo's death, Thomists recovered the translation theory and deployed it against totalitarian regimes.[172] We may doubt that Leo subscribed to the translation theory, just as we may doubt that this axiomatic principle of neo-Thomism is very clearly rooted in Thomas's own work. Yet

---

election. Cajetan's commentary was included in the 1895 Leonine edition of the *Opera S. Thomae*. Undoubtedly, Thomas thought that authority is the predicate of a political community, but this is about all that can be concluded from the texts.

169. The history of the debate is considered most judiciously by Jeremiah Newman, *Studies in Political Morality* (Dublin: Scepter, 1962). For the thought of Leo's mentors, such as Taparelli, who clearly rejected the translation theory, see Jacquin, *Taparelli*, appendix K, 259–65.

170. In *Au milieu*, Leo says in light of Rom 13:1 that "all the novelty is limited to the political form of civil power or to its mode of transmission; it in no way affects the power considered in itself" (§18, *Acta Leonis* 12, 32). This remark can be interpreted either way. At the time, Cardinal Billot explained that Leo denied what has "always been denied with unanimous consent by Catholic theologians," namely, that the people create the *principatus*. For Billot's response, see Alfred O'Rahilly, "The Sovereignty of the People," *Studies: An Irish Quarterly Review* 10 (1921): 39–56, 277–87. At 280, O'Rahilly cites Cardinal Billot: "What is denied is what has always been denied with unanimous consent by Catholic theologians." O'Rahilly lists some 139 scholastic thinkers who held the translation theory. The roll call is assessed somewhat more carefully by Gabriel Bowe, *The Origin of Political Authority: An Essay in Catholic Political Philosophy* (Dublin: Clonmore & Reynolds, 1955).

171. But see Pius XII's address to the Roman Rota, October 2, 1945, *AAS* 37, 258ff.: "We bear in mind the favorite thesis of democracy—a doctrine which great Christian thinkers have proclaimed in all ages—namely, that the original subject of civil power derived from God is the people (not the 'masses')."

172. Rommen, *The State in Catholic Thought*, 380–470; Maritain, *Man and the State*; and Yves R. Simon, *Philosophy of Democratic Government* (Chicago: University of Chicago Press, 1951), who called it "transmission theory."

Leo certainly triggered the issue by opening up three lines of thought. Against the conservatives, he allowed human prudence to invent regimes. Against the Enlightenment, he denied a merely anthropocentric ground for the *principatus*. And finally, he denied that any human being has a natural right to bind another. We should not be surprised that the tension would be resolved in favor of a divine blessing on popular sovereignty.

VIII. THE LEONINE LEGACY

Leo's immediate successor, Pius X (1903–14), directed his energies to internal matters of the Church. While he took some important practical steps in the relationship between church and state during the French separationist crisis (1905) and undertook a reform of canon law that took into account the post-1870 changes in the Church's law, Pius was content to leave the Leonine teachings untouched. So untouched, indeed, that he did not once refer to Leo's favorite theme of eternal law.[173] The pope most responsible for developing the Leonine tradition was Pius XI (1922–39), who cited Leo more than one hundred times in his encyclicals. Ordained a priest in the first full year of Leo's pontificate, and eventually taking three doctorates, Ambrogio Achille Ratti studied under Leo's Thomist colleagues. Like Leo, Ratti looked to Thomas for the twofold pedagogy of "the natural and the supernatural order."[174] When Ratti was elected pope in 1922, he faced a world ruined by World War I; in a few years' time, he faced virulent totalitarian regimes and the onset of the Great Depression. In the midst of these crises, Pius XI reworked the Leonine legacy and rendered to social doctrine a sophisticated and supple body of thought. He was the first pontiff to speak of social teachings as a single body of "social doctrine." On his watch emerged the now familiar concepts of "social justice" and "subsidiarity." Though Pius regarded himself as reaching the "true and exact mind of Leo," most scholars would judge *Quadragesimo anno* (1931) a significant improvement over Leo's *Rerum novarum* in that the later document made clearer the relationship between possession and use of property.[175]

The Leonine understanding of the double pedagogy, the motif in Wisdom 8:1 of God's law "sweetly" moving creatures, the native authority of the family, the intrinsic value of social forms, and the dignity of the human soul radiate through papal letters of the twentieth century. Pius XII's inaugural letter, *Summi pontificatus* (1939), published at the beginning of

---

173. Here, relying on the word count by Elsbernd, "Papal Statements," 406.

174. Pius XI, Encyclical Letter *Studiorum ducem* (June 29, 1923), §20, *AAS* 15, 319.

175. Pius XI, Encyclical Letter *Quadragesimo anno* (May 15, 1931), §44, *AAS* 23, 191.

World War II, was a compendium of Leonine arguments. Yet, in his famous Christmas address of 1944, Pius recommended democracy and thus went well beyond Leo's philosophical rumination on the legitimacy of plural forms of regimes.[176]

The documents of the Second Vatican Council (1962–65) quote Leo more than forty times, and his letters were pivotal in the protracted debate over the Declaration on Religious Liberty, *Dignitatis humanae* (1965). John Courtney Murray's crucial summary of the debate for the drafting committee in 1964 called Leo's letters a *ressourcement* of the program of Gregory VII on the liberty of the Church.[177] That argument, Murray contended, posed no impediment to affirming religious freedom as a civil liberty. John Paul II's *Centesimus annus* (1991), celebrating the centenary of *Rerum novarum*, offered some new and very strong lines of reinterpretation in relation to the situation of peoples at the end of the Cold War. The encyclical *Veritatis splendor* (1993), on the other hand, presented a classic Leonine understanding of how human practical reason is situated in the order of divine providence.

Perhaps the most important development given to Leo's thought concerns the order of special providence. We began this essay with *Annum sacrum*, Leo's Jubilee encyclical on Christological kingship. We saw Leo teaching the pilgrims that the divine sign would not be a new Constantine but the Sacred Heart of Jesus. In *Ubi arcano* (1922), Pius XI dedicated his pontificate to the *Regnum Christi*. In a series of encyclicals on Leo's *Annum sacrum*—*Quas Primas* (1925), *Miserentissimus Redemptor* (1928), *Rappresentanti in terra* (1929), *Caritate Christi* (1932), and *Divini Redemptoris* (1937)—Pius began to explicate the analogies between Christ's kingly office and *munera* of baptized Christians. Although scholars rightly pay attention to the theme of natural law in papal social thought, Catholic political theology has tilted quietly but persistently toward the Christological principle in which the notion of "participation" has much richer content. The Second Vatican Council's constitution on the Church, *Lumen gentium* (1964), gave special importance to participated kingship according to Christ's threefold office of priest, prophet, and king. John Paul II contended that the reinvigorated Christological center is a truly "novel" element of the council, and when he promulgated the 1983 *Code of Canon Law*, he remarked: "In the wake of the Second Vatican Council, at the beginning of my pastoral ministry, my aim

---

176. "Benignitas et humanitas," *AAS* 37, 13: "The democratic form of government appears to many as a postulate of nature imposed upon reason itself."

177. Written and mimeographed for distribution at the council in the fall of 1964, and published under the title John Courtney Murray, "The Problem of Religious Freedom," in *John Courtney Murray, Religious Liberty: Catholic Struggles with Pluralism*, ed. J. Leon Hooper (Louisville, KY: Westminster John Knox Press, 1993), 127–97.

was to emphasize forcefully the priestly, prophetic and kingly dignity of the entire People of God."[178] This Christ-centered understanding of *the princi-patus* (ruling power) indicates how the Leonine project of scouting and marking the sacred perimeter continues apace, now with more emphasis on the laity.[179] Leo's chief legacy is to have prompted the papal magisterium to think, and to think at levels deeper than diplomacy and public policy.

---

178. On the *ratio novitatis*, see John Paul II, Apostolic Constitution *Sacrae disciplinae* (January 25, 1983), *AAS* 75, part 2, xii; for the pledge to devote his pastoral ministry to the idea, see John Paul II, Apostolic Exhortation *Christifideles laici* (December 20, 1988), §14, *AAS* 81, 410ff.

179. The term *périmètre sacré* is from de Maistre's *Du pape*, where it refers to the orbit in which papal authority must prevail.

CHAPTER 6

Two Modernisms, Two Thomisms

Reflections on Pius X's Letter against the Modernists

INTRODUCTION

POPE PIUS X'S CONDEMNATION of Modernism appeared in two documents during the summer of 1907. The Roman Inquisition published the decretum *Lamentabili Sane* (July 3, 1907), containing a syllabus of sixty-five modernist propositions.[1] Two months later, under his own name, Pius X issued the encyclical *Pascendi Dominici Gregis*, On the Doctrines of the Modernists (September 8, 1907). Admitting that his exposition was unusually prolix and didactic, Pius X insisted that such was necessary to deal with Modernism as a "whole system," indeed as "the synthesis of all heresies."[2]

In January 1908, *The Dublin Review* published an editorial on the encyclical.[3] The editor, Wilfrid Ward, immediately proffered obedience to what he called "the act" of the Holy See condemning the doctrine of the Modernists. He was not pleased, however, with what he called "the document." He complained that it left too vague the origin, definition, and scope of Modernism.[4]

---

1. *Lamentabili Sane*, was signed by Pietro Palombelli, Notary of the Supreme Congregation of the Holy Roman and Universal Inquisition, but it contained the notification that Pius X had approved and confirmed the syllabus, and that "every one of the above-listed propositions be held by all as condemned and proscribed." Pii X P.M., *Acta* 5, 76–84.

2. *Pascendi Dominici Gregis*, §39, *Acta* 4, 93: "Iam systema universum . . . ut ominium haereseon conclectum." For Pius X, not just one, but virtually all sectors of sacred doctrine were being reduced to evolving historical constructs.

3. Wilfrid Ward, "The Encyclical Pascendi," *The Dublin Review* 142 (January/April 1908): 1–10.

4. The word *modernismus* had not appeared in the writings of Pius X's predecessors, Pius IX and Leo XIII. In *Aeterni Patris* (1879) Leo rarely used the word *modernus*, much less *modernismus*. Rather, in connection with methods, ideas, and sciences, he used terms like *recentis* (recent) or *hodiernus* (contemporary). One or another variant of the word "modern" did not stand on its own for the purpose of describing, listing, or collecting

163

It was clear enough, Ward conceded, that the pope wished to condemn the principle of "subjectivism in religion." So stated, Modernism would seem to be nothing other than generic Liberalism in matters of religion and theology.[5] If read as a "newspaper article," generalizations and "isolated passages" would too easily furnish partisans with cudgels by which to censure certain books and theologians, not to mention any number of merely half-baked ideas, that were not mentioned in the encyclical itself.

Presciently, he worried that the term could draw into its net a millennium of Catholic intellectual labor devoted to reconciling the *moderni* (the new authors, books, ideas, devotions) with the *antiqui* (with its authors, books, and ideas). For example, Pius X quoted Gregory IX's letter written in 1223 about certain nefarious *moderni* at the University of Paris, suggesting that the precedent for Modernism was the reception of Aristotle among the Parisian masters.[6] In point of fact, Gregory supported Aristotelian scholasticism and had criticized only certain translations and commentaries of an Averroistic bent. Read without qualifications drawn in the rest of the Gregorian letter, the reader of *Pascendi* might conclude that just as the *moderni*

---

errors. The Roman Magisterium had plenty of other words that could be wheeled out, as the occasion required, for indicating errors: e.g., *rationalismus, pantheismus, indifferentismus, socialismus,* or *liberalismus*. All of these can be found in Pius IX's *Syllabus of Errors,* attached to the encyclical *Quanta cura* (1864). But we do not find *modernus* or *modernismus*. But, see three Leonine uses of the term *modernus* which run in the direction of Pius's pejorative sense: (1) "in treating of the so-called modern liberties [*de modernis, uti loquuntur*], distinguished between their good and evil elements; and We have shown that whatsoever is good in those liberties is as ancient as truth itself, and that the Church has always most willingly approved and practiced that good: but whatsoever has been added as new is, to tell the plain truth, of a vitiated kind, the fruit of the disorders of the age, and of an insatiate longing after novelties" (Leo XIII, Encyclical Letter *Libertas praestantissimum* [June 20, 1888], §2, *Acta Leonis* 8, 213); (2) "Substantially the struggle is ever the same: Jesus Christ is always exposed to the contradictions of the world, and the same means are always used by modern enemies of Christianity [*les ennemis modernes du christianisme*], means old in principle and scarcely modified in form" (Leo XIII, Encyclical Letter *Au milieu* [February 16, 1892], §12, *Acta Leonis* 12, 27); (3) "Superficial erudition or merely common knowledge will not suffice for all this—there is need of study, solid, profound and continuous, in a word of a mass of doctrinal knowledge sufficient to cope with the subtlety and remarkable cunning of our modern opponents [*de nos modernes contradicteurs*]" (Leo XIII, Encyclical Letter *Depuis le jour* [September 8, 1899], §48, *Acta Leonis* 19, 187). The last citation is taken from Pecci's pastoral letter (July 19, 1866), written in Perugia in the wake of the *Syllabus*.

5. Ward was referring to the concluding error in the syllabus of *Lamentabili Sane,* no. 65, *Acta* 5, 84: "Contemporary Catholicism can be reconciled with true science only if it is transformed into a non-dogmatic Christianity, that is to say, into a broad and liberal Protestantism" (*Catholicismus hodiernus . . . in protestantismum latum et liberalem*).

6. Pius X, Encyclical Letter *Pascendi* (September 8, 1907), §17, *Acta* 5, 64n8.

of the thirteenth-century schools were once roundly condemned, so too must we reject whatever proves to be modern in theology.

The reader of *The Dublin Review* would have understood the problem raised so delicately by Ward. In 1879 Leo XIII issued *Aeterni Patris*, calling for a revival of scholastic philosophy and theology. He insisted that the Catholic mind ought to do just what the careless reader of *Pascendi* might construe as forbidden. Namely, to harmonize the modern sciences with scholastic philosophy. Leo proclaimed, "The best parent and guardian of liberty amongst men is truth."[7] The proper response to the *moderni* is critical openness to truth and to all of the sciences. Not, of course, openness in a haphazard way. Leo recommended not merely a generic scholasticism as the frame of reference, but a more specific scholasticism culled from Saint Thomas. Thomas's philosophy, he believed, provided the best combination of core principles and synthetic reach on disputed issues in modern times.

Regarding the normativity of Thomas's thought, Leo wrote:

> While, therefore, We hold that every word of wisdom, every useful thing by whomsoever discovered or planned, ought to be received with a willing and grateful mind, We exhort you, venerable brethren, in all earnestness to restore the golden wisdom of St. Thomas and to spread it far and wide for the defense and beauty of the Catholic faith, for the good of society, and for the advantage of all the sciences. The wisdom of St. Thomas, We say; for if anything is taken up with too great subtlety by the Scholastic doctors or too carelessly stated—if there be anything that ill agrees with the discoveries of a later age or, in a word, improbable in whatever way—it does not enter Our mind to propose that for imitation to Our age. Let carefully selected teachers endeavor to implant the doctrine of Thomas Aquinas in the minds of students and set forth clearly his solidity and excellence over others. Let the universities already founded or to be founded by you illustrate and defend this doctrine and use it for the refutation of prevailing errors. But, lest the false for the true or the corrupt for the pure be drunk in, be ye watchful that the doctrine of Thomas be drawn from his own fountains, or at least from those rivulets which, derived from the very fount, have thus far flowed, according to the established agreement of learned men, pure and clear; be careful to guard the minds of youth from those which are said to flow thence, but in reality are gathered from strange and unwholesome streams.[8]

Ward did not mention—and perhaps did not even notice—that Pius X quoted only the sentence regarding the "too great subtlety of the Scholastic

---

7. Leo XIII, Encyclical Letter *Immortale Dei* (November 1, 1885), §40, *Acta Leonis* 5, 144.

8. Leo XIII, Encyclical Letter *Aeterni Patris* (August 4, 1879), §31, *Acta Leonis* 1, 283.

doctors."[9] Left out is the opening exhortation regarding receptivity to truth "by whomsoever discovered or planned." He also elides Leo's explicit recognition that Thomas is mediated by tradition(s), or "rivulets" (*ex iis rivis*), which need to be discerned with regard to the fount (*ab ipso fonte*). In other words, Leo's program looked backward, from the traditions to the original, and forward toward a constructive engagement with modern philosophy and science. For his part, Pius X moves directly to a disciplinary matter. Leo's prescription must be "strictly observed" by all bishops and religious superiors. Seminary professors, he adds, may not disparage or set aside Thomas "especially in metaphysical questions" (*praesertim in re metaphysica*).[10] What began in Leo's encyclical as a program for reckoning with contemporary philosophy and science had been turned into a quite different conversation, emphasizing discipline *ad intra*.

What accounts for these different points of view? Pius X made it clear that the adversaries of Catholicism now are "not from without but from within."[11] Along with its disciplinary apparatus, *Pascendi* treats the *moderni* as an "intestine" disorder to be purged from the bowels of the Church, and then only with great difficulty because this cancer has what Pius X calls a "manifold personality."[12] The *moderni* are shape-shifters and therefore must be astutely diagnosed according to their diverse and often misleading symptoms. Pius X is concerned not merely to distinguish true from false philosophy, but to detect true from false churchmen. Thomism was brought into the center of that diagnostic task. While Leo and Pius X agreed on the practical conclusion, that Thomas ought to be privileged in institutions of ecclesiastical formation, we cannot ignore their quite different conceptions of how the Catholic (and Thomistic) mind ought to situate and dispose itself to modernity.

We will argue that the differences between *Aeterni Patris* and *Pascendi* contain *in nucleo* not only a tension between a constructive and synthetic Thomism on the one hand and a legislated or disciplinary Thomism on the other.[13] Deeper still was another tension—best understood in terms of two different aspects of modernity with which Catholicism had to reckon. The two are interlaced and therefore are not easily separated. But they can be distinguished.

---

9. *Pascendi*, §45, *Acta* 5, 102.

10. *Pascendi*, §45, *Acta* 5, 102.

11. *Pascendi*, §3, *Acta* 5, 48: "Nam non hi extra Ecclesiam, sed intra."

12. *Pascendi*, §5, *Acta* 5, 50: "Modernistarum quemlibet plures agere personas ac veluti in se commiscere."

13. The expression "disciplinary or legislated Thomism" is taken from the magisterial essay by James A. Weisheipl, OP, "Thomism as a Christian Philosophy," in *New Themes in Christian Philosophy*, ed. Ralph M. McInerny (Notre Dame, IN: University of Notre Dame Press, 1968), 184.

For purposes of our inquiry, the first is modernity as social, economic, political, and legal phenomenon. We are speaking of those aspects of modern life that made necessary the development of what came to be called "social doctrine." Pius XI (1922–39) is the first pope to speak explicitly of social doctrine as a unified body of teachings that develop by way of clarity and application.[14] How should Catholics live in a world in which political Christendom is defunct? Both chronologically and in the lived experience of Catholics, this cluster of questions came first. The second theme is modernity as philosophical system that displaced, or at least threatened, what could be called the *praeambula fidei*. Again, for our purposes, these "preambles of faith" include truths known in principle by natural reason, particularly on issues having a propinquity to sacred doctrine.[15] They can be summarized in the pithy remark by Pius X in reference to the obligation of seminary professors to adhere to Thomas *praesertim in re metaphysica*.

The revival of Thomism was closely connected to the search for an adequate social doctrine or, to use the older term, a *doctrina civilis*. But the problem of the *praeambula fidei* was never far behind the curve of political and social questions. It became an especially pressing issue after the First Vatican Council (1869–70), when the Church had the liberty and the will to refashion its internal order—particularly the seminaries—according to Roman norms. Thus, the title of this essay "Two Modernisms, Two Thomisms." Beginning in the nineteenth century there emerged two distinct sets of problems for which Thomism was to provide the remedy.[16] Leo's project included both, but with a decided emphasis upon the social. Pius X's included both, but with an even more decided emphasis upon the philosophy officially needed *ad intra* to buttress sacred doctrine.

To prepare ourselves for this discussion, it is necessary to take a bird's-eye view of the historical events in response to which modernity became a Catholic problem and, what is more, a problem to be understood in Thomistic terms. Among other things, we must consider early efforts by Rome to create lists or syllabi of modern errors. This is of some consequence to our story, because Leo revived Thomism in order to find an alternative to the "lists." The reader will bear in mind that it is not our intention to pass

---

14. Pius XI said that he inherited a "doctrine" handed on from the time of Leo XIII. Pius XI, Encyclical Letter *Quadragesimo Anno*, §§18–21, *AAS* 23, 182–84. See, also, Mary Elsbernd, *Papal Statements on Rights*, 587n1, on the emergence of the term *doctrina*.

15. Debates among Thomists over the status of the *praeambula* is thoroughly covered by Ralph M. McInerny, *Praeambula Fidei: Thomism and the God of the Philosophers* (Washington, DC: The Catholic University of American Press, 2006). Note especially the historical chapters in Part II on the post-Leonine disputes.

16. See note 96 below on Pius XI's understanding of the two modernisms.

judgment on these syllabi and lists as regards their content, at least not on their substantive merit. It will suffice to show how they positioned the Church to fashion two distinct responses to modernity and how Thomism was drawn into the different orbits of the question.[17]

MODERN TIMES

Catholicism was not, as commonly depicted, dragged kicking and screaming into modern times. For several centuries, Catholicism was comfortably—perhaps all too comfortably—adapted to many aspects of modernity. Beginning with the discovery of the New World and the projection of Catholic missions to four continents, many Catholics—clerical and lay—understood that they lived in a new era of exploration, industry, education, art, vernacular literatures, devotions, science, and philosophy. The Reformation and religious wars, culminating in the treaties of Westphalia (1648), destroyed the medieval common law of Christendom by creating a system of states having diverse confessional allegiances. Innocent X declared Westphalia "null, void, invalid, iniquitous, unjust, damnable, reprobate, inane, empty of meaning and effect for all time."[18]

Even so, a *new* common law evolved among the peoples under Catholic rule. It was built upon a complex and evolving set of treaties, informal agreements, and legal fictions through which the Church conceded to Catholic sovereigns rights and obligations over many aspects of ecclesiastical life (the so-called *ius patronatus*), in exchange for which the sovereigns protected the Church from schism and supplied the material resources and governance for the far-flung missions across the world. The sovereigns were deemed junior apostles, entitled to rule "in trust" the quotidian life of the Church in Europe and in her colonies. Innocent X's declaration that Westphalia was "empty of meaning and effect for all time" remained on the books, as it were; but on the ground, Catholicism developed a remarkable symbiosis with the new system of sovereignty—so long as it was in the hands of Catholic families. In fact, the modern state was assembled within the Catholic world, beginning on the Iberian peninsula in 1492, but especially in the bureaucratic system that emerged in the Spanish dominions overseas.[19] It required a deep and

---

17. I have left out of this account the issue of biblical studies and interpretation, which is very important to the modernist controversy.

18. Innocent X, Papal Bull *Zelo Domus Dei* (November 26, 1648).

19. Restricting ourselves only to Spain, Pope Alexander VI issued the bull *Inter Caetera* (1493), conceding to the Spanish monarchs title to the lands discovered and still to be discovered in the Indies. This was followed in 1508 by Julius II's bull *Universalis Ecclesiae*, conceding a universal patronage over the Church in America. Within a century,

extensive cooperation of ecclesiastical and civil authorities. To the very end, on the eve of the French Revolution, this modernity, as it were, was not perceived as a special problem either *ad intra* or *ad extra*. For Catholics it was a political culture involving an intricate minuet of ecclesiastical powers, new religious orders, and ruling dynasties.

I shall not try here to cover these earlier centuries in proper detail, but one story might suffice to convey something of its mindset. On December 15, 1781, Pope Pius VI dispatched from Rome a courier carrying a secret letter to be delivered by the papal nuncio to the Emperor of the Romans, Joseph II. The letter announced the pope's intention to visit Vienna in two months' time to treat with the emperor on issues of ecclesiastical jurisdiction and disputes over territories in the north of Italy. The Crown Cardinal from France, Cardinal de Bernis, warned that the pope would "give the signal of a paper war" with much stronger governments, and thus "give birth to a discussion which the very interest of religion requires you to avoid."[20]

What was a "paper war," and why was it deemed injurious to the "interest of religion"? In sum, paper wars included lists of complaints or errors, or—what was even worse—exercises in speculative theology tending to disturb the common law of Christendom. A serious paper war erupted during the reign of Louis XIV who induced popes to issue six bulls against the Jansenists, the most famous being *Unigenitus* (1713),[21] which condemned some 101 propositions extracted from Pasquier Quesnel's *Réflexions morales sur le Nouveau Testament*. It proved disastrous, not only for the moral authority of the papacy and for the stability of the French crown, but also

---

however, the delegation had been delegated once again. A royal law in 1609 entrusted the *ius patronatus* in cases of lesser ecclesiastical positions to viceroys who came to control the appointment of parish priests. The panoply of Church life, from councils and synods, episcopal chancelleries and ecclesiastical courts, the publications of papal bulls and rescripts, tribunals of the Inquisition, down to the quotidian life of parishes, schools, and hospitals fell to the plenary authority of the king. By concordat in 1753 Benedict XIV extended the patronal right throughout all of Spain. And thus came into existence what was called the *Patronato Real Universal*, which now encompassed Grenada (1486), the Indies (1508), and continental Spain (1753). Rome had never before conceded, nor had any Catholic prince received, such a package of delegated authority. For the legal structure and history of the *Patronato Real*, one can rely on studies by W. Eugene Shiels, *King and Church: The Rise and Fall of the Patronato Real* (Chicago: Loyola University Press, 1961); and on broader historical canvas, the work by J. H. Elliott, *Empires of the Atlantic World* (New Haven, CT: Yale University Press, 2006).

20. Jean Francois Baron de Bourgoing, *Historical and Philosophical Memoirs of Pius the Sixth*, vol. 1 (London: G. G. and J. Robinson, 1799), 221.

21. Clement XI, Papal Bull *Unigenitus Dei Filius* (September 8, 1713); Denzinger-Hünermann (1997), §§2400–2502.

for the Jesuits, who eventually would be expelled from France (1764) and suppressed by the papacy (1773).

The French Revolution's *Civil Constitution of the Clergy* (1790) unilaterally overturned the modern common law of political Christendom. Church governance was handed over *not* to the mischievous but familiar Catholic families, but instead was given to the nation. The clergy became civil servants elected by democratic vote. This model spread to the former colonies, particularly in Latin America. Rights once belonging to the Church had been transferred to kings, and now to the nation. The state was no longer governed by anointed laity, but by a new doctrine of *laicism*. Joseph de Bonald and François-René de Chateaubriand founded the journal *Le Conservateur* in 1818, introducing the term "conservative" into the political idiom of European politics. (Conservative, it should be noted, did not mean the opposite of "modern" but rather of "anarchical.")

What was to be "conserved"? There was more than one answer. Politically, the thing to be conserved was the first modernity, the modern relationship between throne and altar that evolved after the religious wars. Thus, the Congress of Vienna in 1815 attempted to restore the union of throne-and-altar, hoping to contain if not defeat the forces of anarchy. In Rome, Pius VII established in 1801 the Congregation of Extraordinary Affairs. It became a kind of kitchen cabinet that oversaw relations between Rome and the civil powers.[22] Rome went into an emergency mode, resolved to handle the Church-state crisis on an ad hoc basis. But it also signaled that there would be no overarching doctrine to meet the crises. Encyclicals of the era urged Catholics to obey legitimate authority, beginning with the pope's own temporal authority in the papal states. This was the era of Restoration or Legitimism.[23]

Yet there was also a quite different and more radical notion of what had to be conserved. In the aftermath of the Revolution, Catholic reactionaries and liberals disagreed about the proper political response. Reactionaries like Joseph de Maistre, Bonald, and Donoso Cortés argued that the new ideas, new constitutional foundings were inherently unable to master the dynamics of revolution and anarchy. They recommended more rather than less repression by the police powers of state. Liberals, like Lamennais, Montalembert, and Lacordaire argued that the revolutions could be tamed by moderate, liberal constitutions, such as the Belgian Constitution of 1831—the first European

---

22. It would have a long life, lasting with only slight adjustments until 1967. Gregory XVI will make the Secretary of State a member *pro tempore* and executor of the Congregation's resolutions. In 1908, Pius X made it one of three sections of the Secretariat of State.

23. No encyclical better exhibits the principles and the failure of Legitimism than Gregory XVI, Encyclical Letter *Cum Primum* (June 9, 1832) commanding the Poles to obey the czar.

constitution to renounce civil control of the Church. But both camps agreed on one cardinal point: That the common law of modern Christendom was itself the cause of the troubles. Neither side wished to conserve the *ancien régime* just as such. They did not need to read Tocqueville to understand that the so-called *ancien régime* was not medieval, but something quite modern.

So, they returned imaginatively and critically to the work of Gregory VII during the Investiture Controversy of the eleventh and twelfth centuries. It was Joseph de Maistre who first insisted that Gregory VII's work had to be completed in modern times. Maistre criticized the ecclesiology of national churches, and he accused kings and princes of a "great rebellion."[24] For Maistre, Gregory VII was "the genius," the man without whom "all was lost, humanly speaking."[25] Interestingly, in this context, Gregory VII was the "modern" because his reform was put in opposition to the "feudal," which is to say, vassalage of the Church to lay powers. To declare Gregory VII the model for the Church's relations to the restored crowns of 1815 was a most unlikely proposition. But the idea was vigorously and publicly pursued by virtually all of the important Catholic writers in the wake of the Revolution.[26] To speak of the Gregorian reforms as a model for the era of Restoration not only seemed anachronistic, but if put into effect it would mean that the Gregorian critique of the lay control of the Church had to be applied first against the remnants of Catholic temporal authorities, and second against the new, laicist states.

Improbably, this is exactly what found its way into papal rhetoric. From Clement XI (1700) until the election of Pius VI (1775), we find only a single reference in Roman teaching documents to Acts 5:29, "We must obey God

---

24. Joseph de Maistre, *The Pope*, trans. Aeneas M. Dawson (London: C. Dolman, 1850; first published, 1819), III.4, 277.

25. Maistre, *The Pope*, II.12, 199; III.2, 255.

26. Notable works in this genre include: Félicité Robert de Lamennais's notes on the history of the Gregorian reform, *Tradition de l'église sur l'institution des évêques* (Paris, 1814); Dom Guéranger's *Affaire de la Légende de Saint Grégoire VII*, in *Institutions liturgiques*, vol. 2, Ch. 21 (Le Mans/Paris, 1841); Henri Lacordaire's *Éloge Funèbre De Daniel O'Connell* (Paris, February 10, 1848); John Henry Newman's *Present Position of Catholics in England* (1851); Wilhelm Emmanuel von Ketteler's "Freedom, Authority, and the Church in The Social Teachings of Willhelm Emmanuel Von Ketteler," trans. Rupert J. Ederer (Lanham, MD: University Press of America, 1981; first published, 1862); Donoso Cortés, "Letter to Cardinal Fornari on the Errors of Our Times" in *Selected Works of Juan Donoso Cortés*, trans. and ed. Jeffrey P. Johnson (Westport, CT: Greenwood Press, 2000; first published, 1852), which provided notes for an early version of the *Syllabus of Errors*; and Antonio Rosmini, *Delle cinque piaghe della Santa Chiesa* (Napoli, 1832, 1848), a scholarly but passionate compendium of arguments against civil control of the Church. As late as Vatican II, the Gregorian theme was used by John Courtney Murray, SJ. See note 83 below.

rather than men."[27] Then it went into abeyance until after the *Syllabus of Errors* (1864). Recovered from its desuetude by Pius IX, Acts 5:29 became the text by which Roman authorities traced the boundary of Matthew 22:21 regarding the things not owed to Caesar. The Roman Magisterium was ready to critically engage and freely criticize the ruling powers. What had changed?

THE PAPER WAR OF PIUS IX: *SYLLABUS OF ERRORS*

The *Syllabus of Errors* stood on a simple fact of political history. In 1860 Pius IX lost his Italian dominions to the House of Savoy, which installed not merely a lay state, but a laicist state. The Restoration was defunct. Pius's secretary of State, Cardinal Antonelli, confided to a British envoy that "exclusively Catholic governments had virtually ceased to exist."[28] The triumph of the Italian *Risorgimento* had the unintended effect of removing any inhibition of the papacy to speak on matters political. But how should it speak? There had been no systematic political theology for two centuries, since the school at Salamanca. Pius IX and his advisors cobbled together a number of pontifical statements and admonitions, grouped them under various headings, and fired away.

Attached to the encyclical *Quanta Cura* (1864), the *Syllabus* lists eighty propositions. They are somewhat confusing because almost every erroneous proposition is stated in the affirmative. The reader must negate the affirmative proposition. So, for example, proposition 80 states that the Roman Pontiff ought to "reconcile himself to contemporary liberalism," the negation of which *might* be "the pope is not obliged to reconcile himself to contemporary liberalism"; but it could *also* be, "the pope is not obliged to reconcile himself to this or that brand of liberalism, or not obliged to reconcile himself to liberalism as it is understood today." Indeed, the search for a proper set of negations became very important to the Church's response to the problems of the mid-nineteenth century.

From the outset, churchmen understood the problem of promulgating lists of errors. Catholic journals, including *The Dublin Review*, considered republishing the *Syllabus* as a set of negative propositions.[29] In France, there

---

27. In a secret consistory during the Revolution, Pius VI once mentions Acts 5:29. For his remarks at the Quirinal (September 26, 1791), see M. N. S. Guillon, *Collection générale des brefs et instructions de Notre Très-Saint Père le Pape Pie VI, relatifs a la révolution Françoise*, vol. 2 (Paris: Chez Le Clere, 1798), 188–91.

28. See "Lord Odo Russell to Earl of C. (March 7, 1870)," in *The Roman Question, Extracts from the Despatches of Odo Russell from Rome, 1858–1870*, ed. N. Blakiston (London: Chapman and Hall, 1962), 404.

29. See the account by Wilfrid Ward in *William George Ward and the Catholic Revival* (London: Macmillan, 1893), 242f. His father, William George Ward, editor of *The Dublin Review*, was also inclined in this direction, but reluctantly begged off (257).

was talk of making a new catechism out of the *Syllabus*, prompting the Minister of Public Worship to decree on January 1, 1865, that *Quanta Cura* and its appendix could not be addressed from the pulpit. Félix Dupanloup, the bishop of Orléans, wryly responded, "This is done in the name of Gallican liberties, based on two specially liberal Sovereigns, to wit, Louis XIV, and Napoleon I."[30] Dupanloup argued for a sensible principle of interpretation. He contended that the erroneous propositions listed in the *Syllabus* should be read as Liberal theses—Liberal "universals" as it were. A false theory when turned into a universal principle is bound to be bad in a great number of cases, and for that reason must be repudiated. Take proposition 42: "In the case of conflicting laws enacted by the two powers, civil law prevails." This is not always true and therefore must be negated. Or take proposition 39: "The State, as being the origin and source of all rights, is endowed with a certain right not circumscribed by any limits." This proposition is never true. But, alas, Dupanloup's method required considerable sophistication. The ordinary person had to keep fixed in mind that the *Syllabus* lists liberal theses rather than Catholic doctrines, and then had to go in search of just the right negation.[31]

Despite such confusions, Pius IX clearly set forth the purposes and targets of the *Syllabus*. At the beginning of his encyclical, he notes that the errors are "opposed to the eternal natural law engraven by God in all men's hearts, and to right reason; from which almost all other errors have their origin."[32] The chief harm, he says, is to the "good of human society." The ideologues of state power intended nothing less than "to raze the foundations of the Catholic religion and of civil society." This is not a disciplinary encyclical on matters *ad intra*. Rather, it is firmly anchored in the political questions

---

30. Msgr. Felix Dupanloup, *Remarks on the Encyclical, of the 8th of December, A.D. 1864*, trans. William J. M. Hutchinson, 2nd ed. (London: Burns, Lambert, & Oates, 1865), 4.

31. It also caused confusion because Catholics had already converted the (liberal) affirmations into negations, thus making it seem that it was the Catholic thesis that had to be derogated or qualified. On this view, the Catholic thesis (every state must have a religion) could be bent, in hypothesis, to cover certain exceptions from the ideal. See M. Bévenot, SJ, "Thesis and Hypothesis," *Theological Studies* 15 (1954): 440–46. Bévenot points out (443) that the confusion was due, in part, to the fact that one year earlier, in an unsigned article (attributed to C. M. Curci), *Civiltà Cattolica* had reversed the distinction. Fixed principles of ontology were identified with the "thesis," while the "hypothesis" stood for things as they might become by intrusion of accidental circumstances, perhaps regrettable and sometimes criminal (*Civiltà Cattolica*, 5th series, 8, October 2, 1863, 129–49). The *Syllabus* was turned upside-down, but this perspective did not always afford a better view. Confusions about the thesis-hypothesis distinction would haunt Catholic thought for the better part of the next century.

32. Pius IX, Encyclical Letter *Quanta cura* (December 8, 1864), §2, *Acta* 1.3, 689.

following the revolutions of 1848. It would be difficult to imagine a more extroverted encyclical.

For our purposes, three things are important, and each supports our thesis that the social-political problem came first. First, among the *Syllabus*'s eighty propositions only seven are not directly related to the issue of Church and state (but also, by implication, marriage, family, education, sodalities, etc.). Second, only four are culled from papal statements prior to the revolutions of 1848. This is a fact of some importance, because it indicates that Pius IX and his editors knew they were entering a new situation. Third, the core of the document, propositions 19–55, laid waste to the older common law of Christendom.[33] In proposition after proposition, Pius IX flatly denies the rights once exercised by Catholic sovereigns, and now by nation-states. He declares, in effect, the independence of the Church not only in matters of ordinary governance (sacraments and the episcopacy), but also with regard to schools, religious orders, marriage and families, and sodalities. Although he did not intend to inaugurate what came to be known as Catholic social doctrine, many of the rudiments of this tradition are found in the *Syllabus*.

Five years later, parts of the *Syllabus* were reworked into five chapters and twenty-one canons of the first draft of the conciliar document *De Ecclesia Christi*.[34] If conjoined to the doctrine of universal jurisdiction of the pope, the net effect would amount to something like a doctrinalization and enforcement of Gregory VII's reforms, albeit in a completely different time and place. The courts and cabinets of Europe certainly interpreted things in just this way. They were furious that the old fool, the epileptic, the so-called "Oracle of the Tiber," had out-maneuvered them. As it turned out, the chapters and canons drawn from the *Syllabus* had to be dropped because the bishops could not agree on any over-arching theory to unify them. And, of course, they worried about being harassed by their home governments. In July 1870, they gave the papacy universal jurisdiction and went home.

The *Syllabus* and Vatican I laid out the predicates of ecclesiastical order unfettered by civil control. They killed Gallicanism—no more national churches, no Catholicism controlled by local ecclesiastical and lay elites. The theory and the legality of the act were hardly developed or aligned, one with the other. Yet even Catholics like John Henry Newman and Bishop Von Ketteler, who were diffident about the timing of the decrees on papal infallibility and the award of universal jurisdiction, publicly celebrated the result. Newman admitted that "there will be no more of those misunderstandings out of which

---

33. *Syllabus, Acta* 1.3, 701–17.

34. Ioannes Dominicus Mansi, ed., *Sacrorum Conciliorum Nova et Amplissima Collectio*, vol. 51, *Primum Schema Constitutionis de Ecclesia Christi* (Arnhem and Leipzig, 1926), Chs. X–XV, 543–51; canons I–XXI, 551–53.

Jansenism and Gallicanism have arisen, and which in these latter days have begotten here in England the so-called Branch Theory."[35]

THE LEONINE PROJECT: A THOMIST RESPONSE

When Leo was elected in 1878, he inherited an incomplete revolution. Unlike the time of Trent, he had no full set of conciliar doctrines; he had no new catechism; and none of the revolution had been canonically codified (which will await the Pio-Benedictine *Code of Canon Law* of 1917). He inherited a fact, or a deed, rather than a coherent *doctrina civilis*. Therefore, he had to put three things into some kind of synthesis:

> First, the *Syllabus of Errors*, with its eighty propositions, which had to be converted not merely into negations but into an adequate *doctrina civilis*.
>
> Second, Vatican Council I's Constitution *Dei Filius*, ratified unanimously in the spring of 1870, keyed itself to Wisdom 8:1, where Scripture says that divine providence governs all things sweetly [*suaviter*]. *Dei Filius* asserted that God is the "Lord of the Sciences," that faith and reason have distinct objects and ends which are mutually supportive, and that the "assent of faith is by no means a blind movement of the mind."[36] The preambles of the faith needed to be clarified and organized for modern times.
>
> Third, he inherited from the Council authority to directly teach the Catholic world without interference of the state.

The question, then, was how to put these three together. The answer, in part, was to bring his Perugian Academy of St. Thomas Aquinas to Rome, and to make two of its faculty (one of whom was his brother) cardinals. A year later, he issued *Aeterni Patris* (1879).

Before we turn to that encyclical, two points need to be made. First, it should be mentioned that Leo never trusted the Romantic Reactionaries of the early nineteenth century. In his view, they gave a one-sided, and inadequately philosophical, response to the Enlightenment. In his famous *Speech on Dictatorship* (1849), Donoso Cortés asserted that, "[T]here are no more than two possible forms of repression. . . . There is a law of humanity, a law

---

35. John Henry Newman, *Letters and Diaries*, 25:259. In 1883, when the Gladstone government introduced an Affirmation Bill that replaced the oath invoking the name of God, Newman refused to join other church leaders in protest; the God of Christianity, he thought, had long ceased to be the God of Parliament. John Henry Newman, *Letters and Diaries*, 28:206.

36. Vatican Council I, Dogmatic Constitution *Dei Filius* IV and III, respectively (April 24, 1870), in Tanner, *Decrees*, 2:808.

of History."[37] God does not subject creatures only to the natural laws. He is also a dictator in the sense that his decrees can bend or suspend the natural course, and hence by particular Providence history is the theatre of divine admonition and grace.[38] And as God governs in both modes by pure positivity of power, dictatorially, as it were, so too in human societies we see the governance of the state and the Church.[39]

For Leo, the idea of a divine dictator suspending the laws of nature, imposing a twofold order of repression, could not be reconciled with *Dei Filius*, which affirmed a twofold order of providence and a twofold order of knowledge rather than two modes of repression. It was the last thing that modern states needed to hear. It was not, for example, the kind of message that he intended to send to Bismarck, whose *Kulturkampf* was still under way in Prussia and parts of Poland.

Second, Leo was also suspicious of what James Weisheipl aptly calls "nineteenth-century apologetics."[40] Since the eighteenth century, philosophical efforts to defend Catholic doctrine as well as to create bridges to modern thought were not Thomistic. They were inspired rather by Descartes, Christian Wolff, Kant, and Hegel. Education in ecclesiastical institutions, we must remember, was only sporadically under Roman discipline. The new governments suppressed, or at the very least interfered with, Catholic education at every level. There was no "unitary" system of philosophy either at the level of curriculum or discipline. Occasionally, a certain thinker or book or set of ideas was censured by the Roman magisterium—Lamennais, Rosmini, Anton Günther, and George Hermes ran afoul of Roman authorities. Yet there was no over-arching policy of censuring philosophy, certainly nothing like the disciplinary apparatus created by Pius X after Leo's death. Since the French Revolution, the papacy was too distracted by the political issues to land with both feet in the midst of intramural disputes about academic philosophy. The important thing now was the centralization of ecclesiastical jurisdiction after 1870, which gave Leo a window of opportunity to address the problem of philosophical eclecticism in institutions coming under Church discipline.

In *Aeterni Patris*, Leo insisted that a sound philosophy is needed "in order that sacred theology may receive and assume the nature, form, and

---

37. Juan Donoso Cortés, "Speech on Dictatorship (January 4, 1849)," in *Selected Works of Juan Donoso Cortés*, trans. Jeffery P. Johnson (Westport, CT: Greenwood Press, 2000), 53.

38. Cortés, "Speech on Dictatorship," 48: "So gentlemen, when God operates in this way, can it not be said, if human language can be applied to divine things, that he is operating dictatorially?"

39. Interestingly, Donoso was invited to assist with an early draft of the *Syllabus of Errors*. Letter to Cardinal Fornari, "Errors of Our Times (June 19, 1852)," in *Selected Works*, 110.

40. Weisheipl, "Thomism as a Christian Philosophy," 166.

genius of a true science."[41] The faith-reason issues highlighted in *Dei Filius* could not be maintained or advanced on the basis of philosophical eclecticism. Leo complained that since the sixteenth century, philosophical systems have "multiplied beyond measure," and that even Catholic philosophers accommodated themselves to a system "which depends on the authority and choice of any professor."[42] His remark about sixteenth-century "innovators" might be construed as a warning shot, fired in the direction of Baroque-era scholastics, particularly the Suárezians. But this is not quite true. In fact, he praises the schools of sixteenth-century Scholasticism, calling them "homes of human wisdom."[43] He explicitly recognized that Thomas's thought was "unfolded in good time by later masters and with a goodly yield."[44] Leo's immediate target was not intramural debate among scholastics or schools of Thomism. He was speaking of "tottering and feeble" attempts to render modern philosophies user-friendly to Catholic doctrine, but only at the price of creating transitory and eccentric adaptations rather than sound syntheses needed for systematic theology.[45]

It is true, however, that *Aeterni Patris* cannot be read, on its own terms, as an exhortation to a merely generic Scholasticism. Thomas is held out as the "Master," and Leo does not hesitate to admonish churchmen "that nearly all the founders and lawgivers of the religious orders commanded their members to study and religiously adhere to the teachings of St. Thomas, fearful lest any of them should swerve even in the slightest degree from the footsteps of so great a man."[46] Thomas's doctrine must enjoy "excellence over others."[47] Leo did not make a chart of the authentic "rivulets" of interpretation, much less make a list of polluted ones, but it is clear enough that he believed that there is an authentic Thomism.[48]

---

41. Leo XIII, *Aeterni Patris*, §6, *Acta Leonis* 1, 262.

42. *Aeterni Patris*, §24, *Acta Leonis* 1, 278.

43. *Aeterni Patris*, §20, *Acta Leonis* 1, 274f.

44. *Aeterni Patris*, §18, *Acta Leonis* 1, 273.

45. Just what Weisheipl calls "nineteenth-century apologetics," or the attempt to cherry-pick a theme or principle in Descartes, Kant, or Hegel and then to turn it to the apparent advantage of Catholicism. Even here, however, Leo is gentle. *Aeterni Patris*, §24: "In saying this We have no intention of discountenancing the learned and able men who bring their industry and erudition, and, what is more, the wealth of new discoveries, to the service of philosophy; for, of course, We understand that this tends to the development of learning. But one should be very careful lest all or his chief labor be exhausted in these pursuits and in mere erudition."

46. *Aeterni Patris*, §19, *Acta Leonis* 1, 274.

47. *Aeterni Patris*, §31, *Acta Leonis* 1, 283.

48. The subtitle of the encyclical implies as much: *De philosophia Christiana ad mentem Sancti Thomae Aquinatis in scholis catholicis instauranda*.

When we read *Aeterni Patris* as a whole, we see that Leo framed the revival of Christian philosophy chiefly in the context of the ongoing political problems.

> Whosoever turns his attention to the bitter strifes of these days and seeks a reason for the troubles that vex public and private life must come to the conclusion that . . . false conclusions concerning divine and human things, which originated in the schools of philosophy, have now crept into all the orders of the State.[49]

When he enumerates the benefits of reviving scholastic philosophy, and more particularly, the philosophy of Thomas, he speaks first of the social-political issues (and "kindred subjects"), and then of the advance of the physical sciences.[50]

It cannot be doubted that the Leonine revival was motivated by the search for an adequate *doctrina civilis*. Long before *Aeterni Patris*, Leo's mentors were using Thomas for just this purpose. The Jesuits on the editorial staff of *La Civiltà Cattolica*, founded in 1850 to respond to the political and cultural crisis of *Risorgimento*, had already begun to cut this groove. Luigi Taparelli first sketched his theories of social justice and subsidiarity in the cockpit of the journal. His colleague, Matteo Liberatore, who became one of Leo's trusted advisors and a member of the Roman Academy of St. Thomas Aquinas, actually converted to Thomism after joining the staff of *Civiltà Cattolica*. In other words, he came to Thomism through the crucible of the social and political issues. In Leo's own work—in the some 110 encyclicals and other teaching letters—Thomas is rarely discussed or referenced apart from the social-political problems.

These two aims—the systematic and pedagogical, and the search for an adequate *doctrina civilis*—were not without tension. Leo's metaphor of a fountain of doctrine dispersed into certain "rivulets" required an important though subtle distinction. In those subjects having propinquity to sacred doctrine, it is crucial to achieve a rather tightly organized account of the relationship between philosophy and the deposit of faith. Even slight changes in the philosophy will entail new estimations of the doctrine. If Saint Thomas is to be the "Master" on such things, the relationship between the rivulets of interpretation and the source is not something about which the Church could be indifferent. On the bevy of issues which swarm around the social-political problem, the terrain allowed much more room for creative maneuver. As Thomas himself taught, the natural law can change "by addition."[51] The very nature of the subject allows a broad threshold in which principle and prudence conjoin to deliver a suitable conclusion. In the case of Roman encyclicals,

---

49. *Aeterni Patris*, §2, *Acta Leonis* 1, 256f.
50. *Aeterni Patris*, §§29–29, *Acta Leonis* 1, 280f.
51. *ST*, I-II, q. 94, a. 5.

there was also the prudence of papal policies related to governance of the Church, particularly in its dealings with a variety of political situations. Leo explicitly called this level of prudence, concerning "diverse and multiform things," to the attention of the Church.[52] So long as one did not contradict a basic principle, merely plausible lines of interpretation could suffice for fashioning a Thomistic position on such issues as democracy, the social contract, civil toleration of error, and so forth.

To be sure, there is overlap between the two foci. Metaphysical truths about divine providence, the ordination of the soul to a final end, the intelligibility of the good—to mention only a few—stand in both registers. Fundamental issues of anthropology are always Janus-faced, looking in one direction toward preambles of the faith and in another direction toward practical applications in the history of political and economic institutions. Leo wanted Thomism to guide both of these endeavors. But even Leo understood that the social vector had a developmental aspect distinct from the metaphysical and anthropological issues constituting preambles of faith.

Prior to Leo's election to the papacy, Catholic response to the social and political crises were not always Thomistic—not even in a broad, generic sense of the term. As we said, the Romantic reactionaries were anything but "schoolmen." Archbishop Emmanuel von Ketteler used pieces of scholastic philosophy to frame the social question, but he did not have any apparent programmatic interest in Thomism. Dom Guéranger of Solesmes, Antonio Rosmini, and John Henry Newman had much to say about the Church-state problem without relying upon Thomistic, or even scholastic, systematics.

But it is not merely coincidental that the recently restored Society of Jesus would become a kind of sluice gate for Leo's quest to develop a new *doctrina civilis* based upon Thomistic principles. Let us briefly consider why this was so. After their founding in 1640, the Jesuit *ratio studiorum* prescribed the study of Saint Thomas. Although the *Constitutions* of the Society forbade Jesuits from staffing faculties of law,[53] it left them free to teach and publish on the deeper issues of jurisprudence and political philosophy. Thus began the

---

52. "The like disposition and the same order should prevail in the Christian society by so much the more that the political prudence of the Pontiff embraces diverse and multiform things, for it is his charge not only to rule the Church, but generally so to regulate the actions of Christian citizens that these may be in apt conformity to their hope of gaining eternal salvation. Whence it is clear that, in addition to the complete accordance of thought and deed, the faithful should follow the practical political wisdom of the ecclesiastical authority." Pope Leo XIII, Encyclical Letter *Sapientia Christianae* (January 10, 1890), §37, *Acta* 10, 34f.

53. *Constitutions,* cap. XII-4, Gans 215. This is a fact of some importance. Because they were pulled away from the actual practice of the law, Jesuits gravitated to the philosophical and theological issues in jurisprudence.

first systematic modern "schooling" of Thomas's *De legibus*. Some three hundred years after they were written, Thomas's questions on law were excavated, propounded in lectures, summarized in textbooks, and applied not only to casuistical problems but more importantly to the most controversial issues of the time. Cardinal Bellarmine (1542–1621), Juan de Mariana (1536–1624), Louis de Molina (1535–1600), and Francisco Suárez (1548–1617), and a host of lesser lights, made extensive and astute investigations of political order, economics, and relations between the Church and temporal governance.

Like all schools of thought, this neo-Thomism eventually declined in vigor and creativity. Among other reasons, the Jesuits sometimes sailed much too close to the shores of politics. In 1547, the books of Bellarmine and Vitoria were put on the *Index* (only temporarily) for suggesting that the pope did not enjoy *de iure* direct power in matters temporal. Jesuits more often ran afoul of Catholic sovereigns by speculating that political authority is vested inchoately in the body politic, that the original form of government was by nature democratic, that there are, in principle, plural forms of legitimate government; indeed, they argued that heathen peoples have a natural capacity and right of self-governance—rights that include not only standing at private law but also at international law. Yet they were the first to understand and to discuss in print the idea that the emerging common law of modern Catholic Christendom was weakly founded. The principle of Absolutism was not suitable for addressing either the Church-state problems in Europe or the problems of colonization abroad. Canon law did not immediately apply to heathen polities. Despite their support of both the papal and temporal monarchies, the Jesuits' search for a new *doctrina civilis* was potentially subversive.[54] But it was there to be plucked by a new generation of Thomists.

The Jesuits Taparelli and Liberatore had a stake in the systematic and educational reform issues; yet in their quest for a *doctrina civilis*, they rather freely adapted Thomas to contemporary questions of natural rights, private property, and the social principle of subsidiarity—all of which had purchase once one considers the organization and disposition of the modern state, the dislocation of labor, and the suppression of Catholic social institutions.[55] In America, Orestes

---

54. For example, when Rome was enveloped by revolutions of 1848, Pius IX took refuge in the kingdom of Naples. On April 6, 1850, there appeared in Naples the first issue of *Civiltà Cattolica*. The Jesuit editors, however, made the mistake of arguing in one issue that Saint Thomas and the Thomists taught that there are plural, legitimate forms of government. The king of Naples promptly expelled the journal in 1854 on the grounds that it taught doctrines subversive to the state.

55. According to Ernest Fortin, they took on board too much of the modern project. Ernest L. Fortin, "'Sacred and Inviolable': *Rerum Novarum* and Natural Rights," *Theological Studies* 53 (1992): 202–33.

Brownson's *The American Republic* (1865) resourced the ideas of the early modern scholastics to understand and defend the American experiment in republican government and the rule of law. So, too, did Archbishop John Ireland, who used the modern scholastic authors to understand the natural-law foundations of limited government. Ireland took it for granted that the thought of Baroque scholasticism, as applied to the problems of the late nineteenth century, is what the recently elected Pope Leo had in mind. The lesson to be drawn is that Catholics did not view Thomas's political thought as something unmediated by commentators, polemicists, and schools of philosophy, including different schools of Thomism. Catholics were reglossing ideas that had already been once glossed in the sixteenth century, and were being glossed once again.[56]

Thus there emerged a kind of broad Thomism suitable for the political and social issues. When Leo spoke of the "rivulets which [are] derived from the very fount" of the Angelic Doctor, it was often the "rivulets" that seemed especially important. At least in this respect, there is some truth to Lord Acton's claim that Thomas was the "first Whig."[57] He should have said that the Thomists were Whiggish because they developed rather free-wheeling interpretations of the master on disputed issues of political, economic, legal, and social order in modern times, and they showed considerable ingenuity in making their adaptations look continuous with the work of the Angelic Doctor. This penchant for novel interpretations and applications was in full view in Leo's own encyclicals. To take but one example, in *Rerum Novarum* (1891), Leo audaciously used Thomas's *Contra impugnantes*—originally written to defend mendicant poverty and preaching—as the basis for understanding the natural right of laborers to form associations.[58] This is not to mention the point that Ernest Fortin has made regarding Leo's rather interesting

---

56. See Orestes Brownson, *The American Republic* (1865), esp. parts V–VII, for his appropriation of Baroque-era scholasticism, in *The Works of Orestes A. Brownson* (Detroit: Thorndike Nourse, 1885), vol. 18. See, also, Bishop John Ireland's speech at the opening of the Third Plenary Council of Baltimore (November 10, 1884), later published under the title "The Catholic Church and Civil Society," and collected in *John Ireland, The Church and Modern Society: Lectures and Addresses* (Chicago: D. H. McBride & Co., 1896), 7–47. Here I put to one side the debate between historical purists and innovators in order to make the point that it is historically naive to believe that Thomas's political thought was suddenly hijacked by twentieth-century Catholic liberals. See Heinrich Rommen's rather pointed remarks on this subject in his review of Jacques Maritain's "Man and the State," *Commonweal* 54 (1951): 239–42.

57. John Dalberg-Acton, *Selected Writings of Lord Acton*, vol. 3, *Essays in Religion, Politics, and Morality*, ed. J. Rufus Fears (Indianapolis: Liberty Classics, 1988), 536; and vol. 1, *Essays in the History of Liberty*, 34. Acton was here thinking of the doctrine of liberty and just revolution.

58. *Rerum Novarum*, §§51–53, *Acta* 11, 134–37.

incorporation of a Lockean understanding of property rights (to possession and not merely private use) according to a labor theory of value.[59]

None of this should suggest that Leo or his advisors were uninterested in the authentic teachings of Thomas on matters social and political. While Leo never made a list of core doctrines, there were certain principles that framed what could count as plausible interpretations. Chief among these were the teaching on the eternal law, the participation in that law by natural reason, the harmony of faith and reason, the twofold order of divine providence, the priority of intellect to the will in practical reasoning, the common good as the measure of the political order, the penultimacy of political society, and so forth. All of these, and more, had solid foundation in Thomas. Equipped with only a few principles properly delineated and connected, one could go on to make considerable headway in developing a social doctrine.

We should bear in mind that in this sector of the Leonine program the aim was not to produce a pure Thomism to which social doctrine could be appended as so many conclusions; rather it was a quest, lasting over several pontificates, for a social doctrine. Moving from the mid-nineteenth to the mid-twentieth century, the problems continued to change along with the political, legal, and economic facts on the ground. Thomism was a resource for the project, but not its end. Beginning with the Jesuit editors at *Civiltà Cattolica* who cobbled together pieces of Thomism for a wide array of public policy problems, the Thomism in social thought was pluralistic and somewhat eclectic in the order of application.[60] Liberatore was a Suárezian of sorts, Taparelli was not, even though his systematics in social questions reached far beyond the original texts of Thomas.[61]

Convinced that a new *doctrina civilis* was long overdue, Leo gave his Thomists permission to do four things. First, to resurrect the doctrine of plural legitimate forms of regimes. This was the sore spot of the Baroque tradition, and in Leo's time it was still a neuralgic issue for the remnants of the Catholic right-wing, particularly in France. Second, to speculatively reengage the so-called translation theory of authority, according to which God, by the natural law, vests authority originally though inchoately in the body politic. This seemed to be a promising way to give a scholastic foundation to political consent, and brought the Thomist tradition to the vestibule of democratic theory. Leo himself did not officially take a position one way or the other on the

---

59. See Fortin, "'Sacred and Inviolable,'" 203–33.

60. See Walter T. Odell, "The Political Theory of Civiltà Cattolica from 1850 to 1870" (PhD diss., Georgetown University, 1969).

61. On Liberatore, see Gerald McCool, *The Neo-Thomists* (Milwaukee: Marquette University Press, 1994), 33. On Taparelli, see Robert Jacquin, *Taparelli* (Paris: P. Lethielleux, 1943).

matter, but he made it clear that he would not rule out the so-called "translation" theory.[62] Third, to integrate natural law and natural rights. Fourth, to
allow analysis of historical change to play a role in the prudence of state-
making.[63] All of these matters were discussed in Leo's encyclicals, but the Leonine vector of thought was completed in the work of a generation of thinkers
who were born in the waning years of his pontificate: Luigi Sturzo (b. 1881),
Jacques Maritain (b. 1882), Charles Journet (b. 1891), Heinrich Rommen (b.
1897), Yves Simon (b. 1903), and John Courtney Murray (b. 1904).[64]

---

62. No issue better displays the plurality of opinions and different schools of Thomism
in the area of political philosophy. Translation theorists held that political authority is vested
by God implicitly in the body politic, which then, by implicit or express consent "translates"
that authority into a particular form or regime. Designation theorists held that while political authority comes from God, the human act of consent does not transfer or translate
power to command from its original bearer, but rather designates the incumbent. There is
no *ex professo* treatment of the issue in Thomas. The history of the debate is considered
carefully by Jeremiah Newman, who makes the sensible point that translation theory
achieved its first elaboration during the struggle against absolute monarchs, while the designation theory was devised to put a brake upon democratic extremism during the age of
revolutions. See Jeremiah Newman, *Studies in Political Morality* (Dublin: Scepter, 1962),
19. With the collapse of the papal states, and with Leo's decision to adopt a more creative
stance toward the new states, the translation theory came back in vogue. Cardinal Cajetan
(1480–1547), in his commentary on *ST*, II-II, q. 50, a. 1, ad 3, introduced the notion of
the people translating authority to a king (*potestatem in eum transtulerunt*), and then went
on to speculate about a primordial election. Cajetan's commentary was included in the
1895 Leonine edition of the *Opera S. Thomae*. During Leo's time, Cardinal Billot explained
that Leo denied what has "always been denied with unanimous consent by Catholic theologians," namely, that the people create the *principatus*. This left the question entirely
open, for both sides held the premise that political power, as such, is not a human construct.
For Billot's response, see Alfred O'Rahilly, "The Sovereignty of the People," *Studies: An
Irish Quarterly Review* 10 (1921): 39–56, 277–87. Elsewhere, O'Rahilly lists some 139
scholastic thinkers who held the translation theory. See his "Theology of Tyranny," *Irish
Theological Quarterly* 15 (1920): 301–20. After the rise of the totalitarian regimes in the
1920s, the translation theory commanded the consent of virtually all Thomists working
the area of social doctrine. See Pius XII's *Address to the Roman Rota*, October 2, 1945:
"We bear in mind the favorite thesis of democracy—a doctrine which great Christian
thinkers have proclaimed in all ages—namely, that the original subject of civil power derived
from God is the people (not the 'masses')" (*AAS*, 37, 258ff.). What we learn from this fas-
cinating and somewhat exasperating tangle of interpretations is that Thomists had quite
different opinions on the role of human consent in matters political, that they changed
opinions over time, and that the evolution of opinion tracked very closely the evolving character of Catholic social thought in light of current political conditions. It is but one case in
point for appreciating how Leo launched a Thomism "in motion" as it were.

63. Regarding these permissions, see Ch. 5 of this collection.

64. By the 1940s it was not so easy to distinguish Thomas and the Thomists on matters of political philosophy. The ever-astute Leo Strauss expressed bewilderment at the

Leo was engaged in a new kind of "paper war." He took the outmoded structure of a medieval scholastic "article" (for example, what we find in the *Summa theologiae*, with the question, the objections, the *sed contra*, the response, and replies to objections), then he changed the questions and rebuilt the "article" in the prose of an encyclical teaching. It was in part dialectic, in part systematic, and in part apologetic. There was no need to make lists of errors that left Catholics scratching their heads about what had to be affirmed or negated. For example, if we take the most controversial proposition of Pius IX's *Syllabus*—"The Roman Pontiff can, and ought to, reconcile himself, and come to terms with progress, liberalism, and recent civilization"—we convert it into a negation: "The Roman Pontiff need not reconcile himself with progress, liberalism, and recent civilization." The negation is then converted into an affirmation: "By natural right, workers and their families may justly claim to organize and to bargain for living wages, the doctrines of *laissez-faire* liberalism notwithstanding." Hence, we have the encyclical *Rerum Novarum*. All of Leo's major encyclicals on social and political questions can be read in just this fashion. He begins with a question, surveys the authorities, affirms the harmony of faith and reason, and then goes on to construct a teaching on the question at hand.

LEO'S *PHARMAKON* AND PIUS X'S PRESCRIPTIONS

Leo's response to the political and social aspects of modernity proved very successful. For one thing, there was no living memory of a pope doing this kind of work—namely, doing something more than issuing ad hoc complaints or making lists of errors. At least on questions of political and social order— the role of consent, the importance of historical change, the proper role of human creativity in exercising prudence in political foundings, the quest of the third estate for natural rights limiting the state—Leo made use of the *pharmakon*, the thing that is both the disease and the cure. The subversive questions of the Enlightenment were brought within the purview of the Catholic tradition, where they were corrected and harmonized with Catholic truth.

---

extent to which Thomists were revising medieval terms to fit contemporary discussions. See, for example, his generally favorable review of Heinrich A. Rommen: Leo Strauss, "Review of Heinrich A. Rommen, *The State in Catholic Thought: A Treatise in Political Philosophy*," *Social Research* 13 (1946): 250–52; see also Leo Strauss, *What Is Political Philosophy? and Other Studies* (Chicago: University of Chicago Press, 1988), 281–84. But see also his more critical evaluation of Yves Simon (pp. 306–11) and Anton Pegis (pp. 284–86) in that same collection. Interestingly, Strauss recognized the difference between adaptations in political-institutional questions and fundamental principles in the philosophy of nature. In his review of Pegis, he was unforgiving where he detected compromise on the systematic issues.

From philosophers like Marsilius of Padua to Locke to Rousseau, and on issues running from Church-state relations to the origin of authority, and from problems of class warfare to international law, Leo believed that social doctrine enabled the Church to be something more than the outsider in modern life.[65]

The underlying scholastic doctrine gave the body of work at least the appearance of coherence; and as Leo's successors, as well as lay and clerical scholars, continued the project, there emerged a remarkably structured but evolving body of social doctrine. In many respects, it was more sophisticated than its secular rivals. It proved successful because the Leonine project was ready to ascertain what is open or closed in the secular mind, and to use the right mixture of dialectics and systematics to move the latter toward the former. Finally, it proved successful because his lengthy pontificate was the seedbed for six future popes.[66] This allowed a virtually contemporaneous communication of the method and its application to new issues. By 1950, the Leonine project had established itself as a different kind of liberalism that survived the crises of the twentieth century. It was robust and confident. After the Second Vatican Council, the only significant resistances to this vector of doctrine were the neo-Gallicans in France (Marcel Lefevre) and Liberationists in Latin America.

But this brings us back to *Pascendi* and to our over-arching theme of "Two Modernisms, Two Thomisms." Pius X went back into the mode of making lists of errors. *Lamentabili Sane* listed sixty-five errors. To complicate matters, Pius also referenced the encyclical *Auctorem Fidei* (1794), which condemned a list of another eighty-five propositions in connection with Jansenism.[67] A scrupulous scholar under ecclesiastical discipline now found himself reckoning with 150 propositions; and if we include the *Syllabus of Errors*, 230 erroneous propositions. Who could keep track of all these errors?

Charity of interpretation requires us to concede that Leo had the advantage of dealing with a different sector of Liberalism, and in Catholic affairs,

---

65. As John Paul II said in *Centesimus Annus*, §5: "*Rerum novarum* gave the Church citizenship status."

66. Pius X (b. 1835), Benedict XIV (b. 1854), Pius XI (1857), Pius XII (b. 1876), John XXIII (b. 1881), Paul VI (b. 1897).

67. Pius X, *Pascendi*, §24, *Acta* 5, 73. From the Synod of Pistoia, a schismatic synod held in Tuscany in 1786. See Denzinger-Hünermann (1997), §§2600–2700. During the turmoil of the French Revolution, while the Catholic sovereigns were distracted by the war, Pius VI condemned propositions tinctured with Febronian (Jansenist) principles on ecclesiastical and civil relations. Interestingly, by 1907 those propositions had been condemned and rendered defunct not only by Pius VI, but by the *Syllabus* of Pius IX, by the decrees of the First Vatican Council, but also in several of Leo's encyclicals. Why would Pius X want to resurrect a battle that had already been won by the Church of Rome? The answer probably lies in the few passages in *Lamentabili* and *Pascendi* touching upon the analogies and disanalogies between ecclesiological and political order. See note 69 below.

with a different species of Liberal. Montalembert, Lacordaire, Lamennais (through his mid-career, before he defected), and Rosmini were liberal but pro-papal. Montalembert's most famous work was his multivolume *The Monks of the West*, dedicated to Pope Pius IX—he was hardly a Hans Küng in-the-making.[68] These men had no interest in impeaching the deposit of sacred doctrine or of appealing to history in order to suggest profound discontinuity in theology proper. Pius X was dealing with an entirely different kind of theological liberal who resented the post-1870 Roman authority emancipated from civil or democratic control, and who rejected not only Leo's Thomism but scholasticism itself.

Leo also had the advantage of focusing upon the institutional survival of the Church, as well as the array of social institutions clustered around it. Even though it had taken more than three hundred years to develop an adequate *doctrina civilis*, once Rome recovered its bearings, this task played to the strong suit of Church unity against external threats. More often than not the misbehavior of the nation-states only reinforced the perception among Catholics (and non-Catholics) that Leo's teachings were well measured. Disciplinary action *ad intra* could be handled within the ordinary politics and prudence of the pontifical office as well as through the usual instrument of Vatican diplomacy. Clearly, this was an easier battle than tracking down heretical professors in one's own seminaries, where the Church would seem to play the role of the bully. The Oath Against Modernism (*Sacrorum Antistitum*, 1910) and the institution of committees of vigilance at the parish levels certainly distracted attention from the serious theological issues discussed in *Pascendi*.

Pius X turned inward and fixed upon the other set of issues that stood close to sacred doctrine. In *Lamentabili*, only six of the sixty-five propositions remotely touch upon the social questions. In *Pascendi*, we find perhaps three paragraphs in the sphere of social-political thought.[69] Interestingly, in all of Pius X's teaching letters, the favorite Leonine theme of the "eternal law," which constituted the synthetic fulcrum of his social teaching, is mentioned but once.[70] For Pius X, the "synthesis of all heresies" was a different sort of

---

68. Here, paraphrasing Marvin R. O'Connell's insight, in *Critics on Trial: An Introduction to the Catholic Modernist Crisis* (Washington, DC: The Catholic University of America Press, 1994), 14.

69. In *Lamentabili*, §§52, 53, 56–59, *Acta* 5, 83, attack the idea that the Church should be understood primarily in social and historical terms. In *Pascendi*, Pius X criticizes the reduction of the Church to a democratic form (§23, *Acta* 5, 71f.), the inferiority of the Church to the state on *mixti quaestionibus*, on issues of overlapping jurisdiction such as marriage and education (§24, *Acta* 5, 72), and the notion that religion is purely spiritual, without authority in the order of external acts (§25, *Acta* 5, 73f.). All of these were fighting issues for Pius IX and Leo XIII.

70. I rely on the word count by Elsbernd, *Papal Statements on Rights*, 406.

Modernism. At least in the sphere of sacred doctrine and the metaphysical principles conjoined to it by way of preambles, there could be no compromise, nor could there be a development analogous to what was already underway in social teaching. Inevitably, Thomism would be put in a defensive role not only with regard to the deployment of its philosophical theology but also in terms of ecclesiastical discipline.

The apparatus of ecclesiastical discipline consisted not merely of what had accrued from the decretum *Lamentabili*, the encyclical *Pascendi*, and *motu proprio Sacrorum Antistitum* (the Oath Against Modernism, 1910). Some of the impetus for internal discipline arose from questions not quite settled by Leo. In the first year of his pontificate, Pius X sent a brief to the Roman Academy of St. Thomas, noting that Leo's plan for installing Thomism in the seminaries was not moving along satisfactorily.[71] Institutional resistance began not with the Modernists, but inside the Society of Jesus during Leo's own pontificate. Four years after *Aeterni Patris*, at their XXIII General Congregation (1883), the Jesuits pledged their allegiance to the plan of the encyclical, but at the same time expressed esteem for their own scholastics and masters, such as Suárez. This prompted a mild but clear admonition from Leo concerning any derogation from the unity of doctrine. A decade later, the General of the Society, Luis Martín, inquired whether Jesuit teachers were required to follow Thomas's "real distinction" between essence and the act of existence in creatures. Again, Leo replied that the Society's *Constitutions* required the teaching of Thomas's doctrines, though he added that adherence to the Angelic Doctor did not imply any lack of esteem for the erudition and profundity of the Jesuit doctors. This was a delicate situation indeed; for in the sphere of social, political, and legal thought, the Baroque-era Jesuit thinkers provided useful resources for the development of political theory. Moreover, the minds of some of Leo's own teachers and colleagues were more than a little tinctured with Suárezianism. But the social doctrine was not the problem. Rather, at issue was the unity of the metaphysical theses constituting the *praeambula fidei*. Leo made his *mind* clear on this matter. Seminarians were not to be trained in plural metaphysical systems, which at this point in time meant plural Thomisms.

Pius X intended to supply something more than exhortation. The sure sign of Modernism was derogation from, or even disparagement of, Scholasticism.

---

71. Pius X, *In Praecipuous Laudibus*, Acta Sanctae Sedis 36, 654 (1903–1904). For the controversy over Thomism during the pontificate of Pius X and for the precise sequence of events leading to the publication of the XXIV theses in 1914, I rely on the fine work of Jesús Villagrasa, LC, "Origin, Nature and Initial Reception of the XXIV Thomistic Theses in the Light of the Controversy Between Neo-Thomism and Suarezianism," *Doctor Angelicus* 6 (2006): 193–230. See, also, the collection he recently edited, Jesús Villagrasa, LC, ed., *Neotomismo & Suarezismo* (Roma: Ateneo Pontificio Regina Apostolorum, 2006).

Whether it is ignorance or fear, or both, that inspires this conduct in them, certain it is that the passion for novelty is always united in them with hatred of scholasticism, and there is no surer sign that a man is tending to Modernism than when he begins to show his dislike for the scholastic method.[72]

To be heard "carping" (*carpendo*) at Scholasticism was a ground for dismissing either faculty or administrators in ecclesiastical schools.[73] Lest there be any doubt what is meant by Scholasticism, Pius X issued a *motu proprio Doctoris Angelici* (1914), putting the Thomistic norm for studies (in degree-granting ecclesiastical schools) explicitly under precept from the Holy See. In order to curb the private opinions of professors, Pius X ordered that the text of the *Summa theologiae* be used as the text of the lectures and that professorial comments be restricted to Latin (*et latino sermone explicent*).[74] Understanding how unlikely it would be that the entirety of the *Summa* would be so taught, Pius X added: "It goes without saying that Our intention was to be understood as referring above all to those principles upon which that philosophy is based as its foundations [*principiis maxime hoc intelligi voluisse, quibus, tamquam fundamentis*]."[75] These principles, fundaments, or "capital theses" (*capita*) are not to be "placed in the category of opinions capable of being debated one way or the other."[76] Importantly, none of the social and political issues, which were already being vigorously debated and expounded, appear among the principles targeted in the *motu proprio*.

History teaches that to even hint at a list of core principles requires one to say more. Hence, a few weeks later, virtually on the eve of Pius X's death in 1914, Cardinal Lorenzelli, Prefect of the Sacred Congregation for Studies, published a list of XXIV theses.[77] These include, at the outset of the list, an affirmation of the divine being as pure act, in contrast to the admixture of potency in creatures.[78] They comprise metaphysical theses of just the sort that Pius X said cannot be placed "in the category of opinions capable of being debated." Everyone understood that the XXIV theses were aimed in the direction of Suárez, beginning with the doctrine of the real distinction between essence and existence in creatures, which was not generally held by the

---

72. Pius X, *Pascendi*, §42, *Acta* 5, 98.
73. *Pascendi*, §48, *Acta* 5, 104.
74. Pius X, Motu Proprio *Doctoris Angelici* (June 29, 1914), *AAS* 6, 340.
75. *Doctoris Angelici*, *AAS* 6, 337.
76. *Doctoris Angelici*, *AAS* 6, 338.
77. *Decretum*, *AAS* 6, 383–86; Denzinger-Hünermann (1997), §§3601–3624.
78. On the context and effects of the theses, see Fergus Kerr, *Twentieth-Century Catholic Theologians: From Neoscholasticism to Nuptial Mysticism* (Oxford: Blackwell Publishing, 2007), 3–4, 21–24.

Suárezians. The advisors who labored on the list did, in fact, worry that another summary list of truths (or corresponding errors) would be received as a compendium, and thus might suggest that Thomistic principles are to be found simply within the four corners of the list. Editors at *La Civiltà Cattolica* noted that the subtlety of interpretations is built in the questions themselves. The editors were too discreet to draw the obvious conclusion: that learning to think Thomistically requires the student to learn how to grapple with very complex and subtle metaphysical issues. Still other churchmen worried that the new list would appear to be a "piece of propaganda" that might impugn the seriousness and authority of Thomas.[79]

TWO THOMISMS

When Pius X died on August 20, 1914, there were "two Thomisms," one broadly devised and oriented to social questions, the other narrow and consisting of *capita* which could not be debated. The former was ensconced in the ordinary prose and philosophical expositions within the encyclical tradition, the latter in the newly framed lists of errors and truths. In 1917 there was planned an international Congress in Granada, celebrating the third centenary of the death of Suárez. The Catholic press, of course, noted that the XXIV theses had impeached the reliability of Suárez on certain questions of metaphysics.[80] Moreover, the newly drafted, soon to be promulgated *Code of Canon Law* (1917) required those in charge of religious and clerical formation to teach the "principles of the Angelic Doctor and hold to them religiously."[81] The Congress did not juridically fall under the disciplinary decretals, but it was an awkward moment nonetheless. Apparently, Rome recommended that the Congress focus upon the social, political, and international-law aspects of Suárez's thought. On these matters, one was permitted to avow an evolving line of thought and to celebrate its utility in handling modern problems.

We have highlighted only a few important moments and problems in the emergence of these two foci of modernity to which Thomism was applied. At least in passing, we should say that the field of social doctrine was not wide open. Political programs and movements could run afoul of Roman authority, as did Marc Sangnier's *Le Sillon* (1910), and on the other end of the political

---

79. See Villagrasa, "Origin, Nature and Initial Reception," 229.

80. On the Granada Congress, see Villagrasa, "Origin, Nature and Initial Reception," 225–26. It should also be noted that the Congress provided Fr. Luis Alonso Getino with a timely opportunity to correlate the XXIV authentically Thomist theses with the errors of Suárez. This work, in parallel columns, is included in *Neotomisimo & Suarezismo*. See the appendix titled, "Tesi di Tommaso d'Aquino e di Francisco Suárez," 165–78.

81. *Code of Canon Law* (1917), can. 1366, §2. See also can. 595, §1.

spectrum, *L'Action Française* (1926). Moreover, significant differences between Thomas and Suárez on both the epistemological and metaphysical foundations of law were well-known both to clerical and lay scholars. But our general point holds true. So long as one did not advocate Bolshevism or state control of the Church or reduction of ecclesiological principles to match those of (democratic) civil government, one had to rather egregiously run afoul of Roman diplomatic or political policies to be censured in the area of social theory. Important, if subtle, differences within the Thomistic schools were aired and debated at an academic level.[82] Undoubtedly, these debates could have a practical impact within a particular school, faculty, or religious order. Even so, opinions were not put completely out of bounds in the same way as the Pian disciplinary actions. Decades later, John Courtney Murray, SJ, was censured for his opinions on Church-state questions, but this had nothing immediately to do with Thomism. Rather, his troubles ensued upon a spitting match with Cardinal Ottaviani, then the dean of ecclesiastical public law.[83]

---

82. Suárez taught that command (*imperium*) is chiefly an act of the will rather than of intellect. This had implications for the doctrine on the Eternal Law, and could not be reasonably accommodated either to Thomas's teaching or to Leo's stout intellectualism in matters of law (and kindred aspects of practical reason). The best treatment of the similarities and differences between Thomas and Suárez on natural law and metaphysics of participation is the doctoral thesis written at the University of Fribourg by Walter Farrell, OP, *The Natural Moral Law According to St. Thomas and Suarez* (Ditchling: St. Dominic's Press, 1930). Like Fr. Getino's 1917 article on the XXIV theses, Farrell puts the Thomistic and Suárezian theses on law into parallel columns (148–52). Farrell is at pains to explain why and how the most important differences are subtle. He does not invoke ecclesiastical discipline to make his argument. Only in the conclusion does he discreetly observe that Suárez's voluntaristic bent comports with "a decidedly popular theory in modern statecraft." In effect, he suggests that Suárez cannot deliver the foundations for which Thomism was being revived in matters legal and political. On this score, see Vernon Bourke's obituary for Heinrich Rommen, "In Memoriam: Heinrich Albert Rommen (1897–1967)," *Natural Law Forum* 12 (1967): vii-viii. A Thomist of the more strict observance, Bourke explicitly notes that Rommen's Suárezian studies never led him into some of the more disputable voluntaristic theses.

83. John Courtney Murray, SJ, first cut his teeth on the Baroque-era scholastics and on the post-1789 reactionaries: "St. Robert Bellarmine on the Indirect Power," *Theological Studies* 9 (1948): 491–535; and John Courtney Murray, "Political Thought of Joseph de Maistre," *Review of Politics* 11 (1949): 63–86. On Thomas's social, legal, and political thought, Murray's opinions were mostly derivative of work already finished. See, for example, Heinrich Rommen's *The State in Catholic Thought* (German 1935, English 1945). Murray and Rommen admired one another, but Rommen was the senior scholar, and it was to Rommen rather than Murray that the *New Catholic Encyclopedia* turned in the early 1960s for its entry on the State. "The State," *New Catholic Encyclopedia*, vol. XIII (New York: McGraw-Hill Book Co., 1967), 644–54. Relying on work already done by others, Murray's genius was not as a commentator on Thomas but rather his uncanny ability to

In the summer of 1914, it was clear that intramural disputes among Thomists had been brought into the Modernist controversy. Popes soon began to have second thoughts about this strange and potentially crippling consequence. Beginning with Benedict XV, they were unwilling to strictly enforce Pius X's "official" Thomism within the seminaries and the ranks of religious orders. While the exhortations of Leo and the precepts of Pius X were duly noted by Benedict and his successors, rigorous enforcement proved to be the exception rather than the rule. Indeed, only five months after Pius X's death, Benedict conceded that there is room "for divergent opinions" so long as they constitute no "harm to faith or discipline" and so long as they are expressed "with due moderation."[84] He explicitly warned that no one should take upon himself the role of impugning the orthodoxy of others and affixing "the stigma of disloyalty to faith or to discipline." His successors adopted the same policy, insisting on the normativity of Thomas *in re metaphysica*, while at the same time quietly acting to prevent the in-house educational system from becoming politically suffocating.[85] Yet this prudent policy could not remove the sense among faculty and students that in the systematic area it was necessary to tread carefully. As James Weisheipl concluded many years later:

> Not even the ardent efforts of Pius X, Benedict XV, Pius XI, or Pius XII were able to effect anything more than a closed, safe, and sterile

---

discern developmental threads in papal teachings. He carefully studied the magisterial documents from Pius IX up to John XXIII, and was able to cite chapter-and-verse, as it were, the "growing end" of the tradition. In the summer of 1964, he circulated a brief that was later published under the title "The Problem of Religious Freedom" (1964, 1993). Tracing the crisis through the *Syllabus of Errors* and the letters of Leo XIII, Murray showed why the crisis called for a recovery of "the Gregorian state of the question of public care of religion," as well as a new discernment of the "'growing end' of the tradition." The brief circulated at the Council: John Courtney Murray, "The Problem of Religious Freedom," in *Religious Liberty: Catholic Struggles with Pluralism*, ed. J. Leon Hooper, SJ. (Louisville, KY: Westminster John Knox Press, 1993), 165, 188.

84. Benedict XV, Encyclical Letter *Ad beatissimi* (November 1, 1914), §23, *AAS* 6, 576f.

85. On the gradual amelioration of the disciplinary decretals, one can read José Pereira, "Thomism and the Magisterium: From *Aeterni Patris* to *Veritatis Splendor*," *Logos* 5 (2002): 147–83. He does not distinguish, as we do, between the different sectors of Thomism (social-political and metaphysical), and is concerned entirely with the problem and, in his estimation, the inanity of an officially imposed philosophy. Pereira would seem to make the canonical and disciplinary actions the measure of the papal esteem for Thomism. This confusion is answered by Steven Long's keynote address, "The Thomistic Meta-Structure of John Paul II's Doctrinal Initiatives" (Lilly Foundation sponsored seminar on "The Vocation of the Catholic Intellectual," Center for Catholic Studies, University of St. Thomas, St. Paul, MN, 2003).

Thomism, imposed by legislative authority. Legislation did not stimulate a return to the authentic thought and spirit of St. Thomas. Legislation led rather to the production of safe textbooks.[86]

Weisheipl correctly distinguishes this in-house Thomism from the more creative Thomism developed in social thought: "on social problems, government, human liberty, sacred scripture, Catholic Action, marriage, and education."[87]

Benedict's amelioration of the decretals was motivated by a desire to prevent the Modernism crisis from engulfing the internal order with unnecessary disputes and accusations. However, another factor was in play. With the disaster of the Great War and the rise of the totalitarian regimes, the papacy's attention was funneled back into the social and political issues. The shift of magisterial attention back to political modernity is particularly evident during the pontificate of Pius XI (Achille Ratti). As a young cleric, Ratti had been trained by Leo's Thomistic colleagues in Rome. In two encyclicals he weighed in on the issue of the program of ecclesiastical studies and formation.

In *Studiorum Ducem* (1923), Pius XI extolled the virtues of Thomas: "[I]t will be sufficient perhaps to point out that Thomas wrote under the inspiration of the supernatural spirit which animated his life and that his writings, which contain the principles of, and the laws governing, all sacred studies, must be said to possess a universal character."[88] He approvingly quotes Pius X's admonition that there must be no deviation from Thomas, *praesertim in re metaphysica*,[89] and he very clearly reiterates the conviction that the organization and presentation of sacred doctrine require the preambles, or "reasons for belief" drawn from philosophy.[90] This core of metaphysical systematics must be preserved intact, even while allowing the "lovers of Thomas" (*amatores sancti Thomae*) to engage in "honorable rivalry in a just and proper freedom which is the life-blood of studies."[91]

But what is most striking about *Studiorum Ducem* is Pius XI's interest in the social and political issues. One might think of a team that had trouble running the ball but still knew how to throw the pass and make the big play in social doctrine. In the section on the preambles, for example, he includes Thomas's contributions "in the science of morals, in sociology and law, by laying down sound principles of legal and social, commutative and distributive

---

86. Weisheipl, "Thomism as a Christian Philosophy," 184. He is speaking of the official Thomism within ecclesiastical institutions.

87. Weisheipl, "Thomism as a Christian Philosophy," 177.

88. Pius XI, Encyclical Letter *Studiorum Ducem* (June 29, 1923), §11, *AAS* 15, 314f.

89. *Studiorum Ducem*, §16, *AAS* 15, 317.

90. *Studiorum Ducem*, §27, *AAS* 15, 322.

91. *Studiorum Ducem*, §30, *AAS* 15, 323.

justice and explaining the relations between justice and charity."[92] The over-arching theme of the Pian pontificate, the rule of Christ the King, also needed preambles drawn from the natural order. He writes:

> He [Thomas] also composed a substantial moral theology, capable of directing all human acts in accordance with the supernatural last end of man. And as he is, as We have said, the perfect theologian, so he gives infallible rules and precepts of life not only for individuals, but also for civil and domestic society which is the object also of moral science, both economic and politic. Hence those superb chapters in the second part of the *Summa Theologica* on paternal or domestic government, the lawful power of the State or the nation, natural and international law, peace and war, justice and property, laws and the obedience they command, the duty of helping individual citizens in their need and cooperating with all to secure the prosperity of the State, both in the natural and the supernatural order. If these precepts were religiously and inviolably observed in private life and public affairs, and in the duties of mutual obligation between nations, nothing else would be required to secure mankind that "peace of Christ in the Kingdom of Christ" which the world so ardently longs for. It is therefore to be wished that the teachings of Aquinas, *more particularly* his exposition [*praesertim explicando*] of international law and the laws governing the mutual relations of peoples, became more and more studied, for it contains the foundations of a genuine "League of Nations."[93]

While adhering to Pius X's prescriptions regarding what must be adhered to (*praesertim in re metaphysica*), he returns to the Leonine project of what especially needs to be explicated (*praestertim explicando*). Interestingly, it is not the *prima pars*, with its metaphysical armature, but rather the *secunda pars* of the *Summa*, on human conduct. This line of thought is repeated in *Divini Illius Magistri* (1929), which takes up the problem of education, chiefly *ad extra*—in families, in schools, and particularly in the face of claims by governments to enjoy a monopoly on education. Here, Pius recommends Luigi Taparelli's work on natural right—"a work never sufficiently praised and recommended to university students."[94] *Divini Illius* is also the first encyclical to cite an American Supreme Court decision, *Pierce* v. *Society of Sisters* (1925), in which the Court insisted that "the child is not the mere creature of the State."[95]

---

92. *Studiorum Ducem*, §27, *AAS* 15, 322.

93. *Studiorum Ducem*, §20, *AAS* 15, 319.

94. Luigi Taparelli, *Saggio teoretico di Diritto Naturale, Appoggiato sul fatto* [A Theoretical Treatise on Natural Right, Based on Fact] (Roma, 1840–1843); Pius XI, Encyclical Letter *Divini Illius Magistri* (December 31, 1929), *AAS* 22, 65n27.

95. Pius XI, *Divini Illius Magistri*, §37, citing *Pierce* v. *Society of Sisters* (1925), 268 US, 534–35.

On balance, Pius XI held together the two Thomisms, but with the broad and synthetic Leonine approach to the social and political issues put front and center, because he believed that political modernism was by no means rendered defunct by the Great War. In his first encyclical, Pius had distinguished two modernisms: "There is a species of moral, legal, and social modernism which We condemn, no less decidedly than We condemn theological modernism."[96] As the political crises mounted in Europe and Latin America, Pius XI gave a certain cachet to this broad Thomism by canonizing Robert Bellarmine in 1931, and by making him a Doctor of the Church the following year. It was Bellarmine's social and political thought that was held up as exemplary for the Church's struggle against state absolutism.

SOME CONCLUSIONS

We set out to show how Thomas's thought was resurrected and put into play with respect to problems posed by political modernity and then by the philosophical and theological issues related to the Modernism crisis of the early twentieth century. We looked at these two foci primarily from the standpoint and documents of the Roman Magisterium. All of these matters need to be delineated at a more detailed and complete level. But if our narrative is generally correct, we can draw four conclusions. The first two would seem to follow rather directly from our exposition; the second two are more hypothetical, needing careful thought beyond the bounds of this essay.

First, the Roman attempt for issuing syllabi and lists of errors (and truths) did not necessarily achieve the results for which the lists were designed. Whether in response to political or philosophical modernity, from the early lists in the Jansenist controversy, such as *Unigenitus* (1713), through the *Syllabus of Errors* (1864), and then up to *Lamentabili* (1907) and the XXIV theses (1914), the lists sparked confusions. On balance, the Leonine practice of encyclical teaching was more effective, both *ad extra* and *ad intra*. Encyclicals provided magisterial models that could be completed by scholars.

Second, the list-making approach did not play to the strong suit of Thomism, which requires not only definitions and conclusions but also a deeply textured set of questions and distinctions. Particularly on social

---

96. *Ubi arcano* (1922), §61, *AAS* 14, 696: "In quo genus quoddam modernismi moralis, iuridici ac socialis est agnoscendum; quod quidem, una cum modernismo illo dogmatico." Interestingly, Pius's citations of Thomas and Augustine, as well as his citations of the pronouncements of his immediate predecessors (Leo XIII, Pius X, and Benedict XV), are concerned exclusively with the *genus moralis/socialis*.

questions, the developmental curve entails an exquisite balance of principles and facts. On the one hand, it is dependent upon ever-changing historical events. On the other hand, the post-1789 questions could hardly be answered just by repairing to Thomas's treatment of political matters in the thirteenth century. These questions had been glossed by several centuries of scholastic commentary and, after the election of Leo, by the tradition of papal encyclicals that provided a new template for bringing Thomas's thought to modern problems. Skill in this area required one to know Thomas (and Aristotle), the commentators, and the new applications forged in the crucible of magisterial teachings. As we explained, the vector of social thought got a head start over the recovery of Thomas's metaphysics. For nearly a generation, therefore, the recovery of the systematics and its deployment in the curricula of schools had to play catch-up; and it had to do so while laboring under the disadvantage of trying to forge a consensus among different schools of Thomism, which had crystallized their opinions over the course of several centuries. Opinions were hardened, too, by loyalties within religious orders and their lay associates. In social thought, however, the "schooling" of Thomism allowed more consensus because the material was permeable to the politico-ecclesiastical needs and policies of Leo and his successors.

For their part, the metaphysical issues were complex and subtle. They are difficult on their own terms, never mind the practical questions of how to instantiate and to enforce them in educational institutions. The XXIV theses were not strictly juridical in nature, though it was perhaps naive to think that they would not be regarded as glosses on the canonical and other disciplinary *apparatus*. The theses rather tried to expose the deep veins of Thomas's metaphysics. By and large, these veins were much deeper than what many faculty or students could have mastered even under the best conditions. A slight and passing familiarity with Thomas's system, usually acquired secondhand, was almost bound to breed that kind of contempt that comes from knowing a little but not enough. Leo and his successors certainly wanted to keep Thomism in the intelligible rather than in the merely canonical or disciplinary order.[97] Just how to enkindle Thomism as a living pattern of thought, and by what combination of exhortation and precept, proved to be a very difficult problem.

Third, although it would take us far beyond the bounds of our present essay, it would be useful to ask whether Leo's aim for a systematic Thomism

---

97. As Thomas himself wrote in *Contra retrahentes*, c. 13: "It is unseemly and rather ridiculous for professors of sacred doctrine to cite the little glosses of canon lawyers as theological authorities, or to make them the basis of argument" (*quamvis inconsonum et derisibile videatur quod sacrae doctrinae professores, iuristarum glossulas in auctoritatem inducant, vel de eis disceptent*). I thank Steven Long for calling my attention to this gem.

in re metaphysica did not harbor a tension. On the one hand, he discerned the need for a careful exposition of the preambles needed for a scientific organization of sacred doctrine. On the other hand, he wanted systematic Thomism to build a bridge of discourse with contemporary philosophies and sciences. The two are related, of course, but they are not exactly the same kind of work, nor do they include (in the context of modern academics and scholarship) exactly the same audience.

The official discipline, though duly relaxed after 1914, created disgruntlement within clerical ranks. Academicians began to question the need for philosophically organized *praeambula fidei*. Such dissatisfaction could take the route of wanting to make the preambles entirely a matter of theology and history. One could repair, for example, to the history of the early Church and to patristic thinking, or to the theory that Thomas's philosophy was chiefly a work of theology. These lines of inquiry had the seeming advantage of bypassing not only the bewildering welter of medieval disputes, but also the forbidden zone of opinion carved out by the official Thomism. They also had the advantage of a thoroughly theological answer to modernity: The deep calling upon the deep, as it were. It had the promise of a new, and less philosophically constrained, apologetics.[98] At the same time, truly novel and perhaps heterodox philosophical theologies could be developed if one was clever enough to drape the philosophy in the officially approved terminology.

As ecclesiastical discipline declined precipitously in the 1950s and 1960s, and as the drapes were removed, systematic Thomism underwent a kind of defenestration. No longer privileged in the curriculum of either seminaries or Catholic schools (which, by then, chiefly was about the education of the laity), systematic Thomism became a historical specialty. It is ironic that it was Pius X's fear that modernists "wish the scholastic philosophy to be relegated to the history of philosophy."[99] But after the curricular defenestration, this is just where it was deposited. The quest for a pure and official Thomism in systematic questions became a historical specialty charged with the responsibility to deliver, according to contemporary methods of research, just what Thomas said, but often without the systematic or apologetical project for putting that information to good use.[100]

Fourth, the Thomistic contribution to social doctrine was never meant to be a complete Thomism, but rather an adaptation for the purposes at

---

98. On a more direct theological investigation that is not constrained by the long ramp of philosophical preambles, see Fergus Kerr, *Twentieth-Century Catholic Theologians*, 168 and 191.

99. Pius X, *Pascendi*, §38, *Acta* 5, 91.

100. Which is not to disparage the value of historical research, nor the painstaking labor needed to assemble critical editions of Thomas's *opera*.

hand. Social doctrine had its own momentum, seemingly unaffected by the institutional demise of systematic Thomism. Most everyone understood that the great encyclical teachings were wound together by various and sundry threads of Thomistic thinking. For several decades, both progressives and conservatives could affirm the general profile of teachings on the common good, subsidiarity, social justice, and human rights. The gradual separation of the social doctrine from the overall system of Thomas, however, began to create the impression that the philosophy of practical reason was free-standing, a kind of *prima philosophia* having connection to the metaphysical system only by way of dotted lines. This could prove attractive not only for progressives but for moral conservatives as well. The frayed edges between metaphysics and practical reason were particularly evident in the diverse conceptions of natural law, a subject that became a kind of "public reason" detached from the Leonine teachings about participation in the Eternal Law, divine providence, and the *finis ultimis*—detached even from teleology and the rudiments of philosophy of nature. Such issues really did stand close to the preambles.

Leo's revival made "natural law" a common coin of discourse and exposition. Given the fact that natural-law thinking had gone into abeyance in Catholic thinking during the eighteenth century and the subsequent era of Legitimism, it was quite an accomplishment to have brought it back so late in the game of modern debates over political philosophy. But the coin came in different denominations. As early as 1930, Walter Farrell took note of the fact that standard textbooks on moral and social thought could contain as many as six different opinions on natural law. "Evidently," he remarked, "it is time that some definite, well established ideas be proposed on this subject."[101] Farrell detected that the chief term in social doctrine was being used very loosely and confusedly, and that it was necessary to locate the subject more securely in Thomas's own doctrine.

Perhaps we should conclude that the Leonine and Pian insistence upon adherence to Thomas *praesertim in re metaphysica* turned out to be the more important issue. Leo certainly wanted to preserve the proper analogies and systematic connections between the two foci of metaphysics and politics. A century after *Pascendi*, however, the two Thomisms are not at peace. To some degree, this is due to the fact that the *secunda pars* (on human action) is not always adequately integrated with the *prima pars* of the *Summa theologiae*. We need only survey the chronic and significant differences of opinion over the systematic grounding of natural law today, and the extraordinarily complicated

---

101. Farrell, introduction to *The Natural Moral Law*. Here, referring to L. Lehu, OP, *Philosophia Moralis et Socialis* (Paris: Gabalda, 1914).

and controversial skirmish lines over questions of moral theology to see that this is so. As the legislated Thomism in metaphysics retreated in our time, the issues of discipline and Church authority migrated from metaphysics and the preambles of faith into sectors of practical reasoning, particularly the life issues. How strange, but true. But it is not our aim here to complete this circle. We set out to show how the different orbits of Modernism and the Thomistic revival began and how they developed both in and out of tandem through the *Pascendi* era.

PART II

Natural Law

CHAPTER 7

Yves R. Simon on Natural Law and Practical Reason

I.

IN HIS 1958 LECTURES at The University of Chicago, later published under the title *The Tradition of Natural Law: A Philosopher's Reflections* (1965), Yves R. Simon remarks that the subject of natural law "is difficult because it is engaged in an overwhelming diversity of doctrinal contexts and of historical accidents. It is doubtful that this double diversity, doctrinal and historical, can so be mastered as to make possible a completely orderly exposition of the subject of natural law."[1] A "thorough analysis of natural law," he goes on to say, requires "an elaborate technique and sharp philosophical instruments."[2]

But to what should the instruments be applied? What is a theory of natural law a theory of? In the first place, natural law can be regarded as an issue of propositions that are first in the order of practical cognition. On this view, a philosophical account of natural law endeavors to bring into focus those "reasons for action" antecedent to reasons yielded through practical deliberation and judgment. In the second place, natural law can also be regarded as an issue of nature or human nature, in which case natural law is not only a problem of the logic and epistemology of practical reason, but also a problem of how practical reason is situated in a broader order of causality. Finally, natural law can be approached not only as order in the mind or in nature, but as the ordinance of a divine lawgiver.

Simon held that all three foci—law first in propositions, law first in things, and law ultimately in the mind of a divine lawgiver—provide distinct grounds for philosophical reflection.[3] For this reason, the study of natural law cannot be a simple endeavor. Even apart from complications of history and the great variety of doctrinal contexts, the subject is inherently multifaceted. Philosophers

---

1. Yves R. Simon, *The Tradition of Natural Law: A Philosopher's Reflections*, ed. V. Kuic, with an introduction by Russell Hittinger (New York: Fordham University Press, 1992), 5.

2. Simon, *Tradition of Natural Law*, 15.

3. Simon, *Tradition of Natural Law*, 145.

who have focused variously, if sometimes myopically, on natural law chiefly as a problem of moral epistemology, or of nature, or of divine legislation can claim to address some legitimate piece of the subject. As we will see later, Simon insisted that all three foci need to be integrated.[4]

At the same time, he understood, and indeed warned his students of, the difficulties that beset the philosopher who would try to give a full and proper account of natural law. Some of the difficulties are philosophical, about which we will have more to say in due course. Others, however, are extra-philosophical, arising from practical problems in institutions of law, politics, and culture. It is at least paradoxical that the persistent sociological and political sources of interest in the concept of a natural law also tend to militate against full and proper philosophical accounts of the subject. Doctrines are cut and trimmed to serve practical ends of institutional justice—and of course to remediate injustices. Undeniably, the rhetoric of natural law and natural rights has proved to be a powerful and sometimes very effective tool in debates over politics and law. There is hardly a movement of social justice in American history that has not been activated, often on more than one side of the issue, by a concept of natural law.

Despite the fact that modern philosophy has steadily eroded the theoretical grounds for natural law in nature or proceeding from the mind of a divine legislator, we find more rather than less exuberance for framing debates in the language of natural law or natural rights. Simon worried that the concept of natural law would be reduced to its function as a practical tool—in short, that natural law, especially in its modern setting, would become increasingly more difficult to separate from ideology. Therefore, before we turn to Simon's philosophical reflections on natural law, we should discuss his assessment of these extra-philosophical contexts.

II.

Simon refers to the "eternal return" of natural law thinking.[5] The idea of a natural law is irrepressible, because it arises from experience rather than from philosophical doctrines and debates. Moral and legal philosophers exercise their analytical tools on an idea that is rather sturdily shaped in the course of practical affairs. In its most rudimentary form, the idea of natural law arises from the contrast between what is right by nature and what is made right by convention or contract.

---

4. For further discussion of these three foci and their integration in natural law theory, see Scott Roniger, "Natural Law and the Imitation of Nature: A Thomistic Development of Human Ecology," *Lex Naturalis* 2 (2016): 111–30.

5. Simon, *Tradition of Natural Law*, 4.

Thomas Aquinas summarizes a millennium of legal dicta in pointing out that what is due to a person in the order of justice can issue from two different sources.

> First by the nature of the thing [*ex ipsa natura rei*], as when a man gives so much that he may receive equal value in return, and this is called "the natural right." In another way a thing is adjusted or commensurated to another person, by agreement, or by common consent [*ex condicto, sive ex communi placito*], as when a man deems himself satisfied if he receive so much. This can be done in two ways: first by private agreement [*per aliquod privatum condictum*], as that which is confirmed by an agreement between private individuals; second, by public agreement [*ex condicto publico*], as when the whole community agrees that something should be deemed as though it were adjusted and commensurated to another person; or when this is decreed by the prince who is placed over the people, and acts in its stead. And this is called "the positive right."[6]

Some things are owed to persons because of the very nature of the thing; other things are owed to persons because of tacit or explicit agreements, or because of the determination of a legislator that such and such be the case.

The idea of a *ius naturale* expresses the conviction that not all terms of justice are artifactual.[7] What is right is not exclusively the creature of what is "made" to be right. It is true, of course, that some theorists, notably Thomas Hobbes, have challenged the ontological grounds of this distinction. Prior to the political covenant establishing the authority of the sovereign there is no obligation, for by natural right "every man has a Right to every thing; even to one another's body."[8] In *De homine*, Hobbes explains:

> Politics and ethics (that is, the sciences of just and unjust, of equity and inequity) can be demonstrated *a priori*, because we ourselves make the principles—that is, the causes of justice (namely, laws and covenants)—whereby it is known what justice and equity, and their opposites injustice and inequity, are. For before covenants and laws were drawn up, neither

---

6. *ST*, II-II, q. 57, a. 2.

7. Aquinas, *In V Eth.*, lec. 12, no. 1017: "The Philosopher here calls justice political or civil from the usage the citizens are accustomed to, but the jurists call the right political or civil from the cause [*juristae autem nominant ius politicum vel civile ex causa*], viz., that some city has decreed for itself. . . . Political justice then is properly divided by means of these two, for the citizens use justice to the extent that it is imparted to the human mind by nature and to the extent that it is posited by law [*eo quod natura menti humanae indidit, et eo quod est positum lege*]."

8. Thomas Hobbes, *Leviathan*, I, c. 14.

justice nor injustice, neither public good nor public evil, was natural among men any more than it was among beasts.[9]

Hobbes's denial of the traditional concept of *ius naturale* includes two propositions: (*a*) that all moral norms of justice are conventional; and (*b*) that these conventions are nothing other than the artifacts of positive law—or, as Hobbes has it, the commands of the sovereign.

But it should be noted that most of his successors, who could be classified in some broad way as legal positivists, have retreated from directly assailing the distinction between *ius naturale* and *ius positivum*, preferring instead to defend the autonomy of positive law and its logical independence from requirements of morality. Even if they reach the same result, it is one thing to deny *ius naturale* (which is to say that nothing is owed to persons prior to contract or statute), and quite another thing to hold that the *ius positivum* is (legally) valid whatever its moral properties.

H. L. A. Hart, for example, emphasizes that the celebrated "separation thesis" between law and morality only asserts that a norm can be legally valid and at the same time morally unjust; the thesis does not, however, suggest that society does not have a moral reason or even obligation to change the law.[10] After all, modern positivism in the English-speaking world began as a movement to reform the penal laws. The positivist bid to sharpen our perception of the difference between what law is and what law ought to be only reinforces the pre-philosophical intuition that the right (or the *ius*) is not merely artifactual, and that what is "made" to be right by legal enactment may not be morally right.

Here, our business is not to examine, much less refute, all the species of conventionalism and positivism. We are interested in Simon's remark about the "eternal return" of natural law thinking. It returns because theories that would deny it face the daunting challenge of explaining away the notion that there are things to be distributed and owed to persons on grounds other than those made by positive ordinances.

Whenever a polity finds itself debating which laws ought to be made or changed, some distinction between the moral and the legal terms of justice is presupposed. The presupposition, however, is usually brought to mind in the

---

9. Thomas Hobbes, *De homine*, as it appears in *Man and Citizen (De Homine and De Cive)*, ed. Bernard Gert, trans. Charles T. Wook, et al. (Indianapolis: Hackett Publishing Company, 1991), 10.5, 42–43.

10. See H. L. A. Hart, "Positivism and the Separation of Law and Morality," *Harvard Law Review* 71 (1958): 593–629; Neil MacCormick, "Natural Law and the Separation of Law and Morals," in *Natural Law Theory: Contemporary Essays*, ed. R. P. George (Oxford: The Clarendon Press, 1992), 105–33.

context of a problem that forces a polity to doubt the justice of a custom or positive law.[11] Wherever war exists, or the maldistribution of economic resources, or political despotism, or disputes that attend the litigation of rights—in short, wherever a serious imperfection is perceived in human practices and institutions—questions leading to natural law will emerge. If we take historical experience as our guide, it is difficult to imagine a legal or political culture in which such questions would never arise.

Indeed, the persistence of various concepts of natural law in modern politics is due in no small part to the material fact of the abundance of rules that have no other proximate source than human decree. In pre-modern society, law resided chiefly in a customary order. Legal officials periodically attempted to codify the customs, and, of course, to apply them. But the law was more grown than made. In such case, the contrast between nature and convention is more difficult to draw, for the customs not only have no distinct origin in terms of legislative pedigree, but also constitute a kind of second nature. In modernity, however, there is virtually no area of human conduct that is not regulated by public law, particularly by administrative law.

Although it is a virtue of a modern legal culture that citizens and legal officials can discreetly trace a rule to a human mind, for that very reason the positive law is rendered more rather than less vulnerable to a critical contrast between nature and legal convention. The more positive, as it were, a system of positive law, the more we can pinpoint "official" responsibility, and the more we can use moral reasoning to make or unmake the law. If it is a paradox of written law that seeking to make the pedigree and meaning of laws clearer tends to provoke doubts and debates over how texts are to be interpreted, it is also a curious upshot of the law of modern states that, in relying so heavily upon positive law, the "law" appears inherently changeable and, where changeable, amenable to moral criticism and emendation. When we add to this picture the enormous power of modern states, we can understand why the idea of natural law is perhaps more prominent today than it was in previous cultures which had a more favorable intellectual and religious climate for the notion of natural justice.

In *The Tradition of Natural Law*, Simon sets out "to see the difficulties where they are and to puncture a few myths."[12] He worries that the problem

---

11. Simon, *Tradition of Natural Law*, 112–16. For a discussion of the way the problem of natural law is disclosed in the contrast between nature and custom, see Robert Sokolowski, "Knowing Natural Law," in *Pictures, Quotations, and Distinctions* (Notre Dame, IN: University of Notre Dame Press, 1992), 277–92. For a thorough treatment of the larger issue of the promulgation of natural law, see Scott Roniger, "How Is Natural Law Promulgated? A Phenomenological Approach to Aquinas's Natural Law Theory" (PhD diss., The Catholic University of America, 2017).

12. Simon, *Tradition of Natural Law*, 13.

of natural law in our times is not so much the need to defend the idea against its cultured critics as the need to prevent it from being ensconced in ideologies formed under the practical pressure of responding to the various intellectual and institutional felonies of modern life.

> Our time has witnessed a new birth of belief in natural law concomitantly with the success of existentialism, which represents the most thorough criticism of natural law ever voiced by philosophers. Against such powers of destruction we feel the need for an ideology of natural law. The current interest in this subject certainly expresses an aspiration of our society at a time when the foundations of common life and of just relations are subjected to radical threats. No matter how sound these aspirations may be, they are quite likely to distort philosophic treatments. For a number of years we have been witnessing a tendency, in teachers and preachers, to assume that natural law decides, with the universality proper to the necessity of essences, incomparably more issues than it is actually able to decide. There is a tendency to treat in terms of natural law questions which call for treatment in terms of prudence. It should be clear that any concession to this tendency is bound promptly to cause disappointment and skepticism.[13]

Simon observes that natural law is a "subject of direct, intense, daily, and tragic interest to all sorts of people whose philosophic tools may well be primitive."[14] For this reason, he proposes that "when the theory of natural law seems to be commonly accepted and works as a factor of agreement, there are good reasons to suspect that it is embodied in an ideology."[15] By "ideology" Simon means a "system of propositions" that refers not so much to any real state of affairs as to the "aspirations" of a society at a certain time.[16] In political debates, doctrines of first things are liable to be reduced to policy aspirations regarding things quite contingent. In a situation marked not only by diminishing moral and cultural consensus, but also by the reduction of authority to the ever-expanding apparatus of the state, there exists a climate favorable to natural law as a solvent for moral crises.[17] For what else is "natural" law than a body of moral premises untainted by the human will and by the vagaries of political compromise? For Simon, the "great example" in American history

---

13. Simon, *Tradition of Natural Law*, 23.
14. Simon, *Tradition of Natural Law*, 14.
15. Simon, *Tradition of Natural Law*, 66.
16. Simon, *Tradition of Natural Law*, 16–17.
17. In *Practical Knowledge*, Simon contends that one of the reasons for the immoderate expectation with respect to any kind of moral theory is the "breakdown of tradition." See Yves R. Simon, *Practical Knowledge*, ed. R. J. Mulvaney (New York: Fordham University Press, 1991), 97.

of "timely aspirations" assuming the "language of everlasting truth" is the nineteenth-century debate over slavery.[18] Everyone wanted the problem resolved. But the crisis involved exceedingly complicated social, economic, and political compromises, not to mention the legal issues concerning how the positive law of the Constitution distributed shares of authority to deal with the problem. As the controversy escalated, what began as a legal accommodation of slavery on pragmatic grounds became a "universal law" for some Southern apologists. What was once acknowledged to be solely the creature of positive law—the right to property in slaves—became in the opinion of Justice Taney in *Dred Scott* v. *Sandford* (1857) the most natural and inflexible of rights. Of course, both sides invoked natural law and the authority of the Declaration of Independence.[19]

History is replete with examples of natural law used for the purpose of defending a political, economic, or social status quo. Arrangements of prudence are made to look like the dispensations of nature. Simon points out, however, that in modernity appeals to a natural order of justice are usually made "against constituted authority."[20] Modern discourse of natural law and natural rights tends toward a "belligerent universalism." Indeed, in the courts of a constitutional polity as relatively stable as the United States the governments are repeatedly sued by individuals who claim to possess a certain status, goods, or liberties prior—even superordinate to—the terms of justice "made" by the state or "made" by parties at private law. Whether the issue concerns race, gender, age, or a miscellany of lifestyle concerns, it is widely believed that things are owed *ex ipsa natura rei*, by the nature of the thing itself.[21]

In our time, no contest over natural justice has proved more controversial than abortion, where we find natural law and natural rights invoked once

---

18. Simon, *Tradition of Natural Law*, 17.

19. In the twilight of his life, Jefferson Davis insisted that the Southern case for the original Constitutional order depended all along not merely on the written Constitution but also on natural law. In the final pages of his apology for the Confederacy, Davis invoked the Declaration of Independence with respect to "the inalienable rights of man," and wrote that the demise of the South augured the demise of the more universal cause of the natural rights of man. Davis was speaking here not of any natural right to hold slaves, but of a right to political self-determination. See Jefferson Davis, *The Rise and Fall of the Confederate Government* II (New York: De Capo Press, 1990), Ch. 57, 645.

20. Simon, *Tradition of Natural Law*, 8.

21. For a sense of how many different kinds of issues are discussed today under the rubric of "natural law," see my essay, "Liberalism and the American Natural Law Tradition," *Wake Forest Law Review* 25 (1990): 429–99. For a consideration of whether natural law requires judges to settle disputes about positive law on grounds of natural law, see my essay, "Natural Law in the Positive Laws: A Legislative or Adjudicative Issue?" *The Review of Politics* 55, no. 1 (1993): 5–34.

again on both sides of the argument. In 1991, on the eve of the Senate hearings on the nomination of Clarence Thomas to the Supreme Court, Senator Joseph Biden took the position that the Judiciary Committee explore whether Judge Thomas held a "good" or "bad" theory of natural law. A bad theory of natural law, on Biden's view, would seek to expound a "code of behavior . . . suggesting that natural law dictates morality to us, instead of leaving matters to individual choice."[22] A good theory, on the other hand, would support rights of immunity against government on matters of personal sexual conduct and abortion. Senator Biden's remarks, of course, were made with a kind of naive simplicity. But they are useful for illustrating Simon's point about ideology. For Biden, the true and false are to be seen as nothing other than the good or bad outcomes of applying a particular concept of natural law.

One year after the nomination of Judge Thomas, the Supreme Court made yet another bid to settle the abortion issue by issuing what is perhaps the strongest and most unqualified statement of natural right in our judicial history. With respect to the word "liberty" in the due process clause of the Fourteenth Amendment, the authors of the joint opinion explain that: "At the heart of liberty is the right to define one's own concept of existence, of meaning, of the universe, and of the mystery of human life. Beliefs about these matters could not define the attributes of personhood were they formed under compulsion of the State."[23] To be sure, this dictum might include a kernel of truth. It is by nature, not merely by custom and positive law, that human persons have a competence to make morally responsible choices, and to constitute their character by so doing. For the sake of argument, we might stipulate that some zone of decision-making belongs, of right, to human persons. An order of positive law presupposes that principle. But so stated, the proposition requires much more specification if anything is to be resolved about the justice or injustice of abortion. Unfortunately, the judicial use of such rudimentary propositions about natural rights is expected to stop a debate precisely where it has to begin: namely, with carefully drawn specifications of concepts, both in terms of moral and in terms of legal reasoning. Indeed, if consistently applied, the Court's dictum would guarantee a natural right to immunity against virtually any positive law that peremptorily binds the individual to conform his action to the state's definition of things—including the Court's own resolution of disputes.

---

22. Senator Joseph Biden, "Law and Natural Law," *The Washington Post*, September 8, 1991. Senator Biden, it can be recalled, voted against the confirmation of Robert Bork, among other reasons, because Bork expressly rejected judicial uses of natural law. Against Bork, Biden declared, "I have certain inalienable rights because I exist."

23. *Planned Parenthood of Southeastern Pennsylvania v. Casey*, 112 US Supreme Court, S.Ct. 2791, at 2807 (1992).

Of course, since it is one of the tasks of positive law to "hold men together, organize their cooperation, bring about uniformity in the behavior of indefinitely many individuals," Simon notes that "it is highly desirable that these formulas should command the assent of all persons concerned or most of them. We must, accordingly, expect the jurists to evidence an eagerness to keep away from issues on which minds are irretrievably divided."[24]

Simon characterizes the problem as a kind of "antinomy." On the one hand, the positive lawyer is concerned with explaining the relationship between the *determinatio* of the positive law and its moral premise(s). In varying degrees, positive law secures unanimity of action; yet unanimity of action cannot be created wholly out of the cloth of positive law, for positive laws (again in varying degrees) presuppose consensus about some principles and facts of the moral order. Hence, to the extent that the positive lawyer regards his work as explaining the relationship between law and morality, he is liable to ignite philosophical disagreements—the more remote the linkage between absolutely first premises of morality and the law or policy at hand, the more likely that the explanation will be disputed.

On the other hand, insofar as the positive lawyer is immediately interested in governing the community, rather than merely explaining a set of entailments for action, he frequently must abstract from these areas of disagreement. Prudential compromises will have to be made. The positive lawyer, then, could be tempted to use the rhetoric of natural law to split the difference. That is to say, he will insinuate (often in the language of natural rights) an order of moral necessity that undergirds the law, even though (*a*) the law at issue really rests upon quite contingent premises and facts, or (*b*) no such moral consensus really obtains within the political community, or (*c*) no such consensus would obtain if the rhetoric were connected to the philosophical issues which are being glossed over.

III.

Simon's uneasiness about the ideological face of natural law discourse is meant to foster caution rather than skepticism about natural law. He concedes that a "philosophy unaffected by any ideological feature would involve a degree of perfection that human affairs do not admit of."[25] As he says, "for a thorough analysis of natural law an elaborate technique and sharp philosophical instruments are needed." What are the philosophical issues which tend to be submerged in the practical and institutional discourse? Simon pinpoints at least three sets of issues: (1) the relation of law to practical reasoning; (2) the ways that law differs from authority and individual prudence; (3) and the

24. Simon, *Tradition of Natural Law*, 65.
25. Simon, *Tradition of Natural Law*, 22.

lingering, difficult issue of whether order in the human mind or in nature constitutes in some non-metaphorical manner a natural "law."

"Practical science," he wrote, "is pledged to reconcile the opposite features of intelligible necessity and contingent determination."[26] In the sphere of the contingent, where reason must judge and choose amid a welter of options, the perfection of practical reason is exemplified in the cardinal virtues, primarily in prudence. Here, the attunement of the intellect and will to objects cannot be reduplicated, or even completely communicated, by way of general propositions and injunctions. If we ask the prudent agent to explain with the clarity of abstract, general terms the *ratio* of his deliberation, judgment, and choice with respect to the contingent singular, the answer will disappoint.

In the sphere of necessity, however, law plays a principal role in directing practical reason. In contrast to prudence, law has the opposite, though complementary, traits of necessity, generality, and publicity. In matters of lawmaking, we might not expect the clarity of a demonstration, but we do expect a fair degree of clarity in the order of communication. Those to be governed by a law must know what it is, and those responsible for enforcing and adjudicating it must be able to cognize and debate it in public settings. Although law must be treated analogically, one can say that "the more a law is universal, natural and impersonal, the more it has the character of a law."[27] Law, Simon says, "is a premise rather than a conclusion."[28] To the extent that the premises represent what is universal and necessary, the more they bespeak the character of law.[29] "Law is more at home in the realm of necessity. If any law is so grounded in a necessary state of affairs as to be unqualifiedly immutable, this is a law in the most excellent sense of the term."[30]

The concept of natural law, in both its authentic and its ideologically distorted senses, derives from the notion of "prior premises" of action—prior, that is, to terms of action which are constructed by practical reason, either in its individual office of prudence or in its more public office of laying down positive laws.[31] Those absolutely prior were traditionally called the "first precepts" or "common principles" of the natural law, which are always reasoned from rather than to; while those derived as implications of the first precepts were called "conclusions" or "secondary precepts."[32]

---

26. Simon, *Practical Knowledge*, 41.
27. Yves R. Simon, *A General Theory of Authority* (Notre Dame, IN: University of Notre Dame Press, 1962; rev. 1980), 20.
28. Simon, *Tradition of Natural Law*, 85.
29. Simon, *General Theory of Authority*, 20.
30. Simon, *Tradition of Natural Law*, 84.
31. Simon, *Tradition of Natural Law*, 86, 129, 151.
32. *ST*, I-II, q. 94, a. 2; q. 95, a. 2.

From a first premise, it might be possible to generate a demonstration of what is entailed in a particular matter of action—at least for those minds prepared to understand and give assent to a train of argument. So, from the premise that we must always act in accord with the good of life, the practical reason can draw the conclusion that murder is wrong. The more proximate the conclusion to the premise, the more likely the mind will give assent to the entailment.

The inferences from premises that have a high degree of certitude are usually expressed in the form of negative precepts or injunctions. These express "acts wrong by essence."[33] Traditionally, these have included such acts as murder, adultery, and theft.[34] No external circumstance, no subjective element of motivation, can ever make these acts right, for they are inherently inapt for bringing about justice. They are said to be contrary to nature, or wrong by the very nature of the case.[35] As for natural law in the mind, Simon notes that only a few moral problems are resolvable into necessities expressed by first precepts. These would be problems amenable to the negative precepts which can be stated universally and are always relevant to specific choices, circumstances and other complications notwithstanding.

The natural law "is known by way of inclination before it is known by way of cognition."[36] The distinction between knowledge *per modum inclinationis* and *per modum cognitionis* is taken from Thomas Aquinas.[37] Lest the distinction

---

33. Simon, *Tradition of Natural Law*, 146.

34. See, for example, the papal encyclical *Veritatis Splendor* (1993), §52: "The 'negative precepts' of the natural law are universally valid. They oblige each and every individual, always and in every circumstance. It is a matter of prohibitions which forbid a given action 'semper et pro semper,' without exception, because the choice of this kind of behavior is in no case compatible with the goodness of the will of the acting person, with his vocation to life with God and to communion with his neighbor. It is prohibited—to everyone and in every case—to violate these precepts. They oblige everyone, regardless of the cost, never to offend in anyone, beginning with oneself, the personal dignity common to all."

35. As Aristotle said, adultery is an act that admits of no "mean"; which is to say that adultery is something that cannot be done well or ill. Morally considered, it cannot be done at all, which is to say there is no authentic prudence about the act. *Nicomachean Ethics*, II.6, 1107a15.

36. Simon, *Tradition of Natural Law*, 132.

37. *ST*, I, q. 1, a. 6, ad 3: "A man may judge in one way by inclination [*per modum inclinationis*], as whoever has the habit of a virtue judges rightly of what concerns that virtue by his very inclination towards it. Hence it is the virtuous man, as we read, who is the measure and rule of human acts. In another way, by knowledge [*per modum cognitionis*], just as a man learned in moral science might be able to judge rightly about virtuous acts [*de actibus virtutis*], though he had not the virtue. . . . The second manner of judging belongs to this doctrine, which is acquired by study [*per studium*], though its principles are obtained by revelation."

be misconstrued, it should be noted that it expresses a difference, not between intellective and non-intellective acts, but rather between two ways of knowing: knowing something because of a connatural avidity for an end, in contrast to enjoying a term of knowledge by virtue of reasoning it out.

Thomas used this distinction between connatural and reasoned-out knowledge for more than one purpose. He used it to explain how an agent having a virtuous inclination to right acts "knows" the rectitude of a virtue differently from someone who knows it from an outsider's perspective, by dint of having figured it out.[38] He also used it to explain what happens at the other end of the spectrum of cognition from acquired habits.

Some terms of action are understood by exercising one's nature. For example, one does not know that life and bodily integrity are good, and worth pursuing, by argument. Indeed, it is hard to imagine what kind of argument could make such knowledge known *ab initio*. Thomas usually summarizes this most rudimentary knowledge of terms of action as the natural assent "to be, to live, and to know"—and this is nothing other than the tripartite scheme of integral goods that are expressed by the first precepts of natural law.[39]

As Thomas proposed, the inclinations are the *seminalia* or "seeds" of both the common principles of law and the virtues.[40] Both the order of precepts and the order of virtue stem from the order of inclinations. These inclinations are the first way we recognize both the objectives of action (the good of life, friendship, etc.) and, in a simple and uncomplicated manner, the actions that are congruent with those objectives. Before a rational creature moves himself through acts of practical reasoning and measuring, God moves the human intellect and will by instilling a principle of natural movement. This is what Thomas called *lex indita*, or instilled law.[41]

But the knowledge furnished by these inclinations is not sufficient either for a body of law or for fully practical judgments about action. As premises given to cognition via the inclinations, they need to be spelled out in the form of conclusions, applied to individual cases, and eventually complemented and

---

38. *ST*, II-II, q. 45, a. 2: "Now, rectitude of judgment is twofold: first, on account of perfect use of reason; second, on account of a certain connaturality with the matter about which one has to judge. Thus, about matters of chastity, a man after inquiring with his reason forms a right judgment, if he has learned the science of morals, while he who has the habit of chastity judges of such matters by a kind of connaturality."

39. See *ST*, I-II, q. 10, a. 1. In *ST*, II-II, q. 34, a. 1, Thomas speaks of these three integral goods in the course of answering the question whether it is possible to hate God: "Moreover some of His effects are such that they can nowise be contrary to the human will, since 'to be, to live, to understand,' which are effects of God, are desirable and lovable to all."

40. *ST*, I-II, q. 51, a. 1.

41. *ST*, I-II, q. 90, a. 4 ad 1.

made effective through determinations of positive law. Simon points out that considerable time can elapse between what is grasped by affective connaturality and what is understood in the way of explanatory reasons.[42] The first premises of natural law are not always clear either in the psychological sense[43] or in the sense of what can be communicated by demonstration.[44] Hence, we can see why debates about natural law are more difficult than debates about positive laws. As premises of action, positive laws command a less vigorous assent, but (as long as they are artfully framed) evince considerable prepositional clarity; the elementary precepts of natural law, on the other hand, generate strong assent, but are relatively less "clear." And whereas a positive law can be located along a train of other propositions, allowing the mind to reason back and forth, the first precepts of natural law are always reasoned from.

It is a mistake, then, to look to the absolutely first premises as terms of a conclusion about difficult issues in morality. The vigorous assent given to first principles is not to be confused with the consent of many minds to the conclusion of an argument that proceeds, at least tacitly, from those principles. Those whose job is to win consensus in the public arena (policy-makers, lawyers, political officials) need to be on guard against trying to reduplicate through arts of persuasion those modes of assent and consent which stem from nature.

Simon understood that the concept of natural law has always been Janus-faced. From one point of view, it presents the notion of premises of action prior to the constructions of practical reason. This theme is typically brought into view when we notice a problematic contrast between what is right by nature and a convention that seems wrong or unjust. The mind moves back, as it were, to things that are first. From a different point of view, however, we can consider how to make the natural law effective. Here, the chief theme is not reconnecting a convention to a first principle, but using a first principle to create a convention. Although considerable attention is given to the first theme, Simon was more interested in the second.

Simon notes, "[n]ot every rule of human action is a law."[45] If rationalism is the price paid for reducing all the premises of action back into first principles, legalism is the price paid for trying to depict all the operations of practical reason as laws. In the *Summa Theologiae*, Thomas remarks that a rule of action, such as what appears in the first premise of a practical syllogism, is a necessary condition for the exercise of prudence. The human mind is a measured measure: it can actively measure action only if it is first measured; and it

---

42. Simon, *Tradition of Natural Law*, 158; see also Simon, *Practical Knowledge*, 34.
43. Simon, *Tradition of Natural Law*, 77.
44. Simon, *Tradition of Natural Law*, 133.
45. Simon, *Tradition of Natural Law*, 86.

is first measured by law, though of course not first by positive law. When Thomas speaks of the natural law as our "participation" in the eternal law,[46] he not only means that we participate in an order of law by receiving and knowing a law; he also means that from the divine exemplar the human mind can go on to do something more: namely, to be "provident for itself and others."[47] The knowledge of things for an end is in God called providence, in human agents, prudence.[48] Prudence is not merely obedient and receptive, but also creative.[49]

But there is more than one species of prudence. Thomas mentions individual, domestic, and political (or jurisprudential) prudence.[50] When practical reason deliberates and measures an act, it can be said to act lawfully (in reference to a primordial rule), but its measures are not necessarily laws. Legislative prudence aside for a moment, human prudence exhibits traits quite different from those we ordinarily associate with law-making. Simon writes:

> [I]t is the privilege of prudence to deal with the singular and to answer unprecedented questions. Prudence is often defined by this privilege: this is perfectly fitting as long as we realize that answering general questions is also a proper function of prudence whenever, by reason of contingency, the general answer cannot be logically connected with any essential necessity. But at this point the psychological situation is almost inevitably obscure. When the answer of prudence is relative to strictly singular circumstances, it can be put in print without much danger of confusion; all understand that they are presented with a case history. On the contrary, when the question answered by prudence has a character of generality, its treatment normally assumes a systematic and doctrinal form which may, if we are not on our guard, deceptively imitate the ways of science.[51]

In matters of practical reason, Simon emphasizes the difference between legislative reason, which issues the premises for action, and practical reason in the strict sense of the term, which regards action as the conclusion of its discourse. The "conclusion of the practical discourse implies, in the most

---

46. *ST*, I-II, q. 91, a. 2.

47. *ST*, I-II, q. 91, a. 2.

48. *ST*, q. 22, a. 1; *ST*, I-II, q. 19, a. 4.

49. Aquinas, *SCG*, III, c. 129: "Again men receive from divine providence a natural capacity for rational judgment, as a principle for their proper operations. Now, natural principles are ordered to natural results. So, there are certain operations that are naturally suitable for man, and they are right in themselves, not merely because they are prescribed by (positive) law."

50. *ST*, II-II, q. 47, a. 11.

51. Simon, *Practical Knowledge*, 31.

essential fashion, a trait opposed to the rational character of law": right reason in the singular and contingent matter of action.[52]

The function of law as a premise and the fully practical judgments of action by an individual are not reducible to each other. A traffic code, for example, posits certain binding directives for a multitude as to how vehicles are to be operated. However, if such a code is to bring about uniformity of action, it cannot regulate every singular action, in every contingent circumstance, for every single driver (considered in his singularity). Good positive law is under the imperative to achieve adequate generality, and it is precisely this virtue of legislative reason that can prove to be a vice if it is confused with other operations of practical reasoning, in which generalities are never adequate to concrete judgments. The positive law is no substitute for the myriad of intelligent judgments that have to be made on the part of drivers. On the other hand, if there is to be any common order in this regard, individual judgments and actions must be brought under general rules. "The principle of government law," Simon contends, "is subject to such precarious conditions that, if it were not constantly reasserted, it soon would be destroyed by the opposite and complementary principle, viz., that of adequacy to contingent, changing, and unique circumstances."[53]

The first premises of natural law are the foundation for both prudence and legislative prudence, but differently. Legislative prudence is under the burden of ordering a multitude of agents, according to general classes of actions, with a level of publicity and communicability that is rarely appropriate to individual prudence. In other words, the way positive laws are related to natural law overlaps with, but is not exactly the same as, the way individual prudence stands toward those first premises. Now, both species of prudence share common premises. The moral law forbids murder and theft regardless of the distinction between species of prudence, for whether one ought to steal or murder is not a question of prudence. But when we move beyond the question of acts that are adjudged wrong by their nature to consider acts adjudged right, there can be a considerable difference between the measuring to be done by positive law and the measuring of individual prudence. On this score, Simon was concerned that the proposition (i) that *practical reason is ultimately rooted in a law* would be conflated with the proposition (ii) that *all practical measures are laws*. If conflated, it would seem to follow not only that natural law gives birth to positive law, but also that all moral discourse is essentially legal discourse—not merely lawful, but legal as well.

What marks off the sphere of legislative prudence? Let us return for a moment to what marks off prudence from first premises of action. If there is

---

52. Simon, *Tradition of Natural Law*, 83.
53. Simon, *Tradition of Natural Law*, 84.

a per se order of necessity between an act and an end, there is no issue for prudence. The negative precepts of the natural law, for example, express such relations of acts and ends. Prudence comes into its own when there is something contingent or variable about the relation. Thomas held that "practical reason not only apprehends but causes,"[54] and where there is something variable or indeterminate in the relation of acts to ends, we can say that reason rather than nature is (proximately) causative of the act.

The ends of being, living, and knowing win our natural assent; as such, we do not need to deliberate and to issue a command in order to move toward these ends.[55] Although interpreters have been vexed by the Ulpinian dictum at the outset of the *Institutes*, that the *ius naturale* is "what nature teaches all animals," there is a relatively simple and plausible way to construe the dictum.[56] When the Roman governor goes to Asia Minor, he understands that the ordinances of Roman positive law are not needed to move the inhabitants to copulate, procreate, and educate the young. Nor is the competence of man and woman to engage in such acts solely the creature of positive law. No doubt, commands of law or custom might be required for a myriad of details pertaining to these acts and ends. Individuals will deliberate and command themselves with regard to particulars. By the same token, it would be ludicrous to think that the ordering of acts to ends in this regard is caused by positive law, or that it is in any primary sense an artifact of practical reason.

Thus, on the question of whether prudence is from nature, Thomas argues: "Now the right ends of human life are fixed; wherefore there can be a natural inclination in respect of these ends. . . . [S]ome, from a natural inclination, have certain virtues whereby they are inclined to right ends; and consequently they also have naturally a right judgment about such like ends. But the means to the end, in human concerns, far from being fixed, are of manifold variety according to the variety of persons and affairs."[57] As Simon contends, the more the right option is found among a welter of contingencies, and the more the right option is expressed in its very singularity, the more it expresses the rectitude characteristic of prudence. Once we move beyond the things that are known and desired naturally, acquired habits of intellect and will are needed for picking out the right relation and for rectitude of will in the choice.

Legislative prudence also deals with the variable and contingent in relations between acts and ends. It differs from individual prudence insofar as

54. *ST*, II-II, q. 83, a. 1.
55. Although considerable deliberation might be required for the choosing of these goods in particular contexts.
56. *Iustiniani Institutiones*, 1.2, cited by Thomas at *ST*, I-II, q. 94, a. 2.
57. *ST*, II-II, q. 47, a. 15.

law-making establishes a rule of action for a multitude of agents. It is widely agreed that one of Simon's chief contributions is his distinction between authority and law. Because these two notions are interrelated, they need to be sorted out. Let us begin with what they have in common. Given a field of indetermination with regard to things to be done communally, the question is how to achieve unity of action.[58]

Simon writes: "Now unity of action depends upon unity of judgment, and unity of judgment can be procured either by way of unanimity or by way of authority; no third possibility is conceivable. Either we all think that we should act in a certain way, or it is understood among us that, no matter how diverse our preferences, we shall all assent to one judgment and follow the line of action that it prescribes."[59] Of course, the unanimity of judgment has some basis in nature, reason, and custom prior to the application of authority or positive law. Thus, in extreme situations, such as when the community is threatened, individuals are often quickly mobilized to see what needs to be done in concert.[60] Here, unanimity rests upon common inclinations and habits, and consensus about the common terms of action is readily achieved—usually, however, only temporarily. Given any sizable community, beginning perhaps with the tribe, "unanimity is a precarious principle of united action whenever the common good can be attained in more than one way."[61] Whenever there is a plurality of "genuine means," the community cannot rely simply upon the "fortuitous" intersubjective, affective attunement of wills.[62]

Simon observes that law and authority differ, among other respects, in their manner of directing action. "[W]hereas law is attracted by an ideal of rational impersonality, acts of authority tend toward a state of concreteness involving the personalities of men, and all the contingencies to which human wills are subject."[63] Or, as he puts the same distinction elsewhere: "[A]uthority and law evidence opposite intelligible tendencies inasmuch as the more a proposition is expressive of necessity, the more it participates—other things being equal—in the character of law, whereas there is nothing in the concept of authority that expresses aversion to contingency."[64]

---

58. For a clear exposition of Thomas's understanding of the derivation of positive law from natural law, see John Finnis, *Natural Law and Natural Rights* (Oxford: The Clarendon Press, 1980), 281–90.

59. Yves R. Simon, *Philosophy of Democratic Government*, rev. ed. (Notre Dame, IN: University of Notre Dame Press, 1993), 19.

60. Simon, *Philosophy of Democratic Government*, 29.

61. Simon, *General Theory of Authority*, 40.

62. Simon, *General Theory of Authority*, 45.

63. Simon, *General Theory of Authority*, 20.

64. Simon, *Tradition of Natural Law*, 83.

Given the plurality of ways that united action can be achieved, the exercise of moral authority can be very effective, precisely because it is not encumbered by the somewhat artificial contrivances and offices of positive law. Governance by authority thrives on our perception of the personal virtues and skills of a person, which seem to have a promptness and adequacy to the situation. We can think, for example, of the collective consent to the despot because he appears to be "the man of the moment." Governance by law, on the other hand, has the trait of "rational impersonality."

While legislation always requires competent authority, authority does not always require a juridical office. There is no principle that absolutely forbids a community from being organized around an authority who gives particularized commands rather than general standing laws. Whenever a judgment has to be supplied, the authority supplies it. In its ideal form, such an order resembles what Aristotle called "animate justice."[65]

Thus, when some matter of common interest must be decided, the dispute or problem is taken to whoever has virtue or charisma that commands the respect of those to be governed. At first glance, this would seem like a reasonable procedure. Whoever has virtue has the requisite habit of attunement to the contingencies of action. His animated virtue is more apt to reach the right result than the inanimate directives of general standing laws will. In *A General Theory of Authority*, however, Simon points out that when an authority gives directives, out of the saddle as it were, the political order can be called "authoritarian." Rather than distinguishing in some clear institutional way between individual, familial, and political dictates of prudence, the executive powers are permitted "to manage the concrete circumstances by connecting the conclusions of their choice with premises that have no other source than their good judgment, since no positive enactment ever gave these premises any juridical existence."[66]

The precepts of natural law are realized in the contingencies of human action in more than one way. The task of being provident for oneself, for small, affective communities, and for a city require significantly different uses of practical reason. The precision and clarity of the judgments derived from natural law in one case are not necessarily appropriate to the others. Prudential rules of action for an individual require little in the way of art, for the end of action is not a product external to the agent. Prudential rules of action for a family are secured chiefly through common affection, and the main art is education by way of rhetoric. But the rules of action appropriate to a city not only depend on the ability to see what is right and useful, but are secured especially by the ability to artfully create external institutions which govern a great multiplicity of acts and agents.

---

65. *Nicomachean Ethics*, V.4, 1132a22.
66. Simon, *General Theory of Authority*, 48–49n11.

Political prudence causes a harmony of action from a distance, as it were. When it is tailored to the model of individual or familial prudence, the goods it seeks to secure are usually endangered. Indeed, it is characteristic of political prudence to "make" artificial limits on its own effort to make natural law effective. In a host of ways, including rules of evidence in criminal proceedings, limited terms of office, and requirements that ordinances be written, political prudence prudentially limits itself for the sake of the common good. Many of the limits characteristic of a system of positive law would be inappropriate, if not destructive, of prudence in individual and familial settings.

Given these important differences between individual, familial, and political prudence, Simon thought that the problem of natural law is best discussed not exclusively as a regression to first premises, but prospectively toward the distinct ways that the first premises are made effective.

IV.

There is, however, one philosophical problem concerning natural law that Simon thought required the regression to first principles. It is one sufficiently difficult as to incline even the metaphysician "to economy of words on the subject."[67] Why call natural law "law"? Simon insisted that the issue of God's existence is unavoidable once we raise the problem of the natural "law" in the order of being. "There are a hundred reasons for opposition to natural law," he remarked, "but this is one of them and at certain times it may be the strongest: obligation in natural law does not hold unless the natural law exists in a state which is actually prior, but which is ultimate in the order of discovery—'this law is an aspect of God.'"[68]

In yet another passage, he writes:

> There is no question of denying the connection between the problem of natural law and the problem of God. But it is not easy to show precisely what this connection is. One may wonder whether the study of moral nature and of natural law is a way to the knowledge of God or whether the knowledge of God must be had before the proposition that there exists a natural law of the moral world is established. We may be able to show that the truth is better expressed by the first part of this alternative. . . . But from this logical priority in the order of discovery it does not follow that the understanding of natural law can be logically preserved in the case of failure to recognize in God the ultimate foundation of all laws.[69]

---

67. Simon, *Tradition of Natural Law*, 28.
68. Simon, *Tradition of Natural Law*, 139.
69. Simon, *Tradition of Natural Law*, 62.

Let us recall the *definitio legis* given by Saint Thomas. It is the framework for Simon's reflections. Something is called law if it is an ordinance of reason (form), for the common good (end or *telos*), made by a competent authority (efficient), and promulgated (material).[70] Simon notes that this is the real or "scientific" definition of law because it articulates the four causes of law. The real definition of law is a completion, a specification or development of its nominal definition, which serves as an intellectual starting point because the nominal definition is gathered from the way we ordinarily speak about law.[71] According to Saint Thomas, the nominal definition is as follows: "Law is a certain rule and measure of acts in accord with which one is either induced to act or restrained from acting."[72] In the order of names, it should be clear that we first speak about the familiar traits of positive law, its being a rule and measure for human acts that induces or restrains those subject to it. While it is obvious that in the path of discovery we start with the data of positive law, this surely will not suffice for reaching a real, rather than a provisional or merely nominal, definition of natural law. For any alert philosopher, the following problem comes to mind. It is perhaps true that positive law has antecedent premises. Positive laws are *determinationes*, inasmuch as they render determinate what is left indeterminate. This cannot begin from scratch, for something has to be made determinate.

A traffic ordinance, for example, enjoins motorists to drive on the right-hand side of the road. Thus, in the fashion of all laws, something is taken out of the sphere of prudence, and is made binding by virtue of the legal ordinance. Yet there is nothing in the nature of the thing itself—driving on this or that side of the road—that imposes any moral necessity on our choices. This would seem to be a clear case of something that is made just simply by being posited.[73] Presumably, the legal posit is connected, though not reducible to, moral obligations to act in accord with the common good, to obey properly constituted authority, etc. It is not so clear, however, that the antecedent moral premise(s) should be called law. If the moral premises are to be called "law" without equivocation or metaphor, they have to satisfy, in

---

70. See *ST*, I-II, q. 90.

71. Simon, *Tradition of Natural Law*, 70ff.

72. *ST*, I-II, q. 90, a. 1. For a philosophical discussion of the manner in which the distinction between the nominal and real definition of law can be understood in the case of natural law, see Scott Roniger, "How Is Natural Law Promulgated? A Phenomenological Approach to Aquinas's Natural Law Theory" (PhD diss., The Catholic University of America, 2017), 52–67, 174–216.

73. *ST*, II-II, q. 57, a. 2, ad 2: "In the case of the legal just, it does not matter in the first instance whether it takes one form or another, it only matters when once it is posited"; citing *Nicomachean Ethics* V.7, 1134b20.

some analogous fashion, all four traits of law, including the legislative point of origin in a lawgiver. To summarize: it is one thing to say that laws are like premises; it is quite another thing to propose that all premises of action are laws. What is called natural "law" leaves a question about the ontological ground of the name.

Simon maintains that the resolution of this problem involves at least two things. First, it is necessary to distinguish between what is first in the order of discovery and what is first in the order of being. For natural law to be "law" it is not necessary for the order of knowledge that the moral norms or *iura* be immediately cognized as effects of some ultimate legislative act. Rather, what is first in cognition would have to include some evidence that, upon inquiry and reflection, leads the mind to assent to the existence of a first, legislative cause. In short, there would have to be grounds for a traditional *a posteriori* inference leading the mind from things to God.

Simon surely recognized the difficulty here. In the first place, Thomas himself attempted no such formal argument in the questions on law. The eternal law, in relation to which the natural law is defined,[74] is itself defined *supposito quod mundus divina providentia regatur . . . quod tota communitas universi gubernatur ratione divina*, that is to say, granting that the world is regulated by divine providence and that the entire community of the universe is governed by the divine mind.[75] Thomas assumed that this supposition had been verified elsewhere in the *Summa*. In the second place, Simon understood not only the difficulty posed by textual loose ends in the tradition, but also the inherent difficulty of convincing minds tutored by modern philosophy to grapple with the problem as anything other than one concerning the order of propositions in the mind. He commented that if the order of propositions is examined in view of order in things, the next move is made more favorable. "In our scheme of natural law existing—in the order of discovery—first in our minds, secondly in things, and thirdly as an aspect of God, the distance between the second and third stages is of minor relevance, even if not completely irrelevant."[76]

Second, the definitional effort will require a logic of analogy. Precisely what kind of analogy is a difficult matter, for in constructing the analogy it will be necessary that the primary analogate cannot turn out to be positive

---

74. In *ST*, I-II, q. 91, a. 2, ad 1, Thomas insists that the natural law is not diverse from the eternal law. Laws are said to be different according to the active principle, which is the legislative reason. Therefore, the eternal and natural laws are not different laws. In I-II, q. 91, Thomas seems to admit of only two different laws: namely, those traceable to a human mind (temporal laws) and those traceable to the divine mind.

75. *ST*, I-II, q. 91, a. 1.

76. Simon, *Tradition of Natural Law*, 142.

law, even though that is where one has to begin. If, at the end of the day, positive law stands as the primary analogate, then the moral premises can be called law only by the logic of extrinsic attribution. So, for example, food can be called "healthy" only because it is a cause of health in the body. Properly, however, the property of health can be predicated only of the body. In the case of law, this would mean that law can be properly predicated only of positive law.

Take away the relation of the moral norms to positive law, and you remove the ground for speaking of those premises as laws—not indeed in the order of names, for in this order we move from the name "law" in reference to positive law, to the name "law" in reference to its moral antecedents. There is no question that in this order of naming the notion of moral law is dependent upon the notion of positive law, which is in this restricted sense the prime analogate. But with respect to priority and dependence in the order of being, Simon saw very clearly that the logic of extrinsic attribution will save some of the appearances, but will not rescue natural "law."[77] Although he did some closely reasoned work on the logic of analogy, Simon did not systematically apply it to the problem of the definition of natural law.[78] Rather, he suggested that there ought to be an argument from obligation to God,[79] and that not only the order of names and legal usages concerning natural "law" but also the very structure of political authority presuppose at least the de jure possibility of a complete metaphysical grounding.[80]

What does it matter whether the prior moral premises of positive legislation are called "laws"? Simon writes:

> The depth of this difficulty is clearly seen when we once again point out that natural law, in the very meaning of that expression, exists ontologically before it exists rationally in our minds; it is embodied in things before it is thought out, thought through, understood, intelligently grasped. Plainly, it is because natural law is first embodied in things that we declare such and such an action to be right, and such and such an action to be wrong, under circumstances which may have to be defined with great attention and particularity. And here we find ourselves face to

---

77. Simon, *Tradition of Natural Law*, 69–70n. On the theological part of the problem generally, and on the analogy of attribution particularly, see my article, "Natural Law as 'Law'," *American Journal of Jurisprudence* 39 (1994): 1–32. But the most complete examination of the problem in Thomas is Stephen L. Brock, *The Light that Binds: A Study in Thomas Aquinas's Metaphysics of Natural Law* (Eugene, OR: Pickwick Publications, 2020).

78. The preliminary work that Simon did can be found in his "On Order in Analogical Sets," *The New Scholasticism* 34, no. 1 (1960): 1–42.

79. Simon, *Tradition of Natural Law*, 14, 142.

80. Simon, *Philosophy of Democratic Government*, 167. But see also his comment at p. 154 on Leo XIII's encyclical *Diuturnum* (1881).

face with the real problem of obligation. It is clear what happens if we stop here. If we stop here, the last word does not belong to the reason, the last word does not belong to that which is intelligent. The last word belongs to things.[81]

The legality of natural law inevitably raises some of the most profound issues of philosophy and theology. Once we see the need to appeal to some standard or measure of action other than those rules posited by the human mind, we are poised to ask questions about first things. These questions are as interesting as they are difficult. Simon believed that if the last word about moral order belongs to the human mind, it will be difficult to surmount the ancient challenge of Protagoras that the human mind is a measuring measure, measured by nothing but itself. If this were so, then perhaps the political order can rest on nothing more than the rules of "rational" artificers who endeavor to make their decrees "fair" according to a set of procedures which are themselves artifacts of human practical reason. Yet, there is also something unsatisfactory about the notion that the last word belongs to things—to an order of nature that is somehow "there," bespeaking no ordering intelligence. If this were the case, the traditional concept of natural law would have to be reduced to the so-called laws of nature—to lower "laws" which express structural rather than moral or properly legal limitations on human rule-making. The question is whether the political and legal cultures founded in modernity on convictions about a "higher law" have closed themselves to the inquiry into first things.

---

81. Simon, *Philosophy of Democratic Government,* 137. For a useful discussion of this passage, see the review essay by Steven A. Long, "Yves R. Simon's Approach to Natural Law," *The Thomist* 59, no. 1 (1995): 125–35.

CHAPTER 8

Reflections on Natural Law in
Pacem in Terris

INTRODUCTION

BEGINNING ON THE FEAST OF CHRIST THE KING (Oct. 1942) Archbishop Angelo Roncalli made his annual retreat in Istanbul. The retreat master for the Apostolic delegate to Turkey and Greece was the Jesuit Father Rene Follet, who preached on the image of the perfect bishop according to Isidore of Seville. Roncalli wrote in his diary:

> The Bishop must be distinguished by his own understanding, and his adequate explanation to others, of the philosophy of history, even the history that is now, before our eyes, adding pages of blood to pages of political and social disorders. I want to re-read St. Augustine's *City of God*, and draw from his doctrine the necessary material to form my own judgment.[1]

And so it was here, in Istanbul during the Second World War, while reflecting on the problem of nationalism, and while reflecting on the bishop as an image of the supranationalism of the Church, that Roncalli resolved to re-read Saint Augustine's *City of God*. It gave birth to a pattern of themes that would bear fruit exactly twenty years later.

In December 1962, the fourth year of his pontificate, Pope John assembled a drafting committee for a new encyclical, which would be titled *Pacem in terris* (Peace on Earth). He typed the following instructions to Msgr. Pietro Pavan of the Lateran, who headed the team of writers:

> Peace is tranquility in the order of things, ordered obedience in fidelity to the eternal law. Order is giving each thing its place. The Peace of mankind is ordered harmony in the home, in the city, in man. Wretched, therefore, is the people that is alienated from God.[2]

---

1. John XXIII, *Journey of a Soul*, trans. Dorothy White (New York: Image Doubleday, 1999), 260–61.
2. Peter Hebblethwaite, *Pope John XXIII: Shepherd of the Modern World; The Definitive Biography of Angelo Roncalli* (New York: Image Doubleday, 1987), 470.

These three sentences paraphrase Book XIX of Saint Augustine's *City of God*: "peace is the tranquility of order."[3] They also express Roncalli's understanding of the perennial task of the bishop, which he derived from his retreat in Istanbul twenty years earlier: namely, to discern the signs of the times according to the deeper patterns of history, and the still deeper principles of order which ought to inform it. As we shall see, peace as tranquility of order is a paradigm of singular importance for his encyclical, especially its teaching on human rights.

Pope John XXIII's encyclical *Pacem in terris: On Establishing Peace in Truth, Justice, Charity, and Liberty* remains, to this day, a kind of magna carta of the Catholic Church's position on human rights and natural law. As such, it is good to ruminate on this teaching: first, looking back; then, looking around; and briefly, looking ahead.

LOOKING BACK

Issued on 11 April 1963, *Pacem in terris* reflected an acute sense of its own historical moment, both sacred and secular. In about two months' time (from October–December 1962), Pope John:

- Convened the Second Vatican Council
- Wrote an address in French to "all men of good will" only twenty-four hours after American military forces had gone to DEFCON 2 during the Cuban missile crisis
- Then, having appeared on the cover of *Time Magazine* as the "Man of the Year," he learned from his physicians of a cancer that would soon kill him.

---

3. Augustine, *De civitate Dei* [The City of God against the Pagans], trans. R. W. Dyson (Cambridge: Cambridge University Press, 1998), XIX, c. 13:

The peace of the body then consists in the duly proportioned arrangement of its parts. The peace of the irrational soul is the harmonious repose of the appetites, and that of the rational soul the harmony of knowledge and action. The peace of body and soul is the well-ordered and harmonious life and health of the living creature. Peace between man and God is the well-ordered obedience of faith to eternal law. Peace between man and man is well-ordered concord. Domestic peace is the well-ordered concord between those of the family who rule and those who obey. Civil peace is a similar concord among the citizens. The peace of the celestial city is the perfectly ordered and harmonious enjoyment of God, and of one another in God. The peace of all things is the tranquility of order. Order is the distribution which allots things equal and unequal, each to its own place. And hence, though the miserable, in so far as they are such, do certainly not enjoy peace, but are severed from that tranquility of order in which there is no disturbance, nevertheless, inasmuch as they are deservedly and justly miserable, they are by their very misery connected with order.

After receiving the medical report, he set up a drafting committee for the new encyclical. The team of drafters understood they had only weeks or a couple of months, at best, to finish their work.[4] Published on Holy Thursday, Pope John christened it his "Easter gift."[5]

So, let us look back.

In the winter of 1962–1963, two issues galvanized the attention of the global commons. The first was the division between two highly armed "blocs," a division that began in Europe just after the War, but which had rapidly spread to the rest of the world—to the former colonies, where the "cold war" was actually a complex skirmish line of civil wars, revolutions, and from Southeast Asia and to sub-Saharan Africa hot wars by proxies. Interestingly, although Pope John bemoaned the global fear of a nuclear conflagration, calling instead for gradual disarmament and for non-coercive means of resolving disputes, there is relatively little said in *Pacem in Terris* about issues of war. Except for the very significant admonition that use of nuclear weapons is not a fit instrument for the vindication of justice, the encyclical does not conduct arguments *within* or *about* the criteria of just war.[6]

The other great issue of the global commons—which, in fact, occupies the far greater part of *Pacem in Terris*—was the urgent problem of how to achieve political order in an era of very rapid and confusing decolonization. When the U.N. was established in 1945, 750 million people lived in territories

---

4. See Pavan's letter to Loris Francesco Capovilla, the pope's personal secretary, dated November 23, 1962. Pavan disclosed his first line of thought, which was "to reestablish the great line of encyclicals in argomento di Leone XIII" (mentioning *Sapientia Christianae, Diuturnum,* and *Libertas,* the same trilogy that would become so important for John Paul II). But, Pavan mused, it could be aimed at the entire global situation, teaching not only Catholics, but also other Christians and non-Christians. Documento 1, in Alberto Melloni, *Pacem in terris: Storia dell'ultima enciclica di Papa Giovanni* (Roma: GLF, Editori Laterza, 2010), 103–4. At its inception in Pavan's mind, therefore, *Pacem in Terris* would take the great Leonine teachings on the eternal law, together with the changing tides of history, and allow them to resonate with a much wider audience (*avrebbe una vasta risonanza in tutto il mondo e in tutti gli ambienti*). Drew Christiansen's argument that *Pacem in Terris* is a kind of "Copernican" revolution turning papal teachings out of their scholastic grounding, and that "natural law is turned upside down," has no basis in either the constitutive history of the document, nor in the encyclical itself, which devotes more attention to Aquinas's notion of the Eternal Law than any encyclical between Leo XIII and John Paul II's *Veritatis splendor.* See Drew Christiansen, SJ, "Commentary on *Pacem in terris,*" in *Modern Catholic Social Teaching,* ed. K. Hines, OFM (Washington, DC: Georgetown University Press, 2005), 225–26.

5. John XXIII, "Message of 13 April 1963," *AAS* 55, 400. When Cardinal Suenens delivered a copy to the United Nations, he called it "an open letter to the world."

6. On the need for gradual disarmament, see *Pacem in Terris,* §§111–16; for the admonition against the use of nuclear weapons, see *Pacem in Terris,* §§111 and 127.

that were not self-governing. By 1960, two thirds of the new member states were former colonies. In that very year the General Assembly declared that all peoples have a "right to self-determination," and decreed that "immediate steps shall be taken, in Trust and Non-Self Governing Territories or all other territories which have not yet gained independence, to transfer all powers to the peoples of those territories."[7]

This was the problem of the so-called Third World—the peoples who belonged neither to the First World of the West nor to the Second World of the Communist bloc. The third world needed to achieve political and economic development within a wider international order. In many cases, these peoples had de jure states, with flags and stamps and currencies, but they barely functioned with respect to the minimal requirements of political and juridical order. Indeed, it was in 1963 that the long American nightmare in Vietnam began. The Republic of South Vietnam was not able to make the transition from being a French colony to being a successful polity.

In both the secular and ecclesiastical press, much attention was given to the policy of *aggiornamento*—a bringing-up-to-date. The controversial issue was not (yet) what was going on theologically at the Vatican Council, but rather political collaboration between Catholics and parties on the Left. For all practical purposes, *aggiornamento* was interpreted as "the opening to the Left." In the encyclical, the Pope expressed his hope that Catholics might cooperate not only with non-believers but also with adherents of a patently false ideology *insofar as* the cooperation involves "morally lawful aspirations,"[8] especially collaboration in defense of "man's natural rights."[9] The encyclical did not spell out exactly what this meant politically in any particular country.

While it is quite true that *Pacem in Terris* was an "open letter to the world," it was also an important letter to the recently convened Council in Rome. The first meeting of the Council was quickly adjourned for the purpose of electing commissioners who would oversee a new set of schemata. In view of the fact that his earlier encyclical, *Mater et Magistra*, was rather tepidly received, the Pope and Msgr. Pavan "would have to sharpen the message of *Mater et Magistra* so that the Council would pay attention."[10] Since the Council was called not to resolve internal disputes about doctrine, but chiefly in order to facilitate the Church's mission in the world, *Pacem in Terris* signaled that problems in the global commons needed to be put front and center.

7. UN Resolution 1514 (XV), 14 Dec. 1960.

8. *Pacem in Terris*, §159.

9. *Pacem in Terris*, §157.

10. Here, quoting E. E. Y. Hales, *Pope John and His Revolution* (New York: Doubleday & Co., 1965), 156. Hales's point about the implicit message to the Council is certainly suggested by Pavan's letter to Loris Francesco Capovilla.

Although the theme of *aggiornamento* was prominent in *Humanae salutis*, the bull of indictment convening Vatican II, and in the pope's opening address to the Council, *Pacem in Terris* truly did sharpen the message, leaving its stamp upon several conciliar documents: *Lumen Gentium* on the Church as a sacrament of unity; the decree *Ad Gentes* on missionary work; the decree *Unitatis Redintegratio* on ecumenism; and even more indelibly on *Gaudium et spes* and *Dignitatis humanae*.[11]

The pope and his drafting committee understood that one sentence in particular would have a direct effect on the schemata being drawn by the commissioners: "Also among man's rights is that of being able to worship God in accordance with the right dictates of his own conscience, and to profess his religion both in private and in public."[12] The sentences on the right of religious conscience received more internal discussion and debate than any other theme of the encyclical during its drafting process.[13] In order to allow the Council to exercise its full deliberative weight, however, the sentences on religious liberty were written carefully, even somewhat ambiguously.

It was celebrated and criticized both for what it said, for what it didn't say, as well as for what people imagined it must have said or not said. To wit, the doggerel:

> By now we know the simple trick;
> Of how to read Pope John's encyc.;
> To play the game, you choose your snippet;
> Of "Peace on Earth" and boldly clip it.[14]

By and large, the politics of the cold war determined the way *Pacem in Terris* was first received.[15] *The New York Times* (for the first and the last time) printed

---

11. John Courtney Murray, "Things Old and New in '*Pacem in Terris*'," *America* 107, April 27, 1963, 612: "It is obvious, in the first instance, that the Pope here offers a shining example of everything that he means by his own word, *aggiornamento*. He situates himself squarely in the year 1963. There is not the slightest bit of nostalgia, nor of lament over the past course of history or over the current situation that history has evoked here on earth."

12. *Pacem in Terris*, §14.

13. See Alberto Melloni, *Pacem in terris: Storia*, 100–105 and the appendices. See also Jeremiah Newman, *Principles of Peace: A Commentary on John XXIII's Pacem in terris* (Oxford: Catholic Social Guild, 1964), 77–81.

14. John Cogley, *America*, May 18, 1963. Quoted in Newman, *Principles of Peace*, 60.

15. Catholics should do nothing that compromises morality and religion (§157), that one must not forget the possibility and need for conversion (§158), that fruitful cooperation is not a foregone conclusion but must be discerned according to prudence which is itself measured by the principles of natural law and the directives of ecclesiastical authority (§160), and that gradual growth is better than the impetuosity of political revolution (§§161–62).

a papal encyclical in its entirety. The Catholic world was made more than a little nervous by Pope John's words about "collaboration." After all, in 1963 some 55 million Catholics were behind the Iron Curtain. The first Catholic president,

---

In many countries, the debate seems in retrospect to have amounted to little more than what we would call political "spin." *National Review* dismissed *Pacem in Terris* as "a venture in triviality." See Richard Brookhiser, *Right Time, Right Place: Coming of Age with William F. Buckley and the Conservative Movement* (New York: Basic Books, 2009), 47. There was also philosophical hand-wringing of a more serious nature, chiefly on the question of whether the pope was too lenient on Communists and naïve about the aggressive intentions of the Communist ideology. This, in tandem with *Pacem in Terris*'s seemingly ambiguous and soft position on just war, led important Protestant thinkers like Paul Tillich, Reinhold Niebuhr, and Paul Ramsey to ask whether the encyclical was an exercise in "philosophical anarchism," "natural law optimism," perhaps "breathing a Pelagian, rather than an Augustinian, spirit." These remarks in Paul Ramsey, "*Pacem in terris,*" *Religion in Life* 33 (1963–1964): 116–35; repr. in *The Just War: Force and Political Responsibility* (Lanham: Rowan & Littlefield, 2002), 70–90. The latter, on Pelagianism, quoting Reinhold Niebuhr in *Christianity and Crisis* (1963): 83.

See also Peter Steinfels, "*Pacem in Terris*: A Retrospective" (Vincentian Convocation speech, Vincentian Center for Church and Society, St. John's University, Queens, NY, January 30, 2003). Also worth noting is Steinfels's passing remarks about how the encyclical was kept at arm's length by some elements of the Left.

In two countries, however, the encyclical's bid for more collaboration had significant implications for domestic politics. In Italy, for example, the Church had taken a very strong stance against such collaboration in the elections of 1946 and 1948. The Communist party actively recruited Catholics, arguing that in the practical order there was no necessary contradiction between supporting desirable political polices and reforms and following the faith and morals of the Catholic Church. It is still debated whether *Pacem in Terris* did more harm than good in the context of Italian politics. See Elisa A. Carrillo, "The Italian Catholic Church and Communism, 1943–1963," *The Catholic Historical Review* 77, no. 4 (1991): 644–57.

In Czechoslovakia, the high-minded notion of a modus vivendi between Catholics and Communists was cynically manipulated by the government. In 1951 the government attempted to create a schismatic church, like the one in China, under the rubric of "The Peace Movement of the Catholic Clergy." Under the chairmanship of an excommunicate priest, Josef Plojhar, the aim of the organization was to reduce Christianity to a Social Gospel, which, not surprisingly, turned out to be congruent with the policies of the Communist government. Unable to establish ecclesiastical credibility, it was re-established as "*Pacem in Terris.*" Eventually, the government made it clear that any attack on "*Pacem in Terris*" was an indirect attach on the socialist system. See Alexander Tomsky "*Pacem in Terris*: Between Church and State in Czechoslovakia," *Religion in Communist Lands*, Keston Institute, 10, no. 3 (1982): 275–82.

In only a few years, this question of collaboration and compromise would return not as a conflict between the rivals of the Cold War, but as a conflict between Catholics and secularists over public morality. With *Humanae vitae*, legal abortion, and the collapse of the Warsaw Pact, the terms of this debate will become profoundly reconfigured for a new era of liberalism and public reason.

John F. Kennedy was notably restrained in his public comments about this part of the encyclical. Italy had the largest Communist party in western Europe, and so the Christian Democratic Party was not at all pleased with the Pope's remarks. For its part, the Communist government of Czechoslovakia tried to erect a puppet church called "*Pacem in Terris.*" As the strange decade of the 1960s unfolded, the encyclical became a kind of icon of the peace and youth movement, and its actual teaching receded from public view, hardly discussed.

It is all the more necessary for us, a generation later, to look carefully at what the encyclical said about human rights.

LOOKING AROUND (IN THE ENCYCLICAL)

I shall now leave behind the historical context and the contemporary events surrounding *Pacem in Terris*, in order to look around in the document itself—particularly its treatment of human or natural rights. And I intend to do so by returning to the Augustinian themes with which we began. Let us therefore recall Augustine's succinct and profound definitions of peace and order: "The peace of all things is the tranquility of order. Order is the distribution which allots things equal and unequal, each to its own place."[16] We will see that this understanding of peace and order is the proper framework for the integration of justice as human rights and justice as right order.

I count some twenty-five discrete rights in sections 11–27. In his preface to these sections, the pope asserts that these are rights which flow inalienably from human nature.[17] So far as I can discern, the terms "natural" and "human" rights are used interchangeably.[18] They include the right to life, to bodily integrity, to the means which are necessary and suitable for the proper development of life, including the right to security when otherwise deprived of the means to it through no fault of one's own; the right to respect for one's person and reputation, to freedom in seeking truth, and in expressing and communicating one's opinion, to pursuing art within the limits of morality and the common good, and to being informed truthfully about public events. They include too the right to share in the benefits of culture and, therefore, to both a basic education and a technical training in accordance with the educational development of one's country; the right to worship God, both privately and publicly, in accordance with one's conscience; the right to choose freely one's state in life, including the right to set up a family or to follow a religious vocation; and the prior right of parents to support and educate their children. They also include the right to free initiative in the economic field,

---

16. Augustine, *De civitate Dei*, XIX, c. 13.
17. See *Pacem in Terris*, §9.
18. Natural rights (§§12, 13, 20, 28, 30, 157); human rights (§§30, 61, 63, 75, 143).

embracing the right to work; the right to satisfactory working conditions, both physical and moral, and taking account of their special requirements in the case of women; the right to carry on economic activities to the degree of responsibility of which one is capable; the right to a just wage and the right to private property. Finally, they include the right of assembly and association, the right of freedom of movement within one's own country and, when there are just reasons for it, the right to emigrate to other countries; the right to take an active part in public affairs (including women) and the right to juridical protection of one's rights.[19]

This was not a sudden eruption of rights talk in magisterial documents. Of the twenty-five rights, the citations are to Saint Paul, Church fathers, Thomas Aquinas, and to the encyclicals of modern popes. Only two of the rights have an aspect of novelty: the right of religious conscience, which is unmistakably an effort to develop reflection on this issue, and rights of women in the contemporary world.[20]

Mary Ann Glendon has convincingly argued that the 1948 *Declaration of Human Rights* should be read not merely as a list of rights, but read also according to René Cassin's elegantly structured order, which was based upon the portico of a Greek temple. Explaining the structure of the Declaration for the benefit of persons accustomed to simple lists or "bills" of rights, René Cassin compared it to the portico of a temple. The seven clauses of the Preamble are the steps leading up to the entrance. The basic principles of dignity, liberty, equality, and brotherhood, proclaimed in the first two articles, are the foundation blocks for four columns of rights: rights pertaining to individuals as such; rights of individuals in relation to each other and to various groups; spiritual, public, and political rights; and, finally, economic, social, and cultural rights. Crowning the portico is a pediment consisting of three concluding articles that place rights in the context of limits, duties, and the social and political order in which they are to be realized.[21]

A similar approach should be taken when we read *Pacem in Terris*'s doctrine of rights. The interpretive key is to be found in the organization of the

---

19. Here, I use the very succinct and useful summary by Newman, *Principles of Peace*, 69–70. My summary leaves to one side the very important corporate rights: Church, family, nation, as well as a myriad of other groups which enjoy rightful dignity both in themselves and insofar as they stand toward others according to the principle of subsidiarity. Especially important is *Pacem in Terris*, §52, where the pope explicitly affirms the right of peoples to choose their own form of government.

20. On the right of religious conscience, see *Pacem in Terris*, §14; on the rights of women in the contemporary world, see §§19, 41, and 153.

21. See Mary Ann Glendon, "The Rule of Law in The Universal Declaration of Human Rights," *Northwestern University Journal of International Human Rights* 2 (2004): 2–19.

encyclical itself. For the encyclical is not organized according to the four prin-ciples in the subtitle: truth, justice, love, and liberty. Instead, these principles are interwoven according to *six modes of order*. To my knowledge *Pacem in Terris* is the only important human rights document that explicitly takes this approach. In doing so, Pope John XXIII integrates justice as rights and justice as right order.

The encyclical teaches that peace is richly textured and multi-layered order(s):

1. Order in the universe (§§2–3)
2. Order in freedom and conscience that flows from an individual's partici-pation in the eternal law (§§4–7)
3. Order among individual human persons (§§8–10)

(§§11–15 begin list of Rights)

4. Order between members of a political community and its authorities (§§46–79)
5. Order between political communities (§§80–129)
6. Order that ought to obtain between individuals, social groups, and states to a worldwide community. (§§130–45)

In his World Day of Peace Address in 2003, marking the fortieth anniversary of *Pacem in Terris*, Pope John Paul II said:

> Boldly, but with all humility, I would like to suggest that the Church's fifteen-hundred-year-old teaching on peace as *"tranquillitas ordinis—the tranquility of order"* as Saint Augustine called it (*De Civitate Dei*, 19.13), which was brought to a new level of development forty years ago by *Pacem in Terris*, has a deep relevance for the world today, for the leaders of nations as well as for individuals.[22]

John Paul is just right, and he brings us back to the Augustinian themes I mentioned earlier. They must be brought back, front and center, not only because the encyclical was designed just so, but also because the over-arch-ing theme of order was ignored, and sometimes outright dismissed, by the generation that first read *Pacem in Terris*. For that generation, *order* sum-moned all of the boogey-men of their time and place. Politically, it suggested "law and order," the opposite of social and political change. Socially, it sug-gested authoritarianism, in the Church, in the family, and in the wider society.

---

22. John Paul II, "Message for the Celebration of the World Day of Peace," January 1, 2003, §6.

Philosophically, it suggested cosmological order, and nature herself, which speaks an authoritative word apart from, or even contrary to human freedom. Order for that generation usually suggested something imposed, despotic, non-participatory and dismissive of human freedom and subjectivity.

Almost immediately, the encyclical was read as a declaration of human rights stripped of the broader context of natural, divine, anthropological, political, and legal modes of order. To take but one example, let us consider Maurice Cardinal Roy's remarks sent to Paul VI in 1973 on the "Occasion of the Tenth Anniversary of the Encyclical *Pacem in Terris*." Cardinal Roy was a distinguished churchman of his time, to say the least. At the time he was the President of the Pontifical Council on Justice and Peace.[23] In a section entitled "A Method for Our Times," the cardinal admits to being somewhat puzzled by John XXIII's theme of order, especially as it relates to cosmological, metaphysical, and anthropological matters.

Perhaps he was only playing the Devil's advocate, for an astute churchman would not have asked, in his own voice, whether such principles could have become invalid only ten years later. For whatever reason he asked, "Is this answer still valid, ten years later?"

> For today, this idea of nature is very much questioned, if not rejected. . . . The concept also seems too "essentialist" to people of our time, who challenge, as being a relic of Greek philosophy, the term "Natural Law," which they consider anachronistic, conservative and defensive. . . . Although the term "nature" does in fact lend itself to serious mis-understandings, the reality intended has lost nothing of its forcefulness when it is replaced by modern synonyms. . . . Such synonyms are: man, human being, human person, dignity, the rights of man or the rights of peoples, conscience, humaneness (in conduct), the struggle for justice, and, more recently, "the duty of being," the "quality of life." Could they not all be summarized in the concept of "values," which is very much used today?

Admitting that the very first sentence of *Pacem in Terris* asserts that peace is "diligent observance of the divinely established order," Cardinal Roy observed, "this word jars the modern mentality, as does, even more, the idea that it summons up: a sort of complicated organic scheme or gigantic genealogical tree, in which each being and group has its predetermined

---

23. Pope Paul VI addressed his Apostolic Letter *Octogesima Adveniens* (May 14, 1971), on the Eightieth Anniversary of *Rerum Novarum*, to Cardinal Roy, who in turn addressed his thoughts to the pope on the subject of *Pacem in Terris*. He was the former Archbishop of Quebec, the first President of the Pontifical Council on the Laity, then, and finally the President of the Pontifical Council on the Family.

place."[24] For Roy, the dialogical imperative was hampered by the traditional vocabulary of the doctrinal content. In other words, *Pacem in Terris* was too restricted by the outmoded line of encyclicals going back to Leo XIII.

I shall use Cardinal Roy's questions as an occasion, some years later, to say what is correct about the theme of order in *Pacem in Terris*: namely, that justice as rights and justice as right order cannot be in opposition and need to be discussed in tandem. In the first place, we can recall Thomas Jefferson's much-quoted sentence, written to the Danbury Baptist Association in 1801, fourteen years after the adoption of the Bill of Rights. "Adhering to this expression of the supreme will of the nation in behalf of the rights of conscience, I shall see with sincere satisfaction the progress of those sentiments which tend to restore to man all his natural rights, convinced he has no natural right in opposition to his social duties."[25] Jefferson acknowledges the long recognized tension between *ius* as individual right and *ius* as law—and, by extension, justice as right order and justice as the satisfaction of inherent rights. Jefferson anticipated debates of our own century. On one extreme is the position that rights are "trumps" with regard to social order, or at the least, to the policies of political authority intended to protect order. On the other extreme is the complaint that what are claimed as natural (or human) rights turn out to be—by virtue of the nature of the claim itself, or by virtue of its exercise, or by virtue of circumstances—contrary to justice as right order. Apart from right order a right is not, as it were, rightful. Therefore, rights are possessed only as implications or conferrals of right social order.

The extreme version of the "right order" position has been explored and criticized by Nicholas Wolterstorff in his book, *Justice: Rights and Wrongs*.[26] I do not intend to rehearse here his thoughts and arguments at a proper level of detail and complexity. Rather, I want to underscore one point that seems correct, at least with regard to natural rights. "Natural rights (properly understood) are not the rights of asocial beings but the rights of social beings that have not been socially conferred on them."[27] Put in just

---

24. Maurice Roy, "Reflections by Cardinal Maurice Roy on the Occasion of the Tenth Anniversary of the Encyclical *Pacem in Terris* of Pope John XXIII (April 11, 1973)," in *The Gospel of Peace and Justice: Catholic Social Teaching since Pope John*, presented by Joseph Gremillion (New York: Orbis Books, 1976), 556–58.

25. Thomas Jefferson, Letter to Messrs. Nehemiah Dodge and Others, a Committee of the Danbury Baptist Association, in the State of Connecticut (January 1, 1802), https://www.loc.gov/loc/lcib/9806/danpre.html.

26. See Nicholas Wolterstorff, *Justice: Rights and Wrongs* (Princeton, NJ: Princeton University Press, 2008), 27. Here, he is citing Plato's *Republic*, 441d-e. "In such a social order," he writes, "everybody will be doing their 'proper work'. . . their 'proper function.'"

27. Wolterstorff, *Justice: Rights and Wrongs*, 33. Indeed, the very structure of a rights claim indicates a claim to a certain order: X owes Y to Z. Unless and until we achieve the

this way, we can understand that *if* there are natural rights then there is order prior to, and distinct from, the orders we construct or confer. It is a "straw man" to oppose natural rights and right order. Thus, the importance of the word "endowed." Endowment contains *in nucleo* both rights and right order. In ordinary language and in philosophical parlance, endowment implies order rather than a merely subjective claim or evaluation. Prior to the practical deliberations and policies of a human community stands a good to be recognized, honored. Social efforts to construct and maintain order and rights claims on the part of persons have the same source in an anthropological and moral meaning of "endowment." The encyclical proposes that they are integrally related. A lack of rightness in one is bound to impair the rightness of the other.

Now, turning to the encyclical, we find that the charter of human rights (§§8–36) stands between two discussions of divinely created order (§§2–7, 37–38), which serve as bookends. The first is a substantive prelude, while the second is a forceful reminder and admonition. In the prelude, the pope speaks of the whole created universe, marked by order, intelligibility and beauty.[28] What emerges "first and foremost" from the progress of scientific discovery, the pope asserts, is the splendor of creation as an endowment, making possible discovery. It is the same man, made unto the image and likeness of God, who is a part of a vast created order, and who is capable of appreciating and appropriating that order.

As for order *in* human beings, the pope insists that our participation in divinely established order is more perfect, by virtue of intelligence and a law written in the heart. Human peace, therefore, requires something more than the harmony of physical laws. It requires the tranquility of moral order. The principles of moral order are already reflected, inscribed, instilled in human beings endowed with intellect and will. Everyone can understand, albeit in a rudimentary way, that the true governs reason, and that reason governs the passions. First, we are endowed, not merely with random and sporadic powers, but with order.

Wrapping up the encyclical, the pope again quotes St. Augustine:

> The world will never be the dwelling place of peace, till peace has found a home in the heart of each and every man, till every man preserves in himself the order ordained by God to be preserved. That is why St. Augustine asks the question: "Does your mind desire the strength to

---

correct order of relation between these three factors—the giver, the thing given, and the recipient—justice is not done. This seems true of any right claim, whether the foundation is something endowed or socially conferred.

28. Reminiscent of the favorite triad of Augustine: measure, number, order.

gain the mastery over your passions? Let it submit to a greater power, and it will conquer all beneath it. And peace will be in you—true, sure, most ordered peace. What is that order? God as ruler of the mind; the mind as ruler of the body. Nothing could be more orderly."[29]

Some commentators have suggested that in *Pacem in Terris* "natural law is turned upside down," because the pope is swapping out the older scholastic notion of natural order for human moral order.[30] This is nonsense, for Pope John is doing nothing other than using Aquinas's very distinction between how providence is received and participated in nonrational and in rational creatures.[31] If anything, these paragraphs are aimed at Marxist materialism and at various species of modern constructivism, neither of which can allow moral order to be endowed in human beings.

Pacem in Terris not only deploys the older scholastic tradition but does so in its strongest terms. In section 38, which concludes the charter of rights, we read:

> But such an order—universal, absolute and immutable in its principles— finds its source in the true, personal and transcendent God. He is the first truth, the sovereign good, and as such the deepest source from which human society, if it is to be properly constituted, creative, and worthy of man's dignity, draws its genuine vitality. This is what St. Thomas means when he says: "Human reason is the standard which measures the degree of goodness of the human will, and as such it derives from the eternal law, which is divine reason. . . . Hence it is clear that the goodness of the human will depends much more on the eternal law than on human reason."[32]

Consider this passage as well:

> Governmental authority, therefore, is a postulate of the moral order and derives from God. Consequently, laws and decrees passed in contravention of the moral order, and hence of the divine will, can have no binding force in conscience, since "it is right to obey God rather than men" (Acts 5:29). Indeed, the passing of such laws undermines the very nature of authority and results in shameful abuse. As St. Thomas teaches, "In regard to the second proposition, we maintain that human law has the rationale of law in so far as it is in accordance with right reason, and as

---

29. *Pacem in Terris*, §165.

30. See Drew Christenson, "Commentary on *Pacem in terris*." See also Murray, "Things Old and New," 612. The debate already smoldering over contraception perhaps is being read into the encyclical.

31. *ST*, I-II, q. 91, a. 2, ad 3.

32. *Pacem in Terris*, §38. John XXIII cites *ST*, I-II, q. 19, a. 4.

such it obviously derives from eternal law. A law which is at variance with reason is to that extent unjust and has no longer the rationale of law. It is rather an act of violence."[33]

John XXIII draws the following conclusion from this line of reasoning: "Thus, any government which refused to recognize human rights or acted in violation of them, would not only fail in its duty; its decrees would be wholly lacking in binding force."[34]

Interestingly, this is precisely the passage that Dr. Martin L. King, Jr. quoted from Saint Thomas in his *Letter From Birmingham Jail* (16 April 1963).[35] The day after *Pacem in Terris* was issued, eight white Alabama clergymen signed a document entitled "Call for Unity," affirming the goals of the civil rights movement against legal segregation, but complained about the tactic of civil disobedience. Dr. King countered that one has a moral responsibility not to obey unjust laws, and promptly issued his famous *Letter* five days after Pope John's encyclical. Whether or not King was influenced by the recent encyclical is not important. For our purposes, the important thing is that King argued for an integral unity of rights and right order. Along one front, he chastised white moderates "more devoted to 'order' than to justice." Partisans of "law and order," he said, consider order much too narrowly as

33. *Pacem in Terris*, §51, citing *ST*, I-II, q. 93, a. 3, ad 2. See also section 60 of *Pacem in Terris*, which reads, "It is generally accepted today that the common good is best safeguarded when personal rights and duties are guaranteed. The chief concern of civil authorities must therefore be to ensure that these rights are recognized, respected, co-ordinated, defended and promoted, and that each individual is enabled to perform his duties more easily." Both of these texts are quoted verbatim by John Paul II in *Evangelium Vitae*, §§71–72.

34. *Pacem in Terris*, §61. In section 60, John XXIII cites Pope Pius XII's Pentecost Message of 1941: "to safeguard the inviolable rights of the human person, and to facilitate the performance of his duties, is the principal duty of every public authority." See Pius XII's broadcast message, Pentecost, June 1, 1941, *AAS* 33, 200. Further, we should not overlook the bracing passages quoted from Saint Augustine. Section 92 of *Pacem in Terris* says, "And just as individual men may not pursue their own private interests in a way that is unfair and detrimental to others, so too it would be criminal in a State to aim at improving itself by the use of methods which involve other nations in injury and unjust oppression. There is a saying of St. Augustine which has particular relevance in this context: 'Take away justice, and what are kingdoms but mighty bands of robbers.'" The text from Augustine is taken from *De civitate Dei*, IV, c. 4. Striking yet another Augustinian theme, *Mater et Magistra*, having just cited the *Confessions* on the inquietude of the human heart, includes this admonitory sentence: "Separated from God a man is but a monster, in himself and toward others; for the right ordering of human society presupposes the right ordering of man's conscience with God, who is Himself the source of all justice, truth and love." *Mater et Magistra*, §215.

35. See Martin Luther King, Jr., "Letter from Birmingham City Jail," in *A Testament of Hope: The Essential Writings and Speeches of Martin Luther King, Jr.*, ed. James M. Washington (San Francisco: HarperOne, 2003), 289–302.

the absence of conflict. His audience in the spring of 1963 would have readily understood that the use of force to achieve such a narrow notion of "order" at the Berlin Wall and in streets of cities in Alabama did not have the presumption of justice in its favor. The order to which law pertains cannot be found simply in an uncontested result, but in a result compatible with equity and suitable for a common good. Law moves human agents primarily through obligation, and a law that fails to move its citizens through obligation is scarcely distinguishable from force. A human community moved to and fro chiefly by force is a disordered community.

Dr. King therefore carefully defended rights as having their foundation in law, and in so doing he avoided the trap of putting rights and right order into opposition. Indeed, it is quite telling that in the *Letter* Dr. King was not anxious about a list of rights so much as a spectacle of disorders. Among these that he mentions: the corruption of individual and corporate conscience—and especially of the churches—the use of brutal and arbitrary police powers, the refusal to allow peaceful public assembly, the refusal of political representation at the voting booth, and, finally, the appalling history of using human law to compel both public officials and private citizens to treat one another chiefly on the basis of skin pigmentation, thus reducing *Pacem in Terris*'s second and third modes of order to the first one. Racial segregation is nothing other than government decree compelling citizens (third order), to ignore the endowment that constitutes human beings (second order), and to take as normative the endowments which characterize physical nature (first order). One hardly needs to appeal to a subjective right in order to see that the putative "order" of the law of segregation is a disorder.

It was not my purpose to claim that Dr. King wrote a philosophical treatise, nor that he set out in any conscious way to respond to Pope John's *Pacem in Terris*. Pope John's encyclical, for that matter, hardly counts as a philosophical treatise. Even so, the convergence of the two letters (issued only a week apart) expose the truth that it is nonsense to think that either presented some new understanding of natural law, much less that they subordinated natural law to subjective rights. Each letter summarized a common moral teaching, inherited, in its Christian form, by the Pope and Dr. King alike. Each shared the conviction that authentic rights claims and right order are co-implicates rather than opposites, and that the nucleus of both is the anthropological endowment. Doesn't this indicate that, circa the spring of 1963, the common moral teaching could not easily be dismissed (*pace* Cardinal Roy) as an antique relic that "jars the modern mentality"? Quite to the contrary, these two letters—arguably the two most revered statements on natural law of the 1960s—were delivered and received without out the need of technical philosophical or lawyerly argument. I will come back to this point in the conclusion.

Right order requires respect for the nature of human fellowship. The social principle is one human life participating in that of another, according to various kinds of common good: the family, voluntary societies, the nation state, to a family of peoples.[36] The term "common good" is used forty-six times in *Pacem in Terris*. "Now the order which prevails in human society is wholly incorporeal in nature. Its foundation is truth, and it must be brought into effect by justice. It needs to be animated and perfected by men's love for one another, and, while preserving freedom intact, it must make for an equilibrium in society which is increasingly more human in character."[37] Just as the dignity of a human person is reducible neither to the forces of nature nor the constructions of human art, but rather is *open to reality as a whole*, so too human societies are not reducible to the elemental forces of race, class, or historical determinism.

Just as the human person is open to reality as a whole, so too are human societies open to wider orders—to a global order, and to a fully transcendent happiness.[38]

> We must bear in mind that of its very nature civil authority exists, not to confine men within the frontiers of their own nations, but primarily to protect the common good of the State, which certainly cannot be divorced from the common good of the entire human family.[39]

Here, indeed, we reach one of the most controversial teaching of the encyclical—both then and now. Namely, the need for an authority that has "structure and efficacy" for realizing a global tranquility of order in the human family.[40]

Our sobriety and dubiety about the immediate prospects for such an order today should not cause us to impatiently dismiss the principle. It must be discerned, as Archbishop Minnerath says, *"travers l'epaisseur de l'histoire humaine*

---

36. See *Pacem in Terris*, §36: "And so, dearest sons and brothers, we must think of human society as being primarily a spiritual reality. By its means enlightened men can share their knowledge of the truth, can claim their rights and fulfill their duties, receive encouragement in their aspirations for the goods of the spirit, share their enjoyment of all the wholesome pleasures of the world, and strive continually to pass on to others all that is best in themselves and to make their own the spiritual riches of others. It is these spiritual values which exert a guiding influence on culture, economics, social institutions, political movements and forms, laws, and all the other components which go to make up the external community of men and its continual development."

37. *Pacem in Terris*, §37.

38. Even if there were an authority competent for ruling a global family, man's perfection would not stop there.

39. *Pacem in Terris*, §98.

40. See *Pacem in Terris*, §136.

[through the thickness of human history]."[41] The principle is not imposed from the outside, but is detected within other experiences and principles with which we are familiar. The human person is open to reality as a whole. He is not imprisoned either by physical forces or by his own art. Human rights flow from this anthropological principle. And so does the social principle. No true or valid society can pretend to order a human person exclusively to itself. Marriages, families, voluntary societies, nation-states, and so forth, would be grotesque prisons if they made their particular membership the finality of human life. (It was precisely this upon which Roncalli meditated when he considered the problem of nationalism during his retreat in October 1942.) We need to notice that the expanding modes of order continue to track the anthropological principle. Man is open to a universal order—this is his endowment. Therefore, rightful liberties and responsibilities do not begin or stop at the gates of the family or the state.

The human person is capable of plural memberships without prejudice to the others. That one society is not the whole of human sociability is not a defect in man, but an excellence. *Pacem in Terris* therefore asserts that it is "a postulate of the moral order" that there be authority adequate to coordinating and maintaining the common good.[42] Since human action increasingly pushes beyond the confines of the nation-state and treaties between states, there is need of a module of government to protect the rights and right order of that common good.

LOOKING AHEAD: SIGNS OF THE TIMES

It might come as a surprise, but John XXIII did not use *signa temporum* or "signs of the times" in *Pacem in Terris*.[43] He did, however, use it in the

---

41. See Roland Minnerath, "*Pacem in Terris: Quid Novi?*" in *Proceedings of the Pontifical Academy of the Social Sciences: The Global Quest for Tranquillitas Ordinis;* Pacem in Terris, *Fifty Years Later*, Acta 18 (2013): 34–35, available at vatican.va.

42. See *Pacem in Terris*, §136

43. *Gaudium et spes*, §4, uses it without reference to *Pacem in Terris*. As it happened, *segni dei tempi* was inserted as a section heading (above *Pacem in Terris*, §126). It is not in the autograph, *AAS* 55, 291. In §126 (English translation and numbering), the pope speaks of "more and more, men today are convinced that . . ." The section headings appear to come from an earlier Italian draft. See Melloni's table of drafts in *Pacem in terris: Storia*, 134–219. Eager to quickly issue polyglot translations (based upon the Italian not the Latin typical), the Vatican Press inserted the "signs of the times" heading after each of the four parts of *Pacem in Terris*. See Jeremiah Newman, *Principles of Peace*, 51. Thus, *signa temporum* was detached from its original context in Mt 16:3. Rather than the richly ambiguous and the pointedly admonitory meanings of both the scripture and Pope John's use of it in 1961, the phrase seemed to be an empty placeholder for organizing pronouncements about

Apostolic Constitution *Humanae salutis*—the bull of indiction calling the Second Vatican Council (25 Dec. 1961). The context and purpose of the scriptural source deserves attention. The scriptural pericope, of course, is Mt 16:1–5:

> And there came to him the Pharisees and Sadducees tempting: and they asked him to show them a sign from heaven. But he answered and said to them: When it is evening, you say, It will be fair weather, for the sky is red. And in the morning: Today there will be a storm, for the sky is red and lowering. You know then how to discern the face of the sky: and can you not know the signs of the times? A wicked and adulterous generation seeketh after a sign: and a sign shall not be given it, but the sign of Jonas the prophet. And he left them, and went away. And when his disciples came over the water, they had forgotten to take bread.

In the bull of indiction for the council, Pope John uses this strange Matthean pericope to do two things. First and foremost, Christ's admonition was meant to situate the ecumenical council. This Apostolic Constitution, after all, was written for the bishops. "Signs of the times" in this respect should be taken in an immediately theological sense. It pertains to the mission of the Church, sowing the seeds of the Gospel in a particular time. Indeed, the last sentence of the pericope is a wonderfully ambiguous report about the disciples themselves at verses 5–9. In the second place, the pericope was intended to situate more broadly the dialogue between the Church and the world. Accordingly, the pope emphasized that the atrocities of war, the ruin of minds by ideologies, the fear and anxieties which attend scientific technologies, were not without "warning signs." Because these warning signs had been confirmed in experience of this very generation, he proposed that the Church's mission in the contemporary world had reached a moment of teaching and learning "by experience."[44] By *experience*, he did not mean a pontifical commentary on current events; nor did he suggest that current events presented much more than a "murky haze" needing discernment. Rather he meant to remind the bishops that a common experience can facilitate inquiry into, and appropriation of, the principles governing a work to-be-done.[45]

---

current affairs. In this case, journalistic convenience obscured important dimensions of the encyclical: not only the scriptural source of *signa temporum* but also the structural organization of the six facets of order.

44. John XXIII, Papal Bull *Humanae salutis* (December 25, 1961), *AAS* 54, 6–7.

45. Admonitory signs in *Pacem in Terris*, §85, *AAS* 55, 280-81: "But one of the principal imperatives of the common good is the recognition of the moral order and the unfailing observance of its precepts." "A firmly established order between political communities must be founded on the unshakable and unmoving rock of the moral law, that law which

In his opening allocution to the Second Vatican Council, Pope John once again reminded the bishops that "history is the teacher of life."[46] A common historical experience can have a useful winnowing effect for interlocutors of good will. Some options are recognized almost immediately as dead ends, while others remain what William James called "live options." Thus, discerning the "signs of the times" helps one to know where, *in medias res*, a dialogue ought to begin. For Pope John, the experience of the postwar generation provided an opportune moment for setting forth natural law principles governing peace as tranquility of order. The pathologies of totalitarian states were in full evidence; western Europe was still being rebuilt from the devastation of the war; the Cuban missile crisis had made everyone aware of the need for at least some limits to use of lethal force, even in defense of a good cause; and the rapid pace of decolonization made it imperative that the new polities be founded on the four principles comprising the encyclical's subtitle.

Pacem in Terris is both dialogical and doctrinal. It is the first papal encyclical to treat natural law in general terms for a general audience—for men of good will—and even more significantly for the express purpose of instigating collaboration along a wide front of moral, social, and political issues. Importantly, it assumes that the things-to-be-done are already, though inchoately and incompletely, under way. The Pope takes note of contemporary *desiderata*—what men want and hope to achieve regarding justice and peace. The word "value" (*valor*) is not in the encyclical.[47] Instead, we find *animorum appetitiones* and other such phrases to indicate what people are trying to accomplish.[48] In this respect, we are reminded of Jacques Maritain's comment on the drafts in process for a U.N. Declaration of the Rights of Man: "the perspectives open to men, both on the planes of history and of philosophy, are wider and richer than before."[49] Both assent and consent (truth and feasibility of agreement) sometimes are more favorable under certain conditions of shared experience.

---

is revealed in the order of nature by the Creator Himself, and engraved indelibly on men's hearts. . . . Its principles are beacon lights to guide the policies of men and nations. They are also warning lights– providential signs—which men must heed if their laborious efforts to establish a new order are not to encounter perilous storms and shipwreck [*qui quidem ex eius monitoriis, salutaribus providisque signis*]"; quoting Pius XII, *Christmas Broadcast Message*, 1941, *AAS* 34, 16.

46. *Gaudet Mater*, October 11, 1962, Sacrosanctum Oecumenicum Concilium Vatican II, Constitutiones, Decreta, Declarationes (Vatican City: Libreria Editrice Vaticana, 1993), 858.

47. The *valori* were superimposed, first in Italian, as headings for newspapers, and through this venue entered into other translations.

48. See *Pacem in Terris*, §§79, 159.

49. Jacques Maritain, introduction to the UNESCO document, *Human Rights: Comments and Interpretations* (London & New York: Allan Wingate, 1949).

I propose that this is the way we ought to interpret Pope John's use of *signa temporum*. It should be understood in light of his notes during the 1942 retreat when he wrote: "The Bishop must be distinguished by his own understanding, and his adequate explanation to others, of the philosophy of history, even the history that is now, before our eyes, adding pages of blood to pages of political and social disorders. I want to re-read St. Augustine's *City of God*, and draw from his doctrine the necessary material to form my own judgment." As is so often the case, the end was in the beginning.

While I do not insist that my interpretation is the only valid one, it has the virtue of following the rather bright thread of Roncalli's interest in Saint Augustine. It corresponds to the actual organization of the encyclical and the theme of "tranquility of order." It also moderates a tendency from fifty years ago to retreat from doctrinal content and to reduce "signs of the times" to a kind of weathervane of dialogue.

Archbishop Minnerath makes the interesting point that in *Pacem in Terris* the order of nature "is not merely essential; it is also existential."[50] This seems exactly right. My guess is that this double dimension arises from Pope John's early and abiding interest in Augustine's theology of history and Thomas's doctrine of natural law as participation in the eternal law. In any case, the scheme of order, signs, and interpretations is very prominent in Augustine. Consider the following passage in the *Confessions*:

> Is not this beauty apparent to all men whose senses are sound and whole? Why then does it not speak the same to all men? Animals both great and small see it, but they cannot question it. In them, reason has not been placed in judgment over the senses and their reports. But men can ask questions, so that they may clearly see the invisible things of God, "being understood by the things that are made." However, through love for such things they become subject to them, and in subjection they cannot pass judgment on them. Nor do things answer those who ask unless they are men of judgment. They do not change their voice, that is, their beauty, when one man merely looks at them and another both looks and questions, so as to appear one thing to this man, another to that. It appears the same to both: it is silent to one, but speaks to the other. Nay rather, it speaks to all, but only those understand who compare its voice taken in from outside with the truth within them.[51]

Across the ocean of human affairs, things change, along with the signs and interpretations. The cultural and social *signa temporum* are not always

---

50. Roland Minnerath, "*Pacem in Terris*," 35. Indeed, this is the language of *Humanae salutis: inter tot taetricas caligines*, amid the gloomy mists.

51. Augustine, *Confessions*, trans. John K. Ryan (New York: Doubleday, 1960), X, c. 6.

favorable, and human persons are not always favorable to reckoning with the signs they see. The decades from 1945–1965 provided a crucible of shared experience, generating palpable expectations for political liberty, a common order of rights, and economic development. In the ordinary course of things, moral consensus tied to such moments does not last very long. We have good reasons to think that this accounts for Pope John's sense of urgency when he summoned the council and issued instructions to his team of writers shortly before his death.

In 1988, Cardinal Joseph Ratzinger traveled to England to give the annual Fischer Lecture for the Catholic Chaplaincy at Cambridge University. With a paper entitled "Consumer Materialism and Christian Hope," he came prepared to speak about the "characteristic signs of the times." The most troubling sign, he averred, is that "what is moral has lost its evidence."[52] "What was first of all common to all of pre-modern mankind, however, lies really along the self-same line: the conviction that in man's being there lies an imperative, the conviction that man does not devise morality itself by calculating expediencies; rather he comes upon it in the being of things."[53]

The key point is reached at the conclusion of the Cardinal's prepared remarks. Referring to wisdom traditions in general, he proposed that "morality is not man's prison; it is rather the divine in him."[54] This conviction implies that the whole man is open to reality as a whole. Were this not true, the order of nature would amount to a mere aggregation of "details," and man's own interpretation of these details would amount to partial constructions of his own subjectivity—or, what is more likely, the constructions of social, political, and legal forces. Morality, then, would be a "prison." Perhaps we should go even further to say that whatever is "divine" in man would demand that the individual be emancipated from this prison of mere partialities, which can force but only pretend to bind his conduct. Thus, for the modern person, "morality has lost its evidence." He can "see through" all things but not "see."[55]

---

52. Cardinal Joseph Ratzinger, "Consumer Materialism and Christian Hope," in *Teachers of the Faith: Speeches and Lectures by Catholic Bishops*, foreword by Cardinal Cormac Murphy-O'Connor, ed. T. Horwood (London: Catholic Bishop's Conference of England and Wales, 2002), 78–94.

53. Ratzinger, "Consumer Materialism and Christian Hope," 87. The Cardinal's speech is an important documentary antecedent to the International Theological Commissions report, *The Search for a Universal Ethics: A New Look at Natural Law* (2008), available at vatican.va. This document is notable for its serious attempt to re-adapt the dialogical to the doctrinal facets of natural law and human rights.

54. Ratzinger, "Consumer Materialism and Christian Hope," 92.

55. Ratzinger, "Consumer Materialism and Christian Hope," 90; quoting C. S. Lewis, *The Abolition of Man* (New York: HarperCollins, 1947).

And so we have two prelates, both devotees of Augustine with strong interest in the theology of history, interpreting the signs under quite different historical skies. In the spring of 1963 Pope John and Dr. King could communicate a perennial moral logic because persons of "good will" were disposed in their own action and hopes to secure a certain order of rights. They taught what people were already trying to see and understand.

Perhaps the first sign of a changing historical sky was three years later, when in 1966 the U.N. could reach no moral consensus on a Covenant of Rights, and so it issued two: one on Civil and Political Rights, another on Cultural and Economic Rights. The problem was not so much different lists of human rights, but different orders that could not be integrated into a single, complex scheme. René Cassin's model of the portico had not been fully accomplished in history, but his vision had the mark of unity and coherence. After 1966 it became easier to imagine at least two different temples, having different foundations, steps, columns, and pediments. Perhaps there are more. Can there be tranquility of order if human goods, aspirations, and rights are arrayed in such different orders? It is one thing to have a diversity of political regimes—forms of government—but quite another thing to have different temples, which is to say different normativities.

In whichever temple of rights, there is little consensus reflecting what *Pacem in Terris* proposed as the first two modes of order: order in creation and order in human beings. While *Pacem in Terris* was under no illusions concerning the problems of clarifying and instantiating the fifth and sixth orders (between nations and then with respect to a still-to-be-determined global authority), the first two were of a different status. For in these, we are dealing with endowments to be discovered and honored. This constitutes the anthropological and moral foundation of human rights, which came to be perceived as a "prison." One way out of that "prison" is to leave *Pacem in Terris*'s first two modes of order to private opinion. Perhaps the human rights project can continue, but its foundation can be no deeper than the fourth order, between citizens and their government. Thus, the foundations will appear to be the changeable policies and legal instruments of governments.

In his Address to the U.N. General Assembly in 2008, Pope Benedict returned to this problem. Speaking of the 1948 Declaration, he said:

> However, the results still have not been as high as the hopes. Certain countries have challenged the universality of these rights, judged to be too western, inspiring a search for a more inclusive formulation. Moreover, a certain propensity towards multiplying more human rights according to the disordered desires of the consumerist individual or from sectarian demands rather than the objective requirements of the common good of humanity have, in no small way, contributed to devaluing them. Disconnected from the moral sense of values, which transcend particular

interests, the multiplication of procedures and juridical regulations can only wind up in a quagmire, which in the end only serves the interests of the most powerful. Above all, this reveals a tendency to reinterpret human rights, separating them from the ethical and rational dimension—which constitutes their foundation and end—in favor of a pure utilitarian legalism.

"Today," he concluded, "efforts need to be redoubled in the face of pressure to reinterpret the foundations of the *Declaration* and to compromise its inner unity."[56]

This would seem to be a different historical sky, requiring a new dialogical tactic rather than a new teaching. Nonetheless, nearly sixty years later we have good reason to appreciate the encyclical's bid to present rights and right order as integrally related. In this sense, *Pacem in Terris* was prescient, for it underscored the very issue that would become the stumbling block.

---

56. Pope Benedict XVI, "Discourse before the General Assembly of the United Nations," April 18, 2008, *AAS* 100, 335.

CHAPTER 9

Human Nature and States of Nature in John Paul II's Theological Anthropology

CRISIS OF ANTHROPOLOGY

As WE HAVE SEEN, Pius XI (1923–29) is the first pope to speak of social doctrine as a unified body of teachings that develop by way of clarity and application.[1] In *Quadragesimo Anno* (1931), Pius said that he inherited a "doctrine" handed on from the time of Leo XIII.[2] Although it is doubtful that Leo deliberately intended to launch a new doctrinal specialty per se, he certainly laid its foundations. No one expected this sixty-eight-year-old man, who was elected in 1878, exactly one century before John Paul II, to write some 110 teaching letters. Until his death in 1903, Leo averaged about four every year. By any measure, he incited a prodigious stream of magisterial work. When John Paul II was elected in 1978, modern popes had already issued 309 encyclicals and other teaching letters, including some 120 encyclicals on the state and social problems. No government, political party, encyclopedia, or university has produced such a continuous, not to say voluminous, commentary on social issues.

Surveying a century of tradition, Pope John Paul II insists that social doctrine belongs essentially to the "field of theology."

> As such, it proclaims God and his mystery of salvation in Christ to every human being, and for that very reason reveals man to himself. In this light, and only in this light, does it concern itself with everything else: the human rights of the individual, and in particular of the "working class," the family and education, the duties of the State, the ordering of

---

1. Mary Elsbernd, "Papal Statements on Rights: A Historical Contextual Study of Encyclical Teaching from Pius VI–Pius XI (1791–1939)" (PhD diss., Catholic University of Louvain, 1985), 587n1, on the emergence on the term *doctrina*.

2. Pius XI, Encyclical Letter *Quadragesimo Anno* (May 15, 1931), §§18–21, *AAS* 23, 182–84.

national and international society, economic life, culture, war and peace, and respect for life from the moment of conception until death.[3]

For Christians, the *revelata* (revealed things) center upon Christ, who, as new and mature Adam, "reveals man to himself."[4] "Christian anthropology," he goes on to say, is the "chapter of theology" in which revelation is applied to the human person and his works.[5] On the other hand, an "adequate anthropology" must also consider "human experience" as interpreted by philosophy and the specialized sciences.[6]

John Paul II's contribution to the tradition of social doctrine chiefly is in the area of anthropology, both philosophical and theological, but especially along the boundary where the two touch upon one another. From his earliest dramatic works, written in Krakow under German occupation from 1931–45, to the 1976 Lenten conferences given for Pope Paul VI shortly before his own election to the papacy, Karol Wojtyła increasingly came to believe that the crisis of the twentieth century is anthropological. For Wojtyła, the distinctive mark of the age is what can be called "negative anthropology."[7]

The crisis is manifest in the ready affirmation of what man *is not* combined with a deep-seated reluctance to affirm normative anthropological content. To the Roman Rota, the pope speaks of anthropologies that regard the "human," given by nature, as raw data, a prolepsis or outline of what man might be when he is made "specifically human" in the "historical and cultural sphere."[8] Georges Cottier, theologian of the papal household, points out that on this view we are no longer speaking of nature "but of a state of nature'" of "an order of myth." Although told in different ways, it is the myth of a proto-man who awaits humanization through the efficacy of culture, a sphere of freedom in which a multiplicity of forms can be imparted to the *proto-humanum*.[9] Rarely explicated in clear and rigorous philosophical systems, negative anthropology is elusive precisely because it crosses disciplines. Only with

---

3. *Centesimus Annus* (1991), §54.

4. Citing *Gaudium et Spes*, §22.

5. *Centesimus Annus*, §55.

6. See Pope John Paul II, *Theology of the Body* (Boston: Daughters of St. Paul, 1997), 97n23.

7. The term "negative anthropology" is taken from Rocco Buttiglione, *Karol Wojtyła: The Thought of the Man Who Became Pope John Paul II* (Grand Rapids, MI: Eerdmans, 1997), 53.

8. Pope John Paul II, *Address to the Roman Rota* (January 1, 2001), in *Papal Allocutions to the Roman Rota, 1939–2002*, ed. William H. Woestman, OMI (Ottawa: Faculty of Canon Law, St. Paul University, 2002), 261.

9. Georges Cottier, OP, "Reflections on Marriage and the Family," *Nova et Vetera* 1, no. 1 (2003): 18, 20.

that the peoples of Europe and her former colonies were prepared to make almost any sacrifice to transform their polities into *states*. The task of state-making overshadowed any particular ideology, creed, or class: partisans of monarchy and democracy alike—even Marxists dedicated to the withering away of the state—all had to have a state. States claimed a monopoly over family life and marriage, military, technology, education, the arts, national culture, language and dictionaries, calendars, the economy; and through administrative law and the so-called ministries of "cults" states did not hesitate to supervise, or to outright control, the public estate of the Church, from seminaries to graveyards.

Upon his election in 1878 Leo had no useful script with which to work on these institutional problems. Catholic doctrine had undergone virtually no refurbishment since the Council of Trent three centuries earlier. Neither churchmen nor statesmen were sure how to sort out what belongs to the jurisdiction of the Church, what belongs to the jurisdiction of the state, and what indeed belongs to a social order not reducible to either. Canon law on issues *mixti iuris*, overlapping jurisdiction in areas such as marriage, family, education, and ecclesial endowments, had evolved in the context of political Christendom, not secular states; indeed, canon law would not be codified until 1917. Unlike Wojtyła a century later, Leo did not have the armature of a conciliar diagnosis, much less a detailed mandate from his bishops. When the Vatican Council I began on 8 December 1869, the working draft of *De Ecclesia Dei* contained five chapters and twenty-one canons on Church and state, which ranged across the heart of the institutional crisis.[17] The bishops, however, could not reach consensus about these things, and by April 1870 the council turned its attention to papal infallibility and jurisdiction, both of which were affirmed in *Pastor aeternus* (1870). Universal jurisdiction of the papacy removed the option of national churches, and so gave Leo a platform to mold Church policy. But it conveyed little about the content of that policy. The doctrine of infallibility was an important moment in ecclesiology, but it had no purchase upon most of the social and political problems that fell, by degrees, more in the sphere of prudence than of revealed doctrine. Leo would never have reason to invoke it. With the possible exception of John Paul II's statements on abortion and euthanasia in *Evangelium Vitae*, no pope would have occasion to solemnly invoke Petrine authority on an issue related to social doctrine.[18]

---

17. Ionnes Dominicus Mansi, ed., *Sacrorum Conciliorum*, vol. 51 (Arnheim (Pays-Bas) and Leipzig: H. Welter, 1926). Primum Schema Constitutionis, *De Ecclesia Christi*, 539–54. Chs. X–XV, 543–51; canons I–XXI, 551–53. This material in the original schema is the surge of encyclicals on the state after Leo XIII is elected in 1878. Although the chapters and canons were set aside, Leo recovers them for his encyclicals.

18. *Evangelium Vitae*, §57.

The council also ratified *Dei Filius*, which very broadly treated the relationship and harmony between faith and reason. In the *Syllabus of Errors* (1864), Pius IX condemned a list of some eighty propositions of modern thought. To achieve balance, *Dei Filius* elaborated the affirmative propositions missing from, but presupposed by the *Syllabus*. Leo used *Dei Filius* to fashion a twofold pedagogy. Disputed issues would be treated on the one hand according to the evidence afforded by natural reason, including history, custom, science, and, increasingly, natural law. At the same time, disputed issues would be accessed in light of positive revelation, including Scripture, tradition, and doctrine. At every step, the Church would show the harmony between the two perspectives. Leo looked to Saint Thomas to supply the method for this twofold pedagogy. Thomas "pushed his philosophic inquiry into the reasons and principles of things," but more importantly developed the analogies between "things naturally known" and the theological "mysteries."[19] Leo believed that Thomism is uniquely suitable for affirming the dignity of the human intellect with respect to its natural resources even while showing how it is open-textured with respect to revelation. Above all, he recommends the teachings of Saint Thomas for the "true meaning of liberty" and for the "divine origin of all authority."[20] As this prayer indicates, the *ressourcement* of Thomas had the political and social issues in view.

Catholic social doctrine was born in this historical matrix. The initiative for developing a body of thought fell, by default, to the papacy. Beginning with Leo, the arcane papal bull was transformed into teaching letters on a wide array of institutional problems. With the rise of totalitarian regimes, it became all the more important to give reasons for believing that man is something more than a citizen, or a member of a party or a class. The anthropological issues always track the institutional crises. The question of workers' associations calls forth a disquisition on the nature of human work; state-imposed youth fellowships triggers teaching on the rights of the family; civil marriage and divorce lead to a teaching on the nature of matrimony. In the space of fourteen days in March 1937, Pius XI issued encyclicals against fascism in Germany, communism in the Soviet Union, and atheistic liberalism in Mexico.[21]

Ideas that float free of institutional crises and political regimes sometimes are noted, but usually are not commented upon in detail.[22] Modern

---

19. *Aeterni Patris*, §18.

20. *Aeterni Patris*, §29.

21. Pius XI, Encyclical Letter *Mit brennender Sorge* (March 14, 1937); Pius XI, Encyclical Letter *Divinae Redemtoris* (March 19, 1937); and Pius XI, Encyclical Letter *Firmissimam Constantium* (March 28, 1937).

22. An important exception to this pattern is the cluster of the issues pertaining to marriage: purely civil marriage, divorce, abortion, and contraception. Here, Leo XIII and

anthropological myths (Enlightenment-era renditions of the "state of nature") are also duly noted, but once again for the purpose of teaching on the limits of a "social contract."[23] Two things help to explain why the popes did not dwell on problems of anthropology. First, the crises were most manifest in transgressions of public order. Second, and more important for our purposes, the laicist regimes of the nineteenth century and the totalitarian regimes of the twentieth did not publicly avow theses of negative anthropology. To be sure, wherever man is reduced to the state, class, or race there is the seed of such negation. But the industrial era nation-state did not hesitate to legislate, or, in any event, to enforce normative views of the human good. Catholic social thought and doctrine sometimes responded to these forces as mistaken or reductive, but nonetheless positive anthropologies. Finally, it should be said that, after World War II, there appeared a moment of consensus that man is prior to, and in some sense transcends, the political organization of the state. The Protestant theologian Karl Barth aptly called this the era of "disillusioned sovereignty."[24] Too much blood had gone down the gutters of the project of man as citizen, species, or class not to affirm man as individually human.

Every pope since 1775 had written his inaugural encyclical on the problem of political order. When Wojtyła was elected in 1978, it would have surprised no one had he issued immediately an encyclical on political order. As a Pole, he came from the most politically fraught sector of Europe, still under a totalitarian regime. In fact, he would not undertake a full-dress rehearsal on the political aspects of Catholic social teaching for another thirteen years, when he issued *Centesimus annus* (1991). The question for Wojtyła was whether, at this historical moment, the wide and deeply felt disillusionment with modern political ideologies and systems would lead to an affirmation of the predicates of human dignity, or whether it would curve back upon itself as an occasion for negative anthropology.

John Paul II's inaugural encyclical was *Redemptor hominis* (1979): not on the problem of the state, the *deus mortalis*, but rather on Jesus Christ as *salvator hominis*. Where his predecessors asked *Quid est Caesar* (what is Caesar), *Redemptor hominis* begins with the question posed by Psalm 8: "[W]hat is man [*quid est homo*] that you should be mindful of him, or the son

---

Pius XI wrote at some length on the thesis that the human body is a datum of the zoological order, awaiting the reception of a specifically human form by contracts and positive law. Adam stands to his own body and the body of his partner in the same way he exercises dominion over the beasts. See *Arcanum*, §7; *Sapientia Christianae*, §12; *Casti Connubii*, §§7, 49–50.

23. On the myth ("fiction") of the social contract inventing authority from scratch, see, for example, *Diuturnum illud*, §12, *Acta Leonis* 2, 275.

24. *Church Dogmatics*, vol. 3, part 4 (German 467, English 410).

of man that you should care for him? You have made him a little less than the angels, and crowned him with glory and honor. You have given him rule over the works of your hands."[25] To the question, "What is man?" the Pope answers, the "mature humanity in each one of us" made possible by the new Adam.[26] The old Adam, created in the image of God, and capacitated to rule himself and render service to others, is given a new invitation to "be a king," to exercise the virtue of *regalitas*. In his first trip to Poland after being elected Pope—a trip that would forever change the history of central Europe—he called the Poles *piasts*, sovereigns, or those who are crowned.[27]

At least by way of emphasis, here was the reversal of the historic pattern of magisterial teachings, for in this case it was the anthropological premise that proved politically explosive. First, assert the anthropological truth; then allow the issues of external (institutional) liberty to emerge. In Poland, he was hailed as a prophet. Six months earlier, during his trip to the Puebla Episcopal Conference in Mexico, he had been regarded by some Catholics as propounding an unimaginative doctrine of the status quo. But his message in Mexico was virtually identical to the one in Poland. "The primordial assertion of [the Church's] anthropology," he said, "is that the human being is the image of God and cannot be reduced to a mere fragment of nature or to an anonymous element in the human city."[28] He warned that political issues are subsequent, rather than prior to, understanding human persons in terms of their "whole being."[29] As we will now show, the priority of anthropology in

---

25. See *Redemptor hominis*, §8 (March 4, 1979), *AAS* 71, 272.

26. *Redemptor hominis*, §88. Kenneth Schmitz remarks: "The mention of 'maturity' takes the word out of the very mouth of the enlightenment." Kenneth L. Schmitz, *At the Center of the Human Drama: The Philosophical Anthropology of Karol Wojtyła/Pope John Paul II* (Washington, DC: The Catholic University of America Press, 1993), 117.

27. Address at Gniezno (June 3, 1979). See *L'OR*, Eng. Ed., 11 June 1979, 7–9. Piast was the name of the Polish dynasty that converted to Catholicism in 966. So, too, in his trip to Cameroon, he referred to the African youth as "being crowned" according to Ps. 8:4–6. Given at Yaounde, Cameroon, 14 September 1995 on the Feast of the Triumph of the Cross. See *Ecclesia in Africa*, §82. For his use of Ps 8:4–6: *Evangelium Vitae*, §§35, 82, 84; *Letter to Families*, §10; *Mulieris Dignitatem*, §§10–11. For Wojtyła's political theology, see George Hunston Williams, *The Contours of Church and State in the Thought of John Paul II* (Waco, TX: Institute of Church-State Studies, Baylor University, 1983).

28. Delivered in Seminario Palafoxiano, Puebla De Los Angeles, Mexico, 28 January 1979. John Eagleson and Philip Scharper, eds., *Puebla and Beyond* (Maryknoll, NY: Orbis Books, 1979), I.9.

29. This orientation toward theological anthropology was already evident in his decision, after becoming pope, to retain the coat of arms he had borne as archbishop of Krakow. Msgr. Jacques Martin, the prefect of the papal household in 1978, several years later reported that John Paul was pressured to adopt a conventional coat of arms. Critics apparently objected to the papal blazon. Completely missing are the typical symbols of his

Wojtyła's thought was not an exercise of political quietism. Rather, it reflected a carefully considered reading of the *signa temporis*, the signs of the time.

PROMETHEUS IN THE SOIL OF GENESIS

In 1976, Cardinal Karol Wojtyła was summoned to Rome to give the annual Lenten retreat for Pope Paul VI and select members of the Curia. Beginning on 7 March, Wojtyła gave twenty-two addresses in the Mathilda chapel of the Apostolic Palace. Paul VI, then seventy-eight years old, was seated by himself just off the sanctuary, wearing his white cassock over a customary Lenten hair shirt; several senior members of the Curia sat in front.[30] The rhetorical style of these pieces does not neatly correspond to either lectures or sermons; they are perhaps closer to what the medievals called *collationes*, conferences. They were gathered together, with footnotes, and published under the title *Sign of Contradiction*. The conferences are an invaluable window onto Wojtyła's understanding of the anthropological crisis just two years before his election to the papacy. "Careful study of human origins," he proposes, is "particularly important today if we are to understand the crucial problems of anthropology and ethics."[31] One cannot "understand either Sartre or Marx without having first read and pondered very deeply the first three chapters of Genesis."[32] The problem of human origins is not immediately a question of historical chronology, but rather a way to imagine and to experimentally explore experiences that undergird the proposition of negative anthropology that "man is an unknown being";[33] or, as Cardinal Wojtyła put it, that "man is alone, and his greatness requires that this be so."[34] For some years prior to his conferences in the Mathilda chapel, Wojtyła had worked and reworked this theme of Adamic loneliness, both in order to understand it and to rescue it from modern atheism. His play, "The Radiation of Fatherhood,"

---

predecessors: the fleur-de-lis, the castles, the stars, shooting comets, the eagles—all representing princely, familial, and, in any case, human symbols of authority to rule. In their place we find a blue shield, with a slightly off-centered gold Latin cross; and under this cross is the letter *M*, for Mary, who represents the Church at the foot of the cross. In answer to the question *Quid est homo*, the armorial shield answers, *Ecce homo*—Behold the Man. Jacques Martin, *Heraldry in the Vatican* (1987), 257f. See his 1976 Lenten conference on the third sorrowful mystery. Wojtyła, *Sign of Contradiction* (New York: Seabury Press, 1979), 77: "Here we have before us the Christ in truth of his kingship. Pilate says 'Here is the man.' Precisely . . . Jesus came in order to reveal the kingliness of man."

30. George Weigel, *Witness to Hope* (New York: HarperCollins, 1999), 223f.
31. *Sign of Contradiction*, 56.
32. *Sign of Contradiction*, 24.
33. *Sign of Contradiction*, 102.
34. *Sign of Contradiction*, 35.

first published in a Krakow monthly in 1964, is the monologue of an Everyman, who claims to "know who Adam was and who he is"—namely a being "on the frontier between fatherhood and loneliness."[35] The play considers the human condition depicted in Genesis 2:15–20: the Adam who is neither God Father, nor an animal placed alongside other animals; the Adam prior to Eve and the matrimonial covenant related in Genesis 2:22–25; the Adam who is still to discover what Paul in Ephesians 5:31–32 calls "the great mystery" of the union of one flesh. Hence, the deliberate ambiguity of the plays subtitle, "A Mystery."[36]

When it was published in Krakow, Archbishop Wojtyła was at the Second Vatican Council, where he would work on the anthropological sections for the pastoral constitution entitled *Gaudium et Spes*.[37] In a debate over how the document should address atheism, the archbishop insisted that atheism is not merely an academic, ideological, or political system, but also "a problem of the human person." "The human being who is an atheist," he continued, "is one persuaded of his own end—if I may so speak—of his 'eschatological' aloneness."[38] Wojtyła's intervention moved the drafters to distinguish between the external or systematic aspects of atheism (what we have called the institutional crises) and its anthropological premises.[39] Wojtyła was convinced that the exaltation of "Adam" through a negation of his natural and religious aspects has a mythic structure that overlaps with, and subverts, what sacred Scripture reports about the "frontier" of Adam who is resolvable into neither

---

35. Karol Wojtyła, "The Radiation of Fatherhood," in *The Collected Plays and Writings on Theatre*, trans. Boleslaw Taborski (Berkeley: University of California Press, 1987), 336. The play begins at p. 335: "For many years I have lived like a man exiled from my deeper personality yet condemned to probe it. During those years I have toiled to reach it but have often thought with horror that it was disappearing, blurred among the processes of history, in which what is numbers, mass. All this is connected with the name Adam given to me."

36. Sent by Cardinal Adam Sapieha to Rome in 1946 to pursue theological studies, Wojtyła was exposed to the different schools of scholastic Thomism. Although he did his doctoral thesis under Garrigou-Lagrange, the doyen of traditional Thomism, Wojtyła made no effort to reconcile the different philosophical schools. Rather, he wrote on *Faith according to St. John of the Cross*, which he finished in 1948. For our purposes, it is important to note that John of the Cross explored the negative moment of Christian mysticism, the so-called "dark night of the soul." Here can be probed and tested, within the bounds of the Catholic orthodoxy, how the "frontier" of Adam is resolved vertically, in absolute transcendence. Covered in Buttiglione, *Karol Wojtyła*, 44–53.

37. *Gaudum et Spes*; the anthropological sections include §§11–39.

38. *Acta Synodalia Sacrosancti Concilii Oecumenici Vaticani Secundi*, 6 vols. (Vatican City: Typis polyglottis Vaticanis, 1970–1978), IV: II, pp. 660f.

39. *Gaudium et Spes*, §§19–20. For Wojtyła's influence, see especially, §19: "Some so exalt the human as to empty faith in God of all content, being apparently more preoccupied with the affirmation of human beings than denial of God."

God nor beast. Adam knows what he is *not*. According to Wojtyła's reading of modern culture, the negative moment becomes the principal item of interest, and indeed the experience to be universalized.

In the Mathilda chapel, Wojtyła observes that modern anthropology transplants "the Prometheus myth into the soil of Genesis."[40] Told by Protagoras, this myth imagines a *humanum* that differentiates itself from the rest of the animals only by the extrinsic addition of technological art (stolen from Hephaestus and Athena), which is used to invent the world of culture, but most significantly the civil measures of good and evil.[41] In a number of ways, it is distinctly different from the two creation narratives of Genesis. Genesis 1:28 and 2:19–20 report that dominion is a natural endowment, the inscription of *imago Dei*; it suggests an ontological threshold between the natural succession of animals and the creation of man. Furthermore, Genesis 2 reports that man does more than control the animals; he also rules himself, becoming through his actions morally good or evil. Unlike dominion, self-ruling is not a transitive art, but rather what Wojtyła calls an intransitive perfection, for it is the very person who is both the cause of the action and the bearer of the moral predicates, good or evil.[42] Adam, according to Wojtyła, is kingly (having *regalitas*), partially by dominion over the animals, but principally by the capacity to act.[43] Still more, Genesis 2:21–25 relates that Adam did not stand to Eve in the mode of dominion. She is not the animal "other" but "flesh of my flesh."[44]

The mythic and dramatic resources of Genesis were exploited by Enlightenment philosophers. The heuristic scenario of a state of nature was espoused in different ways by Spinoza, Hobbes, and above all Rousseau, who said that Genesis entitles us to consider human nature as "if it had been left to itself."[45] So stranded, man is not distinct from the rest of the zoological order. He is alone, but not lonely. "His desires do not go beyond his physical needs. The only goods he knows in the universe are nourishment, a woman and rest; the only evils he fears are pain and hunger. I say pain and not death because an animal will never know what it is to die."[46] The "fall" of Adam follows upon

---

40. Wojtyła, *Sign of Contradiction*, 32. He returns to the interpretation of Genesis via the Promethean myth in *Evangelium Vitae*, §15.

41. Plato, *Protagorus*, 320d–326.

42. See his discussion of "intransitive efficacy," in Karol Wojtyła, *The Acting Person*, trans. Andrzej Potocki, ed. Anna-Teresa Tymieniecka, Analecta Husserliana 10 (Dordrecht: D. Reidel, 1979), 150f. See also his distinction between control and moral rule at p. 107.

43. *Sign of Contradiction*, 32. He returns to the interpretation of Genesis via the Promethean myth in *Evangelium Vitae*, §15.

44. Wojtyła, *Sign of Contradiction*, 55–56, 97.

45. Jean-Jacques Rousseau, *Discourse on the Origin of Inequality*, trans. Donald A. Cress (Indianapolis: Hackett, 1992), preface, p. 15.

46. Rousseau, *Discourse*, 26.

the trickery of the woman who extols monogamy, stirring in the male imagination the notion of property and exclusivity, both of which establish a distinction in species between himself and the animals.[47] Thus, the two properties that distinguish the Adam of Genesis, dominion over the animals and one flesh matrimony, are the elements of the fall of the Rousseauvian savage. Hobbes's "Lawes of Nature," which conserve "men in multitudes,"[48] and Kant's notion of the "voice of nature" and the "call of nature," as the "limits that bind all animals," represented "natural" man bereft of the endowments of men as we know them.[49] For Hobbes, in the condition of "mere nature" there are no matrimonial laws, only claims to dominion.[50]

Although travel accounts of explorers, especially in the New World and the South Pacific, aroused curiosity and speculation that the state-of-nature scenario converges with natural history,[51] the Enlightenment thinkers usually did not take the "state of nature" to be either natural or human history. Rather, it was a philosophical effort, akin to Protagoras's telling of the Greek myths of origins, to tame the biblical myth, and to render it "speculatively" amenable to the notion that man causes himself to be distinct from his zoological fundaments. Not once upon a time, but even now, Adam stands to his original endowment in the mode of dominion. Like the animals that serve man, the proto-human must be tamed, shaped, and humanized. Of course, the proto-human is knowable in terms of physical and psycho-somatic structures; in another, and more important sense, however, it is not knowable as specifically or normatively human.[52] The latter knowledge is a function of freedom and culture that supplies the experimental constructions of what is indeterminate in the original of nature.

---

47. Rousseau, *Discourse*, 39, 46.

48. Hobbes, *Leviathan*, I, c. 15. See *Leviathan: With Selected Variants from the Latin Edition of 1668*, ed. Edwin Curley (Indianapolis: Hackett, 1994).

49 Immanuel Kant, "Speculative Beginning of Human History (1795)," in *Perpetual Peace and Other Essays*, trans. Ted Humphrey (Indianapolis: Hackett, 1983), 112–13.

50. See *Leviathan*, II, c. 20.

51. The convergence of the state-of-nature scenario and natural history was of prime interest to Captain James Cook and his scientist during his three expeditions to the South Pacific (1768–1779). For the Rousseauvian speculations of Cook, see Nicholas Thomas, *Cook: The Extraordinary Voyages of Captain James Cook* (New York: Walker, 2003).

52. While Kant, like Rousseau, certainly used Genesis subversively to suggest that a "fall" mythically represents man's acquisition of a moral sensibility, Kant says, "The history of nature, therefore, begins with good, for it is God's work; the history of freedom begins with badness, for it is man's work." See Kant, "Speculative Beginning," 54. Wojtyła thought that Kant's is the superior position—philosophically, not exegetically. For Kant locates in the morally good will a human property that transcends instrumental reason. See Wojtyła, *Love and Responsibilty*, trans. H. T. Willetts (San Francisco: Ignatius Press, 1993), 27f.

Thus, the historical succession of human cultures (the story of man humanized by various constructions) is the template imposed over the natural succession of animals studied by the physical sciences. Variants of this "humanism" were the stock-in-trade of European intellectual life, and were well known to Wojtyła. When he proposed to the pope and the Curia that one cannot understand "Sartre or Marx without having first read and pondered very deeply the first three chapters of Genesis," he spoke from experience as an intellectual, but also as a bishop whose city and nation was occupied by a political power that told its own version of the myth.

DISCERNING THE SIGNS OF THE TIME

Why did Cardinal Wojtyła believe that the pope and the Curia would benefit from Lenten lessons on Protagoras and his modern counterparts? The biographer of Paul VI, Peter Hebblethwaite, characterizes the *Sign of Contradiction* as "an austere, pessimistic work, very conscious of the power of evil, and [it] marks a break with the optimism of *Gaudium et Spes*."[53] Hebblethwaite is correct on one score. Wojtyła expressly said that he intended to interpret the "signs of our times" by counterposing the anthropology of *Gaudium et Spes* and that of modern humanisms that rework the Genesis myth.[54] He was interested in a dialogue between Christian and secular anthropologies broken, or at least frayed, since the Enlightenment.

In the first place, the anthropologies that assign man dominion over proto-human material are not merely a curious chapter of the Enlightenment. It is true that for thinkers such as Hobbes, Rousseau, Kant, and Feuerbach the state-of-nature scenarios were devised for a purpose of showing the basis of the civilizing mission of the state. The transition from animal to man, from laws of nature to the sovereignty of law, correlate with the movement from pre-political to citizen. Here, we can pass over the interesting question of how the "state of nature" could prepare the way for such different programs of political power, from class dictatorships to republican regimes. The key point for our purposes is that after the Second World War the myth of origins was released from its earlier function of justifying the state, and turned toward the sovereignty of the individual.

This is the contemporary site of Wojtyła's investigation of "eschatological aloneness." Given the radical indeterminacy of human nature, the Enlightenment theorists tended to conclude, all the more reason for civilizing task of the state;[55]

---

53. Peter Hebblethwaite, *Paul VI, The First Modern Pope* (New York: Paulist Press, 1993), 658.

54. Wojtyła, *Sign of Contradiction*, 35.

55. Authority will have to make its appearance *ab initio* as the voice of man—as Rousseau said, the voice of a divine-like human legislator. But given the fact that nature

the contemporary mind concludes, all the more reason for individual liberty. As the French philosopher Pierre Manent puts it, human nature is a cipher, an "efficacious indetermination" allowing a zone of liberty in which the individual can "affirm himself without knowing himself."[56] How the individual is the bearer of rights is deeply perplexing.[57] Before and after becoming pope, Wojtyła was determined to understand the anthropological grounds of human freedom, for this is the seam along which positive and negative anthropologies are joined. It is important to discern, for example, the difference between a doctrine of negative liberty (as against the state) and a negative anthropology (man is only liberty).[58] Catholic social doctrine, with its affirmation of human rights and its elaboration of the plural spheres of liberty and authority, stands or falls on negative liberty's not being confused with negative anthropology. Discerning the difference between the two is one of the main issues animating John Paul's encyclical *Centesimus annus*, written to interpret the fall of Marxist states after 1989.

In the second place, Wojtyła was acutely aware that Christian anthropology is not immune to a subversion of Genesis. The bellwether of the problem is marriage and procreation, issues simmering in Catholic thought since the 1920s. Previous popes had written extensively and in considerable detail on the subject of marriage. As mentioned earlier, these teachings were prompted by the problem of state-enforced civil marriage and divorce. At the same time, debate over the public status of marriage also brought into the open a version of the thesis that marriage is constructed out of psychosomatic seeds and given different forms according to historical and cultural time and place. Here, we cannot rehearse in detail the history of the debate. One point, however, is very important because of the attention Wojtyła will give to it. From Leo XIII through John XXIII, popes contended that there are natural limits to the marriage contract: between man and woman (uncontested at that time), exclusively monogamous (somewhat contested), and unto perpetuity (greatly contested). Undergirding these so-called *essentiales* of marriage is another principle that has application beyond marriage. No one has a moral right to dominion over the human body.

Thomas, for example, contended that:

---

imparts no titles to rule, on what ground can a man issue a binding word? Who has a natural right to bind another member of the species? The answer, of course, is that men give their consent. They command a commanding voice.

56. Pierre Manent, *The City of Man*, trans. Marc A. LePain, with foreword by Jean Elshtain (Princeton, NJ: Princeton University Press), 129.

57. Perplexities covered masterfully by Hadley Arkes, *Natural Rights and the Right to Choose* (Cambridge: Cambridge University Press, 2002).

58. This is the meaning of his seemingly paradoxical remarks in §86 of *Veritatis Splendor*, "freedom itself needs to be set free."

[M]an is bound to obey his fellow-man in things that have to be done externally by means of the body: and yet, since by nature all men are equal, he is not bound to obey another man in matters touching the nature of the body, for instance in those relating to the support of his body or the begetting of his children. Wherefore servants are not bound to obey their masters, nor children their parents, in the question of contracting marriage or of remaining in the state of virginity or the like.[59]

He concludes that on such matters, man is "immediately under God, by Whom he is taught either by the natural or by the written law."[60] For Thomas, use of the body does fall to the decisions and free acts of a human agent; but only according to the natural and supernatural orders established by divine providence. One may claim a rightful freedom to bodily acts with regard to human authorities precisely because the order of such acts, as well as the "state" of the body vocationally, is already enmeshed in divine providence that is not established by the contract of spouses, by familial or cultural orders, nor indeed by the civil authorities.

"The Supreme Author of all things," said Leo XIII, "so decreed that man should exercise a sort of royal dominion over beasts and cattle and fish and fowl, but never that men should exercise a like dominion over their fellow men."[61] If the human body is an object of dominion in the case of individuals, there is no absolute reason why dominion over the same bodies cannot be transferred as a proprietary right to non-matrimonial agents such as corporations or to the state.

In *Casti connubii* (1930), Pius XI insisted that "[p]ublic magistrates have no direct power over the bodies of their subjects; therefore, where no crime has taken place and there is no cause present for grave punishment, they can never directly harm, or tamper with the integrity of the body, either for the reasons of eugenics or for any other reason."[62] Nor can such immediate right over the body be derived from the matrimonial contract, for "Christian doctrine establishes, and the light of human reason makes it most clear, that private individuals have no other power over the members of their bodies than that which pertains to their natural ends."[63] The human body is not property

---

59. *ST*, II-II, q. 104, a. 5.

60. *ST*, II-II, q. 104, a. 5, ad 2. For a discussion of the relationship between natural law and friendship with God, see Scott Roniger, "Natural Law and Friendship with God," *The Thomist* Vol. 83, no. 2 (2019): 237–76.

61. Leo XIII, Encyclical Letter *In Plurimus* (May 5, 1888), §3; Leo XIII, Encyclical Letter *Arcanum Divinae* (February 10, 1880), §§7, 14.

62. *Casti Cannubii*, §70.

63. *Casti Cannubii*, §71.

but a person, and the moral right of spouses to one another's body is that of usufruct.[64] On this view, man does not own himself, but rather enjoys dominion (of the will) over his actions (operations) according to the norms of the moral law.

After the council, Archbishop Wojtyła was appointed to a pontifical commission originally charged in 1963 with studying questions of population control. At the time of his appointment by Paul VI, the mandate of the commission was expanded to include not only issues of public policy but questions of moral theology. Very quickly, the debate moved from considerations of demography and pharmacology, to principles of moral method, and to anthropological issues—specifically, the scope of human dominion in the light of Genesis and natural law.[65]

The majority argued that "what is given in physical nature" reflects an order of dynamisms and processes that it is the duty of human agents to "humanize and bring to greater perfection."[66] The specifically human in "given [material] nature" is for the sake of man. "The true opposition is not sought between some material conformity to the physiological processes of nature and some artificial intervention," for it is "natural to man to put under human control what is given by physical nature."[67] The majority averred that the inherent finalities, which Genesis says are "good," permit us to conclude that their negation is a "physical evil." But the humanization of nature can permit, and perhaps require, a negation of pre-moral goods for the affirmation of what is specifically human in marriage. Challenged by four members of the minority to show how this view comports with the traditional understanding of Scripture and natural law, the majority responded:

> But an unconditional respect for nature as it is in itself (as if nature in its physical existence were the expression of the will of God) pertains to a vision of man which sees something mysterious and sacred in nature, and because of this fears that any human intervention tends to destroy rather than perfect this very nature. . . . The very dignity of man created to the image of God consists in this: that God wished man to share in his dominion. God has left man in the hands of his own counsel. To take

---

64. For a survey of the distinction between proprietary and usufructory meanings of the traditional expression *ius in corpus*, see John C. Ford, SJ, and Gerald Kelly, SJ, *Contemporary Moral Theology*, vol. 2, *Marriage Questions* (Westminster, MD: Newman Press, 1963), 63–74.

65. A record of the final stage of the debate is summarized in two working papers of the majority of the commission, one working paper of the minority, and the final report. Published in *The Tablet*, April 22, 1967; April 29, 1967; May 6, 1967; September 21, 1968.

66. First working paper of the majority, p. 451.

67. First working paper of the majority, p. 452.

his life or another's life is a sin not because life is under the exclusive dominion of God but because it is contrary to right reason unless there is question of a good of a higher order.[68]

Due to problems with the Polish government, Wojtyła was unable to attend the commission's final meeting in Rome. However, an alert reader will appreciate the alarm taken back in Krakow. The final report of the commission advocated change of Church teaching on contraception. To be sure, the report buffered the blow by embroidering its text with Scripture and with otherwise unobjectionable truisms. But the working papers of the majority are more serious because they made clear that the moral teaching is changeable because of the indeterminacy of the anthropological structure. Here, a group of notable moral theologians had spelled out a position nearly identical to what Archbishop Wojtyła, at the council, had attributed to modern atheism: namely, that the greatness of man requires eschatological aloneness; man left in the hands of his own counsel, now interpreted by theologians as dominion over his "given" nature. Surely, even God demands that this be so.

Paul VI refused to adopt the recommendation of the commission, and in the summer of 1968 issued the controversial encyclical *Humanae Vitae*. Stung by the criticism, he would not write another encyclical. Eight years later, when the aging Pope listened to Wojtyła's conferences in the Mathilda chapel on human nature, states of nature, and Genesis—when he heard the young cardinal insist that, "particularly in our own day," it is necessary to meditate upon the "first and fundamental covenant" offered to Adam, "our humanity"—he surely understood where this line of thought was heading.[69] In *Humanae Vitae*, Pope Paul addressed the problem of dominion from Scripture and from natural law.[70] His discussion, however, is tersely worded, and the reader who is unaware of the background debate of the commission might not have a clear sense of what is at stake.

To return now to the question that motivates and informs Wojtyła's meditations on Genesis, previewed in the 1976 Lenten conferences, but soon to

---

68. Second working paper of the majority, p. 511. The method of "proportionalism," the weighing of pre-moral goods and evils, was not merely an issue of moral reasoning, but also one of anthropology. For the method seems to presuppose a radical indeterminacy of the human body.

69. *Sign of Contradiction*, 19.

70. *Humanae Vitae*, §§10, 13. Compare to *Casti Connubii*, §§63–71, where dominion is treated in a more full-orbed manner; and to Cardinal Ratzinger, Instruction *Donum Vitae* (February 22, 1987), *AAS* 80, 70–102, which explains with considerable precision why dominion (in contrast to moral mastery) over the human body affects not only the reproductive facet, but also the nature of the matrimonial relationship and the moral status of progeny.

be elaborated in remarkable detail in his magisterial teachings, we can mention three points. First, he believed that the anthropological propositions in *Gaudium et Spes* are liable to be interpreted too flatly and unimaginatively unless they are brought into close proximity to the modern myth of man "left to himself."[71] The lawless Adam. This, rather than politics, constitutes the primary site of the anthropological dialogue. The Church's social doctrine on human dignity, natural rights, indeed, the ontological social relations, will be brittle unless the disputed anthropological fundaments are brought into the open. Second, the chief thesis of negative anthropology, the humanization of proto-human material, including the concrete human body, has found its way into Christian moral theology. Here, too, it is necessary to bring into the open what reason and revelation can know about the scope of human dominion. Third, the anthropological premises of Vatican II require at least partial intelligibility of the first Adam. For this Adam is the natural reality, and therefore the natural "sign" of Christian mysteries. So, while it is true that "without its creator the creature simply disappears,"[72] it is also true that deconstruction of the first Adam will cancel the second. Christian anthropology, and all of the social teachings that flow from it, would be a "sectarian" construction of the indeterminate *humanum*.

ASPECTS OF WOJTYŁA'S METHOD

It is not easy to sort out where Wojtyła intends his anthropological reflections to constitute a ground of dialogue between Christianity and modern humanism and where the same reflections expound a theological anthropology drawn from revelation. From the time of his earliest dramatic work, he has used Scripture for both purposes. Scripture can provide an experimental, dramatic context for asking anthropological questions. On the other hand, Scripture can provide evidence for what faith must affirm about the essential dignities and eschatological promise of the *humanum*.

Wojtyła did write at least one academic work, *The Acting Person*, that qualifies as purely philosophical, in which Scripture is not deployed in either of the senses just mentioned. "Man," he begins, "is the first, closest, and most frequent object of experience, and so he is in danger of becoming usual and

---

71. Particularly the following: Man is *imago Dei*, the center and culmination of which things lower than man are ordered, and that dominion does not render man solitary (§12); that what is known through revelation is consonant with our experience (§13); that pursuit of truth and moral responsibility are a "sign" of the *imago Dei* (§§15–16); that Christ is the last Adam, fully revealing man to himself (§22); that man is the only terrestrial creature that God wills for its own sake (§24); that without the Creator the creature disappears (§36).

72. *Gaudium et Spes*, §36.

commonplace; he risks becoming too ordinary even for himself."[73] Wojtyła goes on to locate what must be affirmed about man if we are to be true to experience. The exercise is of a piece with his other work, because it attempts to overcome any self-engulfing negative anthropology. Wojtyła concludes that man is a person. "We experience man as a person," he contends, "and we are convinced of it because he performs actions."[74] The man-act—in Thomistic parlance, the *actus humanus*—consists of knowing, judging, deciding, acting. In such acts, he not only knows himself to be the cause of action, but he also knows himself to be the very person who becomes (morally) good or evil. Whatever else can be said about man, or the "Adam," it cannot be said that he is beyond good or evil.[75]

Although he draws the point in more detail elsewhere, Wojtyła believes he has uncovered one sturdy piece of evidence confirming the fact that man is *ad imaginem Dei*. Namely, that he is unrepeatable, inalienable, and incommunicable.[76] By "incommunicable" (*alteri incommunicabilis*) he means something that cannot be absorbed, transferred, or ceded as property.[77] Even better, the incommunicable denotes what cannot be outsourced. Such indeed appears to be the property of a moral act, which, if surrendered, ceases to be what it is. Wojtyła also believed that a philosophical method can confirm that the acting person is not merely noumenal, a pure act bereft of what Thomas called "potency," for this would rule out the coming-to-be of moral deliberation and judgment, as well as the quest for perfectibility, as we experience it.[78]

---

73. Wojtyła, *The Acting Person*, 22.
74. Wojtyła, *The Acting Person*, 11.
75. Wojtyła, *The Acting Person*, 49.
76. Wojtyła, *The Acting Person*, 107.
77. Wojtyła, *Love and Responsibility*, 96.
78. Beyond this, we must be cautious not to attribute more to Wojtyła's philosophical experiments than what he thought he had accomplished. Even in his post-1978 magisterial writings, the works exhibiting conventional philosophical rigor are sections in *Laborem Exercens* (§§4–6), on why work involves more than instrumental rationality, and the sections of *Veritatis Splendor* (§§71–82) devoted to the nature of the moral agent. These correspond closely to his philosophical work. Wojtyła never attempted a systematic review of cosmology and metaphysics (e.g., demonstrations of the existence of God); and though it seems remarkable, he did not systematically tackle Marxism. Such a trusted interpreter of Wojtyła's philosophy as Rocco Buttiglione points out that the phenomenological method does not demonstrate that the soul is the form of the body, but rather seems to confirm it. Buttiglione, *Karol Wojtyła*, 166f. Of course, what Wojtyła didn't explicitly treat in the mode of academic philosophy cannot tell us either (1) what he thought about the upper and lower limits of philosophical inquiry on matters anthropological, or (2) what in principle might be available to experience and human reason beyond modes of demonstration. When he was professor at the Catholic University at Lublin (1954–1958), Wojtyła taught

Wojtyła's earlier habilitation thesis, *An Evaluation of the Possibility of Constructing a Christian Ethics on the Basis of the System of Max Scheler*, worked a similar problem. What can analysis of experience yield about the values of the good and the right in morals? His professed aim is to compare Christian and non-Christian accounts of moral experience, and to reconnoiter "the border at which they touch one another."[79] Strictly considered, the experience of man-acts is neither philosophical nor theological. The borderline of the two disciplines runs through the experience; it is presupposed by both. Even in his more philosophical writings, Wojtyła never strays far from this "border." Wojtyła makes the point that anthropology presupposes a core of common experience. In his *Catechesis on Genesis*, which we will consider in detail later, he takes up the issue of the "convergence" of experience and revelation in questions anthropological. The Christian theological doctrine of the "redemption of the body," he remarks, is not a reality grasped in "ordinary experience." Yet it presupposes a range of experiences in which we can affirm ourselves as bodily. Christian anthropology is unintelligible if the experiential "givens" along the border of reason and revelation are erased. The secularist can say he has no need to consider human things in the light of revelation; the theologian, however, cannot say the same of ordinary experience interpreted by philosophy and the more specialized sciences.[80]

In a recent address to the Roman Rota, John Paul emphasizes, of course, that Christ instituted marriage as a sacrament of the New Covenant, making it an efficacious sign of the New Adam and the Church. From this, however, one cannot conclude that the "properties" of marriage are entirely the construct of grace, or Church law. They are also based "on a foundation of natural law that, if removed, would make incomprehensible the very work of

---

specialized courses in ethics. He did not think it was his job to reproduce the investigations, findings, and systematic expositions of philosophy engaged by the rest of the faculty. The reader should consult, in addition to Buttiglione and Schmitz already cited, two other books: Jaroslaw Kupczak, *Destined for Liberty: The Human Person in the Philosophy of Karol Wojtyła/John Paul II* (Washington, DC: The Catholic University of America Press, 2000); and a work that has the virtues of sweeping narrative and detailed discussion of Wojtyła's thought (up to the late 1970s), George Hunston Williams, *The Mind of John Paul II: Origins of His Thought and Action* (New York: Seabury Press, 1981).

79. This statement from Wojtyła's work on Max Scheler is taken from Buttiglione, *Karol Wojtyla*, 62.

80. John Paul II, "Catechesis on the Book of Genesis," in *Theology of the Body*, 93n8: "In fact, we have the right to raise the problem of their mutual relation, even if for many people there passes between them a line of demarcation which is a line of complete antithesis and radical antinomy. In their opinion, this line must certainly be drawn between faith and science, between theology and philosophy. In the formulation of this point of view, abstract considerations rather than man as a living subject are considered."

salvation."[81] If there is a "betrothed love," at once essential to marriage and distinct from other modes of human friendship, we cannot posit it in the absence of anthropological evidence, however dim contemporary appreciation of the experiential grounds.[82] With regard to the specialized anthropological sciences, such as biology, psychology, sociology, and medicine, he makes the same point. Insights "come first of all from human experience, which, in all its complexity, in some sense both precedes science and follows it."[83]

Finally, we note that Wojtyła usually treats a subject by multiplying rather than narrowing the perspectives. To take but one example: In his conferences on "St. Paul's Teaching on the Human Body," he examines the moral norm forbidding deliberate sundering of the unitive and procreative facets of the marital act. He argues (1) that the norm belongs to the natural law, (2) that it is discovered in the subjective-psychological dimension of marital love as well as in the structure of the body, and (3) that it is contained in divine revelation. He uses Scripture for all three. Scripture is used experimentally, to call attention to human experiences often overlooked, or perhaps siphoned into abstract categories that have lost their dramatic texture. Similarly, Scripture can be used not so much to propound a doctrine *de fide* as to relocate the question that originally led to the doctrine. The harmony of reason and revelation, he proposes, is to be "sought especially in biblical anthropology."[84] Wojtyła's experimental uses of Scripture have no parallel in the work of modern popes, who use sacred texts to anchor, to proof, and sometimes to embroider doctrine, but not to launch or reconnoiter questions, which might lead back to a doctrine.

IN THE BEGINNING, ANTHROPOLOGICAL THRESHOLDS

The best example of Wojtyła's anthropology, undertaken both theologically and experimentally, is *The Theology of the Body*. Originally, the material was neither a book nor an encyclical, but a series of weekly general audiences beginning in September 1979 and continuing through November 1984.[85] These audiences are important for more than one reason. They continue

---

81. John Paul II, "Address to the Roman Rota," January 28, 2002, in Woestman, *Papal Allocutions*, 268.

82. Wojtyła, *Love and Responsibility*, 95–98.

83. *Letter to Families*, §12.

84. *Theology of the Body*, 389.

85. The audiences were divided and published under different titles: "Original Unity of Man and Woman," "Blessed Are the Pure of Heart," "The Theology of Marriage and Celibacy," and "Reflections of *Humanae Vitae*." Gathered together with a foreword by John S. Grabowski, the entire set is published in Pope John Paul II, *The Theology of the Body: Human Love in the Divine Plan* (Boston: Daughters of St. Paul, 1997).

themes presented in the 1976 Lenten conferences, now aired-out and greatly expanded. Because they are not the occasion for formal teaching, the Pope feels especially free to engage the questions experimentally and speculatively. This is one of the few works containing explanatory notes of a scholarly nature on literary types, philosophy, and psychology. Importantly, the audiences contain his most sustained reading and interpretation of the Adamic myth, treated according to the exegetical nexus of Matthew 19:3–12 ("in the beginning it was not so"), Genesis 2:24 ("and they become one flesh"), and Ephesians 5:32 ("this is a great mystery").

The first year's audiences focus upon Genesis 2, the older of the two creation narratives. One reason for preferring Genesis 2 is that this is the text that Jesus interprets in the Gospel ("in the beginning") and the text to which Paul refers in Ephesians. The pope prefers it because its archaic structure affords space for inquiry. "A reflection in depth on this text—through the whole archaic form of the narrative, which manifests its primitive mythical character—provides us *in nucleo* with nearly all of the elements of the analysis of man, to which modern, and especially contemporary philosophical anthropology is sensitive."[86] Its value lies in the fact that it cannot be confused with historical chronology or natural science. The narrative, he says, "forces us, in a way, to reconstruct the elements that constitute man's original experience." The important thing is not locating something pre-historical, but the trans-historical—what stands "at the root of every human experience."[87]

He locates four experiences that are distinct, but not separable. First, according the Genesis 1:26–27, man is created out of the dust and stamped with the divine image, male and female. Upon them is conferred dominion over the animals. Likewise, Genesis 2:7 reports a creation from the ground, but here the man is given a name—'*adam*, the man, not yet considered' *is*, the male. Again, dominion is exerted over the animals. Adam is created a visible body among other bodies, but in neither account is he made "like" the animals. Bound to the visible world, he is nonetheless, and in some important respect, not in a natural succession with the animals he subdues and names.[88]

---

86. *Theology of the Body*, 30; quoting Paul Ricoeur, "The Adamic myth is par excellence the anthropological myth," 91n4.

87. *Theology of the Body*, 51. See also *Laborem Exercens*, §4: "The Church finds in the very first pages of the Book of Genesis the source of her conviction that work is a fundamental dimension of human existence on earth. An analysis of these texts makes us aware that they express—sometimes in an archaic way of manifesting thought—the fundamental truths about man, in the context of the mystery of creation itself. These truths are decisive for man from the very beginning, and at the same time they trace out the main lines of his earthly existence, both in the state of original justice and also after the breaking, caused by sin, of the Creator's original covenant with creation in man."

88. *Theology of the Body*, 28.

The experience of being distinct from the rest of visible world (not to be confused with being "other" than one's own body) is common, that is to say, trans-historical. Different anthropologies might attempt to expand or contract the threshold, but experience teaches that the threshold is not purely arbitrary. Even a radical contraction must begin with it.

Second, in Genesis 2, the Adam is capable of, and limited by, moral good and evil. Not just the dominion mentioned in Genesis 1, but moral stakes applying to his own person. The precept and sanction of Genesis 2:17 indicate that responsibility in the face of moral opposites enters into the definition of Adam—and not merely his subjectivity, but the entire man who is capable of suffering the penalty of death.[89] Here is found a threshold between good and evil that conditions dominion, one that allows a distinction between moral praxis and instrumental rationality, between a consideration of goods that remain in the personal agent and goods effected in an external product.

These two experiences provide a context for considering the common soil of negative anthropology—a moment perhaps elided in Genesis 1 that sees man whole and complete from the beginning. While Genesis 1 establishes the difference between man, male and female, and the animals, Genesis 2 says that the Adam is "alone."[90] The pope remarks: "This man, '*adam*,' might have reached the conclusion, on the basis of the experience of his own body, that he was substantially similar to other living beings (*animalia*). On the contrary, as we read, he did not arrive at this conclusion; he reached the conviction that he was 'alone.'"[91] Given the archaic and mythic structure of the report, the different elements of the *humanum* are not assembled all at once; the narrative cannot be read as a scientific account of the coming-to-be of man. Even so, the pope takes interest in this one aspect of the *imago Dei*. The Adam is constituted in a unique, exclusive, and unrepeatable relationship to God; any attempt to resolve himself into a succession of animals would be his death. It is the first clue why his humanity cannot be a suitable object of dominion. In one direction, it would erase the threshold between man and animal, and thus require treating man as something less than himself; in another direction, it erases the threshold between man and God, for man would have to *create* himself out of pre-human matter, the very dust from which God originally made the *imago*.

According to John Paul, the experience of solitude, mythically represented in Genesis 2, confirms the notion that the human person is the bearer of dignity and rights: a being, he says, that is *alteri incommunicabilis*—someone not transferable, reducible, fungible. However, it also represents an

---

89. *Theology of the Body*, 40–43.
90. On the analogies between God, man, beast, see *Sollicitudo Rei Socialis*, §29.
91. *Theology of the Body*, 38.

experience giving rise to a negative anthropology, one that lingers on this moment of incompletion; or, perhaps better put, the indeterminacy of a man whose completion resides totally in his unique freedom. In Genesis, of course, Adamic solitude is resolved by God, who, noting Adam's loneliness, puts him into a sleep, from which the original Adam awakes, male and female. Adam's solitude is addressed not by assimilation to another natural substance, nor by the creation of a new substance, but by a *communio personarum*—a sexually differentiated community of persons having the same nature.

> If . . . we wish to draw also from the narrative of the Yawhist text the concept of "image of God," we can then deduce that man became the "image and likeness" of God not only through his own humanity, but also through the communion of persons which man and woman form right from the beginning. The function of the image is to reflect the one who is the model, to reproduce its own prototype. Man becomes the image of God not so much in the moment of solitude as in the moment of communion.[92]

The "image" then is twofold. First, capacity for dominion and moral praxis—transitive efficacy over things lower, and intransitive efficacy in self-rule—both discussed mythically under the rubric of Adamic solitude. Second, the *imago* is capacity for communion of persons "in one flesh" without confusion, destruction, or assimilation. What belongs to "man" in the former also belongs to man and woman, equally in the latter. Kenneth Schmitz has characterized this as the "reciprocity of solitudes,"[93] each having the same dignities. Adam's canticle of consent (Gn 2:23)—"at last, bone of my bones and flesh of my flesh"—expresses recognition that Eve is like himself, not a body to be subdued but one to be loved, just as he loves his own. This is what the pope calls the "nuptial" meaning of the body.[94]

The nuptial body is object and subject of Adam's consent. Here, then, is another threshold, given as sexual differentiation of the human being. In experience, it will appear as the beloved, sexually differentiated "man" and "woman." Not animal among animals; not abstract Adam, for in the myth, while this Adam exhibits some essential human predicates, he is not complete, and indeed is not a real concrete person. "In the beginning," man and woman make their appearance in "betrothed love." Human love, of course, manifests itself in more than one way. It covers respect for the dignities of another, benevolence, a general will for the good of others, both individuals and societies. One might even sacrifice his life for friends. But "betrothed love" is

---

92. *Theology of the Body*, 46.
93. Schmitz, *At the Center*, 102.
94. *Theology of the Body*, 61 and 357f.

distinct. In this case, the human body, male and female, is the locus of a personal and exclusive gift, one person to another. Even in ordinary experience we can confirm that this is not what a teacher, doctor, soldier, or pastor does (wills).[95] In nuptial love, attributed to man "in the beginning," we find the ontological and proto-sacramental grandeur of the concrete human being. Here, the distinction between dominion and moral rule is particularly crucial. There is no question but that Adam and Eve reciprocally rule one another. Do they subdue and dominate?

In modern political culture, everyone will agree that the woman is not subordinated, that she shares dominion, and that she has unrepeatable personhood. But this requires a real (specific) difference between man and animal, permitting us to discern what rightfully comes under dominion. If Adam's own body is proto-human material awaiting humanization, so is Eve's; and, by implication, the bodies of the progeny and siblings. What can arrest the escalation of subjection and servitude (in Kantian terms, instrumentalization)? One thesis is the proprietary body, the visible body as transferable property. It does not require a clear threshold between human and animal; nor does it seem to require human sexual differentiation. In this case, the specific "human" difference is constituted by consent.

The problem of the scope of human dominion limited only by consent is posed acutely in the Holy Office's *Donum Vitae*, which traces the social consequences of regarding the human body as a producible object.[96] The pope treats the issue in several letters: in the *Letter to Families*, comparing Adam's matrimonial consent to "neo-Manichean" dualism, for which consent is given to the negation of the body as "person";[97] in *Evangelium Vitae*, on the distinction between dominion and self-rule;[98] and in *Veritatis splendor*, where he gives a detailed consideration of the thesis that the human body is raw material to be shaped according to a mandate of dominion.[99]

In his audiences on the theology of the body, however, the pope proceeds in a different way. By speculative exegesis, he makes the scriptural narrative release its implicit anthropology, to discover how it converges with, and, ultimately tutors, our experience. Do we experience, for example, the thresholds between man and God, man and beast, good and evil, man and woman? In this light, we can recall Rousseau's speculative traversal of the same ground.

---

95. Here, I draw from Wojtyła, *Love and Responsibility*, 98f.

96. See especially the limits of dominion mentioned in Gen 1:28; see *Donum Vitae*, §2; on the distinction between *dominium* (property) and use of the human body *ad utendum et fruendum*, see *Donum Vitae*, §3.

97. *Letter to Families*, §19.

98. *Evangelium Vitae*, §§43, 52.

99. *Veritatis Splendor*, §§46–49.

As a result of "chance encounters," the savage happily and unproblematically has sex without losing his innocence because he is an animal; he does not distinguish either himself or the woman from the rest of the animals. All animals have the same rights, to sympathy in event of desire and need, and to pity in the case of pain. Against Hobbes's depiction of the state of nature as an envious contest for recognition, and against Locke's speculation that natural man is inclined to form a society for the sake of protecting the offspring, Rousseau is at pains to emphasize that in the original condition every man and woman are indefinitely "substitutable," one for the other. In a hypothetical solitude, therefore, matrimony is impossible, or at least unnecessary. It can emerge only with a proprietorial contract to use the other. Man "falls" into matrimony.[100] Thus does savage man become the "men we have before our own eyes." Rousseau tells the story in order to suggest that man needs a social contract to tame private contracts, which are nothing more than agreements to exercise power despotically. Dominion over man begins in marriage, but quickly overflows into dominion over children, laborers, and those made subject to conquest—all, things to be subdued. Yet Rousseau's myth of origins converges upon two of the anthropological thresholds highlighted by the pope: namely, between man and beast, and the relationship between man and woman.

The snake in Rousseau's garden is dominion, and it is man who becomes property, and who organizes himself as a bearer of tools and technologies. He proceeds by negation, locating experiences that permit us to say, this is what man is *not*; the positive anthropology is reached once we can stabilize the negations, and affirm man as citizen. We reach the threshold that stands firm: the community of citizens, free because they are equal in dignity under the Social Contract, and the outliers who still assert individual dominion. As we said, one arrives in the vicinity of the contemporary retelling of the myth if we take away the culminating chapter of man as citizen, but keep in place the negation of anthropological thresholds along the way. The thresholds can be cancelled and reconstituted by individual choice, operating in a sphere of private choice.

To be sure, the pope warns about fables and myths that negate man.[101] In *Veritatis splendor*, he speaks of "obscure riddles of the human condition which today, also, as in the past, profoundly disturb the human heart," leading the soul to "wander in myths."[102] At the same time, it is important to consider

---

100. Rousseau, *Discourse*, 29 (on chance encounters), 14 (on animal rights), 88n4 (on substitutability), 39 and 88 (on the fall into corruption).

101. Particularly, the Promethean myth. See *Evangelium Vitae*, §15.

102. *Veritatis Splendor*, §30. The first part of the quotation is taken from the document of the Second Vatican Council, *Nostra Aetate* (§1) on non-Christian religions. The second part of the quotation is from 2 Tim 4:1–5: "having itching ears they will accumulate for themselves teachers to suit their own likings, and will turn away from listening to the

the experiences corresponding to the negations. The scriptural site, of course, is Genesis 3–4, which begins the story of the human condition *status naturae lapsae*.[103] When Jesus gives the disciples his teaching on Genesis 2, his "appeal to the 'beginning' dismays the disciples." The teaching is inexpedient, cutting across the grain of experience.[104] Put in another way, perhaps we could say, with Rousseau, that the "men we have before our own eyes" have no option but to treat one another as transferable property.

He explains that within sin emerges a "coercion of the body," as though the natural and somatic substructure of sexuality is "driven back to another plane," limiting the freedom of the self-gift. And thus in Genesis 3:16, we read that among the "sorrows" of Eve after sin, she is told "your desire shall be for your husband and he shall rule over you." The proper moral mastery of the body appears to take on the note of external dominion, introducing the possibility of confusion between rule over persons and rule over animals.[105] He carefully says, "as if," and "almost," in order to clarify that the *libido dominandi* cannot completely suffocate the other pole of human experience, in which the body is not an object of lust.[106] But experience of the body "unilaterally and reductively" made an object is common enough.[107] It is not just a postulate of Catholic theology. The welter of instincts seems to break free of moral rule, suggesting no other solution than to be put under control (dominated). It is important to note that the pope speaks not just of Eve's body, but also Adam's and, as reported in Genesis 4, the bodies of their children, who become subject to violent coercion. This, too, needs interpretation. If Christian anthropology is to reconnect its dialogue with the modern telling of the myth, it will be crucial to distinguish which aspects of experience are normal and which are normative.

CONCLUSION

What are the remedies for the problem? There are many answers to this anthropological question. In past generations, political answers seemed most

---

truth and wander into myths (Vulgate: *ad fabulas*)." In the next two sections, §§31–32, he raises the problem of negative anthropologies.

103. *Theology of the Body*, 73. Strictly speaking, there is no such thing as an anthropological "state of nature." In Catholic thought, one speaks of the state of innocence, sin, and redemption. This is not a grid for three different natures, but rather of the "state" or "condition" in which human nature is exercised. Thomas's discussion of the "states" of man are found in *ST*, I, qq. 94–96, and *ST*, I-II, q. 85, a. 1 and q. 109, a. 2.

104. *Veritatis Splendor*, §22.

105. *Theology of the Body*, 125–27.

106. *Theology of the Body*, 126. And see the lengthy discussion of Gen 3:15–16 in *Mulieris Dignitatem*, §§10–11, 20.

107. *Theology of the Body*, 127.

plausible: revolution, the organization of the individual and society by the state, common ownership of the means of production, and even more darkly, the solution attempted by Cain on a mass scale. The events of the twentieth century make less plausible the solution of resolving man "as if he had been left himself" by means of collectivities. In any event, this route is in temporary eclipse. More compelling are the techniques of experimental naturalism, according to which all anthropological phenomena except freedom are put into a natural succession of animals. This option is the most compelling not only because of technological success (prima facie "improvements" in human biological fundaments); it is especially powerful because it summarizes the modern retelling of the myth of origins without the discredited "moral" of the story, which was salvation by the state. In this way, perhaps, dominion can be used to take the sting out of dominion.

For Catholic theology, Genesis 3–4 needs to be read in light of Ephesians 5 and 1 Corinthians 7 ("For the wife does not rule over her own body, but the husband does; likewise the husband does not rule over his own body, but the wife does"), which bring back into view a covenant of reciprocity and love rather than unilateral rule. The grace of the New Covenant begins the restoration of Adam precisely at the original sacramental site of the *imago dei*.[108]

> Thus, in this dimension, a primordial sacrament is constituted, understood as a sign that transmits effectively in the visible world the invisible mystery hidden in God from time immemorial. This is the mystery of truth and love, the mystery of divine life, in which man really participates. In this history of man, original innocence begins this participation. . . . The sacrament, as a visible sign, is constituted with man, as a body, by means of his visible masculinity and femininity. The body, and it alone, is capable of making visible the invisible: the spiritual and the divine. It was created to transfer into the visible reality of the world the mystery hidden since time immemorial in God, and thus to be a sign of it.[109]

On this very point, John Paul II issued his first encyclical, *Redemptor Hominis*. Asking, "what does man fear," the pope answers, making man the object of his own dominion, a "subjection unto futility."[110] The Christian message is that the visible man is a locus of dignities and perfections that are a natural sign of a mystery that transcends him; but, just as importantly, one not requiring that man be greater than himself by negation of his nature.

---

108. *Theology of the Body*, 296–97. For a survey of different notions of "ruling" in this literature, see Ch. 3 of this collection.

109. *Theology of the Body*, 76.

110. See *Redemptor Hominis*, §§8,15, 21.

We have sketched Wojtyła's understanding of the anthropological issues Catholic theology presupposes and explicates. Of key importance are the four thresholds investigated in light of Genesis: man-god, man-beast, good-evil, and male-female. We have also exposed some of Wojtyła's reasons for plunging into anthropological questions, even though the historic tide of Catholic social thought pulled in the direction of political institutions and public policy. What these political issues will look like once informed by Wojtyła's anthropological teachings will have to be the subject of another investigation.

CHAPTER 10

Natural Law and Public Discourse

The Legacies of Joseph Ratzinger

I. INTRODUCTION

IN 1988, CARDINAL JOSEPH RATZINGER traveled to England to give the annual Fischer Lecture for the Catholic Chaplaincy at Cambridge University.[1] The title of his paper was "Consumer Materialism and Christian Hope," suggesting that he would come prepared to speak about problems like drugs, AIDS, terrorism—important topics, to be sure, but relatively safe for a speech by the Prefect of the Congregation of the Doctrine of the Faith. At first, Ratzinger[2] politely tried to give *that* kind speech before abruptly changing course, proposing that the main crisis of our time is that "[w]hat is moral has lost its evidence."[3]

> Now the concept of a personal relationship between God and Creator and each individual person is certainly not missing from the religious and moral history of humanity; but it is limited in its pure form to the realm of biblical religion. *What was first of all common to all of pre-modern mankind*, however, lies really along the self-same line: ⌊was⌋ the conviction that in man's being there lies an imperative, the conviction that man does not devise morality itself by calculating expediencies; rather *he comes upon it in the being of things.*[4]

As it happened, Ratzinger had come to give a lecture on natural law. He put the question of "evidence" into a context where it once received an answer— the common patrimony and primeval testimony of wisdom traditions, which,

---

1. Joseph Ratzinger, "Consumer Materialism and Christian Hope," in *Teachers of the Faith: Speeches and Lectures by Catholic Bishops*, foreword by Cardinal Cormac Murphy-O'Connor, ed. T. Horwood (London: Catholic Bishop's Conference of England and Wales, 2002), 78–94.
2. Henceforth, I shall use the name Ratzinger without his ecclesiastical titles.
3. Ratzinger, "Consumer Materialism and Christian Hope," 87.
4. Ratzinger, "Consumer Materialism and Christian Hope," 87. Emphasis added.

279

in different ways and with different emphases, affirmed "the necessity for harmony between human existence and the message of nature."[5] His audience must have understood that he was revisiting a theme famously developed by the scholar and former resident of Magdalene College (Cambridge), C. S. Lewis, whose *The Abolition of Man* (1943) included an appendix of universal moral propositions modeled on the Chinese Tao.[6] Ratzinger continued: "Actually, the moral vision of Christian faith is not something particularly Christian; it is rather the synthesis of the great moral intuitions of humanity from a new centre which holds them all together."[7]

What Christianity has in common with other wisdom traditions, he gathered, is the conviction that "[m]orality is not man's prison; it is rather the divine in him."[8] This is not merely an ethical so much as an anthropological conviction: namely, that the human person is "open to reality as a whole." Were this not true, the order of nature would amount to a mere aggregation of "details," and our interpretation of these details would be restricted to the domain of scientific materialism. Other evidences might count but only as the partial constructions of subjectivity or, what is more likely, the constructions of social, political, and legal forces. In that scenario, morality would be a "prison."[9]

Ratzinger concluded that, to the modern person, "moral[ity] has lost its evidence."[10] He can "see through" all things but not "see."[11] Christianity has only very awkward points of entry into dialogue with a cultural world that recognizes only one universal, which, for us, is scientific materialism. In late modernity, only scientific materialism promises that human reason opens to reality as whole. But it succeeds at the cost of erasing all of the other "evidences"—not only moral evidence, but even the human knower himself, who is a useless cultural *meme* having no ground or role in nature.

On that scenario, it is better that Christianity dialogue with other moral traditions that have an *hodos*—a road, a way, a Tao, a pathway of evidence—so to speak.[12]

---

5. Ratzinger, "Consumer Materialism and Christian Hope," 88–89.

6. Ratzinger, "Consumer Materialism and Christian Hope," 88.

7. Ratzinger, "Consumer Materialism and Christian Hope," 93.

8. Ratzinger, "Consumer Materialism and Christian Hope," 92.

9. Ratzinger, "Consumer Materialism and Christian Hope," 92: "[T]he moral imperative is not man's imprisonment from which he must make his escape in order finally to be able to do as he wants."

10. Ratzinger, "Consumer Materialism and Christian Hope," 87.

11. Ratzinger, "Consumer Materialism and Christian Hope," 90; quoting C. S. Lewis.

12. If I understand Ratzinger correctly, we are not speaking of raw evidence but of evidence already marked, or mapped for one who wants to search. Properly speaking, this is dialogue—human discourse in the midst of converging pathways of evidence. Put in Thomistic terms, we are not directly concerned with the first and most common principles

Ratzinger's Cambridge paper turned out to be rather important. It was a paradigm for his contribution to two encyclicals (*Veritatis Splendor* and *Fides et Ratio*), it formed the nucleus for the International Theological Commission's study of Natural Law (2008), and Ratzinger reworked it in several of his most important speeches when he became pope. Importantly, the Cambridge lecture represented Ratzinger's conviction that natural law discourse belongs most fruitfully to something along the lines of inter-religious dialogue rather than to the more familiar contexts of public law and politics, which only recognize scientific materialism under the aspect of cost-benefit laws of utility.

I will to return to the issue of dialogue later.

For now, I should point out something surprising about his Cambridge lecture. As far as I can tell, it was the first time that Joseph Ratzinger, speaking in his own name and in the office of theologian, publicly addressed the subject of natural law in any sustained way.

How could that be so?

Ratzinger began serious theological studies after his ordination in 1951, first writing a dissertation on Augustine's ecclesiology at the University of Munich and then his habilitation on Bonaventure's theology of history and revelation.

When he entered the world of academic theology, the brighter students were channeled into dogmatic, scriptural, and historical theology. As it always has been and probably always will be, the politically ambitious clerics took degrees in canon law. Moral theology was not regarded as a speculative and synthetic discipline that tackled big and interesting theological problems. By and large, it was taught and studied by way of manuals and cases—ultimately to serve priests dealing with issues of law and conscience in the confessional. To be sure, it had a natural law foundation, but it expressed neither a full theological nor a philosophical line of thought.

Moral theology, circa 1953, was a half-lit moon in the firmament of theology. Had Ratzinger entered academic theology ten years later, the picture would have looked very different. The sexual and biomedical issues had come to the fore by the late 1950s, and by the late 1960s, sexuality and conscience occupied the center stage of theology. Indeed, moral theology reinvented

---

of natural law, which constitute the condition of the possibility for any evidence whatsoever in practical matters. *ST*, I-II, q. 94, a. 4. Rather, we are interested in different traditions that have derived from the *communia principia rationis*, which Thomas puts into the category "conclusions." Some conclusions are relatively easy to draw while others depend on the experience and discernment of the wise. The main point is that conclusions represent a developed pattern of evidence. The moral precepts of the Decalogue fall into this category, and could be regarded as an *hodos*. *ST*, I-II, q. 100, a. 1–3. The principles of morals that C. S. Lewis compiled in *The Abolition of Man* are nothing other than what Thomas calls "conclusions."

itself as a speculative and virtually freestanding discipline that treated ethical theories rather than cases and laws.

Many years later, Ratzinger would write: "[The] post-conciliar [aim was to go] beyond the natural law system in order to recover a deeper biblical inspiration," and yet "it was precisely moral theology that ended by marginalizing Sacred Scripture even more completely than the pre-conciliar manualist tradition."[13] "[T]he specialists' debate in current moral theology," he lamented, spun around deontological and teleological theories, thus becoming ever more remote from either the order of creation or redemption.[14] Rather than reforming a casuistical legalism operating on the margins of serious philosophy and theology, moral theology had become ethical theories detached from traditions.[15]

At the same time, the pastoral emphasis of the Second Vatican Council seemed to nudge the older speculative theological disciplines in the direction of praxis—sacramental theology, for example, became liturgical praxis. Ratzinger suggested that the modern age is marked by a shift away from a concern for "what is true" to a concern for "what can be done or made."[16] He admonished theologians not to cooperate in "reason's capitulation in the face of almighty praxis."[17]

Systematic theology aspiring to become praxis, and moral theology insisting upon its right to become theory—in effect, Ratzinger's world of academic theology had been turned upside down. Well into the 1970s, while at the peak of his academic career, he wrote and spoke extensively on the situation of systematic theology, but he postponed reckoning with moral theology. That would change in 1981 when he became Prefect of the Congregation of the Doctrine of the Faith (Prefect of CDF). Now an ecclesial theologian, questions of moral theology were unavoidable.

13. Pope Benedict XVI, "The Renewal of Moral Theology: Perspectives of Vatican II and *Veritatis Splendor*," in *Communio: The Unity of the Church*, ed. D. L. Schindler, trans. Michelle K. Borras (Grand Rapids, MI: Eerdmans, 2010), 183, 187. On casuistry and natural law, see also p. 184.

14. Joseph Cardinal Ratzinger, "The Church's Teaching Authority-Faith-Morals," in *Principles of Christian Morality*, trans. Graham Harrison (San Francisco: Ignatius Press, 1986), 45, 65n13.

15. Here, anticipating some of the work that was soon to be done by Alasdair MacIntyre.

16. Joseph Cardinal Ratzinger, *Introduction to Christianity*, trans. J. R. Foster (San Francisco: Ignatius Press, 2004), 57–69.

17. Joseph Cardinal Ratzinger, "Church's Teaching Authority," 72.

II. Three Contexts

In 2004, as Prefect of CDF, Ratzinger invited Catholic educational institutions to organize symposiums or study days "in order to find constructive pointers and convergences for an effective deepening of the doctrine on natural moral law."[18] In the symposium held at Notre Dame, Alasdair MacIntyre made a very astute observation about the relationship between revealed theology and natural law:

> It is not just that the natural law can be known by the exercise of the powers of reason, independently of revelation, but also that the knowledge of divine law afforded by revelation presupposes a prior knowledge of the precepts of the natural law. It is a revealed truth, that is to say, that the truths of the natural law can be known prior to and independently of any revealed truths, including this particular revealed truth.[19]

Even if the institutions of a given culture—universities, courts, the media, other churches and religions—had no further use of natural law either as a supposition or as an explanatory framework, the Church nevertheless would be bound to teach and affirm the natural law—both as doctrine and in terms of the philosophical infrastructure. Theologians presuppose—or better yet, recognize—a source of evidence that is not exclusively revealed by the Gospel.

It is really a double presupposition: (1) evidence open to everyone, and (2) evidence included in the Gospel, forming an organic part of theology. This double presupposition is deployed in Catholic moral theology in three ways—let's call them contexts:

(1) Systematic: The doctrinal theologian works with the double presupposition in terms of the economies of creation and redemption. So put, the systematic theologian is not immediately concerned with making moral arguments, but rather with making coherent the sources of truth, including what is recognized or presupposed about the natural habitat of reason.

(2) Dialectical: This is the province of moral theology strictly defined. Beginning with a disputed question, the mind works dialectically from common premises and authorities to fully practical conclusions

---

18. Here, he refers to the invitations and subsequent history. See the Benedict XVI, "Address of His Holiness Benedict XVI to Members of the International Theological Commission," October 5, 2007, available at vatican.va.

19. Alasdair MacIntyre, "From Answers to Questions: A Response to the Responses," in *Intractable Disputes About the Natural Law: Alasdair MacIntyre and Critics*, ed. L. S. Cunningham (Notre Dame, IN: University of Notre Dame Press, 2009), 313, 341.

about sexual conduct, biomedical practices, warfare, and fundamental rights.

(3) Dialogical: This is the search for common premises across religious and philosophical traditions. As Ratzinger put it in his Cambridge lecture, dialogue is a search for common and converging pathways of evidence.

In this essay, I am most interested in the dialogical discourse. But if we are to accurately estimate Ratzinger's legacy in this context, we need to consider his understanding of the first two contexts, especially systematic theology.

III. SYSTEMATIC AND DIALECTICAL CONTEXTS

Ratzinger was a systematic theologian. The purpose of systematics is *coherence* of truths and teachings.[20] In the Catholic tradition, this work includes the infrastructure of philosophy brought to bear on the ordered inquires and expositions of sacred doctrine. Ratzinger's interest in natural law developed within this context.

In his first encyclical, *Deus Caritas Est*, for example, he insisted that the *humanum*, made unto the image and likeness of God that becomes by grace *imago Christi* "is not simply a matter of morality."[21] He means to say that moral theology presupposes the nature of the human creature, the scope and dignity of conscience, and the participation of human reason in first truth and divine providence. So put, natural law in the creature falls under anthropology before it comes under morality, but as to the source of the law, it first falls under natural theology, just as Thomas Aquinas insisted in the *Summa Theologiae*.[22] Since the systematic theologian incorporates—or as Ratzinger

---

20. See Ratzinger, "Church's Teaching Authority," 72.

21. Benedict XVI, Encyclical Letter *Deus Caritas Est*, §14.

22. This is the *ex professo* definition of natural law given by Thomas at *ST*, I-II, q. 91, a. 2:

> I answer that, As stated above (I-II, q. 90, a. 1, ad 1), law, being a rule and measure, can be in a person in two ways: in one way, as in him that rules and measures; in another way, as in that which is ruled and measured, since a thing is ruled and measured, in so far as it partakes of the rule or measure. Wherefore, since all things subject to Divine providence are ruled and measured by the eternal law, as was stated above; it is evident that all things partake somewhat of the eternal law, in so far as, namely, from its being imprinted on them, they derive their respective inclinations to their proper acts and ends. Now among all others, the rational creature is subject to Divine providence in the most excellent way, in so far as it partakes of a share of providence, by being provident both for itself and for others. Wherefore it has a share of the Eternal Reason, whereby it has a natural inclination to its proper act and end: and this participation of the eternal law in

frequently says, "purifies"—natural theology, the systematic theologian has a stake in natural law quite independent of deliberation and judgment about particular matters of conduct.[23]

Moral theology presupposes human reason tutored by nature and by faith, as well as by wisdom traditions. Hence, Ratzinger's long-standing criticism of the older casuistical-manualist method, which seemed like a piece of legalism detached from the living tradition of theology. But in much the same vein, he now criticizes the more recent bid of moral theology to be ethical theory detached from the deeper tradition of ethical thought.

Ratzinger's generation of theologians (coming of age in the 1940s) wanted to repristinate theology by returning to the sources, chiefly to scripture and patrology. For these *"Ressourcement"* theologians, scholasticism carried a germ of rationalism, which is to say the primacy of dialectics over wisdom. If taken to extremes, their suspicion of scholasticism could subvert a renewal of natural law thinking, among other reasons, because for the better part of a millennium reflection on natural law within Catholicism evolved within various scholasticisms and neo-scholasticisms.

For his part, Ratzinger was a *ressourcement* theologian and a critic of rationalism—he had little confidence in the moral-juridical approach to natural law. That said, he set himself apart from his generational cohort because he was a staunch defender of the creative encounter of Christian faith and philosophy.[24]

---

the rational creature is called the natural law. Hence the Psalmist after saying (Ps 4:6): "Offer up the sacrifice of justice," as though someone asked what the works of justice are, adds: "Many say, Who showeth us good things?" In answer to which question he says: "The light of Thy countenance, O Lord, is signed upon us": thus implying that the light of natural reason, whereby we discern what is good and what is evil, which is the function of the natural law, is nothing else than an imprint on us of the Divine light. It is therefore evident that the natural law is nothing else than the rational creature's participation of the eternal law.

23. In his dissertation, Ratzinger proposed without extensive commentary that just as revealed theology both recognizes and rehabilitates natural theology, revealed theology must do the same with the notion of natural right, which he says is in "crisis" (Krisis des Naturrechts). For the philosophical resources of late modernity are not sufficient to secure deep convictions about natural or human rights. See Joseph Ratzinger, *Volk und Haus Gottes in Augustins Lehre von der Kirche* (Freiburg im Breisgau: Verlag Herder, 2011). I am grateful to Daniel Burns for calling this passage to my attention.

24. In his work *Catholicisme: les aspects sociaux du dogme* (Catholicism: The Social Aspects of Doctrine), Henri de Lubac maintained that:

In this connection the combined influence of Aristotelian logic and Roman law on the formulation of theology during the Middle Ages has been pointed out more than once. These two excellent instruments of precision, which should have

Going back to his Inaugural Lecture at the University of Bonn in 1959, through the subsequent decades of his books and essays, and finally to his famous Regensburg Address in 2006, Ratzinger refused in no uncertain terms to equate "*ressourcement*" theology with dehellenization.[25] Dehellenization stands for the project to emancipate or purify revealed doctrine by evacuating what was taken from philosophy (as well as from other Graeco-Roman patterns of thought—law, politics, art). This imperative crossed denominational boundaries in theology, and it could imply either very conservative or progressive theological agendas.

Ratzinger himself provided the best summary of dehellenization in his lecture at Regensburg.[26] In fact, it was the core of his Regensburg lecture but was unfortunately lost in the controversy over his remarks about Islam. Below, in bullet points, is Ratzinger's schema.

(I) The first phase of dehellenization regards philosophy as a form of thought alien to faith:

> Looking at the tradition of scholastic theology, the Reformers thought they were confronted with a faith system totally conditioned by

---

been the instruments of progress, were not in the event without their dangers. For in the second was inherent the danger of a legal outlook in expounding the mysteries—an outlook entirely foreign to their nature.

Henri de Lubac, *Catholicism: Christ and the Common Destiny of Man*, foreword by Joseph Cardinal Ratzinger, trans. Lancelot C. Sheppard & Sister Elizabeth Englund (San Francisco: Ignatius Press, 1988), 307. Of course, de Lubac allowed that the Church has a mission to remind the world of the "moral law," stating, "Can we reasonably ask of the authority of the Church anything more than the assertion of the moral law, the careful control of private initiative, the support of all those efforts in which she recognizes her own Spirit, and, finally, such interventions as are necessary to settle eventual disagreements and to sanction what proves to be definitive in the solutions adopted?" However, he contends that the Church's main task is to elaborate the social aspects of the Trinitarian image of the Old Adam rehabilitated as *imago Christi*. See de Lubac, *Catholicism*, 363–64. Ratzinger wrote a foreword to the new edition of *Catholicisme*, and mentions it favorably in his encyclical *Spe Salvi*. See Pope Benedict XVI, Encyclical Letter *Spe Salvi*, §§13–14. Interestingly, in his foreword, Ratzinger says nothing about the other side of the coin, namely the wisdom traditions other than Christianity. The original French title was not only ineptly, but disastrously translated into English as *Catholicism: Christ and the Common Destiny of Man*.

25. See Ratzinger's work as Ordinarius of Fundamental Theology, "God of Faith and the God of the Philosophers: A Contribution to the Problem of Natural Theology." This work is newly published with commentary by Heino Sonnemans in Joseph Ratzinger/ Benedikt XVI, *Der Gott Des Glaubens Und Der Gott Der Philosophen: Ein Beitrag Zum Problem Der Theologia Naturalis*, ed. H. Sonnemans, 2nd rev. ed. (Einsiedeln: Johannes-Verlag Leutesdorf, 2004). See also *Spe Salvi*, §§5–6.

26. Pope Benedict XVI, "Address at Regensburg: Faith, Reason and the University: Memories and Reflections," September 12, 2006, www.vatican.va.

philosophy, that is to say an articulation of the faith based on an alien system of thought. As a result, faith no longer appeared as a living historical Word but as one element of an overarching philosophical system. . . . When Kant stated that he needed to set thinking aside in order to make room for faith, he carried this programme forward with a radicalism that the Reformers could never have foreseen. He thus anchored faith exclusively in practical reason, denying it access to reality as a whole.[27]

Incidentally, the phrase "open to reality as a whole" can be traced back to the Cambridge lecture and will reappear in *Fides et Ratio*.[28]

(II) The second phase of dehellenization regards philosophy as alien to both the humanitarian praxis of Christianity and to modern science:

> The liberal theology of the nineteenth and twentieth centuries ushered in a second stage in the process of dehellenization, with Adolf von Harnack. . . . [The] central idea was to return simply to the man Jesus and to his simple message, underneath the accretions of theology and indeed of hellenization: this simple message was seen as the culmination of the religious development of humanity. Jesus was said to have put an end to worship in favour of morality. In the end he was presented as the father of a humanitarian moral message.[29]

Philosophy is thus placed outside of the "humanitarianism" of Christianity, with Christianity now understood simply as, or reduced to, a "moral message."

(III) The third phase regards philosophy as antichrist, or a false religion. As Ratzinger says, "It is well known that in our century Karl Barth sharpened this protest against the presence of philosophy in theology. . . . Against this continuity between philosophy's search for the ultimate causes and theology's appropriation of biblical faith, Barth sets a radical discontinuity."[30] The Ten Commandments and the common moral truths of the Gentiles must "confront each other in a pure paradox."[31] Ratzinger continues:

---

27. Benedict XVI, "Address at Regensburg."

28. See *Fides et Ratio*, §§70, 71, and 97.

29. Benedict XVI, "Address at Regensburg." For example, Friedrich Schleiermacher says, "In order to make quite clear to you what is the original and characteristic possession of religion, it resigns, at once, all claims on anything that belongs either to science or morality. Whether it has been borrowed or bestowed it is now returned." See Friedrich Schleiermacher, *On Religion: Speeches to Its Cultured Despisers*, trans. John Oman (New York: Frederick Ungar, 1955), 27.

30. Joseph Ratzinger, "Faith, Philosophy and Theology," in *The Nature and Mission of Theology: Essays to Orient Theology in Today's Debates*, trans. Adrian Walker (San Francisco: Ignatius Press, 1995), 13 and 19.

31. Ratzinger, "Church's Teaching Authority," 58.

[T]he third stage of dehellenization . . . is [currently] in progress. In the light of our experience with cultural pluralism, it is often said nowadays that the synthesis with Hellenism achieved in the early Church was an initial inculturation which ought not to be binding on other cultures. The latter are said to have the right to return to the simple message of the New Testament prior to *that* inculturation, in order to inculturate it anew in their own particular milieux.[32]

This phase of dehellenization regards culture as superior to philosophy: Ethos over Logos, which Ratzinger regarded as disastrous for natural law discourse.

For his part, Ratzinger refused to go down these rabbit holes. For one thing, he contended that they misunderstand the emergence of Christian theology:

From the beginning, Christianity has understood itself as the religion of the "Logos," as the religion according to reason. In the first place, it has not identified its precursors *in the other religions*, but in that philosophical enlightenment which has cleared the path of traditions to turn to the search of the truth and towards the good, toward the one God who is above all gods.[33]

For another thing, sacred scripture does not lay out a complete system of ethics but rather presupposes a common morality and purifies it.[34] "Scripture does not offer us a theological system, and still less a system of moral theory, with a systematic and orderly presentation of the main principles of action. To the contrary, Scripture is a path, a history, the multiple re-readings of which converge on Christ, who, for his part, cannot adequately be understood without retracing the path of all the narratives converging on his person."[35]

---

32. Ratzinger, "Address at Regensburg." Emphasis added.

33. On April 1, 2005, the day before Pope John Paul died, Cardinal Joseph Ratzinger took a few hours for a short trip out of Rome to fulfill a long-standing engagement. He went to the Benedictine monastery of Santa Scholastica in Subiaco where he delivered an address "On Europe's Crisis of Culture." See Joseph Ratzinger, "On Europe's Crisis of Culture," April 1, 2005, http://chiesa.espresso.repubblica.it/articolo/27262 (trans. ours). Ratzinger points out that ancient Christian art depicts Christ as the philosopher, "the prototype of the *homo christianus.*" See Ratzinger, "Faith, Philosophy and Theology," 14; see also *Spe Salvi*, §6.

34. Pope Benedict XVI, "Renewal of Moral Theology," 185.

35. "Renewal of Moral Theology," 185. Here we have the example of the rich young man, which frames the first part of *Veritatis Splendor*:

Then someone came to him and said, "Teacher, what good deed must I do to have eternal life?" And he said to him, "Why do you ask me about what is good? There is only one who is good. If you wish to enter into life, keep the commandments." He said to him, "Which ones?" And Jesus said, "You shall not murder; You shall not commit adultery; You shall not steal; You shall not bear false witness;

In the third place, "[Christianity] defends philosophy because it needs it."[36] Rather than demanding closure, it encourages faith seeking understanding, reason seeking enlightenment.[37] "The universality of faith, which is a basic presupposition of the missionary task, is both meaningful and morally defensible only if this faith really is oriented beyond the symbolism of religions toward an answer meant for all, an answer which also appeals to the common reason of [all] mankind."[38] To dismiss Christianity's assimilation of Logos traditions does not purify the Gospel but amputates its roots in the natural habitat of reason.[39]

This is how Ratzinger found his groove with regard to natural law. He didn't go through the front door of moral theology, nor was he instigated by any particular moral dilemma. Nor did he get there as so many other Catholic scholars did by studying and reconsidering Thomas's presentation of human action in the *Secunda Pars* of the *Summa*. Instead, he found his way to the topic as a systematic theologian.

After taking the position as Prefect of CDF, he had to render judgment on issues of moral theology. I call this work dialectical because CDF is often tasked to resolve a disputed issue in sacraments, discipline, or morals. Unlike the first context, which draws the mind back toward sources for the purpose of coherence, clarity, and integration, dialectics moves *from* common sources (dogmatic, philosophical) to conclusions proximate to human action. In his position of Prefect, Ratzinger proposed the topic, assigned the team, and signed the finished product. Many of these fell squarely in the area of moral theology, requiring treatment according to

---

Honor your father and mother; also, You shall love your neighbor as yourself." The young man said to him, "I have kept all these; what do I still lack?" Jesus said to him, "If you wish to be perfect, go, sell your possessions, and give the money to the poor, and you will have treasure in heaven; then come, follow me."

Matthew 19:16–21. Thus, to the Bundestag in 2011, Ratzinger insisted that moral bases for dignitarian rights in the German constitution are presupposed both by Church and polity—they are not alien to either party. Benedict XVI, "Address of his Holiness Benedict XVI, The Listening Heart: Reflections on the Foundations of Law," September 22, 2011, www.vatican.va. The Church does not ask temporal governments to legislate the radical call to discipleship, but rather to remain intelligently alert to its own insights regarding human dignity.

36. Ratzinger, "Faith, Philosophy and Theology," 29.

37. Ratzinger, "Faith, Philosophy and Theology," 17, 29.

38. Ratzinger, "Faith, Philosophy and Theology," 25.

39. Far from correcting rationalism, but makes Christianity more vulnerable to it, for rationalism is nothing other than reason that is not open to reality as a whole. That's the gist of his speech at Subiaco (one day before the death of Pope John Paul II), and then a year later his address to the faculty at the University of Regensburg. Christianity and the children of the Enlightenment need philosophy in different, but complimentary ways.

what I called the "double presupposition" of natural law. Here, it is impossible to give an account of his work at a proper level of detail. There are too many documents representing a wide array of issues.[40] For example:

> *Liberty of Conscience* (1986), on why history does not constitute a moral law or the norm proximate to the act of conscience;[41]
> *Gift of Life* (1987), on in vitro fertilization, heterologous fertilization;[42]
> *On Sterilization* (1993);[43]
> *On Legal Recognition of Same-Sex Unions* (2003);[44]
> *On Participation of Catholics in Public Life* (2002).[45]

Here, I only wish to say that these documents are hardly rationalistic in the fashion of the manuals or canonical verdicts. They display a keen attention to multiple premises, complex lines of reasoning, with expositions that are given enough air in which to breathe.

During these decades at CDF, Ratzinger quietly gave considerable work to two encyclicals, each bearing upon natural law from different directions: *Veritatis Splendor* (1993) and *Fides et Ratio* (1998). To better understand the importance of these encyclicals, let us briefly consider the historical context.

---

40. Moreover, he tasked the International Theological Commission to undertake two important studies: *Propositions on the Dignity and Rights of the Human Person*, and *Communion and Stewardship: Human Persons Created in the Image of God*. See International Theological Commission, *Propositions on the Dignity and Rights of the Human Person* (1983), www.vatican.va.; International Theological Commission, *Communion and Stewardship: Human Persons Created in the Image of God* (2004), www.vatican.va.

41. Congregation for the Doctrine of the Faith, *Instruction on Christian Freedom and Liberation*, approved by Pope John Paul II and signed by Prefect Joseph Cardinal Ratzinger and Secretary Alberto Bovone (March 22, 1986), www.vatican.va.

42. Congregation for the Doctrine of the Faith, *Instruction on Respect for Human Life in its Origin and on the Dignity of Procreation, Replies to Certain Questions of the Day*, approved by Pope John Paul II and signed by Prefect Joseph Cardinal Ratzinger and Secretary Alberto Bovone (February 22, 1987), www.vatican.va.

43. Congregation for the Doctrine of the Faith, *Responses to Questions Proposed Concerning "Uterine Isolation" and Related Matters*, approved by Pope John Paul II and signed by Prefect Joseph Cardinal Ratzinger and Secretary Alberto Bovone (July 31, 1993), www.vatican.va.

44. Congregation for the Doctrine of the Faith, *Considerations Regarding Proposals to Give Legal Recognition to Unions Between Homosexual Persons*, approved by Pope John Paul II and signed by Prefect Joseph Cardinal Ratzinger and Secretary Angelo Amato (June 3, 2003), www.vatican.va.

45. Congregation for the Doctrine of the Faith, *Doctrinal Note on Some Questions Regarding the Participation of Catholics in Political Life*, approved by Pope John Paul II and signed by Prefect Joseph Cardinal Ratzinger and Secretary Tarcisio Bertone (November 24, 2002), www.vatican.va.

In 1963, Pope John XXIII issued *Pacem in terris*. Rhetorically, it was a most extravagant appeal to natural law for grounding some twenty-five discrete rights. Inside and outside the Church there was hardly a murmur of complaint. The Pope had taken the 1948 UN Declaration on Human Rights and laid it out in the language of natural law.[46]

Three years later, Pope Paul VI issued *Humanae Vitae*, which made a rather terse natural law argument against contraception. It immediately met with the most severe disapproval, both by Catholics and non-Catholics. And what made the event all the more embarrassing was that the encyclical was addressed to "all men of good will."[47] The teaching was not just politely ignored but resisted. Paul VI would live for ten more years, but he never wrote another encyclical.

Many, if not most, people rejected the natural law argument on the simplest ground: The conclusion—that contraception for whatever purpose is *malum per se*—seemed completely implausible. Criticism from those more learned in philosophy and theology rejected the premises on the ground that the terms nature and law were used equivocally with regard to moral and physical (biological) aspects. Still others—mostly in the Church—complained that the Pope had flaunted the recommendation of the majority of his own committee. It was a perfect storm: a natural law argument rejected on its conclusions, its premises, and as contradicting not only the opinion of experts but the *sensus fidelium*.

The most striking thing, however, was that even those who agreed with the position understood that *Humanae Vitae* exposed a weakness in Catholic moral theology, especially regarding the natural law component. Joseph Ratzinger and Karl Wojtyła were among them. Indeed, the weakness could be detected on the surfaces of the document. It was rather short, one-fifth the length of *Pacem in Terris*. Its entire treatment of matrimonial acts amounts to about 500 words. It had the appearance of a verdict issued in the fashion of the older manualist-casuistical method: almost no theology, philosophy, or anthropology. References to scripture were mostly decorative, except for the conclusion, where the Pope referenced Luke 2: "But it comes as no surprise to the Church that she, no less than her divine Founder, is destined to be a 'sign of contradiction.'"[48]

---

46. The word "sex" was used only once and in reference to equality in the workforce. See *Pacem in Terris*, §43.

47. Pope Paul VI, Encyclical Letter *Humanae Vitae (July 25, 1968)*. The subtitle is "On the Regulation of Birth."

48. *Humanae Vitae*, §18. Cardinal Karol Wojtyła would give a set of Lenten conferences for Paul VI one year before Wojtyła's election as pope. Those conferences were published in 1977 under the title *Sign of Contradiction*. Karol Wojtyła, *Sign of Contradiction* (New York: Seabury Press, 1979).

The use of natural law needed to be reconsidered—not just the issue of contraception, but natural law deployed in its multiple contexts. Ratzinger brought two things to that task: first, his long-standing suspicion that moral theology was legalistic, rationalist, and situated not just in the suburbs but the exurbs of theology; and secondly, his resistance to theological currents that wanted to evacuate a higher tradition of Logos. For his part, John Paul II brought expertise in philosophical and theological anthropology, and much else besides. After his election, he went on to give 129 conferences, amounting to some 160,000 words on the very topic that *Humanae Vitae* attempted to cover tersely in a mere two paragraphs.

This long slog moving toward a deeper and more nuanced understanding of natural law culminated in two encyclicals. *Veritatis*, issued in 1993, took six years to write. *Fides et Ratio*, issued in 1998, took at least six years (reports, which I have been unable to confirm, claim that from first sketch to final draft amounted to twelve years). Going back to the birth of modern magisterial teaching via encyclicals in the nineteenth century, no previous encyclicals took so long to write.

Veritatis is the first encyclical in history to address moral theology as such. It was addressed not to all persons of good will, but to the bishops. *Veritatis* turned to the question of what kind of component natural law is in moral theology, and how it relates to the other sources of doctrine: sacred scripture, Christology, theological anthropology, ascetical theology, and ecclesiology. Because it addressed (according to the subtitle) "fundamental questions" rather than fully practical ones, the encyclical was free to make more explicit and to give a more nuanced account of the assumptions that govern the magisterium's use of natural law theory.[49]

The encyclical explains that moral truths—in principle accessible to human reason—not only constitute a "preparation for the Gospel," but are also situated within it.[50] The moral law, thus understood, is presupposed in

---

49. I shall make no effort to summarize this very rich encyclical. Instead, I call attention to one of the assumptions that *Veritatis* was at pains to clarify. Namely, that natural law forms an organic part of moral theology:

> In their desire, however, to keep the moral life in a Christian context, certain moral theologians have introduced a sharp distinction, contrary to Catholic doctrine, between an "ethical order" which would be human in origin and of value for "this world" alone, and an "order of salvation" for which only certain intentions and interior attitudes regarding God and neighbor would be significant. This has then led to an actual denial that there exists, in Divine Revelation, a specific and determined moral content, universally valid and permanent.

Pope John Paul II, *Veritatis Splendor*, §37.

50. *Veritatis Splendor*, §§3, 29.

two ways by moral theology. First, as principles of moral order derived from human nature; second, as those very same principles clarified and integrated in the teachings of Christ. "[T]he Magisterium does not bring to the Christian conscience truths which are extraneous to it; rather it brings to light the truths which it ought already to possess, developing them from the starting point of the primordial act of faith."[51]

Important, too, is the encyclical's emphasis upon the ethics of an image bearer.[52] The created image bearer participates in God's wisdom and providence. This is a primary theme of Thomas's natural law theory, but, remarkably, just here, where the philosophical and theological aspects of natural law most deeply overlap, *Humanae Vitae* was silent. Imagine an encyclical on procreation failing to deal with created "image and likeness," given that the ethic of procreation is situated prominently in the first command of Genesis to be fruitful and multiply in imitation of the divine creation of multiple goods, and then in the human participation of the divine providence by way of stewardship![53]

For its part, *Fides et Ratio* (1998) is the first encyclical since Leo XIII's *Aeterni Patris* (1879) to treat the relationship between faith and reason. Ratzinger's imprint on this encyclical is even more evident. One needs to look especially at Ch. 4, on the appropriation of philosophy by the Fathers[54] and the treatment of Wisdom literature in Jewish scripture[55] to appreciate Ratzinger's hand. The word "Search," so important to Ratzinger's account of wisdom traditions, is used more than sixty times to characterize the relationship between faith and reason. On this score, we are back to where we began: the 1988 Cambridge lecture runs like dotted lines through *Fides*.[56]

---

51. *Veritatis Splendor*, §64.

52. Indeed, in the opening sentence of the encyclical: "The splendour of truth shines forth in all the works of the Creator and, in a special way, in man, created in the image and likeness of God (cf. Gen 1:26)." It is referred to and discussed more than twenty times. See, *inter alia*, *Veritatis Splendor*, §§1, 10.

53. Genesis 1:26–28. *Veritatis Splendor* also moves the subject of natural law into the ancient and medieval context of wisdom and providence. *Veritatis Splendor*, §41. Providence is mentioned only once in *Humanae Vitae* in §23. Tellingly, this is the mark of Ratzinger's Logos theory that had been steadily developing since 1959. Moreover, Ratzinger tasked the International Theological Commission to undertake two important studies: *Propositions on the Dignity and Rights of the Human Person* (1983), and *Communion and Stewardship: Human Persons Created in the Image of God* (2004).

54. Pope John Paul II, *Fides et Ratio*, §§36–42.

55. *Fides et Ratio*, §§16–23.

56. For one thing, registering Ratzinger's conviction that marks late modernity is not a surfeit but a deficit of reason. "This is why I make this strong and insistent appeal—not, I trust, untimely—that faith and philosophy recover the profound unity which allows them to stand in harmony with their nature without compromising their mutual autonomy. The *parrhesia* of faith must be matched by the boldness of reason." *Fides et Ratio*, §48. At §97 we read:

I say that Ratzinger left the tradition better off than he found it. The estate of moral theology and its presentation of natural law was immeasurably better than it was in 1953 when he began his academic studies. Most people do not appreciate the steady process of upgrading that was funneled into and expressed by those encyclicals. I suspect that this is due to the fact that the learned and the vulgar alike look at the conclusions, which did not change very much from 1953 to 2013 on issues of marriage, sex, life, and death.

Whether you agree or disagree with the conclusions, the Catholic understanding and presentation of natural law during the Wojtyła/Ratzinger era became much deeper and more supple. Not a minimalist ethic of the manualists but rather expositions that display: (1) a proper complexity of sources, reasons for the teachings;[57] and (2) a closer tie to anthropology and theology, along with the new emphasis on natural law not merely as a set of legal prohibitions but also as a search or path.

Ratzinger also left the tradition in a quandary. As the first two contexts of theological reflection on natural law were expanded and deepened, the dialogical context became difficult in the secular public sphere. While the magisterial improvement of natural law discourse was much appreciated by churchmen who were already learned in such matters, the "upgrade" did not make natural law concepts any more accessible or agreeable to either post-modern secularists or to Catholics in-the-pew—especially on issues pertaining to the public square, which, in our time, invariably are magnetized around sex and politics.[58]

If the *intellectus fidei* wishes to integrate all the wealth of the theological tradition, it must turn to the philosophy of being, which should be able to propose anew the problem of being—and this in harmony with the demands and insights of the entire philosophical tradition, including philosophy of more recent times, without lapsing into sterile repetition of antiquated formulas. Set within the Christian metaphysical tradition, the philosophy of being is a dynamic philosophy which views reality in its ontological, causal and communicative structures. It is strong and enduring because it is based upon the very act of being itself, which allows a full and comprehensive openness to reality as a whole, surpassing every limit in order to reach the One who brings all things to fulfilment. In theology, which draws its principles from Revelation as a new source of knowledge, this perspective is confirmed by the intimate relationship which exists between faith and metaphysical reasoning.

See, of course, Ratzinger's final encyclical issued by Pope Francis, *Lumen Fidei*. Francis, Encyclical Letter *Lumen Fidei* (June 29, 2013).

57. According to what *Fides et Ratio* calls the circularity of theology and philosophy. See *Fides et Ratio*, §73.

58. In February 2014, the German bishops mention both facets of this problem in their summary of the responses from German Catholics in preparation for the General Assembly of the Synod of Bishops to be held in Rome in fall of 2014. See Pressemitteilungen Der Deutschen Bischofskonferenz, *Pastoral challenges to the family in the context of*

IV. CAPSIZED—DIALOGICAL QUANDARIES

The quandary was in view during the year leading up to and the year following his election to the papacy in spring 2005. I will flag three papers that represented the 1988 Cambridge lecture *redivivus.*

(a) In 2004, Cardinal Ratzinger had a much celebrated exchange with Jürgen Habermas, published in 2005 under the title *The Dialectics of Secularization.*[59] Ratzinger's essay was titled: "That Which Holds the World Together: the Pre-political Moral Foundations of a Free State."[60] He proposed that reasonable people will agree that the moral foundations of human law cannot be up for a vote carried by the majority, for the human rights project depends upon the principle of "self-subsistent values that flow from the essence of what it is to be a man, and [which] are therefore inviolable."[61] Ratzinger writes:

---

evangelization: Summary of the responses from the German dioceses and archdioceses to the questions contained in the preparatory document for the III Extraordinary General Assembly of the Synod of Bishops 2014, §§2(a)–(c), at pp. 4–5 (Feb. 3, 2014), http://www.thetablet.co. uk/UserFiles/Files/2014–012b-ENG-Fragebogen-Die-patoralen-Herausforderungen-der-Familie.pdf.:

[1] Very few people are familiar with the term "natural law." It has virtually no role to play at institutional and educational level or in everyday culture. The term natural law is also only rarely used in academic ethics and legal justification. At the same time, there is a great deal of sympathy for the general validity of human rights, but this normally takes place without consideration for their theoretical foundation.

[2] Most of the baptised are also not familiar with the term "natural law." Many baptised categorically refused to answer this question in their responses, stating that they simply had never heard the term before.

[3] The natural law dimension is not explained at all in civil institutions. The idea of natural law in the sense of a normativity that can be derived directly from certain natural particularities runs counter to a rather constructivist understanding of reality in the Modern and Post-modern ages. Natural law is also hardly elaborated on or detailed within the Church, and it is frequently decidedly rejected as being historically out of date and not compatible with modern ethical discourses. In particular, there is sharp criticism of a narrow, biological determinism-based view of "natural law" because it is said not to do justice to the Christian understanding of man.

59. Jürgen Habermas and Joseph Cardinal Ratzinger, *The Dialectics of Secularization: On Reason and Religion*, ed. F. Schuller, trans. Brian McNeil (San Francisco: Ignatius Press, 2005).

60. Joseph Cardinal Ratzinger, "That Which Holds the World Together: The Pre-political Moral Foundations of a Free State," in *The Dialectics of Secularization: On Reason and Religion*, ed. Florian Schuller, trans. Brian McNeil (San Francisco: Ignatius Press, 2005), 53.

61. Joseph Cardinal Ratzinger, "That Which Holds the World Together," 61.

The natural law has remained (especially in the Catholic Church) the key issue in dialogues with the secular society and with other communities of faith in order to appeal to the reason we share in common and to seek the basis for a consensus about the ethical principles of law in a secular, pluralistic society. Unfortunately, this instrument has become blunt. Accordingly, I do not intend to appeal to it for support in this conversation. The idea of the natural law presupposed a concept of nature in which nature and reason overlap, since nature itself is rational. . . . [T]his view of nature has *capsized*.[62]

This is a startling remark. What did he mean to say?

In the western tradition, natural law ethics depended upon how we resolved the distinction between nature and convention (*physis/nomos*). Granted that our animality proceeds from the hand of nature, the question is whether the "rational"—to use Aristotelian terms, the specifically "human"—belongs in the first instance to nature or to convention? Clearly, conventions of all sorts (laws, symbols, procedures, policies, machines) proceed from reason, or from implicit or express compacts among those who exercise reason. But reason must have some ground in human nature as a condition for the possibility of rational artifacts, namely conventions. The ancient proponents of natural law (or the natural right, *ius naturale*) advanced the position one further step. Human nature is a norm for what can count as rational in the domain of conduct and conventions or contracts. Conventions, it is plain to see, can also be norms, provided that they do not contradict the implicit and discoverable norm of human nature. Epictetus's famous fragment makes this point clearly enough:

> Were I a swan, I should do after the manner of a swan. But now, since I am a reasonable being, I must sing to God: that is my work: I do it, nor will I desert this my post, as long as it is granted me to hold it; and upon you too I call to join in this self-same hymn.[63]

Human conventions presuppose the rudiments of a natural human dignity consisting in the form, the ends, and the operations of human nature. Only thus can nature be a norm with respect to convention.

For the post-Enlightenment secular world, however, the distinction is turned upside down—Ratzinger says, "capsized"—with the result that the specifically human stands mainly in the domain of convention: cultures, human

---

62. Joseph Cardinal Ratzinger, "That Which Holds the World Together," 69. Emphasis added.
63. Epictetus, *The Harvard Classics*, vol. 2, *The Golden Sayings of Epictetus*, ed. C. W. Eliot, trans. Hastings Crossley (New York: P. F. Collier & Son, 1909), 117.

laws, and "values" which are missing from nature. The "ought" cannot belong to the habitat of "is."[64] If this is the case, then human rights legislation and its various instruments are only another species of human convention, more or less in the fashion of international law, and perhaps with a value-added emphasis on ethical issues. The norms, however, would reside in the agreement, not in the nature of things. Therefore, just as Ratzinger pointed out, to insist upon the adjective "natural" conveys the idea of an order lower, rather than higher to what is specifically human. Usually, this is taken to mean human biological fundaments, which have yet to be humanized by convention.

(b) He made the same point in his 2011 speech to the German Bundestag: "The idea of natural law is today viewed as a specifically Catholic doctrine, not worth bringing into the discussion in a non-Catholic environment, so that one feels almost ashamed even to mention the term."[65] Once again, to the post-modern ear, the "natural" signifies the protohuman—what awaits humanization in the domain of culture and values. It must be shameful, then, to speak of human freedom and rationality as natural, for the natural, in this sense of the term, is not a sign or a pathway of evidence for conduct so much as pre-given material on which we impose "values."

(c) One day before John Paul II died, Cardinal Ratzinger gave a lengthy paper at Saint Scholastica's original convent at Subiaco. Of the many replays of his 1988 Cambridge lecture, this is the most complete reworking of that lecture.[66]

The Enlightenment, he proposes, was a Logos tradition that was not only in dialogue with Christianity but helped to lead Christianity to appreciate more deeply its own tradition of reason:

> In this connection, the Enlightenment is of Christian origin and it is no accident that it was born precisely and exclusively in the realm of the Christian faith, whenever Christianity, against its nature and unfortunately, had become tradition and religion of the state. Notwithstanding the philosophy, in so far as search for rationality also of our faith, was always a prerogative of Christianity, the voice of reason had been too domesticated. It was and is the merit of the Enlightenment to have again

---

64. In this respect, *Humanae Vitae* was the canary in the coal mine. That is to say, *Humanae Vitae* assumed that reason and freedom stand in a natural habitat not bereft of moral norms.

65. Address of His Holiness Benedict XVI, September 22, 2011, *The Listening Heart: Reflections on the Foundations of Law*, vatican.va. We should note Ratzinger's use of the Augustinian theme of listening and the Bonaventurean theme of signs, evidences.

66. Ratzinger, *On Europe's Crisis of Culture*, available at https://www.catholiceducation.org/en/culture/catholic-contributions/cardinal-ratzinger-on-europe-s-crisis-of-culture.html.

proposed these original values of Christianity and of having given back to reason its own voice.[67]

He singled out Hugo Grotius's famous claim about the natural moral law: common moral norms that would be true, valid, even if God did not exist. Ratzinger regards this dictum as an achievement, *at least in this respect*:

> In the opposition of the confessions and in the pending crisis of the image of God, an attempt was made to keep the essential values of morality outside the contradictions and to seek for them an evidence that would render them independent of the many divisions and uncertainties of the different philosophies and confessions. In this way, they wanted to ensure the basis of coexistence and, in general, the foundations of humanity.[68]

The Enlightenment, Ratzinger insists, is not secularism—rather, secularism is the enlightenment *after* it evacuated its Logos tradition. The one universal remaining is the science of matter, all the rest given over to convention, culture. This is what Grotius could not accept—nor could the Church. The Church's appeal to natural law in the public form of modern times had assumed some significant overlap with the Enlightenment, or at least certain sectors of it, which retained a Logos tradition. This assumption can no longer hold.[69]

Remember that, in the three public lectures I have just summarized, Ratzinger was not referring to the first two contexts of natural law discourse, which are internal to the theology of the Church: natural law in the context of systematics and natural law in the context of moral theology. He was speaking rather of the dialogical context in which natural law is used across institutions and traditions. His estimation of the former is confident, but his estimation of the latter is diffident, to say the least, for the least. Indeed, he sounds like the German bishops in their rather bleak report about the understanding that ordinary Catholics have of natural law. Both Ratzinger and the bishops, each in their own way, wonder if the words "natural law" ought to be used.

What is the solution to the quandary of having a high doctrine of natural law for purposes internal to Catholic theology that has almost no useful

---

67. *On Europe's Crisis of Culture.* Not a *hodos* for wisdom, but a mere convention—put in another way, authority without creative reason. *On Europe's Crisis of Culture*: "In the pastoral constitution, On the Church in the Modern World, Vatican Council II underlined again this profound correspondence between Christianity and the Enlightenment, seeking to come to a true conciliation between the Church and modernity, which is the great heritage that both sides must defend."

68. *On Europe's Crisis of Culture.*

69. This, of course, is his Regensburg theme less than one year later.

connection to the discourse of a post-Enlightenment legal and political culture? Perhaps it can be found in inter-religious dialogue, which is what he proposed in his 1988 Cambridge lecture.

We come, finally, to *In Search of a Universal Ethic: A New Look at Natural Law*.[70] As Prefect of the CDF, Ratzinger gave the topic to the International Theological Commission (ITC) in 2004, just when he himself was working on the exchange with Habermas. The ITC labored on the project for two years, from 2006 to 2008. In the meantime, of course, Ratzinger became Pope Benedict XVI and thus ceased to function as the Prefect. So, Cardinal Levada signed the document in 2009. But the purpose and the intellectual "attitude," so to speak, of the document is Ratzingerian to the bone.

The ITC study endeavors to orient and enrich a dialogue outside of the immediate environs of moral theology: "[I]n this document we intend to invite all who ask themselves about the ultimate foundations of ethics and of the juridical and political order, to consider the resources that a renewed presentation of the teaching of the natural law contains."[71]

In Search treats natural law in the light of what the Catholic tradition has cumulatively discovered and formulated over the centuries, including what it has learned from shortcomings in its own experience. On the latter score, the authors note recurring problems: emphasizing too strongly biological nature at the expense of freedom; having in other ways emphasized too strongly reason, with the inevitable pitfall of rationalism; of having made anthropological assumptions, which needed to be adjusted in view of historical and cultural contexts; suggesting that that the precepts of natural law are an already-assembled system, even down to the most proximate level of precepts governing a problem or case; and not always making sufficiently clear the processes of formation needed for a mature appropriation of the natural law.[72]

> Offering our contribution to the search for a universal ethics, and proposing a rationally justifiable foundation, we desire to invite experts and the spokespersons of the great religious, sapiential and philosophical traditions of humanity to proceed to an analogous work, beginning from their sources, to reach a common recognition of the universal moral norms based on a rational approach to reality.[73]

Wisdom traditions, on this view, recognize and make explicit (in different ways and in various degrees): (1) that there is a "common patrimony" of moral

---

70. International Theological Commission, *In Search of a Universal Ethic: A New Look at Natural Law* (2009), www.vatican.va.

71. *In Search*, §9.

72. *In Search*, §§10, 38, 52, 56, 59, 99.

73. *In Search*, §116.

values, (2) that certain moral actions are required by human nature itself, and (3) that human life stands in a "creative and harmonious manner in a cosmic or metaphysical order that surpasses it and gives meaning to his life."[74] Wisdom traditions, in other words, are open to reality as a whole, even if their vision is partial in this or that aspect.[75] In this special sense of the term, "interreligious" means discourse among traditions that are open to reality as a whole.

The document begins by endorsing the 1948 United Nations's *Universal Declaration of Human Rights* as an authentic expression of conscience, but laments that it has now collapsed into a quagmire of revisions, procedures, and moral posturings that avoid reckoning with an anthropological and moral grounding.[76]

In Search does not mean by dialogue either the Habermasian or Rawlsian methods for reaching norms that are mutually acceptable to the parties of the discussion.[77] It eschews dialogue that is a "purely inductive search, on the parliamentary model, of a minimal, already existing consent."[78] This is a dialogue, in fact, without a "search." As *In Search* remarks, the dialogue has not proven adequate either to secure foundations for the post-1948 human rights project or to win support of religions and wisdom traditions, which need more than a "minimal ethic."[79] *In Search* envisages a dialogue different than what is usually meant by "public reason." Rather than holding back one's best-considered reasons, it puts the mature line of reasons on the table, inviting others to do the same.

Although the authors give due weight to the prephilosophical experience and appropriation of the rudiments or seeds of moral truth, they do not limit consensus to what is primitive in experience.[80] Appropriation of the "evidences" of natural law, either by the individual or by a culture, is a slow process requiring action and reflection—in a wisdom tradition, an "apprenticeship."[81]

Whereas a wisdom tradition is open to reality as a whole—a natural transcendence[82]—the modern, western mind does not view nature or the

---

74. *In Search*, §§11, 12.

75. As the ITC recalls, Catholic theology fed upon the bread of sapiential traditions as a *praeparatio evangelicae*, and once assimilated to theology the two to "form a whole" in the Catholic mind. *In Search of a Universal Ethic*, §26; see also *Fides et Ratio*, §§81, 82, which explain that philosophy lacks its sapiential function if it is addressed only to "particular and subordinate aspects of reality—functional, formal or utilitarian."

76. *In Search*, §5.

77. *In Search*, §8.

78. *In Search*, §6.

79. *In Search*, §6.

80. *In Search*, §60.

81. *In Search*, §§38, 53.

82. *In Search*, §97.

"natural" as "impregnated with an immanent wisdom," but rather, to use *In Search*'s own language, it is "stripped of every immanent teleology or finality."[83] This is only to acknowledge that prior to choice and prior to satisfying procedures of consent, "the natural" is *merely* immanent, along the lines of what Charles Taylor has called "closed world structures."[84] Purpose is assigned rather than discovered within the ordinary frame of things.

By shifting the problem of authority to the moral authority of a "common patrimony" implicit in many wisdom traditions, *In Search* does not relieve the problem—at least not for secular interlocutors. For example, when it proposes that there are moral "messages" in the nature of things and that natural law is not imposed on creatures from without but is inscribed in their very nature,[85] it summons a quite different meaning of the "immanent" than what will be obvious to most agents formed in the institutions of western secular culture. For them, nature is not obviously a semiotic (a book or a ladder) in the sense that we have inherited from Paul, Augustine, Bonaventure, or Thomas. The immanent rather is a domain of freedom just for the reason that it does not require transcendent messages, much less messages, which arrive so intimately with authority.[86] The immanent, for all practical purposes, is nothing other than what is bereft of, or perhaps still waiting for, authority.[87] When the ITC expresses the "urgent" need to reach common foundations (of a natural law sort) for the human rights project, it will have to anticipate a response that, on its view, is terribly inadequate if not irrational. Namely, that public reasons for rights, as Rawls would put it, must prescind from "the whole truth."[88] "[P]olitical liberalism," he insists, not only leaves comprehensive theological and moral doctrines to individual rather than public reason but "applies the principle of toleration to philosophy itself."[89]

While the problem of liberty unseated from nature is more likely to be bridged in dialogue with wisdom traditions, it remains the tougher problem in the familiar world of secular modernity. In one place, the ITC remarks: "In order that the notion of natural law can be of use in the elaboration of a

---

83. *In Search*, §72.

84. Charles Taylor, *A Secular Age* (Cambridge, MA: Belknap Press, 2007), 589.

85. *In Search*, §§11–12, 63.

86. Taylor, *A Secular Age*, 543–44: "The immanent order can thus slough off the transcendent. But it doesn't necessarily do so. . . . It is something that permits closure, without demanding it."

87. This is why the sciences and contemporary institutions of civic formation, education, and economic activity are deemed useful, and indeed legitimate. Precisely by not requiring a sapiential philosophy or religion to interpret transcendent "messages," freedom is protected.

88. John Rawls, *Political Liberalism* (New York: Columbia University Press, 1993), 243.

89. Rawls, *Political Liberalism*, 10.

universal ethics in a secularized and pluralistic society such as our own, it is therefore necessary to avoid presenting it in the rigid form that it assumed, particularly in modern rationalism."[90] This prescription strikes me as a good way to facilitate dialogue among wisdom traditions that tend to have a greater affinity for what we in the West would call the intellectualist rather than a rationalist anthropology. It is much harder to see how the prescription has medicinal value for dialogue with a "secularized" society. Its denizens are not bothered by rationalism so much as by appeals in the public order to transcendent values—not only the supernatural, but also what *In Search* means by natural law.[91]

Tellingly, *In Search* makes clear enough that the Church often invokes natural law (moral truths antecedent to faith) defensively, against a belligerent secularism that dismisses a natural law foundation of moral choice and conscience as a purely confessional subversion of civic dialogue.[92]

For instance, take note of §35, where *In Search* outlines four dialogical uses by the Church. Tellingly, two, if not three, are apologetical, defensive, or both. "Today the Catholic Church invokes the natural law in four principal contexts":

> In the first place, facing the spread of a culture that limits rationality to the positive sciences and abandons the moral life to relativism, it insists on the natural capacity of human beings to obtain by reason "the ethical message contained in being . . . [93]
>
> In the second place, in the presence of relativistic individualism, which judges that every individual is the source of his own values, and that society results from a mere contract . . . [94]
>
> In the third place, facing an aggressive secularism that wants to exclude believers from public debate, the Church points out that the interventions of Christians in public life on subjects that regard natural law . . .[95]

---

90. *In Search*, §33.

91. *In Search*, §97. Not surprisingly, C. S. Lewis's illustrations of the *Tao* in *The Abolition of Man* include quotations from only two modern western authors, Hooker and Locke, and only the latter is a modern in the relevant sense of the term.

92. The authors of *In Search* are anything but naïve about who is their main antagonist on questions of natural law.

93. *In Search*, §35. Continuing, "and to know in their main lines the fundamental norms of just action in conformity with their nature and their dignity. The natural law thus responds to the need to provide a basis in reason for the rights of man and makes possible an intercultural and interreligious dialogue capable of fostering universal peace and of avoiding the 'clash of civilizations.'"

94. *In Search*, §35: "In particular, the democratic form of government is intrinsically bound to stable ethical values, which have their source in the requirements of natural law and thus do not depend on the fluctuations of the consent of a numerical majority."

95. *In Search*, §35: "The defence of the rights of the oppressed, justice in international relations, the defence of life and of the family, religious freedom and freedom of education."

are not in themselves of a confessional nature, but derive from the care which every citizen must have for the common good of society. . . . [96] In the fourth place . . . the Church recalls that civil laws do not bind in conscience when they contradict natural law, and asks for the acknowledgment of the right to conscientious objection, as well as the duty of disobedience in the name of obedience to a higher law.[97]

V. CONCLUSION

In Search intelligently and faithfully adjusts the dialogical context of natural law discourse in ways that reflect the deeper upgrade already given to the systematic and dialectical contexts in recent Catholic theology. Catholic natural law theory, especially at the magisterial level, had become more robust, more complex, and more integrated with theology proper. *In Search* answered Ratzinger's question: "[How] to find constructive pointers and convergences for an effective deepening of the doctrine on natural moral law."

The post-Enlightenment, as Ratzinger said, "capsized"—turned upside down—the distinction between nature and convention. *In Search* suggests, perhaps even requires, that the dialogical use of natural law can succeed only in the context of inter-religious dialogue.[98] Recall the double presupposition of Catholicism: evidence available to all, evidence appropriated to become an organic part of the theology. The dialogical partners would have to be other religious traditions that do the same. Absent some surprising philosophical recovery of, or spiritual grounding for, the human rights project, what remains of dialogue with the post-Enlightenment culture would seem to be a defensive maneuver rather than a "search."

Just as post-Enlightenment civic life protects itself from the intrusion of Logos traditions into public policy (other than the science of mathematized

---

96. *In Search*, §35. See also International Theological Commission, *Dio Trinità, Unità Degli Uomini: Il Monoteismo Cristiano Contro La Violenza* (2014), www.vatican.va.

97. *In Search*, §35.

98. Recall MacIntyre's challenge: "Appeals to natural law of what was traditionally one of their two central features, features that gave such appeals their distinctive point and purpose. What the natural law was held to provide was a *shared* and *public* standard, by appeal to which the claims of particular systems of positive law . . . could be evaluated"—evaluated, that is, not just by experts but also by plain persons. MacIntyre, "From Answers to Questions," 103. But MacIntyre himself does not see the full implications. For it is not just natural law discourse that fails to satisfy such requirements, but also what Rawls calls "comprehensive doctrines" (including those of the Enlightenment, such as a comprehensive liberal doctrine). Rawls, *Political Liberalism*, 243. If we rule out, with Rawls, the public authority of any and all comprehensive doctrine, what could experts and plain persons share by way of evaluation? Perhaps the answer is some social-science correlations supplemented by a mild cost-benefit norm of utility?

matter), so too Catholicism will seek to protect its liberty to exist as both a revealed religion and a Logos tradition, and it will do so by appeal to human rights flowing from natural law. This is not a dialogue, or a search oriented toward discovery of truth, so much as a loggerhead. What is worse is that the Church can be seen as adopting the opposite of its own position: namely, using the discourse of human or natural rights as political-cultural tactics of defense of a certain cultural strand of opinion.

So, should the Catholic Church instead engage in inter-religious dialogue as the main forum for natural law discourse *ad extra*? The answer depends on what is meant by "inter-religious."

On Ratzinger's own terms (I am less sure about the ITC), such dialogue is not inter-religious in the usual senses given to the term. It is not, for instance, ecumenical in the fashion of a Catholic-Lutheran dialogue, which depends upon a shared revealed theology. Nor is it "religious" in the ordinary sociological manner of comparing traditions of religious cult and practice. Going back to the Cambridge lecture, when Ratzinger referred to C. S. Lewis's account of the *Tao* as a model for dialogue about natural law, he did not emphasize the specifically religious aspects so much as the Logos component contained in and transmitted by religions, i.e., human reason "open to reality as a whole." Not all religions have this conviction, but those that do share a Logos tradition and therefore have a basis for dialogue.[99]

Recall Ratzinger's understanding of how early Christianity oriented itself with regard to other traditions: "[Christianity] has not identified its precursors *in the other religions*, but in that philosophical enlightenment which has cleared the path of traditions to turn to the search of the truth and towards the good, toward the one God who is above all gods."[100] Ratzinger's understanding of the dialogical context of natural law, therefore, is keyed to the philosophical and sapiential components. This is what Karl Jaspers meant by spiritual movements of the Axial Age arising in the sixth century BCE.[101] This certainly fits the C. S. Lewis theme that Ratzinger developed in his Cambridge lecture and that the ITC emphasized in *In Search*.

---

99. In *Dominus Iesus*, Ratzinger and his team of writers contrast the assent of faith to a revealing God to religious belief. The latter is a search under the aspect of divinity as the Absolute. See the Congregation for the Doctrine of the Faith, *Declaration "Dominus Iesus": On The Unicity and Salvific Universality of Jesus Christ and the Church*, approved by Pope John Paul II and signed by Prefect Joseph Cardinal Ratzinger and Secretary Tarcisio Bertone (August 6, 2000), §7, www.vatican.va.; see also Gerard Bradley, "Pope John Paul II and Religious Liberty," *Ave Maria Law Review* 33 (2007): 36–37.

100. Ratzinger, *On Europe's Crisis of Culture*. Emphasis added.

101. Karl Jaspers, *Way to Wisdom: An Introduction to Philosophy*, trans. Ralph Manheim, 2nd ed. (New Haven, CT: Yale University Press, 2003), 99–100.

This option, however, seems hopelessly antiquarian, at least for any practical purpose, unless we include the European Enlightenment. Ratzinger held the Enlightenment in high esteem but certainly not for its religion. Rather, the Enlightenment, as he understood it, defended and advanced the dignity of human reason. The dialogical context for natural law, therefore, needs to reconnect with that commitment of the Enlightenment rather than the truncated version that he calls scientific materialism. While much diminished today, the dignitarian humanism of the Enlightenment is within living memory and continues to exist as a module in our post-modern institutions and practices. Ever since the pontificate of Leo XIII, Rome has endeavored to integrate this human rights project with natural law. *Pacem in terris* (1963) was the high tide of that ambition. Only a week after the encyclical, Dr. Martin Luther King Jr. issued his Letter from Birmingham Jail, quoting Thomas Aquinas, "an unjust law is no law at all."[102] Ratzinger's speech to the German Bundestag evinces a position of conflict rather than convergence.

Catholic theology can keep alive the first two contexts of natural law discourse simply by using the resources of its own tradition. Discourse about natural law in the public square, however, needs the Enlightenment. The quandary is ironical, to say the least. The Church needs the voice of its former opponent, the voice that declared the rights of man and the dignity of reason. But this is not the first time the Church has found itself on the terrain of such historical irony.[103]

---

102. Martin Luther King, Jr., "Letter from Birmingham City Jail," in *A Testament of Hope: The Essential Writings and Speeches of Martin Luther King, Jr.*, ed. James M. Washington (San Francisco: HarperOne, 2003), 289–302.

103. See Pope Benedict XVI, "Address of His Holiness Benedict XVI at the White House Welcoming Ceremony," April 16, 2008, www.vatican.va.

CHAPTER 11

The Situation of Natural Law in Catholic Theology

As WE SAW IN THE PREVIOUS CHAPTER, natural law thinking is deployed in Catholic moral theology in three ways, or within three contexts: (1) the systematic, (2) the dialectical, and (3) the dialogical. Thus, discussion of natural law in Catholic theology can lean in one of three different directions. When we ask how natural law stands within the economies of creation and redemption, our inquiry points toward the systematic context, toward the foundations of theology. When natural law is used as one of the resources for inquiry about practical matters, inquiry moves toward particular actions, cases, and classes of actions. This is moral theology in its dialectical context, or its fully practical office. When natural law is used as part of a search for common premises across religious and philosophical traditions, inquiry moves toward a discovery of common and converging pathways of evidence. This is moral theology in its dialogical context, or its role in the search for a universal and universally acknowledged wisdom. The question "Does the sacrament of marriage include natural law requirements of marriage?" corresponds to the systematic; the question "Is divorce licit under the natural law?" corresponds to the dialectical; the question "Is there a core of truth recognized by widely diverging religious and philosophical traditions concerning the nature of marriage and family?" corresponds to the dialogical.

Debates about natural law can arise in all three contexts. Not infrequently debates begin in one line only to jump into another. The sexual questions which have captivated moral theologians for the past half century alternated between deeper issues of anthropology, issues concerning precepts, and discussions of commonly accepted or acceptable evidences. This is exactly what we ought to expect for any tradition that takes natural law seriously.

The two documents I shall consider in this essay lean more toward the sources and toward dialogue than toward practical argument. Neither intends to solve a particular moral question. *Veritatis Splendor* (1993) is the first papal encyclical devoted exclusively to moral theology. As its subtitle indicates, the encyclical treats foundational issues—one of which is the natural law component of moral theology.[1] The International Theological Commission's (ITC) study, *In Search of a Universal Ethics: A New Look at the Natural Law*, considers natural law as a common component of the great "wisdom traditions." The exposition is heavily weighted toward perennial anthropological and metaphysical themes. *Veritatis* is in every respect the stronger account because it looks *ad intra* to the coherence of moral theology. *In Search* aims at dialogue with extra-ecclesial parties for purposes, and under terms of dialogue, that are not always clear. But the two documents—one pontifical, the other a curial paper—give us an interesting picture of how natural law is situated in Catholic theology at the half-century mark from Vatican Council II.

First, I want to put the two documents in a specific historical and political context. After the collapse of political Christendom—marked in the Catholic world at 1870, when the Roman communion ceased being a de facto arrangement of national churches superintended in many ways by temporal sovereigns—the magisterium had to develop a Catholic position on a wide array of moral issues and social problems: economic justice, associational liberties, church-state relations, and of course, marriage, which from the beginning was the most intense skirmish line along which Catholic moral teachings conflicted with the laws and public policies of the secular regimes. Addressing these broad issues, encyclicals went beyond the more narrowly tailored decrees about moral conduct in canonical and confessional cases. The older division of labor in Catholic Christendom that informally distinguished between authority in public policy and authority in ecclesiastical order, corresponding to the competence of royal courts on the one hand and ecclesial tribunals on the other, had become defunct.

Rome now had to speak about the moral dimensions of public policy across the board. Leo XIII used natural law as an appeal (and sometimes as an argument) to resituate the problems of society and authority. His use of natural law was elegantly neo-Thomist, and it won the admiration of the Catholic world because Leo succeeded in balancing the disputed moral or political question with the deeper questions about the nature and end of man and the origin of authority. In the twentieth century, however, the list of disputed issues treated at least partially in terms of natural law multiplied, and came to include the "life" issues such as war and peace, abortion, contraception, and sexual conduct generally, as well as the ever-burgeoning sector of problems that spun out of the post-war human rights project (1948). John XXIII's *Pacem in Terris* (1963) enumerated some two dozen human rights grounded in natural law. To accommodate the expanding field of social doctrine, the

---

1. Pope John Paul II, Encyclical Letter *Veritatis Splendor* (August 6, 1993). The subtitle reads: *De Quibusdam Quaestionibus Fundamentalibus Doctrinae Moralis Ecclesiae* [On Certain Fundamental Questions Concerning the Church's Moral Teachings].

revised *Code of Canon Law* (1983) states: "The Church has the right always and everywhere to proclaim moral principles, even in respect of the social order, and to make judgments about any human matter in so far as this is required by fundamental human rights or the salvation of souls."[2]

The cumulative effect of a century of teachings in the arena of moral theology and social doctrine left the subject of natural law feeling rather cluttered at the practical end of the spectrum. It was easy to lose sight of the coherence that ought to obtain between this bevy of particular moral teachings and the principal sources of moral theology. Thus, the problem of coherence needed to be reconsidered and repaired where it was found wanting. This is the context in which we should read *Veritatis Splendor*, which addressed the coherence of moral theology precisely as theology. But knowledge of this history also helps us to understand the ITC paper, which keeps in view a human rights movement that has gone awry, multiplying and changing the content of rights to such extent that only an apophatic universal remains—a "negative anthropology."[3] That is to say, we can affirm what man is not, but not what he is prior to self-defining liberty.

Veritatis turned to the question of what kind of component natural law is in moral theology, and how it relates to the other sources of doctrine: sacred scripture, Christology, theological anthropology, ascetical theology, and ecclesiology. Because it addressed (according to the subtitle) "fundamental questions" rather than fully practical ones, the encyclical was free to make more explicit and to give a more nuanced account of the assumptions that govern the magisterium's use of natural law theory (or pieces thereof). I shall make no effort to summarize this very rich encyclical. Instead, I call attention to one of the assumptions that *Veritatis* was at pains to clarify. Namely, that natural law forms an organic part of moral theology.

Why shouldn't the Church concern itself only with the habits and actions immediately ordained to salvation—for example, the theological virtues, the gifts of the Spirit, the Beatitudes, the works of mercy, and sacramental actions? Some theologians raised the question from a slightly different angle. Why shouldn't the things belonging proximately to the natural law fall within the magisterium of scholars and experts whose expertise pertains to temporal matters? In effect, the two concerns held together rather tersely in the *Code of Canon Law* ("in so far as this is required by fundamental human rights or the salvation of souls") were being pulled from either end, philosophical and pastoral. The encyclical notes:

---

2. CIC (1983), can. 747, §2.

3. The term "negative anthropology" is taken from Rocco Buttiglione, *Karol Wojtyła: The Thought of the Man Who Became Pope John Paul II* (Grand Rapids, MI: Eerdmans, 1997), 53.

In their desire, however, to keep the moral life in a Christian context, certain moral theologians have introduced a sharp distinction, contrary to Catholic doctrine, between an "ethical order" which would be human in origin and of value for "this world" alone, and an "order of salvation" for which only certain intentions and interior attitudes regarding God and neighbor would be significant. This has then led to an actual denial that there exists, in Divine Revelation, a specific and determined moral content, universally valid and permanent.[4]

The encyclical explains that moral truths—in principle accessible to human reason (§29)—not only constitute a "preparation for the Gospel," but are also situated within it (§3). The moral law, thus understood, is presupposed in two ways by moral theology: first, as principles of moral order are derived from human nature; second, as those very same principles are clarified and integrated in the teachings of Christ. "[T]he Magisterium does not bring to the Christian conscience truths which are extraneous to it; rather it brings to light the truths which it ought already to possess, developing them from the starting point of the primordial act of faith."[5]

Thus, the encyclical's lengthy exegesis of Matthew 19 on the query of the rich young man. Jesus's exhortation to discipleship explicitly presupposes knowledge of moral law. Keeping the commandments, beginning with the negative precepts, is a "basic condition" for justice, love of neighbor, and for moral maturity and freedom. This module of morality is not unique to either Jewish law or Christian doctrine. As Saint Paul contends in Romans 2:14–16, the "conflicting thoughts of the gentiles" give witness to the law as the norm of conscience, according to which "God will judge the secrets of men" (§59). This same law is also explicitly presupposed by Christ when he teaches what is necessary to live a life ordered to the kingdom. From this latter perspective, the moral law is incorporated within another starting point—the life of faith. According to the encyclical, the moral theologian cannot leave behind the natural law component for the purpose of a morality of "salvation" without subverting Scripture and "the living tradition."

To be clear, this is not a fideist position. The encyclical is *not* saying that there is a "universally valid and permanent" body of moral truths *because*, according to Matthew 19, Jesus says so or *because* the Church says so. Nor does it suggest that our only access to moral truth is Scripture or tradition (§3). Rather, the encyclical contends that the moral law, as something proportionate to human reason, forms an organic part of Jesus's teaching, and therefore it is already internal to moral action in the light of faith.

---

4. *Veritatis Splendor*, §37.
5. *Veritatis Splendor*, §64.

Alasdair MacIntyre has astutely noticed the importance of at least one prong of this position:

> It is not just that the natural law can be known by the exercise of the powers of reason, independently of revelation, but also that the knowledge of divine law afforded by revelation presupposes a prior knowledge of the precepts of the natural law. It is a revealed truth, that is to say, that the truths of the natural law can be known prior to and independently of any revealed truths, including this particular revealed truth.[6]

MacIntyre assures the reader, "that in holding this I am not being theologically eccentric."[7] He is not at all. MacIntyre, however, is more immediately interested in the purely philosophical aspects of debate over natural law, and therefore he does not draw out all of the implications for moral theology. One of these would surely be the following. Even if the institutions of a given culture—universities, courts, the media, other churches and religions—had no further use of natural law either as a supposition or as an explanatory framework, the Church nevertheless would be bound to teach and affirm the natural law.

Furthermore, it would need to affirm it precisely as the natural, created measure of human acts; that is to say, as truths that conscience "ought already to possess." When we hear the words of Matthew 19:8 "From the beginning . . ." we can grasp both prongs of the commitment to natural law. For the natural sign of the sacrament of marriage is nothing other than marriage "from the beginning." With respect to this sacrament at least, to erase the natural law would erase the sacrament of the New Covenant. The double commitment therefore is embedded in Catholic theology at levels deeper than what come under the concerns of moral theology or philosophy. Indeed, the theological affirmation of natural law in *Veritatis* makes the moral theologian *more* responsible to the natural law than the moral philosopher, and by extension makes the systematic (sacramental) theologian more responsible than the moral theologian.[8]

---

6. Alasdair MacIntyre, "From Answers to Questions," in *Intractable Disputes about the Natural Law: Alasdair MacIntyre and Critics*, ed. L. S. Cunningham (Notre Dame, IN: University of Notre Dame Press, 2009), 341.

7. Indeed, his brief treatment of Romans 2:14–15 is virtually the same as that of *Veritatis Splendor*, §59; see MacIntyre, "From Answers to Questions," 344: "It is also a revealed truth that we human beings all of us stand accused before God of our violations of and rebellion against his law. But we could not be rightly held responsible for those violations and that rebellion if we were not aware of God's law, simply *qua* human beings, and not only aware of the precepts that comprise God's law, but aware of the compelling character of their authority." Put in this way, MacIntyre is suggesting that some precepts are not only known but also known in their compelling authority. This puts the issue in the foyer of law, if not higher law.

8. As we will show in the following pages, Saint Thomas himself can be considered the exemplar of this point.

Admittedly, this does not make the work of moral theology easier. Interestingly, according to the Scripture, the rich young man hesitates but does not offer a serious objection to the proposition that moral rectitude is a necessary condition for pursuing eternal life. He declines radical discipleship. *Veritatis*, on the other hand, deals with the situation in which the moral prerequisites are the stumbling block "for the Christian conscience." Put in this way, the moral of the story has been transposed. What was the easy matter now appears difficult and controversial. This surprising transposition is implied but is not made explicit in the encyclical. Nevertheless, it is an important symptom that needs to be carefully discerned by moral theologians. The proposal that there exist moral norms prior to human construction, consent, and choice is a rather alarming message in our culture. In proof of which, we only need to consider the fact that questions of human nature and moral conduct are much more likely to be church-dividing issues than questions concerning justification, predestination, and the function of sacraments. From one point of view, the "natural" morality presupposed by the Gospel is the easier thing, objectively speaking; from another point of view, it is just the opposite.

The double commitment also makes it necessary for moral theologians to reckon more seriously with philosophy than they have been prepared or inclined to do over the past several decades. When it was issued, *Veritatis* was received in some parts of the Catholic world as a rebuke of progressive-leaning moral theologians. Not very much imagination is required to see that it also cuts the other way—moderating quasi-Barthian currents in Catholic theology that would have nature disappear into grace. If the natural law component is not sustainable without philosophy, it is a daunting responsibility for theologians. For in the institutions of late modernity (not only universities but also in the far greater domain of political, jurisprudential, and corporate life), the major schools of ethics do not explicitly share the same starting points or explanatory framework; indeed, none can be put in any useful way into the category of natural law.[9] Therefore, either theologians need to leave the natural law component without philosophical articulation or they will have to do much of that work themselves. In effect, they will have to wear two hats.

Thomas Aquinas investigated natural law in his dual role as philosopher and theologian, for which there is no equivalent office or craft in our secular institutions, and increasingly less so in ecclesiastical ones. Of course, there has been and will continue to be disagreement over whether Aquinas was primarily a philosopher or a theologian. As Fergus Kerr puts it: "[Thomas] is a philosopher and a theologian, and we are never going to agree on where to put the emphasis."[10] However, it seems correct, both historically and

---

9. MacIntyre, "From Answers to Questions," 51.
10. Fergus Kerr, *After Aquinas: Versions of Thomism* (Oxford: Blackwell, 2002), 210.

intellectually, to say that Saint Thomas was in fact a theologian whose method incorporated philosophy. As Lawrence Dewan says, "The [*Summa theolo-giae*], and in general the work of St. Thomas, is *meta-philosophical*. It is a study and teaching of what has been revealed to us by God himself, and thus surpasses mere human wisdom, i.e. philosophy. However, revelation presupposes the order of nature, and *Thomas's teaching envelops philosophy rather than excluding it.*"[11] Aquinas's work is a paradigm of the double articulation, or double commitment to natural law: philosophical reflection on the naturally-available truth of the moral order used within a theological doctrine that clarifies and deepens those philosophical insights by integrating them within the revelation of Christ. Thus, Saint Thomas's natural law theory was not developed in spite of but rather because of his being a moral and systematic theologian; Aquinas was *more committed* to studying natural law than someone operating solely as a philosopher precisely because of his office as systematic theologian. At the very least, let us point out that the problem of emphasis and ongoing debates about it in interpreting Thomas are set within, and can arise only within, a tradition that is doubly articulate. *Veritatis* requires the natural law component to be treated in just that fashion.[12]

In Search of a Universal Ethic: A New Look at Natural Law (2009) differs from *Veritatis* not only in its curial pedigree and magisterial weight (a study paper allowed to be published by the Cardinal Prefect of the Congregation for the Doctrine of the Faith [CDF]), but more relevantly, for our purposes, in the questions as well as the audience it addresses. *In Search* aims to orient and enrich a dialogue outside of the immediate environs of moral theology: "[I]n this document we intend to invite all who ask themselves about the ultimate foundations of ethics and of the juridical and political order, to consider the resources that a renewed presentation of the teaching of the natural law contains."[13] However, in shifting from sources of moral theology to the resources for dialogue, the ITC moves to even more difficult terrain than the one occupied by *Veritatis*. Of course, *Veritatis* too worries about negative anthropology and exaggerated notions of individual autonomy which disorient the natural law that theology presupposes. But it has the signal advantage of correcting

---

11. Lawrence Dewan, "St Thomas and the Divine Origin of Law: Some Notes," *Civilizar Ciencias Sociales y Humanas* 15 (2008): 123–34, at 124. Emphasis added. See also Stephen Brock, *The Philosophy of Saint Thomas Aquinas: A Sketch* (Eugene, OR: Wipf and Stock Publishers, 2015), xviii-xix.

12. One cannot ignore the fact that the encyclical is shaped by a high, neo-Thomistic rendering of both natural law and the sources of moral theology. *Veritatis Splendor*, §44: "The Church has often made reference to the Thomistic doctrine of natural law, including it in her own teaching on morality."

13. *In Search*, §9.

and moderating claims of autonomy, as well as the array of different understandings of natural law, within the landscape of its own tradition. *In Search* appears to tackle the issues on an open field with recourse only to natural law. It claims no more authority than being one wisdom tradition among others—albeit a tradition with centuries of experience in this field of inquiry.[14]

The subtitle indicates something "new." But in its treatment of the anthropological and cosmological assumptions, *In Search* differs very little from *Veritatis*.[15] For example, the authors do not equate natural law with purely immanent laws of nature (§10); nor do they suggest that natural rights are terms of obligation without natural law (§88). They contend that the relative autonomy of moral truth, and freedom of choice regarding finite goods, already imply a transcendent, though not necessarily a supernatural, end (§§42, 63, 77). Faithful to the Thomistic tradition, they contend that the good of knowing the truth about God is not merely a theoretical, explanatory addendum to natural law, but is contained seedlike in the foundations and experience of moral truth as one of the first precepts (§50).

Apropos of Yves Simon's suggestion that natural law can be discussed in terms of three foci—reason, nature, and God[16]—*In Search* recognizes that while reason, nature, and God each has its own salience, the price paid for hiving off one, to the exclusion of the others, will be a doctrine of natural law that is not open to reality as a whole.

> The vision of the world within which the doctrine of natural law developed and still finds its meaning today, involves therefore the reasoned conviction that there exists a harmony between the three substances

---

14. *In Search* treats natural law in the light of what the Catholic tradition has cumulatively discovered and formulated over the centuries, including what it has learned from shortcomings in its own experience. On the latter score, the authors note recurring problems of emphasizing too strongly biological nature at the expense of freedom; of having in other ways emphasized too strongly reason, with the inevitable pitfall of rationalism; of having made anthropological assumptions which needed to be adjusted in view of historical and cultural contexts; of suggesting that the precepts of natural law are an already-assembled system, even down to the most proximate level of precepts governing a problem or case; and not always making sufficiently clear the processes of formation needed for a mature appropriation of the natural law. See *In Search*, §§10, 38, 52, 56, 59, 81, 99.

15. Including what we have termed the double commitment. Christianity treats the natural law both a preparation for faith and as a teaching within it: "The new Law of the Gospel includes, takes up and brings to fulfillment the requirements of the natural law. The orientations of the natural law are not therefore external normative demands with respect to the new Law." *In Search*, §112. These two are mentioned several times; see §§12, 23–24, 26–27, 69–71, and 101.

16. Yves R. Simon, *Tradition of Natural Law*, ed. V. Kuic, introduction by Russell Hittinger (New York: Fordham University Press, 1992), 129. See Ch. 7 for further discussion.

[sic—bad translation of *ces trois instances*] which are God, man, and nature. In this perspective, the world was perceived as an intelligible whole, united by the common reference of the beings that compose it to a divine founding principle, to a *Logos*.[17]

The authors are surely correct that a discussion of natural law that puts reason, nature, and God into competition (§§74–75), or that refuses to give to each foci the salience that experience and reason will allow, if not demand, falls short of the Catholic tradition.

Interestingly, the ITC does not situate its presentation and its understanding of dialogue in the fashion of a model United Nations plenary session. Rather, it puts its discussion of moral universals in the context of "great wisdom traditions, both religious and philosophical."

> Offering our contribution to the search for a universal ethic and proposing a rationally justifiable foundation, we desire to invite experts and the spokespersons of the great religious, sapiential and philosophical traditions of humanity to proceed to an analogous work, beginning from their sources, to reach a common recognition of the universal moral norms based on a rational approach to reality.[18]

Wisdom traditions, on this view, recognize and make explicit (in different ways and in various degrees) (1) that there is a "common patrimony" of moral values, (2) that certain moral actions are required by human nature itself, and (3) that the human person stands in a "creative and harmonious manner in a cosmic or metaphysical order that surpasses it and gives meaning to his life."[19] Wisdom traditions, in other words, are open to reality as a whole, even if their vision is partial in this or that aspect. Appeal to sapiential traditions is reminiscent of John Paul II's encyclical *Fides et Ratio* (1998).[20] As *In Search* recalls, Catholic theology fed upon the bread of sapiential traditions as a *praeparatio evangelicae*, and once assimilated to theology, the two "form a whole" in the Catholic mind (§26).

The ITC does not mean by dialogue either the Habermasian or Rawlsian methods for reaching norms mutually acceptable to the parties of the discussion (§8). It also eschews dialogue that is "a purely inductive search, on the parliamentary model, of a minimal already-existing consent."[21] This is a dialogue,

---

17. *In Search*, §69.

18. *In Search*, §116.

19. *In Search*, §§11 and 12.

20. Although it is not quoted or cited, see *Fides et Ratio*, esp. §§81–82: "Philosophy lacks its sapiential function if it is addressed only to 'particular and subordinate aspects of reality—function, formal or utilitarian'."

21. *In Search*, §6.

in fact, without a "search." As the authors remark, the dialogue has not proven adequate either to secure foundations for the post-1948 human rights project or to win support of religions and wisdom traditions, which need more than a "minimal ethic" (§6). Apparently, *In Search* envisages a dialogue rather different from what is usually meant by "public reason." Rather than holding back one's best considered reasons, it puts the mature line of reasons on the table, inviting others to do the same. Appropriation of the "evidences" of natural law either by the individual or by a culture is a slow process, requiring action and reflection—in a wisdom tradition, an "apprenticeship" (§53, §38).

This certainly has the aura of an inter-religious rather than a legal or political dialogue. One is reminded of C. S. Lewis's illustrations of the *Tao* in *The Abolition of Man*, albeit with Thomistic glosses. The idea is very attractive. Let those who have non-reductive anthropologies (open to reality as a whole) put their best understanding of human good and flourishing in common view, and then let us see where they "converge." The hope will be that this kind of discussion will achieve more than the "minimal ethic" in a very narrow and completely practical grounding, such as the one stipulated in the UN Declaration of 1948.[22] Even if we are not so naïve as to believe that a dialogue of wisdom traditions could reform, much less replace, the legal and political conventions governing human rights, it would still be of value. A few strong convergences in the fashion of Lewis's *Tao* would speak more effectively to human conscience than the dubiously abstract and highly politicized lists of rights that are continually multiplied and revised. There is nothing more disappointing and demoralizing than false universals in what pertains to human life.

But there are two aspects of the ITC paper that I find disappointing. First, while the document affirms clearly enough, even insistently, the importance of prudence in judgments that make the natural law effective, its depiction of universal moral norms *prior* to prudence is not very clear. Second, it leaves out of the picture what kind of dialogue can be conducted with secular modernity.

Regarding universal moral norms, *In Search* is understandably reluctant to put a system of precepts in front of its proposals about human nature. For one thing, on anthropological grounds alone it rejects the notion of pure practical reason that can generate a priori such a system of norms. Quite reasonably, the authors also want to acknowledge contingencies of culture and history and the effects of sin—"ideology and insidious propaganda, generalized relativism, structures of sin, etc."[23] Furthermore, they are at pains to emphasize that a mature understanding of moral truth is an achievement

---

22. *In Search* notes with alarm the fragmentation of the human rights project since 1948 (§§5–6, 115, and note 42).

23. *In Search*, §52.

dependent upon the agent's formation in sound social institutions and acqui-sition of moral virtue. All of this reflects the paper's strategic decision to dis-cuss natural law within and among time-tested wisdom traditions.

When we ask, however, what precepts of natural law are universally binding in a normative sense of the term, the document wobbles somewhat. The paper quotes Saint Jerome's remark on the Golden Rule: "Who of us does not know that homicide, adultery, theft and every kind of greed is evil, since we do not want them done to ourselves. If we did not know that these things are bad, we would not ever lament if they are inflicted on us."[24] Accordingly, there is no prudence, just as such, about whether to commit adultery. Provided that one can pick out the relevant facts (this is my neighbor's spouse), the negative precept suffices. Granting that negative precepts need to be completed within a larger moral project (§24), it is very important to emphasize that sound moral reasoning of the more complete kind depends upon what agents can know at this simpler level.

To be sure, *In Search* says strongly enough that there are "precepts and values that, at least in their general formulation, can be considered as universal, since they apply to all humanity" precisely because they are derived from anthropological constants.[25] Here, it is the anthropological constant that is immutable, for it is the ground for values and precepts that "can be consid-ered" universal in their "generality." But this doesn't quite capture what Jerome and others wanted to say about the negative precepts. We also read that we must safeguard "the fundamental data expressed by the precepts of the natural law that remain the same throughout cultural variation."[26] It's dif-ficult to know exactly what the paper means, but on my reading the "data" are the anthropological constants, while the precepts seem to be a kind of sign or expression of a good or value. It is less clear that a precept is a sign of a command or obligation. At §59, the paper states:

> There is here a perspective which, within a pluralist society such as our own, has an importance that cannot be underestimated without suffering significant loss. Indeed, it stems from the fact that moral science cannot furnish an agent subject with a norm that may be applied adequately and almost automatically to concrete situations; only the conscience of the subject, the judgment of his practical reason, can formulate the immedi-ate norm of action. But at the same time it can never abandon the con-science to mere subjectivity: the subject needs to acquire the intellectual and affective dispositions that permit it to open itself to moral truth in such a way that its judgment may be adequate. Natural law cannot,

---

24. *In Search*, §51.
25. *In Search*, §52.
26. *In Search*, §54.

therefore, be presented as an already established set of rules that impose themselves *a priori* on the moral subject, but is a source of objective inspiration for his process, eminently personal, of making a decision.

At least some readers will sense that a step is missing in this very condensed account. Assuming that the paper is correct that natural law should not be presented as an already assembled system of moral precepts, it does not necessarily follow that the natural law is only "a source of objective inspiration for [the agent's] process, eminently personal, of making a decision (*mais elle est une source d'inspiration objective*)."[27] In what precise sense are the inspirations *precepts*? Are they just objective indicators *en route* to the discovery of adequate moral norms? These paragraphs seem to suggest the latter. "[O]nly the conscience of the subject, the judgment of his practical reason, can formulate the immediate norm of action."[28] The ITC insists that "prudence is a necessary passageway to authentic moral obligation."[29]

The quotation taken from Saint Jerome however suggests an intermediate step—a small one, and rather thin, but important nevertheless. Between our grasp of the human good (anthropological constants) and fully practical judgments perfected by prudence, there are some moral norms of the natural law upon which even prudence must rely. Precisely in this zone we might expect some initial but sturdy convergence of moral judgment among wisdom traditions regarding the negative precepts of the moral law. Without such convergence, the dialogue is apt to remain in the anthropological sphere of "objective inspirations" that perhaps intimate, without explicitly reaching, specific precepts. If this were true, we would be agreeing about human values, so to speak, but not about morality.

Another conspicuous problem is that the secularized institutions of the West are not organized within a wisdom tradition; nor do they constitute one. Whereas a wisdom tradition is open to reality as a whole—a natural transcendence so to speak (§97)—the modern, western mind does not view nature or the "natural" as "impregnated with an immanent wisdom," but rather, to use *In Search*'s own language, it is "deprived of immanent teleology or finality."[30] This is only to acknowledge that prior to choice and prior to satisfying procedures of consent, "the natural" is *merely* immanent, along the lines of what Charles Taylor has called "closed world structures."[31] Purpose is assigned rather than discovered within the ordinary frame of things.

---

27. *In Search*, §59.
28. *In Search*, §59.
29. *In Search*, §58.
30. *In Search*, §72.
31. Charles Taylor, *A Secular Age* (Cambridge, MA: Belknap Press, 2007), 551.

By shifting the problem of authority from an internal structure of a theological tradition to the moral authority of a "common patrimony" implicit in many wisdom traditions, *In Search* does not relieve the problem—at least not for secular interlocuters. For example, when it proposes that there are moral "messages" in the nature of things and that natural law is not imposed on creatures from without but is inscribed in their very nature (§§11–12, 63), it summons a quite different meaning of the "immanent" than what will be obvious to most agents formed in the institutions of western secular culture. For them, nature is not obviously a semiotic (a book, or a ladder) in the sense that we have inherited from Paul, Bonaventure, or Thomas. The immanent rather is a domain of freedom just for the reason that it does not require transcendent messages, much less messages that arrive so intimately with authority.[32] The immanent, for all practical purposes, is nothing other than what is bereft of, or perhaps still waiting for, authority. This is why the sciences and contemporary institutions of civic formation, education, and economic activity are deemed useful, and indeed legitimate. Precisely by not requiring a sapiential philosophy or religion to interpret transcendent "messages," freedom is protected. When the ITC expresses the "urgent" need to reach common foundations (of a natural law sort) for the human rights project, it will have to anticipate a response that, on its view, is terribly inadequate if not irrational. Namely, the renewed claim of rights to liberty within this indeterminate "immanent" condition. These rights will be invoked against customs, positive laws, and the natural law insofar as they are norms antecedent to choice and consent.[33]

While the problem of liberty unseated from nature is more likely to be bridged in dialogue with wisdom traditions, it remains the tougher problem in the familiar world of secular modernity. In one place, *In Search* remarks: "In order that the notion of natural law may serve the elaboration of a universal ethics in a secularized and pluralistic society such as ours, it is therefore necessary to avoid presenting it in the rigid form that it assumed, particularly in modern rationalism."[34] This prescription strikes me as a good way to facilitate dialogue among wisdom traditions, at least those that already regard modern rationalism as a dead end. In dialogue with Eastern Orthodox Christians, for example, keeping natural law at arm's length from rationalism would count as a sine qua non. The same holds for dialogue with the great religious

---

32. Again, Taylor, *A Secular Age*, 544: "The immanent order can thus slough off the transcendent. But it doesn't necessarily do so. . . . It is something that permits closure, without demanding it."

33. The authors touch upon, but do not adequately grapple with, the problem of natural rights at §§88–90.

34. *In Search*, §33.

traditions, which tend to have a greater affinity for what we in the West would call the intellectualist rather than rationalist anthropology. It is much harder to see how the prescription has medicinal value for dialogue with a "secularized" society. Its denizens are not bothered by rationalism so much as by appeals in the public order to transcendent values—not only the supernatural, but also what the ITC means by natural law (§97). Not surprisingly, C. S. Lewis's illustrations of the *Tao* in *The Abolition of Man* include quotations from only two modern, western authors (Hooker and Locke), and only the latter is a modern in the relevant sense of the term. For its part, *In Search* makes clear enough that the Church often invokes natural law (moral truths antecedent to faith) defensively, against a belligerent secularism that dismisses a natural law foundation of moral choice and conscience as a purely confessional subversion of civic dialogue.[35] The ITC authors are anything but naive about who is their main antagonist on questions of natural law.

The ITC is faithful to untutored common sense and to its own tradition in affirming that "independently of the theoretical justifications of the concept of natural law, it is possible to discover the fundamental elements of the awareness of which it wants to give an account."[36] Some rudiments of moral truth are so close to human experience that they are available to anyone. One can interpret and appropriate these "evidences" even against the grain of one's inherited explanatory frameworks and the institutions which go along with them. Yet the dialogue that an individual person can conduct in what *Gaudium et Spes* calls the "sanctuary" of his own conscience is not a sufficient condition for the broader and more difficult dialogue envisaged by the ITC.[37] By grasping the first precepts of natural law one has already crossed the threshold into a world of social and intellectual formation, and, for good or ill, into informal and formal explanatory frameworks. We return, as we must, to the question of what to do or to say to the modern antagonist. We are speaking of an antagonist who is an apostate from the Catholic wisdom tradition. This is the issue around which *In Search* maneuvers all too carefully, and understandably, but disappointingly.

In a press conference during a recent trip to Portugal, Benedict XVI expressed hope for a dialogue between religion and modern rationality.

> Today we see that this very dialectic represents an opportunity and that we need to develop a synthesis and a forward-looking and profound dialogue. In the multicultural situation in which we all find ourselves, we

---

35. At §35, of the "four principal contexts" in which the Catholic Church invokes natural law today, three are clearly defensive.

36. *In Search*, §37.

37. *Gaudium et Spes*, §16.

see that if European culture were merely rationalist, it would lack a transcendent religious dimension, and not be able to enter into dialogue with the great cultures of humanity all of which have this transcendent religious dimension—which is a dimension of man himself. So to think that there exists a pure, anti-historical reason, solely self-existent, which is "reason" itself, is a mistake; we are finding more and more that it affects only part of man, it expresses a certain historical situation but it is not reason as such. Reason as such is open to transcendence and only in the encounter between transcendent reality and faith and reason does man find himself. So I think that the precise task and mission of Europe in this situation is to create this dialogue, to integrate faith and modern rationality in a single anthropological vision which approaches the human being as a whole and thus also makes human cultures communicable.[38]

Pope Benedict's *obiter dicta* are quite good. The "single anthropological vision" entertained by the Pope requires the secular civilization either to develop a wisdom tradition or to reattach itself to the one it abandoned. The Pope surely has the latter option in mind. This hope moves the question beyond the specific problem of natural law groundings for a common morality to the prospects of what would have to be a profound intellectual, moral, and spiritual conversion. The moral precepts presupposed by the Gospel do not necessarily constitute the easiest step. The urgency of the dialogue will have to be moderated by the virtue of patience.

---

38. Benedict XVI, "Interview of the Holy Father Benedict XVI with the Journalists During the Flight to Portugal," May 11, 2010, vatican.va.

CHAPTER 12

Religion, Human Law, and the Virtue of Religion

The Case of Dignitatis Humanae

I.

POPE JOHN XXIII CONVENED THE FIRST SESSION of the Second Vatican Council on October 11, 1962. In his opening allocution, he reminded the bishops that "history is the teacher of life."[1] There was more than a little history from which to learn lessons. The last ecumenical council that completed all of its work was the Council of Trent, which ended in 1563. The Church had passed through four centuries of modernity by making ad hoc adjustments along the way. The post-Tridentine era was persistently troubled by church-state relations, which, by the nineteenth century, had gone from bad to worse. In the waning decades of the second millennium, it was time for the college of bishops to reckon with the situation of the Church in more than an incremental and politically make-shift manner. Indeed, by the end of the first session of the Council, the Pope was ready to air a new position on religion and civil liberties.

We tend to think backwards, and thus the "lessons of history." But we live toward the future. Vatican II's Declaration on Religious Liberty, *Dignitatis Humanae*, was the sixteenth and final document of the Council, signed by Pope Paul VI on December 7, 1965, only a few hours before the council adjourned. *Dignitatis Humanae* bore an especially heavy burden of thinking backward and living forward. It set out "to develop the doctrine of recent popes on the inviolable rights of the human person and the constitutional order of society."[2] The word "develop" had at least two meanings for the council. First, it meant taking stock of an historical, legal, and social *development* from Catholic political Christendom to a new constitutional order of society. Second, it meant *developing* the teachings of recent popes on the moral-juridical right of human persons to religious liberty.

---

1. John XXIII, "Gaudet Mater," October 11, 1962, vatican.va.
2. Vatican Council II, *Dignitatis Humanae* (December 7, 1965), §1, www.vatican.va.

In this essay, let us reflect upon *Dignitatis Humanae* in the light of the ancient rubric *virtus religionis*. The topic comes to us chiefly through the work of Thomas Aquinas, who channeled ancient wisdoms, testimonies of sacred scripture, patristic writings (especially Augustine), and the debates of the medieval schools in order to understand how acts of religion are situated under natural, divine, and human law. What are the conditions for the virtue of religious acts, what are the causes and remedies for its vices?

Thomas puts acts of religion under the virtue of justice, having a ground in a natural obligation to give due to God according to certain interior and exterior acts.[3] He places religion among the moral virtues rather than the theological virtues because acts of religion do not approach or "touch" God directly. Whereas the proper matter or object of religion is human acts of worship performed out of reverence for God, the formal object of the supernatural virtue of faith is God revealing, and for charity it is God himself.[4] Therefore, the theological virtues also command acts of religion, but on a different plane and with a different formal object.[5]

Thomas's questions on religion are quite extensive. In the *Summa Theologiae* alone he treats the duty of *cultus divini* in the context of the moral and ceremonial precepts of the Old Law (I-II, qq. 98–103). He later devotes some twenty questions to the virtues and vices of religious acts (II-II, qq. 80–100). In due course, I will show that he provides two rather different treatments of religion. In the one, he accounts for religion on the basis of its causes, objects, and ends in order to give proper definitions and to distinguish the various acts of religion; in the other, he accounts for religion in real historical time, according to both divine and mundane testimony.

These two approaches need to be considered in tandem if we are to reflect on *Dignitatis Humanae* in the light afforded by the virtue of religion. For one thing, the Declaration takes up the question of religious acts in reference to the natural law and to the jurisdiction and coercive power of human law—human law is the main issue. The right of human persons to religious liberty is not framed against moral law or divine law, nor against the complex social network of institutions of religious formation.

Thomas recognized as a matter of historical fact that human laws "have devised many institutions relating to Divine matters, according as it seemed expedient for the formation of human morals; as may be seen in the rites of the Gentiles."[6] Moreover, he understood that the normative and prudential grounds for the authority of human law over *cultus divini* were always a vexed

---

3. *ST*, II-II, q. 81.
4. *ST*, II-II, q. 81, a. 5.
5. *ST*, II-II, q. 81, a. 5, ad 1.
6. *ST*, I-II, q. 99, a. 3.

issue, not just for Christendom but for the pagans. In this regard, Cajetan remarked that the issue of subordination of religion to the political common good has given birth to "many fables [*multas fabulas*]."[7]

Before we begin, it is important to understand that the template of "virtue of religion" cannot count for a strict interpretation of *Dignitatis Humanae*. In the first place, "virtue of religion" is used neither in this document nor in any other document of the Second Vatican Council.[8] In the interlude between the first and second sessions of the council, John XXIII issued *Pacem in Terris* (hereafter, *PT*), listing several human rights formulated in familiar terms of natural law: "Also among man's rights is that of being able to worship God in accordance with the right dictates of his own conscience, and to profess his religion both in private and in public."[9] This document, in fact, was the proximate magisterial source for the duty and the right covered by *Dignitatis Humanae*. Although the Pope makes many references to Thomas's doctrine of natural law and on human conscience participating the eternal law, we find no explicit mention of the virtue of religion. Nor is it to be found in the *Compendium of the Social Doctrine of the Church*. With the notable exception of the *Catechism of the Catholic Church*, the rubric "virtue of religion" has gone into a kind of desuetude in magisterial documents.[10] This does not prevent us, however, from reflecting usefully on the virtues and vices of religion, along with a rich set of issues that were once examined in that vein. It only cautions us to distinguish such reflection from strict interpretation of *Dignitatis Humanae*.

One additional caveat is in order. After fifty years, the teaching in *Dignitatis Humanae* is still controversial. Much literature is given to the question whether its doctrinal development is coherent and consistent. Some of this literature is tedious and merely argumentative, but much of it is quite interesting. I shall not directly engage these debates, for to enter into one is to

---

7. See *In ST* I-II, q. 99, a. 3, no. 4, p. 202.

8. *Dignitatis Humanae* cites Leo XIII's encyclical *Libertas* (1888), which includes an explicit and rather forceful discussion of the "virtue of religion" (§§19–20). Rather than citing that section, however, *Dignitatis Humanae* (at §2n2) cites a different paragraph on why the Christian understanding of liberty of conscience can be defended on its own terms without confusing it with the doctrine of indifferentism; see *Libertas*, §30, *Acta Leonis* 8, 237–38: "every man in the State may follow the will of God and, from a consciousness of duty and free from every obstacle, obey His commands. This, indeed, is true liberty, a liberty worthy of the sons of God, which nobly maintains the dignity of man and is stronger than all violence or wrong." For Leo's discussion of the virtue of religion in *Libertas*, §§19–20, see *Pontificis Maximi. Acta Leonis* 8, 229–30 (also available at www.vatican.va).

9. John XIII, *Pacem in Terris*, §14.

10. CCC, §§1807–1813; see also §§2084–2144, where acts of religion and irreligion are enumerated.

enter into them all.[11] What can be said is that interpreting the document is tricky business. The Declaration is the second shortest conciliar document: forty-six hundred words in Latin, which amounts to about eight single-spaced pages in the usual format. During the drafting process, some bishops worried about the strictly philosophical questions (drawing proper distinctions between subjective and objective meanings of "conscience"). Some bishops worried about practical items (the effect of the declaration on concordatory states), while others worried about ideologies (indifferentism and laicism), and still others about how to interrelate canonical, international, and natural rights. Many bishops wanted the document to clearly rehearse and to settle the broken history of church-state relationships going back more than seventeen hundred years.

Gradually, by trial and error, the commission charged with the task of formulating the position, as well as the bishops who debated various drafts on the floor of the council, realized that the declaration could not do all of these things. This editorial process had the good effect of producing an exceedingly tight and carefully reasoned statement. In Roman tradition, a *declaratio* differs from a *constitutio* and a *decretum*. Constitutions and decrees have binding force upon the whole Church. A declaration, on the other hand, is reserved for matters and persons who are not under the public law of the Church. Therefore, *Dignitatis Humanae* was supposed to be short and to the point.

The downside of the council's success in achieving such a succinct and focused document was that a strong line of historical narrative had to be left for another time.[12] So, for example, *Dignitatis Humanae* cites no scholarly philosophical or theological authority for its position between Gregory the Great and late-nineteenth century papal encyclicals. Thomas Aquinas is not cited. The document sidesteps not only authorities crucial to medieval Christendom, but also the Catholic political Christendom that was reconstituted after the Council of Trent. It is completely silent about both the medieval schools and the significant work of later scholastic philosophers, theologians, and jurists. Interestingly, if we mean by "religion" the acts of *cultus divini*, *Dignitatis Humanae* is mostly silent about religion.

---

11. For a useful study of the consistency and coherence of doctrinal development, along with an updated bibliography of disputants, see Barrett H. Turner, "*Dignitatis humanae* and the Development of Moral Doctrine: Assessing Change in Catholic Social Teaching on Religious Liberty" (PhD diss., The Catholic University of America, 2015).

12. The Relator of the Commission, Bishop de Smedt, remarked that the relation of *Dignitatis Humanae* to past popes is "a matter for future theological and historical studies to bring to light more fully"; see "*Congregatio Generalis* CLXIV, 19 Nov. 1965," in *Acta Synodalia Sacrosancti Concilii Oecumenici Vaticani Secundi*, 6 vols. (Vatican City: Typis Polyglottis Vaticanis, 1970–1978), 4 (pt. 8): 719.

Respecting these silences, and without pretending to offer a strict inter-pretation of the document, we can turn to Thomas's treatment of religion. This article is divided into two parts. First, we will consider his twofold approach to the subject, one systematic and the other historical. We want to come rather quickly to perplexities surrounding the place of religion under human law, which come into focus especially in his historical approach. Second, we will return to *Dignitatis Humanae*, attempting to size it up in light of what we found in Thomas.

II.

We shall limit ourselves to two lines of questions about religion in the *Summa Theologiae*. In questions 98–103 of the *Prima Secundae*, acts of reli-gion are treated under the topic of law. Although these questions are organ-ized around the first table of the Decalogue and the determinations of cult according to Mosaic Law, Thomas uses the occasion to comment on the rela-tionship between natural law and divine law, as well as the historical sequence whereby men are "instructed by law" in acts pertaining to religion. In ques-tions 80–100 of the *Secunda Secundae*, Thomas treats religion chiefly under the topic of virtue, namely religion as a potential part of justice. This extensive set of questions on religion and justice represents a continuation of the earlier questions, for law directs human action principally to justice. In both lines of questions, Thomas locates the proximate cause of religion in the human reason's inclination to know the truth about God and to form various con-siderations about the divine (e.g., creator and end of the natural good), which in turn give structure to volitional acts and incipient awareness of moral duties about rendering to God what is his due.

For the purposes of this essay, I want to highlight two main themes that crisscross throughout the two lines of questions. I shall call the first *the stem and its branches*, by which I mean Thomas's examination of the rational incli-nation to know the truth about God and the various practical considerations and acts of religion, principally acts of divine cult, consisting of both interior and exterior acts of worship. This theme counts as a rather conspicuous appli-cation of Thomas's dictum that the common principles of law are the "seeds of the virtues."[13] I shall call the second theme *the historical situation of for-mation* (and deformation) of religious acts, by which I mean the record of how humans have been educated by laws, customs, and higher causes that include demons and God himself. In other words, all those things in real his-torical time that have shaped acts ensuing upon the root inclination to honor God as an end and to tender religious submission. Thomas holds that the

---

13. *Quaestiones disputatae de virtutibus*, q. 8, ad 10.

328 | CHAPTER 12

root inclination is sturdy and vibrant because the seeds or principles of the inclination are causes "more excellent than the virtues acquired through them."[14] It turns out, however, that the vector of the inclination and its acts does not fare very well in the natural habitat of reason, at least not as we find it after sin.

Among the first precepts of natural law are those arising most proximately from our rational nature: "there is in man an inclination to good, according to the nature of his reason, which nature is proper to him: thus man has a natural inclination to know the truth about God, and to live in society: and in this respect, whatever pertains to this inclination belongs to the natural law, for instance, to shun ignorance, to avoid offending those among whom one has to live, and other such things."[15] The entire ensemble of social virtues is implied in this first sketch of natural law. Furthermore, the two great commandments regarding love of God and neighbor are implied—for, the good to be pursued is nothing other than being rightly ordered to God and other men. This much, he insists, is self-evident, having no need of additional promulgation.[16] This inclination—*ordinem ad deum*—is taken by Thomas to be not only an etymological option for the word *religio*, but the correct and proper one.[17]

The very compact article on inclinations and first precepts (*ST* I-II, q. 94, a. 2) also makes reference to a dignitarian principle. In answer to the question of whether man is naturally fit to love God above all things, Thomas answers that this precept of the natural law, after sin, cannot be integrally fulfilled without grace. On the other hand, if the question is put in a different way, as whether man is inclined to things superior to himself, he answers: "When it is said that nature cannot rise above itself, we must not understand this as if it could not be drawn to any object above itself, for it is clear that our intellect by its natural knowledge can know things above itself, as is shown in our natural knowledge of God. But we are to understand that nature cannot rise to an act exceeding the proportion of its strength. Now to love God above all things is not such an act; for it is natural to every creature, as was said above."[18] To think upon what is above oneself (*cognoscere quae sunt supra seipsum*) is an evidence of human dignity, indeed it is mentioned in his definition of natural law:

---

14. *ST*, I-II, q. 63, a. 2, ad 3.

15. *ST*, I-II, 94, a. 2. For further discussion, see Scott Roniger, "Natural Law and Friendship with God," *The Thomist* 83, no. 2 (2019): 237–76.

16. "Fines praeceptorum: dilectionem Dei et Proximi." See *ST*, I-II, q. 99, aa. 1–2; *ST*, I-II, q. 100, a. 5, ad 1 and 11; *ST*, II-II, q. 44, a. 1, ad 3, and a. 6, ad 3.

17. *ST*, II-II, q. 81, a. 1.

18. *ST*, I-II, q. 109, a. 3, ad 2.

Now among all others, the rational creature is subject to Divine providence in the most excellent way, in so far as it partakes of a share of providence, by being provident both for itself and for others. Wherefore it has a share of the Eternal Reason, whereby it has a natural inclination to its proper act and end: and this participation of the eternal law in the rational creature is called the natural law. Hence the Psalmist after saying Ps 4:6: "Offer up the sacrifice of justice," as though someone asked what the works of justice are, adds: "Many say, Who showeth us good things?," in answer to which question he says: "The light of Thy countenance, O Lord, is signed upon us," thus implying that the light of natural reason, whereby we discern what is good and what is evil, which is the function of the natural law, is nothing else than an imprint on us of the Divine light.[19]

Thomas mentions several ways that the human intellect can think of a superior being: 1) in a general and confused way inasmuch as God is man's beatitude (I, q. 2, a. 1, ad 1); and 2) with additional conceptual clarity and inference— as the beginning and the end of natural goods (I-II, q. 109, a. 3, ad 1), as the first principle of the creation and government of things (II-II, q. 81, a. 3), and as implicitly Trinitarian, insofar as God creates and governs by wisdom and love of the good (II-II, q. 81, a. 3, ad 1). These attributes are summarized according to the idea of *excellentia* (II-II, q. 81, a. 3, ad 2). Thus ensue the first stirrings of obligation, which, in the case of religion, are a due response to divine excellence. The act that proceeds from such considerations is one of the will by which man surrenders himself to the service of God: *latria*, having devotion as its internal act and sensible cult of sacrifice as its exterior object.[20] At least this much, he insists, is a dictate of natural reason.

There is one other consideration that should not be overlooked because it pertains not only to the main acts of religion, but also to prayer in general— namely, our indigence, which is also indicated in Thomas's use of Ps 4: "Natural reason tells man that he is subject to a higher being, on account of the defects which he perceives in himself, and in which he needs help and direction from someone above him";[21] "Now man shows reverence to God by means of prayer, in so far as he subjects himself to Him, and by praying confesses that he needs Him as the Author of his goods. Hence it is evident that prayer is properly an act of religion."[22] Our indigence gives us reason to turn to divine excellence from afar, but also as the divine goodness is close at hand as a cause of our moral illumination and instruction.

---

19. *ST*, I-II, q. 91, a. 2.
20. *ST*, II-II, q. 82, a. 3.
21. *ST*, II-II, q. 85, a. 1.
22. *ST*, II-II, q. 83, a. 3.

What the texts above underscore is a recognition that dependence on God stands very close to the stem of rational inclination. First, even after sin, it remains vigorous. For example, the person who gives little attention to religion will *in extremis* offer prayers and make vows for divine assistance. Second, its vigor also sets the stage for acts of irreligion. Religion is a potential part of justice, since, in giving due to God, no creature can achieve equality in the relation, as one who would repay a debt.[23] The religious *debitum* always exceeds the *res iustum*. The strict justice of the cardinal virtue is not possible in religion, at least not rightly understood. In one important sense, religion is the greatest of the moral virtues precisely because of its asymmetry. For, by acts of honor and devotion to an excellence "above us," we implicitly recognize that the relationship transcends strict commutation.[24] Religion is a freely tendered act of submission to God as an end, and the nobility of the virtue consists precisely in this.[25] To a fellow creature we owe love as we love ourselves. To give due to God under that same *ratio* is to fall short of the natural obligation of religion, which is to love God as a superior and most excellent being. Therefore, the quest for a *quid pro quo* is likely to destabilize the order of religious acts. On that scenario, the object of religion, the divine cult, is not ordered to God as an end, but rather to God as an instrument for the city or some other temporal political or private end (rather than to God as the common good of creation).[26]

Putting to one side all the things that complicate or frustrate acts of religion, T. C. O'Brien states the ideal rather well: "The highest conceivable will-relationship to God would necessarily be a relationship of the creature to its fontal cause; and acknowledgement of a debt, an act of justice proper to the virtue of religion."[27] This is what Thomas attributes to the state of innocence: "And hence we must say that in the state of perfect nature man did not need the gift of grace added to his natural endowments, in order to love God above all things naturally, although he needed God's help to move him to it; but in the state of corrupt nature man needs, even for this, the help of grace to heal his nature."[28]

In view of the last comment, it is useful to understand that, for Thomas, there is no natural religion.[29] We can recall that the object of religion is the

---

23. *ST*, II-II, q. 80, a. 1.

24. *ST*, II-II, q. 81, a. 6.

25. On "freely tendered," see *ST*, II-II, q. 81, a. 2, ad 3, and a. 6, ad 3.

26. For a discussion of how these points are connected to the virtue of religion and the act of prayer, see Scott Roniger, "The Metaphysician at Prayer: Thomas Aquinas on Metaphysics and Prayer as 'Interpreters of Desire,'" *Nova et Vetera* 17, no. 4 (2019): 1163–201.

27. See O'Brien's commentary in the Blackfriars edition, vol. 31, 189.

28. *ST*, I, q. 109, a. 3.

29. Thomas's understanding of natural law grounds of religious duties cannot be confused with the Enlightenment's quest to discover, or even to construct, a natural religion.

cult, which is referred to God as an end. The interior act of cult is devotion, the free act of the will in submission to God under one or another consideration of reason. Although we might imagine the natural inclination culminating satisfactorily in that interior act alone, this is not a sufficient condition for the virtue. For, it is also a dictate of reason that there be exterior acts making use of sensible signs.[30] Such are required not only in worship (sacrifices) but also by other acts of religion, like the making of vows.[31] The virtue, therefore, depends on getting both the interior and exterior acts right.

Thomas frequently points out that the dictates of natural reason regarding religious acts need to be determined by human or divine law: "It belongs to the dictate of natural reason that man should do something through reverence for God. But that he should do this or that determinate thing does not belong to the dictate of natural reason, but is established by Divine or human law";[32] "In like manner the offering of sacrifice belongs generically to the natural law, and consequently all are agreed on this point, but the determination of sacrifices is established by God or by man."[33] Whether on account of the obscurity of God to the human mind, or owing to the fact that what is due to God outstrips the strict justice covered by the cardinal virtue of justice—or even to ordinary, non-culpable doubts about the suitability of the external signs in worship—the natural inclination to offer *latria* is immediately in need of *determinationes* after loss of innocence. By determinations, we need to think of more than laws coordinating actions of a multitude, as would be necessary for any community of worship. We need to think more deeply of determinations of the object itself, of the *cultus divini*.

The pressing need for determinations of cult mark off the "stem" of the virtue of religion as being situated rather differently than action guided by the other first, or most common, precepts of natural law. One example suffices to make the point. Thomas cites the dictum of Ulpian regarding what "nature has taught all animals"—indeed, it is a telic arc including sexual intercourse, procreation, and the nurturing and education of offspring. To be sure, the object and end(s) of the conjugal act have been the subject of many moral and social perplexities, and have been enveloped in myriad laws and customs determining issues of property, consanguinity, frequency of the matrimonial debt, adultery, and divorce.[34] Even so, whatever the condition and circumstances of human conjugal acts, and however they are formed by laws and

---

30. *ST*, II-II, q. 81, a. 7; q. 82, a. 3, ad 2; and *ST*, II-II, q. 85, a. 1.

31. *ST*, II-II, q. 89, a. 8.

32. *ST*, II-II, q. 81, a. 2, ad 3.

33. *ST*, II-II, q. 85, a. 1, ad 1. See also *ST*, I-II, q. 99, a. 3.

34. See, for example, the twenty-seven disputed questions on marriage in *ST*, III, Supplementum, qq. 41–68.

customs, people rather quickly get the point of this vector of rational inclination in respect not only of its proximate object, but also of its end(s). However rough and ready, it survives the loss of innocence, and confusions and perversions notwithstanding, people were not at a loss to know what to do either in general or in particular.[35]

In the case of religion, Thomas thinks historically, by which I mean that he considers not only the natural inclination and its natural law requirements, but also how religion plays out over time in institutions. Again, for Thomas there is no natural religion. He does allow, however, for a "time" between the loss of innocence and determinations of religion by law. Some men, gifted with a "spirit of prophesy" and a divinely given "spiritual instinct," enjoyed a so called "private law" prompting them to worship God in a definite way and in keeping with rightly ordered interior worship.[36] And he allows the scenario that "others followed them." Afterwards, men were instructed by outward precepts about these things.[37] There was no idolatry in the first age, he explains, "owing to the recent remembrance of the creation of the world, so that man still retained in his mind the knowledge of one God."[38] But in the time before the Law—and in an historical time of the gentiles[39] outside of the Law—human laws and customs determined the outward acts of religion. By and large, these efforts were unsuccessful. "Thus Augustine (*De civitate Dei* 6.10) quotes Seneca as saying: 'We shall adore,' says he, 'in such a way as to remember that our worship is in accordance with custom rather than with the reality.'"[40] Hence, there is a twofold disruption of religion: 1) disordered in relation of truth about God; 2) disordered by confusing, or worse, perversely reversing the relation between object and end by giving *latria* to a creature (and many other acts of irreligion that ensue upon these disorders).

Thomas's discussion of the ceremonial precepts of the Law is pivotal to his account of the intersection of divine, natural, and human law in matters religious. These questions too often are given short shrift on account of their length and somewhat tedious detail.[41] Yet, it is here that Thomas gives the bridge connecting the natural inclination and first-order dictates of reason with the determinations of outward worship in the *ceremonialia*. What is most

---

35. We could also think of the rational inclination to enter into society under relations of justice. It is not difficult to imagine Aristotle's scenario (in *Politics* II) of matrimonial and domestic orders opening up to tribal relations, and to villages, and to the necessity of political life.

36. *ST*, I-II, q. 103, a. 1.

37. *ST*, II-II, q. 93, a. 1, ad 2. See also *ST*, II-II, q. 87, a. 1, ad 3; and q. 92, a. 1, ad 2.

38. *ST*, II-II, q. 94, a. 2, ad 2.

39. *ST*, I-II, q. 98, aa. 2–6.

40. *ST*, II-II, q. 94, a. 2, corp.

41. *ST*, I-II, qq. 101–3.

interesting is that these determinations, at least those regarding religion, are more than a positive law determination of things left indeterminate by natural law. They are also rectifications of reason as to the moral precepts regarding religion.[42] This is only to say that the first table of the Decalogue is the center of the crisis of the human appropriation of natural law: "[I]t is clear, since the order of reason begins with the end, that, for a man to be inordinately disposed towards his end, is supremely contrary to reason. Now the end of human life and society is God. Consequently it was necessary for the precepts of the Decalogue, first of all, to direct man to God; since the contrary to this is most grievous."[43]

As we already noted, Thomas admits that, in principle, religious cult can be determined by human laws; "Hence human laws have not concerned themselves with the institution of anything relating to Divine worship except as affecting the common good of mankind: and for this reason they have devised many institutions relating to Divine matters."[44] But in the concrete, determination of cult is vulnerable to perversion. Although a political community could restrict its interest in religious acts solely and honestly to the temporal common good, valuing its good consequences for the formation of morals, it is more likely that God will be worshipped for the community, if not for a merely private good. Hence, some consideration of divinity remains in the object of the act (the cult, the vow, etc.), but not in its end.[45] We recall Augustine's reference to

---

42. *ST*, I-II, q. 101, a. 3: "For in that people there were many prone to idolatry; wherefore it was necessary to recall them by means of ceremonial precepts from the worship of idols to the worship of God. And since men served idols in many ways, it was necessary on the other hand to devise many means of repressing every single one: and again, to lay many obligations on such like men, in order that being burdened, as it were, by their duties to the Divine worship, they might have no time for the service of idols. As to those who were inclined to good, it was again necessary that there should be many ceremonial precepts; both because thus their mind turned to God in many ways, and more continually; and because the mystery of Christ, which was foreshadowed by these ceremonial precepts, brought many boons to the world, and afforded men many considerations, which needed to be signified by various ceremonies."

43. *ST*, I-II, q. 100, a. 6.

44. *ST*, I-II, q. 99, a. 3.

45. *ST*, I-II, q. 99, a. 6: "Those who are yet imperfect desire temporal goods, albeit in subordination to God: whereas the perverse place their end in temporalities." But note that, in this article, Thomas maintains that desire for temporal goods is licit specifically in the context of the Jewish cult determined by divine law, which, like a tutor, restrains any reversal of object and end. For this reason, the gentiles were more assuredly ordered in cult by being admitted into Mosaic worship (*ST*, I-II, q. 98, a. 5, ad 3). Interestingly, in *De regno*, Thomas admonishes the king to avoid the pagan determinations of cult, to respect but not to follow the Mosaic determinations, and to be subjected to priests under the New Law. *De regno*, 16.111: "Because the priesthood of the gentiles and the whole worship of

Seneca's dictum: We worship according to custom rather than truth. To underscore the same point, Thomas cites Livy's report that "one who vowed to his idols to suffer death for the safety of his army" was "devout."[46]

The twenty questions on the virtue of religion in the *Secunda Secundae* evince a scholastic and Aristotelian division of virtues and vices. The details, however, are taken mostly from Augustine, especially *De civitate Dei*, *De doctrina christiana*, and *De vera religione*. No section of the *Summa* is more thickly carpeted with quotations of and references to Augustine.[47] The obvious reason is that, by the thirteenth century, paganism stood at the geographical and cultural periphery of western Christendom. Like everyone of his training and station, Thomas encountered the pagans mainly through book learning: Sacred Scripture, Graeco-Roman authors of antiquity, and above all, the works of Augustine. It will be evident to anyone who reads the questions on the virtue of religion that he does not match Augustine's rhetorical prowess, nor does Thomas cover the issues with anything approaching the pastoral urgency that marked Augustine's polemic in *De civitate Dei*, written for the instruction of Christians who misinterpreted the event of Alaric's sack of Rome in 410.

Nonetheless, he follows Augustine assiduously on the nature and implications of religious acts adapted to the ancient city: "All the gods of the gentiles are demons."[48] The human determination of *cultus divini* was a disaster, and not even philosophers were able to produce a religion that prevented the subordination of cult to the temporal ends of the city.

> It seems that the Apostle touches on the three theologies of the Gentiles. First, the civil, which was observed by their priests adoring idols in the temple; in regard to this he says: *they exchanged the glory of the immortal God*. Secondly, the theology of fables, which their poets presented in the theatre. In regard to this he says, *they exchanged the truth about God for a lie*. Thirdly, their natural theology, which the philosophers

---

their gods existed merely for the acquisition of temporal goods (which were all ordained to the common good of the multitude, whose care devolved upon the king), the priests of the gentiles were very properly subject to the kings. Similarly, since in the old law earthly goods were promised to the religious people (not indeed by demons but by the true God), the priests of the old law, we read, were also subject to the kings. But in the new law there is a higher priesthood by which men are guided to heavenly goods. Consequently, in the law of Christ, kings must be subject to priests." (Latin text available in vol. 42 of the Leonine edition, available at www.corpusthomisticum.org/repedleo.html).

46. On the etymology of "devout," see *ST*, II-II, q. 82, a. 1. The religious object was not only given wrongly (to an idol), but also given for the wrong end.

47. I count some 116 references, including 29 to the *City of God*.

48. *ST*, II-II, q. 94, a. 2. See also *ST*, II-II, q. 92, a. 2; q. 95, a. 2; q. 96, a. 3; and q. 122, a. 2, ad 3.

observed in the world, when they worshipped the parts of the world. In regard to this he says, *they worshipped and served the creature rather than the creator.*[49]

Taken altogether, with all of the complications and details, Thomas does not provide strong support for the practice of *cultus divini* determined by human law.[50] He especially adheres to Paul and Augustine, and to the failure of philosophy to produce a religion any better than those rites directed by civil and poetical theologies.[51] Putting to one side the somewhat extraordinary case of holy men inspired by a kind of "private law" of the Spirit, and then the submission of the Jewish cult to the first table of the Decalogue and the ceremonial determinations of Mosaic law, the record of antiquity is marked by confusion and reversal of the object and the end of religion.[52]

In the abstract, however, he does not rule out a role, even a duty, of human law to assist religion by *determinatio* under the *ratio* of good morals. In the first place, all things are ordered to God, including the temporal common good of the city. While religion has a different *ratio* than the honor given to parents and civil authorities or the ordinary reciprocities of justice and love between human persons, it is interwoven with the ensemble of social virtues in the fashion of a "general virtue"—that is, a virtue that directs the other acts of virtues.[53] Therefore, we may not attribute to Thomas the American dicta that "the state has no interest in" or "the state may not take cognizance of" religion. On the other side of the coin, human law must restrict itself to the temporal common good, to religious acts insofar as they are true and profitable to good morals, and inasmuch as nothing deflect the order of *latria*. This is a tough standard, and hence Augustine's judgment is that the "celestial city, on the other hand, knew that one God only was to be worshipped,

---

49. *Super Rom.*, lec. 7, no. 145, in *Commentary on the letter of Saint Paul to the Romans,* trans. Fabian Larcher, ed. J. Holmes (Lander: Aquinas Institute for the Study of Sacred Doctrine, 2012). See also *SCG,* III, c. 38.

50. Here, he also reminds the King that the Christian religion orders temporal persons and things to a supernatural end. *De regno,* 16.113: "And because it was to come to pass that the religion of the Christian priesthood should especially thrive in France, God provided that among the Gauls too their tribal priests, called Druids, should lay down the law of all Gaul, as Julius Caesar relates in the book which he wrote about the Gallic war." His point is not that the pagan religion was free of idolatry and superstition, only that these rites were ruled by priests.

51. *ST,* II-II, q. 94, a. 1.

52. In reply to an objection that the Jews said they have no king but Caesar, and thus would seem to give devotion to men, Thomas rather laconically answers, "devotion of subjects to their temporal masters is of another *ratio.*" *ST,* II-II, q. 82, a. 2, ad 3.

53. *ST,* II-II, q. 81, a. 8, ad 2.

and that to Him alone was due that service which the Greeks call λατρεία, and which can be given only to a god, it has come to pass that the two cities could not have common laws of religion."[54]

The second reason why Thomas does not absolutely rule out some role for human determination in religion is that he writes at the zenith of political Christendom, at which time existed deep and complex comity of jurisdictions. This comity included some limits to human law—for example, limits to temporal authorities directly determining and administering the divine cult and sacraments of the New Covenant. As he said to the King of Cyprus, religion must be subordinate to the authority of priests. Nor can the children of Jews be compelled to baptism, but the latter is premised on the natural law obligation and right of parents to direct the religious formation of their children.[55] But throughout the different phases and configurations of political Christendom, there existed a penumbra in which human and ecclesiastical law intersected in service of religion—from liturgical and civic calendars, property, and punishment of heretics, to treaties regarding joint cooperation in missions. In this penumbra also stood the disputed issue of Jewish rites, which needs to be mentioned, but which we shall pass over because the complexities of the record would take us too far afield.[56]

The practices and opinions about the penumbral issues developed over many centuries—from the early medieval centuries to the post-Westphalian division of western Christendom into the geographical jurisdictions of temporal sovereignty under the formula *cuius regio eius religio*. It will suffice to note that the underlying problem of human law directing religious acts was never neatly settled. Let us return to where we began, with Thomas's general consideration of the issue: "Divine law is instituted chiefly in order to direct men to God; while human law is instituted chiefly in order to direct men in relation to one another. Hence human laws have not concerned themselves

---

54. *De civitate Dei*, XIX, c. 17. He adds that there can be common laws, manners, and institutions whereby terrestrial peace is maintained, so long as "no hindrance to the worship of the one supreme and true God is thus introduced."

55. *ST*, II-II, q. 10, a. 12, ad 4: "Hence a child, before coming to the use of reason, in the natural order of things, is directed to God by its parents' reason, under whose care it lies by nature, and it is for them to dispose of the child in all matters relating to God."

56. *ST*, II-II, q. 10, a. 11: "Though unbelievers sin in their rites, they may be tolerated, either on account of some good that ensues there from, or because of some evil avoided. Thus from the fact that the Jews observe their rites, which, of old, foreshadowed the truth of the faith which we hold, there follows this good—that our very enemies bear witness to our faith, and that our faith is represented in a figure, so to speak. For this reason they are tolerated in the observance of their rites." For the nuances of Thomas's position on Jewish rites, see Matthew A. Tapie, *Aquinas on Israel and the Church* (Eugene, OR: Pickwick Publications, 2014).

with the institution of anything relating to Divine worship except as affecting the common good of mankind: and for this reason they have devised many institutions relating to Divine matters, according as it seemed expedient for the formation of human morals; as may be seen in the rites of the Gentiles."[57] Cajetan comments:

> If human law should propose to subordinate divine worship to the inter-ests of the peace of Society, and if, for example, it saw in that the chief reason for honoring God, it would be perverse. Human law does not do that: although doubtless many impious legislators have attempted it, inventing all kinds of myths [*multas fabulas*] to serve this end, as Aristotle suggests in the second book of the *Metaphysics*. But whereas there are many ways of justifying divine worship, human law, taking account only of those things that concern its own domain, will make them serve the common good, and it abstracts from reasons that do not concern it. Now to abstract is neither to lie nor to sin. And if grace perfects nature instead of destroying it, human law can take the common good of human society for its principal end without thereby being prevented from subordinating it to a higher end in virtue of a higher principle.[58]

Cajetan gives an accurate summary of the article and its implications for the virtue of religion. When the temporal authority uses the instrumentalities of law to subvert the relation between the object and end of religion, it must be counted as irreligious (perverse). This much holds whether we are speaking of religious acts under natural or supernatural specifications. When, on the other hand, the human law abstracts from the end to consider only the advan-tages of religion for the temporal good, Cajetan and a more recent theologian like Charles Journet hold it does not necessarily sin, provided that the divine end remains intact. Both theologians recognize that the ideal boundary was defeated, at least by the gentiles of antiquity. Exactly when in the Christian order it was honest, fudged, or defeated was the pressing question as Chris-tendom itself began its decadent period after Westphalia, and even more urgently after the French Revolution.[59]

---

57. *ST*, I-II, q. 99, a. 3.

58. See *In ST*, I-II, q. 99, a. 3, no. 4, in the Leonine edition of the *Summa* with Caje-tan's commentary (Rome: Ex Typographia Polyglotta, S. C. De Propaganda Fide, 1892), 202.

59. Cardinal Charles Journet cites Cajetan's comment on article 3 of question 99, but he digs into the historical complications. One must admit that, although Cajetan wit-nessed the opening round of the Reformation, he did not see the end of medieval Chris-tendom at Westphalia or the final demise of Christendom in the events that ensued upon 1789. Journet distinguishes two ways in the older regime of Christendom that the temporal power might act for its own benefit in relation to the Church's superior power to direct

In lieu of that historical judgment, we have no direct way to move from Thomas's questions on religion to *Dignitatis Humanae*. Except a brief note— "through the vicissitudes of human history, there has at times appeared a way of acting that was hardly in accord with the spirit of the Gospel or even opposed to it"—*Dignitatis Humanae* is entirely silent about any part of the historical record that might count as controversial.[60] Even so, we can offer some general remarks about the relevance of Thomas's understanding of the virtue of religion.

III.

In our quick traversal of the questions on religion, we saw that, for Thomas, the virtue of religion is rooted in what most pertains to human dignity, which is the rational inclination to know the truth about God. By means of various considerations about God—excellence, the first and final cause of the good, and human indigence and need of divine assistance—the practical intellect understands obligation to give to God his "due." The object of the *free* act of religion is the "due," or the *cultus divini*, consisting of the interior act of devotion and the external act of sacrifice. The end of religious acts is God. However, on account of the obscurity of the divine and the weakness of the human intellect, and on account of the fact that that debt can never repay God in full and according to equality, and because the sensible signs of the external cult are variable, acts of religion need "determinations." This is especially true after the loss of innocence. For Thomas, there is no such thing as a natural religion, at least not if we consider all of the dimensions and facets

---

religious acts. In one mode, the temporal arm allows itself to be used as an instrument for the Church's pursuit of a spiritual end, but in doing so it acts for its own advantage and uses no power except that which properly belongs to the political. In a second way, the secular arm acts on its own initiative "for an intervention whose end is an immediately temporal good considered as conditioning a spiritual good." For example, the human lawgiver acts to suppress schism or heresy. Journet admits that, in the older Christendom, the legal and moral proprieties of these two modes were extraordinarily complex. With the benefit of hindsight, he asks whether either justification was "truly useful" to the Church. My reading of Journet is that he leaves this question open-ended, but with the burden of proof falling on those who defend it on grounds that are more than abstract principle. Journet, of course, also had the benefit of knowing about the demise of political Christendom and the decrees of the First Vatican Council that solemnly ruled out virtually all of the older arrangements by which temporal sovereigns were deputized with apostolic authority. Journet argues that, with the demise of the last phase of political Christendom, it is Saint Augustine's position "to which we shall have finally to return"; see Charles Journet, *Theology of the Word Incarnate*, trans. Alfred Howard Campbell (London: Sheed and Ward, 1955), 221–22.

60. *Dignitatis Humanae*, §12.

of religion. Rather, there is a rather sturdy natural inclination and natural dictate of reason about the obligation in general terms. Finally, we emphasized that Thomas adheres to the judgments of Paul and Augustine regarding the unsteady and often perverse character of human determinations of religion.

Now, in the final part of this essay, I will sketch in a somewhat general way the compatibility between Thomas and the teaching of *Dignitatis Humanae*. My three main points, made briefly and without adequate elaboration, are as follows: 1) The basis of a human right to religious liberty is a rational inclination to search out the truth about God; 2) The obligation to adhere to the truth includes both internal and external acts of religion; and 3) The human law is forbidden to enjoin or forbid religious acts by means of external coercion. This last point is, firstly, in respect of human dignity and what we have called the stem-set, namely those intellective and volitional acts that must be freely engaged as a minimal condition for the virtue of religion, and secondly, in respect of the end of religious acts, which transcends the terrestrial common good. But human law may facilitate religious acts and, in some cases, restrict religious acts injurious to the temporal common good. Importantly, *Dignitatis Humanae* does not mention a right or duty of the state to *determine* religious acts per se. In the second part of the Declaration, dealing with the religion of the Catholic Church in the light of divine revelation, such human determinations are absolutely forbidden with respect to the ordinary and apostolic powers of teaching, sanctifying, and ruling.[61]

Under the heading of religious liberty "in general" (*ratio generalis*), *Dignitatis Humanae* §§2–8 treat of human dignity according to the natural law, but also as it has become "more fully known to human reason through centuries of experience." The lights and the shadows of those centuries of experience are not reported in any detail. The Declaration moves straight away to the anthropological ground of the right and the duty:

> It is in accordance with their dignity as persons—that is, beings endowed with reason and free will and therefore privileged to bear personal responsibility—that all men should be at once impelled by nature and also bound by a moral obligation to seek the truth, especially religious truth. They are also bound to adhere to the truth, once it is known, and to order their whole lives in accord with the demands of truth. However, men

---

61. The *principium fundamentale* of Church liberty (*Dignitatis Humanae*, §13). This is repeated in a document on the episcopal authority of the bishops; see Vatican Council II, *Christus Dominus* (October 28, 1965), §19: "In discharging their apostolic office, which concerns the salvation of souls, bishops per se enjoy full and perfect freedom and independence from any civil authority. Hence, the exercise of their ecclesiastical office may not be hindered, directly or indirectly, nor may they be forbidden to communicate freely with the Apostolic See, or ecclesiastical authorities, or their subjects."

cannot discharge these obligations in a manner in keeping with their own nature unless they enjoy immunity from external coercion as well as psychological freedom. Therefore the right to religious freedom has its foundation not in the subjective disposition of the person, but in his very nature.[62]

Although it is not elaborated in philosophical detail, the ground of the right is a fair replication of Thomas's inclinational stem-set, which as we saw, has three components: 1) a participation of the human intellect in the eternal law, 2) a search, consideration, and affirmation of the truth about God, and 3) a recognition of duty. The Declaration reads: "[T]he highest norm of human life is the divine law—eternal, objective and universal—whereby God orders, directs and governs the entire universe and all the ways of the human community by a plan conceived in wisdom and love. Man has been made by God to participate in this law, with the result that, under the gentle disposition of divine Providence, he can come to perceive ever more fully the truth that is unchanging."[63] *Gaudium et Spes* puts it this way: "The root reason for human dignity lies in man's call to communion with God. From the very circumstance of his origin man is already invited to converse with God [*ad colloquium cum Deo*]."[64]

These are familiar Thomistic themes, especially the dictum that divine providence disposes things gently, according to their nature. That the Eternal Law sweetly (*suaviter*) disposes people to fulfill their duty to know and to assent to the truth, which is taken from Wisdom 8:1, has a long history in Catholic theology. It was one of Saint Thomas's favorite biblical texts for describing divine governance.[65] Thomas is not directly cited by the Declaration, but there are more than enough indirect clues, including the frequent references to *Pacem in Terris* where John XXIII cites and quotes Thomas's doctrine of natural law.[66]

On Thomas's rendition, the inclinational stem-set includes natural duty with regard to external and sensible acts of religion. Just so, in addition to divine worship, *Dignitatis Humanae* includes the human duty, and therefore the right, to give expression to and communications about religious truths, as well as to maintain institutions of religious formation:[67]

---

62. *Dignitatis Humanae*, §2.
63. *Dignitatis Humanae*, §3.
64. Vatican Council II, *Gaudium et Spes* (December 7, 1965), §19.
65. On the many uses of Wisdom 8:1 by Thomas, see *SCG*, III, c. 97; *ST*, I, q. 22, a. 2; q. 103, a. 8; I-II, q. 110, a. 2; II-II, q. 23, a. 2; and q. 161, a. 1.
66. On participation, truth, God, and the moral order, see *Pacem in Terris*, §§37–38, in *AAS* 55 (1963): 270–71, referenced in *Dignitatis Humanae*, §3n3. Recall that *Pacem in Terris* was the proximate authority for the right of religious liberty. For an analysis and evaluation of *Pacem in Terris* use of Thomas's doctrine of participation, see Ch. 8.
67. *Dignitatis Humanae*, §3.

Provided the just demands of public order are observed, religious communities rightfully claim freedom in order that they may govern themselves according to their own norms, honor the Supreme Being in public
worship, assist their members in the practice of the religious life,
strengthen them by instruction, and promote institutions in which they
may join together for the purpose of ordering their own lives in accordance with their religious principles.[68]

As Thomas himself argued, the domestic order has a natural duty in the matter
of religious formation—one that stands very close to the stem-set.[69] So, too,
for *Dignitatis Humanae*: "The family, since it is a society in its own original
right, has the right freely to live its own domestic religious life under the guidance of parents. Parents, moreover, have the right to determine, in accordance
with their own religious beliefs, the kind of religious education that their children are to receive."[70]

The picture presented by *Dignitatis Humanae* is that the inclination to
know the truth about God and the dictates of reason regarding the obligation
to give proper due to God are completed in concrete determinations and
institutions of religion by agents other than those of Caesar. This, however,
does not mean that temporal government has no legitimate interest in religion under the limited *ratio* of good morals and the common good: "Government is also to help create conditions favorable to the fostering of religious life, in order that the people may be truly enabled to exercise their
religious rights and to fulfill their religious duties, and also in order that society itself may profit by the moral qualities of justice and peace which have
their origin in men's faithfulness to God and to His holy will."[71] The very
recognition of the duty and right of religion is already to regard religion
under the category of good morals and the common good. Under that same
ratio, government may externally curb religious acts that are injurious to the
common good, including acts that are dishonest, abusive to others, or disruptive to the public order. It may also "show favor" to a particular religion,
provided that the rights of other citizens and religious communities are recognized.[72] Of the many things government might do or not do with regard

---

68. *Dignitatis Humanae*, §4.
69. *ST*, II-II, q. 10, a. 12, ad 4.
70. *Dignitatis Humanae*, §5.
71. *Dignitatis Humanae*, §5.
72. *Dignitatis Humanae*, §5. One thinks, in this respect, of concordats or the syn-
chronization of civil and ecclesiastical calendars. For the variety of legal and constitutional
regimes that might be accommodated by *Dignitatis Humanae*, see my essay, "Political Pluralism and Religious Liberty: The Teaching of *Dignitatis Humanae*," in *The Proceedings of
the 17th Plenary Session on Universal Rights in a World of Diversity: The case of religious*

to religious acts under the *ratio* of the common good, it may not "presume to command or inhibit acts that are religious."[73]

I interpret this to mean that the state may not command or inhibit religious acts from scratch, so to speak, for this much already falls under the natural law—most pointedly in the case of parents and children. Surely, the prohibition also includes temporal government, as Thomas noted about the gentiles, devising many institutions on divine matters—that is to say, determinations *of religion*. Admittedly, we enter a penumbra once again. For it is one thing to say that it is not the proper role of Caesar to command the details of the divine cult, but it is another to say that government may never, under the *ratio* of good morals and the tranquility of the common good, use its authority to facilitate the religious acts freely undertaken by citizens in light of their own determinations of religion.

The big picture is clear enough. *Dignitatis Humanae* gives a moral-juridical teaching on the natural law source of religious acts. It does not treat the different modes of knowledge and assent, running from intuition and inference to belief and faith.[74] It does not intend to be an exercise in comparative religion, much less to survey, as Thomas does, all of the vices afflicting

---

freedom, Pontifical Academy of Social Sciences Acta 17 (Vatican City: The Pontifical Academy of Social Sciences, 2012), 39–55, 677–80, available at vatican.va.

73. *Dignitatis Humanae*, §3.

74. *Dominus Iesus*, §7: "For this reason, the distinction between *theological faith* and *belief* in the other religions must be *firmly held*. If faith is the acceptance in grace of revealed truth, which 'makes it possible to penetrate the mystery in a way that allows us to understand it coherently,' then belief in the other religions is that sum of experience and thought that constitutes the human treasury of wisdom and religious aspiration, which man in his search for truth has conceived and acted upon in his relationship to God and the Absolute"; quoting John Paul II, Encyclical Letter *Fides et Ratio* (September 14, 1998), §13. In *Fides et Ratio*, §30, John Paul observes, "All men and women, as I have noted, are in some sense philosophers and have their own philosophical conceptions with which they direct their lives. In one way or other, they shape a comprehensive vision and an answer to the question of life's meaning; and in the light of this they interpret their own life's course and regulate their behavior." And what is relevant to *Dignitatis Humanae*, Ch. 1 ("General Principals of Religious Freedom," §§2–8) is that they do so both by a personal quest and within communal traditions: "On the one hand, the knowledge acquired through belief can seem an imperfect form of knowledge, to be perfected gradually through personal accumulation of evidence; on the other hand, belief is often humanly richer than mere evidence, because it involves an interpersonal relationship and brings into play not only a person's capacity to know but also the deeper capacity to entrust oneself to others, to enter into a relationship with them which is intimate and enduring" (*Fides et Ratio*, §32). See Gerard V. Bradley, "Pope John Paul II and Religious Liberty," *Ave Maria Law Review* 6, no. 1 (2007): 33–59. Not only is this a very lucid article on *Dignitatis Humanae*, but it alerted me to the importance of Ratzinger's work in *Dominus Iesus*.

religious acts. Importantly, the Declaration mentions only one specific religion: "We believe that this one true religion subsists in the Catholic and Apostolic Church, to which the Lord Jesus committed the duty of spreading it abroad among all men."[75] It does not speak in any detail about the ways that the rational inclination is formed and determined by any other religion. The Declaration can say, with Thomas, that the inclinational stem is sturdy because it is imprinted on our nature and is at the center of our dignity.

To draw out the full force of the two stories, consider the fact that, in defense of the natural right of freedom in religious acts, both John XXIII and the council cite Lactantius, an advisor to the Emperor Constantine who died at about the time of the Council of Nicaea. In the section of the *Divine Institutes* cited by the Pope, Lactantius comments in a general way on ancient wisdom shared by Gentiles, Jews, and Christians—namely, that it belongs to the supreme good of humankind to know and serve God: "Truly religion is the cultivation of the truth." For its part, *Dignitatis Humanae*, Ch. 2, on religion in the light of revelation, cites a different section from the same work, where Lactantius explains that the specifically Christian understanding of the Cross of Christ is the ultimate completion of acts of religion.[76] These two references to Lactantius represent just what we have distinguished as the stemset and its natural apprehension of duties, and what the entire vector will look like when we are taught by divine revelation.

IV.

Let us conclude with Thomas's enumeration of the properties of human law. He helps us to understand how religion, under different aspects, can be situated vis-à-vis human law:

> [I]t should be said that, whenever a thing is for an end, its form must be determined proportionately to that end, as the form of a saw is such as to be suitable for cutting. . . . Again, everything that is ruled and measured must have a form proportionate to its rule and measure. Now both these conditions are met in human law, since it is both something ordained to an end, and is a rule or measure ruled or measured by a higher measure. And this higher measure is twofold, viz., the divine law and the natural law. . . . Now the end of human law is to be useful to

---

75. *Dignitatis Humanae*, §1. The internal point of view of this religion and its congruence with the natural right are covered in the Ch. 2 of the Declaration, "Religious Freedom in the Light of Revelation [*libertas religiosa sub luce revelationis*]," §§9–15.

76. Lactantius, *Divine Institutes*, 4.28 and 5.19. English translation by William Fletcher in *Ante-Nicene Fathers*, vol. 7, ed. A. Roberts, J. Donaldson, and A. Cleveland Coxe (Buffalo, NY: Christian Literature, 1886).

man, as the jurist states. Hence Isidore, determining the nature of law, lays down, at first, three conditions: that it be consistent (*congruat*) with religion, inasmuch as it is proportionate (*proportionata*) to the divine law; that it be helpful (*conveniat*) to discipline, inasmuch as it is proportionate (*proportionata*) to the natural law; and that it further the common good, inasmuch as it is proportionate (*proportionata*) to the utility of mankind.[77]

Human law is not a first rule and measure, for it is ruled and measured by the natural and the divine law. So far, this is standard Thomism. In matters pertaining to human law, both higher laws must be observed. In the first place, human law should be consistent with religion insofar as it is proportioned to divine law. We should construe religion here in the way Thomas presents it in the two series of questions on the subject in the *Summa*—not just the inclinational stem that can be counted as the "seeds of the virtues," but the entire package: inclination, first and secondary precepts, and determinations of *cultus divini* by divine instruction. To use the broad terms of *Dignitatis Humanae*, we are dealing with religion *sub luce revelationis*. The human law is proportioned to divine law inasmuch as no citizen who is also a believer be commanded to offer *latria* contrary to the law of the Gospel and determinations of apostolic authority. This is what Augustine meant in saying that while Christians have many laws and customs in common with non-believers they cannot be brought under a law alien to their religion. By the same token, it is what Thomas meant in saying to the King of Cyprus that the ruler should respect the law of priests.

In the second place, human law should be consistent with (moral) discipline proportionate to the natural law. But it is of the natural law—indeed, in

---

77. *ST*, I-II, q. 95, a. 3. The corpus of the article continues: "All the other conditions mentioned by him are reduced to these three. For it is called virtuous [*honesta*] because it fosters religion. And when he goes on to say that it should be 'just, possible to nature, according to the customs of the country, adapted to place and time,' he implies that it should be helpful to discipline. For human discipline depends first on the order of reason, to which he refers by saying just [*iusta*]; second, it depends on the ability of the agent, because discipline should be adapted to each one according to his ability taking also into account the ability of nature (for the same burdens should be not laid on children as on adults); and should be according to human customs, since man cannot live alone in society, paying no heed to others; third, it depends on certain circumstances, in respect of which he says, 'adapted to place and time' [*loco temporique conveniens*]. The remaining words, 'necessary, useful,' etc., mean that law should expedite well-being. Hence, necessity refers to the removal of evils; usefulness to the attainment of good; and clearness of expression, to the need of preventing any harm ensuing from the law itself. And since, as stated above (q. 90, a. 2), law is ordained to the common good, this is expressed in the last part of the description."

its most fundamental and noble ordering of human action—that rational creatures freely search out the truth about God and render devotion by sensible signs. Prescinding from all other complications, this anthropological core must be respected. In this regard, the saying of Epictetus makes the point: "Were I a swan, I should do after the manner of a swan. But now, since I am a reasonable being, I must sing to God: that is my work: I do it, nor will I desert this my post, as long as it is granted me to hold it; and upon you too I call to join in this self-same hymn."[78] This is a matter not of divine right alone, but also of human right.[79]

In the third place, human law must be useful to the common good. The fontal goods comprised under the first precept most proximate to our rational nature is "a natural inclination to know the truth about God, and to live in society; to shun ignorance, to avoid offending those among whom one has to live, and other such things"—*in nucleo*, all of the natural social virtues. Human law subverts itself if it should thwart the tranquility of social order under law. Coercion of religious acts deepens civil strife, and therefore frustrates not only the rational inclination to give due to God, but our inclination and obligation to love our neighbor in a specifically political order. It is the responsibility of government and citizens to remove impediments to political order and to correct injuries to others. The details of time and place of course put a somewhat different complexion on the institutions in which we achieve an honorable and stable peace. *Dignitatis Humanae* repeatedly uses the word "constitutional." Comprehended on its own terms, the Declaration means the constitutional polities of our time and place, having as their constituency a diversity of people, under a rule of law that makes explicit provision for the honest civil rights of minorities, that sets limits to political powers, that makes government responsible to the people, and that provides remedies for those whose rights are abused or neglected in the ordinary processes of politics.[80]

At the outset, I promised to respect the silences of *Dignitatis Humanae* and to stop short of claiming that Thomas's understanding of the virtue and vices of religion can be used for the purpose of a strict interpretation of the Declaration. The Declaration on Religious Liberty should be read in the very rich historical context of its time and according to the very narrow moral-juridical purposes of the document itself. The position is always in danger of being misunderstood in one direction or the other. Even so, Thomas's treatment of religion offers a useful angle of interpretation for the

---

78. Epictetus, *The Harvard Classics*, vol. 2, *The Golden Sayings of Epictetus*, ed. C. Eliot, trans. Hastings Crossley (New York: Collier & Son, 1909), part 2, no. 1.

79. Repression of this basal and fundamental response to the truth is a violation of both the human person and God. See *Dignitatis Humanae*, §6.

80. *Dignitatis Humanae*, §15.

larger issues at stake. In the first place, there is his account of the source and the intellectual and volitional pulse of the human inclination to know the truth about God and to render service. It frames rather nicely *Dignitatis Humanae*'s declaration of a duty and right based upon human dignity. In the second place, informed by scripture and Augustine, Thomas's historical consideration of the weakness and dangers attending determination of *cultus divini* by human law are truly appropriate to the work of *Dignitatis Humanae*. In the third place, his insistence that the stem-set needs to be instructed by divine law and healed by grace takes us close to the deep rationale of Ch. 2 of *Dignitatis Humanae*.

PART III

First Truths

CHAPTER 13

How to Inherit a Kingdom

Reflections on the Situation of Catholic Political Thought

RUSSELL HITTINGER AND SCOTT RONIGER

I. PRUDENCE

IN 1890, POPE LEO XIII WROTE, "The political prudence of the Pontiff embraces diverse and multiform things, for it is his charge not only to rule the Church, but generally so to regulate the actions of Christian citizens that these may be in apt conformity to their hope of gaining eternal salvation."[1] The letter was entitled *Sapientiae Christianae*—on principles of Christian practical wisdom, the truths concerning the pursuit in this life of our supernatural end. Leo was also referring to the regnative prudence of the pontifical office, directing citizens qua baptized. Even if the direction is about political morality, the prudential directives presuppose sanctifying grace and a supernatural end. In other words, such prudence is here proffered under the formality of the New Law.[2]

In the concrete, directing those who have sanctifying grace to right judgment and action regarding what belongs or does not belong to Caesar is not easily given or received. The lines and entanglements are contingent and fluid. At a consistory immediately after World War II, Pius XII remarked that the triumph of democratic forms of government has at least one advantage: "The

---

Our thanks to the Institute for Human Ecology at The Catholic University of America for sponsoring the public lecture (October 6, 2022) at which an earlier version of this essay was presented, and to Professor Émilie Tardivel and Fr. Aquinas Gilbeau, OP for their papers at the colloquium the next day.

1. Leo XIII, Encyclical Letter *Sapientiae Christianae* (January 10, 1890), §37.

2. As Thomas teaches in *ST*, I-II, q. 106, a. 1: "But that which is most prominent in the Law of the New Covenant and in which its power consists is the grace of the Holy Spirit, which is given through faith in Christ. And so the New Law is in the first instance the very grace of the Holy Spirit that is given to those who believe in Christ."

distinction between the Church and even the democratic State becomes increasingly clear."[3] Divine providence includes two comprehensive communities, polity and ecclesia, which differ in their respective origin and end. In the thick of events they are not always so clear. For the better part of two millennia ecclesial and civil governments look very much alike from an institutional and sociological point of view. They share families, languages, costumes, arts and sciences, banks, moral principles, the same contemporary media—indeed, even sharing the same laws and international protocols. More than half of the European Union countries are under at least one concordat with the Holy See. Yet when we casually speak of "Church and state" it is easy to imagine two teams in the same order of things. Even so, Pius XII acknowledged that democratic government makes clear(er) that the first subject of the polity is the *populus*, the people, whereas the first subject of the *ecclesia* is the Holy Spirit.

Beginning with Leo (1878–1903) pontifical prudence had to reckon with the benefits and challenges of representative governments. Whenever public responsibility is vested in the citizens, the baptized citizens bear a greater burden of distinguishing what properly belongs to the Church and to civil government. For in representative governments the citizens are not vassals or retainers of the king and his court. Therefore it falls more directly upon the people to understand the difference between Church and civil government.[4] Leo understood the world he inhabited. In *Rerum Novarum* (1891), he mused, "Nothing is more useful than to look upon the world as it really is" (§18). This marks an important change in papal letters after 1789. Christian wisdom has to be communicated not merely to Catholics who are subjects but also to Catholics who are citizens: in France, Germany, Italy, Belgium, and so on. Thus, Leo observed in an allocution two years after *Sapientiae Christianae*: "Faith embodied in the conscience of peoples rather than restoration of medieval institutions is the way to final victory."[5]

As it turned out, Leo's greatest problem was the French Church and the Third Republic, which became more aggressively laicist with every passing

---

3. Pius XII, Allocution of October 2, 1945, *AAS* 37, 258f.: "If, on the other hand, we bear in mind the favorite thesis of democracy—a doctrine which great Christian thinkers have proclaimed in all ages—namely, that the original subject of civil power derived from God is the people (not the 'masses'), the distinction between the Church and even the democratic State becomes increasingly clear" (trans. ours).

4. See *ST*, II-II, q. 10, a. 10 on whether an infidel ought to head a civil government whose citizens are baptized. Thomas's answer is complicated. If we remove Thomas's sociological supposition that the baptized are vassals bound to comply with the wishes of their masters, the article might have reached a different conclusion.

5. Leo XIII, Allocution "*Onorare le ceneri*," March 1, 1892.

decade, even though it was still under the 1801 Concordat signed by Napoleon and Pius VII. For Leo much was at stake, chiefly the law of divorce, which had been excised from the Napoleonic Code. Born in 1810, Leo had seen the historical events: the captivity of Pope Pius VII and then his release by the French, the demise of Napoleon, the loss of the papal states (the longest continuous temporal government in western Europe, until the summer of 1870), and Bismarck's *Kulturkampf*. He possessed those chief parts of prudence: such as memory, foresight, circumspection, and above all *caution*!

Writing to the French Church in 1892, he observed that:

> Founded by Him who was, who is, and who will be forever, she has received from Him, since her very origin, all that she requires for the pursuing of her divine mission across the changeable ocean of human affairs. And, far from wishing to transform her essential constitution, she has not the power even to relinquish the conditions of true liberty and sovereign independence with which Providence has endowed her in the general interest of souls. . . . But, in regard to purely human societies, it is an oft-repeated historical fact that time, that great transformer of all things here below, operates great changes in their political institutions.[6]

Unlike the Church founded by Christ, and marriage (both of which have divinely insculpted and fixed form and ends), political order has no fixed form. God the author of nature does not guarantee the perpetuity of a particular political form, monarchical or republican. Thus, Leo counseled the French Catholics to dial down the temperature of debate about the relative merits of monarchical versus republican forms. What was at stake was a laicist crackdown that could endanger the two societies that really *are* divinely insculpted: sacramental marriage and Church. This is exactly what happened a decade later. The Republic dissolved the concordat, expelled religious orders, closed Catholic schools, and provided for civil divorce. Leonine prudence yielded a truce with Bismarck and a rollback of his *Kulturkampf*, but Leo could not direct the disputatious French.

Even *Immortale Dei* (1885), the most doctrinal encyclical on these things, is carefully worded: "Hence, civil society, established for the common welfare, should not only safeguard the well-being of the community, but have also at heart *the interests of its individual members*, in such mode as not in any way to hinder, but in every manner to render as easy as may be, the possession of that highest and unchangeable good for which all should seek. Wherefore, for this purpose, care must especially be taken to preserve

---

6. Leo XIII, Encyclical Letter *Au Milieu* (February 16, 1892), §17.

unharmed and unimpeded the religion whereof the practice is the link connecting man with God."[7]

He was not asking the Third Republic to make laws about religion (the Concordat was still in place), much less to direct citizens to a supernatural end, but rather "not to hinder" and to "preserve unharmed and unimpeded" the religious practices of Catholics.[8] In Italy, on the other hand, Leo insisted upon restoration of the *patrimonium Petri*, the so-called papal states. His protégé Pius XI once dubbed the Chilean law of separation to be an "amicable coexistence," for it allowed society to remain somewhat intact, even though it derogated from Church teachings on separation.[9] Polities that followed the French laicist model, however, held that the state has a monopoly on human fraternity, all else being consigned to private life. Even so, Leo and Pius not only refrained from direct criticism of republican government but indirectly supported it against elements of the Catholic right wing.

Perhaps the strangest, but most interesting, take on separation of Church and state came from Émile Ollivier, a French minister of religious affairs, on the eve of the First Vatican Council and its recognition of the universal jurisdiction of the pope. Pius IX declined to invite Catholic sovereigns to send ambassadors (*oratores*) to the Council. The Secretary of State, Cardinal Giacomo Antonelli, explained that there could be no principle of selection between "good" and "bad" Catholic sovereigns. Privately, he said that "exclusively Catholic Governments had virtually ceased to exist."[10] In France, Ollivier declared in the Chamber of Deputies that the Pope had, in effect, introduced the separation of Church and state: "Yes, this is a new fact, a new deed indeed that the disseverance between the laical society and the religious society is put into effect by the pope's own hand."[11] The ever mischievous ultramontane editor of *L'Univers*, Louis Veuillot, gleefully agreed—princes

---

7. Leo XIII, Encyclical Letter *Immortale Dei* (November 1, 1885), §6. "Individual members," meaning both French citizens and baptized Catholics.

8. Nor does Leo suggest that other Christian denominations, much less non-Christian religions, be kept unharmed and unimpeded. That will be the subject of Vatican Council II, *Dignitatis Humanae* (December 7, 1965).

9. Pius XI, *Iam Annus* (December 14, 1925): "Tuttavia tale provvedimento è applicato in modo così amichevole da sembrare non già una frattura ma piuttosto una convivenza amichevole."

10. See "Lord Odo Russell to Earl of C. (March 7, 1870)," in *The Roman Question: Extracts from the Despatches of Odo Russell from Rome, 1858–1870*, ed. Noel Blakiston (London: Chapman and Hall, 1962), 404.

11. "Speech in Chamber of Deputies on 10 July 1868," in Émile Ollivier, *L'église et l'état au Concile du Vatican*, 3rd ed., vol. 1 (Paris: Gamier Frères, 1877), 400. This work is still the best study of the evolution of church-state relations and Vatican I; see also *L'église et l'état au Concile du Vatican*, 3rd ed., vol. 2 (Paris: Garnier Frères, 1877), 46–48.

are now "outside the Church."[12] It was in this light that Ollivier would make bold to say in the same speech: "Undoubtedly, Gentlemen, I know that Rome earnestly wishes to separate itself from the State, but She does not want the State to separate itself from Her." Rome never refuted that charge.

Indeed, this was exactly the intent of Vatican I: to pull the world's bishops out of civil establishments and quasi-establishments and thus to make clear and effective the sui generis nature of the apostolic college, which does not belong to Caesar—no matter how friendly.[13] Indeed, one-way separations can imply an establishment or restoration of proper order. When the Third Republic enacted its long set of laicist restrictions on the French Church (1881–1905), culminating in the cancellation of the Concordat and the issuance of the law of Separation (1905) the purpose was more akin to an establishment. Perhaps it was not as brutal as the Revolution's Civil Constitution of the Clergy (1790), yet it did attempt to establish the diocesan clergy in a civil order.[14]

Leonine era "pontifical prudence" on relations between the Church and civil governments must be seen like pieces on a chessboard—the tactics constitute a very important context for how the principles are formulated and applied. It was for all practical purposes inevitable that churchmen would in due course strip out the relevant sentences representing a spectrum of prudential judgments and arrange them in lists that might prove useful for purely doctrinal canons. In the 1940s, textbooks that were used to teach clergy, religious, and lay students in universities made such lists that had the ambience of Thomistic, or at least scholastic, propositions.

Take, for example, Henri Grenier's three-volume work *Thomistic Philosophy*.[15] It is one of the better textbooks of that period. The author is prudently short-winded on the subject, which does not amount to more than ten pages, placed at the very end of the three volumes. In the section on Church and state, we find several prescriptions for rightly ordered relations, and all but one are contingent, needing to be read in the sense of conditional clauses, "if . . . then." He distinguishes for example obligations in light of (1) pagan states, not Christian, with no presupposition of baptism or sanctifying grace,

---

12. Fredrik K. Nielsen, *The History of the Papacy in the XIXth Century*, 2 vols. (New York: E. P. Dutton, 1906), 2:296.

13. On one-way separations and other important discussions on the Vatican I era, see Ch. 5 of this collection and *The Teachings of Modern Roman Catholicism: On Law, Politics, & Human Nature*, ed. John Witte and Frank Alexander (New York: Columbia University Press, 2007).

14. See Sarah Shortall, *Soldiers of God in a Secular World: Catholic Theology and Twentieth-Century French Politics* (Cambridge, MA: Harvard University Press, 2021), 24–25.

15. Henri Grenier, *Thomistic Philosophy*, vol. 3, 3rd ed., Cursus Philosophiae (Charlottetown: St Dunstan's University, 1949), §§1158–1171.

which means that pagan political authority is intact under natural law, for neither sin nor grace takes away the natural avidity of human persons to form political society, (2) apostate Christian peoples, actively schismatic or rebellious Christian peoples, the conditions of which must be further delineated, (3) liberal states marked by the right of liberty of conscience or by one or another constitutional prohibition on the making of laws respecting religion.[16] The categories can be expanded or contracted, but they could not provide a roadmap for a late twentieth-century student. An alert reader today will understand, at least in retrospect, why it was necessary to locate a *principium fundamentale*.[17]

Whoever does not have a stomach for such historical and social contingencies—not to mention reversals of fortune—on an issue of such magnitude, perhaps should not attempt to handle questions of Church and state.

In what follows we want to locate a fundamental principle that can serve as a light—not at the end of the tunnel of contingencies, but one that illuminates our path at the very beginning.

II. SEPARATED BY THE HAND OF GOD

A truly *first* principle is that the kingdom of Christ is separated both in ordinary human time and eschatologically. We use the term "separate" in just the way Joseph Ratzinger does, both as scholar and pope. "Jesus had actually achieved a *separation* of the religious from the political, thereby changing the world: this is what truly marks the essence of his new path. . . . This brings us back to the question of the interweaving and the separation of religion and politics. In his teaching and in his whole ministry, Jesus had inaugurated a non-political Messianic kingdom and had begun to detach these two hitherto inseparable realities from one another."[18] So, too, for Wojtyła as scholar and

---

16. Which calls to mind the US Constitution VI.3, which prohibits any religious test for the holding office or trust, but which never uses the word "separation."

17. The freedom of the Church "is the fundamental principle [*principium fundamentale*] in what concerns the relationships between the Church and governments and the whole civil order." *Dignitatis Humanae*, §13. This is laid down in the second part of the document, *sub luce revelationis*, which concerns the eschatological framework. The moral principles based upon reason and the natural ordination to discover and hold the truth about God is developed in the first part.

18. Joseph Ratzinger, *Jesus of Nazareth*, vol. 2, *Holy Week from the Entrance into Jerusalem to the Resurrection* (San Francisco: Ignatius Press, 2011), 169–70. Ratzinger uses forms of the German nouns "Trennung" ("separation") and "Lösung" ("solution," "unfastening," "severance," or even "a solution or resolution by decoupling") to describe Jesus's separation of the political from the religious, and he also uses forms of the verbs "trennen" ("to separate") and "lösen" ("to unfasten," "to sever," or "to uncouple"). These words

pope: "Christ's entry into the world reveals an economy *altogether sui generis*, proper to God alone. It is a divine economy, with its source in the Father, the Son and the Holy Spirit."[19]

For our purposes in this essay, separated is the equivalent of being "set aside," not only as something holy, but just as importantly something accomplished by a divine rather than a human act.[20] Hence, we put to one side the usual spectrum of juridical and moral meanings of separation, which, however varied and interesting, are events attributed to human choices and decrees.

The title of our essay is "How to Inherit a Kingdom." Christ's teaching "my kingdom is not of this world" (Jn 18:36) has always proved difficult to hearers of the Word, beginning with Jesus's own disciples prior to Pentecost. It is one thing to understand that a kingdom divided against itself cannot stand (Mk 3:24), but quite another to understand two kingdoms that are not commensurate in their form, finality, or authority. While Caesar may represent and serve as a practical coadjutor of the natural law, he does not represent or govern the Church.

Take, for example, Augustine's pastoral and theological challenge after Alaric's sack of Rome (410). While Saint Jerome bemoaned that the "whole world is perishing in one city," Augustine was annoyed that so many Christians blamed the catastrophe on Christ. From time immemorial deities were expected to protect the safety and prosperity of the city. By a virtually universal custom, religion bound men and women not so much to their gods, but their gods to the public common good. So, if the Empire is now overseen by Christian emperors, *Ubi est Christus?* For weak and for recently converted Christians the sack of 410 suggested that an incompetent deity was on duty. Just when Christians had some political grip on imperial power, Rome itself was being shattered. Augustine understood that this complaint suggested that some of his flock had not understood Christianity.

His main homiletic theme became "How to Inherit a Kingdom." For example, in Sermon 113A, he quotes Matthew 25, "Come blessed of my Father, receive the kingdom." Throughout these "catastrophe" sermons, Augustine admonishes his flock to give heed to the teaching of the Lord and his ministers who are preparing those who hear to receive a kingdom not of

---

are distinct from and, in this context, stronger than "Unterschied" ("distinction"). See Joseph Ratzinger/Benedikt XVI, *Jesus von Nazareth, Zweiter Teil, Vom Einzug in Jerusalem bis zur Auferstehung* (Freiburg: Herder, 2011).

19. Karol Wojtyła, *Sign of Contradiction* (New York: The Seabury Press, 1979), 49.

20. See Aquinas, *Super Ioannis*, Ch. 18, lec. 6, no. 2351. See also *ST*, I-II, q. 112, a. 1 (esp. ad. 1); *ST*, II-II, q. 23, a. 2.

this world rather than grieve for the stones of Rome.[21] Augustine was insistent that they learn the dominical words, "My kingdom is not of this world." In his tracts on the Gospel of John, he restates the words of Christ before Pilate: "Listen therefore Jews and gentiles; listen, circumcision; listen uncircumcision; listen, all earthly kingdoms: I am no hindrance to your dominion in this world. . . . What more do you want? Come to the kingdom that is not of the world by believing."[22] As for those who govern the Church, Augustine admonishes them to imitate Noah, Daniel, and Job, for each symbolizes faith that the Lord God delivers the faithful from tribulation.[23]

These sermons were swiftly reworked into Book I of *De civitate Dei*. This is the sole book of *The City of God* that criticizes Christians, on grounds of both weak morals and even weaker faith. It is also worth remarking that between Sermon 113A (September 410) and his writing of book I of *De civitate Dei* in 412, Pelagius appeared in North Africa after taking flight from his now uncomfortable habitation in Rome. Indeed, he becomes an object of the main question: How can one here below inherit the kingdom, except by supernatural faith? This is the central question of the last decade of Augustine's life.

In making sense of Church and world (including the political powers), separation is a first-order term because it describes what is essential to the kingdom: being set apart, having a supernatural end as well as supernatural capacities for achieving that end. More than seven centuries later Thomas Aquinas relied heavily on Augustine's understanding of what belongs to this world in contrast to the kingdom. Here is Saint Thomas on John 18: "*My kingdom is not of this world*, that is, *does not have its origin in earthly causes and human choice*."[24]

---

21. On those who grumble, see Augustine, Sermon 296, no. 9. See also Sermons 113A, nos. 81, 397.

22. Augustine, Sermon 115, no. 2, in *Homilies on the Gospel of John*, trans. Edmund Hill, OP (New York: New City Press, 2020), 477. Augustine worked on the *Tracts on John* (*In evangelium Ioannis*) while writing what we call his books of separation in *De civitate Dei*: XI (angelic); XII (division of the human will); XIII–XIV (separation of body and soul); XV (Cain and Abel); XX–XXII (Noah and the rest, up to final judgment).

23. Augustine, Sermon 397 (late 411?): "But Noah represents good leaders, who govern and direct the Church, just as Noah captained and steered the ark in the flood. Daniel represents the holy celibates, Job represents all the married people who live good and upright lives. It is these three kinds of people, after all, that God will deliver from that tribulation." See *Sermons 341–400*, trans. Edmund Hill, OP (New York: New York City Press, 1995), Sermon 397, no. 1, p. 435. To put it in another way, tribulation does not contradict Christian vocation. See also *De civitate Dei*, XIX, c. 27 for the development on Job.

24. Aquinas, *Super Ioannis*, Ch. 18, lec. 6, no. 2351.

Leo XIII relies on this tradition: "It cannot be doubted, under safeguard of the faith, that the governance of souls was committed to the Church alone, in such wise that powers of the political order have no share whatever in it."[25] As does Grenier, who contends that temporal happiness secured by rightly ordered politics is not, strictly speaking, a means to the end of eternal happiness, because no natural operation can be a part or direct means to the supernatural end. He puts it this way: "not as a *means or a part*, but only as a good inferior in nature to the good of a higher order." Indeed, "[t]he Church does not embrace all other societies as its parts—civil society is not a part of the Church."[26] Such is true even when Christians are members of the civil community. So far forth, they bring with them a wisdom about moral precepts and virtues that are common to human life. In due course, we will examine this distinction between morals and eschatology.

Grenier makes a critical point. We never say that the civitas, polis or imperium is separate from the families and associations that compose it. Rather, we affirm that the government is distinguished but not separated from the component parts—the living stones so to speak. For common sense, we say that when some thing or group is integral we affirm that its elements can be distinguished (even qualitatively) but not separated. The kingdom in pilgrimage, however, does not consist of other societies as integral parts.[27]

It is difficult *not* to think of the Church as the highest region of a single differentiated society—perhaps as an international one for the progressives, and often a national one for conservatives.[28] This is understandable, but

---

25. *Sapientiae Christianae*, §27.

26. Grenier, *Thomistic Philosophy*, vol. 3, §1165.

27. Except for one, namely marriage, which (bearing in mind Mt 22:20) for the baptized is a sacrament that includes all the natural elements of matrimony. This is why the contest between temporal regimes and the Church will always come back around to marriage. See Russell Hittinger, "Popes Leo XIII and Pius XI," in *Christianity and Family Law: An Introduction*, ed. Gary S. Hauk and John Witte (Cambridge: Cambridge University Press, 2017), 323–43.

28. For modern progressives, it is difficult not to think of the Church as a lower part of a single society, in the fashion of the Social Gospel inspiring but not determining the unfolding of history. On these issues, Ratzinger is once again helpful. In his discussion of John the Baptist's preaching and baptizing as a preparation for Christ's teaching and mission, Ratzinger describes the differences between the Zealots, the Pharisees, the Sadducees, and the so-called Essenes. He says: (1) the Zealots "were prepared to resort to terror and violence in order to restore Israel's freedom," (2) the Pharisees were akin to recalcitrant conservatives who "endeavored to live with the greatest possible exactness according to the instructions of the Torah" and who "refused conformity to the hegemony of Hellenistic-Roman culture, which . . . was now threatening to force Israel's assimilation to the pagan peoples' way of life," (3) the Sadducees were akin to elite liberals "most of whom belonged to the aristocracy and the priestly class" and who "attempted to practice an enlightened

wrong. The Church here below is set aside, separated, sanctified as a sign and preparation of its full eschatological union with the resurrected Christ. Supernatural union is not a superior version of temporal and natural happiness; nor is temporal happiness an inferior version of heaven. Therefore the word "integral" is not fit to do the work of describing the kingdom vis-à-vis the temporal powers. To attempt to do so puts us into trouble even before we start.

Take, for example, Leo XIII's remark in *Immortale Dei*: "There must, accordingly, exist between these two powers a certain orderly connection, which may be compared to the union of the soul and body in man" (§14). Of course, soul to body "in man" is a substantial form. Societies on the other hand are unities of order. In a unity of order, each member possesses what is individually proper to himself—namely, certain operations and acts not reducible to the commonality.[29] So Leo cannot have meant a strict analogy of substantial form. Political society does not have the "form" of the Church. This is proved by reading the next sentences:

> The nature and scope of that connection can be determined only, as We have laid down, by having regard to the nature of each power, and by taking account of the relative excellence and nobleness of their purpose. One of the two has for its proximate and chief object the well-being of this mortal life; the other, the everlasting joys of heaven. Whatever, therefore in things human is of a sacred character, whatever belongs either of its own nature or by reason of the end to which it is referred, to the salvation of souls, or to the worship of God, is subject to the power and

---

Judaism intellectually suited to the times, and so also to come to terms with Roman domination," and (4) the Essenes withdrew to the Judean desert where they created "monastic-style communities, but also a religiously motivated common life for families. [They] also established a productive literary center and instituted distinctive rituals, which included liturgical ablutions and common prayers." He says that "it appears that not only John the Baptist, but possibly Jesus and his family as well, were close to the [Essenes of the] Qumran community." It is not a stretch to say that these four approaches to religion, culture and society, political government, and ultimately to the Messiah determine the way one sees the church-state issue. Contra the Zealots, Ratzinger says that Jesus transformed "the 'zeal' that would serve God through violence . . . into the zeal of the Cross. Thus he definitively established the criterion for true zeal—the zeal of self-giving love. This zeal must become the Christian's goal." In the span of one chapter, Matthew 22, Christ calls the Pharisees hypocrites and teaches them that they must render unto Caesar what belongs to Caesar, and he tells the Sadducees that they "are misled because [they] do not know the scriptures or the power of God," thus stretching their thinking into the eschatological realm, where "at the resurrection they neither marry nor are given in marriage but are like the angels in heaven." See, respectively, Ratzinger, *Jesus of Nazareth*, vol. 1, *From the Baptism in the Jordan to the Transfiguration (Jesus of Nazareth*, trans. Adrian J. Walker (New York: Doubleday, 2007), 12–14 and Ratzinger, *Jesus of Nazareth*, 2:22.

29. See Aquinas, *In I Eth.*, lec. 5.

judgment of the Church. Whatever is to be ranged under the civil and political order is rightly subject to the civil authority. Jesus Christ has Himself given command that what is Caesar's is to be rendered to Caesar, and that what belongs to God is to be rendered to God.[30]

Clearly, Leo does not mean that the two powers are related by substantial form, nor by higher souls or archons ruling lower ones. Stoics sometimes spoke of souls of social organisms. But Leo was not a Stoic, nor was Thomas Aquinas. Perhaps the *Letter to Diognetus* exhibits at least a trace of Stoic rhetoric when it declares: "To speak in general terms, we may say that what the soul is to the body, Christians are in the world." But in that very chapter the author insists that Christians are in the world but not *of* it.[31] The point that the apologist intends is very much like Saint Thomas's note: "Again, in order to dispose our affections, the Gospel contains things which involve that hatred of the world through which a man comes to have a capacity for the grace of the Holy Spirit. For as John 14:17 says, 'The world [read: lovers of the world] cannot take in (*capere*) the Holy Spirit.'"[32]

That his kingdom is not of this world is a dominical saying of supreme importance. Jesus's disciples vehemently resisted this teaching until Pentecost; over the course of Church history many of their successors and our own

---

30. Both this text and the previous quote from Leo XIII are taken from *Immortale Dei*, §14. Leo's use of soul-body is perhaps drawn from a similar comment in St. Thomas's treatment of the judgement that pertains to political judges. See *ST*, II-II, q. 60, a. 6, ad. 3. Aquinas shows that it is unjust to compel someone "to submit to a judgment that is not rendered by the public authority," and he rejects the argument that the spiritual authority's interference in temporal matters justifies usurpation. He says that "it is not a usurpation of judgment if a spiritual prelate inserts himself into temporal affairs to the extent that the secular power is subject to him in those affairs or insofar as the secular power has relinquished them (*non est usurpatum iudicium si spiritualis praelatus se intromittat de temporalibus quantum ad ea in quibus subditur ei saecularis potestas, vel quae ei a saeculari potestate relinquuntur*)." So far forth, this implies nothing of the Church outsourcing its spiritual powers to Caesar.

31. See *Letter to Diognetus*, c. 6. Translation is slightly modified from the one available at www.vatican.va. Even more strongly, Christians "cannot be identified with the world." Perhaps Aquinas's and Leo's soul to body is a metaphor, a meaning carried over to some other thing. The soul's nobility is not diminished by the fact that it is not a bodily part. So too the Church's domain is not limited by saying that it is not a part of the civil jurisdiction. It can inspire and move the members of the body politic without being a "part" in the jurisdictional sense. It is a metaphorical stretch, but see Henri de Lubac, "The Authority of the Church in Temporal Matters," in *Theological Fragments* (San Francisco: Ignatius Press, 1989), 211. For a more critical interpretation of *Immortale Dei*, §14, see John Courtney Murray, SJ, "Leo XIII on Separation of Church and State," *Theological Studies* 14 (1953): 209–10. See also Pius XI, *Quadragesimo Anno*, §88; John Paul II, *Letter to Families*, §17.

32. *ST*, I-II, q. 106, a. 1, ad 1.

brethren have been unnerved by the teaching. Ratzinger explains that "for a long time now, Christians have tended to avoid quoting" the numerous New Testament texts that express the conviction that "our commonwealth is in heaven" (Phil 3:20) and that "here we have no lasting city, but we seek the city which is to come" (Heb 13:14). He says that, especially in the twentieth century, many Christians have neglected this fundamental theme because they have made the mistake of thinking that these texts "appear to alienate man from the earth and prevent him from fulfilling his innerworldly task, which is also a political task."[33] If polity is natural and God-given, why should political authority not be a coadjutor of the kingdom?

The recurrent, perennial position (again, post-peccatum in real historical time) is pagan integralism, which flows in part from the natural human desire for immortality run amok after sin—a distorted expression of the natural desire for immortality.[34] The highest *practical* expression of the desire for immortality is to participate in political life.[35] It outlasts the individual, the family and the tribe. Normal people will grieve the loss of their political society more than even the loss of their own lives. But the temporal regime of political order neither conquers death nor causes resurrection, the truly eschatological premises of the kingdom. It was Christ who had to achieve the separation as a dimension of his overcoming of sin and its effects. We can even say that if the higher life doesn't achieve separation by transcending the political, its activities are not being done badly; rather, they are not being done at all.

Let us sharpen a distinction embedded in the word "separation." First, it can mean *contradictory*, or "separate" can be *contrary*. For example: the reign of sin and death is contradictory to the kingdom even below, and the Church must be separated from it. But we can say that political life, just as such, is a

---

33. Joseph Ratzinger, *Selected Writings: Faith and Politics*, with a foreword by Pope Francis, trans. Michael J. Miller et al. (San Francisco: Ignatius Press, 2018), 148–50. See also Augustine, *De perfectione iustitiae hominis*, 15.35, in *Nicene and Post-Nicene Fathers*, series 1, vol. 5 (Peabody, MA: Hendrickson, 2004), 172: "Because it is not so much when the Church is involved in so many evils, or amidst such offenses, and in so great a mixture of very evil men, and amidst the heavy reproaches of the ungodly, that we ought to say that it is glorious, because kings serve it—a fact which only produces a more perilous and a sorer temptation."

34. See Ratzinger, *Eschatology: Death and Eternal Life*, trans. Michael Waldstein (Washington, DC: The Catholic University of America Press, 1988), 60–66. See also Augustine, *De civitate Dei*, I, where he shows that the political virtues of the Romans mask the fear of death. For a brilliant discussion of counterfeit (political) virtues masking the fear of death, see Robert Dodaro, *Christ and the Just Society in the Thought of Augustine* (Cambridge: Cambridge University Press, 2004), 36–49.

35. See Plato, *Symposium*, 207a–212c, and Yves Simon, *A General Theory of Authority* (South Bend, IN: University of Notre Dame Press, 1980), 29.

good thing—not inherently sinful or death dealing—but even so is *contrary* to (*other than*) the kingdom. As Henri De Lubac helpfully puts it: "Temporal and spiritual power are not opposed as two contradictories."[36] This distinction between separation as signifying otherness and signifying contradiction is propounded by Cardinal Wojtyła in his 1976 Lenten conferences for Pope Paul VI, published in 1979 as *Sign of Contradiction*.

Commenting on the presentation in the temple, where Simeon prophesies that the child will be a sign of contradiction (Lk 2:23–25), Cardinal Wojtyła prays that the light of Christ will "give us strength and make us capable of accepting and loving the whole truth about Christ, *of loving it all the more as the world all the more contradicts it.*" On the other hand, "Christ's entry into the world reveals an economy *altogether sui generis, proper to God alone. It is a divine economy, with its source in the Father, the Son and the Holy Spirit.*"[37] Both senses of separation are distinguished without confusion. Christ initiates a *sui generis* economy that belongs to God alone, and he is a sign of contradiction.[38]

Paradoxically perhaps, if Christians are to fecundate the world, it cannot come by being united to the state, nor by becoming one with the reign of sin and death. Rather, the Church must achieve both kinds of separation as fully as possible. Separate from what is contradictory and separate from what is contrary. Along the lines of the merely contrary, Jesus says that there is no marriage or family in heaven (Mt 22.30). The mode of human fellowship in heaven does not include natural procreation and family. It is not contradictory, only *sui generis*.

Politics, to the contrary, has its foundational principles in morals under natural law, custom, and various species of human law. The capacities and actions deployed to secure this order are connatural to human beings even if a proper political order is difficult to achieve, and even more difficult to maintain. In sharp distinction, however, no person can direct another to the kingdom without presupposing grace. Sacramentally, this means baptism, but more generally it means sanctifying grace.

III. RATZINGER ON MORALS AND ESCHATOLOGY

On these and other related questions, we propose that the most important Catholic thinker of the twentieth century is Joseph Ratzinger, both as bishop-cardinal and as pope. Perhaps the most neglected theological treatise within

---

36. De Lubac, "Authority in the Church," 205.
37. Wojtyła, *Sign of Contradiction*, 8 and 49.
38. See also Benedict XVI, "Christmas Address of His Holiness Benedict XVI to the Roman Curia," December 22, 2005.

the memory of our generation is his work *Eschatology*.[39] Ratzinger treats the fundamental distinction between morals by nature and the formal, efficient and final causes of initiation into the kingdom—properly understood as eschatology. First, the Church imitates Christ, who himself taught the rudiments of the moral law and virtue. Such teaching is given to all the nations. But the kingdom, which is the locus of eschatology, is not an institution or association in the familiar sociological sense. The kingdom is the Person of Christ, and its inhabitants are those who draw close to him by grace. It is not a sphere within other spheres but an event.[40] "[T]he message of the Kingdom of God has something very important to say to politics. It is healthy for politics to learn that its own content is not eschatological. The setting asunder of eschatology and politics is one of the fundamental tasks of Christian theology."[41]

Why call this an eschatological distinction? The true *Basileus* (the temple, the *regnum*) is Christ who is properly called *autobasilea* (self-ruling).[42] For when Christians are moved by the Holy Spirit to make that act of faith, it is truly an eschatological event.[43] This is the sign of Jonah, for Christ's teaching converges upon himself "as the 'now' of God."[44] Faith moves the soul to participate in an eschatological celebration that unites us to Christ and His Church. The Church is, as we have said, properly *sui generis*. Yet, if we are forced to speak very loosely of the "genus" of the Church as a graced, supernatural society in which we participate by faith, then we do well to follow Fr. Benoît-Dominique de la Soujeole, OP, who says that the "sacramentality of the Church . . . gives us, as it were, the genus to which the Church belongs." He repeats this point: "To say that the Church is a sacrament is to specify, as it were, the larger 'genus' to which she belongs." Clearly, Fr. de La Soujeole is using "genus" in a quite extended sense, but understanding the Church as a sacrament, or as sacramental, enables us to see that when we are united to

---

39. See Ratzinger, *Eschatology: Death and Eternal Life*, trans. Michael Waldstein (Washington, DC: The Catholic University of America Press, 1988).

40. Ratzinger, *Eschatology*, 35.

41. Ratzinger, *Eschatology*, 59. Elsewhere he says that "by merging with the state, the Church would destroy both the essence of the state and her own essence. The Church remains something 'outside' the state, for only thus can both Church and state be what they are meant to be. Like the state, the Church too must remain in her own proper place and within her boundaries. She must respect her own being and her own freedom, precisely in order to perform for the state the service that the latter requires." He adds that it is precisely the eschatological premise, or "'eschatological' attitude that guarantees the state its own right while simultaneously resisting absolutism by indicating the boundaries both of the state and of the Church in the world." Ratzinger, *Faith and Politics*, 148–50.

42. Ratzinger, Jesus of Nazareth, 1:49.

43. Ratzinger, *Eschatology*, 35.

44. Ratzinger, *Eschatology*, 32.

Her we are set apart so as to be taken up into an efficacious sign of God's presence in but not of the world.[45]

At the trial, however, Pilate assumed that Jesus was representing something other than himself, just as Pilate represents Caesar. Pilate was confounded.[46] To Pilate he says I am the truth. In other words, I am not a threat to your political rule. I am not raising up an army against which you will have to fight, nor am I delivering a message *from* someone else, or *about* someone else, as do the prophets. I am neither Barabbas nor John the Baptist. This is eschatological. The completion is now, standing before you. Yet Jesus does not impeach Pilate's authority, not even the juridical power in capital cases.[47] Although he has moral worries about the charges made against Jesus, Pilate is entirely clueless about the role of dying in the kingdom. Jesus tells his apostles to take up their cross and follow him, but not even they understood until their faith was confirmed by the Holy Spirit. But Jesus does not tell Pilate to

---

45. This point is beautifully summarized in Vatican Council II, *Sacrosanctum Concilium* (December 4, 1963), §§8–14. For the texts cited, see Fr. Benoît-Dominique de La Soujeole, OP, *Introduction to the Mystery of the Church*, trans. Michael J. Miller (Washington, DC: The Catholic University of America Press, 2014), 451 and 468. One could argue that sacramental incorporation into Christ's Mystical Body includes our supernatural participation in the metaphysical reality that God is radically separate from the world that he creates. It is precisely his infinite transcendence that "allows" God to be present to his creatures in a creative, noncompetitive, and fecundating way without alteration or augmentation on his part. God and the world do not form an integral whole, nor do the Church and the state. See Aquinas, *Expositio libri Peryermeneias*, I, lec. 14, nos. 20–22; *ST*, I, q. 8, a. 1; *ST*, I, q. 105, a. 5.

46. Augustine and Thomas alike are intrigued by Peter's use of the temporal sword in the garden. The servant of the high priest is named Malchus, "king" or "about to reign," according to Augustine, *Super Ioannis*, tract. 112, no. 5. The healing of Malchus's ear is in anticipation of the salvation of the cup that Christ will drink. Thomas emphasizes that Peter and the other disciples were not yet confirmed in their faith (*Super Ioannis*, 18, lec. 2, no. 2289). While Peter's act could be justified as a protection of the innocent (a moral justification), the situation was yet another test of the disciples' ability to live the evangelical life, such as when Christ sent them forth with no purse or bag or sandals (Lk 22:35). They have yet to learn that the kingdom does not make use of the material sword. On this point, Ratzinger says in *Jesus of Nazareth*, 1:39–40: "This temptation to use power to secure the faith has arisen again and again in varied forms throughout the centuries, and again and again faith has risked being suffocated in the embrace of power. The struggle for the freedom of the Church, the struggle to avoid identifying Jesus' Kingdom with any political structure, is one that has to be fought century after century. For the fusion of faith and political power always comes at price: faith becomes the servant of power and must bend to its criteria." See also Ratzinger, *Faith and Politics*, 200–202.

47. See David Lloyd Dusenbury, *The Innocence of Pontius Pilate: How the Roman Trial of Jesus Shaped History* (New York: Oxford University Press, 2021), esp. Ch. 13, entitled "I Obstruct Not Your Dominion." See also Ratzinger, *Jesus of Nazareth*, 2:183–202.

pick up his cross. It is not essential to the role of a political governor to die, whereas it is an act intrinsic to the Christoform order of the New Covenant (Mt 16:24–26).[48]

On this point, Pope Benedict observes:

> The transformation of human nature, and the world with it, is possible only as a miracle of grace. Where it is regarded as being, rather, the building-site where the house of politics is under construction, a rank impossibility is taken as the foundation for all human reality. . . . *The Kingdom of God is not a political norm of political activity, but it is a moral norm of that activity.* . . . In other words, the message of the Kingdom of God is significant for political life not by way of eschatology but by way of political ethics.[49]

Ratzinger stresses that "this separation—essential to Jesus' message—of politics from faith, of God's people from politics, was ultimately possible only through the Cross. Only through the total loss of all external power, through the radical stripping away that led to the Cross, could this new world come into being. Only through faith in the Crucified One, in him who was robbed of all worldly power and thereby exalted, does the new community arise, the new manner of God's dominion in the world."[50] Imitating Christ in his love unto the cross and his proclamation of truth leading to a non-political messianic kingdom will "enable us to situate the temporal order in relation to a transcendent order which gives the temporal order its true measure but without taking away its own nature," and thus the Church "can maintain firmly both the unity and the distinction between evangelization and human promotion. . . . It is thus by pursuing her own finality that the Church sheds the light of the Gospel on earthly realities in order that human beings may be healed of their miseries and raised in dignity."[51]

---

48. For the eschatological and political implications of martyrdom, see Erik Peterson, "Witness to Truth," in *Theological Tractates*, ed. and trans. Michael J. Hollerich (Stanford, CA: Stanford University Press, 2011), 151–81.

49. Ratzinger, *Eschatology*, 59. For a very sharp warning that the political must not be confused with the kingdom, see John Paul II, *Centesimus Annus*, §25: "What Sacred Scripture teaches us about the prospects of the Kingdom of God is not without consequences for the life of temporal societies, which, as the adjective indicates, belong to the realm of time, with all that this implies of imperfection and impermanence. The Kingdom of God, being in the world without being of the world, throws light on the order of human society, while the power of grace penetrates that order and gives it life." See also §§47 and 55.

50. Ratzinger, *Jesus of Nazareth*, 2:170–71.

51. See the Congregation for the Doctrine of the Faith, *Instruction on Christian Freedom and Liberation*, approved by Pope John Paul II and signed by Prefect Joseph Cardinal Ratzinger and Secretary Alberto Bovone (March 22, 1986), §§62 and 65.

He adds: "Nevertheless, we must not be too hasty in condemning the 'purely political' outlook of [Jesus's] opponents. For in the world they inhabited, the two spheres—political and religious—were inseparable. The 'purely' political existed no more than the 'purely' religious."[52] Before Christ integralism has a place in human history insofar as men and women do not understand the radically new kingdom.

IV. Avatars

Last year marked the fiftieth anniversary of Étienne Gilson's Louvain lectures, which were published under the title *The Metamorphoses of the City of God*.[53] His main theme is the problem of achieving a universal human society. He explores the problem through the thoughts of seven Christian, or at least Christian-inspired, thinkers.[54] On this occasion our interests will be given to Gilson's understanding of eschatology.

Let us set the scene. Gilson was addressing the political and ecclesial leaders in the West in the early 1950s. A *kairos*, a new moment had been declared for the terrene city in both its domestic and international tasks. These included: De-colonization, rebuilding of western Europe, the founding of the United Nations and the publication of the Universal Declaration of Human Rights, nuclear disarmament, and of course the readjustment of the Church's evangelical mission. There were two decades of optimism, which subsided rather quickly by the late 1960s. Gilson set out to challenge this moment. These lectures are a tenacious and lucid identification of the principles that we have already marked in this essay.

His thesis and conclusion can be considered in this arresting thought:

> If a lesson emerges about the history of the City of God and the avatars it has assumed during the course of centuries, it is, first of all, that it cannot be metamorphosized. . . . What is common to these attempts is the substitution of a human bond for the bond of faith. . . . This occurs in the hope that [some] human bond will be universalized more easily than faith.[55]

In a 1933 lecture to students at St. Michael's College (Toronto), Gilson summarized this very dilemma at work in *Action Française*. "These men will keep

---

52. Ratzinger, *Jesus of Nazareth*, 2:169.

53. Étienne Gilson, *The Metamorphoses of the City of God*, trans. James G. Colbert (Washington, DC: The Catholic University of America Press, 2020).

54. Roger Bacon, Dante, Nicholas of Cusa, Tommaso Campanella, Abbé of Saint Pierre, Leibniz, Auguste Comte. We will not treat any of these chapters, for we are narrowly interested in Gilson's eschatology, which is found in Chs. 1, 2, and 10.

55. Gilson, *Metamorphoses*, 227.

the Church even though they are at heart pagans. The state cannot live without the Church. . . . Consequently they will stick to the Church as a political means of keeping their own country alive." Just as we pointed out earlier in connection with Ratzinger, Gilson insists that the Church cannot help a society unless it is actually the Church—"that is an entity which in no way can be subordinated to the French State."[56] Elsewhere, Gilson notes that this line of thinking is common among those who are "deeply interested in Rome but not in Jerusalem." In making this point Gilson brings us back around to Augustine's admonition of his flock after 410. How does the Church assist the state? She can do so by teaching and living according to the principles of the moral order. Yet even these principles reflect a natural wisdom that is higher than political order. This in itself is a reminder of what is wrong with *politique d'abord*. Without its eschatology, the Church is not truly itself.[57]

There is no other way to know and to have the kingdom except to participate by faith. On this score, in *Metamorphoses* Gilson cites Thomas Aquinas:

> The Divine Wisdom, that knows all things most fully, has deigned to reveal these her secrets to men, and in proof of them has displayed works beyond the competence of all natural powers, in the wonderful cure of diseases, in the raising of the dead, and what is more wonderful still, in such inspiration of human minds as that simple and ignorant persons, filled with the gift of the Holy Ghost, have gained in an instant the height of wisdom and eloquence. By force of the aforesaid proof, without violence of arms, without promise of pleasures, and, most wonderful thing of all, in the midst of the violence of persecutors, a countless multitude, not only of the uneducated but of the wisest men, flocked to the Christian faith, wherein doctrines are preached that transcend all human understanding, pleasures of sense are restrained, and a contempt is taught of all worldly possessions. That mortal minds should assent to such teaching is the greatest of miracles [*maximum miraculorum*], and a manifest work of divine inspiration leading men to despise the visible and desire only invisible goods.[58]

Gilson remarks that faith is not naturally transmittable by simple rational demonstration, but rather stems from "consent in which the will takes a part,

---

56. Florian Michel, *Étienne Gilson, une biographie intellectuelle et politique* (Paris: Vrin, 2018), 115n3.

57. Gilson calls this fusion of politics and the kingdom a "doctrinal teratology"—combining two things that create a "monster," the opposite of what is integral. See Gilson, *The Philosopher and Theology*, trans. Cecile Gilson (New York: Random House, 1962), 58–59. See also Florian Michel's discussion of *tératologie doctrinale* in Ch. 2 of *Étienne Gilson*, esp. 115–17.

58. *SCG*, I, c. 6.

and this is precisely why the problem is posed of finding how to universalize it."[59] The supernatural virtue of faith is the Holy Spirit moving the will to move the intellect. It is not so much a search as it is an adherence to the divine Word. The kingdom begins in creatures by the adherence to Christ. It is already eschatological. In this sense we should use the term "integral." The human and divine share a life. It is the greatest of miracles. Distinguished, but inseparable in Christ.

The "avatars" of Christendom, Gilson continues, substitute for the theological virtues an intra-mundane task or mission, what Ratzinger calls "building a better world work site." This task comes under morals, the human participation in the eternal law, the fundaments of which are shared by all human beings. But, as Ratzinger suggests, "the entire confession of faith" is brought under the "single theme of hope."[60] Shorn of the "eschatological attitude" flowing from grace, we are left with a Social Gospel that waits upon the evolution of history without the adherence of supernatural faith and remains unmindful of what Gilson calls the "shadow of the Cross."[61]

We will let Chantal Delsol have the last word. "In its pretention to establish itself as a civilization, Christianity ended up producing a monstrous avatar that is at the same time its alter-ego and its mortal enemy." We take her to be saying this: When the Christian Church sloughs off faith, it lets loose phony eschatologies in the world, avatars; but what is worse is that the Church herself becomes an avatar of the temporal powers.[62] And thus separation in the proper theological sense is regarded as an evil. And it would be if we were talking only about social things: marriage and family, polity, international order.

In this essay, however, we are talking about how to inherit a kingdom. Here, being set apart is the beginning of wisdom.

---

59. Gilson, *Metamorphoses*, 220.
60. Ratzinger, *Eschatology*, 59.
61. Gilson, *Metamorphoses*, 235.
62. Chantal Delsol, *La fin de la Chrétienté* (Paris: Cerf, 2021), 149–50.

CHAPTER 14

What Saint Benedict Taught the Dark Ages: His and Ours

THE RENAISSANCE HUMANIST PETRARCH first introduced the term *tempus tenebrae* in the fourteenth century in order to mark and to scorn the time in which the barbaric tribes had defiled Latin language and literature.[1] Later, Enlightenment thinkers would see the dark ages not so much in terms of literary snobbery, but as Immanuel Kant put it, a "self-imposed immaturity." "Immaturity," he explained, "is the inability to use one's understanding without guidance from another."[2] But the Gospel of John (1:9–15) speaks of a deeper darkness and a different light:

> The true light that gives light to everyone was coming into the world. He was in the world, and though the world was made through him, *the world did not recognize him.* He came to that which was his own, but his own did not receive him. Yet to all who did receive him, to those who believed in his name, he gave the right to become children of God— children born not of natural descent, nor of human decision or a husband's will, but born of God. The Word became flesh and made his dwelling among us. We have seen his glory, the glory of the one and only Son, who came from the Father, full of grace and truth. John [as a voice "calling in the desert"] testified concerning him. He cried out, saying, "This is the one I spoke about when I said, 'He who comes after me has surpassed me because he was before me'."

In the wilderness, the Gospel sounds the most profound theme of Christian experience: A Light appears in the darkness of the fallen world. For the Christian imagination formed in Scripture and monastic culture, the Evangelist's "dark age" did not represent a period of cultural history, as it did for the Renaissance.

Rather, for the monastic culture, the notion of a "dark age" was drawn from theological anthropology and Christology. The story was summed up

---

1. Theodore E. Mommsen, "Petrarch's Conception of the 'Dark Ages,'" *Speculum* 17, no. 2 (1942): 226–42.
2. Kant, "An Answer to the Question: What is Enlightenment? (1784)," in *Perpetual Peace and Other Essays*, trans. Ted Humphrey (Indianapolis: Hackett Publishing, 1983), 41.

in the first chapter of John and the fourth chapter of Luke. Adam and his progeny were cast from paradise into a desert—into what Saint Augustine called "a region of dissimilitude"—where the race of men were caught in the brambles of sin, knowing not the Light, and therefore not truly understanding themselves. And so the New Adam went into the desert in search of the old Adam. Praying, fasting and being tempted by the devil for 40 days, the Incarnate Word showed the way back to the house of the Father.

St. Benedict was not the first Christian who went into the desert to discover this Light. But he is justly renowned for molding a simple but sturdy institution for those who are in search of it. At least in this sense—and also in a secondary, historical and cultural sense—Benedict is the patron saint of Lent, the season of the desert and for overcoming darkness.

I would like in this essay to suggest the significance of Saint Benedict for his "dark age" as well as our own by means of four little compositions along the lines of nocturnes. Nocturnes, of course, were the night offices said in a monastery, a spiritual analogue to the nocturnal plant; in biology, a nocturne can mean a plant that flowers in the dark. But in modern times, a nocturne is a musical composition evoking a nighttime theme or being performed at night. And so I offer the following four vignettes: Owl of Minerva, Dark Ages, Curriculum, and Harkening.

THE OWL OF MINERVA: WISDOM IN TWILIGHT

Hegel once wrote:

One more word about giving instruction as to *what the world ought to be*. Philosophy in any case always comes on the scene too late to give it. . . . When philosophy paints its gloomy picture, then a form of life has grown old. It cannot be rejuvenated by the [philosopher's] gloomy picture, but only understood. Only when the dusk starts to fall does the owl of Minerva spread its wings and fly.[3]

Hegel's aphorism can be interpreted in different ways. He probably means to say that life rather than philosophy is prescriptive. The Philosopher can grasp the whole of a thing only when it is complete, in the face of which there is no point legislating what *ought* to be. Perhaps Hegel also means that only when a civilization approaches its demise can the Owl of Wisdom take stock of its essential genius, which Hegel calls its life form (*Gestalt*). *Only at the end of a civilization do its geniuses appear*, like a swan who sings one beautiful song

---

3. George W. F. Hegel, *The Philosophy of Right*, trans. T. M. Knox (Oxford: Oxford University Press, 1967), 12–13.

before it dies. Hence, the Owl of Minerva takes flight not at the morning star or in the noonday sun, but in the dusk.

From a monastic perspective, the Minervian moment is marked at the seventh liturgical office of the day, which Benedict calls Vespers. The word "Vesper" is taken from Greek mythology: *Hesperus* is the personification of the evening star, the planet Venus in its evening appearance; the *Vespera*, then, are prayers at the time of shadows. Measured from the first light of morning-tide, the *vespera* fall sometime between the tenth and the twelfth hours, between 4 and 6 p.m., depending on the season. In C. 41 of the Rule, Benedict prescribes that these prayers are to be chanted before the need of artificial light.

This time is distinguished from the *very* end of the day, which is marked by the office of Compline (from the verb *complere*, to complete). Compline is chanted at about 8:30 p.m. With it, the hours of the day are finished, and the monks, in hope of the resurrection, submit themselves to the Great Silence: to a darkness that swallows all human knowledge, like the tomb that awaits every son of man. *Wisdom therefore must come in the shadows, just as Hegel suggested—in the dusk, rather than the night;* just when things are complete enough for us to take their measure and to consider "what the world ought to be," but not so complete that wisdom itself slips into the oblivion of darkness.

For the monastic tradition, the *vespera* represent a time of judgment—of the hours of the day, of the individual soul, of the people, of the race of man. No less an authority than Saint Augustine himself speculated that after Adam and Eve sinned, and hid from God, He came to find and to judge them at the hour of vespers.[4] Why at this time? God can judge the defendant while there is still light—not just physical light, but more importantly the *lumen synderesis*, the light of conscience, which was already partially in eclipse by the shadows of sin.

---

4. See Augustine, *On Genesis: Two Books on Genesis Against the Manichees; And, On the Literal Interpretation of Genesis, an Unfinished Book*, Fathers of the Church, vol. 84 (Washington, DC: The Catholic University of America Press, 2001), 119:

> Toward evening God was walking in paradise (Gn 3:8), that is, he was coming to judge them. He was still walking in paradise before their punishment, that is, the presence of God still moved among them, when they no longer stood firm in his command. It is fitting [that he comes] toward evening, that is, when the sun was already setting for them, that is, when the interior light of the truth was being taken from them. They heard his voice and hid from his sight. Who hides from the sight of God but he who has abandoned him and is now beginning to love what is his own? . . . For the human soul can be a partaker in the truth, but the truth is the immutable God above it. Hence, whoever turns away from that truth and turns toward himself and does not rejoice in God who rules and enlightens him, but rather in his own seemingly free movements, becomes dark by reason of the lie.

In monasteries under the Rule of Benedict, four consecutive psalms are usually chanted at Vespers: Psalm 109 ("He judgeth among the nations, making their ruin complete"); Psalm 110 ("He hath shown His people the power of his works"); Psalm 111 ("Blessed is the man that feareth the Lord. . . . He shineth to the righteous as a light in darkness"); and Psalm 112 ("From the rising of the sun to its going down let the Name of the Lord be praised"). Then the monks proceed to chant an ancient hymn entitled *Lucis Creator* with its verse: "Creator of Light, who joins morning and the shadows, and for our instruction calls it a day." *Wisdom depends on our ability to know a day and how to take its measure.* Thus were monks enjoined, at Compline, to say with the Psalmist: "So teach us to number our days, that we may apply our hearts unto wisdom" (Ps 90:12).[5]

Let us return, for a moment, to Hegel's image of wisdom arising, phoenix-like, just as a civilization reaches its demise. The *clear* and the *obscure are* mixed together, such that what is clear is all the more intelligible because of the shadows. Applied to history, we see the beginning only at the end—but the *chiaroscuro* consists chiefly in this: that the beginning is the very thing that is ending, and ending is the beginning of something else. The greatest historical figures occupy this time of vespers. They represent with a proper and profound ambiguity the best of what has declined and the seeds of what will come. The Catholic Church of Late Antiquity provides us with two such Minervian figures: Augustine and Benedict.

Augustine was born in 354, the son of a minor official in a provincial town in Roman North Africa. He was formed in the trivium: grammar, rhetoric and logic. Although he complained about the intellectual shallowness and the moral turpitude of his own education, anyone who would pick up his work is bedazzled by what he learned. For elegance of style and for the power of speculative intellect, Augustine was, I dare say, the greatest thinker produced by Roman culture. When he died in 430, his city was surrounded by the Vandals. In retrospect, we are entitled to think that this was the vespers of the ancient world. Augustine himself didn't think so; he believed that he lived in the very cultural-political world of Graeco-Roman civilization. All of Augustine's fathers—which is to say, his teachers—were ancient grammarians, rhetoricians, philosophers, and theologians. And one is always laid to rest with one's fathers, not with one's great-grandchildren.

For his part, Benedict was born in 480, 50 years after Augustine's death. He, too, came from a provincial Roman town, Nursia (today, Norcia), in the

---

5. See *Benedict's Rule: A Translation and Commentary*, trans. Terrence G. Kardong (Collegeville, MN: The Liturgical Press, 1996), Ch. 18. Ps 90 is the only psalm explicitly used by Satan to tempt Christ. See Mt 4:6. Hence, the monastic theme of the night and the ruler of darkness, the dragon.

mountains of Umbria; going back some 1,200 years, this was the borderland of the Etruscans and the Samnite tribes. He too was the son of a Roman civil official. As an adolescent, Benedict was sent, along with his nanny, to Rome to learn the very same trivium studied by Augustine. First, he needed to become a *grammaticus*. What was grammar? The knowledge of words. According to the ancient wisdom: "Everything which does not deserve to pass into oblivion and has been entrusted to writing, belongs necessarily to the province of grammar." Like Augustine, Benedict absorbed himself in grammar but worried that rhetoric was morally corruptive. Augustine did not pray for an emancipation from rhetoric until his was in his mid-30s (indeed, in Bk. 9 of the *Confessions* he describes his baptism as a liberation from rhetoric); in stark contrast, Benedict renounced rhetoric at the age of 16 or 17. So far as we know, he studied only the first segment of the trivium.[6] He never renounced grammar—indeed his Rule requires that the brothers learn to read, in order to appropriate the external word of scripture (1) as it is on the page and (2) as it is expressed as a liturgical word in choir. And thus Benedict represents the via media between the loquacious Augustine and the hermit monk St. Antony, the greatest of monks, who remained illiterate in order to attend only to the *internal word* that manifests itself in the desert and brambles of the soul.

Abandoning his formal education, Benedict tried to live the monastic life as a hermit in caves in the vicinity of Subiaco, not far from Rome. Like the desert father, St. Antony, Benedict learned experimentally. He became so proficient in knowledge of the divine word that other monks asked him to be their master. In the Rule, Benedict says that he intends to found a school— in Latin, a *schola*—for the service of God.

Yet his first attempts to educate and govern other monks were troubled, to say the least. On at least two occasions, his monastic sons tried to murder him—indeed, in the old-fashioned Italian way, which was by poisoning. Benedict was discreet and prudent, eventually learning how to govern monks—he even went so far to allow a bit of wine every day to combat "sadness" and to relieve the temptation of "murmuring."[7] Control over murmuring is a greater achievement than eloquence in letters.

---

6. The hermit Antony, who was a spiritual model and inspiration for both Augustine and Benedict, was illiterate, despite being reared in an affluent family. Saint Athanasius says of the young Antony, "he could not endure to learn letters" (*Life of St. Antony*, §1). The father of Christian monasticism, he was given entirely to the "inner Word." "His memory," Athanasius remarks, "served him for books" (§3). See *Select Works and Letters*, vol. IV, *Nicene and Post-Nicene Fathers, Series II*, ed. P. Schaff and H. Wace (Grand Rapids, MI: Eerdmans, 1980), 195–96.

7. *Rule*, Ch. 40.

Learning by trial and error, he went on to found 13 monasteries. Moving to Cassinum, some 70 miles southwest of Rome, Benedict ascended the 1,800-foot-high Monte Cassino in 529, and there, at the summit, over the top of a demolished temple of Apollo, he laid the altar for his greatest monastery. A year later, he began to write his Rule. Written in vulgar or ordinary Latin, and amounting to fewer than 9,000 words, it is quite different than Augustine's work. It has neither eloquence nor speculative power. Untold thousands of souls have been converted by reading Augustine, but it is hard to imagine anyone being converted merely by reading Benedict's Rule.

If Augustine was the greatest stylist and speculative thinker of the Roman world, Benedict exemplified, in the vespers of that civilization, the genius unique to Rome. Romans always knew that their language and speculative tradition were inferior to the Greeks; that their religion was inferior to the Eastern religions, especially the Egyptians; that their aesthetics were inferior to the Greeks and the Carthaginians. Rome's destiny was different. As Virgil boasted in the *Aeneid:*

> Roman, remember by your strength to rule Earth's peoples
> —for your arts are to be these:
> To pacify, to impose the rule of law,
> To spare the conquered [and] battle down the proud.

The shadows had lengthened since the time of Augustine. Benedict was born 70 years after Alaric and his Vandals sacked Rome, less than 30 years after Attila's Huns had swept through Italy, and only two years after the demise of the last Emperor in the West, Romulus Augustulus. *In this sense—and only in this sense—can Benedict be regarded as a Minervian owl. As Roman civilization collapsed around him, he established a Christian institution that nevertheless carried the stamp of Roman genius.* Albeit in ways unimagined and unanticipated, Benedict's Rule proved to be the greatest pacification program in Western history. Otherwise, there is no evidence that Benedict thought of himself or his monastic Rule as either the end or the beginning of any epoch. As a man of the ancient world, he had no intention to transmit any wisdom other than the ancient one.

After all, Christianity and monasticism first arose and were practiced as an ancient wisdom. Benedict perhaps first learned of monasticism from Syrian hermits who lived in caves around Norcia. These and other monks simply believed that they were imitating Christ and his apostles. The monks had read the scriptures and sought to imitate Luke 4: Led by the Spirit into the wilderness for 40 days, Christ prayed, fasted and was tempted by the Devil. We return again to the story recapitulated by the monastic search. The first Adam sinned and was expelled from the garden of delights—thrown into a wilderness—like the Prodigal Son in the plantation of sorrows, eating food not fit for the swine and not knowing the way back to the house of the Father. As Augustine explained, "For on whatever place one has fallen, on that place he must find support that he may rise again."[8] The new Adam begins where the old Adam fell, Christ went into the desert to confront Adam's nemesis.

Many things and institutions have their origin in the medieval centuries: parliament, romance vernaculars, the heavy plow, tidal mills, cannons, the spinning wheel, universities, glass mirrors, and percussion drilling, invented by Cistercians. But monasticism is not an invention of the Middle Ages. It comes instead from a more ancient light discovered in the desert, from an ancient wisdom molded by Benedict's Roman genius. In the last chapter of the Rule, Cap. 73, entitled, "The Whole of Just Observance Is Not Contained in This Rule," Benedict insists that whatever is taught in this Rule is only a part of what is transmitted from the Holy Fathers. And by the "Fathers" he meant (1) the Apostles, (2) the authors of Holy Writ, (3) the example of the Desert Fathers, and (4) those who have written Institutes for the governance of monks. He concludes: "Whoever you are (*quisquis*) hastening toward your heavenly homeland; fulfill with the help of Christ this little Rule for beginners." And this is perhaps the key sentence in the Rule. *Benedict founds a school for beginners.*

To be sure, it includes rules for reading and writing, for chanting, for using and cleaning farm implements, for greeting strangers, for determining prices for goods sent to market, for the organization of crafts and many other simple, practical details. The school is free—no tuition by way of social class or money. We learn in Cap. 58 that the only thing necessary is a willing heart to seek God (*quaerere deum*) and adherence to the Rule under the Abbot. Benedict's Rule governs a monastery in which the rich and the poor alike begin as beginners. And these beginners begin where the Light first appeared—in the desert.

But Benedict's wisdom, genius, and "legacy," for which history rightly esteems him, certainly extend beyond the modest walls of the monastery or the humble souls of the monks. If one goes to Benedict's hometown of Norcia, a little town of about 4,600 souls nested in the mountains of Umbria, one quickly happens on the Piazza di San Benedetto. On the far end of the piazza stand a church and a monastery built over the top of the Roman-era apartment building in which Benedict was raised. In the center of the piazza is a statue of Benedict, made by Giuseppe Pinzi in the late nineteenth century. The inscription reads:

> Founder and Father of Monasticism in the Western regions, he was driven by the Spirit to a life hidden from society. From whence there arose a renaissance of letters, the useful arts, agriculture, and sciences.

---

8. Augustine, *De Vera Religione*, XXIV, 45.

The inscription is quite astute. Benedict, it suggests, is the patron saint of Europe not so much because of the civilizing of culture accomplished by his monasticism but *because he went into the desert*. This reveals the spiritual root of European culture. Europe's claim to fame, in other words, is not so much that it relearned and perfected the arts and sciences preserved by monks during the Dark Ages, but rather that *Europe is a civilization grown from a cultivated desert*. This is a quite radical claim, made in our own day more than once by Pope Benedict XVI, who suggested that the current crisis of European identity should be understood in terms of what the Benedictines did in the wasteland: Were they merely technicians who invented tools to till the soil, or were they about the business of clearing the weeds growing in the human soul?[9]

If Benedict's Rule established nothing but a trade school for learning the useful arts—slightly eccentric monks who figured out how to build windmills—it quickly would have made itself obsolete. For it is in the very nature of such an enterprise to graduate its students into more advanced skills. This is how humanists in modern times interpreted the story of Benedict's "school." *But* if the monastic school teaches its students to awake from the mortal slumber of the Old Adam, and like the Prodigal to run to the Father, no one (in this life, anyway) can claim to be a graduate, and the capacity of monastic culture to renew culture from within is truly boundless.[10]

How to be "a beginner": This is the first thing Benedict teaches the Dark Ages, his and ours. To be a beginner in this way is not a primitive condition to be outgrown but rather a sign of advancement and the mark of a return to the most essential. It is what everyone needs to relearn each Lent and learn again amid the vespers of our present age.

---

9. Benedict XVI, *Spe Salvi*, §15. See also Benedict XVI, "General Audience," April 9, 2008, and also his "Address to the World of Culture," September 12, 2008.

10. How else can we explain the fact that, over the subsequent centuries, Benedict's sons and daughters created thousands of these schools under the "little rule for beginners"? By the eleventh century, the great Benedictine monastery of Cluny in France had nearly 1,000 daughter houses and affiliated monasteries, constituting a vast, trans-national corporation. Within the Cluniac system alone, there were more Benedictine monasteries than there are McDonalds in France today. A nineteenth-century scholar claimed to have found evidence for the existence of some 37,000 Benedictine houses. (By way of comparison, today there are about 4,100 universities, colleges and two-year colleges in the US.) A mid-nineteenth-century enumeration put it down as follows: 37,000 houses, 30 popes, four emperors, 46 kings, 51 queens, 1,406 princes, 1,600 archbishops, 600 bishops, and 15,000 abbots and learned men. And who knows how many souls who lived in those cloisters whose names and numbers are long forgotten! For Cardinal Newman's counting in the nineteenth century, see Newman, "The Mission of St. Benedict," in *Historical Sketches*, vol. 2 (New York: Longmans, Greens, 1906), 372.

Dark Ages

In 1911, the 11th edition of the *Encyclopedia Britannica* stated that the period from the fifth to the 10th centuries is called "the dark Age."[11] Yet by the time of the Second World War, the 14th edition had a change of heart, now insisting that "the contrast, once so fashionable, between the ages of darkness and the ages of light has no more truth in it than have the idealistic fancies which underlie attempts at medieval revivalism."[12] No self-respecting scholar today, it suggests, would use the term "dark ages" to periodize, categorize or otherwise to mark historical time and events, much less culture.

In my view, however, it is a mistake to drop "dark ages" altogether. The collapse of Roman order in the West *was* devastating.[13] That Roman order was urban and urbane; in the early fifth century it included something like a thousand municipalities, bound together by a civilian, demilitarized aristocracy that spoke Latin and Greek. At its zenith, the city of Rome had more than a million inhabitants; it was served by 11 aqueducts bringing water from as far as 59 miles, over arches 100 feet tall.

These cities, including those of much smaller caliber, were the center of civilization: of business, politics, fine art, patronage, libraries, buildings on a large scale, artisans, diplomacy. The patriarchs and metropolitans of the Christian Church led Christians from the major cities: Rome, Constantinople, Antioch, Alexandria, Milan, Ravenna.

Stationed along the Empire's borders was an army of roughly a half million men, along with a couple hundred thousand auxiliary and part-time units. All told, it was about the same size as the US Army and Marines Corps today. To equip and provision this enormous and highly mobile force required more than 50 state factories, which made swords and arrows, processed leather for various gear and made woolen products such as socks and shirts. About half of the imperial budget went to feeding, equipping and paying the army; another third went to the maintenance of key cities, including the grain and oil handouts to the urban masses; and the rest to the bureaucracy. It is estimated that taxes on agricultural yield from land was

---

11. The so-called monastic centuries (or "Benedictine Centuries") coincide with the Dark Ages. In the West, we are speaking roughly of 500 years, from the sixth century to the end of the eleventh century.

12. *The Encyclopedia Britannica*, 14th ed., ed. James Louis Garvin, Franklin Hooper, and Warren E. Cox, vol. 15 (The Encyclopedia Britannica Company, 1929), 449.

13. In the next few paragraphs I collate data drawn mostly from two recent books: Bryan Ward-Perkins, *The Fall of Rome and the End of Civilization* (Oxford: Oxford University Press, 2005), and Chris Wickham, *Inheritance of Rome: Illuminating the Dark Ages* (New York: Viking Penguin, 2009).

constant at about 25 percent. This was the cash cow that maintained the army and the urban projects.

But when the barbarians penetrated and then overwhelmed the imperial armies beginning in the fifth century, the tax revenue evaporated. The agriculturally rich North Africa, where Augustine lived, was lost to the Vandals in 439, causing an 80 percent reduction in taxes from that region alone by the sixth century. In the aftermath of all this, what emerged in the West was a Libertarian heaven—monies for large public projects would disappear for hundreds of years. But so would cities of more than 50,000 people. By the thirteenth century, only a handful of cities in the West could support 100,000 people: London, Paris, Milan, and perhaps Genoa. Here are just a few things that indicate the "darkness" that fell upon this period:

- Fourth-century levels of maritime trade across the Mediterranean would not be restored until the nineteenth century.
- Drilling through the ice pack in Greenland, scientists have discovered that as the factories closed, the pollution caused by the smelting of lead, copper and silver fell to prehistoric levels, not to be regained until the seventeenth century.
- The art of making pottery on a wheel disappeared from Britain for more than three centuries.
- Abundant coinage disappeared; household utensils, such as cups with glossy surfaces, easy to wash and easy to stack due to standardized shapes, became unknown to men.
- With the demise of cities came the demise of literacy. Consider that Charlemagne, the emperor, circa 800, never could quite get the hang of writing.

It is possible to continue for some time in this vein, simply enumerating all of the things that vanished first from the earth, and then from common human memory.

But what is most important to understand for our present purpose is why the falling dominoes were so hard to put back into place. The answer is that the Empire depended on an extraordinarily far-flung division of labor and knowledge. A northern Italian peasant of the third or fourth century might eat off tableware from Naples, store liquids in amphorae from North Africa, sleep under a roof consisting of tiles from the south of Gaul and be governed by a civil administrator from Tuscany. Along the Tiber as it snakes through Rome is a place called Monte Testaccio. Here, archaeologists discovered the remains of some 53 million amphorae, all imported from Iberia, in which approximately 6 trillion liters of oil were imported from overseas.

It is important to draw the right moral lesson from this story. The Dark Ages were dark not merely because the lights of technology were extinguished, but because *no one knew how to reproduce the whole of the civilization*.

The "light" that was lost was not the tool or *techne* but knowledge and wisdom. And we too are capable of losing that light even in the midst of our highly advanced tools and technology. A "dark" age does not consist merely of technological ignorance; worse yet is having forgotten how to live a good life rather than a life of mere subsistence. Consider all of the things we might not know how to do without sharing in a tradition of wisdom.

- Prepare a corpse for burial.
- Decide whether grandma is dead.
- Adjudicate conflicting legal claims between business enterprises.
- Recite from memory Jewish and Christian scriptures. Throw in the US and state constitutions.
- Remember all of the countries.
- Judge what is an authentic and an inauthentic copy of a book.
- Recall one's paternal ancestors by name five generations back.
- Distinguish carefully between what is established fact and what is mere speculation in any given physical science.
- Distinguish between law and mere force.
- Distinguish what is pleasant to the senses from what is good.
- Distinguish what is good from what is morally good.
- Distinguish between transitory relationships key to survival and enduring memberships, such as one's status in a family or in a polity.

Every day would be a disorganized disaster. It is worth reflecting on the possibility that technology alone is not the only factor that marks civilization from a dark age. The European Dark Ages teach us that the more diversified the functions of a civilization, the more necessary it is that at least some people know what is a life worth living versus a life worth merely enduring. The Dark Ages were dark because people simply forgot what the Owl of Minerva understands— namely, the way the world ought to be or, at least, the way it once was.

As one will discover when reading the Rule, in addition to their commitment to poverty, chastity, and obedience, like other consecrated religious, the Benedictine monks also promise stability (*stabilitas*) and reform of manners (*conversatio morum*). Stability was perhaps the most important vow for the Dark Ages. For when the Benedictines established a community, they were there to stay. Unlike the warrior class, which was mobile and just short of nomadic, the monks would arrive, clear the forests, and irrigate and cultivate the land. Within earshot of the bells, laypeople could begin again to measure time. From the monks they learned how to properly bury the dead, how to read and write—how to do things that transcend a life of mere subsistence. *In summary fashion, this is what Benedict taught the Dark Ages: how to live life as a whole when forces of disintegration and confusion abound.* Not a life of worldly success so much as one of human success. Not only how to divide a day, but how to divide it unto wisdom.

CURRICULUM

If monastic life according to the Rule, as a "school for beginners," can be said to follow any "curriculum," this is because Benedict taught an integrated and integrating knowledge. This he did along three fronts: He taught *materially*, *politically*, and *poetically*. But it is the poetic that suffuses the Benedictine school. All three return us to the fundamentals of knowledge, to the "beginning" of that wisdom and integrity of life still possible in the desert and evening of an age.

First, as regards the *material of life*, nothing is more important than light and dark: namely, an answer to the question, "What suffices for a day?" Infants and very young children are ignorant of what constitutes a day. I am told that even college students have problems in this regard—that a collegiate "day" is a 24/7 flow of flickering images resembling a casino in Nevada. Like the practical wisdom displayed in Genesis, Benedict begins with a Day. A day equally measured: eight hours of prayer, eight hours of labor, eight hours of rest, adjusted for the seasons.

A day having been properly established, the Rule prescribes a unity of things that the ancient world had usually kept apart: on the one hand, the free or liberal arts and sciences, cultivated and practiced by the nobility. This was called a *universitas personarum*, things tending toward one *in and for* the dignity of human persons. On the other hand stood the work of artisans and manual laborers. This was called a *universitas rerum*, a unity for the sake of the things being organized: the bricks, the streets, the monies. Benedict taught the proper order of these things. Tools for the sake of monks, monks for the sake of God—hierarchy of action without distinction by class.

In the ancient world, personal dignity was measured by its remotion or distance from tools and labor. Indeed, the rural warrior class in these centuries of the Middle Ages did not work the land. They killed with their hands, but they did not work with them. Benedict's motto was *Ora et Labora et Lectio*: prayer, work, and reading.[14] The monks therefore are at once contemplatives and laborers.[15]

---

14. The common, shorter version of the motto, *ora et labora*, seems to have been invented rather recently. Paul G. Monson argues that the motto actually originates in America, not Germany, with Martin Marty. See Monson, *"Ora et Labora*: A Benedictine Motto Born in America?"* in *God Has Begun a Great Work in Us: Embodied Love in Consecrated Life and Ecclesial Movements*, ed. J. King and S. Schrein, *College Theology Society Annual*, vol. 60 (Maryknoll, NY: Orbis, 2015), 66–86.

15. Jedis who do the work of artisans and serfs: a very powerful and useful combination. See Jude P. Dougherty, "'Intellectuals with Dirt under Their Fingernails': Attitudes toward Sciences and Technology and the Difference They Make," *Communio* 9 (1982):

Reading is essential in Benedict's school, for it joins together prayer and work. Consider the acts associated with reading, and the materiality involved: speaking, meditating, cogitating, imagining, remembering, understanding, desiring.[16] By summoning so many different mental and physical actions or postures, reading can be profoundly integrative. It forms a clearing in the forest of the sensations of the soul and creates a place for study and prayer. Lent, whether liturgically speaking or culturally speaking, should be a time for reading, at least in the sense understood by the monastic culture.

As regards the *social organization* of human persons in the monastery (political knowledge), three things are extremely important from a sociological perspective: First, it is characterized by easy entrance and difficult exit. The monastery is a voluntary society that is not especially picky about who joins. Within a month or so, the applicant is inside the walls; a few years later he is professed, and solemnly professed a couple of years after that. Yet the learning curve is long—the rest of one's life. Second, each abbey is quasi-autonomous and self-sufficient under the rule of its own abbot. The key to self-sufficiency is the vow of stability. This is the Benedictine understanding of 1 Peter 2:5: "You also, like living stones, are being built into a spiritual house." Third, the Benedictine Rule emphasizes equality among the brothers. For most public purposes, monks are distinguished only by their date of entrance—that is, according to a principle of seniority. Even the youngest monks can vote in an abbatial election.

All of these add up to a sturdy social structure in the wilderness: literate men or women, under a common rule and superior, knowing how to divide a day and how to live a stable life in a certain place, not only within a day but over years, competent to contemplate and to work with their hands, having as their only standard of admission that the novice have a willing heart, and all of them counting themselves as beginners from the day they enter the monastery until they die. From inside the monastic perspective, it does not

---

224–37, and earlier essay by Lynn White, Jr., "Dynamo and Virgin Reconsidered," in *Dynamo and Virgin Reconsidered: Essays in the Dynamism of Western Culture* (Cambridge, MA: MIT Press, 1968), 57–73. Not surprisingly, it would yield great fortunes for some monasteries. Look especially at Cap. 57 of Benedict's Rule on how to price monastic products sent to market (in a spirit of charity and poverty, the monks ought to sell them under the market rate).

16. For the monk, each word is like a hook, catching hold of other words; the monk was like a living concordance. As Dom Jean Leclercq puts it, reminiscences are not quotations, but the words of the person using them. Monastic readers become like a living concordance. Jean Leclercq, *The Love of Learning and the Desire for God: A Study of Monastic Culture* (New York: Fordham University Press, 1982), 77.

really matter too much whether the whole thing is destroyed so long as it starts again—since it can always begin again. It was never meant to be anything but a school for beginners. And there is always another child of the Old Adam who awakes from slumber and will become a brother.

The third of Benedict's ways of teaching, and to my mind the most important, is one fit for a child—or someone seeking to be childlike. One teaches a child through the senses and the imagination—that is, *poetically*. In one of his greatest essays, "The Mission of St. Benedict," John Henry Newman reckoned that the three great paradigms of teaching in Latin Christianity were Benedict, who taught *poetically*, Dominic, who taught *scientifically*, and Ignatius of Loyola, who taught *practically*.[17]

By poetry Newman did not necessarily mean the craft of poetry, which is the craft of constructing metered verse. Rather, he meant a way of learning that arises from sense, experience, and imagination. Its special feature is wonder, or what the Latin speaking peoples called *ad-miratio*. Admiration is taken from the adjective *mirus*, wonderful. We could call it *knowledge touched by the thing being known*. For his part, Aristotle used the word "*thaûma*" (θαῦμα), meaning "miracle" and "*thaumazein*" (θαυμάζειν), which means "to admire." Wonder lies at the root of knowledge, which begins in the senses: "All men by nature desire to know. An indication of this is the delight we take in our senses; for even apart from their usefulness they are loved for themselves; and above all others the sense of sight."[18]

Thus, the genius of the Benedictine method of teaching and learning involves knowledge touched by the thing being known through the senses. Newman contrasts this "poetic" pedagogy to the "scientific" approach:

> Reason investigates, analyzes, numbers, weighs, measures, ascertains, locates, the objects of its contemplation, and thus gains a scientific knowledge of them. Science results in system, which is complex unity; poetry delights in the indefinite and various as contrasted with unity, and in the simple as contrasted with system. The aim of science is to get a hold of things, to grasp them, to handle them, to comprehend them; that is (to use the familiar term), to *master* them, or to be superior to them. . . . But as to the poetical, very different is the frame of mind which is necessary for its perception. It demands, as its primary condition, that we *should not* put ourselves above the objects in which it resides, but at their feet; that we should feel them to be above and beyond us, that we should look up to them, and that, instead of fancying that we can comprehend them, we should take for granted that we are surrounded and comprehended by them ourselves. Hence it is that a child's mind is so

---

17. Newman, "The Mission of St. Benedict," 366.
18. Aristotle, *Metaphysics*, I, 980a21–25.

full of poetry, because he knows so little; and an old man of the world so devoid of poetry, because his experience of facts is so wide.[19]

As Newman sees it, the scientific mentality requires one to stand above the things being studied. Here the dignity of the mind tends to replace the worth of the object.

Poetic learning is for the youth, scientific proof for the mature, and perhaps wisdom for the old. But wisdom itself is more like poetry than proof. In Latin, the word *sapiens* denotes a person who can savor or taste. Wisdom is knowing something that one can savor. In C. 19 of the Rule, Benedict prescribes that psalms are to be chanted *sapienter*, wisely. In his life of St. Benedict, Gregory the Great comments that he was *scienter nescius et sapienter indoctus*, "learnedly ignorant and wisely uninstructed." Benedict did not have a scientific theology of the Psalms, but rather a Rule for savoring them: "My heart and flesh sing for joy to the living God" (Ps 84:2).

The Rule was written for youth in a world grown old. Not the world as it ought to be but, alas, cannot be; rather the world as seen by a youth—which is to say, a world that is admired just the way it appears and is first known through a contact suffused with emotion.

Benedict's "poetic method," moreover, extends to the entire range of material and symbolic culture of the monastery. Newman refers to a "Poetry of life, the poetry of ceremonies—of the cowl, the cloister, and the choir." (Today the power of this "poetry of life" helps explain the enduring fascination children have with the world of *Harry Potter.*) First, the black hood, the cowl, or what was called the *cucullus*—a poncho worn by children in ancient Rome. Then, the cloister—the internal space of the monastery, like a child's house or bedroom. Finally, the choir, which is the place of beauty. Newman notes that in this kind of world, a person can take "each new day as a whole in itself . . . and doing works which cannot be cut short, for they are complete in every portion of them."[20] Imagine, now, chanting all 150 psalms once a week—the variety of images, moods, and emotions. Each psalm is chanted and is complete itself; the one psalm repeatedly is complemented by the next, and by the next office, and the next day without any effort to tie disparate parts together into a scientific system of theology—any synthesis is left to the poetic imagination under the regime of the Holy Spirit.[21]

In view of such poetic, childlike instruction, one becomes aware of the slowness of the good. We may remember what it was like to learn that way, when we were younger: when a summer seemed like a lifetime. Almost

---

19. Newman, "The Mission of St. Benedict," 387.
20. Newman, "The Mission of St. Benedict," 409.
21. *Lectio divina*—a snippet of scripture that suffices unto itself.

effortlessly, a youth can learn more in three months than an adult in three years. The life envisaged by Benedict is not like a five-year plan, or a senior thesis, or a job report. The monk's life is rolled out like the verses of a psalm—little parts that cumulatively become something more.[22] Benedict's poetic teaching calls him to become again like a little child, to begin again.

Again, this is what Benedict taught the Dark Ages, his and ours. The slowness of the good, which is experienced as incredibly rich if one becomes as a child. Tertullian said of the incarnate Christ, that He "suffered Himself to be conceived in a mother's womb . . . [and] wished to be sated with the pleasure of patience."[23] In the Middle Ages, Lent was taken from a Germanic word for *long*; in Benedict's school, however, the Latin adverb *lente* (slowly) is the better term. Life in the Benedictine monastery was to be a perpetual Lent, a linking of patience with poetry.

HARKENING

Finally, and briefly, let me take you to the beginning of the Rule, where, presumably, all of us who read Benedict's Rule begin. The first words: "Harken, my son, and with the ear of your heart hear the precepts of your Master." The poetical approach jumps right off of the page. *Harken!* Not read, study, or merely listen. To harken is to attend to something that is immediate. The notion of a knowledge touched by the thing being known is highlighted (*auscultator*, a hearer who heeds) by means of the scriptural image of the *ear of one's heart* (from Ps 44). One is bidden to incline, to turn toward something as from an inner principle. Benedict continues:

> Readily (*libenter*) accept and faithfully follow the advice of your pious Father (*admonitionem pii patris*), so that through the labor of obedience you may return to Him from whom you have withdrawn because of the laziness of disobedience. My words are meant for you, whoever you are (*quisquis*), who laying aside your own will, take up the all-powerful and righteous arms of obedience.

Here, Benedict embeds the story of the Prodigal Son. The *filius* or *filia* (the son or the daughter) turns to the voice of the Father: "Therefore, let us arise . . . and arising he went unto his Father." (Lk 15:20)

---

22. The longest span of time worth considering is a liturgical season: four weeks of Advent, 40 days of Lent, 50 days between Easter and Pentecost. Again, Ps 90: "So teach us to number our days, that we may apply our hearts unto wisdom." From a point of view within the monastery, it doesn't matter whether one's allotment of time is an hour, a day, a week, a season or many seasons.

23. Tertullian, *On Patience*, c. 3.

The text shifts from the verb *obsculta* (*auscultare*, harken, heed) to its linguistic sister, *ob-dire*, to listen toward a word. Obedience. Benedict's student would have been familiar not only with the story of the Prodigal Son but also with the ideal of the Roman father: the *paterfamilias* who is by right a domestic magistrate, invested with public charge inside his household, including the capital powers of life and death over his wife, sons, slaves, and domestic animals. In the Roman world, what does the son owe to the father, and the father to city, and the city to the protecting gods? *Pietas.* It is a kind of reverence of an inferior to a superior; more precisely, *pietas* is the proper response on the part of someone who can never fully pay back what is received.

Yet it's clear that the Prologue of Benedict's Rule is *not* referring to that kind of daddy. In fact, the word *paterfamilias* is used but once in the Rule (C. 2), and it pertains to Christ as the Good Shepherd. Here's what's important: Benedict is referring to a Father who is Himself Pius—that is, tender. *Pater piissime.* A tender and merciful Father, who has the virtue of piety toward what is lower than himself. To the *humanum* created in his Image. And now we are back to the parable: the Father, who sees from afar the son trying to return, and who takes the initiative. This is not the stern Roman *pater.* The monastery is a school of the Pater Noster, the Our Father. Again, a school for beginners . . . to become childlike again.

Let me take you to one more paragraph into the Prologue to the Rule. We read: "Let us then at last arise, since the Scripture arouses us saying: *It is now time for us to rise from sleep*" (Rom 13:11). Interestingly, Benedict has embedded Lazarus (from John 11, *Lazare veni foras*, Come Out!) into the story of the Prodigal (Come Back), and Easter into the story of the Passion (Arise!). The paragraph continues. "And let us open our eyes to the deifying light; let us attune our ears to what the divine voice admonishes us, daily crying out: *Today if you hear his voice, harden not your hearts.*" Benedict is evoking, along with Scripture, a favorite communion chant of the ancient Church; "Come, O sons, listen. . . . O taste and see . . . and be radiant" (Ps 34). In the Prologue he writes, "*Currite dum lumen vitae habetis*"; hasten while you have the light of life.[24]

Father Benedict teaches through these verbs: "harken," "hasten," "awaken," "arise," "turn," "obey," "leave aside," "listen," "incline." The whole Prologue bristles in this mood, but in a way that is strangely soothing— one reason, perhaps, is that this is precisely what the ear of the heart desires.

---

24. Cf. Jn 12:35. Then Jesus told them, "You are going to have the light just a little while longer. Walk while you have the light, before darkness overtakes you. The man who walks in the dark does not know where he is going."

The most famous monk of the Middle Ages, Bernard of Clairvaux, said that as sin entered the world through sight (beholding the fruit of the tree), so salvation comes first through the ear. Recall Deuteronomy 6:4, "Hear, O Israel, the Lord our god is One." Benedict requires that when the bells summon to prayer, eight times a day, the monk must drop everything, turn toward the sound (incline, awake, arise, harken) and go to prayer. Eight times a day, 56 times a week, 2,912 times a year, one leaves everything behind and turns toward the voice. Here we have a splendidly simple reenactment or recapitulation of the Gospel—*come back, come out, arise*. The Psalms' interior meaning, as well as the Eucharistic liturgy, is the *voice* of Christ. And if you say *Ego* (Prol.)—"I'm the one"—then Benedict says, here is a school for the doing of it. "In instituting it we hope to establish nothing harsh or oppressive." Whatever rules are laid down for correcting vices, maintaining equity, and conserving the order of love will be hard at the beginning but not overwhelming.

CONCLUSION: WHAT BENEDICT TEACHES THE DARK AGES

And so now I can conclude by summing up what Benedict teaches the Dark Ages—not from a standpoint external to the Rule (the judgment of history, economics, aesthetics, agricultural sciences, and arts), but from a point of view internal to the Rule.

The monastic school does not exist for the purpose of surviving the Dark Ages or for helping barbarians to learn to count on something other than their fingers, even if it did have these results. Benedict taught the monks to have a certain contempt for all of that, although not a naïve or callous disregard of the fact of the world's ignorance or misery (read for yourselves the chapters on feeding the poor and welcoming strangers). Rather, *he taught the monks that there is something better to do, something higher and more worthy of their daily labor*. The monastery is nothing other than a school that turns *prodigals* into *pilgrims*. Beginners. That is what we become, once again, each Ash Wednesday, as we commence Lent. In the last stanza of his poem "Ash Wednesday," T. S. Eliot writes:

> I renounce the blessèd face
> And renounce the voice
> Because I cannot hope to turn again
> Consequently I rejoice, having to construct something
> Upon which to rejoice

Eliot's meditation reminds us that the simplest, most natural and supernaturally the most urgent thing always proves to be the most difficult: to begin, to turn once again. This is the "one thing necessary." This is what

Benedict taught then and teaches now: how to begin, how to receive life as Lent and Lent as a new springtime of life, to become young and like a child again, to seek first the Kingdom. Here we discover the fine line, perhaps only a hair's breadth, between the prodigal and the pilgrim. In the end the one infallible "solution" to the new Dark Age upon us would be to address the darkness in ourselves and turn again and again back to Him who is the "true Light" coming into the world, the One who brings us the light, joy, and peace of Easter through patient suffering in the desert, of the Cross.

Select Bibliography

Primary Sources

The Latin texts of the *Acta Sanctae Sedis* and the *Acta Apostolicae* Sedis can be found on the Vatican website: https://www.vatican.va/archive/atti-ufficiali-santa-sede/index_en.htm

Enchiridion delle Encicliche, 8 volumes, edizione bilingue. Bologne: EDB, 1994–98.

Acta Synodalia Sacrosancti Concilii Oecumenici Vaticani Secundi, 6 vols. Vatican City: Typis Polyglottis Vaticanis, 1970–78.

Aristotle. *The Complete Works of Aristotle.* Revised Oxford Translation. Edited by Jonathan Barnes. 2 volumes. Princeton, NJ: Princeton University Press, 1984.

———. *Metaphysics.* Translated by Carnes Lord. Chicago: University of Chicago Press, 1984.

———. *Politics.* Translated by Carnes Lord. Chicago: University of Chicago Press, 2013.

———. *Nicomachean Ethics.* Translated by Robert C. Bartlett and Susan D. Collins. Chicago: University of Chicago Press, 2011.

Thomas Aquinas. *Sancti Thomae Aquinatis opera omnia.* Leonine edition. Rome: Ex Typographia Polyglotta S.C. de Propaganda Fide, 1882–. Available online at https://www.corpus thomisticum.org/

———. *Treatise on law: The Complete Text (Summa Theologiae I-II, Questions 90–108).* Translated by Alfred J. Freddoso. South Bend, IN: St. Augustine's Press, 2009.

———. *An Apology for the Religious Orders.* Edited by John Proctor. London: Sands and Co., 1902.

———. *The Summa Theologiæ of St. Thomas Aquinas.* Translated by the Fathers of the English Dominican Province. New York: Benzinger Brothers, 1948.

———. *Commentary on Aristotle's Physics.* Translated by Richard Blackwell, Richard Spath, and Edmund Thirlkel. Notre Dame, IN: Dumb Ox Books, 1995.

———. *On Creation: Quaestiones Disputatae de Potentia Dei, Q. 3.* Translated by S.C. Selner-Wright. Washington, DC: The Catholic University of America Press, 2011.

———. *On Truth.* Translated by R. Mulligan, B. McGlynn, R. Schmidt. 3 volumes. Chicago: Regnery, 1952–54.

————. *On the Truth of the Catholic Faith (Summa Contra Gentiles)*. Translated by A. Pegis, J. F. Anderson, V. Bourke, C. O'Neil. Garden City, NJ: Doubleday, 1956.

————. *Commentary on Aristotle's Metaphysics*. Translated by J. P. Rowan. Notre Dame, IN: Dumb Ox Books, 1995.

————. *Commentary on Aristotle's De Anima*. Translated by Kenelm Foster and Silvester Humphries. Notre Dame, IN: Dumb Ox Books, 1994.

————. *Commentary on Aristotle's Nicomachean Ethics*. Translated by C. I. Litzinger. Notre Dame, IN: Dumb Ox Books, 1993.

————. *Commentary on the letter of Saint Paul to the Romans*. Translated by Fabian Larcher, and edited by J. Holmes. Lander: Aquinas Institute for the Study of Sacred Doctrine, 2012.

————. *Commentary on Aristotle's Politics*. Translated by Richard J. Regan, SJ. Indianapolis: Hackett Publishing Company, 2007.

————. *Disputed Questions on the Virtues*. Edited by E. M. Atkins and Thomas Williams. Translated by E.M. Atkins. Cambridge: Cambridge University Press, 2005.

Augustine. The Latin texts of Augustine can be found in *Corpus Scriptorum Ecclesiasticorum Latinorum (CSEL)*. Berlin: De Gruyter. Available Online: http://csel.at/en/publikationen/csel/.

————. *The First Catechetical Instruction*. Translated by Joseph P. Christopher. New York: Newman Press, 1946.

————. *Confessions*. Translated by John K. Ryan. New York: Doubleday, 1960.

————. *On The Trinity*. Translated by Edmund Hill, OP. Hyde Park: New City Press, 1991.

————. *Sermons, Volume 6, Sermons 184–229Z*. Translated by Edmund Hill, OP. New Rochelle, NY: New City Press, 1993.

————. *Sermons: Volume 7: Sermons 230–272B*. Translated by Edmund Hill, OP. New Rochelle, NY: New City Press, 1993.

————. *Teaching Christianity*. Translated by Edmund Hill, OP. Hyde Park, NY: New City Press, 1996.

————. *The City of God against the Pagans*. Translated by R. W. Dyson. Cambridge: Cambridge University Press, 1998.

————. *On Genesis. Edited by John E. Rotelle*. Translated by Edmund Hill, OP. Hyde Park, NY: New City Press, 2002.

————. *Homilies on the Gospel of John, 1–40*. Translated by Edmund Hill O. P. Hyde Park, NY: New City Press, 2009.

————. *Homilies on the Gospel of John, 41–124*. Translated by Edmund Hill. New York: New City Press, 2020.

————. *Sermons 341–400*. Translated by Edmund Hill. New York: New York City Press, 1995.

————. *On Genesis: Two Books on Genesis Against the Manichees; And, On the Literal Interpretation of Genesis, an Unfinished Book*. Fathers of the Church, Vol. 84. Washington, DC: The Catholic University of America Press, 2001.

———. *De perfectione iustitiae hominis.* In *Nicene and Post-Nicene Fathers,* series 1, vol. 5. Edited by Phillip Schaff. Peabody, MA: Hendrickson, 2004.

———. *De Vera Religione,* in *On Christian Belief.* Edited by Boniface Ramsey, Edmund Hill, John E. Rotelle. Translated by Edmund Hill. New York: New York City Press, 1990.

———. *On Free Choice of the Will.* Translated by Thomas Williams. Indianapolis: Hackett Publishing Company, 1993.

Code of Canon Law: Latin-English Edition. Washington, DC: Canon Law Society of America, 1999.

Sacrosanctum Oecumenicum Concilium Vatican II, Constitutiones, Decreta, Declarationes. Vatican City: Libreria Editrice Vaticana, 1993.

CLASSICAL AND MODERN SOURCES

A Letter to Diognetus. Translated by Alexander Roberts and James Donaldson. In *Ante-Nicene Fathers,* Vol. 1. Edited by Alexander Roberts, James Donaldson, and A. Cleveland Coxe. Buffalo, NY: Christian Literature Publishing Co., 1885.

Acton, John Emerich Edward Dalberg. *Selected Writings of Lord Acton.* Vol. I: *Essays in the History of Liberty.* Edited by J. Rufus Fears. Indianapolis: Liberty Classics, 1985.

———. *Selected Writings of Lord Acton.* Vol. III: *Essays in Religion, Politics, and Morality.* Edited by J. Rufus Fears. Indianapolis: Liberty Classics, 1988.

Anderson, Gary A. *The Genesis of Perfection: Adam and Eve in the Jewish and Christian Imagination.* Westminster, KY: John Knox Press, 2003.

Arkes, Hadley. *Natural Rights and the Right to Choose.* Cambridge: Cambridge University Press, 2002.

Aubert, Robert. *The Church in the Industrial Age.* Translated by Margit Resch. New York: Crossroad, 1981.

Barth, Karl. *Church Dogmatics.* Edited by G.W. Bromiley and T.F. Torrance. 4 vols. Edinburgh: T&T Clark, 1936–75.

Behr, Thomas C. *Social Justice and Subsidiarity: Luigi Taparelli and the Origins of Modern Catholic Social Thought.* Washington, DC: The Catholic University of America Press, 2019.

———. "Luigi Taparelli D'Azeglio, S.J. (1793–1862) and the Development of Scholastic Natural-Law Thought as a Science of Society and Politics." *Journal of Markets & Morality 6, no. 1* (2003): 99–115.

Bévenot, M. "Thesis and Hypothesis." *Theological Studies* 15 (1954): 440–46.

Bossuet, Jacques-Bénigne. *Politics Drawn from the Very Words of Holy Scripture.* Translated and Edited by Patrick Riley. Cambridge: Cambridge University Press, 1990.

Bourgoing, Jean Francois Baron de. *Historical and Philosophical Memoirs of Pius the Sixth.* Vol. I. London: G. G. and J. Robinson, 1799.

Bourke, Vernon. "In Memoriam: Heinrich Albert Rommen (1897–1967)." *Natural Law Forum* 12 (1967).

Bradley, Gerard. "Pope John Paul II and Religious Liberty." *Ave Maria Law Review* 6 (2007). 33–59.

Bradley, Gerard V. and Brugger, Christian, eds. *Catholic Social Teaching: A Volume of Scholarly Essays.* New York: Cambridge University Press, 2019.

Brock, Stephen. *The Philosophy of Saint Thomas Aquinas: A Sketch.* Eugene, OR: Wipf and Stock, 2015.

———. *The Light That Binds: A Study in Thomas Aquinas's Metaphysics of Natural Law.* Eugene, OR: Pickwick Publications, 2020.

———. "Natural Inclinations and the Intelligibility of the Good in Thomistic Natural Law." *Vera Lex* 6 (2005): 57–78.

———. "Natural Law, the Understanding of Principles, and Universal Good." *Nova et Vetera* 9 (2011): 671–706.

Brownson, Orestes A. *The American Republic: Its Constitution, Tendencies, and Destiny.* Edited with and Introduction by Thomas E. Woods, Jr. Washington, DC: Regnery Publishing, 2003.

Burkle-Young, Francis A. *Papal Elections in the Age of Transition, 1878–1922.* Lanham, MD: Lexington Books, 2000.

Buttiglione, Rocco. *Karol Wojtyla: The Thought of the Man Who Became Pope John Paul II.* Grand Rapids, MI: Eerdmans, 1997.

Calvez, Jean-Yves and Jacques Perrin. *The Church and Social Justice: The Social Teachings of the Popes from Leo XIII to Pius XII (1878–1958).* London: Burns & Oates, 1961.

Cessario, Romanus. *Christian Faith & Theological Life.* Washington, DC: The Catholic University of America Press, 1996.

Chaplin, Jonathan. *Things Old and New: Catholic Social Teaching Revisited.* Edited by F. P. McHugh and S. M. Natale. Lanham. MD: University Press of America, 1993.

———. "Subsidiarity as a Political Norm." In *Political Theory and Christian Vision: Essays in Memory of Bernard Zylstra,* edited by Jonathan Chaplin and P. Marshall, 81–100. Lanham, MD: University Press of America, 1994.

Cicero, Marcus Tullius. *On the Republic. On the Laws.* Translated by Clinton W. Keyes. Loeb Classical Library. Cambridge, MA: Harvard University Press, 1928.

———. *On Invention. The Best Kind of Orator. Topics.* Translated by H. M. Hubbell. Loeb Classical Library 386. Cambridge, MA: Harvard University Press, 1949.

Cottier, Georges. "Reflections on Marriage and the Family." *Nova et Vetera* 1, no. 1 (2003): 11–25.

Cortés, Juan Donoso. *Selected Works.* Edited and translated by Jeffrey P. Johnson. Westport, CT: Greenwood Press, 2000.

Cuddeback, Matthew. "Light and Form in St. Thomas Aquinas's Metaphysics of the Knower." PhD Dissertation. The Catholic University of America, 1998.

D'Azeglio Taparelli, Luigi. *Saggio teoretico di dritto naturale appogiato sul fatto.* 8th ed. Rome, 1949.

de Bonald, Louis. *On Divorce.* Translated and edited by Nicholas Davidson. New Brunswick, NJ: Transaction Publishers, 1992.

De Lamennais, Félicité Robert. *Oeuvres completes de F. de La Mennais.* 12 volumes. Paris: P. Daubrée et Cailleux, 1836–37.

De la Soujeole, Benoît-Dominique. *Introduction to the Mystery of the Church.* Translated by Michael J. Miller. Washington, DC: The Catholic University of America Press, 2014.

De Lubac, Henri. *Catholicism: Christianity and the Common Destiny of Man.* Translated by Lancelot C. Sheppard and Sister Elizabeth Englund, O.C.D., with forward by Joseph Cardinal Ratzinger. San Francisco: Ignatius Press, 1988.

———. *Theological Fragments.* Translated by Rebecca Howell Balinski. San Francisco: Ignatius Press, 1989.

———. *Corpus Mysticum.* Translated by Gemma Simmonds C.J., with Richard Price and Christopher Stephens. Notre Dame, IN: University of Notre Dame Press, 2006.

Delsol, Chantal. *La fin de la Chrétienté.* Paris: Cerf, 2021.

De Maistre, Joseph. *The Pope.* Translation of the 1819 edition of *Du Pape* by Aeneas M. Dawson. London: C. Dolman, 1850.

———. *Considerations on France.* Translated and edited by Richard A. Lebrun. Cambridge: Cambridge University Press, 1994.

De Montalembert, Charles. "Malines Address." August 20, 1863. In *Church and State in the Modern Age: A Documentary History,* edited by J.F. Maclear, 156–162. New York: Oxford University Press, 1995.

De Smedt, Emile-Joseph. "*Congregatio Generalis* CLXIV, 19 Nov. 1965." In *Acta Synodalia Sacrosancti Concilii Oecumenici Vaticani Secundi,* 6 vols. Vatican City: Typis Polyglottis Vaticanis, 1970–1978.

Dewan, Lawrence. "St. Thomas and the Divine Origin of Law: Some Notes." *Civilizar Ciencias Sociales y Humanas* 15 (2008): 123–34.

———. "St. Thomas and the Divinity of the Common Good." In *Ressourcement Thomism: Sacred Doctrine, the Sacraments, and the Moral Life. Essays in Honor of Romanus Cessario, O.P.,* edited by R. Hütter and M. Levering, 211–33. Washington, DC: The Catholic University of America Press, 2010.

———. *Wisdom, Law, and Virtue: Essays in Thomistic Ethics.* New York: Fordham University Press, 2008.

Dodaro, Robert. *Christ and the Just Society in the Thought of Augustine.* Cambridge: Cambridge University Press, 2004.

Ehler, Sidney Z. and Morrall, John B., eds. *Church and State Through the Centuries: A Collection of Historic Documents with Commentaries.* Westminster, MD: Newman Press, 1954.

Elliott, J.H. *Empires of the Atlantic World.* New Haven, CT: Yale University Press, 2006.

Epictetus. *The Golden Sayings of Epictetus.* In *Harvard Classics.* Vol. 2. Edited by C. W. Eliot and Translated by Hastings Crossley. New York: P.F. Collier & Son, 1909.

Eusebius. *Church History, Life of Constantine the Great,* and *Orations in Praise of Constantine.* In *Nicene and Post-Nicene Fathers.* Vol. 1. Edited by P. Schaef and H. Wace. Peabody, MA: Hendricksen Publishers, 1994.

Ford, John C. and Kelly, Gerald. *Contemporary Moral Theology.* Vol. 2: *Marriage Questions.* Westminster, MD: Newman Press, 1963.

Guéranger, Prosper. *Affaire de la Légende De Saint Grégoire VII.* In *Institutions liturgiques,* Vol. II. Paris, 1841.

Dougherty, Jude P. "'Intellectuals with Dirt under Their Fingernails': Attitudes toward Sciences and Technology and the Difference They Make." *Communio* 9 (1982): 224–37.

Dupanloup, Felix. *Remarks on the Encyclical, of the 8th of December, A.D. 1864.* Translated by William J. M. Hutchinson. London: Burns, Lambert, & Oates, 1865.

Dusenbury, David Lloyd. *The Innocence of Pontius Pilate: How the Roman Trial of Jesus Shaped History.* New York: Oxford University Press, 2021.

Durkheim, Emile. *Professional Ethics and Civic Morals.* New York: Free Press, 1958.

Elsbernd, Mary. "Papal Statements on Rights: A historical Contextual Study of Encyclical Teaching From Pius VI–Pius XI (1791–1939)." PhD Dissertation. Catholic University of Louvain, 1985.

Farrell, Walter. *The Natural Moral Law According to St. Thomas and Suarez.* Ditchling: St. Dominic's Press, 1930.

Felici, Pericles. "Nota Explicativa Praevia." In *Sacrosanctum Oecumenicum Concilium Vaticanum II: Constitutiones Decreta Declarationes.* Libreria Editrice Vaticana, 1993.

Finnis, John. *Natural Law and Natural Rights.* Oxford: Oxford University Press, 1980.

———. *Aquinas.* Oxford: Oxford University Press, 1998.

Fortin, Ernest L. "'Sacred and Inviolable': *Rerum Novarum* and Natural Rights." *Theological Studies* 53 (1992): 203–33.

Froelich, Gregory. "The Equivocal Status of Bonum Commune." *The New Scholasticism* 63, no. 1 (1989): 38–57.

Fuller, Lon. L. *The Morality of Law.* Revised Edition. New Haven, CT: Yale University Press, 1969.

Gellner, Ernest. *Conditions of Liberty: Civil Society and its Rivals.* New York: Penguin, 1994.

Gibbon, Edward. *The History of the Decline and Fall of the Roman Empire.* London: Strahan & Cadell, 1776–1789.

Gilson, Étienne. *The Philosopher and Theology.* Translated by Cecile Gilson. New York: Random House, 1962.

———. *The Metamorphoses of the City of God.* Translated by James G. Colbert. Washington, DC: The Catholic University of America Press, 2020.

Glendon, Mary Ann. "The Rule of Law in The Universal Declaration of Human Rights." *Northwestern University Journal of International Human Rights* 2 (2004): 2–19.

Goerner, E.A. *Peter and Caesar: The Catholic Church and Political Authority.* New York: Herder and Herder, 1965.

Goyette, John, Latkovic, Mark S., and Meyers, Richard S., eds. *St. Thomas Aquinas and the Natural Law Tradition: Contemporary Perspectives.* Washington, DC: The Catholic University of America Press, 2004.

Roy, Cardinal Maurice. "Reflections by Cardinal Maurice Roy on the Occasion of the Tenth Anniversary of the Encyclical *Pacem in Terris* of Pope John XXIII." In *The Gospel of Peace and Justice: Catholic Social Teaching Since Pope John,* edited by Joseph Gremillion, 531–68. New York: Orbis Books, 1976.

Grenier, Henri. *Thomistic Philosophy.* Vol. 3, 3rd ed. Charlottetown: St Dunstan's University Press, 1949.

Hales, E. E. Y. *Pope John and His Revolution.* New York: Doubleday & Co., 1965.

———. *Revolution and Papacy: 1769–1846.* Notre Dame, IN: University of Notre Dame Press, 1966.

Hart, H.L.A. "Positivism and the Separation of Law and Morality." *Harvard Law Review* 71 (1958): 593–629.

———. *The Concept of Law.* 2nd Edition. Oxford: Oxford University Press, 1994.

Hallis, Frederick. *Corporate Personality: A Study in Jurisprudence.* Oxford: Oxford University Press, 1930.

Habermas, Jürgen, and Joseph Ratzinger. *The Dialectics of Secularization: On Reason and Religion.* Edited by F. Schuller and translated by Brian McNeil. San Francisco: Ignatius Press, 2005.

Habiger, Matthew. *Papal Teaching on Private Property, 1891–1981.* Lanham, MD: University Press of America, 1990.

Hayek, Friedrich. *The Mirage of Social Justice.* London: Routledge, 1976.

Hebblethwaite, Peter. *Pope John XXIII: Shepherd of the Modern World—The Definitive Biography of Angelo Roncalli.* New York: Image Doubleday, 1987.

Hegel, George W.F. *The Philosophy of Right.* Translated by T.M. Knox. Oxford: Oxford University Press, 1967.

Henkel, Christoph. "The Allocation of Powers in the European Union: A Closer Look at the Principle of Subsidiary." *Berkeley Journal of International Law* 20 (2002): 359–86.

Hittinger, F. Russell. "The Problem of the State in *Centesimus Annus.*" *Fordham International Law Journal* 15 (1992): 952–96.

———. *A Critique of the New Natural Law Theory.* Notre Dame, IN: University of Notre Dame Press, 1987.

———. *The First Grace: Rediscovering the Natural Law in a Post-Christian World.* Wilmington, DE: ISI Books, 2002.

———. "Love, Sustainability and Solidarity: Philosophical and Theological Roots." In *Free Markets, With Solidarity & Sustainability,* edited by Martin

Schlag, 19–31. Washington, DC: The Catholic University of America Press, 2015.

———. "Political Pluralism and Religious Liberty: The Teaching of *Dignitatis Humanae*." In *The Proceedings of the 17th Plenary Session on Universal Rights in a World of Diversity: The case of religious freedom*. Pontifical Academy of Social Sciences Acta 17. Vatican City: The Pontifical Academy of Social Sciences, 2012.

———. "Popes Leo XIII and Pius XI." In *Christianity and Family Law: An Introduction*, edited by Gary S. Hauk and John Witte, 323–43. Cambridge: Cambridge University Press, 2017.

———. "Natural Law and the Human City." In *Contemporary Perspectives on Natural Law: Natural Law as a Limiting Concept*, edited by Ana Marta González, 29–42. New York: Ashgate Publishing, 2008.

———. "A Response to Commentators." In *Ethics Without God? The Divine in Contemporary Moral and Political Thought*, edited by Fulvio Di Blasi, 136–146. South Bend, IN: St. Augustine's Press, 2008.

Hobbes, Thomas. *The Elements of Law, Natural and Politic*. Edited by Ferdinand Tönnies. London: Frank Cass, 1969.

———. *Leviathan*. Edited by Richard Tuck. New York: Cambridge University Press, 1996.

———. *Man and Citizen (De Homine and De Cive)*. Edited by Bernard Gert. Translated Charles T. Wook, et. al. Indianapolis: Hackett Publishing Company, 1991.

Höffner, Joseph Cardinal. *Ordo Socialis: Christian Social Teaching*. Translated by Stephen Wentworth-Arndt. Cologne: Ordo Socialis, 1983.

Iggers, Georg G. "Further Remarks about Early Uses of the Term 'Social Science.'" *Journal of the History of Ideas* 20, no. 3 (1959): 433–36.

International Theological Commission. *Propositions on the Dignity and Rights of the Human Person*. 1983. The Documents for the ITC can be found at: https://www.vatican.va/roman_curia/congregations/cfaith/cti_documents/rc_cti_index-doc-pubbl_en.html.

———. *Memory and Reconciliation: the Church and the Faults of the Past*. 1999.

———. *Communion and Stewardship: Human Persons Created in the Image of God*. 2004.

———. *In Search of a Universal Ethics: A New Look at Natural Law*. 2009.

———. *Dio Trinità, Unità Degli Uomini: Il Monoteismo Cristiano Contro La Violenza*. 2014.

Ireland, John. *The Church and Modern Society: Lectures and Addresses*. 2 vols. Chicago: D. H. McBride, 1896.

Irenaeus of Lyons. *Against Heresies*. In *Ante-Nicene Fathers*, Vol. 1. Edited by Alexander Roberts, James Donaldson, and A. Cleveland Coxe. Buffalo, NY: Christian Literature Publishing Co., 1885.

Jacquin, Robert. *Taparelli*. Paris: P. Lethielleux, 1943.

Jaspers, Karl. *Way to Wisdom: An Introduction to Philosophy*. Translated by Ralph Manheim, 2nd ed. New Haven, CT: Yale University Press, 2003.

Journet, Charles. *Theology of the Word Incarnate.* Translated by Alfred Howard Campbell. London: Sheed and Ward, 1955.

John XXIII. *Journey of a Soul.* Translated by Dorothy White. New York: Image Doubleday, 1999.

Kant, Immanuel. "An Answer to the Question: What is Enlightenment?" In *Perpetual Peace and Other Essays.* Translated by Ted Humphrey. Indianapolis: Hackett Publishing, 1983.

Kantorowicz, Ernst. "Mysteries of State: An Absolutist Concept and Its Late Mediaeval Origins." *Harvard Theological Review* 48 (1955): 65–91.

———. *The King's Two Bodies: A Study in Mediaeval Political Theology.* Princeton, NJ: Princeton University Press, 1957.

Kerr, Fergus. *After Aquinas: Versions of Thomism.* Oxford: Blackwell, 2002.

———. *Twentieth-Century Catholic Theologians: From Neoscholasticism to Nuptial Mysticism.* Oxford: Blackwell Publishing, 2007.

King Jr., Martin Luther. "Letter from Birmingham City Jail." In *A Testament of Hope: The Essential Writings and Speeches of Martin Luther King, Jr.,* edited by James M. Washington, 289–302. San Francisco: HarperOne, 2003.

De Koninck, Charles. *The Writings of Charles De Koninck.* 2 vols. Edited and Translated by Ralph McInerny. Notre Dame, IN: University of Notre Dame Press, 2009–16.

Kupczak, Jaroslaw. "Komunijny wymiar obrazu Bożego w człowieku w soborowej konstytucji Gaudium et spes." *Studia Theologica Varsaviensia* 44 (2006): 139–58.

———. *Destined for Liberty: The Human Person in the Philosophy of Karol Wojtyla/ John Paul II.* Washington, DC: The Catholic University of America Press, 2000.

Kuyper, Abraham. *Lectures on Calvinism.* Grand Rapids, MI: Eerdmans, 1961.

Leclercq, Jean. *The Love of Learning and the Desire for God: A Study of Monastic Culture.* New York: Fordham University Press, 1982.

Lactantius. *Divine Institutes.* Translated by William Fletcher. In *Ante-Nicene Fathers,* vol. 7, edited by A. Roberts, J. Donaldson, and A. Cleveland Coxe. Buffalo: Christian Literature Publishing Co., 1886.

Leff, Lisa Moses. "Jewish Solidarity in Nineteenth-Century France: The Evolution of a Concept." *The Journal of Modern History* 74, no. 1 (2002): 33–61.

Lehu, L. *Philosophia Moralis et Socialis.* Paris: Gabalda, 1914.

Lewis, C. S. *The Abolition of Man.* Oxford: Oxford University Press. 1943.

Locke, John. *Second Treatise of Government.* Indianapolis: Hackett Publishing Company, 1980.

Long, Steven A. "Yves R. Simon's Approach to Natural Law." *The Thomist* 59, no. 1 (1995): 125–35.

Lottin, Dom Odon. "La définition classique de la loi." *Revue Néo-Scolastique de Philosophie* (1925): 129–45.

———. "La valeur des formules de Saint Thomas d'Aquin concernant la loi naturelle." In *Mélanges Joseph Maréchal,* edited by L. Noël, 345–377. Paris: Desclée de Brouwer, 1950.

Lukes, Steven. *Émile Durkheim: His Life and Work*. New York: Penguin Books, 1973.

MacCormick, Neil. "Natural Law and the Separation of Law and Morals." In *Natural Law Theory: Contemporary Essays*, edited by R. P. George, 105–133. Oxford: The Clarendon Press, 1992.

MacIntyre, Alasdair. "From Answers to Questions: A Response to the Responses." In *Intractable Disputes About the Natural Law: Alasdair Macintyre and his Critics*, edited by L. S. Cunningham, 313–51. South Bend, IN: University of Notre Dame Press, 2009.

Maitland, F. W. "Moral Personality and Legal Personality." In *State, Trust and Corporation*, edited by D. Runciman, 62–74. Cambridge: Cambridge University Press, 2003.

Manent, Pierre. "The Contest for Command." In *New French Thought: Political Philosophy*, edited by Mark Lilla, 178–85. Princeton, NJ: Princeton University Press, 1994.

———. *The City of Man*. Translated by Marc LePain, with foreword by Jean Bethke Elshtain. Princeton, NJ: Princeton University Press, 1998.

———. *A World beyond Politics? A Defense of the Nation-State*. Translated by Marc LePain. Princeton, NJ: Princeton University Press, 2006.

Mansi, Ioannes Dominicus. *Sacrorum Conciliorum Nova et Amplissima Collectio*. Vol. 51. Arnhem and Leipzig: Société Nouvelle D'Édition de la Collection Mansi, 1926.

Maritain, Jacques. "Introduction." In *Human Rights: Comments and Interpretations, A Symposium*. Edited by Unesco. London: Allan Wingate, 1949.

———. *The Primacy of the Spiritual: On the Things That Are Not Caesar's*. Translated by J. F. Scanlan. London: Sheed & Ward, 1930.

———. *Man and the State*. Chicago: University of Chicago Press, 1951.

———. *Heraldry in the Vatican*. Gerrards Cross: Van Duren, 1987.

———. *The Collected Works of Jacques Maritain*. Vol. XI, *Integral Humanism, Freedom in the Modern World, and A Letter on Independence*. Edited and Translated by Otto Bird. South Bend, IN: University of Notre Dame Press, 1996.

———. *The Peasant of the Garonne: An Old Layman Questions Himself about the Present Time*. Translated by Michael Cuddihy and Elizabeth Hughes. Eugene, OR: Wipf and Stock, 1968.

Mauss, Marcel. "A Category of the Human Mind: the Notion of Person; the Notion of Self." In *The Category of the Person: Anthropology, Philosophy, History*, edited by M. Carrithers, S. Collins, and S. Lukes, 1–25. Cambridge: Cambridge University Press, 1985.

McCool, Gerald. *The Neo-Thomists*. Milwaukee: Marquette University Press, 1994.

McCormick, William, S.J. *The Christian Structure of Politics: On the "De regno" of Thomas Aquinas*. Washington, DC: The Catholic University of America Press, 2022.

McInerny, Ralph M. *Praeambula Fidei: Thomism and the God of the Philosophers.* Washington, DC: The Catholic University of American Press, 2006.

McLean, Janet. "Personality and Public Law Doctrine." *University of Toronto Law Journal* 49, no. 1 (1999): 123–49.

Mecham, J. Lloyd. *Church and State in Latin America: A History of Politico-Ecclesiastical Relations.* Chapel Hill: University of North Carolina Press, 1966.

Melloni, Alberto. "Documento 1." In *Pacem in terris: Storia dell'ultima enciclica di Papa Giovanni.* Roma: GLF, Editori Laterza, 2010.

Merlin, Hélène and Allison Tait. "Fables of the 'Mystical Body' in Seventeenth-Century France." *Yale French Studies*, no. 86 (1994): 126–42.

Messner, Johannes. *Social Ethics: Natural Law in the Western World.* St. Louis: B. Herder, 1949.

Michel, Florian. *Étienne Gilson, une biographie intellectuelle et politique.* Paris: Vrin, 2018.

Mommsen, Theodore E. "Petrarch's Conception of the 'Dark Ages.'" *Speculum* 17, no. 2 (1942): 226–42.

Monson, Paul G. "*Ora et Labora*: A Benedictine Motto Born in America?" In *God Has Begun a Great Work in Us: Embodied Love in Consecrated Life and Ecclesial Movements*, edited by J. King and S. Schrein, College Theology Society Annual, vol. 60, 66–86. Maryknoll, NY: Orbis, 2015.

Montesquieu, Charles. *The Spirit of the Laws.* Translated by Anne M. Cohler, Basia Carolyn Miller, Harold Samuel Stone. Cambridge: Cambridge University Press, 1989.

Moody, Joseph N., ed. *Church and Society: Catholic Social and Political Thought and Movements, 1789–1950.* New York: Arts, Inc. 1953.

Morrisey, Francis G. *Papal and Curial Pronouncements: Their Canonical Significance in Light of the Code of Canon Law.* 2nd Edition. Revised and Updated by Michel Thériault. Ottawa: Faculty of Canon Law, Saint Paul University, 2001.

Murray, John Courtney. "St. Robert Bellarmine on the Indirect Power." *Theological Studies* 9 (1948): 491–535.

———. "Leo XIII: Separation of Church and State." *Theological Studies* 14 (1953): 145–314.

———. "Things Old and New in '*Pacem in Terris*'." *America* 108 (April 1963): 612–14.

———. *Religious Liberty: Catholic Struggles with Pluralism.* Edited by J. Leon Hooper. Louisville, KY: Westminster John Knox Press, 1993.

———. "Political Thought of Joseph de Maistre," *Review of Politics* 11 (1949): 63–86.

Newman, Jeremiah. *Foundations of Justice.* Cork: Cork University Press, 1954.

———. *Studies in Political Morality.* Dublin: Scepter, 1962.

———. *Principles of Peace: A Commentary on John XXIII's Pacem in terries.* Oxford: Catholic Social Guild, 1964.

Newman, John Henry. *Lectures on the Present Position of Catholics in England.* London: Longmans, Green, 1899.

———. *The Letters and Diaries of John Henry Newman*. Vol. XXV: The Vatican Council, January 1870 to December 1871. Edited by C. S. Dessain and Thomas Gornall, SJ. Oxford: Oxford University Press, 1973.

———. "The Mission of St. Benedict." In *Historical Sketches*, vol. 2, 365–432. New York: Longmans, Greens, 1906.

Nielsen, Fredrik K. *The History of the Papacy in the XIXth Century*. 2 vols. New York, E. P. Dutton, 1906.

Oakley, Francis. "Natural Law, the *Corpus Mysticum*, and Consent in Conciliar Thought from John of Paris to Mattias Ugonius." *Speculum* 56, no. 4 (1981): 786–810.

O'Connell, Marvin R. *Critics on Trial: An Introduction to the Catholic Modernist Crisis*. Washington, DC: The Catholic University of America Press, 1994.

Odell, Walter T. "The Political Theory of Civiltà Cattolica From 1850 to 1870." PhD Dissertation. Georgetown University, 1969.

Ollivier, Émile. "Speech in Chamber of Deputies." July 10, 1868. In *L'église et l'état au Concile du Vatican*. 3d ed., vol. 1. Paris: Gamier Frères, 1877.

———. *L'église et l'état au Concile du Vatican*. 3d ed., vol. 2. Paris: Gamier Frères, 1877.

O'Rahilly, Alfred. "Theology of Tyranny." *Irish Theological Quarterly* 15 (1920).

———. "The Sovereignty of the People." *Studies: An Irish Quarterly Review* (Dublin), 10 (1921): 39–56.

———. *Aquinas versus Marx*. Cork: Cork University Press, 1948.

Paulhus, Normand Joseph. "The Theological and Political Ideals of the Fribourg Union." PhD Dissertation. Boston College, 1983.

Pereira, José. "Thomism and the Magisterium: From *Aeterni Patris* to *Veritatis Splendor*." *Logos* 5 (2002): 147–83.

Perreau-Saussine, Emile. *Catholicism and Democracy: An Essay in the History of Political Thought*. Translated by Richard Rex. Princeton, NJ: Princeton University Press, 2012.

Peterson, Erik. *Theological Tractates*. Edited and Translated by Michael J. Hollerich. Stanford, CA: Stanford University Press, 2011.

Pierson, Christopher. *The Modern State*. London: Routledge, 1996.

Plato. *Plato: Complete Works*. Edited by John M. Cooper and D.S. Hutchinson. Indianapolis: Hackett Publishing Company, 1997.

Pope Pius VI. *Collection générale des brefs et instructions de notre très-saint père le pape Pie VI, relatifs a la Revolution Françoise*. Edited by M. N. S. Guillon, 2 vols. Paris: Chez Le Clere, 1798.

Popović, Petar. *Natural Law and Thomistic Juridical Realism: Prospects for a Dialogue with Contemporary Legal Theory*. Foreword by F. Russell Hittinger. Washington, DC: The Catholic University of America Press, 2022.

Ramsey, Paul. "*Pacem in terris*." In *The Just War: Force and Political Responsibility*, 70–90. Lanham, MD: Rowman & Littlefield, 2002.

Ratzinger, Joseph/Benedict XVI. "The Church's Teaching Authority-Faith-Morals." In *Principles of Christian Morality*, translated by Graham Harrison, 45–74. San Francisco: Ignatius Press, 1986.

———. *Eschatology: Death and Eternal Life*. Translated by Michael Waldstein. Washington, DC: The Catholic University of America Press, 1988.

———. *The Nature and Mission of Theology: Essays to Orient Theology in Today's Debates*. Translated by Adrian Walker. San Francisco: Ignatius Press, 1995.

———. "Consumer Materialism and Christian Hope." In *Teachers of the Faith, Speeches and Lectures by Catholic Bishops,* edited by T. Horwood, 78–94. London: Catholic Bishop's Conference of England and Wales, 2002.

———. *Der Gott Des Glaubens Und Der Gott Der Philosophen: Ein Beitrag Zum Problem Der Theologia Naturalis*. Edited by H. Sonnemans, 2nd rev. Einsiedeln: Johannes-Verlag Leutesdorf, 2004.

———. *Introduction to Christianity*. Translated by J.R. Foster. San Francisco: Ignatius Press, 2004.

———. "That Which Holds the World Together: The Pre-political Moral Foundations of a Free State." In *The Dialectics of Secularization: On Reason and Religion*, edited by Florian Schuller, translated by Brian McNeil, 53–80. San Francisco: Ignatius Press, 2005.

———. *On Europe's Crisis of Culture*. April 1, 2005. http://chiesa.espresso.repubblica.it/articolo/27262.

———. *Jesus of Nazareth, Part One: From the Baptism in the Jordan to the Transfiguration*. Translated by Adrian J. Walker. New York: Doubleday, 2007.

———. *Jesus of Nazareth, Part Two: Holy Week from the Entrance into Jerusalem to the Resurrection*. San Francisco: Ignatius Press, 2011.

———. *Jesus of Nazareth, The Infancy Narratives*. Translated by Philip J. Whitmore. London: Bloomsbury, 2012.

———. *Volk und Haus Gottes in Augustins Lehre von der Kirche*. Freiburg im Breisgau: Verlag Herder, 2011.

———. *Faith and Politics*. Foreword by Pope Francis. Translated by Michael J. Miller and others. San Francisco: Ignatius Press, 2018.

———. "The Renewal of Moral Theology: Perspectives of Vatican II and *Veritatis Splendor*." In *Joseph Ratzinger in Communio: The Unity of the Church*, edited D. L. Schindler, 183–194. Grand Rapids, MI: Eerdmans, 2010.

Rawls, John. *Political Liberalism*. New York: Columbia University Press, 1993.

Rommen, Heinrich. *The State in Catholic Thought: A Treatise in Political Philosophy*. 2nd English ed., Introduction by Russell Hittinger. Leesburg, VA: Alethes Press, 2008.

———. *The Natural Law: A Study in Legal and Social History and Philosophy*. Translated by Thomas R. Hanley, OSB, Introduction by Russell Hittinger. Indianapolis: Liberty Fund, 1998.

Roniger, Scott. "How is Natural Law Promulgated? A Phenomenological Approach to Thomas Aquinas's Natural Law Theory." PhD Dissertation. The Catholic University of America, 2017.

———. "Natural Law and the Imitation of Nature: A Thomistic Development of Human Ecology." *Lex Naturalis* 2 (2016): 111–30.

———. "Natural Law and Friendship with God." *The Thomist* 83 (2019): 237–76.

———. "Is There a Punishment for Violating the Natural Law?" *American Catholic Philosophical Quarterly* 94 (2020): 273–304.

———. "Prudence as Command Across Presence and Absence." *The Review of Metaphysics* 74 (2021): 577–619.

———. "Self-Knowledge, Friendship, and the Promulgation of the Natural Law." *Nova et Vetera* 21 (2023): 287–333.

Rosanvallon, Pierre. *The Demands of Liberty: Civil Society in France Since The Revolution.* Translated by Arthur Goldhammer. Cambridge, MA: Harvard University Press, 2007.

Rosmini, Antonio. *Delle cinque piaghe della Santa Chiesa, Trattato dedicato al clero cattolico con appendice di alcune lettere sulla elezione de' vescovi a clero e popolo.* Napoli: Stabilimento tipografico del Tramater, 1849.

Rousseau, Jean Jacques. *Discourse on the Origin of Inequality.* Translated by Donald A. Cress. Indianapolis: Hackett Publishing Company, 1992.

———. *The Social Contract and Other Later Political Writings.* Edited and Translated by Victor Gourevitch. Cambridge: Cambridge University Press, 1997.

Ruben, David-Hillel. "Social Wholes and Parts." *Mind*, New Series 92, no. 366 (1983): 219–38.

———. "The Existence of Social Entities." *The Philosophical Quarterly* 32, no. 129 (1982): 295–310.

Russel, Lord Odo. *The Roman Question: Extracts from the Despatches of Odo Russell from Rome, 1858–1870.* Edited by Noel Blakiston. London: Chapman and Hall, 1962.

Schaff, P., and Wace, H., eds. *Select Works and Letters.* Vol. IV. *Nicene and Post-Nicene Fathers*, Series II. Grand Rapids, MI: Eerdmans, 1980.

Schleiermacher, Friedrich. *On Religion: Speeches to Its Cultured Despisers.* Translated by John Oman. New York: Frederick Ungar Publishing Co., 1955.

Schmitt, Frederick F. "Socializing Metaphysics: An Introduction." In *Socializing Metaphysics: The Nature of Social Reality*, edited by F. F. Schmitt, 1–38. Lanham, MD: Rowman & Littlefield, 2003.

Schmitz, Kenneth L. *At the Center of the Human Drama: The Philosophy of Karol Wojtyla/Pope John Paul II.* Washington, DC: The Catholic University of America Press, 1994.

Schuck, Michael J. *That They Be One: The Social Teaching of the Papal Encyclicals 1740–1989.* Washington, DC: Georgetown University Press, 1991.

Shields, Leo W. *The History and Meaning of the Term Social Justice.* Notre Dame, IN: University of Notre Dame Press, 1941.

Shiels, W. Eugene. *King and Church: The Rise and Fall of the Patronato Real.* Chicago: Loyola University Press, 1961.

Shortall, Sarah. *Soldiers of God in a Secular World: Catholic Theology and Twentieth-Century French Politics*. Cambridge, MA: Harvard University Press, 2021.

Simon, Yves. *Philosophy of Democratic Government*. Revised Edition. Notre Dame, IN: University of Notre Dame Press, 1993.

———. *A General Theory of Authority*. Notre Dame, IN: University of Notre Dame Press, 1980.

———. *The Tradition of Natural Law: A Philosopher's Reflections*. Edited by V. Kuic, introduction by Russell Hittinger. New York: Fordham University Press, 1992.

———. *Practical Knowledge*. Edited by R. J. Mulvaney. New York: Fordham University Press, 1991.

Sokolowski, Robert. "Knowing Natural Law." In *Pictures, Quotations, and Distinctions*, 277–92. Washington, DC: The Catholic University of America Press, 2022.

———. "Discovery and Obligation in Natural Law." In *Natural Moral Law in Contemporary Society,* edited by Holger Zaborowski, 24–43. Washington, DC: The Catholic University of America Press, 2010.

———. "What Is Natural Law? Human Purposes and Natural Ends." *The Thomist* 68 (2004): 507–29.

———. *Moral Action: A Phenomenology Study*. Washington, DC: The Catholic University of America Press, 2017.

Spaemann, Robert. *Der Ursprung der Soziologie aus dem Geist der Restauration. Studien über L. G.A. de Bonald*. Munich: Kösel, 1959.

Stewart, John Hall. *A Documentary History of the French Revolution*. New York: Macmillan, 1951.

Stjerno, Steinar. *Solidarity in Europe: The History of an Idea*. Cambridge: Cambridge University Press, 2004.

Story, Joseph. *Commentaries on the Conflict of Laws*. Boston: Hilliard, Gray, and Company, 1834.

Strauss, Leo. *What Is Political Philosophy? and Other Studies*. Chicago: University of Chicago Press, 1988.

Sturzo, Luigi. *Church and State*. New York: Longmans, Green, 1939.

Suetonius. *De vita Caesarum*. Translated by J. C. Rolfe. Loeb Classical Library. Cambridge, MA: Harvard University Press, 1913.

Talmy, Robert. *Aux Sources Du Catholicisme Social: L'École De La Tour Du Pin*. Bibliothèque De Théologie, Série IV, Vol. 3 Tournai, Belgium: Desclée &Co., 1961.

Tapie, Matthew A. *Aquinas on Israel and the Church*. Eugene, OR: Pickwick Publications, 2014.

Taylor, Charles. *Modern Social Imaginaries*. Durham, NC: Duke University Press, 2004.

———. *A Secular Age*. Cambridge: Belknap Press, 2007.

Tertullian. *On Patience*. Translated by S. Thelwall. In *Ante-Nicene Fathers*, Vol. 3. Edited by Alexander Roberts, James Donaldson, and A. Cleveland Coxe. Buffalo, NY: Christian Literature Publishing Co., 1885.

"The Encyclical Pascendi." *The Dublin Review* 142 (January/April 1908): 1–10.

Tocqueville, Alexis de. *Democracy in America*. London: Saunders and Otley, 1835–1840.

Turner, Barrett H. *"Dignitatis humanae* and the Development of Moral Doctrine: Assessing Change in Catholic Social Teaching on Religious Liberty." PhD Dissertation. The Catholic University of America, 2015.

Villagrasa, Jesús. "Origin, Nature, and Initial Reception of XXIV Thomistic Thesis in the Light of Controversy Between Neo-Thomism and Neo-Suarezianism." *Doctor Angelicus: Internationales thomistisches Jahrbuch* 6 (2006): 193–230.

———. Ed. *Neotomismo & Suarezismo*. Roma: Ateneo Pontificio Regina Apostolorum, 2006.

Von Gierke, Otto. *Associations and Law: The Classical and Early Christian Stages*. Edited and translated by George Heiman. Toronto: University of Toronto Press, 1977.

———. *Natural Law and the Theory of Society, 1500 to 1800: With a lecture on the ideas of natural law and humanity by Ernst Troeltsch*. Translated with an introduction by Ernest Barker. Boston: Beacon, 1957.

Von Ketteler, Wilhelm Emmanuel. *The Social Teachings of Wilhelm Emmanuel Von Ketteler*. Translated by Rupert J. Ederer. Lanham, MD: University Press of America, 1981.

Wallace, Lillian Parker. *Leo XIII and the Rise of Socialism*. Durham, NC: Duke University Press, 1966.

Ward, Wilfrid. *William George Ward and the Catholic Revival*. London: Macmillan, 1893.

Ward-Perkins, Byran. *The Fall of Rome and the End of Civilization*. Oxford: Oxford University Press, 2005.

Weigel, George. *Witness to Hope: The Biography of Pope John Paul II*. New York: HarperCollins, 1999.

Weisheipl, James A. "The Revival of Thomism as a Christian Philosophy." In *New Themes in Christian Philosophy*, edited by Ralph M. McInerny, 164–186. Notre Dame, IN: University of Notre Dame Press, 1968.

White, Lynn, Jr. *Dynamo and Virgin Reconsidered: Essays in the Dynamism of Western Culture*. Cambridge, MA: MIT Press, 1968.

Wickham, Chris. *Inheritance of Rome: Illuminating the Dark Ages*. New York: Viking Penguin, 2009.

Williams, George Hunston. *The Contours of Church and State in the Thought of John Paul II*. Waco, TX: Institute of Church-State Studies, Baylor University, 1983.

———. *The Mind of John Paul II: Origins of His Thought and Action*. New York: Seabury Press, 1981.

Witte, John and Alexander, Frank, eds. *The Teachings of Modern Roman Catholicism: On Law, Politics, & Human Nature*. New York: Columbia University Press, 2007.

Woestman, William H, ed. *Papal Allocutions to the Roman Rota, 1939–2002*. Ottawa: Faculty of Canon Law, St. Paul University, 2002.

Wojtyła, Karol/John Paul II. *Sign of Contradiction*. New York: The Seabury Press, 1979.

———. *Man and Woman He Created Them: A Theology of the Body*. Translated by Michael Waldstein. Boston: Pauline Books, 2006.

———. *Memory and Identity: Conversations at the Dawn of a Millenium*. New York: Rizzoli International Publications, 2005.

———. *Love and Responsibilty*. Translated by H.T. Willetts. San Francisco: Ignatius Press, 1993.

———. *The Collected Plays and Writings on Theatre*. Translated by Boleslaw Taborski. Berkeley: University of California Press, 1987.

———. *Person and Act and Related Essays*. Translated by Grzegorz Ignatik. Washington, DC: The Catholic University of America Press, 2021.

Wolterstorff, Nicholas. *Justice, Rights and Wrongs*. Princeton, NJ: Princeton University Press, 2008.

Index

China, 24n47, 106, 230n15
chrematistics, 108
Christianae reipublicae (Clement XIII), 133
Christiansen, Drew, 227n4
Christifideles Laici (John Paul II), 93
citizenship, 49–50, 59–60, 63, 94, 112, 121
Civil Constitution of the Clergy, 32, 170
Civiltà Cattolica, 124–25, 137, 173n31, 178, 180n54, 182, 189
Clement XI, Pope, 171
Clement XIII, Pope, 133
Code of Canon Law, 80, 89, 132, 160, 175, 189, 309
"Coherence of the Four Basic Principles of Catholic Social Doctrine, The: An Interpretation" (Hittinger), xv, xvii, 3–48
Coke, Edward, 23n45
Colombia, 151
common good(s): in Aquinas, 13, 41n79; charity and, 60; of creation, 330; distribution of, 43–44; in Finnis, 41n79; in John XXIII, 240; justice and, 60; in Koninck, 59; law and, 345; partnership and, 19; political, 155; as principle of Catholic social teaching, 4; society and, xviii, 6; state and, 42–43; subsidiarity and, 35, 41–42, 47; virtue and, 39–40, 60
Communion and Stewardship (International Theological Commission), 72–73, 73n61–62, 74n64
commutative justice, 17n36, 18, 37, 40, 83, 84n20, 92, 192–93
Compendium of the Social Doctrine of the Church, 104, 325
concession theory, 22–26, 22n41, 23n44, 29
Conditions of Liberty: Civil Society and its Rivals (Gellner), 30, 77, 78n7
Congregation of Extraordinary Affairs, 170

Congress of Vienna, 116–17
conservativism, 170
"Consumer Materialism and Christian Hope" (Ratzinger), 279
Cook, James, 260n51
Corinthians, First, 91, 150
Cortés, Juan Donoso, 113, 134, 170, 175–76
Cottier, Georges, 250
Council of Nicaea, 119, 343
Council of Trent, 114, 119, 323, 326
Counter-Reformation, 49
creation: in Aquinas, 329; charity and, 59; common good of, 330; dominion and, 259, 270; goodness of, 61; idolatry and, 332; image of God and, 69–70; in John Paul II, 270n87; in Leo XIII, 147; order and, 246, 282; society and, 12–13
Critique of the New Natural Law Theory, A (Hittinger), xiii–xiv
cultural revolution, in 1960s, 104–5
Cum primum (Gregory XVI), 116–17
Czechoslovakia, 230n15, 231

D

Daru, Pierre, 120
Davis, Jefferson, 207n19
Day, Dorothy, 109, 121
Declaration of Independence, 11n16, 207n19
Declaration of the Rights of Man and Citizen, 24
Declaration on Religious Freedom, xxviii–xxix
Decline and Fall of the Roman Empire, The (Gibbon), 26n52
decolonization, 227–28, 253, 365
De Ecclesia Christi, 174
De Ecclesia Dei, 253
dehellenization, 286–88
Dei Filius (Pius IX), 122–23, 175–76, 254
Delsol, Chantal, 367
de Lubac, Henri, 75, 285n24, 359n31, 361

98; God and, 147; importance of, 105; in John Paul II, 73n58, 92; kingship and, 92; law and, 27–28, 64–65; in Leo XIII, 19n37, 146–47; liberalism and, 101; natural law and, 307, 311; as optional, 105; prudence and, 146–47; in Rousseau, 274; as sacrament, 357n27; sacrament and, 147; in Wojtyła, 272–73

Marsilius of Padua, 185

Martin, Jacques, 256n29

Martín, Luis, 187

Martino, Renato Raffaele, 104

Marx, Karl, 9, 257, 261

Mater et Magistra (John XXIII), 39, 228

Matthew, Gospel of, 5, 81, 89, 108, 135, 242, 270, 289n35, 310–11, 355, 357n27, 358n28, 361, 364

Maxentius, 26n52

McCool, Gerald, 123

Meilaender, Gilbert, 51

Messner, J., 86n24

Metamorphoses of the City of God, The (Gilson), 365–66

Mexico, 32

Mill, John Stuart, x

Minncrath, Roland, 240–41, 244

Mirari vos (Gregory XVI), 134

Miserentissimus Redemptor (Pius XI), 160

modernism, xxii, 112, 163–98

Modern Social Imaginaries (Taylor), 106–7

Molina, Luis de, 124, 180

Monson, Paul G., 380n14

Montalembert, Charles de, 118–19, 170, 186

Montesquieu, 28–29, 77, 150

"Moral Personality and Legal Personality" (Maitland), 14

moral theology, ix, xi; Catholic social teaching and, xiv–xv, 3; dialectical context in, 283–94; dialogical context in, 284, 295–303; image

of God and, 55n13; in International Theological Commission, 313–14; *koinonia* and, 10; law and, 292–93; natural law and, xv, xxviii, 309, 311; negative anthropology and, 266; in Pius XI, 193; Ratzinger and, 281–82; reason and, 285; systematic context in, 283–94

Mulieris Dignitatem (John Paul II), 91

munus regale, xx, 79–81, 94

Murray, John Courtney, 113, 121, 152, 160, 183, 190, 190n83, 229n11

Mystici Corporis (Pius XII), 4, 11n17, 68, 69n51, 87n28

N

Napoleonic Code, 351

Napoleonic Wars, 79, 137

nationalism, 103–4, 225, 241

natural law, xi; abortion and, 207–8; action and, 218; in Aquinas, xiv, 58–59, 221n74, 284, 284n22, 312–13, 328–29, 330n29, 333; in Benedict XVI, 284; Biden and, 208n22; cognition and, 211–12; dialectical context, 283–94, 307; dialogical context, xxvii, xxvii–xxviii, 284, 295–303, 305, 307; dignity and, 113, 302n93; faith and, 133–34; God and, 176, 219; government and, 157; Hittinger's essays on, xxiii–xxix; imitation of God and, 56–64; International Theological Commission on, 314–15, 317–18, 320; in John Paul II, 291–92, 292n49, 307–10; in John XXIII, 237, 308–9; justice and, 203; law and, 139–41, 221, 344–45; in Leo XIII, 139–45, 308; Leo XIII and, 56–64; liberty and, 301–2; in MacIntyre, 283, 303n98, 311; marriage and, 307, 311; moral theology and, xv, xxviii, 309, 311; natural rights and, 314;